Health Psychology

Catherine A. Sanderson

WILEY

Photo Credits

Chapter 1 Page 10: Ariel Skelley/Corbis Images. Page 13: ©The New Yorker Collection 1997 Danny Shanahan from cartoonbank.com. Page 15: AFP/Corbis Images. Page 17: Corbis Images.

Chapter 2 Page 26: Sandy Felsenthal/Corbis Images. Page 33 (top): Jacques M. Chenet/Corbis Images. Page 33 (bottom): ©2003 Reprinted with special permission of King Features Syndicate. Page 35: Getty Images News and Sport Services. Page 39: Roger Ressmeyer/Corbis Images. Page 40: EyeWire, Inc./Getty Images. Page 47: Rufus F. Folkks/Corbis Images. Page 48: Bob Rowan/Corbis Images.

Chapter 3 Page 63: Pictor/Image State/Alamy Images. Page 68: Steve Smith/Taxi/Getty Images. Page 71: Kevin Laubacher/Taxi/Getty Images. Page 72: ©The New Yorker Collection 1993 Tom Cheney from cartoonbank.com. All Rights Reserved. Page 78: DigitalVision/Getty Images. Page 86: Paul Barton/Corbis Images.

Chapter 4 Page 93: Ken Fisher/Stone/Getty Images. Page 94: ©2003 David Sipress from cartoonbank.com. All Rights Reserved. Page 96: PhotoDisc, Inc./Getty Images. Page 106: Bob Daemmrich/The Image Works. Page 117: ©Mark Nielsen. Page 126: Jose Luis Pelaez/Corbis Images. Page 136: ©Image Source/Alamy Images. Page 138: Bob Daemmrich/The Image Works.

Chapter 5 Page 147: Paul Souders/Corbis Images. Page 152: ©The New Yorker Collection 1993 Charles Barsotti from cartoonbank.com. All Rights Reserved. Page 154: Daly & Newton/The Image Bank/Getty Images. Page 157: Stu Forster/Allsport/Getty Images. Page 166: Royalty-Free/Corbis Images. Page 171: Chad Ehlers/Alamy Images.

Chapter 6 Page 176: Steven Ruben/The Image Works. Page 180: Chris Collins/Corbis Images. Page 192 (top): Sonda Dawes/The Image Works. Page 192 (bottom): ©2003 Peter Steiner from cartoonbank.com. All Rights Reserved. Page 193: DigitalVision/Getty Images. Page 200: William Findlay/Corbis Images. Page 203: The Image Works.

Chapter 7 Page 216: Tom & Dee Ann/Corbis Images. Page 219: Bob Daemmrich/The Image Works. Page 224: Courtesy Centers of Disease Control. Page 231: Lee Snider/The Image Works. Page 237: Mark Reinstein/The Image Works. Page 242: Sean Murphy/Stone/Getty Images. Page 244: L. Clarke/Corbis Images. Page 251: ©The New Yorker Collection 1988 Michael Crawford from cartoonbank.com. All Rights Reserved.

Chapter 8 Page 274: ©The New Yorker Collection 2001 Mike Twohy from cartoonbank.com. All Rights Reserved. Page 278: Ariel Skelley/Corbis Images. Page 279: Lon C. Diehl/PhotoEdit. Page 281: Jack Hollingsworth/ Corbis Images. Page 283: Michael Newman/PhotoEdit. Page 285 & 289: Photofest. Page 292: Bettman/Corbis Images.

Chapter 9 Page 317: Duomo/Corbis Images. Page 322: Deep Light Productions/Photo Researchers. Page 338: ©The New Yorker Collection 2000 Peter Steiner from cartoonbank.com. All Rights Reserved. Page 339: David W. Hamilton/The Image Bank/Getty Images. Page 340: George Shelley/Corbis Images. Page 351: Gary Bistram/The Image Bank/Getty Images. Page 356: Michael Newman/PhotoEdit. Page 360: Corbis Images.

Chapter 10 Page 368: Leif Skoogfors/Corbis Images. Page 374: ©The New Yorker Collection 2000 Joseph Farris from the cartoonbank.com. All Rights Reserved. Page 376: PhotoDisc, Inc./Getty Images. Page 379: Roger Ressmeyer/Corbis Images. Page 392: Corbis Sygma. Page 399: Getty Images News and Sport Services. Page 414: Rob Lewine/Corbis Images. Page 418: Wally McNamee/Corbis Images.

Chapter 11 Page 428: Getty Images News and Sport Services. Page 433: PhotoDisc, Inc./Getty Images. Page 436: A. Ramey/PhotoEdit. Page 440: Reuters New Media/Corbis Images. Page 458: Alan Oddie/PhotoEdit. Page 460: AFP/Corbis Images. Page 464: ©The New Yorker Collection 2000 Barbara Smaller from cartoonbank.com. All Rights Reserved.

Chapter 12 Page 476 (top): John-Marshall Mantel/Corbis Images. Page 476 (bottom): Lester Lefkowitz/Corbis Images. Page 478: AFP/Corbis Images. Page 485: ©The New Yorker Collection 2000 Robert Mankoff from cartoonbank.com. All Rights Reserved. Page 493: David Young-Wolff/PhotoEdit. Page 507: PhotoDisc, Inc./Getty Images. Page 514 (top): Claudia Kunin/Corbis Images. Page 514 (bottom): Royalty-Free/Corbis Images.

Chapter 13 Page 538: Frederic Lucano/Taxi/Getty Images. Page 546: ©The New Yorker Collection 2001 Jack Ziegler from cartoonbank.com. All Rights Reserved. Page 547: PhotoDisc, Inc./Getty Images.

Chapter 14 Page 561: Bill Aron/PhotoEdit. Page 567: Mike Keefe, The Denver Post. Page 568: David Butow/Corbis SABA. Page 572: Corbis Digital Stock. Page 584: AFP/Corbis Images. Page 587: Robert Harding World Imagery/Alamy Images. Page 591: Jose Luis Pelaez/Corbis Images.

ACQUISITIONS EDITOR Tim Vertovec
ASSISTANT EDITOR Lili DeGrasse
MARKETING MANAGER Kate Stewart
PRODUCTION EDITOR Sandra Dumas

DESIGNER Dawn Stanley
PHOTO EDITOR Sara Wright
PRODUCTION MANAGEMENT SERVICES Argosy
COVER PHOTO Universal Man III, 60 × 60", by Paul Giovanopoulus

This book was typeset in 11/12 Bembo by Argosy and printed and bound by R. R. Donnelly & Sons, Inc. (Crawfordsville). The cover was printed by Lehigh Press.

The paper in this book was manufactured by a mill whose forest management programs include sustained yield harvesting of its timberlands. Sustained yield harvesting principles ensure that the number of trees cut each year does not exceed the amount of new growth.

This book is printed on acid-free paper. ∞

To order books please call 1(800)-225-5945.

Sanderson, Catherine A.
Health Psychology

0-471-15074-6
0-471-45156-8 WIE ISBN

Printed in the United States of America.
10 9 8 7 6 5 4 3 2 1

To Bart

PREFACE

I agreed to write a textbook on health psychology in February 2001. At the time, I was in my fourth year as an assistant professor at Amherst College in Massachusetts, had a 2 1/2-year-old son, and was in my eighth month of pregnancy with my second son. I was spending most mornings working on research studies, most afternoons teaching courses, and most evenings answering a seemingly endless supply of questions from a toddler ("why is fire hot?" "why don't dogs poop in the toilet?" "why don't cats live with their mothers?"). So, you may be wondering, why in the world would I commit to doing such a major project? I asked myself this question repeatedly in those months—as did my colleagues at Amherst and elsewhere. And, ultimately, I decided that the opportunity to write a textbook that organized and described the exciting field of health psychology in a new and different way was too appealing to pass up. After agreeing to do this book, I was warned by my older (and wiser) colleagues that writing a textbook would be difficult and tedious and that at some point I would regret the decision. Were they right? Yes, in some respects—it was difficult and at times even tedious. However, I never regretted the decision; in fact, I really enjoyed creating this book and I hope my enjoyment is evident to students who read it as well as professors who teach from it.

I have several goals for this book. First, one of the aspects of health psychology that I find most exciting is its basis in research, specifically in research conducted using the scientific method. I am always shocked when students refer to discussions of research methods as "the boring part" that they must suffer through before we move to the more interesting topics of alcohol and eating disorders and AIDS. Therefore, one of my major goals in this book is to show students the exciting aspects of thinking about and conducting research. Chapter 2 focuses entirely on research methods (and I promise, it is not dry or boring—there is even a joke about masturbation), and I describe specific

v

research studies—ones chosen to be interesting to college students—in detail in each of the subsequent chapters. You'll read about one study that examines the influence of drinking alcohol on intentions to use condoms, another study that examines why wearing a swimsuit leads women to do badly on a math test, and still another that examines whether showing children Disney video-tapes while they get immunized eases the pain (it does). I also include graphs of research data in every chapter to show you how research findings are typi-cally presented and samples of actual research questionnaires so that you can see how you score on these measures (aren't you curious to know whether you are "Type A" and how you cope with pain?).

I also want students who read this book to actively think about and even question what I am describing. This is not a book that you should simply read and try to memorize so you can repeat back "the right answer" on an exam or homework assignment. Of course, I'd like you to read and believe what I'm writing, but I'd also like you to think critically about the information presented. In most chapters I include some specific questions about particular research studies for you to try and answer, but you should be asking yourself these same types of questions throughout all the chapters. If I write that married people live longer than single people (which is true), you should think about why this may be so: Is it that being married leads people to engage in healthier behavior, or is it that people who are healthy are more likely to get married, or is it that people who are optimistic are very likely to get married and are also likely to engage in healthy behaviors? All of these are potential explanations for the link between marriage and health—and there are, of course, many others.

Third, I want to give you a sense of the newest and most exciting topics in the field of health psychology. I describe the most current research throughout this book (including many studies that were published in 2000, 2001, and 2002), and I often tell you exactly who conducted that research and where they work. I also end each chapter with two questions that I call "lingering issues." Do you believe that prayer can lead to better health? Do you believe that simply having surgery—even if the physician doesn't do anything besides cut you open and then sew you up—can improve health? This book answers both of these questions, and more.

Fourth, I want you to learn how the topics addressed in this book have real implications for practical and real-world issues. This book provides information about preventing the spread of HIV, the impact of poverty on health-related behaviors, and the costs and benefits of screening for genetic diseases. And it gives you information that you can use now and for the rest of your life—infor-mation about why students often get sick right after they take final exams, strategies for managing the (tremendous) pain of childbirth, and descriptions of the stages of bereavement following the death of a loved one. One of the rea-sons I love teaching health psychology is because the information students can learn by taking this class, and by reading this book, can make a substantial dif-ference in their lives (and perhaps even the lives of their friends and family).

Finally, no matter how much information a textbook provides, it is useless if students choose not to actually read it (yes, professors are aware that students sometimes do not do all of the reading). I therefore worked to make this book interesting and exciting. It includes personal anecdotes (which may humiliate some of my friends, family, and former students), photographs, and even cartoons. A professor who reviewed this book wrote, "This text reads like Professor Sanderson is having a conversation"—and this is exactly the tone I want to take. Although this will be mostly a one-sided conversation, I'd love to hear what you think; please drop me an e-mail message (casanderson@ amherst.edu) and tell me what you learned, what you liked, and even what you didn't like! Let the conversation begin.

Acknowledgments

Writing this book has been a tremendous undertaking, and I want to acknowledge a number of people who have provided considerable assistance at various points along the way. First, Susan Whitbourne and Rich Halgin at the University of Massachusetts – Amherst were both very influential in my decision to write a textbook, and I appreciate their advice at the early stages. Second, I have received considerable assistance from numerous people at Wiley, including Tim Vertovec (editor), Allison Fredette and Ailsa Manny (permissions), Sara Wight (photos), Kristen Babroski (editorial assistance), Lili DeGrasse, Sandra Dumas (production), Kate Stewart (marketing), and especially Anne Smith, who provided invaluable support from literally the beginning to the end. I also wish to thank Kathleen Byrne, Caroline Roop, and Carolyn Toomey from Argosy Publishing for their assistance in producing the final book. And last, but certainly not least, I want to thank Darren Yopyk, who provided considerable assistance in a variety of ways, including locating relevant literature, creating tables and figures, gathering statistics, finding cartoons, and buying coffee.

The book also benefitted from helpful comments from professors as well as students. I wish to acknowledge the careful and constructive feedback provided by the following professors: Elizabeth Sherwin (University of Arkansas – Little Rock), Elise Labbe (University of South Alabama), Suzanne Mazzeo (Virginia Commonwealth University), Timothy G. Heckman (Ohio University), Charles Kaiser (College of Charleston), Joan DiGiovanni (University of Arizona), David Mostofsky (Boston University), Richard J. Contrada (Rutgers University), James E. Snowden (Midwestern State University), and Catherine Stoney (Ohio State University). I also need to acknowledge my own students from Amherst College, Smith College, and the University of Massachusetts at Amherst who reviewed chapters of this book and provided much needed student feedback: Eric Ammann, Marta Baffy, Noemi Baffy, Erin Beaumont, Elana J. Bernstein, Heather Cole, Mary DuVernay, Staci Kman, Paul Larkin, Elinor Lee, Jeannie Limpert, Andrew Merle, Rebecca Norris, Hallison Putnam, Diana Rancourt, Alison Stahl, and Denise Steele.

A final thanks to Bart, for letting me have quiet writing time on the weekends and evenings and allowing me to take over not only the study but also the dining room table, and to Andrew and Robert, for napping (usually) in the afternoons so I could write and reminding me of the distinction between what seems to be important and what is truly important.

CONTENTS

CHAPTER 5
Personality   145

CHAPTER 8
Obesity and Eating Disorders   267

CHAPTER 1

Introduction

- Peyton is a first-year student at a prestigious law school. She is taking four courses and works 10 hours a week as a paralegal to help pay her tuition. Peyton is also busy applying for summer jobs and is a writer for the law review journal. Although Peyton is under pressure, she takes a yoga class three times a week and frequently gets together with friends for dinner. She feels happy and healthy.

- Phillip is a senior in high school and smokes about a pack of cigarettes a day. Although he knows that smoking causes some types of cancer, he intends to quit smoking when he starts college next year, and he doesn't really see how smoking for just a few years can be such a big deal. Most of his friends smoke, and he would feel uncomfortable being the only one at a party not smoking.

- Deirdra is 28 years old and works full-time as a cashier in a drug store. She is a single mother with two small children and has primary custody of the children—her ex-husband has the children only every other weekend. Recently Deirdra has started experiencing severe migraine headaches. Sometimes they are so debilitating that she can't drive and therefore must call in sick to work. Moreover, she had been taking a few ibuprofen tablets to help ease her headache pain, but they don't seem to have much of an effect anymore.

- Annette was diagnosed with breast cancer nearly 1 year ago. She has undergone chemotherapy for the past year and has now lost all of her hair and generally feels tired and weak. Although Annette is married and has many close friends, she feels very isolated and alone. She is uncomfortable getting undressed in front of her husband because of her embarrassment over the changes in her body, and she doubts his assurances that he continues to find her attractive. Annette has tried to talk to her friends, but often finds them steering the conversation to more uplifting topics.

- Dr. Weisz is interested in examining the effectiveness of different types of treatment for back pain. He recruits a pool of back-pain sufferers and obtains their informed consent to participate in an approved research study he has designed. He asks some patients to start a new exercise routine that focuses on increasing back strength and flexibility, and as a comparison, he gives other patients a pill that he tells them will reduce back pain. However, the pill provides no real medication—it is only a sugar pill that should have no physiological effect on pain. Much to his surprise, Dr. Weisz finds that patients in both groups show significant improvement over the next month.

Preview

What do all of these examples have in common? They all illustrate issues addressed by the field of health psychology, including the influence of social pressures on health-related behavior, the impact of stress on health, the impact of chronic diseases on psychological well-being, and the influence of psychological factors on the experience of pain. This chapter first introduces you to the field of health psychology, describes how this field has changed over time, and discusses how health psychology is related to other disciplines. Finally, it gives you a preview of coming attractions by describing the topics covered in each of the remaining chapters.

What Is Health Psychology?

The field of health psychology addresses how one's behavior can influence health, wellness, and illness in a variety of different ways (see Box 1.1). Specifically, health psychology examines how psychological factors influence the experience of stress and people's physiological reactions to stress, affect the promotion and maintenance of health, influence coping with and treating pain and disease as well as the effects of pain and disease on psychological functioning, and affect how individuals respond to health care recommendations as well as health-promotion messages (Matarazzo, 1980). As shown in Figure 1.1, these psychological factors include environmental stressors, personality factors, and social influences, which in turn influence illness and disease through their impact on physiological responses in the body as well as health-related behaviors (Adler & Matthews, 1994). Let's examine each of these factors in turn.

First, psychological factors can have a direct influence on physical health by impacting whether and how much stress a person experiences as well as the impact of stress on various physiological mechanisms in the body. Considerable research demonstrates that people who are experiencing various stressors (e.g., living through a natural disaster, caring for loved ones with Alzheimer's disease, fighting with a spouse, taking exams) show a weakened immune system (Ironson et al., 1997; Kiecolt-Glaser, Fisher et al., 1987; Kiecolt-Glaser, Glaser et al., 1987; McKinnon, Weisse, Reynolds, Bowles, & Baum, 1989). Do you sometimes develop a headache when you are feeling tense? Do you

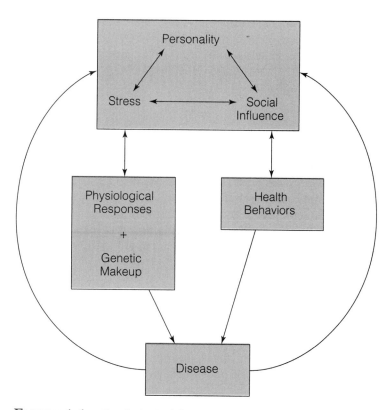

FIGURE 1.1   Psychological factors, including stress, personality, and social influences, impact people's physiological responses as well as their health behaviors, which in turn impact incidence of illness and disease. However, the relationship between psychological factors and physical health is bidirectional: physiological responses, health behaviors, and disease can also influence psychological factors.

sometimes feel nauseous before a "big game" or an important exam? These are all examples of how psychological factors can literally make people sick. But how, you might be wondering, can just taking an exam make you sick? Well, think about the typical behaviors of a college student during exam period. Many students stop exercising, eat more junk food, drink more caffeine, and get less sleep. In other words, the stress of exams leads people to engage in unhealthy behavior, which may ultimately lead to illness. However, people who are able to cope with stress effectively experience fewer health problems than those who find such experiences overwhelming. At the beginning of the chapter, I described how Peyton was experiencing a variety of challenges (e.g., applying for summer jobs, studying for law school exams, working as a paralegal) but was able to manage these stressors by taking yoga classes and spending time with friends.

Personality traits, such as optimism, hostility, and extraversion, are also associated with people's physiological responses as well as their health-related behaviors (Winett, 1995). For example, people who are high in hostility exhibit higher blood pressure and heart rate when they are in virtually any type of "competitive situation" (which could include even a game of Ping-Pong with a friend). Over time, experiencing constant high levels of physiological arousal leads to cardiovascular damage, which may explain why people who are hostile are more likely to experience heart disease (Barefoot, Dodge, Peterson, Dahlstrom, & Williams, 1989; Matthews, Owens, Kuller, Sutton-Tyrrell, & Jansen-McWilliams, 1998; Miller, Smith, Turner, Guijarro, & Hallet, 1996; Smith, 1992). On the other hand, people who are optimistic have about half as many infectious illnesses (e.g., colds, sore throats, flu) and negative physical symptoms (e.g., dizziness, blurred vision, fatigue, muscle soreness) as those who are pessimists (Peterson & Seligman, 1987; Scheier & Carver, 1985). Personality variables also influence the types of health-related behaviors people engage in on a regular basis. People who are high in hostility, for example, may ignore doctor recommendations for treatment and thereby fail to recover—or at least they recover more slowly—from illnesses.

Similarly, social factors, including social support as well as social influences, are associated with individuals' physiological reactions and health-related behaviors. Individuals with high levels of social support have lower blood pressure and a more active immune system compared to those with less support (Uchino, Cacioppo, & Kiecolt-Glaser, 1996). In turn, people who have more social support may be better able to fight off minor illnesses and avoid major ones. People who have high levels of social support may also engage in more health-promoting behavior (e.g., eating nutritiously, exercising regularly), in part because their loved ones encourage such activities. Moreover, because people learn about health behaviors from watching others' behavior, the attitudes and behaviors of family members and friends also influence health-related behavior. Children who have a parent, sibling, or friend who smokes, for example, are much more likely to start smoking themselves later on. As described at the beginning of the chapter, Phillip started smoking because many of his friends smoked, and he continues to smoke as a way of coping with stress.

Box 1.1

Health Psychology in the Real World: Did We Accomplish the Goals of Healthy People 2000?

In 1979, Surgeon General Julius Richmond established a set of specific goals that would help reduce mortality rates in the United States by 1990 (Friedrich, 2000). These goals included decreasing rates of smoking, increasing the use of seat belts, and increasing prenatal care. In 1989, these goals were revised and expanded to form the Healthy People 2000 project, which had a specific focus of improving quality of life as well as life expectancy and reducing health disparities across different groups. As shown in Table 1.1, the United States made much progress toward accomplishing some of the goals, but little (or, in some cases, no) progress in reaching other goals. What is the good news? Although only 15% of the goals have been met or exceeded, including increasing screening for cervical cancer and the wearing of seat belts, we are moving in the right direction for another 44% of the goals, which in some cases are very close to being met. For example, fewer people are smoking cigarettes and more people are exercising. On the other hand, we have moved in a negative direction on 18% of the goals. For example, the number of overweight people in the United States has increased as has the number of people without health insurance.

TABLE 1.1 *How Well Did We Accomplish the Goals of Healthy People 2000?*

Objective	Baseline (%)	Update (%)	Target (%)
More people exercising regularly	22	30	30
Fewer people overweight	26	35	20
Fewer people smoking	29	24	15
More seat belt use	42	67	85
More pregnant women with first-trimester prenatal care	76	83	90
Increase in screening for breast cancer (age 50 and over)	25	64	60
Increase in screening for colon cancer (age 50 and over)	27	35	50
Higher immunization levels (ages 19–35 months)	55	80	90
Fewer people without health insurance (under age 65)	15.7	16.6	0

Note: Although we made great strides in accomplishing some of the nation's health goals, in other areas little change has occurred (Centers for Disease Control, 2003).

Third, psychological factors influence the development and treatment of pain and chronic and terminal disease (Winett, 1995). A number of psychological factors, including response to environmental stressors, personality, and internalization of social modeling, are associated with the experience of pain. As described at the beginning of the chapter, Deirdra's experience of stress led to the development of severe migraine headaches. Psychological factors are also associated with the development of some types of chronic diseases, such as coronary heart disease, cancer, and AIDS. After all, psychological factors influence people's health-related behaviors, which in turn can lead to the prevention or development of such chronic and terminal conditions. A heterosexual college student who believes that only IV drug users and gay men are at risk for HIV infection, for example, is unlikely to use condoms for the prevention of sexually transmitted disease. Psychological factors can also influence the effectiveness of various treatments to manage pain as well as chronic and terminal disease. Many treatments are based in psychological principles, such as reinforcement and social influence. As described at the beginning of the chapter, Dr. Weisz found that people's expectations about the effectiveness of a particular treatment can actually lead to improvements in their physical health and well-being.

Moreover, the experience of pain as well as chronic and terminal disease, not surprisingly, can influence psychological well-being. A person who is constantly in physical pain, for example, may feel depressed and anxious, avoid many social settings, and even withdraw from close family members and friends. People who experience chronic diseases, such as diabetes, cancer, and coronary heart disease, may experience similar negative emotions. For example, at the beginning of the Chapter I described how Annette's struggle with breast cancer led her to feel awkward about engaging in intimate behavior with her husband and has made her feel isolated from her friends. Finally, and not surprisingly, many people who are diagnosed with a terminal illness experience depression and anxiety, and survivors often experience lower levels of psychological and physical well-being.

Health psychology examines how psychological factors influence whether people take steps to identify and treat illnesses early, whether they adhere to medical recommendations, and how they respond to health-promotion messages (Winett, 1995). Behavior that involves detecting illness at an early stage as a way of reducing the illness's potential effects is called *secondary prevention* and can include checking cholesterol, performing a breast self-exam, and following an insulin-taking regimen in the case of diabetes. Secondary prevention is very important because in many cases people have more treatment options and a better likelihood of curing their problem if it is caught early. For example, a woman who practices regular self-exams and finds a small cancerous lump in her breast may have the option of having this lump removed in a simple operation before cancer spreads to other parts of her body, whereas a woman who is found to have a lump in her breast only after the cancer has spread has unknowingly delayed treatment, decreased her treatment options, and will undergo much more difficult treatment, such as invasive surgery (possible removal of both breasts), chemotherapy, and/or radiation. However, psychological factors such as fear and anxiety influence whether someone engages in prevention and health-promotion behavior. For some people, getting tested for HIV is simply too frightening to contemplate (although in reality, ignorance is rarely bliss).

Tertiary prevention refers to actions taken to minimize or slow the damage caused by an illness or disease, such as taking medicine, engaging in regular physical therapy, and following a recommended diet (Winett, 1995). Patients with chronic conditions, such as cancer, AIDS, and heart disease, need to regularly manage their illnesses, cope with pain, and comply with medical regimens. However, some studies suggest that as many as 93% of patients fail to adhere to recommended treatments (Taylor, 1990). When they are sick, why do some people follow doctor recommendations and others ignore these messages? Psychological factors, including people's thoughts about their symptoms and illnesses as well as interactions with health care providers and the medical system in general, influence how people react to treatment plans, and hence whether they recover from illness. For example, think about what happens when a person is hospitalized—they are staying in a room, possibly with one or more strangers, and many different people come into the room at literally any hour of the day or night. They are wearing very little, must eat when food is delivered, and can have visitors only during certain times. Does this sound relaxing? Or, as some research is starting to show, might some aspects of the hospital environment actually impair recovery?

What Factors Led to the Development of Health Psychology?

Health psychology is a relatively new field. In 1973, a task force was created by the American Psychological Association (APA) to study the potential for psychology's role in health research. Although the final report of this task force in 1976 found little evidence that psychologists were examining health-related issues, the task force noted that the potential for psychological factors to influence health was clear (American Psychological Association, 1976). In turn, this report led to the creation in 1978 of a Health Psychology division, with the goal of providing "a scientific, educational, and professional organization for psychologists interested in (or working in) areas at one or another of the interfaces of medicine and psychology" (Matarazzo, 1984, p. 31). The development of this division was followed in 1982 by the creation of the journal *Health Psychology*, in which many research articles on issues in health psychology are published. This section examines various factors that led to the development of the exciting new field of health psychology.

The Nature of Illnesses Has Changed

Until the early 1900s, most people in the United States died from acute infectious diseases, such as tuberculosis, smallpox, measles, pneumonia, and typhoid fever (see Table 1.2; Grob, 1983). These diseases were caused by viruses or bacteria and were typically the result of eating or drinking contaminated water or food, interacting with infected people, or living in unhealthy conditions. Moreover, although people sought treatment for these disorders, doctors often had little knowledge or resources to treat or even manage these illnesses.

Today, in contrast, relatively few people (at least in the United States) die from the major infectious diseases that previously caused such high rates of death. What led to the decrease in the incidence of such diseases? First, changes in technology and lifestyle, such as the development of sewage treatment plants, water purification efforts, and better overall nutrition, led to better overall hygiene. Second, because of the development of vaccines and antibiotics, very few people contract (and even fewer die from) diseases such as smallpox, tuberculosis, and polio (see Figure 1.2). Most children are vaccinated against many of the major infectious diseases, and other diseases can be effectively treated with antibiotics.

The major health problems in the United States today are caused by chronic conditions, such as cancer, cardiovascular disease, obesity, diabetes, and pulmonary diseases, which are caused at least in part by behavioral, psychosocial, and cultural factors (Centers for Disease Control, 2003; see Table 1.2). According to one estimate, about half of the deaths in the United States each year have preventable causes (McGinnis & Foege, 1993). So, what are these preventable causes? Well, tobacco use contributes to about 400,000 deaths per year (19% of all deaths); poor diet and physical inactivity contribute to another 300,000 (14% of all deaths); and other factors, such as alcohol use, unsafe sexual behavior, drug use, and motor vehicles accidents, contribute to another

TABLE 1.2   *The 10 Leading Causes of Death in 1900 versus 2000*

Major Causes of Death In 1900	In 2000
1. Cardiovascular diseases (strokes, heart disease)	1. Cardiovascular diseases (strokes, heart disease)
2. Influenza and pneumonia	2. Cancer
3. Tuberculosis	3. Cerebrovascular disease
4. Gastritis	4. Chronic obstructive pulmonary disease
5. Accidents	5. Accidents
6. Cancer	6. Influenza and pneumonia
7. Diphtheria	7. Diabetes
8. Typhoid fever	8. Suicide
9. Measles	9. Nephritis
10. Chronic liver disease and cirrhosis	10. Chronic liver disease and cirrhosis

Note: In 1900, many people died from infectious diseases; today many of the leading causes of death are chronic conditions that are at least partially caused by lifestyle choices (Centers for Disease Control, 2003).

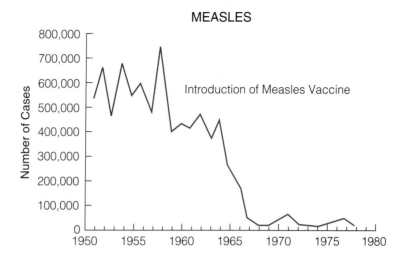

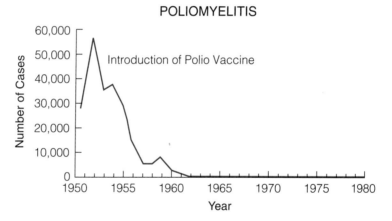

FIGURE 1.2 As these figures clearly illustrate, rates of polio and measles decreased dramatically following the development of vaccinations (data from Matarazzo, 1982).

200,000. We know a lot about factors that lead to heart disease, the leading cause of death in the United States—smoking, high-fat diet, physical inactivity, obesity, and alcohol use (all behavioral choices) as well as psychological variables (e.g., stress) and environmental factors (e.g., social support). Similarly, the major cause of lung cancer—which is the leading cause of cancer deaths for men and women—is cigarette smoking (Ginsberg, Kris, & Armstrong, 1993). Smoking not only contributes to heart disease and cancer, but also to strokes (the third leading cause of death), obstructive pulmonary disorder (the fifth leading cause of death), pneumonia (the sixth leading cause of death), and diabetes (the seventh leading cause of death). In sum, behavioral choices are a major contributor to most of the leading causes of death.

Because of this fact, principles of psychology can be used to try to change people's behavior, such as to increase health-promoting behavior (e.g., wearing seat belts, engaging in regular exercise, using sunscreen) and decrease health-damaging behavior (e.g., smoking, drinking and driving, eating a fatty diet). Psychological principles can be used to promote *primary prevention* behavior, namely, preventing or diminishing the severity of illnesses and diseases. Would influencing changes in everyday behaviors really impact life expectancy? In a word, yes. If the entire population of smokers quit, there would be a 25% reduction in cancer deaths and 350,000 fewer heart attacks each year (Taylor, 1990). Similarly, a 10% weight loss in men ages 35 to 55 would lead to a 20% decrease in coronary artery disease as well as decreases in the rates of stroke, cancer, diabetes, and heart attacks. Yet, influencing peoples' behavior is complex, as you will see throughout this text. Take, for example, disease prevention behavior. Although one of the major ways people can prevent disease is by getting vaccinations against contagious diseases, 24% of American preschool-age children do not have full immunization against currently controllable diseases, and this percentage is even higher in African American and Hispanic children (Centers for Disease Control, 2003; see Photo 1.1). As physician John Knowles (1977) noted, "Over 99 percent of us are born healthy and made sick as a result of personal misbehavior and environmental conditions. The solution to the problems of ill health in modern American society involves individual respon-

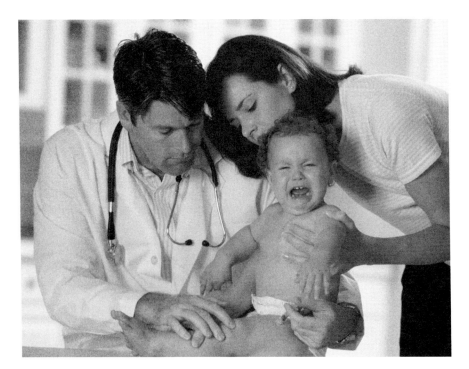

PHOTO 1.1   Although getting vaccinations is one of the most effective ways of preventing illness, a sizeable minority of infants in the United States are not vaccinated against all diseases for which vaccines are currently available.

sibility, in the first instance, and social responsibility through public legislation and private volunteer efforts, in the second instance" (p. 58).

This shift in the pattern of illnesses from acute or infectious diseases to chronic conditions has focused attention on psychological factors related to the treatment and management of such diseases. Although many chronic conditions cannot be cured, people can often live with them for many years. Health psychologists can therefore contribute to the design of treatment programs that help people manage these illnesses, such as ones that encourage patients with heart disease to adopt healthier eating habits and to stop smoking.

The Biomedical Model Is Unable to Fully Account for Health

Another reason for the gain in popularity of health psychology is the failure of the biomedical model to explain many phenomena of health and illness. The biomedical model, which was formed in the 19th and 20th centuries, proposes that illnesses are caused by physical entities or attributes, such as viruses and bacteria, injuries, or biochemical imbalances (Engel, 1977; Schwartz, 1982). According to this perspective, physical health is completely separate from psychological health—the body is a physical entity and the mind is a psychological/mental/spiritual entity, and these operate completely separately. For example, the biomedical model explains a heart attack as caused by characteristics that are physical in nature, such as the blockage of arteries, tissue damage, and so forth, but it ignores the impact of psychological factors, such as hostility and stress, and their influence on the development of physical symptoms. According to this perspective, people must seek medical treatment (e.g., drugs, surgery, chemotherapy) to cure or manage the illness. This model also focuses on disease, not health.

Although the biomedical model has led to a number of benefits for our society, including advancements in immunology, public health policy, pathology, and surgery, increasingly evidence is showing that biological factors alone cannot account for health. First, and as described previously, psychological and behavioral factors are associated with the development of many of the leading causes of deaths such as cancer and heart disease. People with certain personality traits, such as negative affect and hostility, are more likely to develop a variety of physical problems, including ulcers, headaches, asthma, and arthritis (Friedman & Booth-Kewley, 1987a); college students who are in the stress-inducing exam period have weakened immune systems (Jemmott & Magliore, 1988). The biomedical model fails to take into account how psychological factors, such as personality, cognitive beliefs, social support, and the relationship between the patient and the health care practitioner, can influence development of and recovery from illness and disease. Why do *placebos*, drugs or treatments that influence health outcomes purely because of people's expectations of them, lead to improvement of symptoms in a sizeable portion of patients? Why do surgery patients who get more visitors leave the hospital sooner? These are just some of the questions that the biomedical model really cannot answer.

Given these failures of the biomedical model, researchers have turned instead to a model of health that includes biological as well as psychological

Box 1.2

Health Psychology in the Real World: Comparing the Biopsychosocial and Biomedical Models

The biopsychosocial model was developed in the late 1970s and posits that health is affected by both biology and social factors (Engel, 1977, 1980). In this perspective, the physical body is seen as only one aspect of a person; other aspects, such as personality, family, society, also influence the person and his or her health. In contrast, the biomedical model, which was formed in the 19th and 20th centuries, describes health as a function only of physical attributes and sees physical health as completely separate from psychological health. Let's take as an example, a patient, Melanie, who arrives at her doctor's office complaining of recurring heart pain. A physician utilizing the biomedical model would focus almost entirely on physical causes of such pain and would rely primarily on diagnostic tests, such as heart monitor results, temperature, pulse, and so forth, to determine the cause of this symptom. Although the physician might ask Melanie a few questions (when did you last eat? how long have you felt this pain?), the physician would base the diagnosis on the (more objective) test results. Once a physical diagnosis is established, the physician prescribes a treatment regimen for the patient. In contrast, a physician using the biopsychosocial model might start by gathering personal data, such as symptoms, activities, recent behaviors, and social/family relationships. The physician might, for example, ask Melanie whether she was experiencing any particular stressors at home or work, or whether she had experienced significant life changes in the past few months (e.g., loss of job, death of loved one). Although the physician would also use standard diagnostic tests, more emphasis would be put on eliciting psychological factors that could contribute to the symptoms. During this information-gathering phase, the physician also provides information about what is happening and for what reasons to minimize the stress on Melanie of the various medical procedures. Once a diagnosis is made, the physician discusses the treatment options with Melanie, and she has a voice in selecting her own treatment plan. The physician not only works with Melanie to develop a treatment plan, but pays attention to aspects of Melanie's daily life that could influence her adherence to the plan.

factors (see Box 1.2). This model, the biopsychosocial model, views health as determined by individual, social, and cultural factors (Engel, 1977; Schwartz, 1982). As described by Engel:

> To provide a basis for understanding the determinants of disease and arriving at rational treatments and patterns of health care, a medical model must also take into account the patient, the social context in

which he lives and the complementary system devised by society to deal with the disruptive effects of illness, that is, the physician role and the health care system. This requires a biopsychosocial model. (p. 132)

The biopsychosocial model therefore acknowledges that biological factors can and do influence health and illness, and social, cultural, and psychological factors also exert an effect. This model is holistic in that it considers the mind and body as inherently connected. The biopsychosocial model views health as an interactive system in which biological factors (e.g., genetics, physiology) interact with psychological factors (e.g., personality, cognition) and social factors (e.g., community, family, media; Engel, 1980).

Health Care Costs Have Risen Dramatically

Health care costs have risen sharply in the last four decades, therefore there is an increasing focus on the more cost-effective approach of disease prevention. The U.S. population currently spends nearly $1,300 billion a year on health care, which represents 13% of the gross domestic product (Centers for Disease Control, 2003). In contrast, health care costs represented only 5.1% of the gross domestic product in 1960 (see Cartoon 1.1).

One reason for the rise in health care costs is the increase in life expectancy that has occurred over the last 100 years. In the early 1900s, people lived to an

"And, in our continuing effort to minimize surgical costs, I'll be hitting you over the head and tearing you open with my bare hands."

CARTOON 1.1   The increasing cost of health care is one of the factors that has led to the greater interest in the field of health psychology.

Source: ©The New Yorker Collection 1997. Danny Shanahan from cartoonbank.com

average age of 47.3 years; today the mean life expectancy is about 76 years, resulting in part from the drop in infant mortality that has occurred over the last 50 years (Centers for Disease Control, 2003; see Figure 1.3). People today must bear the financial burden of paying for health care into their elder years, when chronic diseases requiring extended (and costly) treatments are likely to occur. Also, a wider variety of treatment options are now available to manage chronic diseases. Today, people are living with conditions that they would have died from in the past.

Another factor contributing to the rising cost of health care is the increasing technological advancements, such as new surgical techniques, chemotherapy, ultrasound, and genetic screening procedures, which require specialized equipment and are very expensive. In fact, while I was writing this textbook, doctors successfully implanted an artificial heart in a patient for the first time (see Photo 1.2). Although these treatments are partially responsible for the increase in life expectancy, they have also greatly increased the cost of health care.

Therefore, there is considerable interest in using principles of psychology to decrease such care costs. So, how can we do this? First, health psychologists try to prevent health problems from developing, for instance, by encouraging healthy eating and the use of constructive methods of managing stress. Psychological principles of persuasion, for example, are commonly used to promote condom use and to prevent smoking (Flay, 1987; Kelly et al., 1991). Similarly, persuasive messages can be used to help people detect health problems earlier, when there are more treatment options available and these options are less expensive. For example, researchers have shown that describing the costs of not conducting breast self-exams is a more effective motivator to women than describing the benefits of conducting such exams (Meyerowitz & Chaiken, 1987). Psychological principles can also be used to help people manage pain and recover from illness. Because research indicates that providing patients with

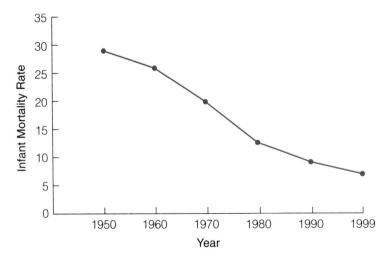

FIGURE 1.3 Infant mortality rates have dropped substantially in the last 50 years (Centers for Disease Control, 2003).

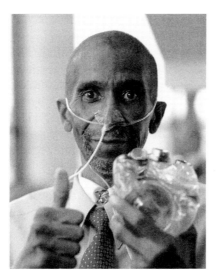

PHOTO 1.2 In the summer of 2001, doctors successfully implanted an artificial heart in a living patient for the first time.

specific psychological strategies to cope with pain leads to use of less pain medicine and faster recovery, some hospitals now provide patients with such training (Bandura, O'Leary, Taylor, Gauthier, & Gossard, 1987). Similarly, while in the hospital, married people who receive more frequent visits from their spouses use less pain medication and show faster recovery times from surgery compared to those who receive few visits (Kulik & Mahler, 1989). Thus, addressing psychological issues can decrease the cost of medical care significantly. All of these psychologically-based strategies for improving health can lead to decreases in health problems and/or minimize the pain and disability caused by such problems, and thereby reduce health care costs.

The Development of New Technology

Although the development of various types of new technology has led to better overall health and longevity, it has also raised new concerns. For example, we now have the capacity to test fetuses for many genetic disorders, including cystic fibrosis, Down's syndrome, and sickle cell anemia. As a result, parents are sometimes faced with very difficult ethical decisions—should they abort a fetus with a life-threatening or highly disabling condition? Other advances in genetics research allow us to identify the particular gene that causes or contributes to the development of a particular disease. For example, there is a gene that causes Huntington's disease and another gene that indicates a woman is at increased risk of developing breast cancer. But what are the psychological consequences of finding out at age 20 or 25 that you are highly likely to (or in some cases, will definitely) contract a fatal disease? Health psychologists are currently conducting research on precisely these issues.

The advances in medical technology also mean that in some cases people are now able to live with serious conditions that in the past would have killed them. For example, infants who are born two or three months premature now have a very good chance of surviving, whereas even 10 years ago their odds were significantly worse. Similarly, people who have suffered a major accident that in earlier years would have led to certain death can sometimes be kept alive through medical means (but we must then consider their quality of life). Family members are forced to make very difficult decisions about the patients' likelihood of recovery as well as whether he or she would prefer to die than to live under such difficult circumstances. Once again, health psychologists are examining how people can best make such decisions and how to help people cope with these most challenging ethical dilemmas.

The Meaning of Health Has Changed

Over the last 100 years, the meaning of health has changed in several ways. We used to think of health as simply the absence of illness or disease, but we now see health and wellness in a much broader way. This change in perspective is also reflected in a relatively new focus within psychology on studying the predictors of happiness and well-being, as opposed to the predictors of depression and poor health (Seligman & Csikszentmihalyi, 2000). The newly developed field of *positive psychology* examines how to help people achieve physical and psychological well-being, including researching the predictors of life satisfaction, altruism, forgiveness, and hope. The World Health Organization now defines *health* as "a state of complete physical, mental and social well-being, and not merely the absence of disease and illness" (World Health Organization, 1964). So, people who are physiologically healthy but who are very depressed might be viewed as unhealthy under the new definition. Similarly, most college students seem healthy—generally they exercise with some regularity and exhibit few obvious signs of disease/serious illness. But can they be viewed as healthy if you look at their eating habits or, even worse, their drinking habits? By the new standard, many college students suddenly seem like they are in worse health. Along the same lines, consider someone who has no obvious signs of illness or disease, but who has a mother and two aunts who have died of breast cancer? Is she healthy?

People in different cultures vary in how they describe health and even in the behaviors that they view as "healthy." People vary considerably, for example, in how they interpret and express physical symptoms, as well as in their willingness to rely on medical professionals as opposed to a "lay referral system" of family and friends for advice regarding medical issues (Bates, Edwards, & Anderson, 1993; Burnum, Timbers, & Hough, 1984; Landrine & Klonoff, 1994; Sanders et al., 1992). Even within a given culture, people differ in how they define health. For example, I don't eat meat, which many physicians see as healthy because eating meat is associated with heart disease and high cholesterol. However, my relatives in Georgia and Alabama regard my vegetarian diet as a sign of unhealthy behavior, and they worry that I am not getting enough iron and protein. In sum, researchers now see health as a continuum, ranging from a healthy level of wellness on one end and illness and even death on the other, and they have found that this continuum is viewed in different ways by different people (Antonovsky, 1987).

How Is Health Psychology Related to Other Disciplines?

Although health psychology is a relatively new discipline, the belief that psychological states can influence physical health has been around for some time (as described in Box 1.3). For example, Sigmund Freud's classic work on phobias and hysteria describes physical problems as manifestations of unconscious symptoms as opposed to a true medical disorder. According to his work on conversion hysteria, Freud believed that unconscious conflicts could lead to various physical symptoms, including paralysis, sudden loss of hearing and sight, and muscle tremors (see Photo 1.3).

Several branches of medicine have also described the role of psychological factors in influencing physical health. *Psychosomatic medicine*, which developed in the 1930s, studies how emotional, social, and psychological factors influence the development and progression of illness (Lipowski, 1986). For example, researchers might study how psychological factors such as anxiety, depression, and stress might lead to physical problems such as ulcers, migraine headaches, arthritis, and asthma. The field of *medical psychology* focuses on teaching physicians how to interact with patients in a tactful and constructive way in order

PHOTO 1.3 Freud's theory about the role of unconscious conflict in leading to physical symptoms is clearly based in the theory that physical health is influenced by psychological factors.

Box 1.3

How Have Views of Health Evolved over Time?

Although health psychology is a relatively new field, the idea that the mind influences the body is a very old one—in fact, historically, most cultures have recognized some type of a connection between how we think, feel, and behave and our health (Ehrewnwald, 1976). Many early cultures viewed illness and disease as caused by evil spirits—and there is some evidence that early medical procedures, at least in some cases, involved such methods as drilling holes in people's skulls to "let out the evil spirits." As early as 400 B.C. Hippocrates described health as the interaction between mind and body, stating, "Health depends on a state of equilibrium among the various internal factors which govern the operation of the body and the mind; the equilibrium in turn is reached only when man lives in harmony with his environment" (Dubus, 1959, p. 114). In line with this view, Hippocrates' humoral theory described disease as caused by an imbalance in the different fluids he believed were circulating in the body: phlegm, blood, black bile, and yellow bile. Despite the faulty theory of the four humors, the emphasis on the interrelation between mind and body is clear.

However, during the 17th century this holistic view of health changed, and for the first time health was seen as purely caused by bodily processes. What led to this change? First, René Descartes's development of the doctrine of mind–body dualism, namely, the view that the mind and body are two separate entities with little interaction, led to the view that the body was basically a machine. Disease was seen as resulting from the physical breakdown of the machine, and it was believed that the physician's job was to fix the machine. Second, advances in other scientific fields such as physics led to the view that science could be used to determine precise physical principles. For example, Isaac Newton's demonstration of an apple falling to the earth because of gravitational pull led other theorists to believe that all physical phenomena could be observed with such ease and explained by concrete laws. Third, various scientific advances, including Giovanni Battista Morgagni's work in autopsy, Rudolf Virchow's work in pathology, and Louis Pasteur's work in bacteriology, led to a focus on how microorganisms cause disease. All of these factors facilitated the focus on a biomedical model.

to best diagnose and manage their illness. Researchers in this discipline might examine how to handle patients who are moody or those who are reluctant to seek or follow medical care. Finally, *behavioral medicine* is an interdisciplinary field that developed in the 1970s and that focuses on the integration of behavioral and biomedical sciences. Specifically, behavioral medicine focuses on developing and applying behavioral techniques to the treatment, management, and rehabilitation of patients (Gentry, 1984). Such techniques are used widely to help people overcome various types of health-damaging behaviors. Correspondingly, the discipline of *behavioral health*, a subdiscipline of behavioral medicine, emphasizes enhancing health and preventing disease in currently healthy people (Matarazzo, 1980). Researchers in this field focus on general strategies of health promotion.

Health psychology is related not only to medical fields, but also to the disciplines of sociology and anthropology. *Medical sociology* examines how social relationships influence illness, cultural and societal reactions to illness, and the organization of health care services (Adler & Stone, 1979). For example, researchers in this field might examine the effects of social stress on health and illness, how attitudes and behaviors influence health and illness, and the negative consequences of labeling someone a "patient." The field of *medical anthropology* examines the differences in how health and illness are viewed by people in different cultures. Cultures, in fact, vary tremendously in how they define health, how they view disease, and, in turn, how they treat illness. Even within a single culture, such as the United States, people in different subcultures vary in how they view health and illness. Certain religious groups, for example, believe illnesses are caused by mental and spiritual processes and they rely entirely on prayer and other nonmedical interventions to treat disease.

What Lies Ahead

As you know by now, Chapter 1 provides a relatively brief description of the field of health psychology as well as the factors that led to its development. Chapters 2 and 3 provide valuable background information needed for understanding and evaluating research in health psychology: Chapter 2 focuses on different research methods used within health psychology, and Chapter 3 describes various theories used in health psychology. Chapter 4 describes the impact of psychological factors on the experience and management of stress. Chapters 5 and 6 examine the impact of two distinct types of psychological factors, personality (Chapter 5) and social support (Chapter 6), on psychological and physical well-being, as well as the potential explanations for this association. Chapters 7 and 8 focus specifically on the impact of psychological factors on health-related behaviors that are often of particular interest to college students—alcohol use, smoking, and eating. Chapters 9, 10, and 11 examine the bidirectional relationship between psychological factors and pain, chronic disease, and terminal illness. Issues of health care utilization and adherence as well as the design of effective health-promotion messages are discussed in Chapters 12 and 13. Finally, Chapter 14 summarizes the main contributions of health psychology, several "hot topics" within this field, and various career options in health-related areas.

Thought Questions

1. Your roommate has started to have frequent headaches. How would the biomedical model explain and treat his problem? How would the biopsychosocial model explain it?

2. Describe two ways that psychological factors can be effective in decreasing health care costs.

3. Your sister has no physical health problems, but is quite depressed—she has trouble getting out of bed, has a poor appetite, and finds little pleasure in spending time with friends. Your brother is a varsity athlete in high school and is in overall good physical health, however, when the team is celebrating their victory most Saturday nights, he typically gets very drunk and engages in unprotected sex. Are your siblings healthy? Why or why not?

4. Describe two distinct factors that led to the development of the field of health psychology.

5. Describe the differences between primary prevention, secondary prevention, and tertiary prevention.

CHAPTER 2

Research Methods

- Dr. Phillips works in the Student Health Center at the College of Connecticut. She has noticed that the health center is pretty quiet for most of the semester, but then gets very busy during midterm week and final exam week. She is interested in examining whether students tend to get sick during exam periods, so she decides to call local drug stores to see whether their sales records indicate that they sell more cold and cough medicine during exam weeks than at other times during the semester.

- Dr. Adams is a cardiologist in San Francisco who sees many patients with coronary heart disease. In talking to his patients, he observes that most of them are very busy: they are often late for their appointments, constantly glance at their watches during office visits, and are quite rude to his receptionist if they are kept waiting. He decides to give his patients a survey to see whether those who are more hostile and time conscious have more severe symptoms of heart disease.

- Brandon and Brenda are student health educators at California University and are trying to decrease the amount of alcohol use on their campus. They want to determine what types of education would be most effective in accomplishing this goal, so they design two different workshops on alcohol abuse. Brenda gives one workshop to students who live in 5 dorms on the east side of campus, and Brandon gives the other workshop to students who live in 5 dorms on the west side of campus. They then plan to measure how much students who live in these 10 dorms drink during the rest of the semester to see which educational workshop was more effective.

- Dr. Ashley is a psychologist who treats patients with eating disorders. She has noticed that many of the women she sees have attended a private high school, and she wonders whether the distinct environment of a private school leads to eating disorders. To examine this question, she obtains their informed consent and then gives surveys to students at several local private and public high schools so that she can compare the rate of anorexia and bulimia at each type of school.

- Dr. Webb, who works at a large pharmaceutical company, has created a drug he thinks will help people cope with hangovers. Before he can market the drug, he must test whether it really works specifically to manage hangovers. After obtaining the necessary approval from the Institutional Review Board of his company, he puts advertisements in several liquor stores in his town to recruit people to try this drug. All people who respond are told that this is a study of new drugs, and that they may or may not receive actual medication. To half of the people who call, Dr. Webb then gives his new drug to take the next time they experience a hangover. He gives the other half a drug that is actually just a sugar pill. He then measures the number of symptoms people in each group report to see whether his drug is effective in treating hangovers.

Preview

This chapter covers a variety of topics related to conducting and evaluating research in health psychology. First, we review the steps involved in conducting research in general. We then describe five specific research methods commonly used in health psychology, with a particular focus on the strengths and weaknesses of each approach. Because health psychology addresses issues in psychology as well as in medicine, it has no distinct methodology, but instead consists of research methods used in both fields. These methods include observational or naturalistic methods, surveys, experiments, quasi-experiments, and clinical studies. Part of the challenge of conducting research is choosing which method is best suited to answer a particular question (and, in fact, most questions can be answered using a variety of different methods). The chapter ends with a description of the ethical issues involved in conducting research in this field, including the specific issues involved in conducting research with animals.

What Is the Scientific Method?

Health psychology is an empirical science, and hence research in this field is based in the scientific method (see Figure 2.1). The general goals of scientific research are to describe a phenomenon, make predictions about it, and explain why it happens. All research in health psychology as well as in other scientific fields starts with a question. Sometimes researchers form these questions based on what they observe in the world. For example, you might notice that you always seem to get a cold right after exam period. Sometimes researchers form questions based on intuition or a "gut feeling." For example, you might have a feeling that people who are happier tend to get sick less often than those who are depressed. These are both examples of *hypotheses*, which are testable predictions about the conditions under which an event will occur.

In other cases researchers generate hypotheses to test a specific *theory*, an organized set of principles used to explain observed phenomena. Although hypotheses are specific predictions about the association between two events (such as exam period and illness, for example), they do not explain how or why these two events are connected. Theories provide potential explanations for particular phenomena, and therefore generate specific ideas for future research. For example, you could have a theory that students don't take care of themselves well during exam period (e.g., they don't sleep enough, don't eat balanced meals), and these poor health behaviors in turn lead to illness. And if you had this theory, you'd be right (as you'll see in Chapter 4).

Once you have formed the particular question that you will attempt to answer through experimentation, you need to form an *operational definition* of how you will study this problem. For example, you need to decide how you will classify illness (is it sneezing and coughing? Is it a diagnosed medical health problem?) and how you will classify exam period (Is it only the time during final exams? Or the time before any test?). Researchers can define their variables in very different ways, which in turn can influence the findings, so it's important to standardize definitions.

Next, you *collect data*. Data could be collected in a number of different ways, including by observation, surveys, or experiments. For example, you could ask people about various symptoms they are experiencing at the beginning of the semester and then ask them the same questions again during exam week. Alternatively, you could track the number of students who visit the health center during the beginning of the semester and then at the end of the semester. If you are really adventurous, you could go to local stores and count how many people standing in line are buying cold medicine or go through students' trash cans and count used tissues!

After the data is collected, the next step is to *analyze the data*. This step is often one of the most exciting parts of conducting research because you get to find out the answers to your questions and write up those responses. (Although issues of data analysis are not covered in this textbook, you can learn more about different approaches to analyzing research findings by taking a

1. Specify a problem or hypothesis.

2. Form an operational definition.

3. Collect data.

4. Analyze data.

5. Form a theory.

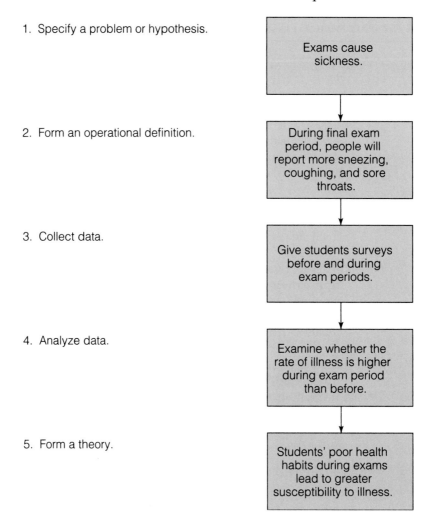

Exams cause sickness.

During final exam period, people will report more sneezing, coughing, and sore throats.

Give students surveys before and during exam periods.

Examine whether the rate of illness is higher during exam period than before.

Students' poor health habits during exams lead to greater susceptibility to illness.

FIGURE 2.1   These are the steps in the research process.

statistics class.) This is my favorite part of conducting research because I get to see whether my hypothesis is right.

The next step in the research process is developing or revising a *theory* based on the findings of the research. If your data supports what you predicted in your hypothesis, you may decide to develop a theory to explain what you found. In other cases your findings may provide additional support for a theory, which gives you confidence that the theory is indeed accurate. However, all researchers sometimes get findings that are unexpected. When this happens, the findings may lead to a revision of the hypothesis or theory, which then of course must be tested again in another research study.

What Are Observational or Naturalistic Methods?

Observational or *naturalistic methods* are used to describe and measure people's and/or animals' behavior in everyday situations. Researchers observe behavior and record some type of systematic measurement of that behavior. The sociologist Emile Durkheim (1951) conducted naturalistic research by examining the records of people who had committed suicide between 1841 and 1872. He found that suicide was more frequent in people who were single rather than married and was more common during the week than on weekends. Through this investigation, he hypothesized that alienation from others was a predictor of suicide.

Epidemiologists, who study how disease occurs or spreads in a population, often use observational methods (Lilienfield & Lilienfield, 1980). Epidemiologists employ two measures: *incidence*, defined as the frequency of new cases of a disease, and *prevalence*, defined as the proportion of a population that has a particular disease. These rates are measured by dividing the number of people in a given population (e.g., those at risk) by those who have the disease (to calculate the prevalence) or those who have developed the disease in a set period of time (to find the incidence). Some diseases, such as asthma, may be very prevalent (e.g., many people in a population have asthma) but have a relatively low incidence (e.g., because new cases do not occur very frequently). On the other hand, other diseases, such as the flu, may have relatively low prevalence (e.g., not many people in a given community have the flu) but have a high incidence, at least at some point during the year (e.g., flu cases are frequently diagnosed in the winter, but people do recover). After assessing the incidence and prevalence of a given disease, epidemiologists then try to examine different behaviors and lifestyles that might lead to the development of a particular disorder or disease. For example, epidemiology studies first noted the relationship between smoking and lung cancer as well as the relationship between Type A behavior and coronary heart disease.

Some researchers use *naturalistic* or *participant observation*, in which they observe a group's behavior and interactions and rate them in various ways. For example, if you were interested in examining the association between obesity and activity level in children, you might observe children at a playground and, after operationally defining the variables, count the amount of physical exertion obese versus nonobese children engaged in (e.g., running, climbing, throwing). If you found that obese children were less active than nonobese children, based upon further analysis, you might conclude that there is a link between activity and obesity. Researchers can also collect naturalistic data without directly observing people's behavior. For example, instead of asking people how much alcohol they drank in the past week, you could, after gaining permission, count the number of beer cans in their garbage (see Photo 2.1). In one study on the factors leading to infection with the common cold researchers gathered and weighed used tissues as a way of measuring mucus produced by subjects (Cohen, Doyle, Skoner, Rabin, & Gwaltney, 1997).

PHOTO 2.1   Counting the number of beer cans and bottles in recycling bins and trash bins is one way to examine alcohol consumption using a naturalistic method.

Another type of observational approach is *archival research* in which researchers use already-recorded behavior, such as divorce rates, disease rates, and death rates. If you were interested in examining whether divorced people die younger than those who are married, you could examine obituaries and note the age of people who died as well as whether they were married. At the beginning of this chapter I described Dr. Phillips's research on testing the link between exam time and illness through gathering drug store records—this is a good example of archival research. In Chapter 5 we examine a clever archival study in which researchers examined newspaper quotes from famous baseball players to form theories about the players' personalities and then measured the players' life expectancies (Peterson & Seligman, 1987).

Finally, some researchers use the *case report* or *case study* to form hypotheses and theories. This research technique relies on studying one or more individuals in great depth to determine the causes of the person's behavior and to predict behavior in others who are similar. Some of you may be familiar with Sigmund Freud's famous descriptions of his patients, such as Dora and "Little Hans," who suffered from psychological difficulties (Freud, 1963). Freud wrote detailed descriptions of his patients' experiences and dreams, and then examined these descriptions to form theories about the causes of their psychological problems. As described in Box 2.1, researchers first determined the existence and transmission of the AIDS virus through case reports.

Although naturalistic or observational methods have many advantages, such approaches also have serious limitations. One problem with the observational approach is that the presence of the observer is likely to influence subjects' behavior. Specifically, people are likely to behave differently when

Box 2.1

Research Focus—The Start of the AIDS Epidemic

The first documented cases of a strange new syndrome were reported in the *Morbidity and Mortality Weekly Report* (*MMWR*) of June 5, 1981 (Foege, 1983). Five young men in Los Angeles were treated for Pneumocystis carinii pneumonia, a rare type of pneumonia that typically affects those with suppressed immune systems. These previously healthy men had developed severe symptoms, including nausea, weight loss, night sweats, and general tiredness. Interestingly, all of these men were homosexuals. At just about the same time, doctors in New York City diagnosed a rare skin cancer, Kaposi's sarcoma, in 20 gay men. Given these unusual cases affecting a particular population, a task force was created by the Centers for Disease Control to interview all patients with these symptoms to determine what factors might have led to these illnesses. By the fall of 1981, epidemiologists determined that patients with these diseases reported having many sexual partners. Researchers then hypothesized that some type of disease was spreading in the gay population, possibly through sexual contact.

Although the first cases of this strange type of pneumonia were found in gay men, doctors soon began seeing similar symptoms in other populations. Doctors in New York noticed similar symptoms in heterosexual men and women who used intravenous drugs. State health departments in New York and New Jersey also reported finding symptoms in prisoners. Nearly 1 year later, in the summer of 1982, three patients with hemophilia, a blood disorder that requires frequent blood transfusions, had developed similar symptoms. This finding finally led public health officials to recognize that this disorder could be transmitted via blood as well as through sexual contact.

they know they are being watched. You might, for example, load your cafeteria tray with more healthy foods if you knew that a health psychologist would be rating the nutritional content of your food as part of her study on eating behavior in college students. To avoid this issue, researchers sometimes remain in an observational environment over an extended period of time to allow people to become accustomed to them before they start to record observations. Also, observers' own biases can influence how they perceive the behavior they observe. For example, one researcher might interpret children on a playground pushing each other as normal behavior, whereas another might view such behavior as a sign of aggression or hostility. To help limit the problems of observer bias, researchers often have at least two people complete the behavior ratings independently, and then they measure how often the raters' data agrees. Although case studies can be very valuable in generating hypotheses and theories, their usefulness is limited because it is always possible that the person (or persons) who was studied is atypical in some way and hence the information cannot be generalized to a larger population. Moreover, case studies can be very vivid in sensory detail, and hence can overwhelm more objective data recorded with other methods. For example, you might have a friend who became quite depressed following his parents' divorce, and therefore you believe strongly that divorce causes depression even if large scientific surveys show no such association.

The most important limitation of observational methods is that while such approaches can describe behavior, they cannot explain or predict it. In other words, while they may correlate two characteristics, two behaviors, or a characteristic with a behavior, they lack the ability to determine causation. Although correlations can tell us about the strength of the association between two variables, they cannot prove that one variable causes the other. For example, if you find that people with more friends live longer than those with few friends (an example of a *positive correlation*; see Figure 2.2), you still cannot determine which of these two variables causes the other. There may be many many possible explanations, and one possibility is that having friends helps buffer people from stressful events and thereby leads to fewer illnesses, and hence a longer life. However, it is also possible that people who are generally healthy have more opportunities to participate in social events, which then leads them to have more friends. Similarly, if you find that people who are more hostile have fewer friends (an example of a negative correlation), you can't tell whether people who are mean to others have trouble making friends or whether people who don't have many friends grow to be hostile over time.

Naturalistic or observational approaches also do not eliminate the possibility of a *third variable* that explains the observed association. For example, in men, hair loss and the death of one's spouse are positively correlated: men who are bald are more likely to experience the death of their spouse. However, it would be inaccurate to say that balding *causes* one's spouse to die

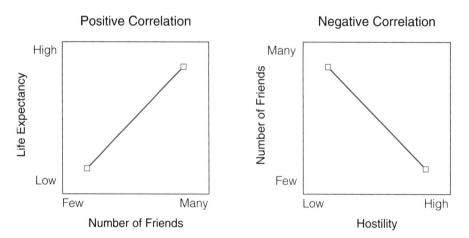

FIGURE 2.2 As optimism increases, so does life expectancy (positive correlation). As amount of social support increases, depression decreases (negative correlation).

because actually both balding and becoming a widow are the result of getting older (the "third variable" in this example). Similarly, the research study proposed by Dr. Ashley at the start of this chapter can test only whether the rates of eating disorders differ in students at public versus private high schools, not whether the type of school attended leads to the development of eating disorders. This is because students are not randomly assigned to attend a particular type of school; so, a third variable, such as drive for perfection or parental pressure or socioeconomic status, could be responsible for any differences in the rate of occurence that she finds. Thus, while observational methods are very useful in describing the association between two variables, they do not allow researchers to determine which variable causes the other.

What Are Survey Methods?

Survey methods rely on asking people questions about their thoughts, feelings, desires, and actions and recording their answers. These questions may be asked directly by the experimenter in a face-to-face or a phone interview, or participants may complete written surveys. For example, the Rosenberg Self-Esteem Scale is one commonly used written measure that assesses whether people generally have positive feelings about themselves (Rosenberg, 1965; see Table 2.1 for an example). Researchers may administer this scale to subjects as well as a questionnaire assessing their health behaviors to determine whether people with high self-esteem engage in more healthy behaviors than those with low self-esteem. Box 2.2 describes a study that uses survey methods to predict whether high school students plan to start smoking. Similarly, the research study Dr. Adams plans to conduct to test the link between hostility and coronary heart disease uses the survey method.

TABLE 2.1 *Test Yourself: Self-Esteem Scale*

Indicate whether you strongly agree, agree, disagree, or strongly disagree with each of these statements.

1. I feel that I'm a person of worth, at least on an equal plane with others.
2. On the whole, I am satisfied with myself.
3. I wish I could have more respect for myself.
4. I certainly feel useless at times.
5. At times I think I am no good at all.
6. I feel that I have a number of good qualities.
7. All in all, I am inclined to feel that I am a failure.
8. I am able to do things as well as most other people.
9. I feel that I do not have much to be proud of.
10. I take a positive attitude toward myself.

Note: For statements 1, 2, 6, 8, and 10, give yourself 4 points for strongly agree, 3 points for agree, 2 points for disagree, and 1 point for strongly disagree. For statements 3, 4, 5, 7, and 9, give yourself 1 point for strongly agree, 2 points for agree, 3 points for disagree, and 4 points for strongly disagree. (Rosenberg, 1965).

Box 2.2

Research Focus—The Link between Self-Image and Smoking in Adolescents

Laurie Chassin and her colleagues at Arizona State University were interested in examining the association between adolescents' self-views, their beliefs about typical male and female smokers, and their attitudes and behavior related to smoking (Chassin, Presson, Sherman, Corty, & Olshavsky, 1981). One hundred and seventy-five 9th and 10th graders completed a series of scales rating their self-image, the type of person they would like to be, and their perceptions of the typical male and female smoker. For example, students rated themselves and others on scales of healthy–unhealthy, beautiful–ugly, and relaxed–nervous. The students also answered questions about whether they currently smoked and whether they intended to "try" smoking in the next month and in the next year.

The findings from this study revealed that adolescents view smokers in a generally negative way. Specifically, smokers are viewed as somewhat unhealthy, nervous, disobedient, not so good at school work, and foolish. However, they were also viewed in some ways that might be considered positive for high school students: they were more likely to drink alcohol, likely to be with a group, and likely to be interested in the opposite sex. Most important, this study revealed that students who didn't currently smoke but saw themselves as fairly similar to typical smokers were much more likely to report intending to try smoking in the next month and next year. In sum, adolescents who saw themselves as tough, liking to be with a group, consumers of alcohol, and interested in the opposite sex were more likely to think about starting to smoke.

Survey measures have many advantages and thus are commonly used to collect information about the link between people's attitudes and behaviors. Using surveys enables researchers to collect data from many subjects at the same time, and hence is a very inexpensive way to gather data. Researchers could, for example, recruit many college students to complete a written survey on their exercise habits and illness rates to gather data on the link between physical fitness and health. Surveys also allow researchers to ask questions about a range of topics, including actions, feelings, attitudes, and thoughts, that could not be assessed simply by observing people's behavior. Finally, because surveys are often completed anonymously, researchers do not have to be concerned about the effects of observer bias, which can be a problem with some types of studies using naturalistic observation.

Although surveys are useful, they have a number of potential problems. First, survey methods introduce the possibility of bias through the use of *leading questions*. Leading questions are those that provide some evidence of the "right answer" based on how the question is phrased. For example, experimenters should ask subjects "do you examine your breasts for cancer?" as opposed to "how often do you examine your breasts?" which implies that everyone engages in this behavior. Similarly, let's say that you want to examine the frequency of drinking and driving in college students. If you ask students, "How often have you driven an automobile after having an alcoholic drink?" you will get more accurate estimates than if you asked students, "How often have you gotten behind the wheel of your car when you have had too much to drink, thereby putting your own and others' lives in danger?" This is an extreme example, but it is not far from what actually happens in some surveys that contain leading questions. Nationwide surveys on abortion, for example, often reveal conflicting results of how Americans feel about legalized abortion. When one examines the questions that researchers use to assess such views (see Table 2.2), however, the reason for this discrepancy is clear.

When researchers provide different *response options*, they must be careful to phrase them in such a way as to avoid getting biased results. The provided responses give people an idea of what the "normal" or "typical" behavior is, and people often don't want to appear very different from others. (And they *really* don't want to appear worse than others.) Respondents are therefore likely to choose one of the midlevel choices as opposed to one of the more extreme (high or low) choices no matter what their actual behavior is. So, if you ask people if they smoke less than 1 cigarette a day, 1 to 2 cigarettes a day, 3 to 5 cigarettes a day, or more than 5 cigarettes a day, they will give lower estimates about their cigarette smoking than if you ask if they smoke fewer than 10, 10 to 20, 20 to 30, or more than 30 cigarettes a day. In this first example, regardless of their actual smoking behavior, people will be likely to report smoking between 1 and 5 cigarettes a day (the two midlevel choices in this set of answers), whereas in the second example, people are likely to report smoking 10 to 30 cigarettes a day, again, because these responses are the midlevel options and many respondents wish to report their behavior in a way that seems to fall within the norm. Table 2.3 provides another example of how response options can influence people's reports of how much television they watch (Schwarz, Hippler, Deutsch, & Strack, 1985). In this case, only 16.2% of people report watching more than 2 1/2 hours of television (the highest response option given) when it is offered as the low-frequency condition, but 37.5% of people report watching this much television when it is offered as the high-frequency condition. From this, you might see how people sometimes tailor their responses to conform to the perceived desired responses.

TABLE 2.2   *Example of Leading Questions in Surveys*

Given the importance to future generations of preserving the environment, do you believe the Clean Air Act should be strengthened, weakened, or left alone?

Given the fact that installing scrubbers at utility plants could increase electricity bills by 25%, do you believe the Clean Air Act should be strengthened, weakened, or left alone?

Source: Taken from Goodwin, 1998.

TABLE **2.3** *Reported Daily Television Watching as a Function of Response Alternatives*

Low-Frequency Alternatives	Daily Consumption Reports	High-Frequency Alternatives	Daily Consumption Reports
Up to 1/2 hour	7.4%	Up to 2 1/2 hours	62.5%
1/2 hour to 1 hour	17.7%	2 1/2 hours to 3 hours	23.4%
1 hour to 1 1/2 hours	26.5%	3 hours to 3 1/2 hours	7.8%
1 1/2 hours to 2 hours	14.7%	3 1/2 hours to 4 hours	4.7%
2 hours to 2 1/2 hours	17.7%	4 hours to 4 1/2 hours	1.6%
More than 2 1/2 hours	16.2%	More than 4 1/2 hours	0.0%

Source: Taken from Schwarz, Hippler, Deutsch, & Strack, 1985.

Although we assume that people can accurately report on their own beliefs, attitudes, and behaviors, people are less accurate than we might think. Thus, survey methods are also limited by the possibility of *inaccurate reporting*. In some cases, people might believe they are telling the truth, but they simply may not be able to accurately recall the necessary information. For example, people may actually not remember when they last visited the dentist, when they first noticed a given symptom, or how long pain lasted. In other cases, people may be motivated to give inaccurate information. When you visit the dentist, you may overestimate the number of times you've flossed recently to avoid reporting behavior you assume might be perceived as negative. In Chapter 12, we examine cases in which people are motivated to inaccurately provide information to their health care provider about how well they follow a prescribed medical regimen. People may be especially likely to give inaccurate information when they are asked about highly personal or sensitive attitudes or behavior. (An old joke goes, 95% of people masturbate, and the other 5% lie. See Photo 2.2).

Finally, another limitation of survey methods is that these methods do not allow researchers to determine causality. Similar to observational or naturalistic methods, survey methods are correlational methods, and hence they do not enable researchers to assess the direction of the effects. For example, one highly publicized study found that people who had higher levels of education had less frequent sex (see Cartoon 2.1). This study does not reveal, however, whether having more education *leads* to having less sex. It may be, for example, that people who have more education also work longer hours, and hence have less time to engage in sex. In this case a third variable (number of hours worked) could be associated with both more education and less sex, and it is this variable that leads to the association between level of education and frequency of sex. Given the limitations of both observational and survey methods in determining the causal direction of associations between variables, researchers often use experimental methods to definitely prove how two variables are associated.

PHOTO 2.2 The number of pornographic magazines purchased based on sales reports of vendors is considerably higher than the number of pornographic magazines reported to be purchased based on surveys of the reading population. Can you guess why?

CARTOON 2.1 Studies show that people with more education have sex less often. But is this causation or correlation?

Source: ©Reprinted with special permission of King Features Syndicate

What Are Experimental Methods?

In conducting experiments, researchers randomly assign people to receive one or more *independent variables*, namely the factor that is being studied to see if and how it will influence attitudes and/or behavior. (A particular type of drug or a particular stressful event could serve as the independent variable.) Then experimenters measure the effect of the independent variable on one or more *dependent variables,* the measured outcome of the experiment. The dependent variable could be an attitude or a behavior, such as beliefs about wearing seat belts or frequency of condom use (see Box 2.3). *Random assignment* means that every participant had an equal chance of being subjected to either of the conditions: the participants did not choose which condition they wanted, nor did the experimenter use any type of nonrandom selection process to assign people to conditions (e.g., putting the first 10 people in one condition and then the next 10 people in the second condition). Random assignment improves the likelihood that there is not a third variable causing some association between the independent and dependent variables, therefore explaining your seemingly significant findings. For example, if you want to test whether doing Tae-Bo (a form of aerobic kick-boxing) leads to weight loss, you could gather a representative sample of a population, obtain their informed consent, weigh them all, and then give half of them the Tae-Bo videotapes and half of them no videotape. If you then weigh these people again 1 month later, you could see whether those in the Tae-Bo group had lost more weight than those in the no-videotape group (see Figure 2.3, Photo 2.3). Similarly, at the beginning of the chapter I described an experiment that Brenda and Brandon conducted to evaluate the effectiveness of different types of alcohol prevention workshops. Because experiments contain multiple conditions or groups (e.g., those who got a video or attended a workshop and those who did not), they can show causality, namely, that the independent variable (having the videotape or attending the workshop) leads to the dependent variable (the loss of weight or decrease in alcohol consumption), and not the other way around. This is therefore an advantage experiments have over the other research methods, which show correlation but not causation.

Why is random assignment so important? Think about what would happen if you ran your experiment on the effects of Tae-Bo but instead of using random assignment, you let people choose whether they'd like to receive the Tae-Bo tape or not. If you then find that those who received the Tae-Bo tape lost more weight than those who didn't get a tape, can you be certain that receiving the Tae-Bo tape caused the weight loss? No, because it is likely that people who *chose* to get the Tae-Bo tape differ from those who chose not to get the viedotape. Perhaps members of the Tae-Bo group are more motivated to lose weight in general, or perhaps they are more interested in exercising, or perhaps they are more helpful (and hence want to give the experimenter the desired results). Although we can't tell whether any of these factors influenced your findings, they are all possible. We therefore can't tell whether your independent variable (receiving the Tae-Bo tape) influenced your dependent vari-

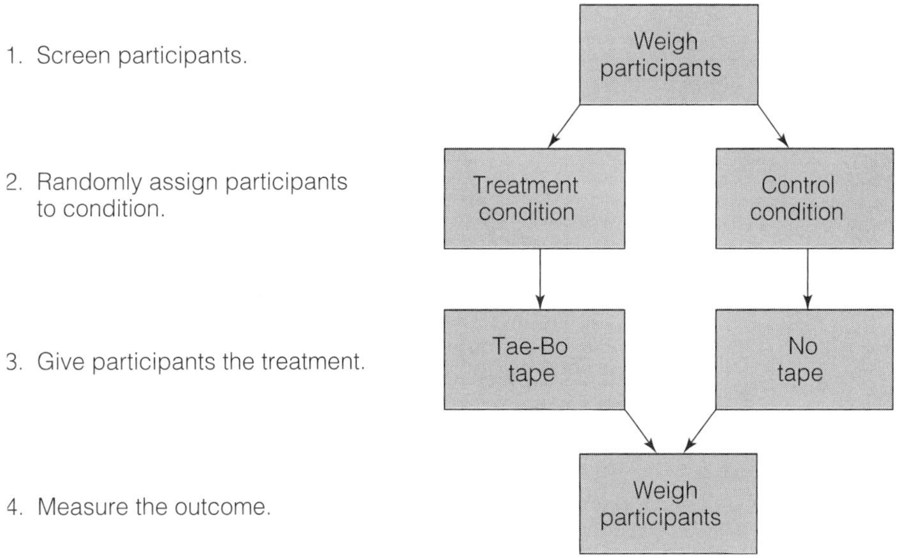

1. Screen participants.

2. Randomly assign participants to condition.

3. Give participants the treatment.

4. Measure the outcome.

```
                    ┌──────────────┐
                    │    Weigh     │
                    │ participants │
                    └──────────────┘
                    ↙              ↘
        ┌──────────────┐      ┌──────────────┐
        │  Treatment   │      │   Control    │
        │  condition   │      │  condition   │
        └──────────────┘      └──────────────┘
               ↓                     ↓
        ┌──────────────┐      ┌──────────────┐
        │   Tae-Bo     │      │     No       │
        │    tape      │      │    tape      │
        └──────────────┘      └──────────────┘
                    ↘              ↙
                    ┌──────────────┐
                    │    Weigh     │
                    │ participants │
                    └──────────────┘
```

FIGURE 2.3   Key elements of experimental design.

able (weight loss). This is why random assignment is so important—to minimize the likelihood of a third variable influencing the results.

Despite their strengths, experiments also have some weaknesses. First, *artificial settings can influence behavior.* Because experiments typically take place in laboratory settings, the participants' attitudes and behavior can sometimes be

PHOTO 2.3   Does Tae-Bo really help people lose weight? Only an experiment can tell.

Box 2.3

Research Focus—An Essay a Day Keeps the Doctor Away

Joshua Smyth and his colleagues at the State University of New York at Stony Brook examined the effects of writing essays about traumatic events on improving health in people with chronic illnesses (Smyth, Stone, Hurewitz, & Kaell, 1999). One hundred and seven people with asthma or rheumatoid arthritis completed a number of physiological measures as baseline information. They were then randomly assigned to either a "treatment group" or a "control group." For 20 minutes each day for 3 consecutive days those in the treatment group were asked to write about their deepest thoughts and feelings regarding the most stressful event they had ever undergone. These events might inclued the death of a loved one, problems in relationships, or disturbing events they had experienced or witnessed (e.g., childhood events, accidents). In contrast, those in the control condition were asked to write about their plans for the day, again, for 20 minutes each day for 3 days. All subjects were then examined 4 months later by a doctor, who measured the severity of their symptoms, their level of pain, and their general psychological well-being.

The researchers found that, comparing baseline health data to the later health checkup, even something as simple as writing about a stressful experience led to better health in patients with these chronic diseases. Of those in the treatment group, who wrote about the traumatic events, 47.1% showed significant improvement, 48.6% showed no change, and 4.3% got worse. In contrast, of those in the control condition, 24.3% showed improvement, 54.1% showed no change, and 21.6% got worse. What factors led to the treatment subjects' dramatic increase in health? Although this study does not provide a definitive answer, it shows that writing about traumatic events may lead to physiological alterations, may assist with coping responses, and/or may improve health-related behaviors. (These issues are addressed in more detail in Chapter 4.)

influenced by such settings, instead of by the independent variable (IV). For example, subjects who are asked to do an unusual procedure in the study setting may act how they think they should act, as opposed to what they would normally do in a real-life situation. Some researchers who study marital interaction, for example, ask couples to reenact a conflict that they have had previously and then they videotape that reenactment. In this study design, it is certainly possible that couples who know their fight will be watched by psychologists will not act naturally in the reenactment; thus, the study results may be less accurate.

To try and overcome this potential weakness, experimenters try to design experimental procedures that are high on *experimental/psychological realism*, namely that subjects are involved in and take seriously, which in turn leads them to behave naturally and spontaneously. The famous Milgram study in which subjects were told to give high levels of shocks to another person, for example, was very high in experimental realism, and therefore it is assumed that participants' behavior was genuine.

Although experiments are the only research method that allows researchers to determine whether one variable *causes* another, there are some cases in which practical and/or ethical concerns make it impossible to conduct true experiments. For example, you can't randomly assign some people to get divorced or to acquire cancer in order to determine whether these types of major stressors lead to illness and mortality. In these cases, researchers conduct *quasi-experiments*. These are research studies in which there are distinct groups of people in different conditions, but unlike in true experiments, the people were not randomly assigned to the groups. A study that compares rate of illness in people who are divorced versus married, for example, includes an independent variable (marital status) that may impact a dependent variable (illness), but people are of course not randomly assigned to the divorced and married groups.

There are several types of quasi-experiments. *Natural experiments* are one type that can be conducted when researchers take advantage of a naturally occurring event, such as an earthquake. For example, after a disaster at the nuclear plant on Three Mile Island, researchers examined how people living near the plant were coping as compared to people living farther away (McKinnon, Weisse, Reynolds, Bowles, & Baum, 1989). Similarly, and as described in Box 2.4, following a major earthquake in northern California, researchers examined the frequency of nightmares in students who lived in areas affected by the quake as compared to students who lived in other areas of the country.

Ex post facto studies are another example of research based in quasi-experimental methods. In this type of study researchers cannot randomly assign people to various conditions or treatments, but instead they select people who differ on a particular variable of interest. This type of study is used very commonly in health psychology because many of the issues of interest in this field cannot be tested practically and ethically using experimental methods. For example, it is impossible to randomly assign women to breast-feed or bottle-feed their infants in order to determine the effects of breast-feeding on infant health. Researchers therefore would compare the health of infants who were breastfed versus bottlefed on various dimensions, such as frequency of childhood illness, IQ, and occurence of obesity, while controlling for various characteristics in the mothers of the sample population.

One type of ex post facto approach is called a *prospective study*, which compare people with a given characteristic to those without it to see whether these groups differ in their development of a disease. These studies, therefore, are prospective because they follow people over time. For example, one prospective study measured Type A behavior in a large group of men and then followed these men over time to determine whether those with higher levels of Type A behavior were more likely to develop heart disease (Rosenman et al., 1975). As predicted, men with Type A behavior were more likely to develop heart disease. *Longitudinal studies*, in which a single group of subjects is followed

Box 2.4

Research Focus—The Effect on Nightmares of Experiencing an Earthquake

James Wood and his colleagues at both the University of Arizona and Stanford University conducted a natural experiment on the influence of experiencing a natural disaster on the frequency of nightmares (Wood, Bootzin, Rosenhan, Nolen-Hoeksema, & Jourden, 1992). Researchers asked a sample of students from three different universities (Stanford University, San Jose State University, and the University of Arizona) to record how many nightmares they had and how intense the nightmares were every day for 3 weeks. Half of these students (those from Stanford and San Jose State) had just experienced the Loma Prieta earthquake of 1989, which measured 7.1 on the Richter scale. This earthquake caused $5.6 million worth of property damage (including the collapse of a freeway) and killed 62 people (see Photo 2.4). Hence, it was a major stressor for students in northern California (including me—I was actually in a psychology class on the fourth floor of a building when this earthquake hit.). Students from Arizona, who had presumably heard about the earthquake through news reports but who did not experience its effects directly, served as the control or comparison group.

As predicted, students who were in California at the time of the earthquake had marked reactions. Specifically, during the first 3 weeks after the earthquake, 74.3% of San Jose State students and 64.9% of Stanford students experienced a nightmare, as compared to only 53.6% of Arizona State students. California students also had more frequent nightmares, with San Jose State students and Stanford students reporting mean frequencies of 3.06 and 2.47, respectively, compared to only 1.50 for the Arizona students. Finally, students who had directly experienced the earthquake were more likely to have nightmares about the earthquake. Forty percent of San Jose State students and 37% of Stanford students reported having a nightmare about the earthquake, whereas only 5% of Arizona students reported having such a nightmare.

over time, are a distinct type of prospective study. These studies are expensive to conduct because they require following many people over a considerable period of time. They can, however, provide valuable information about how specific variables influence health over time.

Another ex post facto approach is called a *retrospective study*, in which researchers examine differences in a group after a disease has occurred and attempt to look back over time to examine what previous factors might have led to the development of the disease. For example, some studies compare those who have cancer to those without cancer in terms of the experience of major life events (e.g., death of a loved one, marital discord; Sklar & Anisman,

PHOTO 2.4 Damage in San Francisco following the 1989 Loma Prieta earthquake.

1981). This research indicates that those with cancer have experienced more significant life events, suggesting that life stressors can lead to the development of cancer. *Cross-sectional studies*, in which researchers compare people of different ages at the same point in time, are a distinct type of retrospective study. You could, for example, compare the rate of cancer in 20-year-olds, 40-year-olds, and 60-year-olds to assess whether older people have higher rates of cancer than younger people in a cross-sectional study.

Although quasi-experimental methods can provide useful information about the effects of an independent variable on a dependent variable, they suffer from some of the same limitations as naturalistic, observational, and survey methods. First, these types of approaches do not randomly assign participants to different conditions or treatments, and hence they do not answer questions about correlation versus causation. If researchers using one of these research methods find that students in fraternities engage in more alcohol abuse than those not in fraternities, can they be sure that fraternity life leads to more drinking or can they conclude that those who like to drink alcohol prefer to join fraternities? Quasi-experimental approaches also do not

PHOTO 2.5 Can breast-feeding influence infant IQ? Quasi-experimental studies may help answer this question.

eliminate the possibility of a *third variable* causing the observed association. For example, if researchers find that breastfed babies have higher IQs than non-breastfed babies, it is possible that a third variable leads to both breast-feeding and high IQ (see Photo 2.5). Perhaps mothers who have a higher IQ are more likely to breast-feed and they are also more likely to pass this high IQ on to their children. Thus, it is possible that the link between breast-feeding and high IQ is actually the result of another variable. Researchers typically try to control for potential third variables by matching participants in control and subject groups on other related variables. For example, researchers might match each woman who chose to breast-feed with a woman who had a similar IQ or income in the control group, and then compare infant IQs between these two groups. Although creating matched groups helps minimize the problem of third-variable effects, researchers obviously can match on only some, not all, variables. Quasi-experimental methods can therefore suggest associations between two or more variables, but researchers must conduct experiments to determine the precise association between the variables.

What Are Clinical Methods?

Researchers who are examining the effectiveness of different drugs or therapies on medical problems often use *clinical studies*. These methods are very similar to experiments in many ways, in that they use random assignment to condition and are often blind or even double-blind studies, meaning the participants or the participants and the experimenter are unaware of which conditions the participants are being subjected to and perhaps are unaware even of the hypothesis of the study. However, because these studies often involve patients who have actively sought help for a given disorder (such as cancer or depression), the practical and ethical issues involved in conducting this type of study can be complex (see Box 2.5).

Well-designed clinical trials must have clear *patient selection* criteria. In other words, researchers must set specific guidelines determining which participants are eligible for participation in the study. For example, if you are conducting a study on the effectiveness of a given therapy or drug on relieving back pain, you must make sure that all patients included in the study actually have back pain as defined for your study, not neck pain or joint pain.

Another issue to consider in conducting a clinical research study is whether participants have *comorbidity* and/or *concomitant treatment*. Clinical studies often involve people with co-morbidity, namely who are suffering from more than one disease, which tends to add variability and make it harder to conduct a controlled experiment. For example, some people could have cardiovascular disease caused by diabetes whereas others may only have cardiovascular disease. Similarly, people may be receiving ongoing treatment for diseases other than the one of the intended treatment they are currently participating in the study to assess. Any change in health could therefore be due to the other treatment they are receiving. Once again, random assignment helps to ensure that any findings will be caused by the effects of the intended treatment and not other factors. Some clinical studies may even exclude participants with comorbidity and/or concomitant treatment to avoid the potential impact of the factors.

Finally, researchers who are conducting clinical research must be sure sure they have *patient cooperation*. Specifically, researchers must involve patients who will precisely follow treatment recommendations. For example, if subjects are instructed to take a particular pill every morning, they must follow the instructions because every deviation affects the accuracy of the study results. This matter of cooperation is a particularly important issue because patients often do not voluntarily disclose a lack of cooperation on their part, and so study design must encourage full cooperation as well as provide a way for participants to honestly report their conformance or nonconformance. (The issue of adherence is addressed in detail in Chapter 12.)

Box 2.5

Psychology in the Real World: Close to the Bone

We all knew the treatment was a gamble. But compassion should have been a sure thing.

A friend called one morning last April to ask if I'd seen the news. The slight catch in her voice made me straighten my back, put me off, made me lie and say I had.

I found the article quickly enough, then read with deliberate slowness, in a state approximating calm. "Breast Cancer Treatment Questioned," the headline said. Four new studies had shown that high-dose master-blaster chemo, also known as bone-marrow transplants, did almost nothing to improve the chances of women with advanced breast cancer. The next great breast-cancer cure wasn't.

But I could have told them that. Of all the women I knew who'd had a transplant, I didn't know a single one whose cancer hadn't come back. Including me.

In the weeks immediately following the report, I was sanguine, even incurious. I did not make further inquiries. I did not call the hospital and rant. Ten years of recurrent breast cancer had made me my own spin artist of disease. Of course it had been a gamble, I concluded, as quickly as if I were a spokeswoman for the hospital. Come on, the doctors never promised that the eight months of warm-up chemotherapy, followed by the four high-dose bombs, would actually work. Hadn't I signed a consent form before even getting started?

So I told my friends that the studies were irrelevant. "They're just statistics," I'd say, the paragon of cool rationality. "Maybe the treatment did help." Maybe it did: three years later, I was still standing; the cancer's recurrence, to my adrenal gland, had been easily treated with hormones.

Or maybe I just couldn't bring myself to think about the unholy ways the transplant had leveled me—the violent, chattering fevers, the suckling weakness, the transformation into something more wormlike than human. And maybe I was still being propelled forward by the same psychic mechanism that kept me going when my red-cell count hit zero and I couldn't stand. This thing would work. It had to. Belief was all I had to go on.

The anger was slow to come, delayed, like radiation burn. But when it did, it was compressed fury, an actual physical sensation that built when I saw there wasn't anyone to aim at. Certainly not my doctors. They'd done what they thought was best, even if it meant taking me to the point of death and back four times. Four times! And for what?

In the cooling anger, the answer formed: for an experiment, that's what. I had given my body to science, had been doing that for 10 years, in fact. Most cancer patients do, for most cancer treatments are experimental. But some more so than others. It's one thing to be a medical guinea pig. It's another, in the case of the transplant, the extreme experiments, to feel like a sacrificial lamb.

(continues)

Not one of the team involved in my bone-marrow transplant—not a doctor, or a social worker, or a med-tech policy maker—even informed me that it had probably been all for naught. I guess they just figured someone else would fax me the news report—if they thought about it at all. That kind of institutional arrogance is something most cancer patients encounter. (To be admitted into one program, for instance, I had to spend two hours having my vertebrae scraped in order to confirm the fact that I—a patient with a file a foot thick—did indeed have cancer.) And that arrogance flares up every six months or so, when yet another next great cure is announced. Despite the fact that 28 years after Nixon declared war on cancer, as my friend Joanne puts it, "500,000 a year still come home in a body bag."

Recently, when I was thinking about all this too late at night, I called my friend Zina, whose cancer returned six months after her bone-marrow transplant. Do you realize that procedure cost about the same as a Ferrari, I asked. If you were buying a Ferrari, you know they'd fawn all over you, she said. And if you spent 120 grand on a car and they found it didn't work, at the very least you'd get a written apology, I snorted.

We were lucky to be alive, we quickly added. But our doctors were fumbling in the dark, and until they found a better path, we were doomed to fumble along with them, like it or not. It wasn't their fault that we were sick. It wasn't even their fault that the treatment that had raised so much hope didn't end up working. But you know what? At that moment, we decided, a single expression of sorrow or regret—one indication that it mattered to them even a fraction as much as it mattered to us—would almost have changed everything. It wouldn't have altered the results. But it would have been a nod toward dignity. And that, for now, would have been change enough.

Source: Russell Rich, K. (1999, December 19). Close to the bone. *New York Times Magazine.*

How Can We Evaluate Research Studies?

Thus far, I have described various research techniques used in health psychology and the particular strengths and limitations of each method. However, all research studies—regardless of the method used—should be evaluated in terms of their internal and external validity. This section describes these two types of validity and explains why they are important.

Internal Validity

One way of evaluating the quality of a research study is to examine whether it is high in *internal validity*, which means that it is highly likely that the effects on the dependent variable were caused by the independent variable. For example, let's say we are conducting an experiment about the effects of a given drug on mood. We randomly assign some consenting participants to get the drug, and others to not get the drug. If the results show that those who received the drug have better mood (as we've defined it) than those who do not receive the drug, we must be sure that this effect is caused by the independent variable (i.e., the drug). Maybe those who didn't receive the drug were disappointed that they didn't get the drug and therefore felt worse. Maybe the experimenter assumed that those who received the drug would be in a better mood and therefore was nicer to those people, affecting their responses. Perhaps those people who received the drug felt better because they were treated well by the experimenter, not because of the effects of the drug. Maybe people who received the drug talked about how great it was to receive the drug, which made those who didn't get the drug feel bad. In other words, there could be a variety of alternative explanations for the findings, which therefore weaken the internal validity of the experiment. However, if all of these effects have been eliminated or minimized in the study design, it is highly likely that the drug actually caused the improvement in mood, and therefore, the design would have high internal validity.

To increase internal validity, researchers must be sure that participants' expectations do not influence the dependent variable. Experiments often use a *placebo*, a treatment added to a research study as a way of controlling for the effects caused by a person's expectations. Placebos are inactive substances that should cause no psychological effects inherently; any effect that they do have, then, may be assumed to be caused by the subject's mental processes. In fact, because people who believe they are receiving a drug that will reduce their symptoms often show improvements—even if they are given only an inert sugar pill—drug companies must demonstrate that the actual drug they are marketing is more effective than a placebo pill at relieving a particular symptom. Another way to minimize the effects caused by participants' expectations about a particular treatment is to keep the participants *blind*, namely, to avoid telling them which condition they are being subjected to (e.g., whether they will experience the "real" condition or the "placebo," or control, condition). Dr. Webb's study on the effectiveness of a new drug includes a placebo condition to help prevent participant expectancy effects. In his study, all participants received some type of pill, but no one knew whether he or she was receiving real medicine or simply an inert sugar pill.

Although people commonly think of placebos as a type of inert drug (as in the preceding example), placebos can also be different types of conditions or procedures that some participants are exposed to in order to provide a comparison for participants in the test condition. For example, in some studies on HIV prevention, those in the treatment condition watch interesting videos and participate in discussions on safe sex led by trained facilitators, whereas those in the *control condition* were given a pamphlet to read by themselves. If the researchers later find that those in the treatment condition are more likely to use condoms, a behavior defined as successful adoption of this study's goals, can they determine that the increase in condom use results from the effectiveness of the information presented or from how the information was presented, with group interaction and personal attention of the facilitator? It is very likely that people learn more when they interact with the material in a fun way over a longer period of time than when they sit alone and briefly skim a brochure.

So, what is a better approach to determine the efficacy of particular HIV-pre-vention information? You may present everyone with information in a fun group format, but some people will receive information on HIV prevention (the treatment condition) and others will receive information on smoking cessation (the control condition). This setup allows researchers to evaluate whether people who received the HIV prevention information were more likely to use condoms than those who received the smoking cessation information, since both groups received their information in the same format, and therefore the effects of group interaction on learning were controlled for.

Researchers must also protect experiments from experimenter expectancy effects to increase internal validity. *Experimenter expectancy effects* are produced when an experimenter's expectations about the results of the experiment influence his or her behavior toward the subjects, and thereby ultimately do affect the results. For example, if you know which patients in a research trial are getting a real drug and which others are getting a placebo, you may treat subjects in these two conditions differently in subtle ways that influence participants' behavior and responses. You might frame questions in particular ways, based on your expectations, which then may elicit your predicted response from subjects. For example, you might ask some people, "How much of a lessening of pain have you experienced?" (a leading question) and others, "Did you experience any lessening of pain?" This may happen even if you are consciously attempting to treat all participants the same.

In fact, experimenter expectancy effects can affect results even in studies with animals. In one clever study, an experimenter told subjects that the purpose of the trial was to replicate a well-established finding that some rats are "maze-bright," whereas others are "maze-dumb," and have more trouble learning to navigate a maze (Rosenthal & Fode, 1963). He told half of the student participants they were working with smart rats and the other half they were working with dumb rats. Each student then had to place his or her rat at the start of the runway and had to time the rat's movement through the maze. On day 1, the times for "smart" and "dumb" rats were pretty close, but over time, the "bright" rats ran faster and faster than the dumb rats (see Figure 2.4), intimating that student handler expectations and behavior somehow influenced the performance of the rats.

To protect against the biases of experimenter expectancy effects, some experiments are conducted *double-blind*, in which neither the participants nor the experimenter knows which participants are in which condition, and, in some cases, the experimenter who is interacting with the participants and collecting the data may not even know the study's hypotheses. This approach decreases the possibility of experimenter expectancy effects influencing the data.

External Validity

External validity refers to the degree to which researchers have reasonable confidence that the same results may be obtained using the same experiment for other people and in other situations; in other words, that the experiment is

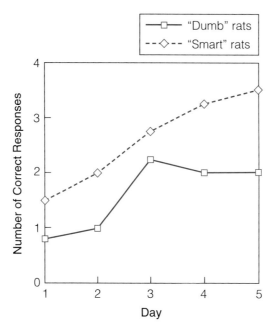

FIGURE 2.4 Students' expectancies about their rats' ability clearly influenced the rats' behavior (Rosenthal & Fode, 1963).

repeatable. For example, one summer before I'd committed to writing a health psychology textbook, I was watching the *Oprah Winfrey Show*, and Oprah was talking about her success with losing weight. Oprah noted that it was really important to keep exercise interesting; hence one shouldn't just get on the Stair Master for 30 minutes a few times a week. Instead, one week Oprah flew to the Grand Canyon and hiked; another week she flew to Vail and skied; and a third week she flew to Bermuda and swam (see Photo 2.6). Now, this exercise regime may indeed have worked wonders for Oprah (at least in the short term), and they might be very effective approaches for perhaps 100 other very rich people, but how effective are these weight-loss tips for the average person? The results of Oprah's exercise program probably would not be replicated widely; therefore, her experiment in finding the best way to keep exercise interesting would be considered to have low external validity.

This problem of low external validity is relatively common. For example, many studies on HIV prevention are conducted on college campuses. However, college students tend to be younger and more educated than the general population, so, if we learn that a given intervention is effective for college students, can we assume that this intervention would work in other populations? Similarly, can we assume that those individuals on a college campus who care to attend an HIV prevention intervention are similar to those who do not come voluntarily? Our findings on a self-selected sample may not generalize to other people in experiments with low external validity.

PHOTO 2.6   Oprah's weight-loss plan may have worked for her (at least temporarily), but how feasible is this plan for most people?

There are, fortunately, several ways of increasing external validity. First, *use a representative sample,* namely, a sample that reflects the characteristics of the target population at large. If you are interested in examining the frequency of drinking alcohol on college campuses, it would be a mistake simply to survey students who live in a fraternity or sorority house, because research shows that these students drink more alcohol than those who live in residence halls or off-campus housing (Wechsler, Dowdall, Davenport, & Castillo, 1995). Instead, you might call every 10th person in the student directory to try to recruit a sample that truly represents all the students on campus (e.g., including an equal mix of males and females, athletes and nonathletes). In contrast, other studies use a *convenience sample*, namely, a sample that is selected because the members are readily accessible to the researcher (such as college sophomores who are taking a psychology course!). Using a convenience sample is not necessarily bad, but other researchers should be made aware of what sample is being used in order to better interpret the results. Results from a study that used only college students as participants, for example, are likely to be most accurate in predicting behavior in other college students, not the general population.

Researchers must also consider that those who take the time to participate in a study might differ from those who choose not to participate, and therefore participant responses may not generalize or be applicable to the general population (Bradburn & Sudman, 1988). For example, a study of sexual behavior was conducted by researchers at the University of Chicago (Michael, Gagnon, Laumann, & Kolata, 1994). It included a number of questions on personal topics, such as frequency of masturbation, marital affairs, and homosexual behavior. Those participants who are relatively comfortable discussing such sensitive issues, and revealing personal information to strangers were likely the ones to decide to participate in the study, knowing its topic at the screening phase—people who lack this comfort may have simply refused to participate. Individuals who are comfortable discussing such topics might also be more likely to engage in such behaviors, and thus this type of survey approach might lead to an overestimation of the frequency of these behaviors in the general population if the composition of the participant group is not considered during the interpretation on the results (see Photo 2.7).

Similarly, those with particularly strong feelings about the topic of a study may be most likely to respond. Let's say you are asked to evaluate the quality of your Health Psychology course. If you really like your professor, you are probably highly motivated to complete the survey to let others know how great this class is. Similarly, if you really hated this course (which, I know, is hard to imagine, but try), you are likely to want to warn others away from this class and would hence complete the survey. However, if you have sort of mixed feelings about the class (you like some parts, you don't like other parts, but you don't generally feel strongly), you may not be very motivated to complete a survey at all.

PHOTO 2.7   Going door to door helps researchers get a random, representative sample of participants.

Researchers can also increase external validity by *making participation in the study as convenient as possible.* If you recruit people to participate in a smoking cessation intervention that requires them to spend every Saturday for a month traveling to a faraway place, you are probably just involving and influencing those who are very motivated to quit and hence the results may not generalize, or be applicable to the average smoker (who likely lacks such extreme motivation). On the other hand, if you find that attending one 2-hour workshop helps people stop smoking, this intervention may be very generalizable to many other smokers. Many people would be willing to attend this type of program, and therefore the researchers should feel more confident that their approach could work with other people.

A third way of increasing external validity is to *conduct the same study in different populations or locations.* As stated previously, many studies on HIV prevention are conducted on college campuses, however, college students tend to be younger and more educated than the general population. If we learn that a given intervention is effective for college students, we cannot assume that this approach would work in other populations. However, if a smoking cessation program is equally effective for students in a suburban private high school, a small rural high school and a large inner-city public high school, then researchers can be confident that the intervention would be effective for most teenagers in the general population. You might not, however, be able to determine whether this program would be effective for college students or for adults.

Finally, researchers must d*esign studies with high mundane realism,* that is, studies that resemble places and events that exist in the real world, in order to be able to apply the findings from an experiment to the real world. For example, some research has examined how susceptible college students are to getting a cold during exam period (Jemmott & Magliore, 1988). Obviously, the exam period occurs several times during the academic year; therefore findings from this type of research approach are likely to provide valuable information about how the regular college exam period impacts health. However, imagine an experiment in which students were asked questions and were given an electric shock each time they gave a wrong answer. Although getting shocked would probably be extremely stressful (as well as ethically questionable) to participants; the design setup has low mundane realism, and hence may not give researchers accurate information about how stress can influence health in real-life situations.

How Do Research Ethics Influence Scientific Studies?

Paying attention to the ethical issues involved in conducting research is now mandatory, in part because of some previous studies that were ethically questionable. For example, a study conducted in Tuskegee, Alabama, from 1934 to 1974, examined the effects of syphilis on 412 African American men. The researchers were aware that the men had syphilis, but they did not tell the subjects they were infected nor did the researchers give subjects penicillin to cure them because the researchers were interested in measuring the long-term effects of syphilis left untreated. The men were asked to return to the clinic periodically (in exchange for free hot meals) so that the researchers could conduct physical exams and blood tests. The researchers even asked local doctors to not provide treatment to these men. What did this study show? That, left untreated, syphilis causes blindness, insanity, and even death (Faden & Beauchamp, 1986). Yet, the Tuskegee experiment is considered totally unethical because, through deception, the men were left untreated and suffered greatly from the effects of the disease. This experiment has had a lasting effect on the perceptions of the health care system in general by many African Americans. As described in Box 2.6, we now know that a number of other studies were conducted on various people, including prison inmates, pregnant women, and low-income children, who were unwittingly subjects in experiments with significant long-term health consequences.

In order to avoid ethically questionable studies, there are now procedures researchers must follow when conducting scientific research (see Box 2.7). First, studies must undergo an extensive *institutional review* before they are implemented. This review by a panel of experts is required by virtually all organizations in the United States, including schools, hospitals, community organizations, and so forth. These boards review whether the potential benefits of the research are justifiable in light of possible risks or harms, and they may force experimenters to make changes in the design or procedure of the research to minimize negative effects. You might wonder about the effects of (falsely) telling your roommate he had cancer or that he had failed out of school, but a research review panel would never allow a study using this type of deception because of the high potential risk of harming your unsuspecting roommate.

Research studies require participants to give *informed consent* (see Box 2.8 for a sample informed consent form). This consent is an individual's deliberate, voluntary decision to participate in research, based on the researcher's description of what such participation will involve. It is not necessary to describe every single aspect of the research to potential participants, but they do need to hear enough to make an educated decision about whether they would like to be involved.

Third, patients' *confidentiality* must be protected from unauthorized disclosure; hence, surveys often use a code number instead of the person's name to preserve anonymity. Data also must be stored in a locked room with restricted access. Reports based on the data must contain only group-level information, not descriptions of results for individual people. You would say that "most students who received the alcohol prevention workshop drank less," instead of "most students who received the alcohol prevention workshop drank less, except for Brad Simpson who surprisingly doubled his beer intake over the following month."

Some research studies use *deception*, in which they give false information to subjects in order to measure their responses to certain stimuli. For example, subjects may be told that they are receiving a drug, but they are actually receiving a placebo. Why would researchers do this? As we discuss in Chapter 9, people who think they are getting a drug actually have more positive results along the trial's measurement scale than those who think they are not getting

Box 2.6

Psychology in the Real World—Atomic Guinea Pigs

Although the Tuskegee syphilis study has received considerable attention in recent years, other studies have also relied on dangerous and unethical approaches. The following cases are all true examples of people's unknowing participation in potentially life-threatening research studies.

Hazardous Oatmeal

In the 1950s, Frederick Boyce was one of about 24 boys at the Fernald School in suburban Boston who were fed radioactive oatmeal as part of a nutrition study. The experiment, financed by the Atomic Energy Commission and the National Institutes of Health, was designed to show how the body absorbs various minerals. The boys were enticed to participate with the prospect of joining a "Science Club." Letters sent to parents by the researchers made no mention of the radiation. In fact, they suggested that the boys would benefit from the experiment and from Science Club activities. "They get a quart of milk daily," one letter says, "and are taken to a baseball game, to the beach and to some outside dinners and they enjoy it greatly."

Poison in the Womb

Emma Craft did not know that the "vitamin cocktail" her doctor gave her in 1946 contained radioactive iron. But 47 years later, when she read newspaper reports about experiments on pregnant women at Vanderbilt University Hospital and about children who had developed cancer, she says, "I knew in my heart that they were writing about me and my baby." At least 820 women consumed radioactive iron as part of this study on nutritional requirements in pregnancy. According to the report of President Bill Clinton's Advisory Committee on Human Radiation Experiments, "There is at least some indication that the women neither gave their consent nor were aware they were participating in an experiment."

"Elmer Allen Was No Hero"

In July 1947, when 36-year-old Elmer Allen arrived at a San Francisco hospital with an injured knee, doctors told him that his leg would have to be amputated. Three days before the surgery, they secretly injected him with plutonium. Like 20 other patients in hospitals around the country, Allen had unknowingly been enrolled in an experiment financed by the Atomic Energy Commission to gather information to help protect workers at A-bomb plants. Although the researchers understood that the injections could cause cancer, Allen was never told that he was at risk. Nor did he know that when he was invited for "metabolism tests" and free trips to Chicago and Rochester in 1973 the doctors were actually studying the long-term effects of radioactivity.

Source: Antonio, M. D. (1977, August 31). Atomic guinea pigs. *New York Times Magazine,* pp. 38, 41, 42.

Box 2.7

APA Guidelines for Conducting Research with Humans

Informed Consent

Using language that is reasonably understandable to participants, psychologists inform participants of the nature of the research; the researchers inform participants that they are free to participate or decline to participate or to withdraw from the research; the researchers explain the foreseeable consequences of declining or withdrawing; the researchers inform participants of significant factors that may be expected to influence their willingness to participate; and the researchers explain other aspects about which the prospective participants inquire.

When psychologists conduct research with individuals such as students or subordinates, psychologists take special care to protect the prospective participants from adverse consequences of declining or withdrawing from participation.

When research participation is a course requirement or opportunity for extra credit, the prospective participant is given the choice of equitable alternative activities.

Deception in Research

Psychologists do not conduct a study involving deception unless they have determined that the use of deceptive techniques is justified by the study's prospective scientific, educational, or applied value and that equally effective alternative procedures that do not use deception are not feasible.

Psychologists never deceive research participants about significant aspects that would affect their willingness to participate, such as physical risks, discomfort, or unpleasant emotional experiences.

Source: Taken from American Psychological Association, 1992.

a drug. Using this type of deception allows researchers to compare the effects of actually getting a particular drug to the effects of subjects simply believing they are getting a drug (e.g., comparing the efficacy of the drug to the power of positive thinking). However, deception is used only in cases in which there is no other reasonable way of studying a particular research question and in which it is extremely unlikely that physical and/or emotional harm could result (see Box 2.9).

Following participation in a research study, participants are given a *debriefing*, disclosure to subjects after research procedures are completed in which the researcher explains the purpose of the study, answers any questions, attempts to resolve any negative feelings, and emphasizes the contributions to science of the research. This is especially important in cases in which deception has been used.

Box 2.8

A Sample Informed Consent Form

Amherst College
Protection of Human Subjects
CONSENT FORM

Title of Study: The effectiveness of HIV prevention videos on increasing condom use in college students

Investigator(s): Professor Catherine A. Sanderson
Darren J. Yopyk

The following informed consent is required for any person involved in a research study. This study has been approved by the Institutional Review Board for the Protection of Human Subjects at Amherst College.

I understand that:

1. My participation is voluntary.

2. I may withdraw my consent and discontinue participation in this study at any time. My refusal to participate will not result in any penalty.

3. You will give me an explanation of the procedures to be followed in the project, and you will answer any inquiries that I have.

4. All of the information will be strictly confidential. No names will be associated with the data in any way. Providing my address to receive a report of this research upon its completion will also not compromise the anonymity of the data. I understand that the data will be stored in locked offices and will be accessible only to members of the researching group.

5. The results of this study will be made part of a final research report and may be used in papers submitted for publication or presented at professional conferences, but under no circumstances will my name or other identifying characteristics be included.

I hereby give my consent to participate in this research. I also agree not to discuss the purposes and procedures of this study with anyone in order that the integrity of this research is not compromised.

_____ Signature
_____ Print Name
_____ Date

Please send a report on the group results of this research upon its completion:
   YES   NO

Address to which the report should be sent:
_____
_____

Box 2.9

The Downside of Using Deception in Psychological Research

I was having a drink with my friend Justin when he spotted an attractive woman sitting at the bar. After an hour of gathering his courage, he approached her and asked, "Would you mind if I chatted with you for a while?" She responded by yelling at the top of her lungs, "No, I won't come over to your place tonight!" With everyone in the restaurant staring, Justin crept back to our table, puzzled and humiliated. A few minutes later, the woman walked over to us and apologized. "I'm sorry if I embarrassed you," she said, "but I'm a graduate student in psychology and I'm studying human reaction to embarrassing situations." At the top of his lungs Justin responded, "What do you mean two hundred dollars?"

Ethical Issues Relevant to Experimentation on Animals

Although the majority of psychological research uses humans as participants, a small minority of research studies (about 7% to 9%) use animals as research subjects (Gallup & Suarez, 1985). Research is conducted with animals for both ethical and practical reasons (Miller, 1985). First, certain types of studies are impossible to conduct on humans, given ethical concerns. Researchers cannot, for example, randomly assign some pregnant women to drink alcohol in order to test the effects of this behavior on the fetus. Research with pregnant animals, however, provides convincing evidence that alcohol has negative effects on the fetus (Sutherland, McDonald, & Savage, 1997). Second, experimenters have much more control over animals' lives than over people's; hence, using animals as subjects allows researchers to come to stronger conclusions about the nature of cause and effect since many extraneous factors can be controlled for. For example, in a trial examining whether people who are under greater stress experience more illness, it is impossible to examine all of the different variables that might lead to this association, such as poor health habits, genetic factors, and lack of social support. Research with animals, however, could control for all of these variables by using genetically similar rats (e.g., rats from the same litter) and providing all rats with the same exact living environment. Researchers could then expose some rats to stress and measure whether they have higher rates of illness than nonstressed rats.

Although some animal rights activists believe that animals should never be used for research purposes, research with animals has given us important information helping to improve people's quality of life. Specifically, research with animals has provided insight into the link between stress and health, methods of treating drug addiction and eating disorders, and strategies for helping premature infants gain weight (Miller, 1985). For example, research using monkeys to show the importance of developing attachments early in life led to changes in the then standard procedure of separating newborn infants from their mothers shortly after birth. Similarly, many people with incurable illnesses such as cancer and AIDS have benefited from drug treatments originally tested on animals.

Researchers who use animals as subjects must adhere to a set of strict guidelines regarding the animals' ethical treatment (see Box 2.10). Researchers must be properly trained in providing care for the animals, must justify the scientific value of the research, and must attempt to minimize stress and harm to the animals whenever possible. Moreover, Miller (1985) points out that many, many animals who are *not* used in research often suffer much more than those who are used to advance scientific research. For example, at least 20 million dogs and cats are abandoned each year in the United States, and of these, approximately half are ultimately euthanized in pounds or shelters, while many others die in painful ways (e.g., are hit by cars, starve to death). Although some people remain strongly opposed to the use of any animals in psychological research, recent studies indicate that over 70% of both psychologists and psychology majors support the use of animals in research (Plous, 1996a, 1996b).

Box 2.10

APA Guidelines for Conducting Research with Animals

Researchers who conduct research involving animals treat them humanely.

Psychologists trained in research methods and experienced in the care of laboratory animals supervise all procedures involving animals and are responsible for ensuring appropriate consideration for their comfort, health, and humane treatment.

Psychologists make reasonable efforts to minimize the discomfort, infection, illness, and pain of animal subjects.

A procedure subjecting animals to pain, stress, or deprivation is used only when an alternative procedure is unavailable and the goal is justified by its prospective scientific, educational, or applied value.

Surgical procedures are performed under appropriate anesthesia; techniques to avoid infection and minimize pain are followed during and after surgery.

When it is appropriate that the animal's life be terminated, it is done rapidly, with an effort to minimize pain, and in accordance with accepted procedures.

Source: Taken from American Psychological Association, 1992.

What Is the Best Approach?

How do you decide which research technique to use to answer a particular question? There is no single best method, and all methods have strengths and weaknesses. Because experiments are the only technique that randomly assigns people to conditions, this approach is the best method for determining which variable definitively causes another. However, because experiments are necessarily somewhat artificial, this approach does not give us as much information about what actually happens in real-life situations. On the other hand, while naturalistic observation methods give us very accurate information about what happens in the real world, they tell us more about how two (or more) different variables are connected than they do about one variable causing the other. In sum, different methods are best for providing certain types of information and for answering particular questions. For example, you might use naturalistic observation or quasi-experimental methods to examine how experiencing the loss of a loved one influences depression, because obviously you could not answer this question using a true experimental design. On the other hand, if you are interested in examining the effectiveness of a particular type of smoking cessation program, conducting a true experiment is probably the best approach. Finally, we can be more confident about scientific findings if researchers using different types of research methods all produce the same results. For example, and as described in Table 2.4, if researchers using a variety of different approaches all examine the link between smoking and health and reach the same conclusion, we can be quite confident in those results.

TABLE 2.4 *Different Research Approaches for Examining the Smoking–Health Link*

Research Method	Research Plan
Observational/Naturalistic	Examine the rate of smoking and lung cancer in a given population
Survey	Examine people's self-reports of smoking frequency and health problems
Experimental	Randomly assign some laboratory rats to breathe cigarette smoke and examine whether these rats are more likely to develop health problems than rats not subjected to cigarette smoke
Quasi-Experimental	Examine rates of health problems in people who smoke versus people who do not smoke

Thought Questions

1. You are interested in examining the association between television watching and obesity in children. How would you test this association using survey methods as compared to experimental methods?

2. Describe two ways to increase internal validity and two ways to increase external validity.

3. Your roommate, Darren, wants to know if his new hypnosis tape is actually effective in helping people to stop smoking. To test its effectiveness, he asks 10 of his close friends to participate in his experiments. He gives his 5 male friends the hypnosis tape and gives his 5 female friends a music tape. Finally, 1 week later he asks each person how many cigarettes he or she is smoking per day. When Darren asks you for your thoughts on his study, what problems do you see?

4. You are interested in examining whether there is an association between alcohol use during pregnancy and birth defects. Describe how to examine this topic using a prospective method and a retrospective method.

5. Dr. Smith is a professor who wants to get feedback from his students on how effective he is as a teacher. He was planning to distribute an anonymous questionnaire with the midterm to get a response from all students in the course, but then decided that this would be too much work. Instead, he's planning to ask students for their thoughts about the course and his teaching methods when they come in to his office for office hours. What is the problem with this approach?

CHAPTER 3

Theories of Health Behavior

- Diana knows she really should insist that her boyfriend wear a condom to protect them both from sexually transmitted diseases (STDs), but somehow she never actually makes that suggestion at the "crucial moment." She has never regularly used condoms before with other sexual partners and has never had an STD, so Diana thinks she might be invulnerable (or at least really lucky in choosing partners). Moreover, Diana heard from some friends that basically all STDs can now be cured with some type of pill or shot and they're not such a big deal anyway. Even though she thinks she might feel more comfortable during sex if she and her partner were using a condom, Diana worries that her boyfriend might be offended by the suggestion and may even end the relationship.

- Steve has read several articles about the health benefits of regular exercise, and he is now planning to join a gym to start weight training a few times a week. He knows that he would feel good about himself if he felt more fit and strong. Steve's roommate already belongs to the local gym and thinks it is a great idea for Steve to start exercising. And Steve's parents have agreed to pay for the first year of gym membership to help him get started on his new plan.

- Hillary knows she should floss her teeth, but just finds it hard to motivate herself to actually do it, particularly when she is tired at the end of a long night. Her dental hygienist suggests that she reward herself for flossing to help enhance her motivation. Hillary decides she will treat herself to a new pair of Nine West shoes every month that she flosses at least 20 times.

- Allen is a college sophomore who is currently on academic probation because of his low grades during the fall semester. Although Allen always intends to focus more effort on classes, he is living in an off-campus apartment with some friends, and they all stay up late drinking and playing cards. Some mornings Allen just can't get up for class because his head is pounding. His academic advisor pressured Allen into attending an alcohol abuse prevention workshop, and even Allen is hoped it would help him stop drinking so much. In the workshop Allen got some advice on how to tell his roommates that he's not going to drink alcohol on weeknights anymore, and he even role-played a few practice dialogues with his friends. He began to weigh the benefits of cutting down a little on his drinking, including losing his "beer belly," having more money to spend on a spring break trip, and getting better grades.

- Maggie is 28 years old and has smoked for 10 years. During college she mostly smoked only at parties and when she was out with friends, and she never even thought about quitting. However, Maggie got married last year and she and her husband have recently begun talking about trying to have a baby. She knows that smoking while pregnant is very dangerous for the developing fetus, so she is trying to stop smoking. Thus far she has gone 9 days without having a single cigarette.

Preview

This chapter introduces the major theoretical perspectives used to predict and influence health-related behavior. First, we examine four continuum models of health behavior; the health belief model, the theories of reasoned action/planned behavior, learning theories, and social cognitive theory. These models all describe people's health-related behavior as the result of some combination of distinct variables, such as vulnerability, attitudes, benefits, and self-efficacy. We then examine two stage models of behavior change: the transtheoretical (stages of change) model and the precaution adoption process model. According to these models, people can be classified into distinct categories that represent their motivation to change their behavior. The six theories discussed in this chapter are often used to predict as well as to change people's health-related behavior.

What Are Continuum Theories of Health Behavior?

Continuum theories identify some set of variables that are thought to influence people's behavior, and then combine those variables to predict the likelihood the person will engage in a given behavior (Weinstein, Rothman, & Sutton, 1998). Thus, these theories predict where a person is on a continuum of action likelihood. For example, the variables included in the theory might include perceived risk or vulnerability, attitudes, and self-efficacy, and these might be summed to predict whether a person will engage in a particular health-related behavior, such as smoking cigarettes, screening for cancer, or using condoms. As you will see, these theories share some common elements, but also differ in terms of the specific components that they use to predict behavior as well as how these components are combined. Before you start reading about these theories, take a minute to think about what factors influence whether or not you engage in a behavior related to health. Is it how much **not** doing the behavior scares you (e.g., the fear of getting AIDS if you don't use a condom)? Is it how much you think doing the behavior is a good idea (e.g., maybe you think exercising regularly to look fit is a good idea, but you aren't convinced that having a tetanus shot is a great benefit)? Is it how confident you feel that you could actually do the behavior (e.g., maybe you know you should give up eating those high-fat fast-food hamburgers, but you don't think you have the willpower to pass by the Golden Arches)? Is it that the negatives about doing the behavior seem more important than the positives (e.g., you know you should stop smoking, but whenever you cut back on cigarettes you feel grouchy and nervous and start snacking all the time, which you hate)? Now read about the variables that each of these models includes and see how well they might predict your own behavior.

Health Belief Model

The health belief model is one of the oldest and most widely used theories to explain people's health-related behavior. A group of social scientists originally developed this model in the 1950s to explain why people often fail to participate in programs to prevent or detect diseases (Rosenstock, 1960). For example, after the government provided free tuberculosis screening conveniently located in various neighborhoods, researchers were surprised that relatively few people took advantage of this opportunity for early detection and treatment. (Professors often feel a similar amazement when they sit waiting for students to stop by during office hours and have no visitors.) An examination of the factors that successfully led to more people using screening formed the basis of the health belief model (see Table 3.1).

The health belief model posits that the likelihood that individuals will take preventive action is a function of four types of factors (see Figure 3.1). First,

TABLE **3.1**   *Test Yourself: Sample Questions Testing Components of the Health Belief Model*

Susceptibility	The possibility of getting wrinkles or age spots worries me.
Severity	It would be terrible to look older than I really am because of too much sun exposure.
Benefits	Wearing sunscreen with an SPF of at least 15 regularly when I am in the sun would reduce my chances of getting skin cancer.
Barriers	How likely is it that the cost of sunscreen would keep me from using it?

Source: Taken from Jackson & Aiken, 2000.

individuals need to believe that they personally are **susceptible** to the condition. Perceived susceptibility can include beliefs about the general risks of engaging in a behavior (e.g., the likelihood of getting cancer if you smoke) as well as beliefs about how likely you personally would be to acquire an illness or disease. For example, you may be generally aware that tanning without sunscreen can lead to skin cancer, but if you've never used sunscreen before and have had no bad results, you might have relatively low motivation to wear sunscreen (see Photo 3.1).

Next, individuals must believe that if they were to acquire a particular illness or disease it would have **severe** consequences. For example, if you believe that having an STD would not be particularly bad ("Hey, I'll just go

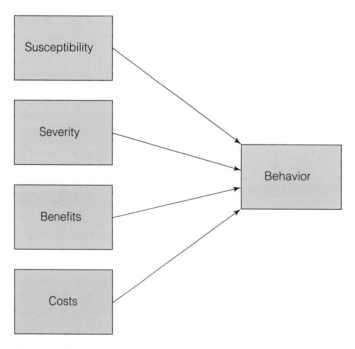

FIGURE **3.1**   The health belief model.

PHOTO 3.1   Although most people know that tanning leads to skin cancer, the perceived benefits of a tan can seem greater than the costs.

get some penicillin at the campus health center"), you will be less motivated to use condoms than if you believe that having an STD would be pretty unpleasant ("Hmm, it will hurt badly when I pee, it will be embarrassing to go to the campus health center for treatments and I might infect someone I care about"). The evaluation of perceived severity can include the consequences we individually would face, such as pain, disability, and even death. For example, if you believe that having a baby as a teenager would hurt your chances of attending college, you will be motivated to either remain abstinent or use effective contraception if you are highly motivated to continue your education. The evaluation of severity can also include the consequences others in our social network would face if we were to experience an illness or disease. Parents who smoke, for example, may be motivated to try to stop this behavior to protect their children from the pain they would encounter having to cope with the death of a parent.

Finally, people must believe that engaging in a particular behavior would be **beneficial** in reducing the threat of a particular illness and that the benefits of taking this preventive action outweigh the **barriers**. The benefits of stopping smoking are pretty clear (longer life expectancy, less expense, whiter teeth, etc.), but for some people, the barriers to quitting, such as the fear of being more tense or of gaining weight, could outweigh the benefits (see Box 3.1). For example, even though I see the long-term benefits of protecting myself from skin cancer, I still sometimes go to the beach without sunscreen in an attempt to acquire a "savage tan" (perhaps from repeatedly hearing my father's mantra, "Brown fat is better than white fat"). Similarly, people who have cancer have to balance the benefits of various treatment options (e.g., chemotherapy, radiation, surgery) with the treatment option costs (e.g., losing hair, risk of death, severe illness). As described at the beginning of the chapter, Diana is relatively unlikely to use condoms because she sees the potential costs of using condoms (conflict with boyfriend) as greater than the benefits she would gain from such behavior (protection from STDs).

Although the original version of the health belief model included only the four components of severity, susceptibility, benefits, and costs, a revised version of this model also includes cues to action (Janz & Becker, 1984). **Cues to action** refers to any type of reminder about a potential health problem that could motivate behavior change. These cues can be internal, such as experiencing a health symptom, or could be external, such as receiving a

---

Box 3.1

Health Psychology in the Real World

When Smoking Is a Matter of Money

Getting people to quit smoking may be hard, but discouraging them from starting, at least when they are young, may be as simple as raising the taxes on cigarettes.

A new study reports a link between the price of a pack of cigarettes and the likelihood that a teenager will start smoking. After surveying a total of 12,000 8th- and 10th-grade students for seven years and taking into account the local price for cigarettes, the researchers concluded that a 10 percent increase in price decreased the odds of teenagers' starting smoking by as much as 10 percent.

The study was conducted by ImpacTeen, a research partnership at the University of Illinois at Chicago, and by researchers from the University of Michigan. Based on data collected by the National Institute on Drug Abuse, the project was part of a long-term study into substance abuse among children.

The researchers said the study helped resolve a debate over whether cigarette prices affect the number of teenagers who begin smoking. Previous studies showed that higher prices did decrease the number of children smoking and the amount they smoked.

The lead author, Dr. John A. Tauras, said the evidence was clear. Indeed, to hear Tauras, an economist, tell it, the study says almost less about public health than it does about basic economics: if you charge too much for something, fewer people are likely to buy it. Noting its addictive nature, other experts have doubted that this would hold true for tobacco.

"Cigarette smoking does actually adhere to the fundamental principles of economics," he said.

The study also illustrates another fundamental of many teenagers' lives.

"Youths have very little disposable income," Tauras said. "They have certain fixed dollars each month to spend."

Source: Nagourney, E. (May 1, 2001). When smoking is a matter of money. **New York Times**, p. F8.

postcard reminder to get your teeth cleaned or watching a public service announcement on television about the dangers of smoking. These cues are just the final push that it sometimes takes to get people to act.

How good is this model at predicting what people do? Overall, the health belief model is a good predictor of whether people engage in health-related behaviors as well as whether they participate in health-screening programs (Rosenstock, 1990). For example, the health belief model can predict behavior related to dental care (Ronis, 1992), breast self-examination (Champion, 1994), condom use (Aspinwall, Kemeny, Taylor, Schneider, & Dudley, 1991), and diet (Becker, Maiman, Kirscht, Haefner, & Drachman, 1977). One recent study examined the predictors of HIV testing among gay, lesbian, and bisexual youth using the health belief model (Maguen, Armistead, & Kalichman, 2000); both barriers to HIV testing and perceived susceptibility to AIDS were significant predictors of HIV testing.

Although the results of studies on the health belief model have generally been favorable, researchers have raised some questions about its usefulness. First, this model does not include the component of self-efficacy, or a person's confidence that he or she can effectively engage in a behavior (Schwarzer, 1992). More recent theories, such as the theory of planned behavior and social cognitive theory, include this component, and research demonstrates that self-efficacy is a consistently strong predictor of health-related behavior. Second, while perceived barriers and perceived susceptibility tend to be the best predictors of behavior, perceived severity is not a very strong predictor of behavior (Janz & Becker, 1984) and may be a particularly poor predictor of health behavior in cases in which health problems are either hard to define in terms of severity (e.g., medical conditions with which people are unfamiliar) or are extremely severe for virtually everyone (e.g., cancer). Third, this model was originally developed to predict whether people would obtain immunizations, and it continues to be more useful in predicting one-time or limited behaviors than in predicting habitual behaviors (Kirscht, 1988). The health belief model may therefore be more useful in describing relatively simple behaviors than in describing complex behaviors.

Theories of Reasoned Action/Planned Behavior

The theory of reasoned action is a general psychological theory that is useful in predicting the link between attitudes, intentions, and behavior across different domains, such as voting, donating money, and choosing a career (Fishbein & Ajzen, 1975). For example, if you want to know how likely individuals are to vote for Al Gore, you must examine their attitudes toward him and their intentions to vote. This theory emphasizes the role of individuals' beliefs about their social world, and therefore includes components assessing individuals' own attitudes as well as their beliefs about others' attitudes toward a given behavior (e.g., how do you think your friends will feel if you vote for Al Gore?).

This theory posits that the key determinant of people's behavior is their **intention** to engage in that behavior. For example, your intentions to brush your teeth every night are probably a very strong predictor of whether you actually do brush your teeth. In turn, according to the theory of reasoned action, intentions are determined by people's **attitudes** toward the behavior as well as their **subjective norms** for the behavior. Steve, described at the beginning of the chapter, has strong intentions to exercise because he has positive attitudes about exercising and believes his friends and parents are supportive of this behavior; his intentions will likely influence his subsequent behavior.

Attitudes are a person's positive or negative feelings about engaging in a particular behavior. You might have a positive attitude about eating breakfast every day, but a negative attitude about avoiding your morning coffee. In turn, individuals' attitudes are a function of their beliefs about the consequences of engaging in a particular behavior as well as their evaluation of these outcomes. For example, a woman's attitudes about dieting will be formed by her beliefs about whether a diet will help her feel thinner and more attractive and her feelings about the benefits of having a thinner body.

Subjective norms refer to individuals' beliefs about whether other people would support them in engaging in a new behavior and whether they are motivated to follow the beliefs of these salient others. Who are these "other people," according to this theory? They might be family members, friends, and romantic partners. For example, an individual's intention to diet could be influenced by his beliefs about whether his family and friends would be supportive of his efforts to diet as well as by whether he is motivated to engage in behaviors these people encourage (see Table 3.2).

A later version of this model, the theory of planned behavior, added the component of **perceived behavioral control**, namely, the extent to which a person believes that he or she can successfully enact a behavior (Ajzen, 1985; see Figure 3.2). You might believe strongly that you can wear your seat belt but doubt whether you can refuse to get in a car driven by a friend whose had a few too many drinks. Perceived behavioral control is a reflection of both past experience with the behavior as well as beliefs about your ability to engage in a particular behavior in the future. For example, if you are trying to lose weight but have failed to resist eating Ben & Jerry's New York Super Fudge Chunk in the past and doubt whether your willpower is strong enough to resist eating it now, your perceived behavioral control will be low.

TABLE 3.2 *Sample Questions Based in the Theory of Reasoned Action*

Attitude Items	Social Norm Items
If I eat fruits and vegetables regularly, I will improve my health.	My parents would like for me to be healthier.
I would feel better about myself if I were healthier.	My friends think I should eat healthier food.

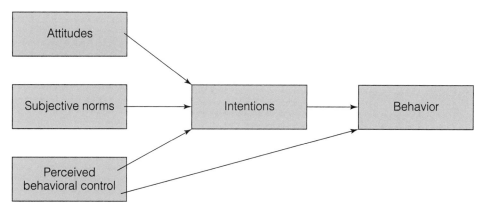

FIGURE 3.2 Model of the theory of reasoned action/planned behavior.

The theories of reasoned action and planned behavior are successful in predicting a range of different types of health behaviors, including engaging in testicular and breast self-examinations (Brubaker & Wickersham, 1990; McCaul, Sandgren, O'Neill, & Hinsz, 1993), using sunscreen (Hillhouse, Stair, & Adler, 1996), wearing seat belts (Budd, North, & Spencer, 1984), smoking cigarettes (Hill, Boudreau, Amyot, Dery, & Godin, 1997), drinking alcohol (Schlegel, Crawford, & Sanborn, 1977), using condoms (Sheeran & Taylor, 1999), screening for health conditions (DeVellis, Blalock, & Sandler, 1990; Sheeran, Conner, & Norman, 2001), breast-feeding (Manstead, Proffitt, & Smart, 1983), and flossing (McCaul et al., 1993). For example, a study on whether doctors successfully talked to their adolescent patients about the importance of STD and HIV prevention revealed that attitudes, social norms, perceived behavioral control, and intentions were all important predictors of the doctors' behavior (Millstein, 1996). Similarly, Box 3.2 describes the effectiveness of the theory of planned behavior in predicting weight loss in college women (Schifter & Ajzen, 1985).

Although the theories of reasoned action and planned behavior are widely used to predict health-related behaviors, they have some limitations. One problem with both theories is that the relevant attitudes, beliefs, and intentions toward a given behavior are typically particular to a given sample (Fishbein & Middlestadt, 1989). For example, the relevant attitudes and subjective norms toward use of condoms in high school students may relate to their parents' attitudes toward condom use, whereas the relevant attitudes and norms in a sample of gay men may relate to their concerns about implying a lack of trust toward their partner. Another limitation of both the theory of reasoned action and the theory of planned behavior is that they fail to include the person's current or past behavior (Manstead et al., 1983). The best predictor of future behavior often is past behavior, and past behavior may influence behavior both directly and indirectly through its influence on intentions. Finally, although these theories posit that individuals' intentions lead directly to behavior, people often intend to do a behavior but fail to actually follow through (Sheppard, Hartwick, & Warshaw, 1988). In fact, you can

Box 3.2

Research Focus—Using the Theory of Planned Behavior to Predict Weight Loss

Deborah Schifter and Icek Ajzen from the University of Massachusetts at Amherst examined the ability of the theory of planned behavior to predict weight loss in college women (Schifter & Ajzen, 1985). Women who considered themselves overweight were encouraged to participate, but women of normal weight were also allowed to participate. Eighty-three female college students completed a series of questionnaires assessing their attitudes toward losing weight ("How good would it be for me to reduce weight during the next 6 weeks?"), their subjective norms for weight loss ("Most people who are important to me think I should reduce my weight over the next 6 weeks"), their perceived control over weight loss ("How likely is it that if I try I will manage to reduce weight over the next 6 weeks?"), and their intentions to lose weight ("I intend to reduce weight over the next 6 weeks"). Participants were then weighed and asked how much weight they expected to lose over the next 6 weeks (see Photo 3.2). Six weeks later, participants again completed a series of assessments and were weighed.

PHOTO 3.2 Strong intentions to lose weight as well as an individual's belief in his or her ability to do greatly influence actual weight loss.

Findings indicate that the theory of planned behavior was quite effective in predicting weight loss. First, a majority of participants (58%) did manage to lose weight, even though the follow-up period was fairly brief. However, women varied considerably in how much weight they lost, and, in fact, some women even gained weight during this period. What factors predicted weight loss? First, there was no significant association between either attitudes or subjective norms and weight loss. These findings indicate that women's attitudes toward losing weight (which were all quite positive) and beliefs about others' attitudes toward their weight loss did not predict whether women actually lost weight. However, both perceived control, namely, the extent to which women believed they could effectively lose weight, and intentions predicted weight loss. In fact, perceived control was the best predictor of weight loss, and women who had high perceived control and strong intentions lost the most weight. In other words, women who strongly intended to lose weight and believed they were very capable of doing so were the most likely to succeed.

probably think of many times in which your intentions to do a behavior did not successfully lead to enacting behavior. In sum, these theories are a good, but not perfect, predictors of behavior.

Learning Theories

Learning theories are based on the assumption that behavior is influenced by basic learning processes, such as association, reinforcement, and modeling (Bandura, 1977; Pavlov, 1927; Skinner, 1938; Thorndike, 1905). People learn health-related behaviors in the same way that they learn other behaviors. The two main types of learning approaches are classical conditioning and operant conditioning.

Classical conditioning/respondent learning occurs when a previously neutral stimulus comes to evoke the same response as another stimulus with which it is paired. You may be familiar with a famous study on classical conditioning conducted by the Russian physiologist Ivan Pavlov (1927). At the start of the study Pavlov noted that dogs normally salivate in response to the presentation of food, but they do not salivate in response to hearing a bell. For several days, he then rang a bell right before delivering food to hungry dogs. Over time, the dogs began to salivate merely at the sound of the bell before the food was presented. This research demonstrates the power of associative learning, in which dogs (and people!) understand that two events are linked (see Figure 3.3).

Classical conditioning can also influence people's health-related behavior. For example, imagine that you are reclining in a seat at your dentist's office

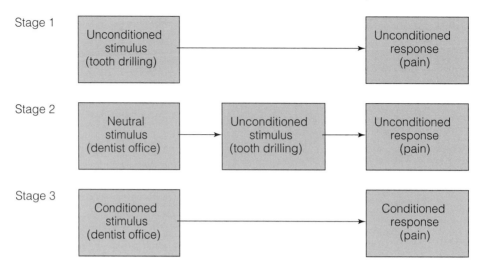

FIGURE 3.3   Model of classical conditioning.

hearing the sound of a dentist's drill coming from the next room. Even though the dentist is not anywhere near you (or your teeth), simply hearing the drill may produce feelings of arousal, anxiety, or pain because over time you have come to associate the noise of the drill with the pain in your mouth. Similarly, patients who have undergone chemotherapy, a treatment that often leaves people feeling nauseous and weak, sometimes develop anticipatory nausea even before they begin receiving a periodic dosage of the drugs (see Photo 3.3). They may start to feel sick when they are sitting in the chair waiting for treatment or in the car as they are driving to the hospital. A recent study by Christine Cameron and her colleagues (2001) demonstrated that cancer patients who had previously received either chemotherapy or radiation reported experiencing nausea or vomiting in response to smells, sights, or tastes that reminded them of their treatment. Thirty percent of the patients reported experiencing nausea in response to smells that reminded them of the treatment, and 17% reported experiencing nausea in response to sights that reminded them of the treatment.

Operant conditioning refers to the idea that behaviors can be increased or decreased as a function of the consequences of engaging in them (Skinner, 1938). On the one hand, desired behaviors can be positively reinforced through rewards, which should lead to their continuation (see Cartoon 3.1). For example, if you are trying to stick to an exercise program, you might decide to give yourself a small reward each week that you run at least 4 days. Similarly, as described at the beginning of the chapter, Hillary should be highly motivated to keep flossing so that she can buy new shoes. On the other hand, the frequency of undesirable behaviors can be decreased through punishment. For example, people who are caught driving under the influence of alcohol typically receive severe punishments, including loss of license, fines, and possibly even jail time. These negative consequences should motivate people to avoid drinking and driving.

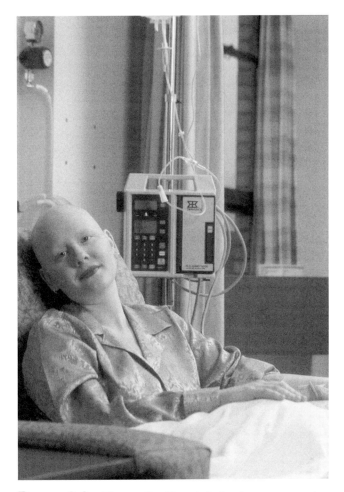

PHOTO 3.3   The smell of hospital cleaning agents, seeing someone else who has cancer, or tasting food eaten while receiving treatment were all enough to stimulate a nauseous response in chemotherapy patients.

Operant conditioning approaches are most effective when people receive rewards for making small steps toward behavior change. Changing behavior is often a long and difficult process; hence, if people receive rewards only after they have completely adopted the behavior, they will likely experience frustration. People should therefore receive rewards simply for taking steps toward adopting the behavior. For example, if you are trying to stop smoking, you might receive a reward for cutting down the number of cigarettes you smoke each day or for delaying smoking your first cigarette each morning. After you have mastered one of these steps toward smoking cessation, you would then receive rewards only for mastering the next step.

Operant conditioning can also occur simply through **observation**, namely, through watching someone else receive rewards or punishment for engaging in a particular behavior (Bandura, 1977, 1986). As described in Box 3.3,

"Oh, not bad. The light comes on, I press the bar, they write me a check. How about you?"

CARTOON 3.1   Money is a very effective reward for desired behavior. (©The New Yorker Collection 1993. Tom Cheney from cartoonbank.com. All Rights Reserved.)

children often form their beliefs about the consequences of various health-related behaviors by watching their parents and older siblings. For example, women whose mothers react with more distress to menstruation report significantly more menstrual symptoms, visits to a health clinic, and disability days because of these symptoms than those with mothers who show less dramatic reactions (Whitehead, Busch, Heller, & Costa, 1986). Similarly, my father is very brave (some would say insane) about pain, and thus he never used novocaine when getting cavities filled. When it was my turn to have cavities filled, I also refused novocaine!

Although learning theories are widely used to predict and influence behavior, these approaches have some important limitations. First, although classical conditioning can be an effective way of influencing health-related behavior, it also has some potential problems. As we examine in detail in Chapter 7, one way to help alcoholics stop drinking is to give them a drug (e.g., Antabuse) that causes them to become violently ill when they drink alcohol. The theory behind this approach is that patients will grow to associate drinking alcohol with nausea and therefore stop drinking. However, patients typically understand that the Antabuse is causing the sickness; therefore, they may simply stop taking the drug instead of avoiding alcohol. Second, operant conditioning can lead people to engage in a behavior simply

Box 3.3

Research Focus—The Effects of Older Siblings on Younger Siblings' Health-Related Behavior

Elizabeth D'Amico and Kim Fromme from the University of Texas at Austin examined the effects of older siblings' outcome expectancies and behavior related to health issues (e.g., drinking, sex without condoms, illicit drug use) on their younger adolescent siblings (D'Amico & Fromme, 1997). One hundred ninety-five students, all of whom had a same-gender younger sibling, completed a series of questionnaires about their own health behaviors, their beliefs about the consequences of engaging in various health risk behaviors, and how often they had engaged in each of these behaviors (e.g., drinking more than five alcoholic drinks on one occasion, smoking marijuana, having sex without a condom). Positive consequences of these behaviors included feeling more sociable and enhancing sexuality, whereas negative consequences included cognitive impairment and aggression. Researchers then mailed a questionnaire assessing these same variables to the participants' younger siblings.

Findings indicated that younger siblings were clearly looking up to their older (though not necessarily wiser) siblings. First, the more younger siblings **believed** their older siblings drank, the more the younger siblings themselves drank and the more the younger siblings believed that positive outcomes would emerge from heavy drinking. This association between younger siblings' perceptions of their older siblings' behaviors and the younger siblings' own behavior was true even though younger siblings were not particularly accurate in their beliefs about their older siblings' behavior. Second, younger siblings' beliefs about their older siblings' positive experiences with other behaviors, such as getting drunk, driving under the influence of alcohol, and having unprotected sex, led the younger adolescents to develop their own positive expectancies about engaging in these behaviors. In sum, younger siblings may learn through modeling and vicarious experience about the consequences of engaging in particular types of health-related behaviors.

to get the reward, but not because of any intrinsic changes in their intentions to engage in the behavior; once the reward is withdrawn, the behavior will stop. In one study, 732 seventh grade boys and girls were asked to use a fluoride mouthwash daily and were given small prizes for doing so (e.g., pencil, pen, yo-yo; Lund & Kegeles, 1984). Children who received rewards were more likely to use the rinse, but once the rewards were eliminated they no longer continued to use the rinse. In sum, learning theories may be effective at changing behavior, but are less effective in maintaining behavior.

Social Cognitive Theory

Social cognitive theory posits that people acquire attitudes through various sources in their immediate social network as well as by observing people presented in the media (Bandura, 1977, 1986). **Direct modeling** occurs when people observe others in their social networks engaging in particular behavior (e.g., watching my foolish father having cavities filled without pain medication), whereas **symbolic modeling** occurs when people observe people portrayed in the media, including magazines, newspapers, and on television. However, whether these attitudes lead to behavior is a function of people's beliefs about their own ability to engage (or not engage) in a particular behavior as well as their beliefs about the consequences of engaging (or not engaging) in a particular behavior. For example, when deciding whether to stop drinking alcohol, individuals might think about whether they realistically would be able to "just say no" and whether they think not drinking would have positive or negative consequences (on their health, social life, etc.). These two components of social cognitive theory are described in detail here.

Social cognitive theory includes the role of an individual's **self-efficacy**, namely, the extent to which one believes he or she can engage in a particular behavior (see Table 3.3). (This concept of self-efficacy is similar to that of perceived behavioral control, as described in the theory of planned behavior.) For example, people who strongly believe they will be able to follow through on their intentions to exercise four times a week will be more likely to successfully carry out this behavior than those who have doubts about their ability to follow through on such intentions. Self-efficacy is seen as a particularly powerful influence on health behavior because it is thought to influence people's behavior in two distinct ways (O'Leary, 1992). First, people who have a strong sense of self-efficacy for a given behavior are likely to exert considerable effort to perform the behavior. A person who has great confidence in her ability to stop smoking, for example, may try harder to resist offers of cigarettes from friends. She may also continue with her goal of quitting even if she experiences a brief lapse in judgment and smokes a cigarette on one occasion. In contrast, someone with low self-efficacy may show little resistance when confronted with tempting offers and may quickly return to regular smoking after smoking a single cigarette. Second, research shows that people with low self-efficacy have a greater physiological response to stressful situations (such as making difficult changes in their behavior), including higher heart rates and blood pressure, than those with high self-efficacy. This greater anxiety response may lead people with low self-efficacy to be less likely to even attempt to engage in behavior change than those with high self-efficacy. Finally, and perhaps most important, people with high self-efficacy show a higher correlation between knowledge and behavior: they are more likely to act on their knowledge (e.g., to eat healthy foods if they understand that healthy foods are good for them; Rimal, 2000).

Social cognitive theory also includes the component of **outcome expectancies**, an individual's beliefs about whether engaging in a particular

T··ɒ·ᴦ 3.3   *Test Yourself: The Condom Use Self-Efficacy Scale*

٠⸃٬᠆ᴧᴜ⸗ using condoms in specific situations. Responses are
ιdecided = 2, agree = 3, strongly agree = 4.

n myself or my partner.
ɔndoms with a new partner.
ι condom even after I have been drinking.
ʃom on myself or my partner even in the heat

rtner to accept using a condom when we have

om correctly.
ι without feeling embarrassed.
ιa with a partner without "breaking the mood."
ιrry a condom with me should I need one.
ιa during intercourse without reducing any sexual

nave a desired outcome. For example, people who believe that
y foods will make them feel good and be healthy are more like-
:h foods than people who believe that nutritious foods taste bad
ɔly aren't going to help their health much anyway. One study of
ιers found that those who chose to breast-feed as opposed to bot-
ιad more positive beliefs about the outcomes of breast-feeding,
ʃ protecting their baby from infection, establishing a close bond with
ɔy, and helping with their own weight loss (Manstead et al., 1983). As
ed in the section on learning theories, outcome expectancies can be
l through direct experience with a behavior, or by observing the con-
ιce someone else experiences as a result of that behavior. You may learn,
ample, that drinking alcohol leads to relaxation by watching the posi-
ɔnsequences your parents experience after drinking a glass of wine after
ʒh day at work.
ial cognitive theory is a good predictor of a variety of different types of
ior, such as smoking cessation (Borrelli & Mermelstein, 1994), eating
ious foods (Sheeshka, Woolcott, & MacKinnon, 1993), lowering choles-
Bandura, 1997), brushing and flossing teeth (Tedesco, Keffer, Davis, &
ɛrsson, 1993), using condoms (Wulfert & Wan, 1993), and exercising
ʃy (Bandura, 1997). As shown in Figure 3.4, one study on the predic-
ʃmoking cessation found that individuals who believed they were able
with stress and that smoking would not be an effective way of cop-
rted having the lowest urges to smoke (Shadel & Mermelstein, 1993).
ʃ, Box 3.4 describes the role of self-efficacy and outcome expectan-
predicting women's ability to withstand pain during childbirth
ιg & Wright, 1983; see Photo 3.4). These studies all suggest that social
ɛ theory is a useful predictor of health-related behavior.

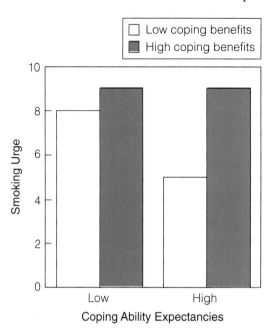

FIGURE 3.4 Smokers who see few benefits of smoking and have strong expectancies about their ability to refuse cigarettes experience the fewest urges to smoke (from Shadel & Mermelstein, 1993).

Given the success of social cognitive theory in predicting health-related behavior, some researchers have examined how to increase and build an individuals' self-efficacy for a given behavior. This work suggests that self-efficacy increases after individuals successfully achieve goals; hence, interventions should help people set attainable subgoals to guide longer-term behavior (Bandura, 1977, 1997). For example, a person who is trying to lose weight might initially fail to reach a very large goal (e.g., "lose 20 pounds"), but might succeed in reaching smaller goals (e.g., "exercise for 30 minutes 3 times this week"). Simply allowing people to believe that they have high self-efficacy can be an effective approach to behavior change as well. One study on smoking cessation informed some participants that they were chosen to participate in the treatment program because they had demonstrated they had strong willpower and a great potential to control their own behavior, whereas others were told they were chosen at random to participate (Blittner, Goldberg, & Merbaum, 1978). After 14 weeks, 67% of those in the "self-efficacy" condition had stopped smoking compared to only 28% of those in the "random" condition (and 6% of those in the control condition), despite the fact that participants with similar senses of self-efficacy made up the study's total population.

As with other theories we've discussed, social cognitive theory also has some limitations. First, interventions should be sensitive to where individuals are in their sense of self-efficacy for a behavior: "cold turkey" approaches may be more

Box 3.4

Research Focus—The Effects of Self-Efficacy and Outcome Expectancies on the Use of Pain Medication during Childbirth

Martha Manning and Thomas Wright from Catholic University examined the role of self-efficacy expectancies, outcome expectancies, and importance as predictors of whether women used pain medication during childbirth (Manning & Wright, 1983). Fifty-two women who were enrolled in childbirth preparation classes with their first pregnancy served as participants in this research. Women completed questionnaires during the third trimester of their pregnancy, the early stages of labor, and several days after delivery. The women were asked about their self-efficacy for controlling pain without medication ("I will be able to control the pain of labor and delivery without pain medication") and their outcome expectancies for using nonmedical approaches to pain control ("The techniques for controlling pain which are taught in prepared childbirth classes will make it possible for a woman to go through labor and delivery without pain medication"). Researchers also called all women following delivery and asked them several questions, including their length of labor, type of delivery, and use of pain medication.

As predicted, both self-efficacy and outcome expectancies were significant predictors of whether women used pain relief medication during childbirth. First, women who were more confident in their ability to withstand the pain of labor and delivery without medical relief were less likely to use medication in general. Even among women who did use medical relief, those who were more confident about their ability to control their pain without drugs used medication later in labor. Similarly, women who had more positive expectancies about childbirth were less likely to use pain medication in general and requested medication later during labor. These findings provide support for the value of both self-efficacy and outcome expectancies in predicting behavior.

effective with those who are high in self-efficacy and less effective for those with less confidence (Mermelstein, 1997). Individuals who lack confidence in their ability to enact a behavior change may need to focus on making small steps toward adopting a behavior in order to gain confidence in their ability to ultimately reach their goal. Second, some researchers believe that social cognitive theory really does not improve on other models of health behavior, such as the theory of planned behavior. For example, a study by McCaul and colleagues (1993) found that the theory of planned behavior was a better predictor of women's breast self-examination than social cognitive theory.

Photo 3.4   A woman's sense of self-efficacy and her outcome expectations can influence her decision whether to use pain medication during childbirth.

What Are Stage Models of Health Behavior Change?

Although the models described thus far have all focused on describing the various components that predict whether people engage in a particular health-related behavior, some researchers believe these models as too simple because they focus only on the outcome behavior of interest (e.g., condom use, smoking cessation). Critics of these models believe that behavior change occurs gradually and in stages, and they have therefore proposed alternative models that focus on the process that leads to behavior change. In turn, these models specify a set of ordered categories, or stages, that people go through as they attempt to change their behavior.

Transtheoretical or Stages of Change Model

According to the transtheoretical, or stages of change, model, making changes in health-related behavior is a complex process, and individuals make such changes only gradually and not necessarily in a linear order (see Figure 3.5; Prochaska, DiClemente, & Norcross, 1992). People move from one stage to another in a spiral fashion, which can include movement to new stages as well as movement back to previous stages, until they have finally completed the process of behavior change. It is likely, for example, that a person who decides to stop smoking will experience several setbacks, or relapses, as he or she attempts to quit.

The first stage in this model is **precontemplation**. Individuals who are in this stage lack an awareness of the problem behavior and have no intentions or plans to change the behavior in the foreseeable future (e.g., "I have no intention to stop smoking"). Basically, they just aren't motivated to make any change in their own behavior, and they may underestimate the benefits of change and overestimate the costs to justify their inaction. People who smoke, for example, may believe that because they exercise regularly they will not suffer the negative health effects of smoking, and that if they stop smoking they will gain weight and hence suffer the (much worse) health consequences of obesity. They may also believe that although other people have suffered negative outcomes from the behavior, they have some unique personal invulnerability. I remember a friend in college telling me he actually believed he drove better while intoxicated. Individuals in this stage may also lack confidence in their ability to successfully engage in the new behavior.

Individuals who are beginning to consider making a change are in the **contemplation** stage (e.g., "I may start to think about how to quit smoking"). This stage is often characterized by a growing awareness of the costs of the negative behavior as well as of their personal susceptibility. People who are in this stage are out of the "ignorance is bliss" stage of precontemplation and are realizing that making a change would probably be a very good idea. At the start of the chapter, I described how Allen's academic problems caused him to think about cutting down on his drinking, although he is not actually taking steps (yet) to carry out this behavior. People in the contemplation stage may start seeking information on the negative effects of their behavior

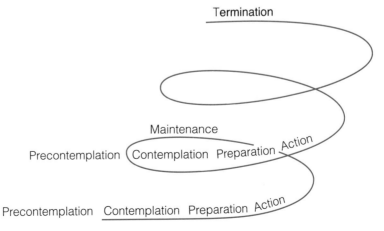

A Spiral Model of the Stages of Change

FIGURE 3.5 Model of stages of change.

and strategies for changing such behavior, although they may still lack confidence in their ability to make the change. This stage is often characterized by ambivalence as well as frustration.

Individuals who have made a commitment to change their behavior are in the stage of **preparation** (e.g., "I will stop smoking within the next 30 days"). They may start making small changes in an attempt to move toward the desired end point, such as decreasing the number of cigarettes they smoke each day or trying to delay the time they have their first cigarette each day. People in this stage are preparing to ultimately change their behavior, but are starting by taking a series of small steps toward the desired behavior change. Although individuals in this stage are often highly motivated to change, they may vary in how confident they are of achieving success.

The stage of **action** is reached when they are actually engaging in a new behavior ("I have stopped smoking"). The behavior change is now public, and the criterion for successfully engaging in it is high. Although the risk of relapse is strong at this stage, people often receive a lot of support from their family and friends during this stage because they have made a public commitment to changing their behavior.

Finally, the **maintenance** stage is reached when people sustain the change over time, typically 6 months ("I will continue to not smoke"). The focus in this stage is on preventing relapse. People receive less social support during this stage because they have already engaged in action, but support is still an important predictor of maintaining the new behavior.

The transtheoretical model predicts the adoption of a variety of health-related behaviors, including ceasing to drink, use drugs, and overeat, and starting behaviors such as condom use, sunscreen use, exercise, and screening for cancer (Prochaska et al., 1994). For example, one recent study with college students found that those who were in the preparation stage in terms of exercising at one time were more likely to be exercising 1 to 3 months later than those who were initially in the stages of precontemplation or contemplation (Rosen, 2000). Considerable research using the transtheoretical model has focused on its effectiveness in predicting smoking cessation (Prochaska et al., 1992). As described in Box 3.5, people who are in different stages of change in terms of their smoking behavior differ in predicted ways on numerous variables, including self-efficacy for smoking cessation, perception of costs and benefits of smoking, and behavioral efforts toward quitting (DiClemente et al., 1991).

What factors influence people to move from one stage to the next? Researchers who developed this theory believe that people go through specific processes of change as they progress through the various stages (Prochaska et al., 1992). At the earliest stages, people must become aware of the problem and to learn effective ways of avoiding it. For some types of health behaviors, such as smoking, people typically already have exposure to information about their negative effects, but in others cases, such as getting a regular tetanus shot, people must be educated about the benefits of engaging in the behavior. **Social liberation**, external forces that facilitate change, can also be effective in moving people along. For example, programs that prohibit smoking in par-

Box 3.5

Research Focus—Using the Stages of Change Model to Predict Smoking Cessation

Carlo DiClemente and his colleagues examined smoking history, processes of change, self-efficacy, and decisional balance for smokers at different stages of change (DiClemente et al., 1991). Participants who smoked but were at different stages of change completed a series of questionnaires, including smoking history, self-efficacy for quitting smoking, physical dependence on nicotine, and the perceived costs and benefits of smoking. Of the participants, 166 were in the stage of precontemplation, 794 were in the contemplation stage, and 506 were in the preparation stage. Researchers then followed up on all participants 1 month later and 6 months later to see whether the participants had successfully stopped smoking.

As predicted, findings indicated that people at different stages of change in terms of smoking also differed in terms of self-efficacy, the perceived benefits and costs of smoking, and, most important, their behavioral efforts in terms of quitting. First, those who were in the stage of preparation had greater self-efficacy to quit than those in the stage of contemplation, who in turn had higher scores than those in the stage of precontemplation. Similarly, while those in the stage of preparation thought that the costs of smoking were greater than their benefits, those in contemplation saw the costs and benefits as equal, and those in precontemplation saw the benefits as greater than the costs. Finally, those in the preparation stage had made more lifetime and last-year quit attempts than those in either contemplation or precontemplation. At the 1-month follow-up, for example, those in the preparation stage were more likely to have made a quit attempt (56% versus 6% for those in the precontemplation stage and 24% for those in the contemplation stage). Findings at the 6-month follow-up also revealed strong differences in quitting behavior, with 80% of those in the preparation stage having made a quit attempt as compared to only 48% of those in the contemplation stage and 26% of those in the precontemplation stage (see Figure 3.6).

ticular buildings can help make the act of smoking less convenient and less comfortable. As people move along to the later stages of the models, they often examine the costs and benefits of changing their behavior. They might, for example, reflect on whether their desire to lose weight is really worth giving up late-night McDonald's trips. Perceived benefits of changing the behavior usually increase as people move from precontemplation to contemplation, and the costs of the new behavior usually decrease between the contemplation and action stages (see Table 3.4). So, behavior-change messages should help people

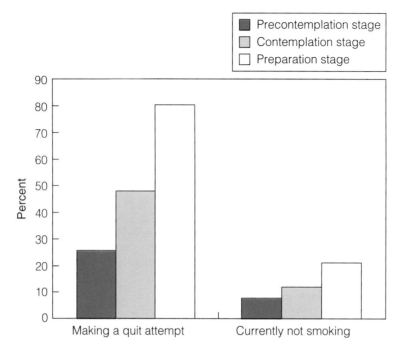

FIGURE 3.6   At the 6-month follow-up, smokers who were in the stage of preparation were much more likely to report having made a quit attempt as well as currently not smoking than those who were in the stages of precontemplation or contemplation (DiClemente et al., 1991).

focus on the costs of continuing the old behavior (e.g., "I have stained teeth because of all of my smoking") and the benefits of adopting the new behavior (e.g., "think about how much money I'll save by not smoking"). Finally, there are a number of strategies that help people move from the action stage to the maintenance stage, such as rewards and substituting new behaviors for the old ones. These methods might include treating oneself to dinner at a favorite restaurant after a week of not smoking or chewing gum instead of smoking. (Issues of relapse are discussed in detail in Chapter 13.)

As with all theories of health behavior, the transtheoretical, or stages of change, model has some limitations. First, although the processes of change by stage have been widely studied with respect to issues of smoking and substance abuse (DiClemente et al., 1992), some research suggests that the cognitive processes involved in leading people to stop certain behaviors (e.g., smoking) may be different than those involved in leading them to start behaviors (e.g., exercise; Rosen, 2000). Specifically, while consciousness raising and social liberation are seen as most useful during the early stages of change toward ceasing a behavior, these processes are used frequently during later stages of change toward adopting a new behavior. Second, although the trans-

TABLE 3.4   *Test Yourself: Decisional Balance Measure for Contraceptive Use: Disease Prevention*

Please rate how important each statement is with respect to your decision whether to use contraceptives to prevent diseases. Answer each question using a scale of 1 to 5, with 1 = not important to 5 = extremely important.

1. I would feel protected against STDs if my partner and I used condoms.
2. My partner would feel more protected against STDs if we used condoms.
3. I would feel more responsible about STDs if I used condoms.
4. Protecting myself from STDs would increase my self-esteem.
5. Using condoms to guard against the transmission of STDs builds trust.
6. Condoms are easy to use.
7. Sex would be more enjoyable if I felt protected from STDs.
8. Methods that protect you from STDs are easy to obtain.
9. Condoms are affordable.
10. If I used condoms to prevent STDs, I would gain my partner's respect.
11. My partner would find sex less exciting if a condom were used.
12. I might hurt my partner's feelings if I suggested we use a condom.
13. It is harder to insist on condom use once a commitment has been made to a partner.
14. I would hurt my partner's feelings if I suggested we use a condom when we were already using the birth control pills.
15. Methods of contraception that prevent STDs are unpleasant to use.
16. I might spoil a sexual encounter if I brought up condom use.
17. Discussing STD prevention makes my partner uncomfortable.
18. Condoms take the spontaneity out of love making.
19. My partner would be angry if I refused to have sex unless a condom were used.
20. I am uncomfortable discussing STD prevention with a partner.

Items 1 to 10 measure the benefits of condom use, whereas items 11 to 20 measure the costs of condom use.

Source: Grimley, Riley, Bellis, & Prochaska, 1993.

theoretical/stages of change model describes how cognitive processes should lead people to move forward in the stages, most of the research testing this model has examined people only at one point in time. However, some recent research indicates that people who are weighing the costs and benefits of smoking at one time are **not** more likely to move to a higher stage one or two years later (Herzog, Abrams, Emmons, Linnan, & Shadel, 1999). These researchers believe that thinking about the costs and benefits of a behavior is not a good predictor of whether people will move further toward change. Finally, are the specific stages described in this model the right ones? As described next, the precaution adoption process model, another stage model, defines the stages of health behavior change in a different way.

Precaution Adoption Process Model

The precaution adoption process model is similar in some ways to the trans-theoretical model—it is also proposes that when individuals consider engaging in new health-related behaviors they go through a series of stages (Weinstein, 1988). As with the transtheoretical model, people do not necessarily move directly from one stage to another, but rather can move backward or forward between stages. For example, you may decide on New Year's Eve that your resolution for the upcoming year is to stop drinking alcohol, but by February 1st, you may have changed your intention to follow through with this behavior. The precaution adoption process model differs from the trans-theoretical model, though, in the number of stages it proposes as well as the process by which it predicts how people progress through the stages.

As shown in Figure 3.7 and Table 3.5, the precaution adoption process model includes seven stages. In stage 1 people are not even aware of the disease or problem. For example, many adolescent girls do not get enough calcium in their daily diet, but often are unaware that this greatly increases their risk of osteoporosis in the future. In stage 2, people are aware generally of the health risk and believe that others might be at risk, but they do not believe that they personally are at risk. In other words, they have an **optimistic bias** about their own level of risk. So, you might know that wearing a seat belt can protect people in car accidents from serious injuries, but you may believe that because you are a safe driver you will never experience an accident anyway. In stage 3, the decision-making stage, people have acquired a belief in their own personal risk, but they still have not decided to take action to protect themselves from that risk. You may know people who understand that lack of exercise puts them at greater risk of developing heart disease, for example, but they haven't decided whether they are going to exercise. From stage 3 people may move to stage 5, in which they decide to take action (e.g., finally do exercise; see Photo 3.5), but they may also move to stage 4, in which they decide that action is unnecessary (e.g., they plan to continue being inactive, at least for the time being). In stage 6, which is similar to the stage of action in the transtheoretical model, people have begun to change their behavior. Finally, in stage 7 people maintain the behavior change over some period of time.

Although the precaution adoption process model is a relatively new theory of predicting health behavior, some research already provides support for it. One study found that this model was a useful predictor of engaging in home radon testing (Weinstein & Sandman, 1992), and other studies demonstrate that this model predicts smoking cessation (Boney McCoy et al., 1992), contraceptive use (Emmett & Ferguson, 1999), and mammography use (Clemow et al., 2000). For example, S. Boney McCoy and colleagues found that although few smokers are at stage 1 (probably because virtually everyone is aware of the health hazards of smoking), many are at stage 2, in which they see smoking as generally dangerous, but still possess an optimistic view of their own risk. For example, many smokers believe that compared to "typical smokers" they were less likely to suffer from smoking-related health consequences.

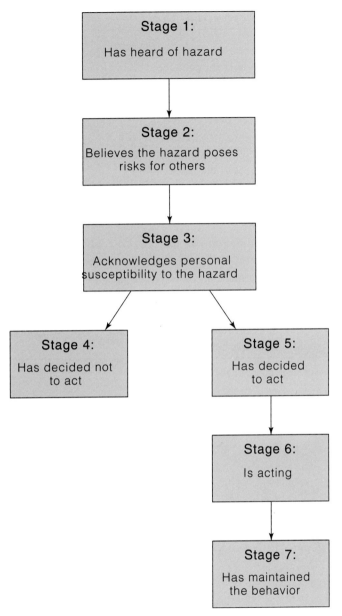

FIGURE 3.7 Precaution adoption process model (taken from Weinstein, 1988).

However, smokers who had recently joined a smoking cessation clinic were typically one or two stages further along: they recognize their own vulnerability to smoking-related health problems and have made a decision to try to quit. Box 3.6 describes a study predicting osteoporosis prevention in young women using the precaution adoption process model (Blalock et al., 1996).

TABLE 3.5   *Examples of the Seven Stages of the Precaution Adoption Process Model*

Statement	Stage Classification
I have never seriously thought about trying to increase the amount that I currently exercise.	Stage 1
I have seriously thought about trying to increase the amount that I exercise but decided against it.	Stage 2
I have seriously thought about trying to increase the amount that I currently exercise, but I have not thought about it in the past 6 months.	Stage 3
I am seriously thinking about trying to increase the amount that I exercise some time within the next 6 months.	Stage 4
I plan to increase the amount that I exercise within the next 6 months.	Stage 5
I am currently doing things to increase the amount that I exercise.	Stage 6
(Women who were already engaging in exercise for at least 45 minutes three times a week and who reported that they had been engaging in exercise for the last 6 months were classified as stage 7.)	

Source: Taken from Blalock et al., 1996.

PHOTO 3.5   According to the precaution adoption process model, people who are currently thinking about increasing their exercise (stage 4) or plan to increase their exercise (stage 5) will be more likely to actually exercise than those in earlier stages.

Box 3.6

Research Focus—Using the Precaution Adoption Process Model to Predict Osteoporosis Prevention

Susan Blalock and her colleagues at the University of North Carolina at Chapel Hill examined the predictors of osteoporosis prevention using the precaution adoption process model (Blalock et al., 1996). Four hundred and fifty-two women between the ages of 35 and 45 were recruited to participate in this study. Women completed a questionnaire assessing their calcium consumption, frequency of exercise, and measures directly related to the precaution adoption process model (e.g., perceived severity of osteoporosis, benefits associated with eating calcium, concern over osteoporosis, and susceptibility to osteoporosis). After women returned the questionnaire, they were sent an order form describing six different types of brochures that they could receive free of charge. This allowed researchers to measure whether women in different stages differed in how interested they were in receiving information about osteoporosis.

The reasearchers found that women who had never engaged in exercise had less knowledge about osteoporosis, saw fewer benefits of exercise, and had lower self-efficacy for exercise than those who were currently engaging in exercise. Second, compared with women who were currently thinking about or planning to increase their exercise frequency, those who had previously engaged in exercise (but who were no longer regularly exercising) reported lower self-efficacy, more exercise inconvenience, and fewer exercise benefits. Finally, while only 7.7% of those who had never engaged in exercise requested one of the free brochures, 22.9% of those who had previously engaged in exercise requested a brochure, and 40.2% of those who were currently exercising requested a brochure. This study provides support for the precaution adoption process model and suggests some strategies for helping women move to a further stage of behavior change.

As with the other models we've discussed, the precaution adoption process model has some important implications for designing health behavior change interventions. First, individuals who are at different stages should be influenced by different types of information. When someone is deciding whether to take action (stage 3), for example, perceptions of vulnerability should predict whether he or she moves to stage 5 (decides to engage in behavior change) or stage 4 (chooses not to engage in behavior change). On the other hand, when someone has decided to engage in behavior change (stage 5), whether that person actually does so (moves to stage 6) should be influenced by obstacles and barriers to such change.

Because the precaution adoption process model is quite new, relatively little research has examined how useful this approach is, and in particular whether it is more useful than the transtheoretical model. The major difference between these two models is that the precaution adoption process model separates people into more distinct categories than the transtheoretical model does (Weinstein et al., 1998). First, the transtheoretical model groups all people who are not currently thinking about behavior change into one stage (precontemplation), whereas the precaution adoption process model separates these people into those who are unaware of a health issue (stage 1) and those who are aware of an issue but do not see themselves as personally vulnerable to it (stage 2). The precaution adoption process model also distinguishes people who have never even thought about changing their behavior (stages 1 and 2) from those who have thought about making a change but have decided against it for the time being (stage 4). Future research must clearly compare the effectiveness of these two stage models in predicting health behavior change.

Lingering Issues

Is one of these models better than others? Although all of the models described in this chapter view health-related behavior as caused by multiple factors, they vary in exactly which factors they include. For example, the health belief model is the only one to include the component of susceptibility, perhaps because this model (unlike most of the others) was originally developed to specifically predict health-related behavior. However, this model ignores the role of individuals' self-efficacy, which other models (theory of planned behavior, social cognitive theory) view as fundamentally important. Although research has not shown which model is the most useful in describing health-related behavior in general, it does suggest that different models may be most useful in describing particular types of behavior. Specifically, a study comparing the theory of reasoned action to the theory of planned behavior found that the component of perceived behavior control was an important predictor of behavior only for those behaviors that are under low personal control (Madden, Ellen, & Ajzen, 1992). For example, students viewed the behavior "getting a good night's sleep" as relatively outside of their control (possibly due to the challenges of getting to sleep in a college dorm), and for this behavior, having a strong belief that one could get a good night's sleep was an important predictor of behavior. On the other hand, students viewed "taking vitamin supplements" as highly under their control, and for this behavior, their personal confidence that they could take vitamins was not a strong predictor of behavior. Similarly, research generally shows that the health belief model is a better predictor of one-time or infrequent behavior, such as getting immunizations or having a mammogram, whereas other models are stronger predictors of more frequent behavior, such as quitting smoking and using condoms.

Are there other variables that should be included in these models? One critique of these models is that they fail to include some factors that may be quite strong predictors of behavior, including race, gender, and socioeconomic status. Rosenstock (1990) has noted that all of these models focus on the individuals' own attitudes, beliefs, and self-efficacy, but largely ignore broader factors that can influence health-related behavior, such as public policy, interpersonal processes, and community norms. For example, although the AIDS epidemic led to a push for monogamous, committed relationships, gay men have no option for entering legally binding relationships and often have no financial incentive to do so (e.g., health care coverage is rarely extended to the partners of gay men; no tax benefits). Similarly, these models are largely based in studies with whites, and often only white men; therefore they may not consider the different values that motivate behavior among members of other ethnic groups (Cochran & Mays, 1993). For example, because the African American community places a stronger priority on interdependence and connection with extended family than does the white community, African Americans may be more influenced in terms of their health-related behavior by the attitudes of their family. Finally, socioeconomic factors can also influence whether people engage in health-related behaviors, but they are entirely ignored in all of these theoretical models. For example, people who have limited financial resources may be strongly motivated to eat healthy foods, but simply lack the money to purchase fresh fruits and vegetables, which are often very expensive—if available at all—in many inner cities (Cochran & Mays, 1993). Similarly, people who lack transportation or health insurance may be unable to take part in regular health screenings and vaccination programs though they may want to.

Thought Questions

1. You are in charge of creating an alcohol abuse prevention workshop at your university. Design one workshop based on the theory of planned behavior and another on the health belief model.

2. What similarities do the theory of planned behavior and social cognitive theory have? What are their differences?

3. Describe two ways that principles of learning theory can be used to help people make changes in their health-related behavior.

4. Your friend Bill never wears his seat belt and claims that because he is a very safe driver he has no need for such a safety device. Your roommate Jamal, on the other hand, never wore his seat belt until after his sister was injured in a car accident; he now tries to use his seat belt more regularly. According to the stages of change model, how could you help Bill and Jamal move to later stages of change?

5. What factors do you think are the most important ones to include in a model predicting whether people wear sunscreen? Are these the same ones or different ones that would be best to include in a model predicting the consistent use of condoms? Why or why not?

CHAPTER 4

Stress

- Robert is a doctor in a busy and crowded emergency room. He feels overwhelmed by his long hours and the huge responsibility he has for saving people's lives. Moreover, this pressure is even worse because he has no control over his work schedule—as a new doctor, Robert must cover other doctors' shifts when they can't come in, with only last-minute notice sometimes. Although Robert has always been very healthy, recently he has developed an ulcer and is experiencing frequent migraine headaches.

- Sara is a sophomore in college and is a pre-med major. She wants very much to be a doctor, but is struggling to keep up with all of the required courses. This semester, Sara is taking chemistry and physics, and neither class is going very well. To make matters worse, even though she puts in long hours studying for her exams, whenever she takes a test her mind simply goes blank.

- Chandler just moved to a new city and started a new job. Because he doesn't really know anyone in his new city, Chandler writes in his journal every night and calls old college friends whenever he is feeling lonely. Although he is under a lot of time pressure at his new job, Chandler knows that he needs to take some time for himself every day to relax. He therefore joins a health club with a pool so that he can swim each day after work. Chandler is enjoying the challenges of his job and looking forward to making some new friends.

- Monica just started college and already is experiencing a lot of stress. Her parents have been fighting a lot and have recently told her that they are separating. Also, she is having trouble keeping up with the reading in her English literature course, and has not even started writing a paper that is due tomorrow. After being encouraged by her aunt, Monica decides to go see a therapist at the college health center to talk about her feelings about her parents' separation. She also decides that she will ask her English professor for a 1-week extension on her paper and will stop going to basketball practice until she is caught up with work.

- Elizabeth has a strong belief in the power of religion. She prays every morning, attends religious services regularly, and has a general belief that "things happen for a reason." Although Elizabeth has suffered from diabetes since she was a child, she regularly takes her medicine, watches her diet, and jogs four times a week, and hence has not experienced any really disabling effects. She feels very lucky that God is watching out for her and keeping her healthy.

Preview

Everyone has experienced stress (you may be feeling it as you read this chapter), and we know what people mean when they say they are "stressed." But what exactly is stress? In the field of health psychology, *stress* refers to a state of challenge or threat that disrupts the normal rhythm and balance of a person's life. This chapter examines a number of issues related to the link between stress and health: first it describes different sources of stress and different ways of measuring stress, and then it examines two different theories about how stress influences physiological responses as well as the physical and psychological consequences of stress. Finally, this chapter describes various strategies for coping with stress, in particular, the use of religion to cope with stress.

What Are the Main Sources of Stress?

Although personal relationships can be a source of support (as we discuss in Chapter 6), they are also a major source of stress. In fact, one third of the stressful events college students experience are caused by relationships (Ptacek, Smith, & Zanas, 1992), and interpersonal conflicts account for as much as 80% of the stress experienced by married couples (Bolger, Delongis, Kessler, &

Schilling, 1989). These conflicts can focus on how to spend money, the balancing of work and family time, and the fair distribution of child care and household tasks. Family issues such as an illness or divorce can also lead to stress, in part because these problems can lead to emotional and financial pressures. For example, caring for a loved one who has a chronic illness can cause financial burdens, such as the cost of in-home nursing care, and emotional problems, such as depression, anxiety, and sadness (Kiecolt-Glaser, Glaser et al., 1987). In fact, research by Karen Rook (1984) suggests that having undermining or disruptive interpersonal relationships can have an even greater impact on health (albeit a negative one) than having supportive and positive relationships. Even seemingly positive events, such as marriage and the arrival of a new baby, can create stress (see Photo 4.1). A couple with a new baby, for example, is likely to experience financial pressure, sleep deprivation, and challenges in balancing time, which can all lead to stress. (In Chapter 10, we examine the particular stresses that are caused by having a chronic illness, and in Chapter 11 we examine the stress associated with experiencing the loss of a loved one.)

Work pressures, including long hours, constant deadlines, and substantial responsibility, can create considerable stress (Spector, 2002). The stressful period that hits most college students at the end of the semester when they must take exams and complete term papers is a good example of this type of stress. People who have jobs that involve a responsibility for saving people's lives, such as doctors, firefighters, and air traffic controllers, often experience particularly high levels of stress because making a mistake can have dire consequences (Shouksmith & Taylor, 1997). As I described at the beginning of the chapter, Robert's position as a doctor in a busy emergency room led to considerable occupational stress for him. But even jobs without the pressure of life and death

PHOTO 4.1   Even positive events can cause stress.

CARTOON 4.1 Work pressures, including long hours, heavy workload, and constant deadlines, can all create stress. (©2003 David Sipress from cartoonbank.com. All Rights Reserved.)

can be stressful. Other aspects of jobs that can create stress include relationships with colleagues or supervisors, lack of resources (e.g., defective equipment, few supplies), and the physical environment (e.g., noise, heat). One recent study found that factory workers who experienced loud noise at work had higher blood pressure, especially if they were working on complex tasks that required concentration (Melamed, Fried, & Froom, 2001). People who have little control over their jobs, such as when, where, and how they complete their work, also experience considerable stress (see Cartoon 4.1) (Spector, 2002). For example, restaurant servers often experience high levels of stress because they must satisfy both customers and their employers, but they have very little control over their work environment (e.g., they do not prepare the food, set prices, determine how fast food is ready; Theorell et al., 1990). Physicians whose work schedule (including number of hours worked as well as when those hours are worked) is not what they prefer experience more burnout (see Photo 4.2, Barnet, Gareis, & Brennan, 1999). On the other hand, while my job as a professor often includes deadlines and long hours, I have a large amount of control over where and even when I do most of my work—I can write lectures and grade papers in my home or office (or even on the beach!) and can choose when I'll focus on each task (see Box 4.1 for a related benefit of this lifestyle). Finally, some recent research suggests that people who achieve greater career success—such as becoming president of a country, winning a Nobel Prize or an

---

Box 4.1

Focus on Women—Why Working Mothers Actually Are Happy

Although the media constantly focuses on the pressures working mothers feel, research in psychology suggests that this "pressure" actually leads to greater psychological and physical well-being. In fact, women who are employed are less depressed than nonemployed women, and this is even true for women with children (Barnett & Hyde, 2001). Moreover, one recent study found that employed men and employed women have similar levels of illnesses, whereas women who are homemakers experience higher levels of illnesses (Weidner, Boughal, Connor, Pieper, & Mendell, 1997). Employed women also show lower levels of cholesterol than homemakers. Why do women benefit from having multiple roles? Negative experiences in one domain can be buffered by experiencing positive effects in another. Some days when my research is not going well, I can recover from my anxiety by playing Candyland with my son. On the other hand, after a weekend in which I scrubbed crayons off the wall and changed 82 diapers, going to the office on a Monday morning can be a real treat! In sum, for women, being employed outside the home may help buffer the effects of stressful conditions in the home, and vice versa.

Oscar, or serving on the Supreme Court—relatively early in their lives tend to have shorter lives than those who attain such success later on possibly because they have experienced large amounts of stress as they focused so intensely on high achievement (McCann, 2001).

People can also experience stress from environmental pressures, such as natural disasters, noise, and crowding. People who experience natural disasters suffer from both psychological and physical distress (Norris & Kaniasty, 1996). For example, after the 1980 eruption of the Mount Saint Helens volcano in Washington, there was an increase in number of phone calls made to a mental health crisis line, referrals to an alcohol treatment program, reports by the police of domestic violence, and visits to hospital emergency rooms (see Table 4.1; Adams & Adams, 1984). People who work in noisy conditions experience increased stress (Evans, Bullinger, & Hygge, 1998), as do those who live in busy cities (see Box 4.2; Levine, 1990). Box 4.3 describes a type of environmental stress that college students may experience: the stress of living in dormitories with long halls! Another major cause of stress is poverty, which is often associated with other stressors, such as crime, overcrowded housing, pollution, and noise (Johnson et al., 1995; Myers, Kagawa-Singer, Kumanika, Lex, & Markides, 1995).

PHOTO 4.2   Although you might think that working mothers suffer from burnout (e.g., having to be too many things to too many people), women who work outside the home benefit in terms of health from having high self-complexity.

TABLE 4.1 *Average Monthly Rates of Emergencies Before and After the Mount Saint Helen's Eruption*

Variable	Predisaster	Postdisaster
Calls to a mental health crisis line	11.14	23.28
Appointments scheduled at a mental health clinic	99.14	126.43
Mental illness diagnoses at a medical clinic	14.8	49.7
Hospital emergency room visits	286.71	384.00
Police reports of domestic violence	6.86	10.57
Clients served by community alcohol center	25.43	34.71

Source: Adams & Adams, 1984.

Box 4.2

Health Psychology in the Real World—Does Your City Cause Stress?

People who have lived in or visited different parts of the United States are likely to have noticed many differences, including differences in accent, dress, and food preference. Robert Levine (1990), a professor at California State University, Fresno, examined another type of difference: the "pace of life." He collected data from nine different cities in four regions of the United States (Northeast, Midwest, South, and West), and within each city he measured four aspects of pace of life. What were these measures? Pace of walking, speed of talking, time it took to complete a bank transaction, and proportion of people who were wearing a wristwatch. You can probably guess the results of his study: people in the Northeast do have a faster pace of life. Specifically, as compared to people in other regions, Northeasterners walk faster, talk faster, complete transactions faster, and are more likely to wear a wristwatch. In contrast, Westerners apparently lived up to their "laid-back" name: they were the slowest at each of the four tasks. What is the impact of pace of life on health? Studies have shown a connection between living a "fast-paced life" and heart disease. In fact, people who are Type A personalities, or those who have a strong sense of time urgency, hostility, and competitiveness, are much more likely to have heart disease and to experience a heart attack. Stressful situations, such as those with great time urgency, can also lead to unhealthy behaviors, such as cigarette smoking and poor eating habits.

Stress can also be caused by pressures from within ourselves. There are many times we are torn between two different goals, and this internal pressure can cause stress (Lewin, 1935). For example, you may want to take a trip to Europe with your family over spring break, but you may also want to spend time hanging out with friends. This type of conflict is called an *approach–approach conflict*, because you are torn between wanting to do two desirable things that are incompatible. In other cases, people experience *approach–avoidance* or *avoidance–avoidance conflicts*. These types of conflicts might include wanting to eat tempting foods (approach) but also wanting to lose weight (avoid), and choosing between chemotherapy (avoid) and radiation (avoid) to treat cancer. What are the consequences of experiencing such internal conflict? Research by Robert Emmons and Laura King (1988) demonstrates that students who experience such conflict have more depression and anxiety as well as more psychosomatic complaints, including headaches, chest pains, and nausea.

Finally, people often experience considerable stress when they are in situations in which they lack control—this is why seemingly minor situations, such

Box 4.3

Research Focus—The Potential Hazards of Dormitory Living

Andrew Baum and Robert Gatchel conducted a series of studies on the effects of living environments on psychological and physical well-being. One study of particular relevance for college students examined the effects of living in different types of dormitory environments in 64 first-year students (Baum & Gatchel, 1981). Half of the participants lived in long-corridor dormitories (those with 32 to 49 residents sharing common spaces such as lounges, halls, and bathrooms) and half lived in short-corridor dormitories (those with 6 to 20 residents sharing common spaces). Participants completed a brief questionnaire prior to moving into their dormitory, and then completed more detailed questionnaires three times during the semester. Questionnaires surveyed students' general adjustment to college life, including their satisfaction with college and dormitory life, their success in making friends, and the types of problems they had experienced.

As predicted, living arrangements had a major impact on students' psychological well-being and patterns of social interaction. First, those who lived in long-corridor dorms felt that their dormitories were less controllable and predictable than those in short-corridor dorms. For example, they were more likely to report problems with predicting who they might see in the hallways, meeting people they did not know well, and avoiding people they did not want to see. Students who lived in long-corridor residence halls were also less satisfied with college and with their dormitories, had fewer friends, and belonged to fewer social groups. These findings suggest that college administrators need to think carefully about the types of housing arrangements they offer students, particularly first-year students who are most likely to leave college if dissatisfied.

as waiting in a slow line at the post office or being put on hold during a phone call, can be so irritating. Lacking control can have a very negative impact on health and well-being. For example, in one study researchers implanted tumorous cancer cells in rats, and then some of the rats were given uncontrollable shocks (those which they could not avoid), other rats were given controllable shocks (those which they could avoid by pressing a bar), and other rats were given no shocks (Visintainer, Volpicelli, & Seligman, 1982). After one month, 73% of the rats who were given uncontrollable shocks had died as compared to 37% of those who were given controllable shocks and 46% of those who did not receive shocks. Similarly, when people are exposed to uncontrollable events, such as problems that can't be solved and loss of personal freedom, they feel distress and physiological arousal. One study exposed people to a loud noise that in some conditions they could avoid and in some conditions they could not (Corah & Boffa, 1970). The noise was seen as much less stressful when people could avoid the noise than when it was unavoidable. Lacking control can lead to long-term health consequences: one recent study found that workers in low-control jobs experienced a 43% increase in chance of death over 10 years (Amick et al., 2002). What's the good news? As described in Box 4.4, giving people a sense of control over their environment can lead to decreases in stress and in turn greater psychological and physical well-being.

Box 4.4

Research Focus—The Effects of Having Control on Health in Nursing Home Residents

Ellen Langer and Judy Rodin (1976) examined the effects of giving people a sense of control on their psychological and physical well-being. Ninety-one adults in a nursing home were randomly assigned to either the control-enhanced group or the comparison group. Residents who were in the control-enhanced group heard a speech from the director of the nursing home that emphasized how much control they had over their own lives (even in this nursing-home setting). For example, the director told residents that they were free to arrange the furniture in their rooms however they would like it, they could visit others or have other residents visit them, and that they would each be given a plant to take care of by themselves. The residents in the comparison group also heard a speech by the director, but this speech emphasized only that he wanted them to be happy. Residents in this group were also given a plant, but were told that the nurses would take care of the plant for them. The residents filled out questionnaires 1 and 3 weeks after the director's speech, and nurses also filled out questionnaires. The researchers also examined several different types of behavioral measures, including whether residents participated in a jelly bean guessing contest, whether they attended evening movies, and their general level of activity (which was cleverly measured by putting tape on the wheels of their wheelchairs to see how much the tape wore down over time).

What were the findings? Those in the control-enhanced group rated themselves as happier, more active, and more alert than those in the comparison condition. For example, 48% of those in the enhanced control condition reported feeling happier as compared to only 25% of those in the comparison condition. The nurses' ratings also suggested that residents benefited from having enhanced feelings of control. According to their ratings, 93% of those in the control-enhanced condition seemed improved as compared to only 21% of

(continues)

those in the comparison group. Those in the control-enhanced group spent more time visiting people in and out of the nursing home and more time talking to the staff, and they spent less time passively watching the staff compared to the other group. Finally, movie attendance was higher in the control-enhanced group as was participation in the jelly bean guessing contest (21% versus 2%). There was no difference, however, in how active people were in the two groups based on wearing down the tape on their wheelchairs.

A follow-up study was conducted 18 months later to examine longer-term effects of the intervention (Rodin & Langer, 1977). This study revealed that those in the control-enhanced group were rated by the nurses as more active, sociable, and vigorous, and as generally healthier. Furthermore, while the average death rate in the nursing home during this time period was 25%, 30% of those in the comparison group had died whereas only 15% of those in the control-enhanced group had died. These findings suggest that providing people with greater control over their environment can have a substantial impact on psychological and physical well-being.

How Is Stress Measured?

Although people commonly use the term *stress* in their daily lives (e.g., "I'm feeling very stressed about my upcoming exams"), it is difficult to measure precisely how much stress a person is experiencing. This section describes the different approaches researchers have used to assess stress, including several different types of self-report inventories as well as various physiological measures.

Life Events

Some researchers measure stress using the Social Readjustment Rating Scale (SRRS), which assesses the number and type of major events that have happened in a person's life in the past year (see Table 4.2; Holmes & Rahe, 1967). This scale was developed based on data from more than 5,000 patients about the various life events that seemed to precede illness. Several studies have demonstrated that those who experience more life events (both prospectively and retrospectively) are more likely to become ill and to experience an accident (Holmes & Masuda, 1974). For example, children with cancer are quite likely to have experienced a number of life changes, such as personal injury and change in the health of a family member, in the year preceding their diagnosis (Jacobs & Charles, 1980).

However, the SRRS has been criticized for several reasons (Schroeder & Costa, 1984). First, it does not take into account the subjective experience of an event for the person. Getting divorced, for example, may be very upsetting for someone whose religion forbids divorce, whereas someone who is leaving

TABLE 4.2 *Test Yourself: Social Readjustment Rating Scale*

Life Event	Mean Value
1. Death of spouse	100
2. Divorce	73
3. Marital separation	65
4. Jail term	63
5. Death of a close family member	63
6. Personal injury or illness	53
7. Marriage	50
8. Fired at work	47
9. Marital reconciliation	45
10. Retirement	45
11. Major change in the health of family member	44
12. Pregnancy	40
13. Sex difficulties	39
14. Gain of a new family member	39
15. Business readjustment	39
16. Change in financial state	38
17. Death of a close friend	37
18. Changing to a different line of work	36
19. Change in the number of arguments with spouse	35
20. Mortgage over $10,000	31
21. Foreclosure on a mortgage or loan	30
22. Change in responsibilities at work	29
23. Son or daughter leaving home	29
24. Trouble with in-laws	29
25. Outstanding personal achievement	28
26. Wife begin or stop work	26
27. Begin or end school	26
28. Change in living conditions	25
29. Revision of personal habits	24
30. Trouble with boss	23
31. Change in work hours or conditions	20
32. Change in residence	20
33. Change in schools	20
34. Change in recreation	19
35. Change in church activities	19
36. Change in social activities	18

(continues)

TABLE 4.2   *(continued)*

Life Event	Mean Value
37. Mortgage or loan for less than $10,000	17
38. Change in sleeping habits	16
39. Change in number of family get-togethers	15
40. Change in eating habits	15
41. Vacation	13
42. Christmas	12
43. Minor violation of the law	11

This scale measures the number of major life events that a person has experienced over the last few months and assigns each life event a point value that expresses the severity of the event. People who experience more stressful life events tend to have poorer health.

Source: Holmes & Rahe, 1967.

an abusive marriage may see divorce as a welcome relief. Similarly, a pregnancy could be a very positive and exciting event for a stable married couple hoping to start a family, but could be extremely negative and upsetting for a high school student. Moreover, some of the events included in this scale are objectively positive (e.g., marriage, outstanding personal achievement, vacation), whereas others are objectively negative (e.g., death of spouse, foreclosure of mortgage, jail term), and still others are ambiguous (e.g., change in job responsibilities, spouse begining or stopping work, revision of personal habits). But experiencing positive personal events, while they may cause some stress, is typically less problematic than experiencing objectively negative events (Sarason, Johnson, & Siegel, 1978). Also, some of the items on this scale are quite vague, such as "change in status at work" and "son or daughter leaving home." Because this scale assumes that change in general is stressful, regardless of whether it is positive or negative, someone who gets fired gets the same score as someone who gets promoted! Finally, some researchers have criticized this scale for focusing on stressful events that are likely to affect those in the middle or upper classes and for ignoring those that may affect people who are poor or members of minority groups (Jackson & Inglehart, 1995). Poverty and racism, for example, may be very stressful, but are not included in this scale.

Daily Hassles and Uplifts

Although the SRRS is a widely used approach to measuring stress, some researchers have argued that many stressors come not from major life events but instead from *daily hassles*, such as losing one's keys, having difficulty paying bills, and having too many things to do (Lazarus, Kanner, & Folkman, 1980). As shown in Table 4.3, the Hassles Scale measures these types of daily

TABLE 4.3   *Test Yourself: The Hassles Scale*

Hassles are irritants that can range from minor annoyances to fairly major pressures, problems, or difficulties. They can occur few or many times. Circle the hassles that have happened to you in the past month. Then indicate how *severe* each of the hassles you experienced has been, with 1 = somewhat severe, 2 = moderately severe, and 3 = extremely severe.

1. Conflicts with boyfriend/girlfriend/spouse
2. Being let down or disappointed by friends
3. Too many things to do at once
4. Getting lower grades than you hoped for
5. Separation from people you care about
6. Not enough leisure time
7. Loneliness
8. Dissatisfaction with your athletic skills
9. Not enough time for sleep
10. Disliking your studies

This scale is designed to test minor hassles that are commonly experienced by many college students. Once again, people who experience more daily hassles show poorer health.

Source: Kanner et al., 1981.

life events. People report concerns about weight, health of a family member, rising prices, home maintenance, having too many things to do, money, crime, and physical appearance as the most frequent hassles they experience. Hassles are a strong predictor of both psychological and physical well-being (Kanner, Coyne, Schaefer, & Lazarus, 1981; Zarski, 1984). Experiencing more hassles also leads to more symptoms for those who are already suffering from an illness (Levy, Cain, Jarrett, & Heitkemper, 1997). Interestingly, hassles are more highly correlated with psychological and physical symptoms than are major life events.

Researchers have also explored whether small uplifting events predict positive outcomes (Kanner et al., 1981). According to this perspective, experiencing even small events that bring you pleasure, such as spending time with friends, having a good night's sleep, and reading a good book, may have beneficial effects on physical health and psychological well-being (see Table 4.4; Lazarus et al., 1980). (Just for the record, note how many of these items focus on social support. We talk more about the role of social support in influencing health in Chapter 6.) In turn, people who experience more uplifts have more positive moods, and women—not men—who have more uplifts have fewer psychological symptoms (Kanner et al., 1981). However, the frequency of uplifts is not a particularly good predictor of physical health (Zarski, 1984).

Although some research suggests that measures of daily hassles (and possibly uplifts) are a better predictor of health than measures of major life events, these self-report measures have some of the same limitations we discussed

TABLE 4.4   *Test Yourself: The Uplifts Scale*

Uplifts are events that make you feel good. They can be sources of peace, satisfaction, or joy. Some occur often; others are relatively rare. Circle the events that have made you feel good in the past month. Then indicate how *often* each of the uplifts has occurred in the last month, with 1 = somewhat often, 2 = moderately often, and 3 = extremely often.

1. Saving money
2. Relating well with your spouse or lover
3. Socializing (parties, being with friends, etc.)
4. Reading
5. Shopping
6. Spending time with family
7. Sex
8. Growing as a person
9. Doing volunteer work
10. Being a "good" listener

This scale measures the frequency of various positive events a person could experience, under the assumption that people who have more positive events show better psychological and physical health.

Source: Kanner et al., 1981.

previously about the SRRS. One problem is that someone who experiences a major life event is also likely to experiences many daily hassles. For example, someone who gets divorced may struggle with daily financial pressures, conflicts with the ex-spouse, and increased household responsibilities. Another problem with these measures is that some scales assessing hassles and uplifts include items that refer to health-related behavior (e.g., drinking, smoking, feeling healthy). Thus, if studies find a correlation between frequency of hassles or uplifts and health, it may be due to the link between a given behavior (such as smoking) and health as opposed to the link between stress and health.

Perceived Stress

Because simply asking people whether they have experienced a given life event or daily hassle does not take into account that different people evaluate such experiences in different ways, other researchers have developed a measure that assesses individuals' perceived stress (Cohen, Kamark, & Mermelstein, 1983). The Perceived Stress Scale (PSS) does not ask people whether they have experienced a particular event, but simply asks how frequently they have felt stressed or upset in the last month. For example, items on this scale include, "In the last month, how often have you found that you could not cope with all the things you had to do?" and "In the last month, how often have you felt nervous and 'stressed'?" PSS predicts psychological and physical symptoms (Hewitt, Flett, & Mosher, 1992), as well as changes in the immune and endocrine systems (Harrell, Kelly, & Stutts, 1996; Maes et al., 1997).

Physiological Measures

Given the various limitations of self-report measures of stress, some researchers have instead relied on measures of physiological measures to assess stress (Baum, Grunberg, & Singer, 1982; Uchino, Cacioppo, Malarkey, & Glaser, 1995). Because a central aspect of stress is the stimulation of the sympathetic nervous system, stress can be measured through various measures of *physiological arousal*, including heart rate, blood pressure, respiration, and changes in the skin's resistance to electrical current (galvanic skin response, or GSR; see Photo 4.3). For example, Joseph Speisman and colleagues (1964) manipulated people's reaction to a particularly graphic film, and then assessed individuals' physiological reaction using heart rate and GSR to measure stress reactions. This film, *Subincision in the Arunta*, shows (in gruesome detail) a puberty rite in which the penises of young adolescent boys are cut with a jagged and rusty knife. Most people (particularly men) find the film quite disturbing and show a high level of physiological arousal while watching it. To examine whether people's thoughts and interpretation of the film would influence their physiological reaction, researchers accompanied the film with different narratives for different groups. While watching the film, one group heard a narration that emphasized the emotionally upsetting aspects of the ceremony, including the pain and mutilation experienced by the boys, the danger of infection, and the jaggedness of the knife. Another narration emphasized the positive aspects of the ceremony, such as the pride the boys felt in demonstrating their bravery and entering adulthood, and denied the painful aspects. A third group heard a detached and intellectual discussion of the history of the tribe and the anthropological aspects of the ceremony. Finally, a fourth group saw the film, but heard no soundtrack at all. How did the interpretation provided by the narration influence people's reactions? As predicted, those who heard about the positive aspects of the ceremony or the intellectual discussion reported feeling less upset and experienced fewer physiological reactions to the film than those who heard the pain narration. For example, skin conductance (a measure of sweating) was 20.08 micromhos for those in the trauma condition and 16.08 for those who watched the silent (control) version, but only 14.77 for those in the positive aspects condition and 13.88 for those in the intellectualized version.

Biochemical measures can be used to assess the presence of particular hormones, such as norepinephrine, epinephrine, and cortisol (Baum et al., 1982). These hormones can be detected in blood or urine tests and are reliable indicators of an individuals experience of stress. Increases in corticosteroids and catecholamines (two types of chemicals, or neurotransmitters, in the body) are found in a variety of different types of stressful situations, including in astronauts during splashdown (Kimzey, 1975), people who are doing challenging mental arithmetic (Uchino et al., 1995), and snake phobics who see a snake (Bandura, Taylor, Williams, Mefford, & Barchas, 1985).

PHOTO 4.3 The polygraph exam is an example of a physiological measure of stress.

Physiological measures have some limitations. First, some people find the use of physiological measures in and of themselves very stressful. If a person is nervous about having blood taken or being hooked up to a machine that is measuring sweat or heart rate, he or she will show higher levels of stress simply because of the use of these techniques. Second, physiological measures can be influenced by factors other than stress, including gender, weight, and physical activity level. Researchers therefore need to be aware of these complicating factors and must interpret the results accordingly. Finally, because physiological measures of stress rely on either equipment or laboratory testing, the use of these measures is very expensive and time-consuming. They also require trained technicians to perform the tests and interpret the results.

How Does Stress Influence Health?

Researchers generally have agreed on the sources of stress but our understanding of how stress influences health has evolved considerably over time. This section describes two theories about how stress leads to physiological reactions, which in turn can impact physical well-being.

Cannon's Fight-or-Flight Response

Imagine that you are walking in a forest with some friends on a sunny afternoon. As you are talking to them, not really paying attention to where you are walking, you suddenly notice movement just in front of your right foot. You quickly glance down and see a large striped snake, coiled and seemingly ready to strike. What is your immediate physiological reaction? Like most people who are afraid of snakes, your heart will start to pound, your muscles will become tense, and you will start to sweat. In fact, you may have experienced mild forms of these reactions while reading this description of the snake.

This type of physiological reaction in response to threat, called the fight-or-flight response, was first described by Walter Cannon, a physiologist at Harvard Medical School in the early 1900s. According to Cannon (1932), people are normally in a state of internal physiological equilibrium or balance called *homeostatsis* (Chrousos & Gold, 1992). When a person (or animal) is threatened, the immediate response is to either fight off the stressor or escape from it. To prepare for either alternative, energy is shifted from the nonessential body systems to those systems necessary to respond to the challenge. So, when someone first notices a threat (such as the snake), the person's sympathetic nervous and endocrine systems are stimulated, which causes a dramatic rise in two types of hormones: epinephrine (adrenaline) and norepinephrine (noradrenaline). The increase in these hormone levels in the bloodstream lead to a number of other physiological responses that prepare someone to either fight off a threat (unlikely, in the case of the snake) or run from it (very likely, in the case of the snake), including increases in heart rate, blood pressure, and breathing, widening of the pupils, and movement of blood toward the muscles. Similarly, the cardiovascular system is activated, so that blood is directed to the brain and muscles. Processes that do not help fight off a threat, such as digestion and reproduction, are stopped or slowed down. This increase in some types of physiological responses and decrease in others allows the body to focus its resources where they are most needed to respond to the challenge.

General Adaptation Syndrome

Hans Selye (1956), an endocrinologist, extended Cannon's work by describing the stages the body goes through when reacting to a stressor. He conducted a series of tests in which laboratory rats were exposed to different types of stressors, such as heat, starvation, and electric shock. Interestingly, he found that regardless of what type of stress the rats were exposed to, they developed similar physiological reactions, including enlarged adrenal glands, shrunken lymph nodes, and bleeding stomach ulcers. This observation led to the development of his General Adaptation Syndrome (GAS), a model to describe how stress can lead to negative health consequences over time (see Figure 4.1).

First, there is the *alarm stage*, in which the body mobilizes to fight off a threat. As shown in Figure 4.2, when a threat is perceived, the hypothalamus (a structure in the brain) activates both the sympathetic nervous system and the endocrine system. The sympathetic nervous system signals the adrenal

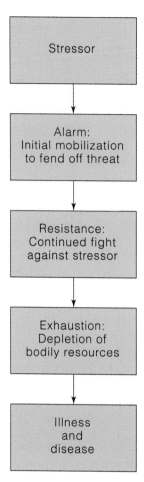

FIGURE 4.1 Model of the General Adaptation Syndrome (GAS).

glands (endocrine glands on the top of each kidney) to release cate-cholamines, such as epinephrine and norepinephrine. As epinephrine and norepinephrine circulate in the bloodstream, they lead to a number of physiological changes, including increases in heart rate, blood pressure, and breathing rate. These changes all help to prepare the body to react to a threat: oxygen is brought to the muscles (to let you run or fight), pupils dilate (allowing more light to enter to see more clearly), and palms sweat (for better gripping). This stage is similar to Cannon's fight-or-flight response. At the same time, the pituitary gland releases adrenocorticotropic hormone (ACTH), which causes the adrenal glands to produce glucocorticoids, such as cortisol. Cortisol increases the production of energy from glucose and inhibits the swelling around injuries and infections. Thus, the body has more energy to respond to threats and is protected from injuries. In this stage, the body is mobilizing all of its resources to do whatever is necessary to fight off (or escape from) the threat, and longer-term functions, such as growth, digestion, reproduction, and operation of the immune system are inhibited. (Astute readers may now be wondering why the immune system, which protects the body from illness and disease, would be inhibited during times of danger. But remember, illness and disease may kill you, but they do so slowly—the alarm stage serves to protect you from immediate threats that could kill you quickly.)

Next, there is the *resistance stage*. After the body mobilizes to fight off the initial threat, it will continue trying to respond. This stage still requires energy, so heart rate, blood pressure, and breathing are still rapid in order to help deliver oxygen and energy quickly throughout the body. Nonessential functions, such as digestion, growth, and reproduction, may operate but at a slower pace than normal, and no new energy is stored during this time. After all, why waste energy where it is not needed? (This is one reason why menstruation may stop in women who are under severe stress.) Although there is less

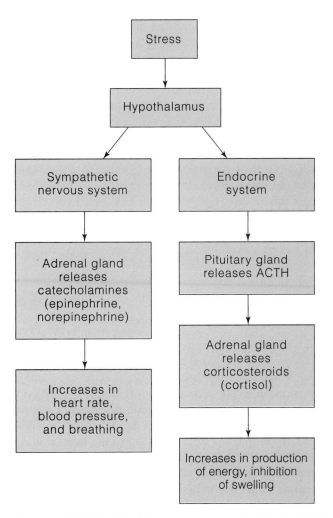

FIGURE 4.2 Model of the organ systems involved in GAS.

of a drain on energy during this stage than during the alarm stage, the body continues to work very hard to resist the stressor on a long-term basis. If the threat is brief, the body will have enough resources to respond to the threat. However, if the threat lasts for some time, and the body stays in a state of physiological arousal for a long time, problems can begin to emerge. Essentially, the body neglects many normal physical and psychological functions during times of stress; over time this neglect takes its toll on the body's resources.

Finally, when the threat continues for a long time, occurs repeatedly, or is very severe, *exhaustion* may set in, the last stage. For example, you may feel OK initially under conditions of high stress, but over time it can be damaging to your body since all of its resources are consumed. Continuing or particularly strong stress therefore creates a situation of imbalance that results in considerable wear and tear on the body. In the exhaustion stage, the body's resources are depleted and thus it becomes very susceptible to physiological damage and disease. Moreover, if epinephrine and cortisol stay at high levels over time, they can damage heart and blood vessels and suppress the immune system. These changes leave the body very susceptible to illness, such as heart disease, high blood pressure, arthritis, and colds and flu (McEwen, 1998). Stress can also lead to particularly negative health consequences in people who are suffering from chronic illnesses, who already have a weakened immune system. For example, HIV-positive men who experience the loss of a partner to AIDS (a major stressor) show signs of more rapid progression of their own AIDS illness (Kemeny et al., 1994).

According to Selye, the GAS is *nonspecific*, which means that all stressors produce the same physiological response. In other words, people will go through this three-stage process in response to any type of stressful event, including taking final exams, losing a loved one, or living in a crowded situation. In fact, although he believed positive stresses (e.g., getting married) would be less harmful than negative ones (e.g., getting divorced), both types of events are seen as causing some stress, potentially leading to the same negative physiological responses. In support of this view, recent research suggests that many different types of stressors can lead to an increase in adrenal hormones (Baum et al., 1982).

Although Selye's GAS has received considerable attention in the field of health psychology, researchers have criticized it for several reasons. First, and contrary to Selye's original model, recent research suggests that different hormones are released, depending on the specific type and intensity of emotion experienced in response to a stressor (Henry, 1990; Mason, 1975). Specifically, people who experience a sudden and unexpected stressor release more hormones than those who experience a gradual and expected stressor. Different types of emotional responses also lead to the release of different types of hormones. For example, anger is associated with an increase in norepinephrine, whereas fear is associated with an increase in epinephrine.

Second, some researchers have argued that because Selye's theory was developed using animals, it does not address the psychological or cognitive responses that humans may have to stressful situations (Scherer, 1986). People can interpret or appraise stressors in different ways: a woman who is married and desperately trying to have a baby may react to conception differently than a woman who is single and still trying to finish college. According to the *transactional, or relational, model,* the meaning a particular event has for a person is a more important predictor of the experience of stress than the actual event (Lazarus & Folkman, 1984). Because people's cognitive interpretations of stressful events influence their reactions, people vary in how stressful they find different experiences. For example, one day when I was a college student I was driving in a car with my boyfriend when we got a flat tire. Because I had no idea how to change a tire, I immediately appraised the situation as a real emergency and panicked ("How much will it cost us to get the car towed? How late will we be for class?"). My boyfriend, however, calmly got the spare tire out of the trunk and within 10 minutes had replaced the bad tire. For me, flat tire equaled emergency. For him, flat tire equaled minor inconvenience.

Lazarus and Folkman (1984) suggest that the cognitive appraisal of a stressful event includes two distinct parts. As shown in Figure 4.3, people engage in *primary appraisal* in which they assess the situation. In this stage people are interpreting the situation and what it will mean for them (e.g., "Am I in danger?"). For example, a person who is fired from his or her job may see it as a stressful event (e.g., "My family will starve") or as a positive opportunity (e.g., "Now I can explore new career options"). People also engage in *secondary appraisal* in which they assess the resources available for coping with the

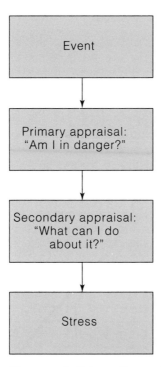

FIGURE 4.3 According to the transactional, or relational, model, whether people experience stress is influenced both by their initial reaction to the particular challenge and the resources they have to cope with this challenge.

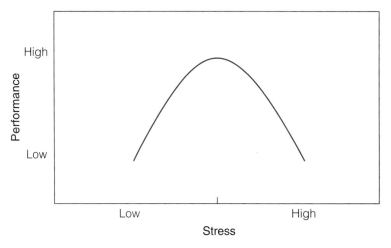

FIGURE 4.4 Moderate levels of stress can actually benefit performance, whereas low or high levels can have detrimental effects.

situation. In this stage people examine their ability to cope with the event based on their resources (e.g., "What can I do about this?"). For example, an individual who has a working spouse may appraise the loss of a job less negatively, because he or she has more financial resources to rely on than someone who is the sole wage earner in a family. The impact of a particular event may therefore have very different consequences, depending on whether it is perceived as high or low in stress.

Finally, although this section focuses on the negative physiological consequences of stress, some researchers have examined the benefits that can come from experiencing stress. Hans Selye (1974) used the term *eustress* to describe beneficial stresses. Moderate levels of stress can actually cause people to experience small amounts of arousal, providing extra energy, and can help them perform at their best. For example, athletes often want to feel somewhat excited as they compete, because this feeling of "getting up for a game" can enhance their performance. As shown in Figure 4.4, a moderate amount of stress can provide enough arousal to help us give our best performance. In contrast, very low and very high levels of arousal can be detrimental to performance, either because they do not motivate us sufficiently (in the case of low levels) or because they create too much anxiety (in the case of high levels).

What Are the Physical Consequences of Stress?

In a nutshell, stress is damaging to your health. People who are under stress have a greater risk of experiencing a number of illnesses and diseases, including ulcers, diabetes, colds and flu, arthritis, appendicitis, gastrointestinal disorders, herpes, asthma, sports injuries, headaches, migraines, eczema, hives, back

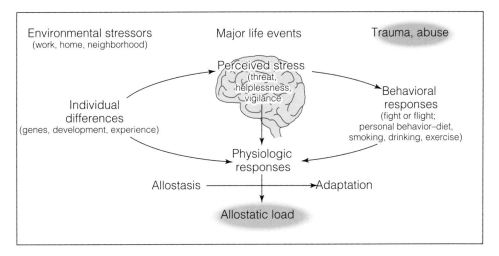

FIGURE 4.5 The impact of perceived stress on physiological reactions (McEwan, 1998).

pain, gastrointestinal disorders, hernias, cancer, and cardiovascular disease (Glaser & Kiecolt-Glaser, 1994). When a person faces a challenge—such as taking a difficult test, walking through a dangerous neighborhood, or giving a public speech—the body turns on an *allostatic* response to adapt to this situation (see Figure 4.5; McEwen, 1998; McEwen & Stellar, 1993). This physiological response includes a number of systems in the body and is shut off as soon as the challenge ends. However, when people experience repeated stress over a long period of time, the allostatic load builds up and can eventually lead to physiological responses that affect nearly every system in the body (Seeman, Singer, Horwitz, & McEwen, 1997). The following section examines the direct impact of such chronic stress on several systems within the body, the interaction of these systems (as described by the field of *psychoneuroimmunology*), and the indirect effects of stress on physiological functioning.

Nervous System

The nervous system, which includes the *central nervous system* as well as the *peripheral nervous system*, controls the body's overall reaction to stress in several ways (see Figure 4.6). The central nervous system consists of the brain and spinal cord, where information processing occurs (e.g., "That's a bear—it could hurt me!"). The peripheral nervous system consists of the neural pathways that bring information to and from the brain. Specialized cells called *neurons* transmit this information, although the *neurotransmitters*, or chemical messengers, released by a particular neuron influence whether the information is transmitted (some neurotransmitters inhibit transmission, and others facilitate it). The peripheral nervous system, includes the *somatic nervous system* and the *autonomic nervous system*. Both of these systems carry messages throughout the body, but they differ in the types of messages they transmit. The somatic nervous system transmits messages regarding sensation, such as touch, pressure, temperature,

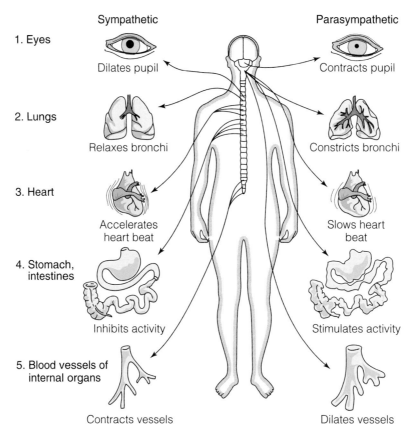

FIGURE 4.6 Model of the nervous system

and pain, and messages regarding the voluntary movement of the body. In contrast, the autonomic nervous system, which consists of the *sympathetic* and *parasympathetic divisions*, carries information that is directly related to survival (for organs that are not under voluntary control). The sympathetic division mobilizes the body to react in the face of a threat, much like the response that occurs in Cannon's fight-or-flight response. This response includes increases in respiration, heart rate, and pulse; decreases in digestion and reproduction; dilation of pupils (for far vision); and movement of blood to the muscles to prepare for action. The parasympathetic division demobilizes the body to conserve energy, which includes increasing digestion; decreasing heart rate, respiration, and pulse; and constricting pupils. These physiological reactions occur because the autonomic nervous system triggers the endocrine system to react in the face of stress, as described in the next section.

Endocrine System

The endocrine system regulates a number of different physiological processes in the body, including physical growth, sexual arousal, metabolism, and stress response. The endocrine system works by releasing hormones from an endocrine gland, such as the pituitary, thyroid, and pancreas, into the blood stream (see Figure 4.7). These hormones then travel though the bloodstream to influence a particular body tissue or organ. For example, when the hormone estrogen is released from a young woman's ovaries, it causes the uterus to grow in preparation for carrying an embryo, the breasts to enlarge in preparation for nursing, and the brain to increase in interest in sexual activity.

During times of stress, the sympathetic nervous system activates two core systems within the endocrine system (Chrousos & Gold, 1992). When the *sympathetic-adrenal medullary (SAM) system* is activated, the hypothalamus triggers the adrenal glands to release epinephrine and norepinephrine (adrenaline and noradrenaline). These hormones act very quickly and lead to a number of physiological effects, including increased heart rate, increased blood flow, and increased sweating. The *hypothalamic-pituitary adrenal (HPA) system* is also activated during times of stress. The HPA system starts by secreting corticotropin-releasing hormone (CRH), which in turn triggers the anterior pituitary gland to release adrenocorticotropic hormone (ACTH). Finally, the presence of ACTH leads the adrenal gland to release glucocorticoids, including cortisol. If stress is maintained over time, the resulting high levels of cortisol can lead to damage in the hippocampus, an area of the brain involved in memory. During times of stress, the endocrine system also inhibits the secretion of growth hormones as well as hormones associated with reproduction

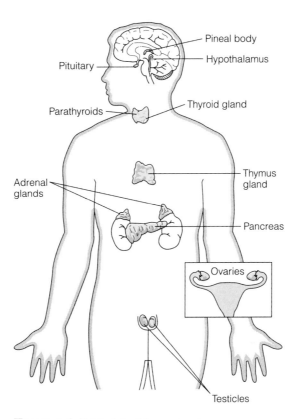

FIGURE 4.7 Model of the endocrine system.

(Chrousos, 1998). This is one reason why women may experience the loss of their menstrual cycle (amenorrhea) during times of high stress.

Several studies have demonstrated the powerful effects of stress on the endocrine system (Frankenhauser, 1975, 1978; Ursin, Baader, & Levine, 1978). One study by Ursin and colleagues (1978), for example, examined how young military recruits reacted physiologically to the stressful situation of their first parachute-training jump. In this first stage of training, recruits climbed to the top of a 40-foot tower and then slid down a wire to the ground, which feels similar to free fall. Most people find this experience stressful, and, as shown in Figure 4.8, levels of epinephrine, norepinephrine, and cortisol were significantly higher on the day of the jump than the day before. Some readers may be thinking, "Well, sure, but how often do people jump from a plane—I want to know how the endocrine system responds to more normal types of threat." You'll be pleased to know that there are similar increases in these hormones following other, more typical stressful situations, including taking oral exams, riding in a crowded commuter train car, and having a repetitive and low-control job (Frankenhauser, 1975, 1978).

Cardiovascular System

The primary function of the cardiovascular system is for the heart to generate the force necessary to pump blood to transport oxygen to and remove carbon dioxide from each cell in the body (see Figure 4.9). The blood travels initially through the larger blood vessels (such as the *aorta*), which in turn branch

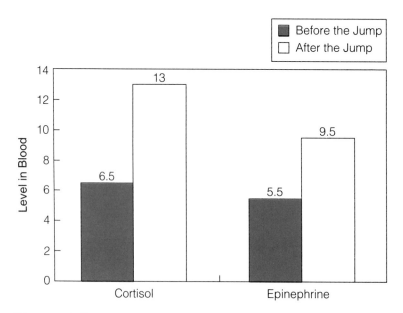

FIGURE 4.8 Levels of cortisol and epinephrine in the blood were higher following the stressful experience of parachute training (data from Ursin et al. 1978).

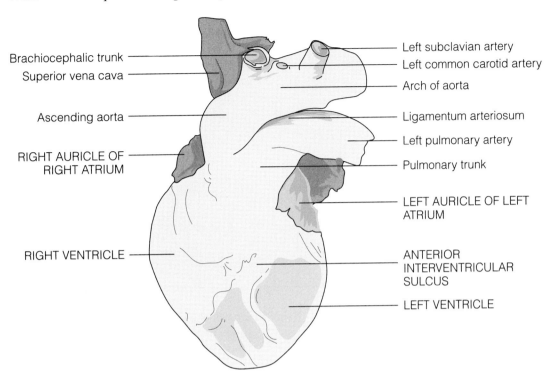

FIGURE 4.9 Model of the cardiovascular system.

into smaller and smaller vessels, and eventually into capillaries. Two major measures to evaluate cardiovascular activity are *heart rate*, the number of beats per minute, and *blood pressure*, the force of blood against the artery walls.

So, what happens to your cardiovascular system when you are feeling stress? Your heart has to work harder—people under stress show heightened cardiovascular reactivity, including high blood pressure and increased heart rate (see Figure 4.10). For example, one study found that women who were asked to complete a series of tricky math problems had faster heart rates and higher blood pressure after this stressor than before (Uchino et al., 1995). People who experience elevated blood pressure during a stressful arithmetic test also show a similar elevation in blood pressure when they are in stressful situations in daily life (Matthews, Owens, Allen, & Stoney, 1992). Research in more natural settings reveals similar findings about the impact of stress on the cardiovascular system: for example, couples with low marital satisfaction show greater heart rate reactivity during conflicts (Kiecolt-Glaser et al., 1988; Manne & Zautra, 1989). Unfortunately, prolonged periods of high blood pressure can lead to a buildup of fatty acids and glucose on blood vessel walls, which forces the heart to work even harder to pump blood through narrowing arteries. Over time, this chronic wear and tear can lead to considerable damage to the heart and arteries. For example, monkeys who are at the

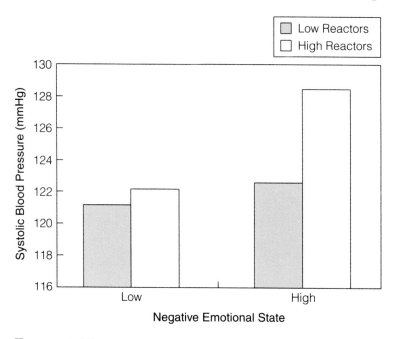

FIGURE 4.10 People who tend to show high levels of reactions to stressful events experience very high blood pressure when they are in highly negative emotional states (e.g., angry, sad, anxious; data from Matthews et al., 1992).

bottom of the dominance hierarchy (and hence are continually under conditions of high stress) are very likely to develop high blood pressure as well as arteriosclerosis (Sapolsky, 1994).

Immune System

The immune system is the body's major line of defense against infections and diseases. It works to eliminate foreign, "nonself" materials, such as bacteria, viruses, and parasites, which contact or enter the body (see Box 4.5). If you get a splinter in your hand, the immune system will trigger a response to fight against this invader (in this case, wood). The blood vessels will dilate to increase blood flow to the site of the injury, which leads to warmth, redness, and swelling, and allows tissue repair to begin. As shown in Figure 4.11, the immune system consists of specialized types of white blood cells called lymphocytes, including B cells and T cells. The B cells, which originate in the bone marrow, control the *humoral immune response system*, in which proteins called antibodies, which bind to foreign toxins and inactivate or destroy them are produced. The T cells, which originate in the thymus, control the *cell-mediated immune response system*, in which they bind to foreign cells to kill them. Other immune system cells include the *natural killer (NK) cells*, which detect and then destroy damaged cells, such as precancerous cells before they develop into tumors, and *macrophages*, which engulf and digest foreign cells, such as bacteria.

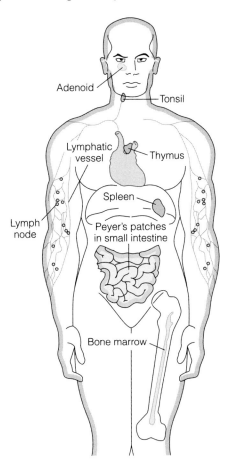

Adenoid
Tonsil
Lymphatic vessel
Thymus
Lymph node
Spleen
Peyer's patches in small intestine
Bone marrow

FIGURE 4.11 Model of the immune system.

Box 4.5

Health Psychology in the Real World—The Immune System in Action

Although you may think of the immune system as fairly abstract, it impacts your life in a variety of ways. First, vaccinations for diseases such as polio and chicken pox were created based on knowledge of how the immune system works. When you get a vaccination, you are actually introducing a weakened form of a virus or bacterium into your body. The body then reacts to this threat by producing antibodies to fight it. When and if you are exposed to the actual disease, your body already has the

(continues)

antibodies ready to respond, and thereby protect you from illness—it is like having a head start on fighting an illness.

However, in some cases doctors must try to suppress, or inactivate, the immune system to help seriously ill patients. People who receive organ transplants, for example, must be given drugs that suppress the immune system so that it does not reject the new (clearly "nonself") organ. Without these immune-suppressing drugs, the immune system would function normally and quickly identify the new heart, liver, or kidney as foreign tissue, and then mobilize to attack this new organ. However, when the immune system is weakened through immune-suppressing drugs, people are very susceptible to infections that they could normally fight off with ease. People who are on immune-suppressing drugs after receiving an organ transplant must therefore be very careful about exposing themselves to any type of illness or disease—even a cold could be life-threatening.

Considerable research with both animals and humans demonstrates that stress has a number of negative effects on the immune system (See Figure 4.12; Jemmott & Locke, 1984; O'Leary, 1992). Individuals who experience a variety of different types of stressors, including divorce, loneliness, unemployment, bereavement, marital conflict, and exams have fewer B, T, and NK cells (see Boxes 4.6 and 4.7; Ironson et al., 1997; Kiecolt-Glaser, Fisher, et al., 1987; Kiecolt-Glaser, Glaser et al., 1987; Kiecolt-Glaser et al., 1984; Kiecolt-Glaser & Glaser, 1989, 1995; Kiecolt-Glaser et al., 1985; Kiecolt-Glaser et al., 1997; McKinnon, Weisse, Reynolds, Bowles, & Baum, 1989). For example, one study by Arthur Stone and colleagues (1994) showed that on days in which people experienced more positive events their bodies produced more antibodies, whereas on days with more negative events, their bodies produced fewer antibodies. Although studies with humans often have difficulty showing that stress—as opposed to some third variable such as personality—causes such physiological reactions, experimental research with animals reveals such findings. For example, rats who are exposed to stressors, including noise, overcrowding, and inescapable shock, show less immune cell activity, as well as the fastest rate of tumor growth compared to those rats not under such stress (Ben-Eliyahu, Yirmiya, Liebeskind, Taylor, & Gale, 1991; Moynihan & Adler, 1996). Finally, the experience of stress can even influence the rate of wound healing (Kiecolt-Glaser et al., 1995; Marucha, Kiecolt-Glaser, & Favayehi et al., 1998). In one study, dental students agreed to have small wounds placed on the roofs of their mouths during two distinct times in the semester, and researchers then measured the rate of wound healing (Marucha et al., 1998). Wound healing took 40% longer during exam period than during summer vacation.

Psychoneuroimmunology

So far, I have described the impact of stress on the nervous, endocrine, cardiovascular, and immune systems as separate and distinct effects, in reality these different body systems all interact to influence health. Careful readers

Box 4.6

Health Psychology in the Real World: Why Zebras Don't Get Ulcers

Although all mammals experience a physiological response to stress, neuroscientist Robert Sapolsky (1994) has pointed out that not all mammals experience the negative health consequences of stress. In fact, humans seem to experience a very high rate of stress-related illnesses, including headaches, ulcers, and coronary heart disease. Sapolsky believes that humans experience more stress (and more illness) because we generate all sorts of stressful things in our heads. The physiological stress reaction characterized by Cannon's fight-or-flight response and Selye's General Adaptation Syndrome is designed to help humans (and animals) respond to true threats of personal safety, such as occurs when you are chased by a large barking dog or when you are in combat during war. These physiological reactions may also be adaptive during other "high-pressure" situations, such as during a job interview or on a first date. However, humans constantly create stressful situations in their minds—people worry about a range of abstract and even hypothetical situations that can cause very real stress, including finding a dating partner, paying bills, and dying. In turn, even these imagined stressors can lead to physiological reactions. This may be why, as Sapolsky cleverly writes, "zebras don't get ulcers," but humans often do.

Box 4.7

Health Psychology in the Real World—The Stress of Caring for an Alzheimer's Patient

Alzheimer's disease afflicts more than 10% of those over the age of 65 and nearly 50% of those over 85 (Plaud, Mosley, & Moberg, 1998). This disease is characterized by substantial problems with thinking, speaking, and memory; hence, people who suffer from Alzheimer's often experience the need for virtually total care, at least in the disease's later stages. Given that people with Alzheimer's disease typically live for 8 to 15 years following diagnosis, caring for such patients becomes a chronic stressor. Caregivers, often the spouses or children of the Alzheimer's patients, face not only the very difficult physical demands of providing care (such as

(continues)

feeding, bathing, and dressing the patient), but also must face the difficult emotional problems associated with caring for someone who does not necessarily appreciate such help (and at times who may not even recognize the caregiver). Not surprisingly, caregivers of Alzheimer's patients often suffer from clinical depression (Drinka & Smith, 1983) as well as poor immune function (Kiecolt-Glaser et al., 1991). For example, one study comparing the health of caregivers of Alzheimer's patients to a matched control group (people of a similar age but without such responsibility) found that caregivers had a weaker immune response and were more likely to develop infectious diseases. Fortunately, however, receiving support from friends and family can help decrease the negative health consequences of caregiving (Kiecolt-Glaser et al., 1988).

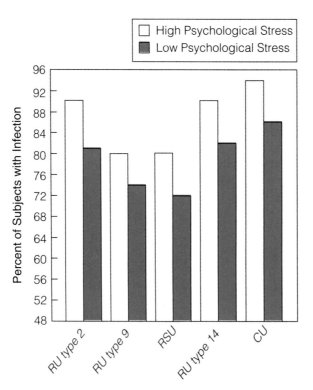

FIGURE 4.12 Sheldon Cohen and his colleagues (1991) examined the influence of stress on illness by injecting 394 people with nasal drops containing a cold virus. Individuals who were experiencing more stress in their daily lives had a greater rate of infection with the cold, even controlling for other factors (e.g., age, gender, personality variables).

Questioning the Research 4.1

Although many studies on the link between stress and health are based on research that assesses college students' health before and after exams, what are some limitations of this approach?

---

may have noticed, for example, that when the endocrine system is activated, it in turn leads to cardiovascular changes, such as increases in heart rate and blood pressure. Activating the endocrine system also leads to the release of glucocorticoids, which hinder the formation of some white blood cells, including NK cells, and which kill other white blood cells (Cohen & Herbert, 1996; Jemmott & Locke, 1984; Kiecolt-Glaser & Glaser, 1986). The field of *psychoneuorimmunology* examines the complex connection between psychosocial factors, such as stress, and the nervous, cardiovascular, endocrine, and immune systems (Adler, 2001).

Although we now fully accept the idea that the mind and body interact in complex ways to influence health, this finding was originally discovered by accident. In 1974, psychologist Robert Ader from the University of Rochester School of Medicine was working on a series of studies designed to show that rats could learn to avoid a sugar-flavored drinking water by using classical conditioning techniques (see Chapter 3 for a quick refresher). First, he gave rats a sugar-flavored water to drink, which, not surprisingly, the rats enjoyed. They he injected the rats with an immune-supressing drug that caused them to feel nauseous. The rats quickly learned that the drink would make them ill, hence, they developed an aversion to the taste that was associated through conditioning with the injection. However, several weeks later Ader found that many of the rats involved in this study on taste aversion became sick and ultimately died. Testing revealed that the immune system in these rats was impaired, apparently due to the drug they had received. But amazingly, the immune system was also impaired in rats that had received only the immune-suppressing drug on one occasion and that on all future trials received only the sugar water (which obviously should have had no effect on their immune system). Apparently, the animals' immune systems associated the taste of the sugar water with the experience of immune-suppression, and hence they developed a conditioned response to this taste in later trials that led to a suppression of their immune response. Ader then conducted a series of studies with Nicholas Cohen, an immunologist, to replicate his surprising findings (Ader & Cohen, 1975, 1985). These studies again demonstrated that immune responses can be conditioned. These studies, which demonstrate that psychological, neural, and immunological processes interact in complex ways, led to the development of the field of psychoneuroimmunology.

Indirect Effects of Stress on Health

Think of yourself during exam period. What types of things do you do to relieve your stress? If you are like most college students, during stressful times you tend to eat junk food, drink coffee and other caffeinated beverages, sleep less, and reduce (or eliminate) exercise. These behaviors are not unusual: people who are experiencing stress engage in numerous behaviors that can impair their health, including eating less-nutritious foods, smoking cigarettes, drinking caffeine, staying up too late, and skipping exercise (Conway, Vickers, Ward, & Rahe, 1981; Kiecolt-Glaser & Glaser, 1988). One study examined health-related behaviors in a sample of medical students both 4 weeks before and in the middle of a stressful exam period (Ogden & Mitandabari, 1997). As predicted, students reported smoking more cigarettes during the exam period than earlier in the semester and doing less exercise. People who are experiencing stress also engage in behaviors that increase the likelihood of injury. For example, one study with college students found that those who were under more stress reported engaging in more reckless behavior and more substance abuse (Wiebe & McCallum, 1986). In turn, and as we discuss in more detail in Chapters 7 and 8, poor eating habits, physical inactivity, and smok-

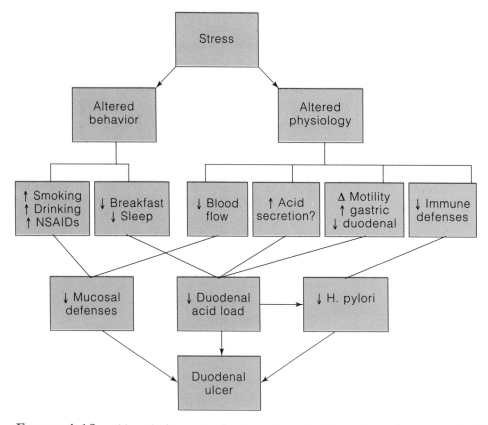

FIGURE 4.13   Although this section has focused on the direct effects of stress on physical health, stress can also have indirect effects on health through its impact on health behaviors. This model postulates that behavioral and psychophysiologic factors may influence the development of peptic ulcers. NSAIDS stands for nonsteroid anti-inflammatory drugs (Levenstein, 2000).

ing could all have a direct negative impact on physical well-being (Conway et al., 1981). For example, one study examined immune cell activity in a group of healthy men who were kept awake between 3 and 7 A.M. (Irwin et al., 1994). As predicted, this type of sleep deprivation led to decreases in immune cell activity that returned only after the men had a good night's sleep. In sum, consciously not taking care of yourself can actually lead to poor health. Similarly, and as shown in Figure 4.13, many of the factors associated with developing an ulcer are behaviors that people choose to engage in, such as skipping breakfast, exacerbating lack of sleep, drinking large amounts of alcohol, and smoking (Levenstein, 2000).

What Are the Psychological Consequences of Stress?

Although thus far we have examined the negative effects of stress on physical health, stress can also have negative effects on psychological health. Stress can lead to *cognitive* problems by impairing people's memory and attention. Have you ever misread a question on an exam and gotten the answer wrong, even though you knew the right answer? People who are under conditions of high stress often have trouble concentrating or focusing on a particular task because other thoughts continue to come into their minds (Lyubomirsky & Nolen-Hoeksema, 1995; Sarason et al., 1986). For example, as you take an exam that is not going well, you may start thinking, "Everyone else seems to be nearly finished," or "If I don't do well on this test, I will get a C in this course," which in turn increases stress and makes it even harder for you to focus (see Photo 4.4). As I described at the beginning of this chapter, Sara experienced this type of cognitive difficulty whenever she sat down to take a final exam. One recent study examined reading and memory skills in children ages 8 to 12 who lived near a noisy airport (Hygge, Evans, & Bullinger, 2002). After the airport was shut down, the children's reading and memory scores improved, whereas children who lived near the new airport showed a decline in scores on these measures.

Stress also increases physiological arousal, which can lead people to make poorer decisions (Keinan, Friedland, & Ben-Porath, 1987). People who are experiencing stress are less likely to consider various options and they tend to make more impulsive decisions. By creating a sense of urgency (e.g., "a limited time offer"), some types of sales techniques rely on this type of pressure to force people to make rushed (and often poor) decisions. Moreover, research with rats and monkeys has shown that long-term exposure to cortisol, a hormone released during times of stress, leads to the loss of neurons in the hippocampus, which in turn disrupts memory (Sapolsky, 1992).

Stress can lead to a variety of negative *emotions*, such as fear, anxiety, and sadness (Rubonis & Bickman, 1991). Posttraumatic stress disorder (PTSD), a particular type of anxiety disorder, is caused by experiencing extreme stressors, such as war, natural disasters, and assault (see Box 4.8). One study by Gail

PHOTO 4.4   Many students find taking exams extremely stressful.

Ironson and colleagues (1997) found that about one-third of people who had experienced a tremendous hurricane showed some symptoms of PTSD even several months after the storms occurence. In cases of extreme stress, these reactions can last for many years. For example, survivors of Nazi concentration camps sometimes report continuing anxiety and fear as long as 50 years after their internment (Valent, 2000). Routine stresses, such as constant pressure at work, can eventually lead to frustration and apathy (Maslach, 1982). This state of emotional exhaustion, or burnout, is particularly common in people who work in helping professions, such as doctors, nurses, police officers, and social workers.

Finally, stress can influence *behavior* in a number of ways. People who experience severe stressors may suffer from continuing behavioral problems (Kessler, Sonnega, Bromet, Hughes, & Nelson, 1995). For example, war veterans often experience severe behavioral symptoms, including sleeplessness, nightmares, and startle reactions (Sutker, Davis, Uddo, & Ditta, 1995). Stress can also lead to negative interpersonal behavior. After the devastating

---

Box 4.8

Focus on Women—Posttraumatic Stress Disorder in Rape Victims

An estimated 172,400 women are raped each year in the United States, and 1 in 4 college women have experienced either rape or attempted rape. Victims of rape often experience a number of emotional and behavioral reactions that are consistent with the diagnosis of posttraumatic stress disorder (PTSD; Steketee & Foa, 1987). First, women who have been raped often have persistent negative emotions, including fear, anxiety, and depression. One study found that 41% of rape survivors reported depression more than a year after the attack (Nadelson, Notman, Zackson, & Gornick, 1982). Persistent fear and anxiety also negatively impact women's social and romantic relationships. Women who have experienced rape are often very hesitant about participating in social functions and may choose to avoid situations in which they will encounter strangers. One study found that more than half of those who had experienced rape reported going out only with friends, even as long as 1 to 2 years after the rape (Nadelson et al., 1982). Not surprisingly, sexual dysfunction is a relatively common side effect of rape, with survivors often reporting both less frequent and less enjoyable sexual interaction. Although women who have been raped experience a number of negative psychological and physical consequences, for many rape victims these effects decline within 3 months. Rape survivors may also benefit from some type of treatment, including various cognitive-behavioral approaches such as desensitization and cognitive therapy.

Hurricane Andrew hit south Florida in 1992, causing high levels of stress in the many people who experienced the destruction of their home and/or other possessions, reports of domestic violence increased dramatically (Polusny & Follette, 1995). Even low levels of stress can have a negative impact on behavior. In one study, researchers measured the helping behavior of people who were shopping in a mall during a stressful or nonstressful time (Cohen & Spacapan, 1978). Some people were sent to the mall to buy difficult-to-find items during a time in which the mall was crowded, whereas others were sent to buy easy-to-find items during a time in which the mall was uncrowded. After subjects finished their errand, they encountered a woman who had "lost" a contact lens. Those who had experienced a stressful shopping trip helped less often and for less time than those who had experienced a more relaxing trip. Sexual drive is also affected by stress. It decreases in men and women during times of stress: women are less likely to ovulate, and men are more likely to have difficulty achieving and maintaining an erection (Saplosky, 1994).

What Are Some Strategies for Coping with Stress?

People who are able to cope with stress effectively do not necessarily experience such negative stress consequences as presented in this chapter. As described by Richard Lazarus and Susan Folkman (1984), *coping* refers to an individual's efforts to manage the stressful demands of a specific situation, such as working to solve a problem, finding a new way to look at the situation, or distracting oneself from the problem. This section describes some of the strategies that help people reduce their feelings of stress and thereby experience better health.

Coping Styles

One common strategy for managing challenging situations is trying to confront and change the stressor. This is called *problem-focused coping* and can include a number of different approaches, such as seeking assistance from others, taking direct action, and planning (Carver, Scheier, & Weintraub, 1989; Folkman & Lazarus, 1980). For example, a person who is feeling stress because of too much work could ask for an extension on a paper or make an effort to stop procrastinating and finish one project each day. Strategies could include active coping (removing the stressor by dropping a class), planning how to cope with the stressor (structuring specific times for studying each day), suppressing other activities to focus on the stressor (eliminating participation in athletic events), and seeking advice or assistance with coping (talking to one's advisor about how to balance work projects). At the beginning of the chapter, I described how Monica used problem-focused coping to manage her feelings of stress by talking to a therapist about her parents' separation and asking her professor for an extension on her paper. This type of coping is often used when something constructive can be done to help solve the problem, or at least make the situation better (Folkman, Lazarus, Dunkel-Schetter, DeLongis, & Gruen, 1986; Folkman & Lazarus, 1980). For example, college students are more likely to use problem-focused coping when preparing for an exam, but are less likely to use this approach when they are nervously waiting for their grades after taking the exams (Folkman & Lazarus, 1985). See Table 4.5.

Is tackling a problem directly beneficial in terms of health? Yes: Most research suggests that people who use problem-focused coping show better adjustment (Dunkel-Schetter, Feinstein, Taylor, & Falke, 1992). Problem-focused coping is likely to be particularly effective because it can help people solve problems. For example, if you are feeling angry about your roommate's lack of help cleaning your apartment, directly talking with her about this issue could lead to her greater assistance. Similarly, one study found that while students who procrastinate experience less stress than other students early in the semester, by the end of the semester (when procrastinating is finally catching up with them), they experience greater stress and have more symptoms of illness (see Figure 4.14; Tice & Baumeister, 1997). Students who directly handle

TABLE 4.5   *Test Yourself: How Do You Cope with Problems?*

Active Coping

I concentrate my efforts on doing something about it.

I take direct action to get around the problem.

Planning

I try to come up with a strategy about what to do.

I make a plan of action.

Suppression of Competing Activities

I put aside other activities in order to concentrate on this.

I keep myself from getting distracted by other thoughts or activities.

Restraint Coping

I force myself to wait for the right time to do something.

I hold off doing anything about it until the situation permits.

Seeking Social Support for Instrumental Reasons

I ask people who have had similar experiences what they did.

I try to get advice from someone about what to do.

Seeking Social Support for Emotional Reasons

I talk to someone about how I feel.

I try to get emotional support from friends or relatives.

Positive Reinterpretation and Growth

I look for something good in what is happening.

I learn something from the experience.

Acceptance

I learn to live with it.

I accept that this has happened and that it can't be changed.

Turning to Religion

I seek God's help.

I try to find comfort in my religion.

Focus on and Venting of Emotion

I get upset and let my emotions out.

I let my feelings out.

Denial

I refuse to believe that it has happened.

I pretend that it hasn't really happened.

(continues)

TABLE **4.5**   *(continued)*

Behavioral Disengagement

I give up the attempt to get what I want.

I just give up trying to reach my goal.
Mental Disengagement

I turn to work or other substitute activities to take my mind off things.

I sleep more than usual.
Alcohol–Drug Disengagement

I drink alcohol or take drugs, in order to think about it less.

This scale assesses 14 different strategies people sometimes use to cope with problems.

Source: Carver, Schierer, & Weintraub, 1989.

their problems by keeping up with regular course reading and assignments thereby avoid the considerable stress faced at the end of the semester by those who have ignored these responsibilities.

On the other hand, *emotion-focused coping* is focused on managing the emotional effects of a stressful situation (Folkman & Lazarus, 1980). This strategy might include a number of different approaches, such as simply not thinking

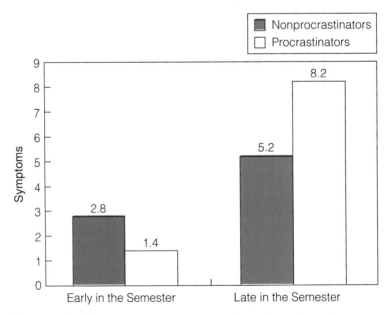

FIGURE 4.14   Although procrastinators have fewer physical symptoms than nonprocrastinators at the beginning of the semester, the tables are turned at the end of the semester.

about the problem (denial or avoidance) as well as venting about the problem to others (seeking social support). For example, someone who has a fight with a close friend could simply try to put it out of his mind as a way of avoiding feeling sad, or could discuss these feelings with another person to try to make sense of the sadness. This type of coping is often used to handle situations that just have to be accepted, such as health problems (Folkman & Lazarus, 1980). For example, Susan Folkman and colleagues (1986) found that when people perceive a problem as unchangeable, they were most likely to use distancing ("tried to forget the whole thing") and escape–avoidance ("slept more than usual"), which allow them to avoid thinking about the problem.

Most research suggests that emotion-focused coping is associated with negative adjustment, in part because denying or avoiding thinking about problems can actually lead to negative psychological and physical well-being (see Box 4.9; Aldwin & Revenson, 1987; Carver et al., 1993; Kelley, Lumley, & Leisen, 1997; King & Miner, 2000). Simply avoiding thinking about a traumatic event prevents individuals from understanding and ultimately coming to terms with the experience (Pennebaker, 1989; Wegner, 1994). One study of breast cancer patients found that those who reported bottling up emotions instead of expressing them were more likely to experience depression and anxiety (Classen, Koopman, Angell, & Speigel, 1996). Similarly, a study by Steve Cole and colleagues (1996) found that among gay men who were HIV-positive, those who were "in the closet" had a more rapid spread of infection—and faster death—than those who were open about their sexual orientation. The use of denial or distraction can even lead people to delay seeking medical care in response to various health symptoms, as we discuss in Chapter 12. Second, deliberately trying to avoid thinking about negative events is very difficult, and thus requires considerable effort (Pennebaker, 1989). Have you ever tried to *not* think about something (an ex-boyfriend, a particularly gruesome scene from a movie, a failed test) and then found that thoughts about this "forbidden" topic dominate your mind? Research by Dan Wegner and his colleagues (1990) at the University of Virginia reveals that asking people to *not* think of something can actually lead them to become preoccupied with the event. Finally, because constantly exerting effort to avoid thinking about something upsetting leads to chronic physiological arousal, relying on this coping strategy can lead to decreases in immune cell activity as well as higher blood pressure and heart rate (Petrie, Booth, & Pennebaker, 1998; Pennebaker, Hughes, & O'Heeron, 1987). For example, James Gross and Robert Levenson (1997) found that women who watched sad films and were asked to conceal their feelings while watching showed a greater cardiovascular reaction than those who were allowed to openly express their feelings.

Questioning the Research 4.2

The study by Steve Cole and his colleagues suggests that HIV-positive gay men who are open about their sexual orientation experience better health and even live longer. But can you think of some alternative explanations for this finding?

Box 4.9

Research Focus—Can Writing in a Journal Improve Your Health?

James Pennebaker and Sandra Beale (1986) examined the health benefits of writing about traumatic events. Forty-six college students were randomly assigned to write for 15 minutes on 4 consecutive nights about either the shoes they were wearing (the control condition), the facts about a trauma they had experienced, their feelings about a traumatic event, or about the facts and their feelings about a traumatic event. Students wrote about very personal subjects in these journals, including the death of a loved one (27%), a relationship breakup (20%), and a major fight with a friend or family member (16%). For example, one student wrote that he had considered suicide because he felt he has disappointed his parents; another wrote about a sailing outing in which her brother drowned. Participants also completed questionnaires on their physical symptoms and moods and had their blood pressure taken.

How did the type of writing they did influence health? Initial findings showed that students who wrote about traumatic events were more upset than those in the control condition—they had larger increases in blood pressure and more negative moods. However, and as predicted, students who wrote about their facts and feelings showed signs of better health at the 4-month follow-up than those in the control condition. For example, students who wrote about their feelings reported having fewer illnesses and minor health problems (e.g., headaches, acne, diarrhea) than those in the control condition. Moreover, students who wrote about both the facts and feelings regarding traumatic events made 0.54 visits to the health center, compared to 1.33 visits for those in the control condition, 1.25 for those in the only-feelings condition, and 1.18 for those in the only-facts condition. These findings provide very strong evidence that writing about traumatic events can lead to improvements in health over time.

Other researchers believe that both problem-focused and emotion-focused coping can be effective, depending on the situation (Forsythe & Compas, 1987; Terry & Hynes, 1998). Specifically, while problem-focused coping is very effective in the case of stressors that you can change by actively confronting them, in cases in which you have no opportunity for improving the situation, the use of problem-focused coping may lead to feelings of frustration and disappointment (Roth & Cohen, 1986). For example, if you are struggling to come to terms with your parents' divorce, trying to use problem-focused coping will be ineffective because this situation is out of your control—you aren't going to be able to fix the problems in their relationship. On the other hand, while emotion-focused coping can be detrimental if you simply refuse to try to fix a manageable problem, this approach may be very effective when there is little that can be done to change a negative situation (Terry & Hynes, 1998). For example, emotion-focused coping is most effective in dealing with failed in–vitro fertilization attempts, a situation over which couples have virtually no control. In sum, the type of coping people use must match the type of situation they are coping with in order for them to experience the greatest benefits. As shown in Figure 4.15, people who cope with events using the "right" type of strategy experience fewer symptoms of anxiety and depression, and subjects who cope using the "wrong" type of strategy experience more symptoms (Forsythe & Compas, 1987). In sum, because different types of situations call for different types of coping, individuals who are comfortable using a number of different coping styles have a higher likelihood of minimizing their stress in a variety of of challenging situations. For example, you may need to use problem-focused coping when trying to constructively resolve a conflict with your dating partner, but must use emotion-focused coping if your efforts to solve the problem fail and the relationship ultimately ends.

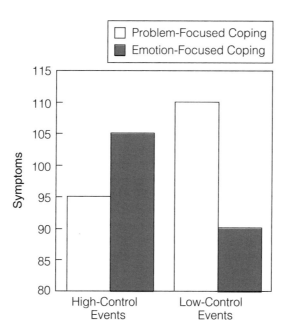

FIGURE 4.15 Students who cope with each type of problem using the "right" strategy experience fewer physical symptoms.

Relaxation

Another way of coping with stress is through the use of various relaxation techniques. In *progressive muscle relaxation*, people focus on tensing and then releasing each part of their body (hands, shoulders, legs, etc.) one at a time (Jacobson, 1938). This helps patients learn to distinguish states of tension from states of relaxation, thereby helping them learn how to calm themselves down in virtually any stressful situation. The technique of biofeedback also helps people distinguish between states of tension and relaxation, but with a particular focus on how these psychological states influence their physiological reactions. Patients are attached to a monitor that shows their physiological response (heart rate, muscle tension, sweat), and they are able to learn how their thoughts and feelings influence their physiological reactions. This technique is also an effective way to help people learn strategies of decreasing stress as well as the impact of stress on their physical reactions. Other relaxation strategies that are effective in decreasing physiological arousal in response to stressful situations include meditation, hypnosis, and yoga.

Systematic desensitization focuses specifically on helping people relax in the face of a particular stressful object or event. In this technique the person is asked to describe the specific causes of his or her anxiety, and then to create a hierarchy of different stimuli associated with that anxiety. As shown in Table 4.6, these fears are ranked such that relatively low-anxiety-causing stimuli fall at the bottom of the hierarchy, and higher-anxiety-provoking stimuli set at the top of the hierarchy. The therapist then asks the patient to focus on the least-anxiety-provoking image, while encouraging the person to relax. Whenever the patient experiences anxiety, the therapist asks him or her to focus on a less-stressful stimulus. Gradually, as the patient is able to think about a low-level stimulus without feeling anxiety, the therapist continues to higher-level (more anxiety-provoking) stimuli; this process, over time, enables people to build up their tolerance to the stressful situation.

TABLE 4.6   *Sample Desensitization Hierarchy for Coping with Fear of Injected Shots*

1. You are reading a magazine and there is a photograph of someone getting a shot.
2. You are watching a television show or movie in which someone gets a shot.
3. You receive a letter from your college stating that before you return in the fall you must have a tetanus vaccine.
4. You call the health center to make an appointment for your vaccination.
5. You leave your room on the morning of your appointment.
6. You park at the health center.
7. You sit in the line to receive your shot.
8. Your name is called by the nurse.
9. You sit in the room as the nurse wipes your arm with alcohol.
10. You watch the nurse approach with the needle.

All of these relaxation techniques can work to reduce the negative effects of stress on psychological and physical health (see Figure 4.16). For example, high school students who learn progressive muscle relaxation during their regular health class show a decrease in blood pressure (Ewart et al., 1987); medical students who are trained in relaxation techniques have better immune system functioning during exams (Kiecolt-Glaser et al., 1986); and patients who are trained in biofeedback show a reduction in their symptoms associated with irritable bowel syndrome (IBS), a gastrointestinal disorder often linked to stress. Adolescents who receive training in meditation show decreases in blood pressure and heart rate compared to those who receive only health education (Barnes, Treiber, & Davis, 2001). Finally, some research suggests that training patients with severe coronary heart disease in relaxation techniques, such as meditation, can even lead to a reversal in the amount of arteriosclerosis present (Ornish et al., 1998).

Humor

Interestingly, having a sense of *humor* can lead to better physical health (see Photo 4.5). In a series of studies at the University of Waterloo, Herbert Lefcourt has shown that after watching various funny videotapes, students show improvements in how well their immune system functions, including

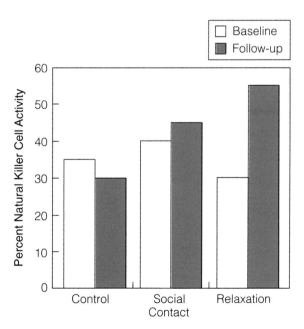

FIGURE 4.16 Senior citizens who received relaxation training had higher immune system responses at the follow-up than those in the control or social contact conditions.

PHOTO 4.5   Research supports the view that laughter can be a good medicine.

producing higher levels of NK cells and lower levels of cortisol (Lefcourt, Davidson-Katz, & Kueneman, 1990). Using humor as a coping mechanism is also associated with lower blood pressure (see Table 4.7; Lefcourt, Davidson, Prkachin, & Mills, 1997). The reason is, humor may help people cope with stressors by distracting them from their problems. For example, one study found that patients who joked and laughed prior to dental surgery experienced less anxiety during the procedure (Trice & Price-Greathouse, 1986). As Dan Shapiro (2000), a clinical psychologist and author, says, "We all have a

TABLE 4.7   *Test Yourself: The Coping Humor Scale*

Please indicate the extent to which you agree or disagree with each statement, with 1 = strongly disagree, 2 = mildly disagree, 3 = mildly agree, 4 = strongly agree.

1. I have often found that my problems have been greatly reduced when I try to find something funny in them.
2. I usually look for something comical to say when I am in tense situations.
3. I have often felt that if I am in a situation where I have to either cry or laugh, it's better to laugh.
4. I can usually find something to laugh or joke about even in trying situations.
5. It has been my experience that humor is often a very effective way of coping with problems.

This scale assesses people's tendency to use humor to cope with problems.

Source: Martin & Lefcourt, 1983.

choice as to how to respond to stressful situations. Take losing one's luggage. We can respond with humor: 'Has my luggage gone somewhere interesting? Is it having a good time?' or we can take it as a calamity."

Exercise

Another technique for coping with stressful events is *exercise*. Exercise improves mood and reduces anxiety and depression (McCann & Holmes, 1984). Moreover, people who exercise more frequently report fewer illnesses (Roth, Wiebe, Fillingim, & Shay, 1990). One study by Jonathon Brown (1991) examined the association between physical fitness, stress, and number of visits to the campus health center. Students who were high in stress and low in physical fitness made the most visits, whereas those who were high in stress but also high in fitness made as few visits as those under low stress. Similarly, at the beginning of the chapter, I described how Chandler managed his job stress by swimming every day after work. So, the next time you are feeling blue, think about going for a jog—or a brisk walk, if even the thought of jogging is stressful!

Social Support

Another factor that can help people manage stress is *social support*. People who have support from friends and family may have more resources to cope with the stressful events and may therefore see these events as less problematic. For example, if you are studying for a very important exam, your roommate's offer to bring you dinner in your room or quiz you on class material might be particularly helpful. (We discuss in detail the very important role of social support in managing stress and thereby predicting health in Chapter 6.)

Can Religion Help People Cope with Stressful Events?

Religion plays a very important role in the lives of many people. More than 90% of American adults consider themselves to be a part of a formal religious tradition (Kosmin & Lachman, 1993), and almost 96% believe in God or some other type of universal spirit (Becker, 2001). More than half of Americans report that prayer is an important part of their daily life, and women, African Americans, older people, and those with lower income are particularly likely to see prayer as an important coping mechanism (see Photo 4.6, 1997; Princeton Religious Research Center, 1990). Although some people distinguish between *religiosity*—a formal link to religious organizations— and *spirituality*—a personal orientation toward religious beliefs—most people see these two concepts as quite similar (George, Larson, Koenig, & McCullough, 2000).

PHOTO 4.6   Many Americans report praying as a way of coping with stressful life events.

    In turn, people who are involved in religion experience better psycholog-
ical and physical health (see Table 4.8; Bergin, Masters, & Richards, 1987;
Koenig, McCullough, & Larson, 2001; McFadden, 1995). One study with
college students at Brigham Young University (a predominantly Mormon
university) found that those with more internalized religious beliefs experienced lower levels of anxiety and better overall mental health (Bergin et al.,
1987). Similarly, among those people who are caregivers for people with
Alzheimer's disease or cancer (a potentially very stressful situation), those who
have strong religious beliefs are less likely to experience depression (Rabins,
Fitting, Eastham, & Zabora, 1990). Moreover, religious involvement, such as
attending religious services and holding strong religious beliefs, is associated
with lower levels of cancer, heart disease, stroke, and suicide (Levin, 1994;
McCullough, Hoyt, Larson, Koenig, & Thoresen, 2000). Finally, and most
important, religious involvement is associated with lower rates of mortality
(Oxman, Freeman, & Manheimer, 1995). For example, one study with 232

TABLE 4.8   *The Use of Religion to Cope with Traumatic Events*

"After the flight attendant explained emergency landing procedures, we were left with our thoughts. That's when I began praying. I closed my eyes and thought, "Dear Lord, I pray that you'll guide the pilot's hands." I also thought that if God wanted to take my life, that it was OK with me. I was full of peace. Here I was sitting on the edge of eternity. I wasn't facing the end of my life."

"The plane smelled like a house after a fire. I was exhilarated to be alive but deeply grieved when I could see and smell death. It was like being at the doorstep of hell. I pulled my Bible out of my bag. That's all I wanted."

"I did what I needed to do to prepare to die. My thought at the time was that I wanted to be reborn into a family where I would be able to hear the teachings of Buddha. I'd done a lot of Buddhist meditation in my life, and this trained me to become one-pointed in my awareness. I was totally focused on the brace position."

These quotes are from survivors of United Flight 232, which made a crash landing in a field in Iowa on its way from Denver to Chicago on July 19, 1989. As you can see, many passengers thought about their religious beliefs during this traumatic event.

Source: Pargament, 1997.

patients who had open heart surgery found that those who experienced strength and comfort from their religious beliefs were less likely to die in the six months following surgery.

There are several potential mechanisms accounting for the greater well-being associated with religiosity and spirituality. (Koenig et al., 2001; Plante & Sherman, 2001; Seybold & Hill, 2001). People who are religious may have stronger and more extensive social networks. As we discuss in Chapter 6, people who are religious may belong to a church, temple, or other organization that brings them together on a regular basis with others who share their general views. One study found that 41% of community members reported they would use their clergy for help with personal problems (Pergament, 1997). Second, many religions directly encourage healthy behavior, such as abstaining from smoking, alcohol/drug use, and risky sexual behaviors (Gorsuch, 1995). The Mormon, Muslim, and Southern Baptists religions for example, forbid the use of alcohol. In turn, religiousness is associated with lower levels of alcohol abuse, marijuana use, smoking, and premarital sexual activity in teenagers (Donahue & Benson, 1995). Similarly, and as described at the beginning of the chapter, Elizabeth has strong religious beliefs and shows a high level of adherence to her diabetes care regimen, which in turn helps her stay in good health. Religious commitment may also lead people to rely on adaptive coping mechanisms (Pargament, 1997). Many people use religion as a way of coping with potentially stressful events, including medical problems, accidents, and problems with loved ones (see Table 4.8; Pargament, 1997). For example, one study of parents who had lost a baby to sudden infant death syndrome found that those parents who felt that religion was important to them engaged in more cognitive processing about the experience, which in turn led to greater well-being later on (McIntosh, Silver, & Wortman, 1993). Finally, people who have strong spiritual beliefs may benefit in terms of health because their religion provides some type of meaning for even seemingly senseless tragedies. Seeing the benefits of a negative experience gives people a chance to confront and cope with thoughts and feelings about the trauma, but with a focus on its positive aspects, which in turn can lead to greater psychological and physical well-being.

Although religiosity and spirituality are generally associated with good health, they also can have some drawbacks (Koenig et al., 2001). Some religions, such as Jehovah's Witnesses and Christian Scientists, forbid some types of medical care, including blood transfusions and immunizations. For example, Jehovah's Witnesses believe that there is no distinction in God's eyes between having a blood transfusion and drinking someone else's blood, and therefore anyone who receives a transfusion will be "turned away" from eternal salvation. People with strong religious beliefs may also delay seeking medical care or refuse life-saving medications and procedures because they believe prayer and other religious methods of managing illnesses will lead to positive outcomes. In line with this view, one study published in the *Journal of the American Medical Association* demonstrated that one reason why more African American women die from breast cancer than white women is because some of their cultural beliefs lead them to delay seeking medical care (Lannin et al., 1998). For example, African American women are much more likely than white women to believe, "If a person prays about cancer, God will heal it without medical treatments." Religious coping strategies can also be detrimental when people rely on them alone, as opposed to using a broader range of strategies (Abernethy, Seidlitz, Evinger, & Duberstein, 2002). Spouses of lung cancer patients who use moderate levels of religious coping are less depressed than those who use either lower or higher levels. In sum, religious beliefs seem to have a beneficial effect on health only when these beliefs are used in conjunction with standard medical care, not as a replacement for such care, and in conjunction with other coping mechanisms.

Lingering Issues

Are there gender differences in how people respond to stress? Although for many years researchers simply accepted Walter Cannon's observation that people respond to stress with heightened arousal (fight-or-flight response), recent research by Shelley Taylor and colleagues suggests that this reaction may not apply to everyone (Taylor et al., 2000). Because the vast majority of research on the stress response has relied on entirely male samples (and often on male rats!), it is not clear whether females show a similar response to stressful situations. Moreover, some research with humans suggests that women prefer to affiliate with others during times of stress, whereas men prefer less social interaction. For example, when women expect that they will be given painful electric shocks, they prefer to wait with other women, whereas men often prefer to wait alone. In sum, while men do typically show the classic fight-or-flight response to stress, women may show what Taylor calls the "tend-and-befriend" response.

Some research by Catherine Stoney also suggests that there are gender differences both in how people respond to stress and the influence of stress on illness (Stoney, Davis, & Mathews, 1987 Stoney, Mathews, McDonald, & Johnson, 1988). First, men tend to have higher blood pressure than women in general and also have a greater change in blood pressure during stressful situations. For example, in one study researchers asked men and women to perform three different types of challenging tasks, including computing a series of subtractions, giving a speech, and evaluating their own videotaped speech. Men showed higher blood pressure increases in each case. This greater physiological responsiveness to stress may partially explain why the rate of coronary heart disease is so much greater for men than women. Specifically, if men are constantly reacting to stress more than women, their hearts are likely to undergo much more wear and tear.

Is praying an effective strategy for coping with stress? Kwang Cha and his colleagues (2001) conducted a study to examine whether prayer could actually impact physical health. One hundred and ninety-nine women in Korea who sought medical help in becoming pregnant were randomly assigned to prayer or no-prayer groups. Pictures of the women in the "prayer group" were then given to people who attended churches in the United States, Canada, and Australia. These people were asked to pray that these women would become pregnant. However, neither the women who were trying to get pregnant nor the medical staff who were caring for them knew about the study. Researchers then assessed whether women who were prayed for were more likely to become pregnant than women without these prayers. To the surprise of even the researchers, women who were prayed for were much more likely to became pregnant than those who were not prayed for. Specifically, 50% of the women who were prayed for became pregnant, as compared to only 26% of those who were not. The rate of pregnancy in the prayer group was also much higher than the standard rate of pregnancy in this clinic, which was 33%. Interestingly, prayer was effective in increasing the rates of pregnancy only for women who were 30 and older—it had no effect on rates of pregnancy for women who were younger than 30 (possibly because the rates of pregnancy in this younger group were already quite high). Because this study included only a small sample of women, these results should be considered preliminary. Nonetheless, this research suggests yet another way that religiosity may lead to better health.

Thought Questions

1. Describe two different ways that you could measure stress and the advantages and disadvantages of each method.

2. Describe the three stages of Selye's General Adaptation Syndrome, and give two critiques of this model.

3. Describe the effects of stress on the cardiovascular, endocrine, and immune systems, using specific examples from research with humans and/or animals.

4. You have recently noticed that you develop some type of minor illness, such as a sore throat or a cold, each time you take final exams at the end of the semester. What are three specific things you could do to decrease your likelihood of getting a cold during exam week this year?

5. Although people with strong religious beliefs generally experience better psychological and physical well-being, are there some cases in which such beliefs could be detrimental to health? Why or why not?

Answers to Questioning the Research

Answer 4.1: Many studies of the effects of stress on health are based on studies of college students who are experiencing the stress of exams. There are many advantages of this type of approach: college students are obviously an easy population for researchers to find, and exams happen regularly and at predictable times, so researchers can readily assess students' health before, during, and after. However, these studies have some substantial limitations. First, exams are predictable—you know from the beginning of the semester that they are going to happen and even when they are going to happen. But many of the most stressful events people experience lack this type of forewarning, which probably makes them even more stressful. Moreover, while exams are clearly stressful, they are not particularly life-altering like some other stressors, including death of a family member, cancer diagnosis, or divorce. These studies also rely on self-report from the college students, so it is impossible to tell whether students are giving accurate information. Many people have the belief that students engage in less healthy behavior during exam periods, so it is possible that students report that their behavior is less healthy than it actually is during exam periods—or that they report engaging in healthier behavior than they really do during other times of the semester. Finally, college students by and large are a very healthy population, so stressful events may not have as much of an impact on their health as they might on less healthy people, such as senior citizens and those with chronic illnesses.

Answer 4.2: Although this study found that HIV-positive gay men who were "in the closet" had a more rapid spread of infection and earlier death, the major limitation of this study is that it shows correlation as opposed to causation. What are some alternative explanations for this finding? One possibility is that men who are open about their sexual orientation are more likely to be in stable, long-term relationships than those who are trying to hide their orientation are. Men who are in relationships may get assistance from their partners that directly benefits their health, including reminders to take their medication, provision of healthy meals, and much-needed social support. These factors could in turn lead to better health and longevity. Another possibility is that gay men who are open about their sexual orientation are more likely to acknowledge their own risk of acquiring HIV; hence, they seek more frequent HIV testing than those who are hiding their sexual orientation. It may be that gay men who are open about their orientation simply find out that they are HIV-positive sooner than who are still "in the closet." In other words, it may not be that gay men who are open live longer with HIV, but rather they live longer *knowing* they have HIV because they get tested more frequently. Finally, gay men who are hiding their sexual orientation may be less comfortable buying condoms or asking their partners to wear condoms than those who are open about their orientation. This higher rate of unprotected sex on the part of some men could therefore lead to more exposure to HIV and other STDs that could have negative health effects, thereby leading to more illness and rapid death.

CHAPTER 5
Personality

- Jason, who is 48 years old, underwent coronary heart surgery last week. Although Jason was initially nervous about having this surgery, he talked to a number of people who had experienced the procedure and became confident that the surgery would go well. In fact, Jason typically approaches upcoming events with a positive attitude—he has a strong belief that "things work out for the best." Following his surgery, Jason received many visitors in the hospital and is making great progress in his recovery. He plans to return to work within a few weeks and has begun taking short walks with his wife in the evening.

- Sue, a junior in college, is outgoing, energetic, and sociable; in fact, she is often described by her friends as "the life of the party." She is also full of energy—Sue is the president of the Student Government Organization, an active member in a campus volunteer organization, and the captain of the women's soccer team. Even though she is very busy with her academic and extracurricular activities, Sue is almost always happy and upbeat. Like most college students, Sue occasionally develops a cold or sore throat, but these symptoms pass quickly and rarely cause any significant disruption in her activities.

- Cindy is 28 years old and is a "rising star" in the public relations firm where she works. Cindy is very efficient at her job, in part because she works very long hours and is constantly doing many things at one time (e.g., responding to e-mail messages while talking on the phone). She tends to skip lunch, or just picks up a hamburger at a drive-in, and typically sleeps no more than 6 hours a night. Cindy is very competitive with her coworkers and prides herself on billing more hours than anyone else at her level. Although she has never experienced any health problems (and in fact plays in several local tennis tournaments each summer), Cindy has recently started experiencing migraine headaches and has developed an ulcer.

- Miles is 52 years old, and is consistently in a "bad mood." Although he is a partner in a large law firm, he is very nervous whenever he must appear in court and generally feels that his job is not going very well. Miles is not married and has few close friends, in part because his anxiety tends to make others around him nervous. He also suffers from a number of recurring physical problems, including back pain, fatigue, and general achiness.

- Debbie, who is 34 years old, has just started a new job at an advertising agency. Although most of her coworkers have tried to make her feel welcome and have offered to answer any of her questions, Debbie thinks they are probably just trying to highlight her ignorance about the new job. She has therefore refused their help in all cases; she, instead, prefers to work alone and has refused to participate in several large group projects. Debbie has smoked for many years, and has received advice from her physician about the importance of quitting. However, Debbie believes the physician is simply trying to "tell her what to do," and she believes she'll decide on her own when—and if—she'll quit smoking.

Preview

This chapter examines how various personality traits, the individual differences in people's tendencies to think, feel, and act in particular ways, influence health behavior. First, we examine how certain personality traits, including optimism, extraversion, and conscientiousness, are positively associated with psychological and physical well-being. We then examine how other personality factors, such as neuroticism/negative affect, Type A behavior, and hostility/disagreeableness, are associated with negative health. Next, we examine a number of different explanations for the personality–health link, including the amount of stress people experience, the strategies they use to cope with stress, the amount of social support they have, their health-related behaviors, their interaction with and adherence to medical regimens, and their physiological responses to stress.

What Personality Factors Lead to Good Health?

As soon as you meet someone for the first time, you notice what they are like. Are they friendly, outgoing, and energetic, or are they anxious, withdrawn, and fearful? If I ask you to describe your closest friends or your siblings, you can probably list a number of these types of personality traits. But why do people differ so much in terms of their personalities, and where do these traits come from? According to personality psychologists, at least some personality traits are strongly influenced by heredity (Eysenck, 1967, 1990). This is why identical twins who are raised apart often show very clear similarities in their personalities, whereas children who are raised together but have no genes in common (e.g., adopted children) may show little or no resemblance in terms of personality to other members of their family. Researchers believe that people inherit variations in their body chemistry that influence how sensitive they are to different types of stimulation as well as the types of moods they generally experience (Diener, 2000; Izard, Libero, Putnam, & Haynes, 1993). For example, some people may be highly sensitive to stress (which can lead them to experience more negative affect or neuroticism), others may need a high level of stimulation (which can lead them to be higher in extraversion), and still others may crave order and routine (which can lead them to be high in conscientiousness). These traits are basic characteristics of the person that are relatively stable across situations and over time. These traits are formed by people's experiences in the world, not just their biology; hence, our personalities reflect the environment in which we were raised (Sarason, Sarason, & Gurung, 1997). This section examines how four personality factors are positively associated with psychological and physical well-being (see Boxes 5.1 and 5.4).

Optimism

Many researchers have examined the role of optimism, the expectation that good things will happen in the future and bad things will not, in predicting behavior (Peterson, 2000). Michael Scheier and Charles Carver (1992), for example, created a scale to assess people's optimistic expectations (see Table 5.1; Scheier & Carver, 1993). When you take a difficult exam, do you typically believe that you did well? If so, you are probably an optimist. Fans of baseball teams with long-standing losing streaks, such as the Boston Red Sox and the Chicago Cubs, often hold a very optimistic view about their team's future chances and think, "Maybe next year." On the other hand, if you tend to approach different situations expecting failure or disappointment, you are probably a pessimist.

Other researchers have described optimism not in terms of people's expectations about whether good or bad events will happen in the future, but rather in terms of how people explain bad events that have already occurred (Peterson, 2000). According to this view, people who explain bad events as resulting from external, unstable, and specific causes are optimistic, whereas

Box 5.1

A New Focus on Positive Psychology

The study of psychology has for some time focused predominantly on understanding and helping people cope with tragedy, adversity, and disease (Seligman & Csikszentmihalyi, 2000). Sigmund Freud, for example, examined how the unconscious led people to experience troubling physical symptoms. Similarly, many more research studies have examined what leads people to experience destructive mood states, such as depression and anxiety, more than what leads people to experience positive mood states, such as happiness and optimism. The field of positive psychology, which examines how to help people achieve healthy physical and psychological well-being, was therefore recently developed in an attempt to focus psychologists on examining more positive aspects of life. Researchers in the field of positive psychology are examining the predictors of well-being, contentment, and satisfaction; the impact on psychological and physical well-being; of positive personality traits, including hope, hardiness, forgiveness, wisdom, and courage; and the factors that lead people to engage in prosocial behavior, including altruism, nurturance, and tolerance. This new focus on positive psychology should help us understand how to help people function in adaptive ways, and therefore help people, communities, and societies flourish and thrive.

those who see these events as resulting from internal, stable, and global causes are pessimistic (Abramson, Metalsky, & Alloy, 1989; Peterson, Sligman, Yurko, Martin, & Friedman, 1998). So, students who are optimistic and do poorly invariably blame the professor (e.g., "The test was totally unfair!"), whereas those with a pessimistic style who do poorly blame themselves (e.g., "I guess I'm just not good at psychology").

TABLE 5.1   *Test Yourself: Sample Items from the Optimism Scale*

1. In uncertain times, I usually expect the best.
2. If something can go wrong for me, it will.
3. I always look on the bright side of things.
4. I'm always optimistic about my future.
5. I hardly ever expect things to go my way.
6. Things never work out the way I want them to.
7. I'm a believer in the idea that "every cloud had a silver lining."
8. I rarely count on good things happening to me.

Items 2, 5, 6, and 8 are reverse-scored so that lower scores indicate greater optimism.

Source: Scheier & Carver, 1985.

Yet another way researchers have described optimism is through people's sense of hope, namely, their expectations that their goals could be achieved (see Box 5.2; Snyder et al., 1996). The hope scale measures people's focus on pursuing their goals (e.g., "I energetically pursue my goals") as well as their belief that these goals can be accomplished (e.g., "There are lots of ways around any problem").

Although researchers have varied in exactly how they describe and measure optimistic beliefs, findings across many different studies indicate that holding such beliefs is associated with psychological well-being (Scheier & Carver, 1993; Taylor et al., 1992). For example, women who are optimistic and high in self-esteem are less likely to experience postpartum depression (Carver & Gaines, 1987), HIV-positive men who are optimistic are less worried about developing AIDS (Taylor et al., 1992), and people who are optimistic are less depressed following unsuccessful attempts at in vitro fertilization (Litt, Tennen, Affleck, & Klock, 1992). Although many studies have assessed optimism and mood at a single point in time (and, therefore, we can't tell whether optimism leads to lower levels of depression or vice versa), longitudinal research studies have assessed optimism at one time and then assessed symptoms later (Scheier & Carver, 1987). For example, Charles Carver and colleagues (1993) interviewed women with breast cancer in order to assess their optimism and negative feelings at the time of diagnosis and then again one day before surgery, 10 days after surgery, and at 3-, 6-, and 12-month follow-up visits. As predicted, optimism at the initial diagnosis was associated with lower distress levels at each of the following dates. Another longitudinal study found that college students with a negative explanatory style during their first year were more likely to experience both major and minor depression during their junior year than those who had a positive explanatory style (see Figure 5.1; Alloy, Abramson, & Francis, 1999). These studies give us some confidence that having a positive outlook does in fact lead to better health.

Box 5.2

The Power of Hope

Hold fast to dreams
For if dreams die
Life is a broken-winged bird
That cannot fly.

This famous poem by Langston Hughes describes the importance of hope in maintaining positive psychological and physical well-being.

Source: Rampersad & Roessel, 1994.

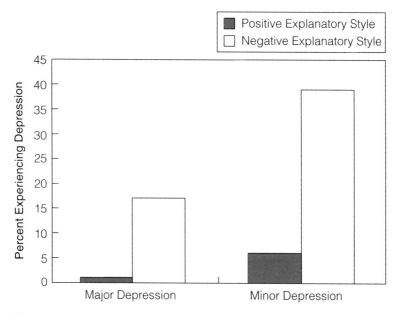

FIGURE 5.1 College students who had a positive explanatory style were much less likely to suffer from minor or major depression than those with a negative explanatory style (Alloy et al., 1999).

People who have a generally optimistic view about themselves and the world also experience better physical well-being (Scheier & Carver, 1993). People who are optimistic have fewer infectious illnesses than do pessimists, and optimists are less likely to develop physical symptoms (e.g., dizziness, blurred vision, fatigue, muscle soreness) even during stressful times (Peterson & Seligman, 1987; Scheier & Carver, 1985). For example, in one study nearly a hundred 25-year-old men were asked to explain negative events in their lives, such as difficulties in their careers and close relationships (Peterson, Seligman, & Vaillant, 1988). Researchers then coded these responses as internal (e.g., "I cannot decide on a career") or external (e.g., "My mother just wouldn't see my side, because she was so stubborn"). When the men were contacted again 35 years later, those who were pessimistic at age 25 had poorer health than did those who were more optimistic, even controlling for initial physical and emotional health. Optimists also recover more quickly from surgery and are less likely to be rehospitalized after surgery (Scheier et al., 1989, 1999). As described at the beginning of the chapter, Jason's optimism helped him make a rapid recovery following coronary heart surgery.

Most important, however, having an optimistic view of oneself and the world leads to a longer life (see Box 5.3; Everson, Goldberg, Kaplan, & Cohen, 1996; Peterson et al., 1998). For example, one study by Susan Everson and colleagues (1996) examined how feeling hopeless was associated with health in a sample of nearly 2,500 middle-age men. The study's findings

---

Box 5.3

Research Focus—Do Optimistic People Live Longer?

In order to examine the effects of optimism on life expectancy, Chris Peterson and Martin Seligman (1987) created a list of all members of the Baseball Hall of Fame who played between 1900 and 1950. They examined quotes from the *New York Times* and the *Philadelphia Inquirer* for these years and wrote down every quote by any one of these 94 players. The researchers then rated the extent to which the quote reflected what type of causal attribution the players made for a good event or a bad one. For example, "These guys were just too good for us" was classified as a global, unstable, external cause. On the other hand, "We don't care who pitches for the Tigers because we are again on our batting stride" was classified as a specific, internal, somewhat stable explanation. Men who gave internal, stable, and global explanations for bad events lived a shorter life, as did those who offered external, unstable, and specific explanations for good events. What does this study suggest in terms of health? If you want to live a longer life, you should take credit for your successes and blame your failures on others.

---

revealed that men who were high in hopelessness were more than twice as likely to die from cancer and more than four times more likely to die from cardiovascular diseases than men who were low in hopelessness (see Figure 5.2). Similarly, people who explain events in an optimistic way are less likely to die from accidental or violent causes than those without this beneficial explanatory style (Peterson et al., 1988). Men who have AIDS and are optimistic live nearly twice as long as those who are pessimistic (Reed, Kemeny, Taylor, Wang, & Visscher, 1994), and cancer patients who are optimistic live longer (Levy, Lee, Bagley, & Lippman, 1988; Schulz, Beckwala, Knapp, Scheier, & Williamson, 1996). Finally, one recent study found that older individuals who have positive attitudes about aging lived an average of 7.5 years longer than those with less positive attitudes (Levy, Slade, Kunkel, & Kasl, 2002).

Extraversion

Extraverted people are outgoing, social, and assertive—they have many friends, show high levels of energy, and often take on leadership roles (Costa & McCrae, 1992). According to Eysenck (1967), extraverts tend to seek a high level of stimulation—they get bored easily, enjoy new challenges, and like to take risks. If you think you'd make a good salesperson, enjoy attending parties and other large gatherings, and like trying exciting new things (e.g., parachuting, bungee jumping), you might be an extravert (see Photo 5.1). In con-

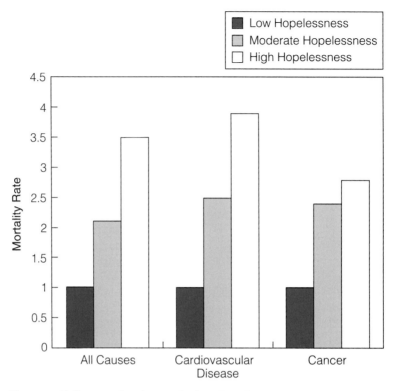

FIGURE 5.2 People who are high in hopelessness have higher rates of general mortality as well as higher rates of mortality from cardiovascular disease and cancer than those who are low in hopelessness (data from Everson et al., 1996).

trast, introverted people are cautious, serious, and low-key. Because people who are high in introversion are easily overaroused, they tend to avoid crowds and other stimulating environments and activities. If you prefer jobs that require more solitary work, carefully deliberate over decisions, and prefer spending time with just a few close friends, you may be an introvert. (See Table 5.2 to test yourself.)

Extraversion is associated with psychological and physical well-being (Costa & McCrae, 1980; Martin et al., 1992; Swindle, 1989). Extraverts experience more positive moods, including higher levels of pride, excitement, and pleasure; simply knowing how extraverted a person is lets you predict how happy they'll be 10 years later (Costa & McCrae, 1980). Extraverts also experience better physical well-being: they have lower rates of both major and minor illnesses, including asthma, arthritis, ulcers, and even coronary heart disease (Friedman & Booth-Kewley, 1987a). For example, one study with over 1,000 men found that those who were high in extraversion reported fewer psychological and physical symptoms (Spiro, Aldwin, Levenson, & Bosse, 1990). As described at the beginning of this chapter, Sue is busy with

TABLE 5.2 *Test Yourself: Sample Items from an Extraversion–Introversion Scale*

1. Are you usually carefree?
2. Do you often long for excitement?
3. Do you often do things on the spur of the moment?
4. Would you do almost anything for a dare?
5. Do you enjoy wild parties?
6. Do you generally prefer reading to meeting people?
7. Are you mostly quiet when you're with others?
8. Are you slow and unhurried in the way you move?
9. Do you hate being in a crowd who plays jokes on one another?
10. Do you like the kind of work you need to pay attention to?

If you answered "yes" to questions 1 through 5 and "no" to questions 6 through 10, you are an extravert. If you answered "no" to questions 1 through 5 and "yes" to questions 6 through 10, you are probably an introvert.

Source: Eysenck & Eysenck, 1964.

PHOTO 5.1 Extraverts often seek out high levels of stimulation and hence are more likely than introverts to enjoy dangerous activities, such as skydiving, mountain climbing, and bungee jumping.

her academic and extracurricular pursuits, but manages to experience high
levels of psychological and physical well-being.

Conscientiousness

Conscientious people are hardworking, motivated, and persistent (Costa &
McCrae, 1987). They show high levels of self-restraint (e.g., may write a term
paper even when they'd rather be watching game 7 of the World Series) and
focus intensely on their goals (e.g., may carefully choose summer internships
that help them achieve their career ambitions). On the other hand, people
who are low in conscientiousness are easygoing and somewhat disorganized;
for example, they may have trouble deciding on a career path and meeting
deadlines.

Although relatively little research has examined the link between conscientiousness and health, one longitudinal study suggests that people who are
high in conscientiousness experience better health and even live longer
(Friedman et al., 1993). In this study over 1,000 children (approximately 11
years old) completed a series of personality assessments in 1922, including
measures of conscientiousness, optimism, self-esteem, sociability, stability of
mood, and energy level, and then completed surveys repeatedly every few
years through 1986. Researchers therefore were able to examine how personality was associated with health over time. Findings indicated that only
conscientiousness was associated with better health over time. For example, a
person in the top 25% on conscientiousness had only 77% of the risk of dying
in a given year compared to someone in the bottom 25% on conscientiousness. In other words, children who were truthful, reliable, hardworking tended to live about 2 years longer than those who were described as impulsive
and lacking in self-control.

Internal Locus of Control/Hardiness

As we discussed in Chapter 4, having a sense of control over events in one's
life is a very important predictor of health. Some researchers have classified
people based on whether they generally have an internal or an external locus
of control over the events in their lives (Rotter, 1966). People who have a
strong internal locus of control believe that their decisions and behaviors
impact their outcomes, and people with such a belief generally experience
better physical and psychological health.

Similarly, according to Suzanne Kobasa and colleagues, a person most likely to stay healthy in the face of stress showed commitment to goals and activities, possessed a sense of control over what happened to him or her and
viewed stressful events as challenging rather than threatening (Kobasa, Maddi,
& Kahn, 1982). Such individuals are committed to their work and their families and believe that what they do is important and under their own control.
In fact, demanding situations can lead hardy people to perform particularly

TABLE 5.3 *Quotes from People Who Are High or Low in Hardiness*

High Hardiness

"I realize that setbacks are a part of the game. I've had 'em, I have them now, and I've got plenty more ahead of me. Seeing this—the big picture—puts it all in perspective, no matter how bad things get."

"I had a sense of peace inside that assured me that this loss would pass just as all of life passes. . . . At the funeral I knelt in front of him and the same peace came over me. The next day I was out back chopping wood, just as three generations of family had done on this land before me."

"The key to dealing with loss is not obvious. One must take the problem, the void, the loneliness, the sorrow, and put it on the back of your neck and use it as a driving force. Don't let such problems sit out there in front of you, blocking your vision. . . . Use hardships in a positive way."

Low Hardiness

"I was certain I would die on the table . . . never wake up. . . . I felt sure it was the end. The I woke up with a colostomy and figured I have to stay inside the house the rest of my life. Now I'm afraid to go back to the doctor's and keep putting off my checkups."

"I was apprehensive all the time—he was sick for years and each day that I got out of bed, I was thinking that he was going to die. It was always in the back of my mind, always. Another fear I have is of falling. Therefore, I never go anywhere for fear I'll fall in a strange place."

"I have arthritis and every day I feel stiffer than the day before. Simple jobs around the house look so big to me and I feel fatigued oftentimes before I begin them. Sometimes I stay in bed for much longer than I should and get up feeling worse. I worry too much. . . . Life has never been a rose garden."

Note: These quotes illustrate differences in how people who are high in hardiness think about the potentially stressful events of their lives compared to those low in hardiness.

Source: Colerick, 1985.

well. Table 5.3 provides some examples of perspectives of those high versus low in hardiness.

As predicted, people who are hardy and those with an internal locus of control experience better psychological and physical well-being (Florian, Mikulincer, & Taubman, 1995; Funk & Houston, 1987; Kobasa & Puccetti, 1983; Lakey, 1988). For example, those who believe they have control suffer less depression in response to major illnesses, such as kidney failure, coronary heart disease, and cancer (Helgeson, 1992; Marks, Richardson, Graham, & Levine, 1986; Taylor, Lichtman, & Wood, 1984). Similarly, cancer patients who have greater perceptions of control (over their illness, interpersonal relationships, and symptoms) are less depressed than those who have low perceived control (Thompson, Sobolew-Shubin, Galbraith, Schwankovsky, & Cruzen, 1993). The perception of control may be particularly important for helping people cope—and thereby stay healthy—during times of high stress. For example, Suzanne Kobasa and colleagues (1982) conducted a study with 259 business executives to examine the association between hardiness, stress, and level of illness. Those who were low in hardiness and who experienced many stressful life events reported experiencing high levels of illness; those who were high in hardiness remained healthy even when they experienced many stressful life events (see Figure 5.3).

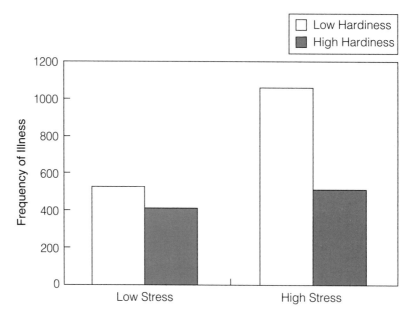

FIGURE 5.3 Although people who experience relatively few stressful life events have a low rate of illness regardless of how hardy they are, those who experience many stressful life events and who are high in hardiness also show low rates of illness. In contrast, people who experience many stressful life events and who are low in hardiness experience extremely high rates of illness (Kobasa et al., 1982).

Questioning the Research 5.1

What do you think of the hardiness personality trait? Are all of its components equally important?

Box 5.4

Research Focus—If You're Happy and You Know It . . .

Deborah Danner and her colleagues at the University of Kentucky examined whether people who generally experience more positive emotion also experienced better health (Danner, Snowdon, & Friesen, 2001). To test this question, they read the autobiographies of 180 Catholic nuns, and then coded the writing to measure its emotional content. For example, researchers counted the number of words and number of sentences describing positive emotions, such as happiness, love, and pride. They then examined survival rates of these nuns when they were 75 to 95 years old. This study provided very strong evidence that women who experience more positive emotion actually live longer lives. Specifically, 55% of those who used few positive emotion words (in the bottom quarter) had died, as compared to 21% of those who used very many positive emotion words. Similarly, 54% of those who wrote relatively few positive emotion sentences had died, as compared to 24% of those who wrote many positive emotion sentences. This research, using a very unique sample of women, suggests that experiencing more positive emotions—or at least writing about such emotions— leads to better health and longevity.

What Personality Factors Lead to Unhealthy Behavior?

Some personality factors are associated with poor psychological and physical health. This section examines the impact of neuroticism/negative affect, Type A behavior, and hostility/disagreeableness on health.

Neuroticism/Negative Affect

Neuroticism, or *negative affect*, is a broad personality dimension that refers to the tendency of some people to experience negative emotions, such as distress, anxiety, nervousness, fear, shame, anger, and guilt, often (Watson & Clark, 1984). Although everyone experiences these feelings at times, people who are high in negative affect are in a "bad mood" quite frequently. They are likely to worry about upcoming events, dwell on failures and shortcomings, and have a less favorable view of themselves and others.

People who are high in neuroticism describe themselves as having a greater number of physical symptoms as well as more severe and uncomfortable symptoms (see Cartoon 5.1; Affleck, Tennen, Urrows, & Higgins, 1992; Aldwin, Levenson, Spiro, & Bosse, 1989; Costa & McCrae, 1987; Watson,

1988; Watson & Pennebaker, 1989). One study of 347 women ages 18 to 94 years found that neuroticism was associated with reports of a number of physical symptoms, including frequency of illness, cardiovascular problems, digestive problems, and fatigue (Costa & McCrae, 1987). Although this study was cross-sectional (hence, it can't distinguish between correlation and causation), other researchers have examined how negative affect influences psychological and physical health over time. For example, Elaine Leventhal and her colleagues examined negative affect in a sample of older adults (ages 62 to 73), and then followed up with the participants over 6 months (Leventhal, Hansell, Diefenback, Leventhal, & Glass, 1996). People who were higher in negative affect were more likely to report experiencing a variety of physical symptoms, including fatigue, dizziness, sleep disturbance, and energy loss. Similarly, college students who experience high levels of negative affect report more physical complaints, such as headaches, diarrhea, and sore throat (Watson, 1988; Watson & Pennebaker, 1989).

Type A Behavior

In 1956, cardiologists Meyer Friedman and Ray Rosenman were studying the association of diet and heart disease in married couples. Although women consumed as much cholesterol and fat as did their spouses (probably because couples tended to eat the same types of foods), men were much more susceptible to heart disease. One woman suggested that men's increased likelihood of heart attacks was because of the constant stress they experienced in the business world—at the time this study was conducted, many women were

"No, no, that's not a sin, either. My goodness, you must have worried yourself to death."

CARTOON 5.1   People with high levels of negative affect, including anxiety, fearfulness, and guilt, do experience more health problems. (©The New Yorker Collection 1993 Charles Barsotti from cartoonbank.com. All Rights Reserved.)

not involved in work outside the home. The researchers therefore interviewed 3,000 healthy middle-aged men, and then followed these men over 9 years to determine which would develop heart disease. These interviews revealed that the men varied in their personalities. While some of the men were generally easygoing, relaxed, and laid-back, others were quite impatient, competitive, time-conscious, and quick to anger. Friedman and Rosenman classified these two different personality types as Type B and Type A, respectively. Moreover, of the 258 men who experienced a heart attack during the time of this study, 69% were classified as Type A, and only 31% were classified as Type B (Rosenman et al., 1975).

As shown in Table 5.4, the Type A behavior pattern is characterized by three features (Friedman & Booth-Kewley, 1987b; Matthews, 1988). First, Type A people experience high levels of time urgency—they are irritated by and impatient with time delays and constantly try to do more than one thing at a time (see Photo 5.2). If you walk and talk fast, interrupt slow speakers (or finish their sentences), race through yellow lights, and hate waiting in line, you may have a tendency toward Type A behavior. Second, Type A's have a strong competitive drive and are focused on doing better than other people in all sorts of situations (work and play). For example, Type A's engage in competitive leisure activities more than Type B's—they may prefer playing tennis (in which there is a clear winner and loser) to doing aerobics (Kelly & Houston, 1985). Finally, Type A's are prone to experiencing anger and hostility (e.g., they are more irritable when frustrated in their goal pursuit, are easily aroused to anger). Like people who are high in hostility, Type A people are quick to experience anger and may lash out at others in frustration.

Although the Friedman and Rosenman study was the first to suggest an association between Type A behavior and health, other studies have also shown this link (see Figure 5.4). For example, Type A's report experiencing more minor illnesses, such as coughs, allergies, headaches, and asthma attacks,

TABLE 5.4   *Test Yourself: Sample Items from the Framington Type A Scale*

Answer true or false to the following questions.

1. I want to be the best at everything.
2. I can be described as domineering.
3. I like to compete.
4. I eat too quickly.
5. I often feel stressed.
6. I have often thought about work after work.
7. I feel mentally and physically exhausted after work.
8. I get impatient when I have to wait.
9. I have often felt stressed at the end of the working day.
10. I have often felt uncertain, worried, and dissatisfied with how well I have accomplished my tasks at work.

More true answers indicate higher levels of Type A behavior.

Source: Haynes, Levine, Scotch, Feinleib, & Kanner, 1978.

PHOTO 5.2 People with Type A behavior pattern perceive time delays as very stressful.

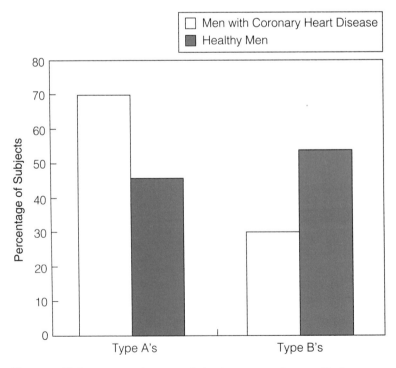

FIGURE 5.4 Men with Type A behavior are much more likely to experience coronary heart disease than men with Type B behavior (data from Miller, Turner, Tindale, Posavac, & Dugon, 1991).

as well as more gastrointestinal problems, such as ulcers, indigestion, and nausea, than Type B's (Suls & Marco, 1990; Woods & Burns, 1984; Woods, Morgan, Day, Jefferson, & Harris, 1984). Similarly, as described at the beginning of the chapter, Cindy, who has the characteristics of a Type A personality, experiences frequent migraine headaches and has developed an ulcer. People with Type A behavior are also more likely to experience major health problems. One study found that middle-aged Type A men were more than six times as likely to experience a heart attack as Type B men (Suinn, 1975). Similarly, while only 4.5% of Type B women show signs of hypertension, 35% of Type A women show such symptoms (Rosenman & Friedman, 1961). (However, see Box 5.5 to learn some benefits of Type A behavior.)

Although the Type A concept has received much attention, some more recent studies suggest that there is little or no relationship between Type A behavior and coronary heart disease. David Ragland and Richard Brand (1988), for example, found that Type A's had a mortality rate of 19.2% as compared to 31.7% among Type B's! One explanation for the discrepancy in study results is that some researchers have measured Type A behavior using a self-report scale and others have used an interview method. The structured interview is more accurate at assessing Type A behavior, in part because this behavior is more apparent during an interview than on a self-report questionnaire (Friedman & Booth-Kewley, 1987b). For example, an interviewer is likely to notice pace of speech, checking of the wrist-watch, and interruptions.

Box 5.5

Health Psychology in the Real World—The Benefits of Type A Behavior

For all of you Type A's who are reading this (and that includes me), let me assure you that there are some advantages to this type of behavior. In fact, people with Type A behavior pattern do actually achieve more: they are more likely to earn honors in college, are more productive in work, have higher GPAs in college, prefer working alone on tasks, are more likely to push themselves (e.g., they report studying more hours, playing football while injured, exerting more effort even when exhausted; Kliewer, Lepore, & Evans, 1990). One study of 132 college students found that Type A students took more credit hours and more volunteer hours per week, worked more hours, viewed grades as more important, achieved higher GPAs, and focused more on their classes and career goals (Ovcharchyn, Johnson, & Petzel, 1981). Why do people with Type A behavior manage to achieve better than Type B's? Apparently, Type A's can focus attention on an important task and avoid thinking about peripheral factors (e.g., pain, fatigue, other distractions), given their drive for success.

Moreover, some features of the structured interview (a commonly used measure of Type A behavior) are designed to test how people react to potentially stressful situations. For example, the interviewer might use slow and hesitating speech to see whether the person interrupts or finishes the interviewer's sentences. Or the interviewer may rudely interrupt the subject to challenge an answer to see how he or she responds (Chesney, Eagleston, & Rosenman, 1980; Tallmer et al., 1990).

Second, although researchers often refer to "Type A behavior" as representing a single type of behavior, Type A behavior actually has three distinct types: impatience/speed, job involvement, and hard-driving. While the link between hostility and coronary heart disease is quite strong, the link between other components of Type A behavior and health is much weaker. Howard Friedman and colleagues suggest that some people who are labeled Type A are simply expressive, efficient, and ambitious people who are coping well with their personal and professional lives and that these people are actually not at increased risk of experiencing health problems (Friedman, Hall, & Harris, 1985). In contrast, and as we discuss next, "real Type A's," namely, those who are tense, repressed, and hostile, are the ones most likely to experience physical problems.

Hostility/Disagreeableness

Like those who are high in neuroticism, people who are high in hostility have more negative moods and fewer positive moods (Cook & Medley, 1954; Smith, Pope, Sanders, Allred, & O'Keefe, 1988). But this personality trait focuses specifically on people's expectations about and interactions within their interpersonal relationships. People who are hostile or disagreeable believe that others are motivated by selfish concerns and expect that other people will deliberately try to hurt them (see Table 5.5; Miller, Smith, Turner, Guijarro, & Hallet, 1996). In turn, because of their general mistrust and cyn-

TABLE 5.5   *Test Yourself: Sample Items from the Hostility–Guilt Inventory*

1. Once in a while I cannot control my urge to harm others.
2. I can't help being a little rude to people I don't like.
3. When someone makes a rule I don't like I am tempted to break it.
4. Other people always seem to get the breaks.
5. I commonly wonder what hidden reason another person may have for doing something nice for me.
6. I can't help getting into arguments when people disagree with me.
7. Unless someone asks me in a nice way, I won't do what that person wants.
8. My motto is "Never trust strangers."
9. Whoever insults me or my family is asking for a fight.
10. If somebody annoys me, I am apt to tell him what I think of him.

This scale assesses a person's general level of hostility, including feelings of antagonism, cynicism, and aggression.

Source: Buss & Durkee, 1957.

PHOTO 5.3   People who are hostile experience high levels of conflict in their work, family, and marital relationships.

icism about other people's motivations, hostile people don't hesitate to express these feelings—they are often uncooperative, rude, argumentative, condescending, and aggressive (see Photo 5.3).

People who are hostile have poorer health, including higher rates of hypertension, coronary heart disease (CHD), and even death (see Box 5.6; Barefoot, Dodge, Peterson, Dahlstrom, & Williams, 1989; Miller et al., 1996; Smith, 1992). One prospective study assessed hostility in 200 healthy women and then followed these women over 10 years (Matthews, Owens, Kuller, Sutton-Tyrrell, & Jansen-McWilliams, 1998). Even controlling for variables such as smoking, women who had higher hostility scores in the earlier testing were more likely to show symptoms of cardiovascular disease 10 years later. Similarly, Raymond Niaura and his colleagues (2002) found that older men with the highest levels of hostility were at the greatest risk of experiencing CHD (see Figure 5.5). What accounts for these higher rates of cardiovascular disease symptoms? One study found that people who were high in hostility were much more likely to experience coronary artery blockage than those who were low in hostility (Iribarren et al., 2000). For example, for those with the lowest levels of hostility, only 8% showed some artery blockage as compared to 18% of those with the highest levels of hostility. Given these rates of blockage, it is not surprising that people who are high in hostility have rates of mortality nearly four times as high as those who are less hostile (Barefoot et al., 1989).

Although the trait of hostility describes people's general negative feelings toward others, the expression of such feelings is also associated with negative health outcomes (Jorgensen, Johnson, Kolodziej, & Schreer, 1996; Kiecolt-Glaser et al., 1993; Lai & Linden, 1992; Siegman, Anderson, Herbst, Boyle, & Wilkinson, 1992; Siegman, 1993; Williams et al., 2000). People who both experience higher levels of anger (e.g., "I control my temper," "I withdraw from people") and express such anger through aggressive physical and/or verbal behavior (e.g., "I say nasty things," "I strike out at whatever infuriates me") are particularly at risk of developing cardiovascular problems. In fact, people who frequently experience anger are three times as likely to suffer a heart attack as

Box 5.6

Research Focus—Do Only the Hostile Die Young?

John Barefoot and his colleagues at the University of North Carolina were interested in examining whether people who are hostile are more likely to experience coronary heart disease and early mortality as compared to those who are more agreeable (Barefoot, Dahlstrom, & Williams, 1983). To examine this question, in the fall of 1981 researchers sent a questionnaire to all alumni of the University of North Carolina Medical School in the classes of 1954 to 1959. This questionnaire asked about their current health. Because all medical students had taken a standard personality inventory during school, researchers had baseline measures of hostility. They therefore classified men into one of four groups based on their level of hostility as assessed when they were medical students. Researchers also asked for death certificates from the families of those who had died prior to the follow-up.

As predicted, hostility was a stronger predictor of health and mortality. First, men who were high in hostility were five times more likely to have experienced coronary heart disease than those who were low in hostility. Specifically, 4.5% of those who were high in hostility had experienced either angina or a myocardial infarction as compared to only 1% of those who were low in hostility. Men who were high in hostility were also nearly seven times as likely to have died before the time of the follow-up than men who were low in hostility. As shown in Figure 5.5, about 6% of the men in the high-hostility group had died by the time of the follow-up compared to less than 1% of those in the low-hostility group. Although this study does not indicate why men who are hostile die at younger ages than those who are not hostile, it clearly suggests that hostility matters.

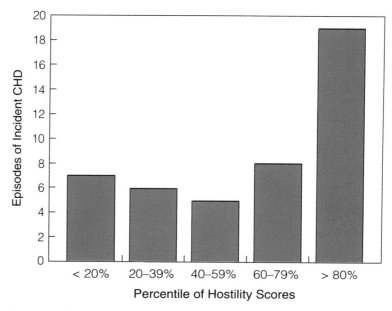

FIGURE 5.5 Men who are in the highest 80% in hostility are much more likely to develop CHD than those who are lower in hostility (data from Niaura et al., 2002).

those who rarely experience anger (Williams et al., 2000). For example, Janice Kiecolt-Glaser and colleagues (1993) videotaped 90 newlywed couples discussing several marital conflicts, and then coded the interactions as low or high in anger. High-anger couples showed significant declines in immune system activity compared to low-anger couples. Think about what happens to your body when you yell at someone—your heart rate probably increases, and, although you may not be aware of it, so does your blood pressure. People who regularly experience this higher level of physiological arousal may be at greater risk of developing cardiovascular problems because they exert so much wear and tear on their blood vessels and heart (Siegman et al., 1992).

What Factors Lead to the Personality–Health Link?

Thus far, we have examined the link between many different personality variables and psychological and physical well-being; we have not discussed, however, the factors that may lead to this association. This section describes several possible pathways that may account for the association between personality and health (see Figure 5.6).

First, individuals' personalities may influence how much stress they experience—or how much stress they perceive they are experiencing (Hemenover, 2001; Hemenover & Dienstbier, 1996; Watson, 1988). For example, people who are high on negative affect, or neuroticism perceive events as

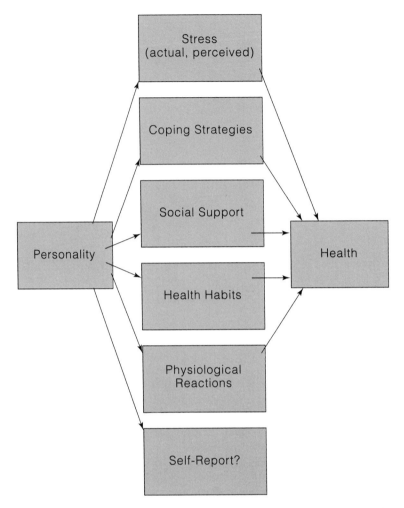

FIGURE 5.6   Researchers have examined a number of different pathways that may explain the link between personality and health.

more stressful and difficult to cope with than do those who are low on this dimension; they tend to focus on the negative features of the situation (Hemenover, 2001; Watson, 1988). People's personalities can also influence whether they create stressful situations. For example, one study found that people who were high in negative affect at one point in time experienced more stressful life events as well as greater psychological distress even 6 years later (Ormel & Wohlfarth, 1991). Similarly, hostile people who anticipate that others will act aggressively toward them may behave antagonistically first, which in turn elicits the aggressive behavior they expected (Smith, 1992). People who are high in hostility experience more frequent and severe daily hassles and major life events, and they report more conflict in their jobs, marriages, and families than those who are low in hostility (Smith et al., 1988).

People with Type A behavior may also appraise challenging situations as more stressful and behave in ways that increase stress (Ortega & Pipal, 1984; Rhodewalt, Hayes, Chemers, & Wysocki, 1984; Sorensen et al., 1987). For example, they are more involved in academic and extracurricular activities in school, work longer hours, and choose tasks of greater difficulty. Similarly, when playing games, Type A's view their opponents as more competitive and hard-driving than Type B's do, and not surprisingly, they elicit more competitive and aggressive responses from others. In contrast, people who are high in hardiness, optimism, and extraversion perceive potentially stressful life events as less threatening, perhaps because they tend to view such events as challenging as opposed to threatening and tend to focus on the positive features of the situation (Florian et al., 1995; Hemenover, 2001).

Second, personality factors may influence the use of different coping strategies. People who are high in optimism, hope, hardiness, extraversion, and internal control use more adaptive and functional strategies for coping with problems, including acceptance, rational thinking, social support, and positive reframing, and use destructive coping strategies less frequently, such as denial and behavioral disengagement (see Box 5.7; Anderson, 1977; Carver et al., 1993; Drach-Zahavy & Somech, 2002; McCrae & Costa, 1986; Taylor et al., 1992; Williams, Wiebe, & Smith, 1992). In one study, college students read a number of hypothetical scenarios that described stressful situations (e.g., finding out that they have three exams on the same day), were asked to imagine the events were happening to them, and were instructed to write about how they would cope with each one (Scheier et al., 1986). As shown in Figure 5.7, optimists tended to use constructive strategies, including making a plan of action and following it, focusing intently on the problem, and seeking social support. On the other hand, they were less likely to simply distract themselves from thinking about the problem. Similarly, a study with 276 Israeli army recruits found that those who were high in hardiness were more likely to use problem-focused coping and less likely to use emotion-focused coping, which in turn led to more positive psychological well-being at the end of training 4 months later (Florian et al., 1995). In contrast, people who are high in neuroticism and have an external locus of control tend to rely on maladaptive coping strategies (Hewitt & Flett, 1996). For example, one study of people who were coping with a major environmental disaster (an accident at a nuclear power plant) found that people who were high in neuroticism were more likely to use maladaptive coping mechanisms, such as self-blame, and less likely to use constructive coping strategies, such as problem solving (Costa & McCrae, 1990). The use of more constructive coping strategies can result in better health in part by leading people to experience fewer negative life events. By confronting problems earlier and more effectively, people with certain personality traits "nip problems in the bud," and thereby avoid allowing small issues to become larger ones.

Third, personality factors may influence how much social support a person has (as we discuss in Chapter 6; Lepore, 1995; Smith, 1992). People who are hostile, neurotic, and pessimistic may have trouble forming close relationships and may experience high levels of interpersonal conflict, in part because

Box 5.7

Research Focus—Why Do Optimists Demonstrate Faster Recovery from Surgery?

Michael Scheier and his colleagues (1989) conducted a study to examine whether optimists recover from surgery faster than pessimists. Fifty-one middle-aged men scheduled for coronary artery bypass surgery answered a series of questions the day before their surgery, including measures of optimism, mood, and coping strategies. One week after their surgery, they again answered questions on mood, coping, social support, expectations about recovery, and general satisfaction with the level of medical care. Finally, 6 weeks and 6 months after the surgery, patients completed measures of satisfaction with various life domains. Members of the hospital team also contributed their observations to the data.

This study shows that optimists had a better recovery from surgery than pessimists in a number of ways. First, optimists were judged by members of the medical team to reach each of the markers of recovery more rapidly, including sitting up in bed and walking around the room, than pessimists did. Second, optimists themselves reported that their recovery went more smoothly than pessimists reported. For example, 6 months after surgery, optimists were more likely than pessimists to have resumed physical exercise, returned to work full-time, and returned to recreational activities. The researchers hypothesized a number of different factors leading optimists to improved recovery, including greater satisfaction with the amount of social support they received from family and friends and the use of more effective coping strategies. Optimists did report less hostility and less depression before surgery, had a stronger base of social support, made plans and set goals for recovery sooner, and were less likely to dwell on negative aspects of the experience. For example, pessimists tended to block out thoughts of the recovery process, whereas optimists were likely to try to get as much information as possible about what to expect and how to cope. Researchers believe that the use of these more constructive coping styles may at least partially explain why optimists experience better health.

they are likely to treat others in an antagonistic way (Sarason, Sarason, & Shearin, 1986; Smith, 1992). As described at the beginning of the chapter, because Miles's consistent anxiety makes other people uncomfortable, he has few social relationships. In line with this view, people who are high in negative affect and those who are Type A personalities have lower marital satisfaction (Burke, Weir, & DuWors, 1979, 1980; Schaefer & Burnett, 1987). People who are high in hostility also have difficulty seeking and accepting social support (Houston & Vavak, 1991). For example, one study found that people who are low in hostility experience less stress when they have a friend with them

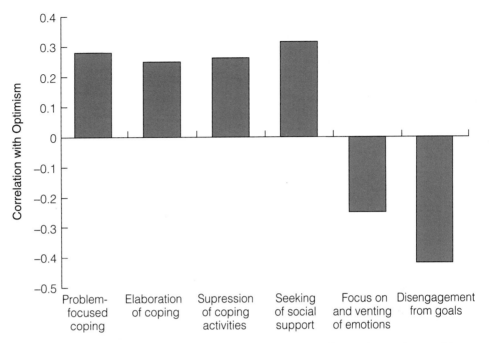

FIGURE 5.7 Optimists tend to use constructive strategies for coping, such as problem-focused coping and seeking of social support, and they avoid destructive strategies, such as denial and rumination. The use of these coping strategies may lead optimists to experience better health.

while they give a difficult speech, whereas people who are high in hostility do not show any benefit from the presence of such support (Lepore, 1995).

Fourth, personality factors may influence individuals' health habits (Houston & Vavak, 1991; Leiker & Hailey, 1988; Seeman & Seeman, 1983). People who are high in traits such as neuroticism, hostility, and Type A behavior are more likely to smoke, abuse alcohol, eat less healthy foods, avoid exercise, sleep less, and drink caffeine (see Photo 5.4; Booth-Kewley & Vickers, 1994; Costa & McCrae, 1987; Folsom et al., 1985; Houston & Vavak, 1991; Howard, Cunningham, & Rechnitzer, 1976; Leiker & Hailey, 1988; Miller et al., 1996). For example, one study of 103 male military personnel found that neuroticism was associated with fewer wellness behaviors, less accident control behavior, and more traffic risk-taking behavior (Booth-Kewley & Vickers, 1994). This is true even for dental hygiene and driving under the influence. People who are hostile and Type A may, for example, run red lights, tailgate,

---

Questioning the Research 5.2

This section discusses how personality factors such as hostility and negative affect may lead to lower levels of social support. What are some alternative explanations for this association between personality and social support?

cut off other cars, or pass unsafely. This type of careless behavior may explain why people who have pessimistic explanatory styles have higher rates of death from accidents and violence, but not from cancer or cardiovascular disease (Peterson et al., 1998). In contrast, people who are high in conscientiousness, optimism, and extraversion and who have an internal locus of control, are more likely to engage in health-promoting behaviors, including taking vitamins, regular exercise, healthy eating, cigarette smoking and drug avoidance, and safe driving (see Figure 5.8; Blumenthal, Sanders, Wallace, Williams, & Needles, 1982; Booth-Kewley & Vickers, 1994; Robbins, Spence, & Clark, 1991; Scheier & Carver, 1992; Seeman & Seeman, 1983; Taylor et al., 1992).

Personality factors may also influence whether individuals take preventive steps to modify their behavior following illness, such as following a prescribed medical regimen or altering behaviors that produce illness (Christensen & Smith, 1995; Seeman & Seeman, 1983; Wiebe & Christensen, 1997). In line with this view, conscientious people, who have the self-control to overcome potential barriers (e.g., fear) and to complete difficult, aversive, and stressful tasks (e.g., getting a mammogram, having an HIV test) tend to follow health care advice, whereas those who are low in conscientiousness simply abandon medical regimens that are distasteful in some way (see Figure 5.9; Christensen & Smith, 1995; Schwartz et al., 1999). For example, one study of patients who were undergoing dialysis found that those who were conscientious were more likely to adhere to the medical recommendations of their doctors (Christensen & Smith, 1995). Similarly, dialysis patients who are high in internal locus of control are more likely to follow recommended diets and participate in rehabilitation (Poll & Kaplan De-Nour, 1980). People with high levels of perceived control and optimistic expectations may also promote their own rehabilitation, whereas those who believe that illnesses are caused by internal, global, and stable factors may become passive in the face of illness and may not seek or follow medical advice. For example, cardiac patients who are optimistic are more likely to take vitamins, eat low-fat foods, enroll in a rehabilitation program, successfully reduce their weight, follow a recommended diet, and start exercising (Maroto, Shepperd, & Pbert, 1996; Scheier et al., 1989). Similarly, one study of 54 men in treatment for alcohol abuse found that optimists were more likely to successfully complete a 90-day inpatient program than pessimists were (the pessimists were less likely to be discharged from the program because of renewed drinkin;g Strack, Carver, & Blaney, 1987).

On the other hand, hostile people and those with Type A behavior patterns may fail to adhere to medical regimens and may even react against doctors' orders to exert their independence (Lee et al., 1992; Rhodewalt & Smith, 1991). As described at the beginning of the chapter, Debbie was irritated by her physician's advice to quit smoking and believes she's the only one who should decide about her own health-related behavior. Type A's may ignore early signs of a heart attack, suppress or ignore symptoms, and exert themselves too hard (Carver, Coleman, & Glass, 1976). They are especially likely to deny symptoms when they are focusing on a challenging task, which can lead them to delay treatment. For example, Type B's report more symptoms when they are working on a challenging task, whereas Type A's report fewer

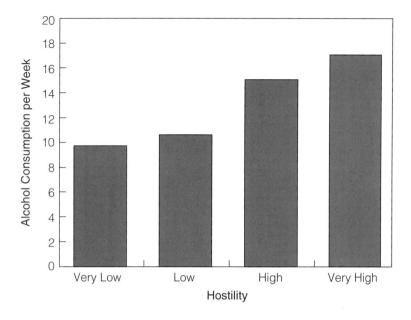

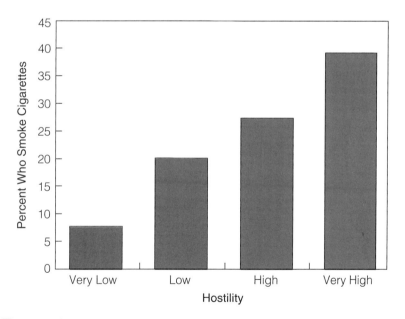

FIGURE 5.8 As shown in this figure, people who are high in hostility drink more alcohol and are more likely to smoke cigarettes than those who are low in hostility (Iribarren et al., 2000).

(Rhodewalt & Smith, 1991). This tendency to deny early symptoms increases a person's likelihood of dying from a heart attack.

PHOTO 5.4   People with certain personality traits, such as neuroticism, hostility, and Type A behavior, may engage in unhealthy behaviors, which in turn leads to poorer health.

Fifth, personality factors may influence people's physiological reactions to stress, including their immune functioning and cardiovascular response (Scheier & Carver, 1987). For example, people who have a pessimistic explanatory style or who are low in perceived control have weaker immune responses and poorer DNA repair than those with a more optimistic view of the world and those who are high in perceived control (Kamen-Siegel, Rodin, Seligman, & Dwyer, 1991; Segerstrom, Taylor, Kameny, & Fahey, 1998). Physiological reactions may also explain why people who are high in hostility tend to have worse health—hostile people have consistently higher heart rates and blood pressure than those who are low in hostility, they show extreme cardiovascular reactions to stressful situations, and it takes longer for their bodies to return to normal functioning following a stressful interaction (see Box 5.8 and Figure 5.10; Raikkonen, Matthews, Flory, & Owens, 1999; Smith, 1992; Suarez, Kuhn, Schanberg, Williams, & Zimmerman, 1998). People who are hostile experience such high levels of physiological arousal in part because they are distrustful of others, so they are constantly on guard against slights from others. Similarly, people who are Type A show a distinct physiological reaction to potentially stressful tasks, particularly those involving time urgency and competition—when they are in situations in which they feel threatened or challenged, they show greater changes in heart rate,

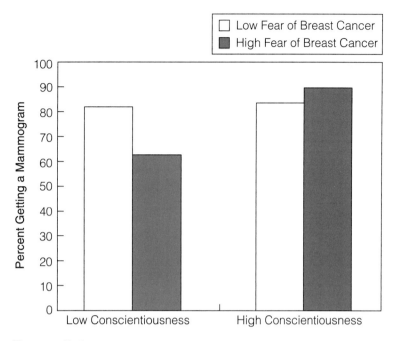

FIGURE 5.9   Although women who were afraid of breast cancer and low in conscientiousness were the least likely to obtain a mammogram, fear of breast cancer had no impact on likelihood of having a mammogram for those who were high in conscientiousness (data from Schwartz et al., 1999).

blood pressure, and adrenaline levels than Type B's (Contrada, 1989; Lyness, 1993). In one study, men played a competitive game with a partner, who, in some conditions, harassed and insulted them (Glass et al., 1980). Although both Type A's and Type B's showed signs of physiological arousal (probably because of the competition), Type A's showed particularly high levels of arousal when they were harassed by their partner. These increased reactions to stress lead to wear and tear on the heart over time. Finally, some researchers believe that people who are high in negative affect consistently experience high levels of anxiety, tension, and anger, which in turn leads to health problems such as headaches, nausea, ulcers, asthma, arthritis, and even coronary heart disease (Watson, 1988; Watson & Pennebaker, 1989).

Finally, the link between personality and health could be a function of self-report—in other words, personality traits may influence how much a person notices or complains about symptoms, but not how many symptoms that person experiences (Watson & Pennebaker, 1989). To test this possibility, research has included physiological tests of health, such as immune system functioning, cardiovascular fitness, and measures of cholesterol levels (Costa & McCrae, 1987; Watson & Pennebaker, 1989). This work generally suggests that there is little association between personality traits and actual physical measures of health. For example, in one study Stanley Cohen and his colleagues (1995) asked people about their cold symptoms (e.g., runny nose, congestion)

Box 5.8

Research Focus—Hostile People Get Really Mad Really Fast

Because most of the research on hostility and health has included only men, Irene Powch and Kent Houston (1996) were interested in examining whether women who are high in hostility would also experience greater reactivity to stressful situations. To examine this question, they asked 109 college women to discuss an issue with a partner (who was really a confederate hired by the experimenter to express a particular view). In the low-interpersonal-stress condition, participants were asked to discuss an issue in which they had no particularly strong opinion, and their partner always agreed with them. However, in the high-interpersonal-stress condition, the participant was asked to discuss an issue that was important to her, and the confederate always disagreed strongly. Researchers then measured the participants' blood pressure and heart rate during the discussion in order to see how participants would respond. The discussions were videotaped and later coded for incidents of hostile and friendly behavior. For example, statements that reflected sarcasm, criticism, and anger were coded as hostile behavior (e.g., "Can't you see that that doesn't make any sense?"), whereas statements that reflected pleasantness and agreeableness were coded as friendly behavior (e.g., "You know a lot about this topic").

As predicted, women who were high in hostility did indeed show a stronger physiological response—but only if they were in the high-interpersonal-stress condition. Blood pressure readings after this interaction revealed that high-hostility women who participated in the high-conflict role-play had higher diastolic blood pressure. In contrast, low-hostility women had relatively low blood pressure regardless of whether they had participated in the low- or high-conflict role-play. This study therefore suggests that people who are high in hostility become more physiologically aroused than people who are low in hostility when they are in difficult interpersonal situations.

and also gathered more objective data (e.g., mucus output). Although people who were high in negative affect complained more about various health problems (e.g., headaches, chest pains, stomachaches), there was no evidence that they actually experienced more health problems (e.g., elevated blood pressure, serum lipids). Personality traits may also influence how focused people are on their physical health, and hence how likely they are to notice various aches, pains, and symptoms. Those who are high in negative affect, for example, may interpret relatively minor and normal symptoms as more painful and problematic than those people with low negative affect (Watson,

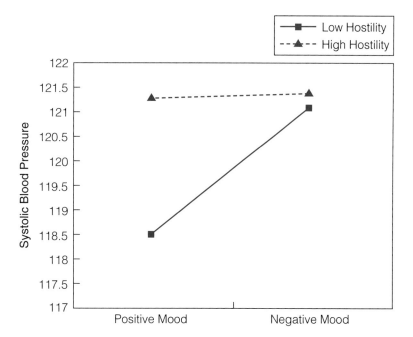

FIGURE 5.10   Regardless of their level of hostility, people who are in a bad mood show higher blood pressure. However, people who are high in hostility show similarly high levels of blood pressure even when they are in a positive mood. Over time, this constantly high blood pressure could lead to cardiovascular problems (data from Raikkonen et al., 1999).

1988; Watson & Pennebaker, 1989). In line with this view, a study by Lee Ellington and Deborah Wiebe (1999) presented subjects with a vignette describing an illness and asked them to pretend they were patients presenting these symptoms to a doctor. Students who were high in neuroticism presented more elaborate and detailed symptoms, regardless of whether the illness was low in severity (e.g., strep throat) or high in severity (e.g., acute appendicitis). In fact, research shows that people who are high in negative affect complain of all kinds of physical problems and symptoms, but do not actually show evidence of increased health problems or earlier mortality—there is no evidence from biological tests that they experience more problems, visit the doctor more often, take medicine more often, or miss school/work more often.

In sum, although the model suggests that each pathway between personality and health is separate and distinct from all others, clearly these pathways could be, and probably often are, interrelated. Personality factors are likely to influence the type of coping strategy used, which in turn influences the amount of stress experienced. Similarly, the amount of social support a person receives may impact the amount of stress he or she experiences, the coping strategies used, and even the person's health habits, any or all of which could in turn influence health.

Lingering Issues

Can health promotion interventions lead to personality change, which in turn leads to better health? In an effort to improve health, several studies have attempted to do just this, influence personality. Meyer Friedman and his colleagues have conducted a series of studies on people who have experienced a heart attack, focusing on reducing Type A behavior. For example, one study assigned over 800 heart attack survivors to receive either a cardiology counseling condition or an intervention that included cardiology counseling as well as information on changing Type A behavior (e.g., relaxation training, modification of Type A–related beliefs and attitudes, role-playing of Type B behavior; Friedman et al., 1986). Thirty-five percent of patients in the behavioral treatment group reduced their Type A behavior, as compared to only 9.8% of those in the cardiology-counseling group. Moreover, the recurrence of heart attacks over the next 4 1/2 years was 12.9% for those in the behavioral intervention group as compared to 21.2% for those in the cardiology-counseling-only condition. This study provides some compelling evidence that at least some people can modify their Type A behavior, which in turn can lead to better health. These interventions may be particularly effective if they focus on reducing hostility (probably the most important contributor to unhealthy behavior in Type A's), and concentrate on helping people maintain positive self-esteem (by not criticizing personality styles too much, which can lead to reactance). Similarly, people who receive anxiety-anger management training show reductions in their levels of anger, which in turn should lead to health benefits (Suinn, 2001).

Another health-promotion study trained managers in hardiness or relaxation (Maddi, Kahn, & Maddi, 1998). Specifically, managers in a utilities company participated in 10 sessions in which they described stressful situations they were experiencing and learned techniques for coping with them. They were taught how to understand their stressors and to think about them in new, more positive ways. Managers who received hardiness training experienced more job satisfaction and social support as well as fewer illnesses and physical symptoms over the next 2 1/2 months than those who received other types of information (e.g., relaxation training, social support). Although the follow-up period in this study was relatively brief, the preliminary findings suggest that this type of training may indeed be effective in increasing hardiness, and thereby improving health.

Is there a downside to optimism? Although optimism is generally associated with better health, some intriguing studies suggest that optimism can also have costs. Specifically, research by Neil Weinstein (1984, 1987) indicates that people who are unrealistically optimistic about their risk of various health problems can actually put their health at risk. For example, people generally believe they are at less risk of experiencing many different types of problems than other people are, including car accidents, alcohol problems, sexually transmitted diseases, and drug addiction. Basically, people tend to believe that although risks do exist in the world, "it won't happen to me." And this ten-

PHOTO 5.5 The invulnerability often felt by college students can lead them to some very risky health-related behavior, including drug use, unprotected sex, and driving while intoxicated.

dency may be especially common in college students, who generally believe (wrongly!) that they are invulnerable to all sorts of problems (see Photo 5.5). Unfortunately, these unrealistically positive beliefs can lead people to fail to protect themselves adequately from such problems. In fact, one longitudinal study by Howard Friedman and colleagues (1993) found that optimists had a higher mortality rate, and other research suggests that optimistic children grow up to be more careless about their health (Martin et al., 2002). It may be that while optimism in general is good for health, too much optimism can be bad for health.

Thought Questions

1. Your roommate is a classic extravert—outgoing, sociable, and always looking for new and exciting challenges. On the other hand, his step-brother is moody, antagonistic, and pessimistic. What might you predict about the psychological and physical well-being of each person?

2. Describe two ways that Type A behavior might lead to health problems, and describe two problems with the Type A construct.

3. Describe three factors that may lead optimists to experience better health.

4. Linda is very conscientious in virtually everything she does—she completes her work on time, is never late for appointments, and is extremely

responsible and reliable. Based on your knowledge of health psychology, how would Linda respond to learning she has breast cancer? What steps would she take following this diagnosis?

Answers to Questioning the Research

Answer 5.1: Although several studies have shown that the general personality trait of hardiness is associated with psychological and physical well-being, more recent research indicates that the specific components of hardiness are not all equally useful in predicting health-related behavior (Hull, Van Treuren, & Virnelli, 1987). Specifically, both commitment and control are systematically linked to health, but there is little evidence that challenge is a consistent predictor of health.

Answer 5.2: Although research shows that people who are high in negative affect experience lower marital satisfaction, this study shows only correlation, not causation. How do you think you'd grow to feel over time if you were in an unhappy and conflict-ridden marriage? It could easily lead you to feel bad about yourself and hence to experience high levels of guilt, anxiety, and depression. It may be that participating in a dysfunctional marriage *leads* to negative affect as opposed to the reverse. Another possibility is that a third variable leads to both negative affect and lower marital satisfaction. For example, people who are struggling with many negative life events, such as poverty, natural disasters, and/or major illnesses, might develop negative feelings about themselves, and, because of the pressures of their situation, they may argue more frequently with their spouses. Just remember, *correlation* does not necessarily mean *causation*.

CHAPTER 6

Social Support

- Betty's town of West Palm Beach, Florida, was struck two days ago by Hurricane Andrew. Her house is still standing, but the roof was badly damaged and her car was totaled. Luckily several members of Betty's church have volunteered to loan her a car while hers is in the shop, and some of her neighbors have already started to work on patching her roof. Although Betty is still very shaken, she is relieved to have such a strong network of social support.

- Mark is 58 years old and is undergoing heart surgery tomorrow. His hospital roommate, Sam, underwent the same surgery 1 week ago and is making good progress on his recovery. Mark has many questions for Sam about the surgery, concerning the procedure itself and the recovery process. As Sam speaks, Mark can almost feel his heartbeat slowing down and his anxiety subsiding. Somehow just knowing what to expect—and knowing that Sam came through the same surgery with flying colors—has made a huge difference in Mark's feelings about the procedure.

- Annie just gave birth to her first child, Daniel. She had felt very nervous about the pain of labor, and therefore she and her husband Bill had attended a series of childbirth preparation classes. While Annie was in labor, Bill held her hand and helped her focus on her breathing exercises. He also gave her small sips of water and told her what a great job she was doing. Annie gave birth after only 8 hours of labor and even managed to avoid having an epidural for pain relief. She left the hospital within 24 hours of giving birth, and she and Bill are now having fun with Daniel at home.

- Arturo is feeling anxious because he is in the midst of a difficult exam period at school. He is having trouble sleeping and has started having headaches several times a day. However, his parents sent him a care package containing fresh fruit, and Arturo's roommate has volunteered to substitute for him at his tutoring job this week to free up time for Arturo to study. Arturo now feels more confident that he can get through the exam period OK, and his headaches have already disappeared.

- Diana's husband, Bill, just died following a long battle with lung cancer. Although Diana wants very much to talk about how much she misses her husband and would like to share her fond memories with other people who knew him, she finds that her friends avoid bringing up Bill's name. Moreover, when her friends try to console her by saying, "Well, at least you had many good years together," Diana just feels like they don't understand at all what she is going through. Even though she knows her friends mean well, Diana sometimes just prefers to be alone.

Preview

This chapter describes the connection between health and social support, the social interactions or relationships that provide people with actual assistance in times of need or that enable them to believe that such assistance is available. We start by examining different ways of defining social support, and then describe research that shows the link between social support and both psychological and physical well-being as well as various explanations for this association. We then examine how gender and sociocultural factors may influence the link between social support and health. Finally, we describe some potential negative effects of social support as well as ways to increase support.

What Is Social Support?

One of the major challenges in examining the link between social support and health is determining how to measure social support. Different researchers have defined *social support* in different ways, such as the existence or quantity of social relationships, the amount of assistance individuals believe is available to them, and the amount of assistance individuals receive (House & Kahn, 1985). Is social support simply having many casual friendships? Is social support a single construct or are there different types of social support? Is social support a reflection of what support you *think* is available or the amount of support you actually *receive*? This section examines different approaches to measuring social support.

Social Network

Some researchers have examined social support in terms of the structure of people's social relationships, namely, the number and types of such relationships (House & Kahn, 1985). These measures take into account whether a person is married or single, and whether he or she lives alone or with others, as well as the person's membership in various social organizations, such as houses of worship and clubs. The social network can also include the frequency of contact with friends and relatives.

Several large-scale surveys have assessed social support based on the existence and quantity of social relationships. For example, in a survey of people living in Alameda County, California, researchers examined four types of social ties: marriage, contacts with extended family and friends, church or temple membership, and other formal and informal group affiliations (Berkman & Syme, 1979). They created a social network index by combining these four types of social ties, and then used this measure to predict mortality (see Photo 6.1). Similarly, other researchers have measured different types of social relationships, such as intimate social relationships (relationships with one's spouse, friends, and family), formal nonwork organization relationships (e.g., church), and active leisure pursuits that include social contacts (e.g., attending classes; House, Robbins, & Metzner, 1982). These approaches assess the number of social relationships as well as individuals' participation in various social activities.

Although these surveys allow researchers to discover how many relationships a person has, they do not capture the structure and complexity of social relationships. Other approaches have assessed social support in terms of the web of social relationships (as opposed to their mere existence); hence, they include not only a person's friends but also the friends of these friends. These approaches may measure other factors, such as the density of one's social relationships (the extent to which members of a network are linked to each other), durability (the duration of relationships over time), reciprocity (the extent to which support is both given and received), and dispersion (the geographic distance between network members). For example, the Social Network List (Stokes, 1983) asks people to list up to 20 people who are important to them and with whom they have contact at least once a month. As a way of assessing density, the assessor then must indicate which network members are significant in each other's lives and who has contact with each other at least once a month. Researchers have hypothesized that more-dense social networks (those in which people are very interconnected with one another) might be particularly useful in times of stress because people could better

PHOTO 6.1 People who have larger social networks, which may include membership in social and religious organizations as well as contact with family and friends, experience better health.

coordinate different types of support (Wortman, 1984). For example, if you needed help after surgery, nearby friends might work together to divide up various tasks they could do to help you, such as cooking, cleaning, and running errands. Similarly, at the start of the chapter, I described how Betty's social network assisted her in recovering from the devastation of Hurricane Andrew; her dense social network supported her in a time of need.

Although several large-scale studies connecting social support and health have used social network measures (Berkman & Syme, 1979; House et al., 1982), their use has been criticized for several reasons. First, the mere existence of a relationship does not mean that relationship is actually supportive (Antonucci, 1990). You may have friends and relatives, for example, with whom you speak every month, but these people may not provide you with any real support. Second, assessing various characteristics of a social network (reciprocity, density, etc.) is quite time-consuming and may not be particularly accurate. In fact, some studies have found that individuals often do not even agree with whether they are in each other's social networks; the rate of agreement is as low as 36% in some studies (Shulman, 1976).

Perceived Social Support

Given the weaknesses of social network measures of social support, other research on the link between social support and health has focused on people's perceptions of the different types of support various relationships provide (Cohen, 1988; House, 1981; see Table 6.1 for an example of one measure assessing different types of support). Although researchers vary in how they categorize the different types of support, they generally agree on the types of support described in the following paragraphs.

Emotional support refers to the expression of caring, concern, and empathy for a person as well as the provision of comfort, reassurance, and love to that person. Most people who are confronted with stressful life events want to be able to talk about these events with others, and having a "listening ear" can be very valuable. One study of cancer patients found that more than 90% saw

---

TABLE 6.1   *Test Yourself: Sample Items from the Interpersonal Support Evaluation List*

Please rate whether each of the following items is true or false.

1. If I had to go out of town for a few weeks, someone I know would look after my home, such as watering the plants or taking care of the pets.
2. If I were sick and needed someone to drive me to the doctor, I would have trouble finding someone.
3. If I were sick, I would have trouble finding someone to help me with my daily chores.
4. If I needed help moving, I would be able to find someone to help me.
5. If I needed a place to stay for a week because of an emergency, such as the water or electricity being out in my home, I could easily find someone who would put me up.
6. There is at least one person I know whose advice I really trust.
7. There is no one I know who will tell me honestly how I am handling my problems.
8. When I need suggestions about how to deal with a personal problem, there is someone I can turn to.
9. There isn't anyone I feel comfortable talking to about intimate personal problems.
10. There is no one I trust to give me good advice about money matters.
11. I am usually invited to do things with others.
12. When I feel lonely, there are several people I could talk to.
13. I regularly meet or talk with my friends or members of my family.
14. I often feel left out by my circle of friends.
15. There are several different people I enjoy spending time with.

Give yourself one point for each of the following items answered true: 1, 4, 5, 6, 8, 11, 12, 13, 15, and one point for each of the following items answered false: 2, 3, 7, 9, 10, 14. Items 1 to 5 assess tangible support, items 6 to 10 assess appraisal support, and items 11 to 15 assess belongingness support.

Source: Cohen et al., 1985.

emotional support as one of the most valuable types of support (Dunkel-Schetter & Wortman, 1982; Dunkel-Schetter, 1984). Similarly, college students may need emotional support to cope with the stress of a relationship breakup, a poor exam grade, or the divorce of their parents.

Belongingness support is similar to emotional support in that it too includes a focus on being able to talk to others, but this type of support refers primarily to the availability of social companionship (Cohen, Mermelstein, Karmarck, & Hoberman, 1985). People are interested in having others with whom they can engage in social activities, such as people with whom they can go out to dinner, see a movie, and attend a party; and this type of support is an important predictor of well-being. People who are unemployed (hence, they lose one valuable type of social integration) particularly benefit from having belongingness support, and they experience more psychological symptoms when they do not have this type of support (Cutrona & Russell, 1990).

Instrumental, or *tangible, support* refers to the provision of concrete assistance, such as financial aid, material resources, or needed services. For example, you may need instrumental support from your parents to pay for textbooks and from your friends to help carry your belongings when you move to a new apartment. Victims of natural disasters, such as hurricanes, floods, and earthquakes, particularly benefit from receiving tangible support, (see Box 6.1 and Photo 6.2; Norris & Kaniasty, 1996).

Informational, or *appraisal, support* refers to advice and guidance about how to cope with a particular problem. For example, you may depend on your professors for informational support when you are trying to find a summer internship and depend on your friends for such support when choosing classes to take. Victims of natural disasters, who need advice about how to organize cleanup efforts and arrange to receive government aid, also benefit from this type of support.

People also benefit from receiving *esteem,* or *validational, support*, the affirmation of self-worth. This type of support gives a person feedback that he or she is valued and respected by others. One study on long-term recovery from heart surgery found that patients who believed they received considerable esteem support from their spouses had the highest levels of emotional well-being and were the least likely to experience disruption of their everyday lives (e.g., problems with social interaction, recreation activities, sleep, walking) or symptoms of heart trouble even as long as 1 year after surgery (King, Reis, Porter, & Norsen, 1993).

Received Social Support

Although some researchers have focused on the *perceived* availability of different types of social support (i.e., how much support would be available if needed), other researchers have instead focused on assessing the amount of support that is *received* in a particular period of time. As with perceived social support, received support could also be divided into various types. For example, the Inventory of Socially Supportive Behaviors asks people to indicate how often in the last 4 weeks they have received various types of supportive behaviors, such as when someone "gave you information on how to do something"

Box 6.1

Health Psychology in the Real World—Coping with Natural Disasters

Several research studies have examined the mobilization of social support for people who have experienced a natural disaster, such as a hurricane, flood, or earthquake (Kaniasty & Norris, 1995; Norris & Kaniasty, 1996). This work reveals several important findings. First, and not surprisingly, people who have the greatest loss from the disaster receive the most aid. As described by the *rule of relative needs*, people who suffer more losses in terms of property and personal injury receive more assistance than those who experience fewer losses. However, the amount of support people receive is also a function of the *rule of relative advantage*: those who are female, young, married, white, or more educated typically receive higher levels of support than those who are male, older, single, black, or less educated. In fact, those who are the most in need of assistance (elderly people, the poor) are sometimes the least likely to receive it. Second, although family members are the most utilized source of support, people also receive considerable support from other sources, including friends, neighbors, and religious groups. These informal sources of support are particularly important in providing help in cases in which people do not have strong family connections. Third, although people who have experienced a natural disaster particularly benefit from receiving practical types of aid, such as tangible and informational support, many survivors of natural disasters are also in need of emotional support. People may have witnessed friends and family members dying, lost their homes and/or property, and experienced considerable fear about their own survival. One study of victims of Hurricane Hugo, a storm that devastated large parts of North and South Carolina in the fall of 1990, found that emotional support was the type of support most frequently exchanged.

(cognitive-informational), "gave you over $25" (tangible) or "talked with you about some interests of yours" (emotional; Barrera, Sandler, & Ramsey, 1981).

Although these types of measures have an advantage in that they assess actual support received and not just individuals' perceptions of the support available, they also have some disadvantages. One problem with assessing received social support is that individuals are most likely to receive support during times of need; hence, the amount of received support is often correlated with negative health symptoms (Stroebe & Stroebe, 1996). For example, individuals who are very sick may need—and may receive—more social support, but this does not mean that having this support *caused* the illness. Another problem with assessing received support is that individuals may not have needed a particular type of

PHOTO 6.2   Following the tragic terrorist attacks of September 11, 2001, Mayor Rudy Guiliani of New York City set up a family center where families who had lost a loved one in the attacks could learn about opportunities for financial assistance.

support during the month prior to the assessment, even though it was available. If you didn't need to borrow money from your parents in the past month, it may still have helped you simply to know that you could have received a loan if needed. Finally, and somewhat surprisingly, there is often little or no association between actual and perceived support (Lakey & Heller, 1988), and some research indicates that perceived support is a stronger predictor of well-being than received support (Cohen & Wills, 1985).

What Is the Link between Social Support and Health?

The first published study on the link between social support and mortality was conducted by Berkman and Syme (1979). They collected data from a representative sample of nearly 7,000 men and women living in Alameda County, California, in 1965. Respondents completed measures of four types of social ties (marriage, contacts with extended family and friends, church membership, and other formal and informal group affiliations) and the state of their physical health. Researchers then collected mortality data from 1965 to 1974 to examine death rates as a function of social ties. Overall, people who lacked social ties were two to three times more likely to die during this period than those with social ties (see Figure 6.1). This association between support and health was true not only for the combined index of the four different types of social ties, but independently for each of the separate measures of social ties. Moreover, the number of social ties predicted each of the separate causes of death, including heart disease, cancer, and circulatory disease. This study therefore provides compelling evidence about the importance of social relationships.

Another large-scale study of the connection between social support and health was conducted by House and colleagues (1982). This study included nearly 3,000 participants who were 35 to 69 years of age when the study began. Participants were interviewed about their social activities and relationships, completed several biomedical measures (e.g., cholesterol, hypertension, blood glucose levels), and were followed for a 10- to 12-year period. Once

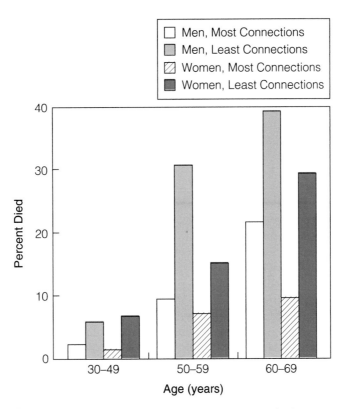

FIGURE 6.1 At every age, men and women with the most social support are less likely to die than those with the least social support (data from Berkman & Syme, 1979).

Questioning the Research 6.1

Note the four categories of social ties that form the social network index. What weaknesses do you see in the categories as they are set up?

---

again, the study results indicate that greater involvement in social activities and relationships predict longer life expectancies for both men and women.

Following the publication of these first studies, researchers became interested in examining the connection between social support and health. As it turns out, having greater social support is associated with a variety of positive health outcomes, including greater psychological well-being, greater physical well-being, faster recovery from illness, and, most important, lower rates of mortality (Stroebe & Stroebe, 1996).

Psychological Well-Being

The advantages of social support to psychological well-being are clear: individuals with greater social support are less likely to suffer from various psychological disorders (Schwarzer & Leppin, 1992). Depressed people report having fewer friends, fewer close relationships, and less supportive family interactions than nondepressed people (Billings & Moos, 1985). Similarly, college students who perceive greater support from their families are less likely to report neurotic symptoms (Procidano & Heller, 1983). The link between social support and psychological well-being occurs in the United States as well as in other countries: for example, one recent study with older adults in Japan and in the United States found that having strong social ties, such as a spouse or frequent contact with children, friends, neighbors, or relatives, was associated with fewer symptoms of depression in both samples (Sugisawa, Shibata, Hougham, Sugihara, & Liang, 2002).

However, studies that measure people's level of social support and psychological well-being at the same time are correlational and therefore do not tell us how these two variables are linked. Fortunately, some researchers have examined people over time, which allows them to study causal effects. For example, a study of HIV-positive gay men found that those who were satisfied with the social support they received were less likely to be depressed 1 year later than men who were not satisfied with their amount of social support (Hays, Turner, & Coates, 1992). Similarly, in a study of patients with a chronic disease, those who perceived different types of social support as readily available had less anxiety and more positive affect as long as 1 year later (Sherbourne & Hays, 1990). Another study revealed that college students who had more and higher-quality social interactions had fewer health problems and visits to the campus infirmary (Reis, Wheeler, Kernis, Spiegel, & Nezlek, 1985). Because these studies are prospective (that is, they measure social support at one time and health at a later time), they give us some confidence that greater social support *leads* to better psychological well-being and not the reverse.

Physical Well-Being

Individuals with more social support experience better physical well-being as well as better psychological well-being (Hays et al., 1992; Holahan, Moos, Holahan, & Brennan, 1997; House, Landis, & Umberson, 1988). One study of 3,809 Japanese American men in California found that the risk of suffering from coronary heart disease (CHD) was nearly twice as large for those who had the lowest levels of support compared to those with the highest amount of support (Berkman, 1985); similar findings are seen for women (Blumenthal et al., 1987). Similarly, men who receive low levels of social support are twice as likely to have high levels of prostate-specific antigen (PSA), a marker of prostate cancer, than those with high levels of support (Stone, Mezzacappa, Donatone, & Gonder, 1999). In fact, the impact on health of having low levels of support is similar in magnitude to the effect of smoking (House et al., 1988).

Pregnant women who have high levels of social support experience a number of benefits, including fewer pregnancy complications, heavier and healthier babies, and lower rates of postpartum depression (Collins, Dunkel-Schetter, Lobel, & Scrimshaw, 1993; Norbeck & Tilden, 1983). In one study, 117 women completed measures of life stresses and social support during the second trimester of their pregnancies, and then later completed measures about their experiences with pregnancy, labor, and delivery (Norbek & Tilden, 1983). Among women who experienced a lot of life change during their pregnancies (e.g., being robbed, moving, having a loved one die), receiving little support was associated with more complications during pregnancy as well as more complications with the infant shortly after birth. Having support during labor and delivery is also associated with shorter labor and fewer complications—as described at the beginning of the chapter, support from her husband Bill during childbirth helped Annie have a natural childbirth (see Box 6.2). Women who have high levels of social support during pregnancy probably are encouraged toward healthier behaviors (e.g., eating nutritious meals, having regular prenatal care), receive assistance with household tasks (e.g., cleaning, running errands), and receive emotional support.

Rapid Recovery from Illness

People with high levels of social support recover more quickly from illnesses when they do get sick. For example, those with greater social support recover more rapidly from kidney disease (Dimond, 1979), leukemia (Magni, Silvestro, Tamiello, Zanesco, & Carl, 1988), and stroke (Robertson & Suinn, 1968). One study of patients who had heart surgery examined the association between spousal support and recovery (Helgeson, 1991). The findings indicate that perceiving greater social support from one's spouse predicted less chest pain and a lower likelihood of returning to the hospital. Similarly, individuals who receive more social support from their spouses use less pain medication and show a faster recovery time from surgery (see Box 6.3; Kulik & Mahler, 1989). Those with more social support also report experiencing fewer symptoms of angina and less functional disruption of their usual activities as long as 1 year after surgery (King et al., 1993).

Box 6.2

Focus on Women: The Effects of Having a Supportive Companion during the Experience of Childbirth

Although in most cases childbirth represents an exciting and joyful time for women and their partners, it also involves both physical and psychological stresses—which can be reduced by the presence of social support. Pregnant women who have a supportive companion during labor have significantly fewer complications during delivery (Kennell, Klaus, McGrath, Robertson, & Hinckley, 1991; Sosa, Kennell, Klaus, Robertson, & Urrutia, 1980). For example, one study found that 8% of women who were assisted by a trained supportive companion had a cesarean section compared to 18% of the matched control group who did not have such a companion present (Kennell et al., 1991). These women were also less likely to use anesthetics: 55% of women in the control group had an epidural to block pain versus 8% of those with a supportive companion. Similar results were found for other measures of the experience of childbirth, including duration of labor, length of infant hospitalization, and maternal fever. For example, in one study of 40 mothers, those who had a supportive companion had a mean length of labor of 8.7 hours as compared to 19.3 hours for those without such support (Sosa et al., 1980). Those who had a supportive companion also interacted with their infant more positively following delivery. The presence of a supportive person may help with the pain of labor both psychologically and physiologically. For example, having this support may help reduce women's anxiety, which in turn may facilitate uterine contractions and blood flow.

Lower Mortality Rate

Most important, greater social support is associated with lower rates of mortality (Berkman & Syme, 1979; House et al., 1982; Kaplan et al., 1988; Rosengren, Orth-Comer, Wedel, & Wilhemlmsen, 1993; Welin et al., 1985). For example, Rosengren and colleagues examined the impact of social support on mortality on a sample of 752 fifty-year-old men in Sweden. Emotional support (having significant intimate relationships), not social integration (simply having large social networks), was associated with lower mortality over the next decade. Moreover, while men with many stressful life events had greater mortality in general, this effect was true only for those who received low levels of emotional support: apparently receiving high levels of emotional support buffered these men from the negative health consequences of stressful life events.

The association between social support and life expectancy is found even in people who are critically ill (Berkman, Leo-Summers, & Horowitz, 1992; Ruberman, Weinblatt, Goldberg, & Chaudhary, 1984; Williams, Barefoot, et al.,

Box 6.3

Research Focus—The Effects of Spousal Support on Recovery from Surgery

James Kulik and Heike Mahler (1989) examined the link between social support and speed of recovery from coronary bypass surgery. Fifty-six male heart patients were interviewed prior to their surgery about the quality of their marriage and their current anxiety levels. Following surgery, researchers assessed how often the patients took pain medication, the amount of walking they performed, and the number of hours between the end of surgery and their release from the intensive care unit to the general ward of the hospital. Participants were divided into groups based on the quality of their marital relationships (high versus low) as well as the amount of social support they received from their wives following their surgery (based on the number of visits from their wives). The researchers also examined recovery in a set of 16 unmarried patients as a comparison group.

As predicted, having greater social support led to faster recovery from heart surgery. Although the men in both the high- and low-marital-quality groups were relatively similar in terms of health indicators prior to the surgery and did not differ in the amount of anxiety they experienced, those who received more support following surgery requested less pain medication and recovered more quickly than those with low support. For example, married patients who received high support were released an average of 1.26 days sooner than those who received low support. While the quality of the marital relationship was not a strong predictor of speed of recovery, individuals who were married and received low support had slower recoveries than even those who were single. This finding suggests that while receiving high levels of social support from one's spouse is beneficial in terms of recovery from major surgery, being in an unsupportive marriage can actually have a negative impact on recovery.

1992). For example, twice as many single people die from coronary heart disease than do married people (Schwarzer & Leppin, 1992). One study of over 1,000 patients with confirmed heart disease found that those with greater social support, as defined by having a spouse or close confidant, had lower rates of mortality (Williams, Barefoot, et al., 1992). Eighty-two percent of those who were married or had a close confidant lived for at least 5 years, compared to only 50% of those without such support. Similarly, people who have cancer survive longer if they have extensive social support (Helgeson, Cohen, & Fritz, 1998; Spiegel & Kato, 1996). A study of breast cancer patients, for example, found that participation in a weekly social support group was associated with living longer (Spiegel, Bloom, Kraemer, & Gottheil, 1989). Specifically, women who participated in this support group lived for an average of 36.6 months following the intervention versus 18.9 months for those in the control group. However, more recent research has not replicated these findings. (We talk more about the role of social support in helping people cope with chronic and terminal illness in Chapter 10).

But Is This Effect Correlation or Causation?

Multiple studies demonstrate a link between social support and health, but for ethical reasons virtually all of this research is correlational: it is obviously impossible to randomly assign people to receive different levels of social support and then to assess the consequences of such support on well-being over time. Thus, we can tell that social support and health are correlated, but we can't tell whether having social support *causes* better health. Some researchers have therefore proposed alternatives to explain the link between social support and health.

One possible explanation for the association between social support and health is that illness leads to disruption in social support. People who are suffering from a chronic and/or debilitating illness are likely to have trouble engaging in social and recreational activities; hence, they may have difficulty making and maintaining interpersonal relationships. For example, individuals who are disabled, such as through spinal cord injury or a stroke, often report having smaller social networks than those who are of similar age but not disabled (Schulz & Decker, 1985; Schulz & Tompkins, 1990). People sometimes hold negative stereotypes about those who have a chronic illness and may even blame ill persons for acquiring the disease. These beliefs can lead people to avoid spending time with someone who has a chronic or terminal illness. Also having a chronic illness can cause people to feel alienated from family and friends, which thereby disrupts normal levels of social support (Dakof & Taylor, 1990; Wortman & Dunkel-Schetter, 1979). One study found that 75% of breast cancer patients reported that people treated them differently after learning of their disease (Peters-Golden, 1982). All of these factors could lead people who are in poor physical health to experience decreases in the amount of social support they receive.

Another possible explanation for the link between social support and health is that a third variable causes this association. For example, people who are very hostile may have few friends and may also experience greater cardiovascular stress during interpersonal interactions. If researchers then found that people who have few friends have worse health, they wouldn't be able to tell if the poor health was the result of having low levels of social support or the result of having more cardiovascular reactivity, which leads to wear and tear on the heart over time. In this case, the supposed association between social support and health would simply be a reflection of hostility leading to both low levels of social support and poor health.

Although both of these alternative explanations for the link between social support and health are possible, research suggests that they are unlikely for several reasons. First, studies that follow people over time still show an association between social support and rates of mortality (House et al., 1988). For example, researchers in the Alameda County study measured social support at one point in time, and then measured death rates over the next 9 years (Berkman & Syme, 1979), and other large-scale studies that followed people over time reveal similar findings (Blazer, 1982; House et al., 1982; Kaplan et al., 1988; Ruberman et al., 1984; Williams et al., 1992). These prospective studies suggest that social support leads to well-being as opposed to the reverse.

Second, studies show a link between social support and health even when they take into account other variables, such as social class and personality, that might predict both support and health. For example, in the Alameda County study the link between social support and mortality was found to be independent of socioeconomic status as well as other health-related behaviors, such as smoking, alcohol use, obesity, and physical inactivity (Berkman & Syme, 1979). This means that none of these other variables explains the link between social support and health. Similarly, in a study examining whether people with more social support are less susceptible to getting a cold, researchers considered a number of other variables that could explain this relationship, including smoking, poor sleep quality, alcohol abstinence, and low levels of intake of vitamin C (Cohen, Doyle, Skoner, Rabin, & Gwaltney, 1997). However, the association between social support and health remained even when these other factors were considered. Nonetheless, the vast majority of research showing a link between support and health is correlational; hence, it is important to remember that this association could be interpreted in different ways.

When Does Social Support Lead to Better Health?

Research indicates that social support leads to better health, but has not specified whether support is always beneficial or whether it is particularly important during times of high stress. This section discussed two hypotheses that describe the link between social support and well-being in different ways.

Buffering Hypothesis

As discussed in Chapter 4, considerable research demonstrates that stress affects health (Selye, 1976). In turn, having social support may provide a buffer from the daily life stress that people experience, which in turn protects them against illness. For example, when one spouse is particularly busy at work, the other spouse may do more housework and "pick up the slack" to reduce his or her partner's responsibilities and thereby reduce the spouse's experience of stress. Similarly, as described at the beginning of this chapter, Arturo benefited during the difficult exam period from receiving a care package from his parents as well as assistance from his roommate. This hypothesis, the *buffering hypothesis*, depicted in Figure 6.2., suggests that social support leads to better health by protecting people from the negative effects of high stress (Wills, 1984).

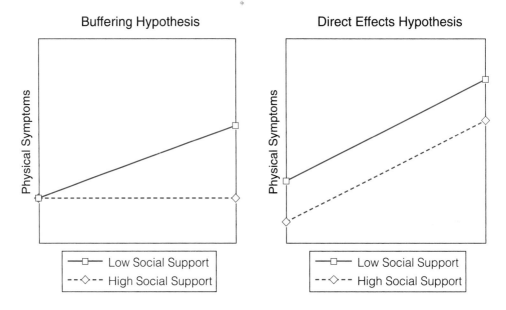

FIGURE 6.2 The buffering hypothesis suggests that social support is particularly beneficial to health during times of stress, whereas the direct effects hypothesis suggests that social
support is always beneficial.

Several research studies provide support for the buffering hypothesis by
showing that the benefits of social support are greatest for people who are
experiencing high levels of stress, including those involved in military combat
(Solomon, Mikulincer, & Hobfoll, 1986), those with AIDS (Hays et al., 1992),
those experiencing natural disasters (Fleming, Baum, Gisriel, & Gatchel, 1982;
Kaniasty & Norris, 1993), and those who are unemployed (Schwarzer,
Jerusalem, & Hahn, 1994). In one study by Schwarzer and colleagues (1994),
235 people completed questionnaires about their amount of social support,
employment status, and health. Social support had only a small effect on health
for those who were employed, but had a large effect on health for those who
were unemployed (and who were presumably under conditions of greater
stress). In fact, those who were unemployed and who had low levels of support
reported having the worst health. Similarly, a study of soldiers who fought in
the Israel–Lebanon War compared those who experienced a psychological
breakdown to those who did not and found that those who experienced such
a breakdown received lower levels of social support from the officers in their
company (Solomon et al., 1986). The soldiers may have benefited from both
instrumental support, such as receiving information that helped them stay safe
during intense battle conditions, as well as emotional support, such as feeling
cared for and connected to others. In sum, numerous research studies suggest
that social support is particularly beneficial in terms of health for people who
are undergoing high levels of stress.

One possibility explaining how social support may buffer people from stress is that people with high levels of social support think about difficult situations more positively than those with low levels of support. People with high levels of social support know that others will be there to help them during times of need, and thus they may perceive potentially stressful events as less impactful. For example, a person who receives little support from a spouse may see the loss of employment as a very negative event posing substantial problems for the family. In contrast, a person who receives high levels of support from a spouse could interpret the loss of a job as a somewhat negative event, but also as an opportunity to investigate a new career path; the loss of a job might then be perceived as less stressful.

Individuals with high levels of social support may also be able to cope more effectively with potentially stressful events. First, receiving various types of social support could help someone directly eliminate, or at least lessen, the negative effects of potentially stressful situations. For example, if your car breaks down and you can't get to work, having a friend who will drive you or loan you a car could substantially reduce your concern about your car breaking down. One research study with over 1,000 participants found that people who were under considerable financial stress but who received high levels of tangible support were less likely to engage in heavy drinking, whereas those who received low levels of support were particularly likely to demonstrate such behavior (see Figure 6.3; Peirce, Frone, Russell, & Cooper, 1996). Simply talking to other people may help relieve stress, even if these people can't help you fix or solve the problem. In fact, even talking to one's pet can help people cope with life stressors (see Box 6.4 and Photo 6.3)! These factors may help people with high levels of support experience better health.

Direct Effects Hypothesis

The buffering hypothesis suggests that social support benefits health only during times of high stress, but other researchers believe that social support benefits health regardless of the amount of stress individuals are experiencing (Wills, 1984). According to this perspective, individuals benefit from having social support during stressful and low-stress times. For example, you may be helped by having emotional support from your friends when you are under a lot of stress at exam time, but you may also be helped from having this support during low-stress times. This hypothesis, the *direct effects hypothesis*, posits that social support can help people experiencing both low and high levels of stress; hence, having high levels of social support is always advantageous to health (see Figure 6.2).

Individuals' social relationships could influence their attitudes and behaviors related to health (Stroebe & Stroebe, 1996). For example, significant others can encourage people to exercise, stop smoking, and eat a balanced diet (see Photo 6.4 and Cartoon 6.1). In line with this view, people who have more social connections are less likely to engage in unhealthy behaviors, such as smoking and using alcohol, and are more likely to engage in health-promoting behaviors, such as wearing a seat belt (Barrerra, Chassin, & Rogosch, 1993; Maton &

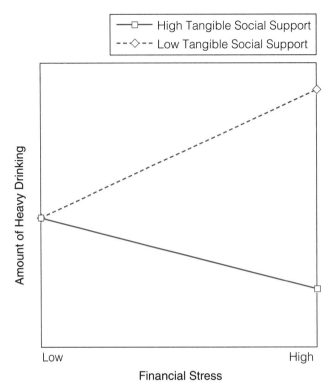

FIGURE 6.3 While people who have high levels of tangible support decrease their frequency of alcohol use when they experience financial pressure, people with low levels of such support increase their frequency of alcohol use (data from Peirce et al., 1996).

Zimmerman, 1992; Windle, 1992). Significant others might also encourage people to use health care services and follow medical regimens to help manage existing illnesses (e.g., reminding a diabetic to monitor blood sugar levels). In fact, individuals with high levels of social support are more likely to use health care services (Wallston, Alagna, DeVellis, & DeVellis, 1983) and adhere to medical regimens (Christensen et al., 1992; Wallston et al., 1983).

The absence of social companionship such as that provided by marriage or friendship is likely to lead to loneliness, which in turn is associated with distress, depression, and negative physical symptoms (Peplua, 1985; Stroebe & Stroebe, 1996). To study the impact of companionship on health, Rook (1987) measured levels of stress, social support, companionship, and physical symptoms in a sample of over 1,000 California residents. This study distinguished between social support, defined as having people to talk to about personal issues, help with household tasks, and consult when making important decisions, and social companionship, defined as having people with whom you can eat meals, visit, and engage in recreational activities. Rook's findings indicate

Box 6.4

Research Focus—The Health Benefits of Pet Ownership

Some research reveals that pets can provide people with valuable social support, which in turn can lead to better health. In one study, 938 people age 65 years or older were interviewed by telephone about their health status, social support, pet ownership, and frequency of doctor visits (Siegel, 1990). The researchers then reinterviewed the participants every 2 months for 1 year to examine whether having a pet was associated with fewer trips to the doctor. As predicted, they found that people with pets had fewer doctor visits: those who had experienced many stressful events and did not have a pet had an average of 10.37 doctor visits during the year compared to 8.38 for pet owners.

Siegel (1990) also examined the effects of owning different types of pets. Interestingly, the effect between pet ownership and doctor visits was true only for those who owned a dog; having a cat or a bird did not seem to produce the same beneficial effects. (There were too few people with other types of pets to examine their relative benefits.) The particular benefit of owning a dog might be a function of the different types of relationships people have with different types of pets. For example, dog owners spend more time outdoors with their pets (an average of 1.43 hours per day versus 0.59 hours for owners of other types of pets), and spend more time talking to their pets (an average of 1.48 hours per day versus 1.14 hours for other pet owners). Dog owners were also more likely than those who owned other pets to report that their pets provide love and make them feel secure.

One factor that might lead to this link between pet ownership (in particular dog ownership) and health is that owning a pet gives people some of the same types of support that they get from human companionship. People clearly form deep attachments to their pets and may view their pets as members of their family. In fact, 75% reported that their pet provided them with companionship. Another possibility is that owning a pet, particularly a dog, leads people to exercise more. As described earlier, dog owners spend more time outdoors with their pets than those who owned cats or birds. People who have a dog may therefore live longer because they are engaging in regular exercise. Finally, people who own a dog may interact more with other people, as anyone who has ever walked a dog knows—people talk to those who are with a dog!

that social support assisted people in times of stress (in line with the buffering hypothesis), and social companionship led to positive well-being regardless of stress levels (in line with the direct effects hypothesis). This work suggests that researchers must distinguish between practical types of support, such as direct

PHOTO 6.3   For senior citizens, having a pet can lead to better health.

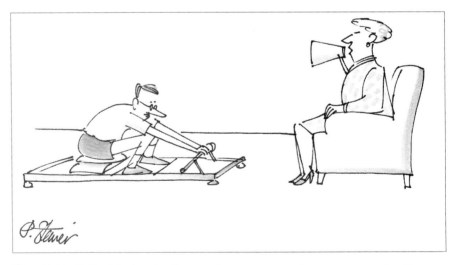

CARTOON 6.1   Having significant others support and encourage our health-related behaviors is very helpful (©2003 Peter Steiner from cartoonbank.com. All Rights Reserved).

help with problem solving and assisstance with tasks, which may be particularly beneficial to health when people are experiencing stress, and companionate support, such as listening to people's problems and providing emotional support, which may be beneficial to health in general.

PHOTO 6.4   People with higher amounts of social support may take better care of themselves, including eating well, exercising, and adhering to medical regimens.

Who Benefits from What Support?

The buffering and the direct effects hypotheses differ on whether social support is viewed as beneficial for health at all times or only during times of stress. Other hypotheses suggest certain types of social support are helpful following particular types of stresses. For example, if your car breaks down and you need a ride to an appointment, getting a ride or borrowing a car will be helpful, whereas simply talking about your feelings regarding your broken car will not be very helpful. On the other hand, if you are sad following a fight with your girlfriend, it may be quite helpful to talk about your feelings with a close friend. According to the *matching hypothesis*, individuals benefit from receiving the type of social support that fits their particular problem (Cohen & Wills, 1985; Cutrona & Russell, 1990).

Several studies suggest that people in different situations do benefit from having different types of support. Specifically, in the case of controllable events, namely, those that can be solved or fixed, people benefit most from receiving practical types of support (Cutrona & Russell, 1990). For example, instrumental support is consistently associated with better psychological and physical well-being for new parents. Pregnancy, childbirth, and caring for an infant are challenging events that people may initially have trouble managing. However, tangible and instrumental support, such as advice on infant care, financial assistance, and assistance with child care tasks, can help to ease this stress, and in turn benefit both physical and mental health of the new parent. Similarly, victims of natural disasters particularly benefit from receiving tangible support (Norris & Kaniasty, 1996).

On the other hand, in the case of uncontrollable events, such as the loss of a spouse, practical types of support will not be as effective because they will not help people solve or eliminate the stressor. Emotional support should therefore be more valuable in these cases. In support of this view, one study of patients with a chronic disease found that family support was associated with better morale as well as fewer medical complications (Dimond, 1979). Similarly, breast cancer patients benefit from having emotional support but not from instrumental support (Helgeson & Cohen, 1996). This research all points to the importance of receiving the "right type" of support for a given problem.

People also benefit more from receiving support from people who have faced a similar situation. Similar others can provide a person with information about useful coping strategies as well as standards for judging one's own reaction (Thoits, 1986). Contact with similar others may also allow individuals to vent their feelings to those who are likely to understand, and who thus can provide important emotional support. One study of patients scheduled for heart surgery found that those who had a hospital roommate who had already undergone the same type of surgery reported feeling less anxiety, and they left the hospital sooner after surgery (Kulik, Mahler, & Moore, 1996). Those with an "experienced roommate" left the hospital more quickly after their own surgery than those whose roommate had had a different surgery—8.04 days as compared to 9.17 days respectively. As described at the beginning of the chapter, Mark felt calmer and more comfortable after receiving information about what to expect during and following heart surgery from his roommate Sam.

How Does Social Support Lead to Better Health?

Recent research has examined the influence of social support on physiological processes that can lead to various diseases (Kennedy, Kiecolt-Glaser, & Glaser, 1990; Uchino, Cacioppo, & Kiecolt-Glaser, 1996; Uchino, Uno, & Holt-Lunstad, 1999). As a person experiences repeated stressors, and their accompanying physiological reactions, his or her body may experience a state of *allostatic load*, which leads to great susceptibility to illness and disease (this phenomenon is described in more detail in Chapter 4). Social support, however, may protect against such health problems by reducing the impact of potential stressors and thereby the body's physiological response. Specifically, social support may influence individuals' appraisal of stressors, coping strategies, and health behaviors, which can all lead to physiological effects that impact health (see Figure 6.4). This section examines the impact of social support on the cardiovascular system, the immune system, and the neuroendocrine system.

Cardiovascular System

As described in Chapter 4, the cardiovascular system is responsible for transporting oxygen to and removing carbon dioxide from all the cells in the body. When the heart pumps blood, it generates the force necessary to accomplish this important transportation throughout the body. The number of times the

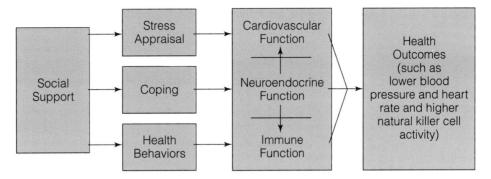

FIGURE 6.4 Social support may lead to better health through a variety of different pathways (adapted from Uchino et al., 1999).

heart beats per minute is the *heart rate*, one measure of cardiovascular reactivity, and the force of the blood against the artery walls is *blood pressure*, another such measure. The majority of research on the link between social support and physiological processes has focused on the effects of support on these two measures of cardiovascular function (Uchino et al., 1996).

The evidence overwhelmingly points to a link between social support and cardiovascular function (Uchino et al., 1996). Specifically, people who have higher levels of social support have lower heart rates and blood pressure than those without this support (Bland, Krogh, Winkelstein, & Trevisan, 1991; Linden, Chambers, Maurice, & Lenz, 1993; Unden, Orth-Gomer, & Elofsson, 1991). For example, Unden and colleagues (1991) found that individuals who had high social support at work had lower mean heart rates as well as lower blood pressure. Because elevated blood pressure can be a risk factor for cardiovascular disease, this association between social support and blood pressure suggests one pathway by which greater support leads to better health. Individuals with more social support are also less reactive to stressful situations (Gerin, Pieper, Levy, & Pickering, 1992; Kamarck et al., 1996; Lepore, Mata Allen, & Evans, 1993). For example, Kamarck and colleagues (1996) examined whether social support can reduce cardiovascular reactivity during stressful tasks by asking female college students to complete various arithmetic tasks either alone or in the presence of a friend. Women who had a friend with them had a significantly lower heart rate than those who completed the questionnaires alone. One recent study even found that pet owners who take a math test in the presence of their pet experience lower heart rates and blood pressure reactivity than those whose pets are not present (Allen, Blasovich, & Mendes, 2002)! These findings—from both correlational and experimental studies—all suggest that individuals who have more social support have better cardiovascular function.

Immune System

Again, as described in Chapter 4, the immune system helps defend the body against viruses and foreign bacteria, hence, it plays an important role in protecting us from many diseases, including HIV, cancer, and arthritis. The immune system consists of specialized types of white blood cells called lymphocytes, which include B cells, T cells, and natural killer (NK) cells. These cells respond to threats to the body in a variety of ways, such as by producing antibodies that bind to—and thereby inactivate—foreign cells, engulfing and destroying foreign cells, and detecting and destroying damaged cells.

Greater social support is strongly related to better immune functioning (Jemmott & Locke, 1984; Uchino et al., 1996). Specifically, people with higher levels of social support have more effective immune systems, hence, they are better able to fight off major and minor illnesses. For example, people whose spouses have cancer (a clearly stressful situation) and who have high levels of perceived social support show greater NK cell activity, namely, a greater ability to kill off tumor cells, than those who have low levels of social support (see Figure 6.5; Baron, Cutrona, Hicklin, Russell, & Lubaroff, 1990). Similarly, concentrations of secretory immunoglobulin A, which provides a first line of defense against infections, are higher among college students who feel they have an adequate amount of social support (Jemmott & Magliore, 1988), whereas NK cell activity is lower in people who are depressed (Kiecolt-Glaser et al., 1984). Individuals who have a larger social network—those who talk to more people on a regular basis—are even less susceptible to the common cold (see Box 6.5; Cohen et al., 1997). On the other hand, people who experience an extreme loss of social support, such as the loss of their spouse through death

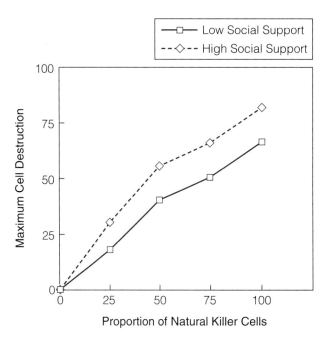

FIGURE 6.5 People who receive high levels of social support show greater immune responsiveness, indicating they are better able to fight off illnesses (data from Baron et al., 1990).

or divorce, typically show substantial deficits in their immune functioning (Kiecolt-Glaser, et al., 1987; Kiecolt-Glaser et al., 1988; Schleifer, Keller, Camerino, Thornton, & Stein, 1983).

Although for ethical and practical reasons most of this research is correlational, some research with animals has used more controlled, experimental studies. Such work has shown that stressful social circumstances lead to negative effects on the immune system (Moynihan & Ader, 1996). For example,

Box 6.5

Research Focus—The Benefits of Social Support on Susceptibility to the Common Cold

Although individuals with social support experience benefits in terms of physical health, we know relatively little about the processes leading to this link. To examine this issue, Sheldon Cohen and his colleagues (1997) conducted a study to assess whether individuals who had more social support were at less risk of developing the common cold. Two hundred seventy-six healthy participants completed a series of questionnaires, including measures of life stressors, health practices, and the number of distinct social roles they played (e.g., parent, friend, child, sister). They also underwent blood tests to rate their levels of natural killer cell activity and antibodies to a standard cold virus. Participants were then given nasal drops that exposed them to one of two cold viruses. (As described in Chapter 2, for ethical reasons all participants clearly were informed about this aspect of the study and agreed to undergo this exposure.) All participants were then housed together for 1 week to avoid exposure to any additional viruses. This method allowed researchers to assess whether individuals with higher levels of social support had greater resistance to the cold viruses. The researchers collected several different types of data: at the end of each day, participants rated their own symptoms (sneezing, coughing, headache, etc.), and researchers collected all of the tissues used by each participant in order to measure the amount of mucus produced.

As predicted, individuals with more social roles were less susceptible to the common cold: those who reported having only 1 to 3 roles were four times more likely to get sick than those who reported having 6 or more roles. Specifically, those with more social ties reported feeling less sick and also produced less mucus. The researchers also examined many other health practices in order to determine whether the link between social support and health was a result of another variable. Although smoking, poor sleep quality, alcohol use, and low levels of intake of vitamin C were all associated with greater susceptibility to colds, these factors could account only partially for the relationship between social support and colds. These findings suggest that individuals with more diverse social networks are less susceptible to the common cold.

monkeys who are separated from their peers have an altered lymphocyte response (Reite, Harbeck, & Hoffman, 1981). Similarly, monkey infants who are separated from their mothers show decreases in antibody production (Coe, Wiener, Rosenberg, & Levine, 1985). These studies provide additional evidence that social support impacts physiological functioning.

Neuroendocrine System

The endocrine system works by releasing hormones from various endocrine glands, such as the pituitary gland, thyroid, and pancreas, which then travel though the bloodstream to act on a particular body tissue or organ. During times of stress, the sympathetic nervous system activates two core systems within the endocrine system (Chrousos & Gold, 1992). When the *sympathetic-adrenal medullary (SAM) system* is activated, the hypothalamus triggers the adrenal glands to release epinephrine and norepinephrine, which leads to a number of cardiovascular effects (e.g., increased heart rate and blood pressure). The *hypothalamic-pituitary adrenal (HPA) system* is also activated during times of stress, which in turn leads to the release of cortisol (which decreases the effectiveness of the immune system). (These processes are described in more detail in Chapter 4.)

Although relatively little research has examined the influence of social support specifically on the neuroendocrine system, some evidence suggests that support may also enhance this system (Uchino et al., 1996). A study by Seeman and colleagues, for example, found that older adults who had more and better social relationships had lower levels of various hormones, including epinephrine, norepinephrine, and cortisol in their blood (Seeman, Berkman, Blazer, & Rowe, 1994). Similarly, Fleming and colleagues (1982) found that people who had less social support had higher levels of norepinephrine. Some experimental evidence also points to the importance of social support in influencing the neuroendocrine system (Kirschbaum, Klaver, Filipp, & Hellhammer, 1995). For example, the presence of a supportive companion during a difficult public speech led to a lower cortisol response.

Does Social Support Benefit Men and Women Equally?

Some researchers have examined whether men or women benefit more in terms of health from having social support (Schwarzer & Leppin, 1989). On the one hand, women tend to receive more support than men (Cohen, McGowan, Fooskas, & Rose, 1984). Women typically have a broader social network and more people in whom they confide (Depner & Ingersoll, 1982). College women get more support from their friends and roommates than do men in college (Lepore, 1992). Women are also more likely than men to have a close confidant: one study found that two-thirds of women report having a "best friend" compared to 25% of men (Rubin, 1986). However, these broader social networks not only provide women with more support, but also give women more people they are supposed to provide support to, which in turn can cause stress (Cohen et al., 1984; Flaherty & Richman, 1989; Kessler, McLeod, & Wethington, 1985). Women are more oriented toward the needs of others (Eisenberg & Lennon, 1983; Gilligan, 1982) and are more likely than men to provide support to their aging parents, children, and friends (Kessler et al., 1985).

Women not only give and receive more social support than men, but they also tend to benefit more psychologically and physically from having social support (Antonucci & Akiyama, 1987; Schwarzer & Leppin, 1989). Women with less support are more likely to experience both depression and anxiety (Flaherty & Richman, 1989), and those who do not have a confidant are more likely to report symptoms of psychological and physical distress (Miller & Ingham, 1976). In both of the preceeding studies there was no association between social support and health for men. Similarly, one study examined level of stress, social support, and physical symptoms in a sample of 115 undergraduate men and women (Wohlgemuth & Betz, 1991). Although social support had no impact on physical symptoms for men, the amount of and satisfaction with social support was a significant predictor of symptoms for women. Finally, research also shows that women benefit more in terms of life expectancy than men from having a large social network. Findings from the Alameda County study, for example, indicated that women with few social connections had a rate of mortality 2.8 times greater than those with many social connections, whereas men with few social connections had a mortality rate only 2.3 times greater than those with many social connections (Berkman & Syme, 1979).

Interestingly, although women in general benefit more from social support than men do, men benefit more from marriage (Chesney & Darbes, 1998). Although the death of a spouse is associated with increased risk of mortality for both men and women, losing a spouse is particularly impactful for men (Martikainen & Valkomen, 1996; Stroebe & Stroebe, 1983). One study examined death rates in about 8,000 people who were married or widowed (Helsing & Szklo, 1981). Although there was no difference in death rates for women who were married as compared to those who were widowed (23.2% and 24.1%, respectively), widowed men were at much greater risk of dying from various causes, including infectious diseases, accidents, and suicide, than were men whose spouse was still living (65.3% versus 51.8% respectively). This difference in death rate for married versus widowed men was particularly large in men who were 55 years and older.

One reason women who experience the death of a spouse do not suffer from the same negative health consequences as men may be that women's generally larger social networks enable them to receive more social support following the death of their spouse (see Photo 6.5). For example, women are likely to have more friends available to talk with about their loss, and this emotional support can lead to better health (Stroebe & Stroebe, 1983). Moreover, men generally rely on their wives for emotional support, but women are likely to rely on their children, friends, and other family members for support (Kohen, 1983). Married men may also have relied on their wives to maintain contact with friends and family members; hence, they may feel the loss of support not only from their

PHOTO 6.5   Women may experience better health than men because they are more likely to confide in others.

wives but also from their lost contact with others. Finally, because women tend to live longer than men, women who lose a spouse are likely to find a much larger support group of similar others than are men (Stroebe & Stroebe, 1983). In fact, many community-based support groups for those who have lost a spouse are focused primarily on serving the needs of women.

Another possibility is that because the woman in a married couple tends to take responsibility for much of the day-to-day functioning of the household, men who experience the death of their wife find themselves newly burdened with many household responsibilities. For example, one study of married couples found that wives reported an increase in the time they spent doing housework on days that their husbands had stressful workdays, whereas there was no association between wives' level of work stress and their husbands' participation in household tasks (Bolger, DeLongis, Kessler, & Schilling, 1989).

Are There Sociocultural Differences in the Benefits of Social Support?

Although relatively little research has examined the association of ethnicity with both social support and health, ethnic groups may vary in the amount of social support their members provide and expect. At least in the United States, African Americans and Hispanic Americans tend to have larger family networks than European American families (Berkman, 1986; Neighbors, 1997). Compared to Caucasians, African Americans have more interdependence and a greater frequency of contact with their extended families (Chatters & Taylor,

1993; Dressler, 1985). For example, Timmer and colleagues found that African American newlywed couples visited their families on a more frequent basis than Caucasians (Timmer, Veroff, & Hatchett, 1996).

Similarly, some studies have examined whether individuals who live in countries that place a high priority on interdependence and connection with one's social group experience better health (Bond, 1991; Triandis, Bontempo, Villareal, Asai, & Luca, 1988). Countries with social norms of connection could promote better health in a variety of ways, including giving more support to elderly relatives and encouraging people to openly discuss their problems (Bond, 1991). Living in a culture that provides more social support could therefore protect people from stress, hence leading to lower rates of disease as well as longer life expectancy. For instance, the Japanese culture places a high priority on connection to one's family and social group, and, in turn, the rate of heart disease in Japan is quite low (Reed, McGee, Yano, & Feinlab, 1983). This lower rate of heart disease does not seem to be simply a function of genetics because Japanese people who live in the United States experience higher rates of heart disease than those living in Japan. The difference in rate of heart disease also cannot be explained by other likely factors, such as smoking, diet, and blood pressure. This research suggests that people who live in cultures that emphasize interdependence are generally healthier than those who live in self-focused countries, such as the United States.

Within the United States there is some evidence that people who live in more cohesive and supportive communities experience better health. One 25-year study conducted in Roseto, Pennsylvania, found that the although residents in this town were similar to those in nearby towns in terms of health-related behaviors, such as smoking, exercise, and eating patterns, they had much lower rates of heart attacks, other stress-related disorders, and death (Wolf, 1969). Researchers found that almost all of the town's residents were of Italian descent and that relationships within families and among neighbors were very close and cohesive. Apparently, having this type of social support buffered the negative effects of stress on health.

Questioning the Research 6.2

Wolf's 1969 study suggested that the cohesive family relationships in Roseto were responsible for the low mortality rates in this town. What other explanations might there be for these rates? Which interpretations do you find most convincing, and why?

What Are the Negative Effects of Social Support?

Social support can also have negative implications for psychological and physical well-being. In some cases people receive social support that is intended to be helpful, but that is actually detrimental to physical and psychological health (see Table 6.2; Dakof & Taylor, 1990; Thoits, Hohmann, Harvey, & Fletcher, 2000; Wortman & Lehman, 1985). For example, if you are depressed about a recent relationship breakup, friends may encourage you to "drown your sorrows" by drinking alcohol, which obviously is not a great strategy for enhancing your health. Similarly, people can give unwanted advice, discourage open discussion of the problem, and push for a too rapid recovery following an illness or negative event (see photo 6.6; Dakof & Taylor, 1990; Dunkel-Schetter & Wortman, 1982). As described at the start of the chapter, Diana longs to talk about the loss of her husband, but frequently finds that her friends avoid mentioning him. For example, people might tell a woman who has had a miscarriage, "It's a good thing you have other children" or, "You can always have another baby," which most women do not find helpful. Moreover, people who experience more problematic, or undermining, social support are at greater risk of experiencing coronary heart disease (Davis & Swan, 1999).

To provide effective support, people must have a realistic sense of the challenges a person is facing. People who underestimate the amount of stress someone is experiencing are less helpful than those who are more accurate in their estimations (Chapman, Hobfoll, & Ritter, 1997). In one study, 68 pregnant women were interviewed about their stressful life events and their partner's support. In order to assess their accuracy, the partners were also interviewed about how many stressful events the women had experienced. Overall, women who experienced more negative life events had greater depression, but this effect was particularly strong for women whose partners thought they had experienced relatively few stressful events (see Figure 6.6). In sum, women with partners who underestimated the amount of social support they needed were more depressed.

TABLE **6.2** *Test Yourself: Sample Items from the Negative Interactions Scale*

Sometimes even when people may have good intentions, they say or do something that upsets you. I am going to list some of these things. Think about the period of time since you were diagnosed up until today. How often did the following situations arise with your family or friends (1 = never and 5 = very often).

1. Change the subject when I try to discuss my illness
2. Tell negative stories about other people who have cancer
3. Doesn't understand my situation
4. Avoids me
5. Appears afraid to be around me
6. Minimizes my problems
7. Seems to be hiding feelings
8. Acts uncomfortable when I talk about my illness
9. Trivializes my problems
10. Tells me I look well when I don't

Source: Helgeson, Cohen, Schulz, & Yasko, 2000.

PHOTO 6.6   Although having the support of friends is generally beneficial to health, sometimes friends encourage people to do things that are actually detrimental to physical well-being.

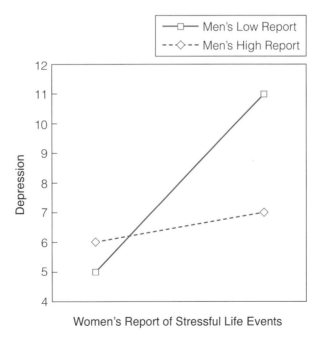

FIGURE 6.6   Women who experience many stressful life events and who have a partner who misunderstands these stresses show the highest rates of depression (data from Chapman et al., 1997).

How Can You Increase Social Support?

Given the benefits of social support in terms of health and longevity, what can you do to increase your own support? First, you can attempt to form larger social networks. Having more people to rely on increases the likelihood of having a particular type of support available when you need it. So, form new friendships. This might be a particularly important strategy to use when you are in new environments (e.g., starting college, moving to a new city), which may be stressful and in which you may not already have many sources of support. You can also try to maintain closer contact with old friends. Cunningham and Barbee (2000) suggest that women may be better at maintaining regular contact with friends than men, which again may help explain why losing a spouse has more impact on men's health than women's.

Second, people can participate in organized social support groups that include others who are facing or have faced a similar crisis. People who have experienced the loss of a child, who are taking care of a spouse with Alzheimer's disease, or who are themselves suffering from a chronic or terminal illness might particularly benefit in terms of psychological and physical well-being from participating in such a group (Gottlieb, 1985), which allow people an opportunity to share their feelings with others who are likely to understand and accept what they are going through. Moreover, because these groups consist of similar others, they provide not only emotional support but also tangible and informational support. For example, individuals who are coping with cancer could learn effective techniques of managing the side effects of chemotherapy. Recent research indicates that even computer bulletin board support groups can provide valued support to those with health problems (Weinberg et al., 1996). We talk in more detail about the value of social support groups in helping people cope with chronic diseases and terminal illness in Chapters 10 and 11.

Lingering Issues

Is social support a personality characteristic? As we saw in Chapter 5, personality characteristics such as optimism, self-esteem, and hostility influence health in a variety of ways. Some researchers therefore suggest that individuals' perceptions of how much social support they have could simply be a reflection of their beliefs about whether others care about and love them (Sarason, Pierce, & Sarason, 1990). As Irwin Sarason and colleagues point out, how a person thinks about and interacts with people probably has a major impact on how much social support they *think* they receive as well as how much social support they *actually* receive (Sarason, Sarason, & Shearin, 1986). And, in fact, individuals' perceptions about the amount of social support they receive are relative stable over time (up to 3 years), and these perceptions are often more highly correlated with health than are other measures of social support. Research also indicates that people vary in how effective they are at both eliciting and giving social support (Connell & D'Augelli, 1990). For example, one study of first-year college students found that those who were high in social competence and self-disclosure and low in social anxiety were more likely to develop close friendships (Cohen, Sherrod, & Clark, 1986). Similarly, people who believe they receive high levels of social support are judged by observers to be more competent leaders and problem solvers than those who believe they receive low levels of support (Sarason et al., 1986). Future research should clearly examine whether the amount of social support a person receives (or believes he or she is receiving) is really a reflection of one or more personality dimensions.

Can people have too much social support? According to the buffering hypothesis, social support helps individuals cope with problems, which in turn reduces stress and its negative effects on health. This model therefore assumes that social support is useful to the extent that it allows people to handle such problems, but is not necessary if they are already able to cope. Some researchers suggest that receiving more social support than is needed could even be detrimental in terms of health (Stroebe & Stroebe, 1996) because excessive amounts of support could lead people to become overly dependent on others and could impact feelings of self-worth. For example, although you may feel quite capable of working at a part-time job and keeping up with your classes, if you received constant financial assistance from your parents, you could begin to feel more reliant on them and less confident in your own ability to establish independence. One study of physically disabled people found that nearly 40% had experienced emotional distress as a result of receiving unwanted help from their spouses (Newsom & Schultz, 1998). In this case, overprotection, even though well-intentioned, was associated with depression even as long as a year later. Similarly, a study with patients recovering from a heart attack found that families' concern sometimes led patients loved ones to do things that actually harmed patients, such as not letting him or her exercise and thereby strengthen the heart muscle (Garrity, 1973). Future research should therefore examine whether in some cases individuals can receive excessive amounts of support.

Thought Questions

1. You notice that your friends who are in dating relationships seem to get sick less often than your friends who are single. Describe how both the direct effects and buffering hypotheses would explain this observation.

2. Describe two different ways that social support may influence physiological processes.

3. Describe the advantages and disadvantages of assessing social support using social network measures versus perceived social support measures.

4. You are feeling overwhelmed with the amount of work you have as finals week approaches. What are two helpful things your roommate could do? What are two detrimental things he or she could do?

5. Although the bulk of the evidence suggests that greater social support leads to better psychological and physical well-being, it is certainly conceivable that other factors account for the support–health link. Describe two such alternative explanations and the evidence that disproves these views.

Answers to Questioning the Research

Question 6.1: Although this study assessed four different categories of social ties, namely marriage, contacts with extended family and friends, church or temple membership, and other formal and informal group affiliations, these do not represent the only types of social ties people could have. For example, people who are not married but who have a close relationship with a live-in partner probably experience the same benefits of social support as those who are married. These researchers also give equal weight to the four different types of social support, and thus simply count how many different types of support people have. But it is probably more important in terms of health to have close connections (e.g., with family and friends) than to have more distant contacts (e.g., casual relationships with work colleagues).

Question 6.2: One alternative explanation for these findings is that genetic factors influenced health. Specifically, because many of the residents of Roseto, Pennsylvania, were of Italian descent, it is possible that genetic factors (e.g., less risk of heart disease) protected them from health problems. Another possibility is that living in a small town is simply less stressful than living in a big city. In fact, people who live in urban areas are exposed to greater stresses, such as pollution, crowding, and noise, than those who live in more rural areas.

CHAPTER 7

Smoking and Alcohol Abuse

- Jack is 25 years old and started smoking in high school. Back then he would smoke only when he was with friends at parties and mostly when he was drinking. However, during college Jack started smoking more frequently and smoking more cigarettes—the one or two cigarettes he used to have in an evening just didn't have the same good effects. Jack also found that smoking helped him relax during stressful times and even seemed to help his concentration when he was studying. Although he knows the health risks of smoking, Jack finds that whenever he tries to quit, he feels anxious and has trouble focusing at work.

- Annabelle is 11 years old and in 6th grade. As part of her school health education class, she has participated in several smoking prevention programs. These programs have provided information about how cigarette companies try to trick kids into buying cigarettes, how cigarettes make your teeth turn yellow and your breath smell bad, and how many teenagers aren't interested in dating someone who smokes. Although her older sister smokes, Annabelle now thinks smoking is a pretty disgusting habit.

- Diana is 30 years old and has smoked since her sophomore year of college. She knows smoking is bad for her health and therefore has tried to stop smoking three or four times. But each time, Diana has gained weight, which then leads her back to smoking. Recently, Diana and her husband, Mark have decided to have a baby. Because of the many negative effects that smoking can have on a developing fetus, Diana has made the decision to quit smoking. She is working with a therapist to identify the factors that lead her to crave a cigarette and has started chewing nicotine gum.

- Biff is the starting quarterback on his college football team and is a proud member of the Phi Delta Theta fraternity. However, he is now on academic probation because of his low GPA. Although he always plans to go to class, Biff finds it difficult to wake up in time for his classes when he has been out late drinking the night before. He knows that his drinking is a little out of control, but Biff believes that he is much funnier and more relaxed when he has been drinking. Moreover, because he's now living in the fraternity house, there is always someone around to drink with.

- Jenny is 48 years old and has had a problem with alcohol use for as long as she can remember. Although she usually drinks only on the weekends, Jenny sometimes experiences memory loss after drinking and sometimes finds herself in bed with a stranger the next morning. She has been arrested three times for driving under the influence. After her most recent arrest, Jenny lost her driver's license for 60 days and was ordered to enter an in-patient treatment for alcohol abuse and to attend daily Alcoholics Anonymous meetings for the next 90 days.

Preview

Smoking and alcohol use are two of the most common health-compromising behaviors, and often they are used in combination (Sher, Gotham, Erickson, & Wood, 1996; Shiffman et al., 1994). These two behaviors also lead to many of the major health problems, as well as causes of death, in the United States today, including cancer, coronary heart disease, accidents/unintentional injuries, and even homicides and suicides. This chapter therefore addresses the psychological factors that influence these health-compromising behaviors. First, we examine the health consequences of smoking as well as the distinct psychological and physiological factors that lead to people to start smoking as well as to continue smoking. We then examine some strategies for preventing smoking and for helping people quit smoking. Next, we examine the health consequences of alcohol abuse and the influence of biological and psychological factors on alcohol use. Finally, we examine strategies for preventing and treating alcohol abuse.

Smoking

Who Smokes?

Most recent estimates suggest that 23.5% of American adults smoke, including roughly equal proportions of men and women (see Figure 7.1; Centers for Disease Control, 2003). Although this is a drop from the mid-1960s, it still represents about 46.5 million smokers in the United States alone. Both whites and African Americans are more likely to smoke than Hispanic Americans (24.3% versus 19.8%), who in turn are more likely to smoke than Asian Americans (15%). Smoking is much more common in people who have lower levels of education than among those with higher levels (see Figure 7.2). Smoking is also more common among people with lower income: one recent study found that 75% of young men and 60% of young women in low socioeconomic homes smoke (Winkleby, Robinson, Sundquist, & Kraemer, 1999).

Most smokers acquire the habit at a relatively young age, typically before age 21 (Chen & Kandel, 1995). Among those who smoke regularly during adolescence, 70% become regular adult smokers. National statistics indicate that 30% of high school sophomores and 37% of high school seniors have

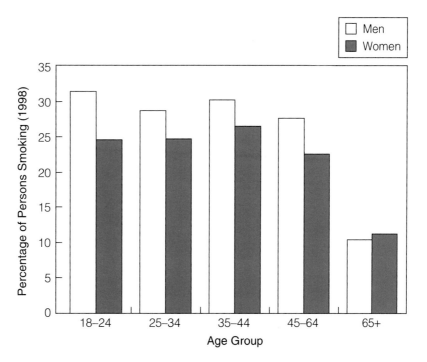

FIGURE 7.1 Although men are still more likely to smoke than women, this gap has become increasingly smaller over the last 20 years (Centers for Disease Control, 2003).

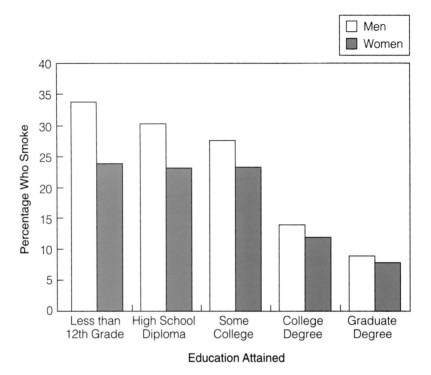

FIGURE 7.2   Smoking is much more prevalent in both men and women with low levels of education than those with high levels of education (Centers for Disease Control, 2003). Can you think about some possible explanations?

smoked a cigarette during the past 30 days (Johnston, O'Malley, & Bachman, 1998). The majority of students (60%) has smoked a cigarette before high school graduation, and more than 20% of students smoke daily. Although most teenagers would like to quit and believe that quitting smoking would be fairly easy, only 16% of adolescents had quit smoking when they were contacted again 4 years later (Zhu, Sun, Billings, Choi, & Malarcher, 1999).

What Are the Health Consequences of Smoking?

Smoking is the leading cause of preventable mortality in the United States, causing 440,000 deaths per year in the United States alone (Centers for Disease Control, 2003). In fact, more people die as a result of cigarette smoking than as a result of car accidents, fires, suicides, and homicides combined (see Figure 7.3; Kaplan, Orleans, Perkins, & Pierce, 1995). Smoking is clearly linked with a number of types of cancer, including cancer of the lung, mouth, pharynx, esophagus, and bladder (Thun, Day-Lally, Calle, Flanders, & Heath, 1995). Lung cancer alone accounts for more than 140,000 deaths each year in the United States, and over 90% of these are related to smoking (Mattson, Pollack, & Cullen, 1987). Furthermore, the risk of developing coronary heart disease

Box 7.1

Health Psychology in the Real World—Is Smokeless Tobacco Better than Cigarettes?

Although the health hazards of cigarette smoking are clear, using other forms of tobacco, such as chewing tobacco and snuff, is also bad. One study examined the frequency of smokeless tobacco use in over 11,000 high school students in Georgia, Tennessee, South Carolina, and Florida (Riley, Barenie, Woodard, & Mabe, 1996). Thirty-four percent of the students reported having tried smokeless tobacco, and one-third of them had used for 1 year or longer. The use of smokeless tobacco is most common in white boys, especially those who are involved in organized athletics, probably because of the frequent role modeling of this behavior among professional athletes (Tomar & Giovino, 1998). Although the risk associated with chewing tobacco is not as great as that associated with smoking, chewing tobacco is associated with oral cancer as well as cardiovascular disease (Bolinder, Alfredsson, Englund, & deFaire, 1994; Winn et al., 1981). For example, one study found that men who chewed tobacco had twice the risk of dying from coronary heart disease compared to those who did not use tobacco.

and stroke, which is the leading cause of death in the United States, is twice as high for smokers than for nonsmokers for those under the age of 65 (see Box 7.1; Thun et al., 1995). Smoking can also lead to a range of other major illnesses, such as emphysema, bronchitis, and respiratory infections, as well as relatively minor health problems, such as impotence (Mannino, Klevens, & Flanders, 1994) and the common cold (Cohen, Tyrell, Russell, Jarvis, & Smith, 1993). Finally, smoking by pregnant women is associated with a number of negative consequences on the fetus, including lower birthrate and miscarriage (Grunberg, Brown, & Klein, 1997). Children whose mothers smoked during pregnancy are also at increased risk of attention deficit disorders, hyperactivity, and sudden infant death syndrome (MacDorman, Cnattingius, Hoffman, Kramer, & Haglund, 1997).

Passive smoking, or environmental tobacco smoke, is a serious problem, particularly for infants and young children. Current estimates suggest that 43% of children ages 2 months to 11 years live in a home with at least one smoker (Pirkle et al., 1996). Passive smoking is a major cause of respiratory problems in children, including pneumonia and bronchitis. Exposure to smoke also increases a child's risk of developing asthma and increases the severity of symptoms of asthma. Most important, passive smoking can even lead to death—an estimated 3,000 lung cancer deaths each year in the United States alone are caused by passive smoking. Maternal smoking also contributes to an estimated

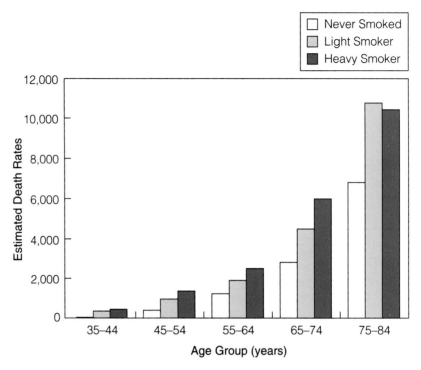

FIGURE 7.3 At every age group smokers have a higher death rate than non-smokers (Centers for Disease Control, 2003).

700 deaths due to sudden infant death syndrome in the United States alone (Grunberg et al., 1997).

What causes the numerous health consequences of smoking? First, nicotine constricts blood vessels and increases heart rate, cardiac output, and blood pressure, so the heart becomes overworked. Cigarette smoke contains high levels of carbon monoxide, which reduces the amount of oxygen in the blood and thereby leads to arteriosclerosis (hardening of the arteries). Again, this increased buildup of plaque in the arteries forces the heart to work harder to pump blood. Also, tars, small particles of residue in smoke, contain carcinogens, or cancer-causing agents, that lead to abnormal growth of cells in the mouth, throat, and lungs. Moreover, as smoke repeatedly passes through the bronchial tubes, it disrupts the ability of the cilia (fine, hairlike structures that line the bronchial tubes) to effectively clear the lungs of foreign particles. The carcinogens therefore have consistent contact with the bronchial tubes, which is why lung cancer is one of the most common types of cancer caused by smoking.

Given the many negative health consequences of smoking, it is not surprising that an estimated 30% of smokers make a quit attempt each year (Fiore et al., 1990). However, smoking is a hard habit to break—two-thirds of people who quit on their own return to smoking within 2 days, and 97% return to smoking within 6 months (Hughes et al., 1992). These rates of returning to smoking are slightly lower for people who participate in formal smoking cessation programs, but even these programs only lead to long-term quitting in 20 to 30% of smokers (Cohen et al., 1989). Even people who are highly motivated to quit smoking have great trouble stopping. Forty percent of people who have had a laryngectomy (which is typically performed to treat throat cancer) continue to smoke, as do more than 50% of those who have experienced a heart attack or surgery resulting from lung cancer (Stolerman & Jarvis, 1995).

How Do Psychological Factors Lead to the Initiation of Smoking?

As described previously, most adult smokers started smoking when they were teenagers or young adults—very few 40- and 50-year-olds suddenly decide to start smoking for the first time. What leads young people to smoke their first cigarette? First, teenagers may start to smoke as a way of trying out a new identity. Although teenagers may hold some negative views about smokers, such as they are unhealthy and foolish, they also see smokers as tough, cool, rebellious, mature, socially precocious, and more interested in the opposite sex (Aloise-Young, Hennigan, & Graham, 1996; Dinh, Sarason, Peterson, & Onstad, 1995). One study found that 5th and 7th graders who saw smokers in a positive way, viewing them as cool, good at sports, independent, and good-looking, were more likely to start smoking later (Dinh et al., 1995). Not coincidentally, advertisements for cigarettes often promote smokers as having precisely these qualities. Teenagers may therefore start smoking to try to seem glamorous, older, or more mature. Celebrities can also serve as role models—seeing actors, athletes, and rock stars smoke can promote that behavior in adolescents (Grunberg et al., 1997).

The media contributes to smoking, in part by portraying smoking as glamorous and cool (see Box 7.2; Goldstein, Sobel, & Newman, 1999; Pechmann & Shih, 1999). This presentation of smoking as desirable occurs even in films targeted to very young children. One recent study in the *Journal of the American Medical Association* examined the presence of tobacco products (cigarettes, cigars, and pipes) in 50 G-rated animated children's films, including *Bambi*, *Lady and the Tramp*, and *The Lion King* (Goldstein et al., 1999). Tobacco use was portrayed in 56% of the films, including all seven films released in 1996 and 1997 (the latest years included in the study), and "good characters" are as likely to use tobacco as "bad" ones. Moreover, after exposure to smoking in feature films, teenagers see smokers as higher in social status and their intentions to smoke increased (Pechmann & Shih, 1999).

Teenagers who smoke also seem to have distinct types of personalities (Burt, Dinh, Peterson, & Sarason, 2000; Windle & Windle, 2001). Adolescents who smoke often engage in other risk-taking behaviors, such as alcohol and drug use and sexual activity with multiple partners (Emmons, Wechsler, Dowdall, & Abraham, 1998). Although they may be less academically oriented and less involved in school sports, they are not antisocial—in fact, adolescents who smoke tend to be extraverted and spend considerable time socializing with friends (Stein, Newcomb, & Bentler, 1996). However, adolescents who smoke do show higher rates of depression (Windle & Windle, 2001). Another factor that may prompt smoking in girls is a concern about weight. As we examine

Box 7.2

Health Psychology in the Real World

Hollywood's Responsibility for Smoking Deaths

I've written 14 movies. My characters smoke in many of them and they look cool and glamorous doing it. Smoking was an integral part of many of my screenplays because I was a militant smoker. It was part of a bad-boy image I'd cultivated for a long time—smoking, drinking, partying, rock 'n' roll.

Smoking, I once believed, was every person's right. Efforts to stop it were politcally correct, a Big Brother assault on personal freedoms. Secondhand smoke was a nonexistent problem invented by professional do-gooders. I put all these views into my scripts.

In one of my movies, "Basic Instinct," smoking is part of a sexual subtext. Sharon Stone's character smokes; Michael Douglas's is trying to quit. She seduces him with literal and figurative smoke that she blows into his face. In the movie's most controversial scene, she even has a cigarette in her hand.

I'm sure the tobacco companies loved "Basic Instinct." One of them even launched a brand of "Basic" cigarettes not long after the movie became a worldwide hit, perhaps inspired by my cigarette-friendly work. My movie made a lot of money; so did their new cigarette.

Remembering all this, I find it hard to forgive myself. I have been an accomplice to the murders of untold numbers of human beings. I am admitting this only because I have made a deal with God. Spare me, I said, and I will try to stop others from committing the same crimes I did.

Eighteen months ago I was diagnosed with throat cancer, the result of a lifetime of smoking. I am alive but maimed. Much of my larnyx is gone. I have some difficulty speaking; others have some difficulty understanding me. I no longer have the excruciating difficulty swallowing or breathing that I experienced in the first months after my surgery.

I haven't smoked or drank for 18 months now, though I still take it day-to-day and pray for help. I believe in prayer and exercise. I have walked five miles a day for a year, without missing even one day. Quitting smoking and drinking has taught me the hardest lesson I've ever learned about my own weakness; it has also given me the greatest affection and empathy for those still addicted.

I have spent some time in the past year and a half in cancer wards. I have seen people gasp for air as a suctioning device cleaned their tracheas. I have heard myself wheezing horribly, unable to catch my breath, as a nurse begged me to breathe. I have seen an 18-year-old with throat cancer who had never smoked a single cigarette in his life. (His mother was a chain smoker.) I have tried not to cry as my wife fitted the trachea tube that I had coughed out back into my throat. (Thankfully, I no longer need it.)

(continues)

I don't think smoking is every person's right anymore. I think smoking should be as illegal as heroin. I'm no longer such a bad boy. I go to church on Sunday. I'm desperate to see my four boys grow up. I want to do everything I can to undo the damage I have done with my own big-screen words and images.

So I say to my colleagues in Hollywood: what we are doing by showing larger-than-life movie stars smoking onscreen is glamorizing smoking. What we are doing by glamorizing smoking is unconscionable.

Hollywood films have long championed civil rights and gay rights and commonly call for an end to racism and intolerance. Hollywood films espouse a belief in goodness and redemption. Yet we are the advertising agency and sales force for an industry that kills nearly 10,000 people daily.

A cigarette in the hands of a Hollywood star onscreen is a gun aimed at a 12- or 14-year-old. (I was 12 when I started to smoke, a geeky immigrant kid who wanted so very much to be cool.) The gun will go off when that kid is an adult. We in Hollywood know the gun will go off, yet we hide behind a smoke screen of phrases like "creative freedom" and "artistic expression." Those lofty words are lies designed, at best, to obscure laziness. I know. I have told those lies. The truth is that there are 1,000 better and more original ways to reveal a character's personality.

Screenwriters know, too, that some movie stars are more likely to play a part if they can smoke—because they are so addicted to smoking that they have difficulty stopping even during the shooting of a scene. The screenwriter writing smoking scenes for the smoking star is part of a vicious and deadly circle.

My hands are bloody; so are Hollywood's. My cancer has caused me to attempt to cleanse mine. I don't wish my fate upon anyone in Hollywood, but I beg that Hollywood stop imposing it upon millions of others.

Source: Eszterhaus, Joe. (2002, August 9). Hollywood's responsibilty for smoking deaths. *New York Times*, p. A15.

in Chapter 8, many girls and women, including those who are of normal weight, are concerned about body shape and size. One study of over a thousand 7th- to 10th-grade girls found that girls who were trying to lose weight and who had symptoms of eating disorders were much more likely to smoke than those without such concerns (French, Perry, Leon, & Fulkerson, 1994).

Social factors, including modeling and peer pressure, may contribute to smoking. Most first smoking occurs in the presence of a peer, and adolescents who start smoking usually have friends—or siblings—who smoke (Ary & Biglan, 1988). One study that followed over 2,000 seventh- to eleventh-grade students in Minnesota for 2 years found that students who began smoking were far more likely to have friends who smoked than those who did not smoke (Mittelmark et al., 1987). How does having friends who smoke lead to smoking? One possibility is that teenagers who see smoking in a positive way choose to have friends who also see the benefits of smoking (appearing cool,

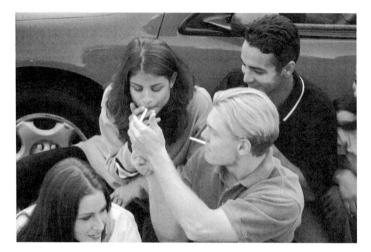

PHOTO 7.1   Social pressures often lead teenagers to begin smoking.

mature, etc.). Teenagers may also feel pressure to smoke in order to fit in with particular peer groups (see Photo 7.1). Having friends who smoke can also encourage smoking simply by providing more access to cigarettes. One study of over a thousand middle and high school students found that nonsmokers receive an average of 0.16 offers of cigarettes per week as compared to 4.22 offers for smokers (Ary & Bigland, 1988).

Although social modeling by and pressures from peers are particularly powerful influences during adolescence, parents' attitudes and behaviors also influence whether teenagers smoke. Among those with a family history of smoking, 26.6% become adult smokers as compared to 12.5% of those whose parents did not smoke (Chassin, Presson, Rose & Sherman, 1996). In contrast, children who see their parents as strongly antismoking are seven times less likely to smoke than those who see their parents as not strongly against smoking (Murray, Johnson, Luepker, & Mittelmark, 1984). A recent study by Laurie Chassin and colleagues found that mothers who smoke themselves were more likely to have teenagers who smoke, whereas mothers who discuss and punish smoking are less likely to have teenagers who smoke (Chassin, Presson, Todd, Rose, & Sherman, 1998).

What Factors Lead to Continued Smoking?

Addiction refers to the condition in which a person has a physical and psychological dependence on a given substance, such as cigarettes, alcohol, or caffeine (my own personal addiction). Addiction is caused by repeatedly consuming the substance, which over time leads the body to adjust to the substance and to incorporate it into the "normal" functioning of the body's tissues. People who are dependent on a given substance also develop *tolerance*, in which their bodies no longer respond at the same level to a particular dose, but rather need larger and larger doses to experience the same effects. They also experience unpleasant withdrawal symptoms, such as irritability, difficulty concentrating, fatigue, nausea, and weight gain, when they discontinue using the substance (Hughes & Hatsukami, 1986).

People become physically dependent on tobacco because of the nicotine they ingest. Nicotine leads to a number of physiological reactions, such as increasing alertness, blood pressure, and heart rate. However, these effects are maintained only while there is nicotine in the bloodstream—when it decays, these effects are gone. So, maybe a person starts out smoking just 2 or 3 or 4 cigarettes when he or she feels nervous. After all, the person thinks, how much harm can a couple of cigarettes once a month really do? But the problem is that the body builds up a tolerance to nicotine and so smoking just 2 or 3 or even 4 cigarettes begins to have no effect. Over time, smokers need 20 or 30 or 40 cigarettes to get the same positive effects. People don't start smoking and say, "I think I'll smoke 3 packs a day now and see how that works"; they gradually get to that point as their tolerance for nicotine increases. Although smoking is clearly an addiction, the precise processes that lead to nicotine addiction are unclear. This section describes the three different types of theories to explain it: nicotine-based models, affect-based models, and combined models.

Nicotine-Based Models

According to the *nicotine fixed-effect model*, nicotine stimulates reward-inducing centers in the nervous system (Leventhal & Cleary, 1980). Nicotine increases the levels of neuroregulators, such as dopamine, norepinephrine, and endogenous opioids, which in turn lead to better memory and concentration and reduced feelings of anxiety and tension. Nicotine has a number of reinforcing physiological effects, including speeding up the heart and relaxing the skeletal muscles. These physiological effects lead to simultaneous mental alertness and physical relaxation. These positive effects are reinforcing, so people are motivated to continue smoking in order to experience these physiological benefits. This model is very simple—it basically proposes that smoking feels good, so people are motivated to continue the behavior.

The *nicotine regulation model* extends the fixed-effect model by predicting that smoking is rewarding only when the level of nicotine is above a certain "set point" in the body (Leventhal & Cleary, 1980). In other words, individuals need to smoke enough cigarettes to maintain a certain amount of nicotine in the bloodstream or they do not experience the physiological effects of smoking. One study by Stanley Schachter and his colleagues (1977) provided smokers with either low- or high-nicotine cigarettes; researchers then counted how many cigarettes the smokers consumed during a 2-week period. Heavy smokers liked the high-nicotine cigarettes much more than the low-nicotine cigarettes, and they also smoked more of the low-nicotine cigarettes than the high-nicotine ones (see Figure 7.4). In contrast, light smokers liked both types of cigarettes equally and showed no difference in the number of cigarettes they smoked. Moreover, Stanley Schachter (1977) observed that many of the heavy smokers who were (unknowingly) given low-nicotine cigarettes reported feeling especially irritable and anxious—one man whose wife was participating in the study remarked, "If you don't get her off those cigarettes soon, she's going

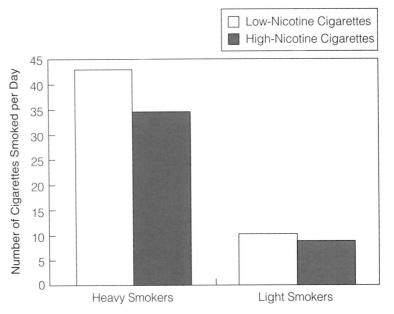

FIGURE 7.4 Although there is virtually no difference in the number of high-versus low-nicotine cigarettes smoked by light smokers (who probably are not addicted to nicotine), heavy smokers smoke many more low-nicotine than high-nicotine cigarettes (graph data from Schachter et al., 1977).

to get herself another husband" (p. 9). This finding suggests that the amount of nicotine does matter, at least for heavy smokers.

Although there is some evidence that smokers do try to maintain a certain level of nicotine in the body, both of these nicotine-based models have several limitations. First, because nicotine disappears from the blood a few days after smoking ceases, quitting should not be that difficult. However, ex-smokers often continue to crave cigarettes even after they have not smoked for some time. Second, these models ignore environmental pressures that can prompt smoking, such as stress and anxiety. In fact, smokers who are undergoing stress have a much more difficult time quitting (Shiffman et al., 1996). Finally, even heavy smokers do not smoke enough to compensate for the decline in nicotine resulting from tolerance, and although nicotine replacement methods (e.g., the patch, nicotine gum) ease some withdrawal symptoms, they do not end smokers' cravings for cigarettes.

Affect-Regulation Model

One of the earliest models predicting smoking focused on the ability of smoking to help with affect or mood regulation (Tomkins, 1966, 1968). Tomkins's *affect-regulation model* proposes that people smoke to attain positive affect or to avoid (or reduce) negative affect (see Box 7.3). Positive-affect smokers may smoke as a way of enhancing the pleasure associated with other events, such as eating a great meal or having sex (as movies so often portray). These people find smoking extremely pleasurable and smoke only when they are already feeling good. To test this theory of smoking, Howard Leventhal and Nancy Avis (1976) dipped cigarettes in vinegar (to make them taste bad) and then measured how many cigarettes people would smoke. As predicted, people who smoked primarily for its pleasure smoked significantly fewer bad-tasting cigarettes than they normally smoked, whereas those whose smoking was not motivated by pleasure smoked the same number of cigarettes they usually did.

Tomkins's affect-regulation model also proposes that people smoke as a way of coping with negative affect, to reduce anxiety, tension, and frustration (see Photo 7.2). Relaxation is one of the most common motivations for smoking (Spielberger, 1986). The first time I taught health psychology one of my students came to me during the final exam with a very important question—she was feeling very nervous and wanted permission to go outside and smoke a cigarette to calm herself down! (Although I reluctantly agreed to her request, I had to wonder what she had really learned in the course about the dangers of smoking.) Frederick Ikard and Silvan Tomkins (1973) tested the hypothesis that some people smoke to cope with anxiety by counting the number of smokers at various points during a horse race. About 17.5% of people were smoking before the race; the number climbed to 23.7% during the race (when people are nervously waiting to see if their horse wins) and then drops to 13.2% after the race ends. Although some people may smoke occasionally to manage negative affect, over time they may become addicted to cigarettes if they come to rely on smoking as their only effective strategy for coping with unpleasant emotions. One large national health study found that smokers who were depressed were 40% less likely to quit than those who were not depressed (Anda et al., 1990).

PHOTO 7.2 Many smokers report that cigarettes help them concentrate and ease tension during times of stress.

Box 7.3

Research Focus—"I'm Nervous—I Need a Cigarette!"

Stanley Schachter and his colleagues (1977) conducted a study to examine the effects of stress on smoking. Forty-eight students who were all smokers were recruited to participate in a study on "tactile stimulation." Subjects who were randomly assigned to the low-stress condition were told they would experience a weak electrical current that "will not be painful; it will feel like a tickle or a tingle, that's all. You will barely be able to notice it." In contrast, subjects who were in the high-stress condition were told they would receive a series of quite painful electrical shocks and that they would continue to increase "until you tell me that they have become so painful that you want me to stop." Subjects then received either the low or high shocks. Next, the experimenter told them that the first testing period was over and that they should simply wait in the room until the next testing session began. During this time, subjects were free to drink water or smoke cigarettes. Experimenters behind a one-way mirror then counted how many cigarettes each subject smoked as well as how many puffs on each cigarette each subject took.

The findings from this study provide strong evidence that stress leads to smoking. First, those in the high-stress group smoked an average of 2.57 cigarettes compared to only 2.05 cigarettes for those in the low-stress condition. Moreover, while low-stress subjects took an average of 15.09 puffs on a cigarette, those in the high-stress condition took an average of 22.74 puffs. These differences are even more profound for heavy smokers (those who have smoked a pack or more per day for at least 4 years). Heavy smokers who were in the high-stress condition took 66% more puffs on cigarettes and smoked 26% more cigarettes than did heavy smokers in the low-stress condition. It seems stress can indeed lead to smoking, especially for long-time smokers.

Combined Models

According to the *multiple regulation model*, the combination of physiological and psychological factors leads to addiction. This model predicts that smoking is initially used to regulate emotions (in line with Tomkins's model), but over time how smokers feel becomes linked with how much nicotine they have in their blood (Leventhal & Cleary, 1980). For example, an individual who is anxious may initially smoke a cigarette to feel more comfortable (the act of holding something in his or her hand, the feeling of fitting in with others, etc.). In this case external stresses (e.g., taking a difficult exam, attending a party) lead to the desire to smoke. Over time, however, the repeated pairing of smoking and reduction in anxiety becomes linked (remember our discussion of classical conditioning in Chapter 3?). At this point, low levels of nicotine in the blood trigger feelings of anxiety (and a craving for cigarettes), even if the person is not in a stressful situation. So, people learn to smoke as a way of reducing the negative feelings that result from a drop in nicotine levels. Because smoking can be used both to reduce arousal (and thereby reduce stress) and create arousal (and thereby increase stimulation), nicotine can easily become paired with positive as well as negative states.

The *biobehavioral model* proposed by Ovide Pomerleau and Cynthia Pomerleau (1989) also suggests that both psychological and physiological factors lead people to continue to smoke over time. This model proposes that nicotine has a number of physiological effects that make people feel good (e.g., improves memory and concentration, reduces anxiety and tension), which leads people to readily become dependent on smoking. Smokers then become dependent (both physically and psychologically) on using nicotine to experience these positive effects. In fact, smokers who are trying to quit often return to smoking precisely because they find it difficult to concentrate and relax without having a cigarette (and, most important, the nicotine that it provides). As described at the beginning of the chapter, Jack found that whenever he tried to stop smoking, he felt anxious and distracted at work, which in turn led him to return to smoking.

What Are Some Strategies for Preventing Smoking?

Because most people who smoke start at an early age, efforts to prevent smoking must target adolescents before they begin smoking; these are primary prevention strategies. Although initial efforts to prevent smoking focused on the negative long-term effects of this behavior (e.g., dying of lung cancer), these approaches were basically unsuccessful for several reasons. First, many teenagers who begin to smoke are already aware of these dangers—but perceive them as not personally relevant, in part because teenagers usually intend to quit before they experience the longer-term consequences. Second, even those who believe they are at risk of various health consequences may perceive the shorter-term benefits of smoking (e.g., looking "mature," feeling relaxed) as more important than the distant, long-term consequences. Emphasizing the long-term consequences of smoking can even backfire by making teenagers think there are no negative short-term effects. More recent smoking prevention programs have therefore focused on providing social influence and/or life skills training (Flay, 1987).

Social influence programs include a number of components designed to make them effective in keeping adolescents away from smoking (Flay, 1987). First, these programs inform teenagers of the immediate physiological and social consequences of smoking, such as the financial cost of smoking, rejection by potential dating partners who don't like the smell of smoke, and having stained teeth and bad breath. In fact, emphasizing minor but short-term consequences is more effective in changing attitudes toward smoking than emphasizing the serious long-term health consequences (Pechmann, 1997)! These programs also appeal to adolescents' desire for independence by pointing out the manipulative nature of cigarette ads. The underlying message is that people who buy cigarettes are giving in to advertising slogans, whereas those who refuse to smoke are independent and self-reliant (very appealing traits to most teenagers). Third, because peers play a major role in the initiation and maintenance of smoking, these programs often emphasize that many adolescents are against smoking. Adolescents tend to overestimate the number of others who are engaging in risky behaviors, and they believe that others have more favorable perceptions of the behaviors and those who engage in them (Graham, Marks, & Hansen, 1991; Marks, Graham, & Hansen, 1992). Finally, social influence programs are typically presented by desirable role models, namely, slightly older students (e.g., high school students leading groups for junior high school students). These peer leaders demonstrate strategies for resisting peer pressure to smoke and allow participants to role-play various situations to practice their responses. For example, students might be asked to show how they would respond if someone said, "Come on, everyone is having a cigarette."

One study with 6th-grade students in Canada revealed that students who received a social influence program were significantly less likely to try cigarettes by the end of 8th grade than those who did not receive such a program (47% versus 60%, respectively; Best et al., 1984). Moreover, this program was even effective in helping students who were already smoking occasionally—at the 2-year follow-up 63% of those who received this program had quit smoking as compared to only 28% of those who did not receive this program. As described at the beginning of this chapter, Annabelle's health-promotion class emphasizing the negative social and short-term physical consequences of smoking led her to form a very negative attitude toward cigarettes.

Life skills training programs are based on the assumption that adolescents who lack self-esteem and self-confidence are at greater risk of smoking (Flay, 1987). These adolescents may turn to smoking both as a way of feeling better about themselves and because they lack the skills necessary to stand up to peer pressure influencing them to smoke. These programs may include some of the same components as social influence programs, such as information about the negative short-term consequences of smoking and the impact of media on smoking, but they also provide adolescents with general assistance in enhancing self-esteem and social competence, techniques for resisting persuasive appeals, and skills for verbal and nonverbal communication. One study by Gil Botvin and his colleagues (1984) demonstrated that 7th-grade students in New York who received 15 sessions of life skills training over 4 to 6 weeks were less likely to report smoking than those who did not receive such training, even as long as 1 year later (10% versus 22%, respectively).

Although psychosocial approaches to prevent smoking may be effective, some programs have had good initial success, which then disappears as time passes (Flay et al., 1989). Moreover, because students as young as 5th grade may have already formed positive attitudes about smokers (possibly based on images in movies or television), smoking prevention programs may need to start even earlier (Dinh et al., 1995). Students in high school are particularly likely to start

---

Questioning the Research 7.1

Can this study really tell us whether social influence programs are effective in reducing teenage smoking? What are some limitations of this research?

smoking, and receiving a program 3 to 4 years earlier seems to have little effect. Effective programs probably need to include "booster" sessions in high school, focus attention on those who have already smoked occasionally and are therefore at high risk, and assess and provide more personal attention based on students' distinct psychological needs. It is also important to offer smoking prevention messages to those who smoke, but who are not yet regular (and addicted) smokers; this is an easier time to intervene than after the habit is firmly entrenched (Ary & Biglan, 1988).

A number of mass media approaches, including television, magazine, and billboard ads, have been used to try to prevent smoking (see Box 7.4). Although some large-scale programs may help prevent smoking by reducing cues for smoking and decreasing the often-prevalent view of smokers as "cool," these approaches are largely ineffective for several reasons (although see Box 7.5; Pechmann, 1997). Television networks, which don't receive money for running public service ads, are likely to run such ads during low-viewing times (e.g., 56% occur late at night). Moreover, research suggests that in order to be effective, viewers must see at least 1 nonsmoking ad for every 4 smoking ads they see. However, the U.S. tobacco industry spends about $7.12 per person in advertising each year (ads in magazines and on buses, highway billboards, event sponsorships, etc.), whereas antismoking campaigns spend well under $0.50 per person. Advertising prompts smoking—one study found that Joe Camel (a now discontinued character featured on a brand of cigarettes) was second only to Mickey Mouse in face recognition among American children (Grunberg et al., 1997). But you could advertise during prime-time hours (4 to 9 P.M.), on television stations teenagers watch (e.g., MTV) and on radio stations they listen to, with a focus on short-term social costs of smoking (see Photo 7.3; Pechmann, 1997).

Finally, large-scale government programs are also used in an attempt to prevent teenage smoking. These programs use a variety of strategies, such as increasing the cost of cigarettes, restricting cigarette advertising, banning smoking in public places, and denying teenagers the opportunity to buy cigarettes. For example, ex-President Bill Clinton initiated several government programs designed to prevent smoking, including increasing the tax on cigarettes, providing Medicaid patients with medication that helps in smoking cessation, and providing money to the Food and Drug Administration to help enforce youth access laws. But these approaches are not generally very successful—teenagers typically have little difficulty buying cigarettes either through vending machines or stores, and even when they are unable to buy cigarettes at some stores, they go to other stores or ask smokers of legal age to buy cigarettes for them. Increasing the cost of cigarettes, however, can be quite effective in decreasing smoking in teenagers, probably because teenagers have relatively little disposable income (Tauras, O'Malley, & Johnston, 2001). In fact, one recent study found that increasing the cost of cigarettes by 10% would lead to a 10% decrease in smoking among teenagers.

What Are Some Strategies for Quitting Smoking?

Although an estimated 30% of the smokers in the United States attempt to quit at least once each year (Fiore et al., 1990), only 19% of these attempts are

PHOTO 7.3   Notice how this ad focuses on one of the short-term consequences of smoking—impotence. This approach is more effective at preventing smoking in teenagers than an approach that focuses on the long-term health consequences.

effective for even a month (Hughes et al., 1992). People who smoke less than a pack a day (e.g., have less nicotine dependence) have fewer smoking friends, have less stress, have higher levels of education and are employed, have self-confidence in their ability, perceive the negative effects of smoking, have intrinsic motivation and are more successful in quitting (Shiffman et al., 1996). Having support from others, including family, friends, and coworkers, is helpful (Cohen & Lichtenstein, 1990b). Women seem to have more trouble quitting than men (see Box 7.5 for one potential explanation for this gender difference; Perkins, 1996). People who are more concerned about gaining weight following smoking cessation are, not surprisingly, less likely to successfully quit: one study found that women who were not concerned about gaining weight had a quit rate of 21% compared to 13.1% for those who were extremely concerned about gaining weight (Jeffery, Hennrikus, Lando, Murray, & Liu, 2000). Quitting smoking is a process—most people who successfully quit have tried to do so on repeated occasions before they are successful.

Because one of the major problems of quitting smoking is the experience of nicotine withdrawal symptoms, many approaches to smoking cessation rely on some type of nicotine replacement (Wetter et al., 1998). Some people use nicotine-fading strategies, such as reducing smoking by switching to low-

Box 7.4

Research Focus—The Influence of Antismoking Ads on Decreasing Rates of Smoking

Brian Flynn and colleagues (1992) were interested in examining whether adding media antismoking ads would increase the effectiveness of school-based smoking prevention programs. To test this hypothesis, researchers selected approximately 2,000 students in grades 5 to 7 in four different communities in Vermont and Montana. All of these students attended at least three special antismoking classes in their schools. Moreover, researchers ran special antismoking ads in two of the community newspapers (one in Vermont, one in Montana) for 5 months initially, and then again for 1 month each year for 3 years. These ads emphasized the short-term costs of smoking, such as smelly breath and clothes, demonstrated how to refuse offers of cigarettes, and emphasized that most teenagers did not smoke. Researchers then measured the rate of smoking in each of the 4 communities over 4 years.

Adding the media components was more effective in preventing teenage smoking than simply providing school-based antismoking education. Although the smoking rates increased over time in all communities as the students got older, those who were in communities that were exposed to the ad campaigns had less smoking than in the communities that received only the school program. For example, 2 years after the intervention 9.3% of students who received only the school-based program smoked as compared to 5% of those who also received media ads (see Figure 7.5). These lower rates of smoking remained as long as 6 years later, indicating that including media antismoking ads can be a very important tool in preventing teenage smoking.

nicotine cigarettes, and then slowly weaning themselves off of nicotine. One study found that 44% of those who gradually reduced the number of cigarettes they smoked were still abstaining 1 year later, as opposed to only 22% of those who quit "cold turkey" (Cinciripni et al., 1995). Others use nicotine-replacement strategies, such as gum and nicotine patches, which are effective in decreasing withdrawal symptoms and helping to achieve short- and long-term success (although see Box 7.6 for a humorous description of a drawback to nicotine gum). For example, one study with 173 people who were attempting to stop smoking found that 33% of highly dependent smokers had stopped smoking even 2 years after participation in group counseling and receiving nicotine gum (Tonnesen et al., 1988). Nicotine-replacement approaches are especially effective if they are used in combination with behavioral therapy (Wetter et al., 1998) and for smokers who are highly dependent on nicotine.

Aversion strategies for smoking cessation are based on principles of classical conditioning—these approaches try to reduce smoking by pairing smoking

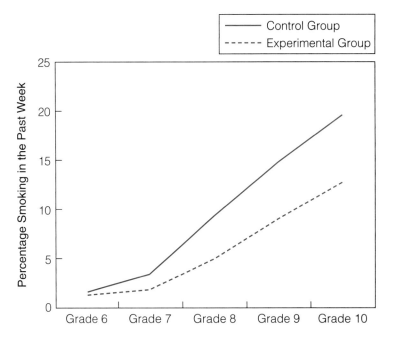

FIGURE 7.5 Although smoking rates increased as children got older, the rates remained significantly lower for those who received the media-based campaign in addition to the school-based campaign even as long as 5 years later (data from Flynn et al., 1992).

with some type of unpleasant stimulus. In the rapid-smoking technique patients smoke rapidly and continuously so as to exceed their tolerance for cigarette smoke and thereby experience an unpleasant sensation (Lichtenstein & Mermelstein, 1984). For example, patients may be told to take a puff every 6 seconds until they literally cannot stand it anymore. Aversion strategies may also work by pairing smoking with unpleasant or upsetting images to create negative connections. For example, people may be told to take a puff of smoke and hold it in their mouths while thinking about vomit or excrement (Kamarck & Lichtenstein, 1985). Other aversive treatments include pairing smoking with electric shocks—every time a smoker takes a drag on the cigarette a slightly painful electric shock is given. A recent review of the effectiveness of various smoking cessation programs indicates that aversive smoking leads to significant increases in smoking cessation rates (Wetter et al., 1998). Aversion strategies are especially effective for smokers who are low on physical dependence on nicotine and for those who smoke for pleasure (Zelman, Brandon, Jorenby, & Baker, 1992). The most effective strategies involve actual smoke (e.g., smoke holding), as opposed to electric shock or imagined scenes.

Self-management strategies focus on identifying those situations that lead people to smoke and then teaching people strategies to resist temptation (see Box 7.7; Lichtenstein & Mermelstein, 1984). In the initial stages, the emphasis is on strengthening the motivation to quit, setting a date to quit, and monitor-

Box 7.5

Focus on Women—Gender Differences in the Effectiveness of Smoking Cessation Treatments

Some recent research suggests that nicotine may be a more important factor in predicting men's smoking, whereas psychological/situational factors (e.g., the smell of cigarettes, the act of holding a cigarette) may be a more important factor in predicting women's smoking (Perkins, 1996). For example, women are less accurate than men in detecting different doses of nicotine and whether a particular substance even is nicotine. This difference in sensitivity to nicotine would help explain why women often have more trouble stopping smoking than men—the often-used nicotine replacement therapies aren't as helpful for people whose smoking is driven by psychological factors. On the other hand, research indicates that women experience much more comfort and relaxation from smoking cigarettes than men, and women are more motivated to smoke by the opportunity to hold cigarettes and "bring them to their mouths." This may also be why women are more influenced than men by smoking advertisements, which promote particular social and cultural images of smoking (e.g., thinness, relaxation). Women may also have more weight issues that lead to continued smoking. The popular image of women who smoke is that they are attractive and thin—it is no accident that one of the best-selling brands for women is Virginia Slims (Grunberg, Winders, & Wewers, 1991). And research indicates that concern about weight can both lead to smoking and make smoking cessation more difficult. What's the good news for women? One recent study found that 21% of women who received cognitive-behavioral therapy for smoking cessation that included information on possible slight weight gains had stopped smoking 1 year later, as compared to only 9% of women who received standard smoking cessation therapy (Perkins et al., 2001).

ing one's smoking patterns. Once people understand the situations that lead them to want to smoke, they can then start to avoid these situations (a technique called *stimulus control*). For example, people are often tempted to smoke when they are with others who are smoking and when they are drinking alcohol (Shiffman et al., 1996). They might therefore make a decision to avoid socializing with other smokers and to avoid drinking alcohol, at least initially. Some stimulus control methods can be very small, such as removing the ashtrays in your home and only going to nonsmoking restaurants. It is impossible to avoid all situations that prompt a cigarette craving, so people also must practice *response substitution*, or choosing another way to handle situations that lead them to want to smoke. A person might go for a walk after dinner instead of smoking or chew gum whenever he or she feels like smoking. Because many smokers crave cigarettes when they are under some type of stress, self-

Box 7.6

The Down Side of Nicotine Gum

Well, here we are at the start of a fresh century, and I am pleased to announce that I recently had my own little victory in the new-beginnings department. After a life-time of cravenly addiction, I quit smoking with the help of Nicorettes, a nicotine-enhanced chewing gum.

Truth be told, the new beginning was my new addiction—to Nicorettes.

The earliest moments of my cigarette-free life were deeply gratifying. As I sat at my desk noisily chomping gum, I believed that my days as a weakling were over. I had simply to follow the step-by-step instructions in the Nicorettes pamphlet, a gradual process that ideally leaves you purged of all nicotine urges within a mere 12 weeks.

That was two years ago. Need I add that I am chewing a Nicorette as I write this?

So much for fresh starts. So much for my formidable self-control.

I must get off Nicorettes.

The idea of recovery is central to our therapeutic culture, but not every weakness can be conquered overnight. Perhaps the best we can ever do is to replace one addiction with another. Or so it seems as I sit at my desk, staring at a sheet of Nicorettes—a swatch of silver foil divided into 12 little squares, each containing a piece of beige gum—and actually talking aloud to it. "I am through with you!" I exclaim defiantly. The next thing I know I'm back at my neighborhood drugstore, replenishing my supply and murmuring to myself: "Oh, so what? If life isn't about enjoying gum, what is it about?"

A few months ago at the drugstore, I was in the checkout line when I noticed and elderly woman in a frayed red coat who was holding a box of Nicorettes. Feeling the instant surge of empathy that fellow addicts do, I asked her it she had just quit smoking. "No," she said with a chuckle, "I quit seven years ago."

Seven years? It was shocking to contemplate, and in my nicotine-stimulated mind I saw myself stooped and gray-haired, traipsing to the drugstore week after week, year after year, a broken woman who had alienated her family, lost the respect of her friends and nullified her achievements, a woman who had sunk her energy, her spirit and her money into the support of an ignominious addiction. My habit now runs about $9 a day for 24 pieces of gum, more than cigarettes ever cost me.

Perhaps you find me melodramatic. Gum, after all, might seem innocuous compared with the notorious evils of cigarettes; and it's true that Nicorettes offer genuine advantages over cancer sticks. For instance, Nicorettes do not burn holes in your terry-cloth bathrode. Better yet, they do not encourage strangers in bars to start conversations with you. No one has ever bummed a Nicorette from me.

(continues)

Still, who would deny that Nicorettes have unsavory features all their own? Chewing gum is an unattractive habit, and unless you are under the age of 16 you cannot do it with any real style or elegance. Did Bette Davis chomp gum in "All About Eve"? Of course not. The sound alone is right up there with car-theft sirens on the list of audibly irritating phenomena. Last summer, I was on the phone trying to purchase a plane ticket to London when the ticket agent suddenly shouted, "I can't stand the sound of your gum," and slammed down the receiver. It was one of countless small humiliations in my gum-besotted life.

Nicorettes also pose home-décor problems. In an effort to cut back on my nicotine intake, I often save a chewed piece of gum with the intention of using it later, but invariably I forget about it. As a result, I can't pick up a book in my house without finding a wad of gum stuck to the cover.

Naturally, I have sought help in ridding myself of my habit, but to little avail. I once called the 800 consumer-health number for SmithKline Beecham, the manufacturer of Nicorettes. A taped voice informed me that anyone who swallows more that the normal dosage should get assistance by calling "your local poison-control center." How reassuring. A few seconds later, an actual human being answered the phone, and when I asked her if Nicorettes are addictive, she said: "They can be habit-forming. We recommend weaning."

Every so often I scan the shelves in my local bookstore hoping to find a self-help book for the gum-addicted and afflicted. One good thing about living in America is that there is no neurosis too insignificant to merit its own paperback. Or so I thought. Amazingly enough, there are no books currently in print for women who love Nicorettes too much and can't stop chewing them.

Maybe I should write one. Or a whole series. I could turn Nicorettes self-help books into my next addiction.

Source: Solomon, Deborah. (2000, January 23). Chain chewer. *New York Times Magazine*, p. 82.

management approaches may also include training in stress management, relaxation, and coping skills (Wetter et al., 1998). As described at the beginning of the chapter, Diana worked with a therapist to identify factors that led her to want a cigarette, and then she tried to avoid these situations or alternatively to cope with them in a new way. Finally, *contingency-contracting approaches* can be used to give smokers additional motivation to stop. In this technique smokers give some money to a friend (or therapist), with the understanding that if they are not smoking 6 months later, they get the money back. This technique therefore uses the promise of a reward to encourage smoking cessation (an operant-conditioning approach).

Given the widespread problem of smoking, a variety of relatively large-scale plans to decrease smoking have been attempted. One approach is to ban smoking in particular situations, such as in the workplace, in school, and on airplanes. Although these types of programs certainly help prevent the problems associated with passive smoking, smokers can just smoke more in other places to compensate (see Photo 7.4). For example, one study of the effects of a

Box 7.7

Research Focus—"I Would Quit If I Knew How"

Victor Stevens and Jack Hollis (1989) conducted a study to examine the effectiveness of a skills-training program on smoking cessation. Seven hundred forty-four smokers interested in quitting attended an intensive series of 2-hour meetings over 4 days. These meetings provided training in a variety of quitting strategies, such as chewing gum instead of smoking, using deep-breathing methods to cope with stress, and cognitive restructuring. Participants were then randomly assigned to one of three follow-up conditions: a skills condition, a discussion condition, or a no-treatment control condition. People in the skills condition identified "high-risk" situations (that is, those that could prompt a desire to smoke), discussed strategies for coping with these situations, and then rehearsed their response to these situations until they felt confident using them. In contrast, people in the discussion condition simply described their experiences related to smoking in the past week and discussed the benefits and problems they were having in quitting. Both the skills and discussion conditions met three times over the next month for 2 hours each time. Participants in the no-treatment condition did not receive additional follow-up meetings. Researchers then contacted participants each month for 1 year in order to measure whether they were smoking, and if so, how many cigarettes. Finally, at the 1-year follow-up researchers collected a saliva sample from each subject to measure whether nicotine was present in their bodies.

People who attended the skills-training follow-up sessions were significantly more likely to not be smoking than those in either of the other two groups at the 1-year follow-up. Specifically, 41.3% of those in the skills condition were not smoking at the 1-year follow-up as compared to 34.1% of those in the discussion condition and 33.3% of those who received no follow-up. This finding suggests that simply providing social support for smoking cessation is not enough—people also need ongoing training in specific coping strategies in order to maintain their new behavior over time.

workplace ban on smoking found that although there was an initial decrease of levels of nicotine in the bloodstream of smoking employees 1 week after the ban was enacted, 6 weeks later nicotine levels were nearly back to baseline levels (Gomel, Oldenburg, Lemon, Owen, & Westbrook, 1993). However, there is some evidence that providing smoking cessation programs at work can be at least somewhat effective (Lichtenstein & Glasgow, 1992). Some efforts have been made to reach large groups of individuals in a given community by providing media information (e.g., through radio, television, newspapers) as well as extensive individual education on quitting smoking (Farquhar et al., 1990).

Box 7.8

Information You Can Use: What Can You Do to Help Someone Stop Smoking?

Let's say your mother or boyfriend or sister smokes, and you'd like to help him or her quit. What types of things should you do to try to help them? Most research suggests that giving positive support, such as congratulating them on their decision to quit, celebrating their quitting attempt, and expressing confidence in their ability to quit, can be quite effective (Cohen & Lichtenstein, 1990b). Direct assistance such as doing an activity (e.g., walking) that prevents them for smoking and helping them relieve stress in other ways can be especially helpful. So, if your friend always smokes when he or she is nervous about exams, you could suggest going for a run or watching a movie together as an alternative method of relaxation. On the other hand, negative strategies, such as criticizing smoking and pressuring the person to quit, are less constructive and can even backfire. People need to feel that they have made their own decision to quit (not that they were forced to quit by someone else), or they may return to smoking in part as a way of demonstrating their freedom to make that choice. Similarly, strategies such as commenting on their lack of willpower and expressing doubt in their ability to quit, can be quite detrimental. Virtually all former smokers will at times experience intense cravings for cigarettes, and during these times they need to feel confident that they can successfully overcome their desire to smoke.

PHOTO 7.4   Although workplace smoking bans do decrease smoking in the office, smokers often just choose to smoke in other places to compensate.

In the Stanford Five City Project, for example, cities with this type of intensive education showed a 13% reduction in smoking over 2 to 5 years compared to rates in similar cities without such instruction.

Alcohol Use

Who Drinks?

Most adults drink alcohol at least occasionally—about 52% of Americans ages 12 and over report having had at least one drink in the past 30 days (Centers for Disease Control, 2003). Rates of alcohol use also vary as a function of gender, ethnicity, and education. As you might guess, men are more likely than women to drink (69% versus 56%, respectively), binge drink (30% versus 12%, respectively), and binge drink at least 12 times in the past year (15% versus 4%, respectively). How is ethnicity associated with alcohol use? Drinking is more common among European Americans than Hispanic Americans, African Americans, and Asian Americans (see Figure 7.6). Interestingly, although smoking is more common among people with lower levels of education, the reverse is true in terms of alcohol use. More than two-thirds of college graduates drink

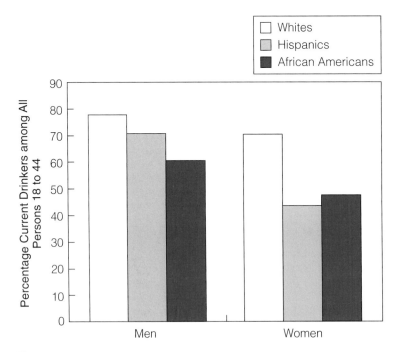

FIGURE 7.6 As this graph shows, more men tend to drink alcohol than women, and whites drink more than Hispanics and African Americans (Centers for Disease Control, 2003).

alcohol on a regular basis, as compared to only 38% of those with less than a high school education. And even though alcohol use is illegal for those under age 21, large-scale national surveys reveal that 79% of high school seniors have tried alcohol, 51% have had a drink in the past month, and 33% have had five or more drinks of alcohol on at least one occasion in the past month (Centers for Disease Control, 2003). It's not just kids in large cities who drink—both alcohol use and binge drinking are actually more common in high school seniors who live in rural areas as opposed to urban ones (Cronk & Sarvela, 1997).

What Is Problem Drinking?

Although most people who try alcohol or drink occasionally never develop problems with alcohol abuse, about 20% engage in binge drinking (having five or more drinks on the same occasion at least once in the past year), and 9% are heavy drinkers (having five or more drinks on the same occasion on at least 12 different days in the past year; Centers for Disease Control, 2001). See Tables 7.1 and 7.2. As you might expect, binge drinking and heavy drinking are much more common among young people than among older adults—32% of people ages 18 to 24 years who drink are binge drinkers and 15% are heavy drinkers (see Figure 7.7). This type of alcohol abuse is also much more common in men than women. For example, 41% of men ages 18 to 24 years who drink are binge drinkers and 23% are heavy drinkers, whereas only 23% of women in that age category are binge drinkers and only 8% are heavy drinkers.

People who have a problem with alcohol drink heavily on a regular basis, are psychologically dependent on alcohol, experience loss of memory while drinking, and suffer social and occupational impairments from their drinking (Mayer, 1983). They may drink often, drink alone frequently, drink during the day (including when going to work), and drive under the influence. Of those who are problem drinkers, about half are alcoholics (Davidson, 1985). *Alcoholism* is defined as alcohol consumption that is compulsive and uncontrollable, physically addictive, or habitual and that results in serious threats to a person's health and well-being. Alcoholics have a very high tolerance for alcohol, suffer blackouts or memory losses, and experience withdrawal symptoms such as delirium tremens (hallucinations, impaired motor coordination, cognitive disruption) when they stop drinking. Thus, alcoholism involves both psychological and physical dependence, whereas problem drinking involves only psychological dependence.

What Are the Health Consequences of Alcohol Abuse?

Alcohol use has a number of negative health consequences. The most well known is liver damage caused when fat accumulates in the liver and blocks blood flow, which can eventually lead to cirrhosis, a buildup of scar tissue in the liver (Eckhardt et al., 1981). Alcohol abuse can also have negative effects on the brain and on neuropsychological functioning (Delin & Lee, 1992). About 10% of alcoholics are affected by Wernicke-Korsakoff syndrome; symptoms

TABLE 7.1 *How to Calculate Your Estimated Blood-Alcohol Content*

Body Weight	1	2	3	4	5	6	7	8	9	10	11	12
100 lb.	.038	.075	.113	.150	.188	.225	.263	.300	.338	.375	.413	.450
110 lb.	.034	.066	.103	.137	.172	.207	.241	.275	.309	.344	.379	.412
120 lb.	.031	.063	.094	.125	.156	.188	.219	.250	.281	.313	.344	.375
130 lb.	.029	.058	.087	.116	.145	.174	.203	.232	.261	.290	.320	.348
140 lb.	.027	.054	.080	.107	.134	.161	.188	.214	.241	.268	.295	.321
150 lb.	.025	.050	.075	.100	.125	.151	.176	.201	.226	.261	.276	.301
160 lb.	.023	.047	.070	.094	.117	.141	.164	.188	.211	.234	.258	.281
170 lb.	.022	.045	.066	.088	.110	.132	.155	.178	.200	.221	.244	.265
180 lb.	.021	.042	.063	.083	.104	.125	.146	.167	.188	.208	.228	.250
190 lb.	.020	.040	.059	.079	.099	.119	.138	.158	.179	.198	.217	.237
200 lb.	.019	.038	.056	.075	.094	.113	.131	.150	.169	.188	.206	.225
210 lb.	.018	.036	.053	.071	.090	.107	.125	.143	.161	.179	.197	.215
220 lb.	.017	.034	.051	.068	.085	.102	.119	.136	.153	.170	.188	.205
230 lb.	.016	.032	.049	.065	.081	.098	.115	.130	.147	.163	.180	.196
240 lb.	.016	.031	.047	.063	.078	.094	.109	.125	.141	.156	.172	.188

How to calculate your estimated blood-alcohol content (BAC):

Showing estimated percentage of alcohol in the blood by number of drinks in relation to body weight. This percentage can be estimated by doing the following:

1. Count your drinks (1 drink *equals* 1 ounce of 100-proof liquor, one 5-ounce glass of table wine, or one 12-ounce bottle of regular beer).
2. Use the chart to find the number of drinks opposite body weight, then find the percentage of blood alcohol listed.
3. Subtract from this number the percentage of alcohol "burned up" during the time elapsed since your first drink. This figure is 0.015% per hour. (Example: 180-lb. man has 8 drinks in 4 hours equals 0.167% minus (0.015 × 4) = 0.107%.

Source: Created from NHTSA chart, with modifications.

include severe memory problems, disorientation, and drowsiness (Parsons, 1977). Heavy drinking can also lead to the development of some types of cancer, including cancer of the liver, esophagus, or larynx (Levy, 1985). Excessive alcohol use by pregnant women has a number of negative effects on the growing fetus (Larroque et al., 1995). Fetal alcohol syndrome, which is caused by insufficient protein in the mother's diet, can be caused by excessive drinking during pregnancy and may result in significant problems for the fetus, including mental retardation, growth problems, and nervous system problems.

Alcohol use can also lead indirectly to a number of other health problems (see Figure 7.8). First, alcohol use reduces the association between attitudes and behavior, so people are more likely to engage in behaviors that are not in

TABLE 7.2   *Test Yourself: Are You a Problem Drinker?*

Answer yes or no to the following questions.

1. Have you found that the same amount of alcohol had less effect than before?
2. Have you found that you had to drink more than you once did to get the same effect?
3. Have you been sick or vomited after drinking?
4. Have you felt depressed, irritable, or nervous after drinking?
5. Have you found yourself sweating heavily or shaking after drinking?
6. Have you heard or seen things that weren't really there after drinking?
7. Have you taken a drink to keep yourself from shaking or feeling sick?
8. Have you ended up drinking much more than you intended to?
9. Have you found it difficult to stop drinking once you started?
10. Have you kept drinking for a longer period of time than you intended to?
11. Have you tried to cut down or stop drinking and found you couldn't do it?
12. Have you wanted to cut down or stop your drinking and found you couldn't do it?
13. Have you continued to drink even though it was a threat to your health?
14. Have you kept on drinking even though it caused you emotional problems?
15. Have you been arrested or had trouble with the police because of your drinking?
16. Have you kept drinking even though it caused you problems at home, school, or work?
17. Did a spouse or someone you lived with threaten to leave you because of your drinking?
18. Have you driven a car after having too much to drink?
19. Have you done things when drinking that could have caused you to be hurt?
20. Have you done things when drinking that could have caused someone else to be hurt?

Give yourself a point for every yes answer. What is your score? Higher scores indicate more problems with alcohol use.

Source: Dawson, Grant, &, Harford, 1995.

line with their actual beliefs (Steele & Josephs, 1990). Sometimes such uninhibited behavior might simply make you feel silly—imagine dancing on a table wearing a lamp shade, for example. But alcohol use can also lead to behavior that has more dangerous consequences, including unsafe sex, drunk driving, and accidents (see Boxes 7.9 and 7.10; Gordon, Carey, & Carey, 1997; MacDonald, MacDonald, Zanna, & Fong, 2000). As described at the beginning of the chapter, Jenny's alcohol abuse led her to repeatedly drive under the influence of alcohol and to engage in sexual activity with assorted random partners—two highly risky behaviors. Drunk-driving accidents cause about nearly half of the automobile accidents each year—about 20,000 deaths each year—and alcohol is associated with 30% of suicides and 50% of homicides (see Photo 7.5). Alcoholics have higher rates of automobile accidents, partial drownings, electrical shocks, and communicable diseases than do nonalcoholics (Glenn, Parsons, & Stevens, 1989). Alcohol use even increases the likelihood of death while bicycling and swimming. During my first year of college, my Friday afternoon sailing class was canceled so that a dive team could search the small pond for the body of a student who had last been seen walking home (drunk) from a fraternity party the night before; the student's body was recovered from the pond that afternoon.

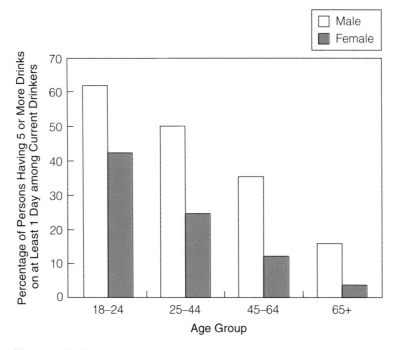

FIGURE 7.7 Binge drinking is most common in people ages 18 to 24 years, and decreases steadily with age (Centers for Disease Control, 2003).

One reason people who are drunk do such stupid things is that alcohol use impairs judgment, so people aren't able to think rationally as they could when sober. For example, a study by Shelia Murphy and her colleagues (1998) demonstrated that women who were drunk saw attractive but promiscuous men as much higher in "relationship potential" than did women who were sober. So, a sober woman might recognize that an attractive man who reports consistent sexual promiscuity is probably not interested in having a long-term relationship, but a drunk woman might misjudge the situation. Another reason for alcohol's impact on behavior is that drinking leads to what Steele and Josephs (1990) refer to as *drunken invincibility*, a feeling that a person is invulnerable to the dangers he or she might normally experience. This is why people who know that driving while intoxicated is not a good idea, may believe they are able to drive "even better" when drunk. One study by William Hansen and colleagues (1991) demonstrated that heavy drinkers view the potential negative consequences of drinking, such as being arrested for driving under the influence and doing embarrassing things, as much less serious than do light drinkers. People who are drunk are also less effective at negotiating condom use and are more likely to consent to unprotected sex (Gordon et al., 1997).

Although we've focused thus far on all the negative consequences of alcohol abuse, there is growing evidence that alcohol use in moderation can actually have some benefits. Several studies have shown that the link between alcohol use and health is a U-shaped curve—people who drink light to mod-

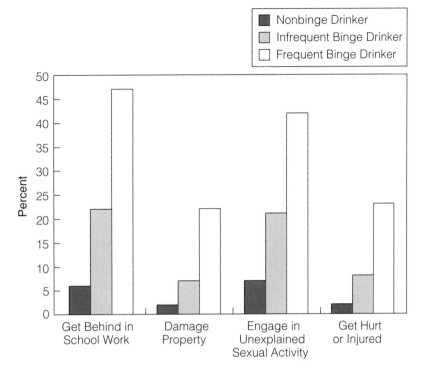

FIGURE 7.8 One study by Harry Wechsler and his colleagues at the Harvard School of Public Health demonstrated the consequences of "binge drinking" in a sample of nearly 30,000 college students (Wechsler, Davenport, Dowdall, Moeykens, & Castillo, 1994).

PHOTO 7.5 Drunk-driving accidents cause nearly half of all automobile accidents each year.

Box 7.9

Students Are Dying: Colleges Can Do More

Drunk driving isn't a new problem, but it continues to ravage our campuses. I know we can change that.

Unfortunately, I am an expert on drinking and driving. As a high-school freshman in Wayland, Mass., I suffered through the death of a classmate on my hockey team who was killed in an alcohol-related crash. Two years later I attended the funeral of another classmate who died while driving under the influence. Twelve months after that a wrestling teammate returning to Wayland from a college break totaled his car in a drunk-driving accident, partially paralyzing himself and causing permanent brain damage. His father, a town firefighter responding to a 911 call, was the one to find him on the roadside near death.

After all that, I thought I knew the worst about drunk driving. I was wrong. Three years ago my brother, Ryan, a Middlebury College senior, drove 70-100 miles an hour on a rainy rural road into a tree, ending his life. His blood-alcohol level was nearly three times the legal limit. Witnesses later recounted that he was swerving and speeding on a nearby road.

It was one of the worst accidents that officers at the crash site had ever seen. The two policemen assigned to wipe Ryan's blood and tissue off the car's broken windshield found it impossible even to talk to us about the details of what they found. According to the police report, before officers could transport Ryan to the funeral home, they had to remove a small branch that pierced his permanently flattened lips.

Ryan was last seen drinking on campus at a fraternity house that was serving vodka punch. He left the party intending to drive to his off-campus apartment three miles away to pick up a toga for yet another event. He never made it home. After his death, we found out that Ryan had developed a drinking problem while away at college. But even though he drank to excess at nearly every social function, usually three to four times a week, many of his friends never realized he was on his way to becoming an alcoholic.

It turns out that one of the staff members in the student-activities office where Ryan often came to register his fraternity's parties had suspected that he had a drinking problem. And Ryan isn't the only Middlebury student to be involved in a dangerous alcohol-related incident: in the year before his death one of Ryan's fellow students nearly died in a binge-drinking incident, saved only because the hospital pumped her stomach as she lay unconscious. Her blood-alcohol level was .425 percent.

(continues)

What should we do about the Ryans of the world? I know that my brother was ultimately responsible for his own death, but in my view, college administrators can work harder to keep kids like Ryan from getting behind the wheel.

But many schools have been reluctant to address the problem. Why? Perhaps because taking responsibility for drinking and driving will make trustees and college presidents legally liable for college students' drunk-driving behavior. If administrators accepted this responsibility, they might ask themselves the following questions: Should we expel students who receive a D.U.I.? Has the president of our university met with the mayor to create a unified policy toward drunk driving within our town? Have we contacted organizations like M.A.D.D. and S.A.D.D. to help us implement alcohol- and driving-education programs?

On campuses like Middlebury's, where many students own cars, administrators can use more aggressive methods to combat drinking and driving. Yet after Ryan's death his university ignored my family's request to fund a Middlebury town officer to patrol the main entry into campus for out-of-control drivers on weekend evenings. This, despite the fact that the Middlebury College director of health services informed me and my family that approximately 15 percent of the school's freshmen were so intoxicated at some point during the last year that a classmate had to bring them to the infirmary.

Why does the problem of drunk driving persist? It's not easy to solve. College students are young and irresponsible, and drinking is part of their culture. Administrators have not wanted to abolish social houses and fraternities for fear that ending such beloved college traditions would lower alumni donations.

To college presidents, trustees and all college officials, I ask that you go home tonight and consider your love for your own son or daughter, your own brother or sister. Imagine the knock on your door at 3 a.m. when a uniformed police officer announces that your loved one has died. Then go to a mirror and look deep into your own eyes. Ask yourself the question: have I done enough to help solve this problem?

The choice is simple. You can choose to be a leader and an agent of change on a controversial issue. Or you can continue the annual practice of authoring one of your student's eulogies. My family, in its grief, begs you to do the former.

Source: Waldron, Rob. (2003, October 30). Students are dying; colleges can do more. *Newsweek*, p. 16.

erate amounts of alcohol have better health than those who drink heavily (not surprising) and those who do not drink at all (very surprising). For example, one study followed over 2,000 people over a 10-year period and divided participants into four groups based on their drinking habits—nondrinkers, light drinkers (two or fewer drinks per day), moderate drinkers (three to five drinks per day), and heavy drinkers (six or more drinks per day; Klatsky, Friedman, & Sigelaub, 1981). Nondrinkers and moderate drinkers had a similar death rate; heavy drinkers had the highest death rate, and light drinkers had the lowest

Box 7.10

Research Focus—Why Drunk People Don't Use Condoms

Tara MacDonald and her colleagues at the University of Waterloo conducted a study on a topic that is very near and dear to the hearts (well, maybe not exactly the hearts) of many college students—the effects of alcohol use on intentions to use condoms (MacDonald et al., 1995). Fifty-four male undergraduates were randomly assigned to either the sober or the intoxicated condition. Those in both conditions watched a video and then answered some questions, but those in the intoxicated condition were first given three alcoholic drinks. (For those of you who are suddenly very interested in participating in psychology research, let me assure you that this study was conducted in Ontario, Canada, where the drinking age is 19.) The 10-minute video featured a couple of undergraduates, Mike and Rebecca, who meet at a campus bar, dance and drink with friends, and then walk home to Rebecca's apartment. Mike and Rebecca then begin "hooking up," at which point they discuss the fact that neither of them has condoms, and the only store close by has closed for the night. Rebecca discloses that she is on the Pill, so pregnancy prevention is not the issue. At this point the video stops, and students are then asked to answer a series of questions as if they were experiencing the situations in the video.

The findings of this study provide strong (and scary) evidence for how alcohol impairs decision making. First, both sober and intoxicated students viewed having unprotected sex in this situation as foolish. On a scale of 1 to 9, sober students rated this behavior as extremely foolish (8.08) as did intoxicated students (7.67). Similarly, sober students rated this behavior as extremely irresponsible (8.04) as did intoxicated students (7.83). However, while sober participants were fairly unlikely to report that they would engage in sex in this situation (3.83), drunk students were very likely to report that they would indeed have sex in this situation (6.78). In fact, only 21% of the sober participants reported that they were even fairly likely to have sex in this situation, whereas 77% of the drunk participants did so. Although this study does not obviously test what students would actually do in a similar situation, it certainly suggests that alcohol use may lead people to engage in behavior that they recognize as foolish and irresponsible.

death rate (nearly half the rate of the heavy drinkers). Similarly, one study of female nurses found that those who consumed a moderate number of drinks had a lower risk of death than those who consumed no alcohol or those who consumed higher rates of alcohol (Fuchs et al., 1995). One reason drinking moderate amounts of alcohol may be beneficial is that alcohol increases the rate of high-density lipoprotein cholesterol (HDLC), which in turn helps protect people from heart disease (Gaziano et al., 1993; Linn et al., 1993). Other research suggests that moderate alcohol use can lead to other benefits, including increased bone density (Felson, Zhang, Hannan, Kannel, & Kiel, 1995), protection from heart attacks and blood clots (Ridker, Vaughan, Stampfer, Glynn, & Hennekens, 1994), and lower rates of depression (Lipton, 1994).

How Do Psychological Factors Lead to Alcohol Abuse?

Many researchers believe that people learn to abuse alcohol the same way that they learn other behaviors, by reinforcement and modeling (Maisto, Carey, & Bradizza, 1999). This section describes several psychological theories of drinking and alcoholism.

Tension-Reduction Theory

According to tension-reduction theory, people drink alcohol to cope with or regulate negative moods, including feelings of tension, anxiety, and nervousness (Cooper, Russell, Skinner, Frone, & Mudar, 1992; Greely & Oei, 1999; Swendsen et al., 2000). In other words, a person feeling nervous or anxious may reduce the unpleasant tension by drinking alcohol, the moderation of negative affect then reinforces his or her drinking behavior. In line with this theory, rats who are exposed to social stressors (e.g., forced isolation) increase their consumption of alcohol (Roske, Baeger, Frenzel, & Oehme, 1994). Similarly, a recent study by Margaret Carney and colleagues (2000) found that people who experienced more negative interpersonal events, such as conflicts with family and friends, reported more frequent alcohol use. Although this study was correlational (and therefore can't tell us whether these negative events lead to drinking), experimental research reveals similar results. For example, Claude Steele and Robert Josephs (1988) found that, compared to those who were sober, students who performed a distracting task and were intoxicated had significantly less anxiety about an upcoming stressful speech they would supposedly deliver on "what I don't like about my body" than those who were not intoxicated.

Although tension-reduction theory was one of the first theories describing the link between psychological factors and alcohol use, overall research provides only mixed support for its usefulness in predicting drinking (Greeley & Oei, 1999). First, most evidence suggests that some people do indeed consume alcohol to reduce tension, but many others do not. This reliance on alcohol to cope with negative events is particularly likely for men and for those who have fewer other coping skills (Cooper et al., 1992). This theory also ignores the often powerful role of people's expectations about the consequences of alcohol use, which, at least in some cases, may have a greater impact on behavior than actual alcohol use. For example, people who think they are drinking alcohol show a greater loss of control, regardless of whether they are truly drinking alcohol (see Figure 7.9; Lang, Goeckner, Adesso, & Marlatt, 1975). Finally, this theory focuses only on the use of alcohol to cope with negative events (e.g., tension, stress) and thereby fails to explain the use of alcohol to celebrate positive events; people

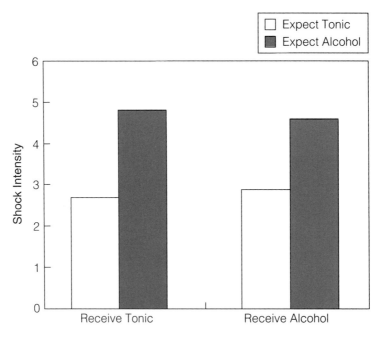

FIGURE 7.9 Participants in this study were told they were given alcohol or tonic water, and in some cases received what they expected but in other cases received the reverse. They were then given the opportunity to shock another person. As you can see in the figure, the expectation that they received alcohol regardless of its accuracy, led to significantly higher shocks than the expectation they received tonic water (data from Lang et al., 1975).

often report drinking to enhance or intensify positive emotions as well as drinking more on days with positive interpersonal events, such as being complimented and feeling cared for (Carney et al., 2000; Mohr et al., 2001).

Social Learning Theory

According to Bandura's social learning theory (1969), children learn the norms for alcohol use by watching others, including their parents, siblings, peers, and media figures (Maisto et al., 1999). Children are likely to see people relaxing with a cocktail after a long day at the office, celebrating with a champagne toast at a wedding or graduation, and drinking beer while socializing at a party. Even if children don't directly observe these models for alcohol use in their daily lives, television and movies provide numerous examples of the link between fun and drinking (Goldstein et al., 1999; Grube & Wallach, 1994). Alcohol advertisements typically show young, attractive people drinking in appealing settings (at parties, on the beach, etc.) and having a very good time—ads don't show senior citizens drinking while they play shuffleboard. One study with 5th and 6th graders found that kids who had more awareness of television beer advertisements (e.g., could identify the type of beer advertised even when its name was blocked) had more favorable beliefs about the consequences of drinking and higher intentions to drink as an adult (Grube & Wallach, 1994). Alcohol use is frequently portrayed even in films marketed to children, including G-rated animated films such as *Pinocchio*, *Pocahontas*, and *Beauty and the Beast* (Goldstein et al., 1999).

Watching people drink also creates norms that alcohol use is appropriate and desirable. People drink more when they are part of a group than when alone, especially when they are with people who are drinking heavily (Maisto et al., 1999). They also drink more when they have friends who drink heavily. One longitudinal study with adolescents ages 10 to 15 years old revealed that friends' drinking behavior was a strong predictor of individuals' own future alcohol use, with adolescents who reported higher alcohol use in their friends showing particularly steep increases in their own alcohol use (Curran, Stice, & Chassin, 1997). Interestingly, the mere belief that other people are drinking heavily can lead people to drink more—even if this belief is wrong (see Photo 7.6). A series of studies at Princeton University by Deborah Prentice and Dale Miller (1993) demonstrated that college students often believe that there is too much alcohol use on campus but believe other students like the amount of alcohol use. Moreover, the mere perception of a "heavy drinking norm" can lead students to have more positive attitudes about alcohol and even to drink more (see Box 7.11; Baer & Carney, 1993; Baer, Stacy & Larimer, 1991; Marks et al., 1992).

Social learning theory also describes the role played by people's expectations about the consequences of alcohol use, which often develop even before the onset of drinking, in leading to alcohol use (Cooper, Frone, Russell, &

PHOTO 7.6 College students' alcohol use is often influenced by how much they think other students are drinking.

Box 7.11

Drinking to Belong

No one wanted me when I was an undergraduate at Princeton. Ivy Club didn't want me. Cap and Gown didn't want me. Tiger Inn didn't want me, either. These were a few of Princeton's eating clubs, the university's genteel equivalent of fraternities and sororities, and not to be wanted by them was a miserable, humiliating experience.

Still missing home but too proud to say so, barely 18, too studious by half, and the son of a Princeton alumnus who had belonged to the rip-roaringest club of his day, I would have done almost anything then to win the clubs' attention and approval. I recalled this need when I read about the deaths of two college freshmen, at the Massachsetts Institute of Technology, and Louisiana State University, who drank themselves to death during fraternity pledge week.

On Monday, 18-year-old Scott Kreuger died after attending an M.I.T. fraternity party at which freshmen were supposedly required to collectively consume a certain amount of liquor. It has been reported that he didn't even like to drink, and I have no trouble believing that. No one can know his state of mind. But I know from my college friends' experience that the strange thing about drinking oneself into unconciousness while fraternity brothers are standing by offering support and shot glasses is that most people are not drinking to get drunk. They think they are doing something more meaningful: vowing their loyalty to new friends, winning the respect of others, building a zany memory they'll later cherish.

Fraternities and selective social clubs exploit students' desperate hunger to fit in. The problem isn't only the drinking these clubs encourage, but also the pressurized social climate they serve the drinks in.

I remember how it was at Princeton, a lofty academic preserve where it wasn't uncommon on weekend nights to spot a few dozen ashen Wunderkinds vomiting into the bushes, and where everyone talked about trees and trolls, some drunken wrestling match I never experienced because, thank goodness, no club wanted me.

How miserable it all was. How sad and stupid. To get into Princeton, the first school in my life where I didn't feel like a nerd for loving books, and find out that silly cliques still topped the social pyramid. Am I surprised by studies showing that fraternity members consume more alcohol than other students and are more likely to take part in binge drinking? Get real. What surprises me is that a study was needed to prove this.

Simply banning alcohol from college campuses isn't the way to prevent more tragedies. Scott Kreuger was legally too young to drink anywhere in Massachusetts, but did that protect him? Did it stop his friends?

(continues)

> What's more, his drinking took place at an off-campus fraternity, out of the practical reach of any ban. And even if such a rule could be enforced, it's a fair bet that new initiation rituals, just as perilous, just as sadistic, would take the place of assisted heavy drinking.
>
> The answer, I think, is for colleges and universities to do away with the selective campus fraternities and sororities that have bullied, insulted and hazed their students for generations. It's not the clubs' liquor licenses, but their status, their promise of social elevation, their ability to prey on the insecurities of young adults that need to be revoked, and then, if possible, filled by other, less destructive means. Ever heard of a chess-club hazing?
>
> *Source:* Kirn, Walter. (October 3, 1997). Drinking to belong. *New York Times*, p. A15.

Mudar, 1995; Goldman, Del Boca, & Darkes, 1999; Maisto et al., 1999). In fact, children as young as preschool and elementary school have expectations about the effects of alcohol, based on parental modeling as well as the portrayal of alcohol use in the media. Although these expectations are initially negative (e.g., they see alcohol as having unpleasant consequences), they get increasingly positive as children mature. As shown in Table 7.3, these expectations include the belief that alcohol use enhances social situations and interpersonal encounters in various ways, including increasing social expressiveness (e.g., "makes me more friendly") as well as "sexual prowess" (see Photo 7.7; Goldman et al., 1999). As described at the beginning of the chapter, Biff sees himself as funnier and more relaxed when he is drinking, and he therefore finds it hard to stop drinking even though it is having a negative impact on his academic performance. Most important, people who have more positive expectations about alcohol are more likely to drink (Sher et al., 1996; Smith, Goldman, Greenbaum, & Christiansen, 1995; Stacy, Newcomb, & Bentler, 1991). For example, teenagers' expectations about the social benefits of alcohol use predicted their frequency of drinking 1 year later (Smith et al., 1995).

Cognitive Theory

According to cognitive theory, alcohol's effect on psychological states and interpersonal interactions is caused at least in part by the physiological effects of alcohol (Sayette, 1999). First, by impairing information processing, alcohol use reduces self-awareness and in turn reduces anxiety for cases in which such awareness would reveal negative self-relevant information. For example, Jay Hull and Richard Young (1983) gave college students either negative or positive feedback about their IQ and then asked them to taste and rate different kinds of wine. As predicted, students who were told they had low IQ scores drank more wine, presumably in an attempt to reduce self-awareness, than those who received positive feedback. Because alcohol use frees people from the normal inhibitions that may guide their words and actions, drinking may lead people to engage in more extreme or excessive behavior (Bailey, Leonard, Cranston, &

TABLE 7.3   *Motives for Alcohol Use*

As a way to celebrate

Because it is what most of your friends do when you get together

To be sociable

Because it is customary on special occasions

Because it makes a social gathering more enjoyable

To relax

To forget your worries

Because you feel more self-confident or sure of yourself

Because it helps when you feel depressed or nervous

To cheer up when you're in a bad mood

Because you like the feeling

Because it's exciting

To get high

Because it's fun

Because it makes you feel good

The first five items describe social motives, the next five items describe coping motives, and the last five items describe enhancement motives. If you drink, why do you do it?

Source: Cooper et al., 1992.

PHOTO 7.7   Alcohol is often used to enhance celebrations.

Taylor, 1983; Steele & Josephs, 1990). For example, alcohol use often increases antisocial or aggressive behavior (Bailey et al., 1983; Leonard, 1989).

The most influential cognitive theory about alcohol use is that of *alcohol myopia*, the state in which individuals under the influence of alcohol make decisions based on salient short-term concerns while ignoring longer-term consequences of their behavior (Steele & Josephs, 1990). In other words, people who are intoxicated may "see the tree, albeit more dimly, but miss the forest altogether" (Steele & Josephs, 1990, p. 923). This state occurs because individuals are unable to engage in the complex cognitive processing required to consider the more distant consequences, and instead they base decisions primarily on the most salient and immediate cues. For example, people who are sober may recognize that engaging in unprotected sex could have substantial long-term consequences (e.g., unintended pregnancy, transmission of STD/AIDS) and therefore refuse to have sex without a condom, whereas those who are intoxicated may act based entirely on the immediate situation (e.g., their desire to engage in sex) and may ignore the more distant consequences of this decision (MacDonald, Zanna, & Fong, 1995). Alcohol myopia theory also describes the effects of alcohol on a person's self-evaluation. Specifically, people who are intoxicated often experience "drunken self-inflation," meaning that people who are drinking see themselves in an idealized way (Steele & Josephs, 1990). In one test of this hypothesis, students were asked to first rate themselves on a number of traits (friendly, intelligent, independent, sincere, etc.), then drink some alcohol, and finally to rerate themselves on the same traits (Banaji & Steele, 1989). Can you guess how drinking influenced self-ratings? As predicted, students' ratings of their most valued traits increased after drinking, particularly for those traits that they had not felt that good about previously.

Personality

Many studies have examined whether certain personality traits, including neuroticism/negative affect, impulsivity/disinhibition, and extraversion/sociability, are associated with alcoholism (Sher, Trull, Bartholow, & Vieth, 1999). Support for the link between personality traits and alcoholism is primarily found in correlational studies. For example, alcoholism is associated with high rates of anxiety (Kessler et al., 1997; Kushner et al., 1996), antisocial and borderline personality disorder (Regier et al., 1990), and extraversion. However, many of these studies suffer from a major flaw: they examined people at a single point in time; hence, they simply can't determine whether personality traits lead to alcohol abuse, whether alcohol abuse over time leads to changes in personality traits, or whether a third variable leads to personality traits as well as alcohol abuse.

Although relatively little research has examined the link between personality traits and alcoholism over time, results from several longitudinal studies do indicate that personality traits can predict future alcohol abuse (Bates & Labouvie, 1995; Caspi et al., 1997; Chassin et al., 1996; Zucker & Gomberg, 1986). For example, adolescents who at age 18 had lower scores on harm avoidance (e.g., choosing to avoid danger, preference for safe activities) and control (measure of cautiousness and rationality) were more likely to engage in alcohol abuse at age 21 (Caspi et al., 1997). Similarly, several studies suggest that high extraversion scores are associated with alcohol problems later on, especially in women (Kilbey, Downey, & Breslau, 1998; Prescott, Neale, Corey, & Kendler., 1997). But even longitudinal studies do not tell us whether a third variable is involved. As described in the next section, biological and genetic factors may in fact influence both personality and alcoholism.

Biological/Genetic Factors

A number of researchers have examined whether certain people are born with some type of predisposition for alcohol abuse (McGue, 1999). Because studies involving children born and raised with their biological parents do not allow researchers to distinguish whether alcohol problems are the reflection of genetic factors or environmental factors, researchers usually conduct twin studies (in which they compare rates of alcohol abuse in identical twins—who share all their genes—as compared to fraternal twins—who share half their genes) or adoption studies (in which they compare rates of alcohol abuse in children's biological parents and adoptive parents), which reveal a genetic influence in the development of drinking problems (Schuckit, 1985). For example, if one member of a same-sex twin pair is an alcoholic, the risk of the other twin being alcoholic is twice as great if the twin is identical as opposed to fraternal. Similarly, adopted children with an alcoholic biological parent are four times more likely to become problem drinkers than other adoptees. A series of studies indicates that people with a particular gene are more likely to become alcoholics than those without this gene, although not everyone with this gene develops alcoholism—about 45% of alcoholics have this gene, as compared to only 26% of nonalcoholics (Cloninger, 1991). Having this gene does not mean that a person will definitely become an alcoholic, but it increases the likelihood. Interestingly, this link between genes and alcoholism is stronger for men than for women (McGue, 1999).

One reason how this genetic predisposition may lead someone to have problems with alcohol is because they are less sensitive to the effects of alcohol, which then leads to overdrinking (Newlin & Thomson, 1990). In several studies Marc Schukit has shown that men who are at high risk of developing alcoholism (based on their family history) are not as sensitive to the early effects of alcohol as those without such a history (Schuckit & Smith, 1996). For example, after consuming a set amount of alcohol, high-risk subjects report feeling less drunk and show less impairment on various tasks than low-risk subjects. People with a family history of alcoholism may also find alcohol more rewarding and less anxiety provoking than those without this predisposition (Newlin & Thomson, 1990). In other words, genetic factors may lead people to experience more positive effects of alcohol use and fewer negative consequences. Finally, some research suggests that genetic factors may influence personality, which in turn leads to alcohol abuse (McGue, 1999). As described previously, alcoholics differ from nonalcoholics in a number of ways, including impulsivity, sensation-seeking, extraversion, and neuroticism (Sher et al., 1999). Some researchers therefore believe that alcoholics are more likely to experience problems with mood regulation, and then turn to alcohol in attempts to make themselves feel better.

Although many studies have shown that parents' drinking behavior predicts their children's drinking behavior, these studies usually cannot separate issues of biology (e.g., parents' drinking predicts their children's drinking because of genetic factors) and environment (e.g., children model their drinking on their parents' behavior). However, even adoption studies show that people drink more when they are raised with people who drink heavily (McGue, 1999). For example, 48% of adopted males raised in families with an alcoholic parent develop alcoholism, as compared to only 24.5% of those raised in families without alcoholic role models.

What Are Some Strategies for Preventing Alcohol Abuse?

Early-intervention programs focus on detecting people who are at risk of experiencing problems with alcohol use, and then providing them with information about its dangers and strategies for decreasing alcohol use. Most programs target college students. For example, one study assigned problem drinkers to either a skills-training group, an information-only group, or a no-treatment group (Kivilan, Marlatt, Fromme, Coppel, & Williams, 1990). Those in the skills-training group received information about strategies for drinking moderately as well as training in relaxation and assertiveness skills. They were specifically given the goal of drinking just to get blood-alcohol content (BAC) to 0.055 and were given information about how to set drinking limits to reach (but not exceed) this level. In contrast, those in the information-only condition received information about the effects of alcohol, the alcohol industry, and alcoholism. Findings at the 1-year follow-up indicated that those in the skills-training condition reported having only 7.6 drinks in the past month, as compared to 16.8 drinks for those in the information-only condition (and 15.4 drinks for those in the control condition).

Other prevention programs have focused on challenging individuals' beliefs about alcohol use. One study by Jack Darkes and Mark Goldman (1993) randomly assigned 218 heavy-drinking college males to one of two alcohol abuse workshops or a no-treatment control condition. One workshop focused on the physical, social, and personal consequences of alcohol use, and the other focused on challenging individuals' expectations about the consequences of alcohol use. For example, students were given real alcohol or a placebo drink designed to taste like alcohol, and then had to guess based on their own and other people's behavior who had actually received alcohol (a very difficult task, meaning that all subjects made some errors). How effective was this approach? As shown in Figure 7.10, only those in the expectancy condition decreased their drinking over the next month.

Early-intervention approaches may also try to influence people's perceptions about how common drinking is among their peers. As we discussed earlier, the perception that most other people drink heavily can lead to increased alcohol abuse, even if this perception is wrong. In one study incoming "high-risk" first-year students (those who were already heavy drinkers) met individually with a

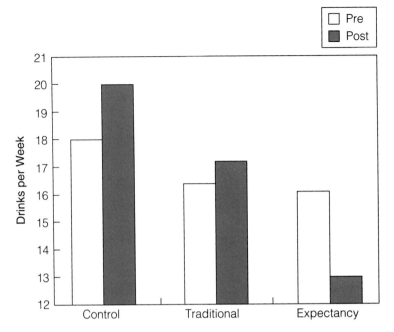

FIGURE 7.10   Although there was no change in frequency of drinking for students in the control and traditional groups, students who were in the expectancy group showed a significant decrease in their drinking (data from Darkes & Golden 1993).

clinical psychologist who gave them personal feedback, including how much more they drank than most students, the health consequences of heavy alcohol use, and environmental risk factors for heavy drinking, such as belonging to a sorority or fraternity and having heavy-drinking friends (Marlatt et al., 1998). Although these heavy-drinking students continued to experience more alcohol-related problems than the average college student, at the end of 22 years only 11% of those who received this feedback were judged alcohol-dependent as compared to 27% of heavy drinkers who did not receive this type of feedback. Similarly, a study by Brian Borsari and Kate Carcy (2000) challenged students' beliefs about alcohol use as normative by giving students accurate information about the frequency (which was lower than they expected) of drinking among their peers. Students who received this intervention reported drinking an average of 11.4 drinks in the past week, as compared to 15.78 drinks for those who were in the control condition. Box 7.12 also describes

---

Questioning the Research 7.2

Although the Borsari and Carey (2000) study shows that providing information about the real frequency of drinking (which is lower than students believe) led to decreased alcohol use, can we apply the results from this study to all students with alcohol problems? Why or why not?

Box 7.12

Research Focus—"They Don't Drink as Much as You Think They Do"

Christine Schroeder and Deborah Prentice (1998) examined the effectiveness of giving college students accurate information about the frequency of alcohol use on campus. One hundred forty-three first-year college students were randomly assigned to participate in either an individual-focused discussion on alcohol use or a peer-oriented discussion on alcohol use. The individual-focused group focused on how individuals make decisions about alcohol use, people's options in drinking situations, and the personal and social consequences of various choices people might make in terms of drinking. In contrast, the peer-oriented condition focused on how people often think that others are more positive about alcohol use than they actually are and how these misperceptions influence campus life. Researchers then measured students' frequency of drinking again 4 to 6 months later to measure the effects of participating in these discussion groups.

The findings from this study reveal that students who received information about how frequently (or rather infrequently) others students drink alcohol drank less alcohol than those who received standard education about alcohol use. Specifically, students who had participated in the peer-oriented discussion reported drinking about 3.10 alcoholic drinks per week, whereas those in the individual-focused discussion reported drinking about 5.05 drinks in past week. This study suggests that providing students with education about the real amount of alcohol use on campus (which is often lower than they think) is one effective way of reducing alcohol abuse.

another effective alcohol program for college students based on the goal of challenging students' beliefs about the prevalence of drinking.

Public policy and legal approaches to prevent alcohol abuse attempt to limit the purchase of alcohol or make such abuse seem less desirable in an effort to decrease problem drinking (Ashley & Rankin, 1988). One of the most obvious approaches is the enforcement of the drinking age, which prohibits people who are under 21 years of age from purchasing alcohol. Other approaches include limiting the number of places where and the times in which alcohol can be bought. For example, in Massachusetts, alcohol is not sold on Sundays. Unfortunately, these approaches are generally ineffective in decreasing problem drinking. As you probably know, most college students are under 21, yet, often they report having little trouble gaining access to alcohol. Other drinking prevention programs focus on promoting the negative effects of alcohol abuse. You have probably seen television and magazines ads that portray the negative consequences of drunk driving.

What Are Some Strategies for Treating Alcohol Abuse?

Although a recent large-scale survey revealed that 75% of people who recovered from alcohol problems did so on their own, many people do need assistance in quitting drinking (see Cartoon 7.1; Sobell, Cunningham, & Sobell, 1996). The first step for all alcoholics is detoxification, the drying out process in which the person withdraws from alcohol completely. This process takes about a month and can include severe symptoms, such as intense anxiety, tremors, and hallucinations (Miller & Hester, 1980). Detoxification may take place in a hospital or rehabilitation center with the use of medication in cases in which the symptoms of alcohol withdrawal are particularly severe (most often when the person has a long history of alcohol abuse), but it can sometimes take place in an out-patient setting.

Alcoholics Anonymous (AA) is the most widely known self-help program for alcohol abuse and is attended more often than any other alcohol program (Weisner, Greenfield, & Room, 1995). AA was started in the 1930s by people with drinking problems who found that sharing their problems and experiences with alcohol with others helped them remain sober. The process they used eventually evolved into 12 steps (see Table 7.4). People who are trying to stop drinking attend frequent meetings (daily, at least initially) in which members talk about their experiences with alcohol and their difficulty in quitting. The general AA philosophy is based on two principles. First, people who abuse alcohol are alcoholics and will remain that way for life, even if they never drink

"Tomorrow night let's switch back to gin."

CARTOON 7.1   It is very hard to make changes in your behavior when you are in environments that prompt the old behavior (even when you have the social support of a friend). ©The New Yorker Collection 1988. Michael Crawford from cartoonbank.com. All Rights Reserved.

TABLE 7.4 *The 12 Steps of Alcoholics Anonymous*

1. We admitted we were powerless over alcohol—that our lives had become unmanageable.
2. Came to believe that a power greater than ourselves could restore us to sanity.
3. Made a decision to turn our will and our lives over to the care of God as we understood Him.
4. Made a searching and fearless oral inventory of ourselves.
5. Admitted to God, to ourselves, and to another human being the exact nature of our wrongs.
6. Were entirely ready to have God remove all these defects of character.
7. Humbly ask Him to remove our shortcomings.
8. Made a list of all persons we had harmed and became willing to make amends to them all.
9. Made direct amends to such people whenever possible, except when to do so would injure them or others.
10. Continued to take personal inventory and, when we were wrong, promptly admitted it.
11. Sought through prayer and meditation to improve our conscious contact with God as we understand Him, praying only for knowledge of His will for us and the power to carry that out.
12. Having had a spiritual awakening as the result of these steps, we tried to carry this message to alcoholics and to practice these principles in all our affairs.

These 12 steps are the core of the Alcoholics Anonymous approach to drinking problems.

Source: Alcoholics Anonymous, 1977.

again. Second, taking even a single drink after being abstinent can set off an alcoholic binge; therefore, the goal is total abstinence from alcohol. Although AA claims a success rate of 75% "for those who really tried," it is difficult to systematically track its success rate given its anonymous nature (Peele, 1984). Moreover, many people who attend AA meetings in an attempt to quit drinking eventually drop out. However, some people are clearly helped by this form of therapy, with men, those with less education, and those who are highly sociable showing the greatest benefits (Miller & Hester, 1980).

Aversion strategies attempt to create associations between alcohol use and some type of stimulus, such as electric shock or nausea (Miller & Hester, 1980). As with similar types of therapy used to help people quit smoking, the theory behind this approach is that after repeated pairings of alcohol use and some unpleasant outcome, people will begin to associate drinking with negative consequences. For example, patients may be given an injection of emetine, which causes vomiting, and then are quickly given an alcoholic beverage. Patients go through several of these sessions and may also receive booster sessions after they are discharged from the hospital or clinic. As shown in Figure 7.11, one study found that approximately 63% of those who received this type of treatment remained abstinent 1 year later, although half of these then returned to drinking in the second year (Wiens & Menustik, 1983). Similarly, patients may be given Antabuse to take every day, which will then cause them to experience extreme nausea if they drink alcohol. Unfortunately, these programs are not very effective, perhaps because alcoholics can avoid the treatments so as to not experience the negative consequences. For example, patients can easily stop taking Antabuse, thereby avoid feeling sick when they drink.

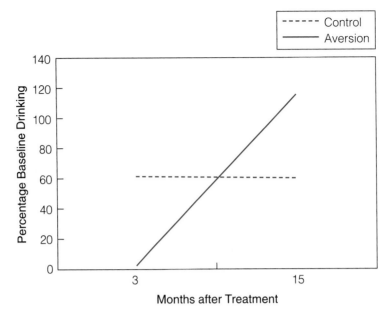

FIGURE 7.11   Although aversion therapy is initially quite effective in decreasing drinking, its effectiveness decreases steadily over time. (Marlatt, 1983).

Cognitive-behavioral programs view alcohol abuse as a learned behavior that can be changed using various behavioral techniques, such as self-monitoring, stimulus control, response substitution, and contingency contracting (Fletcher, 2001; Lang & Marlatt, 1982). These programs focus on helping people become aware of their expectations about the benefits of drinking, the factors that lead them to drink, and the situations that lead them to drink. Then people are trained to avoid these situations. For example, if you used to drink whenever you were hanging around with high school friends in a bar, in a cognitive-behavior program you might be taught to suggest other activities (e.g., going to a movie, playing basketball) to substitute. Some recovered alcoholics report that they avoid any situations in which alcohol may be served, such as weddings and cocktail parties. One study with successful recovered alcoholics found that 25% had to abandon some old friends in their efforts to stop problem drinking.

Other cognitive-behavioral approaches train people to respond in new ways to tempting situations, such as bringing nonalcoholic drinks with them or eating food instead of drinking. In one study people who were dependent on alcohol had to spend 40 minutes a day for 10 days in a "tempting situation"—holding, picking up, smelling, and thinking about drinking a desirable alcoholic drink, but they could not actually drink it (Drummond & Glautier, 1994). The goal of this training was to help people learn that they can control their urge to drink, even when they are in very tempting situations. Follow-up results show that this program was more effective than a relaxation-training condition in helping people reduce their alcohol use. Because alcoholics often use drinking as a way of coping with tension and anxiety, they might learn new methods for handling stress, such as relaxation, meditation, and exercise (Miller & Hester, 1980). For example, they could learn to hit a pillow, take a warm bath, or write in a journal whenever they feel the urge to drink as a way of coping. These approaches could also help people develop specific skills for refusing alcohol, because alcoholics are typically less skillful in and comfortable with turning down offers for drinks (Maisto et al., 1999). Telling friends that they will be the "designated driver" or that they are on medication that interacts with alcohol can be effective, for example, because they give people an "acceptable out" for not drinking and thereby reduce peer pressure to drink (see Table 7.5). Although cognitive-behavioral approaches can be effective, particularly if they train people in specific skills in drink refusal (Sobell, Sobell, & Gavin, 1995), some programs may be effective while they are in force (e.g., contingency contracting), but when the reinforcement or program disappears, so might the sobriety.

Insight-oriented psychotherapy focuses on helping people understand their motivations for drinking, such as feeling negatively about themselves or coping with various problems in their lives (Miller & Hester, 1980). A therapist might then work with them to change the problems that lead them to drink, to help them gain self-esteem, to understand the factors that lead them to drink, and to learn new methods of coping with such problems. One recent study of 222 former abusive drinkers found that two-thirds reported benefiting from such therapy (Fletcher, 2001). Both individual and group methods of therapy have had some modest success in treating drinking problems (Emrick & Hansen, 1983).

Although there are many different approaches to treating alcohol abuse, more than 50% of alcoholics drop out of treatment; even among those who continue, fewer than half of these remain successful over the long term (Stark, 1992). Typically, those who are older, have a higher socioeconomic status, have stable employment and social relationships, and have little or no history of other types of substance abuse are successful in stopping their alcohol abuse. We will discuss issues of relapse in more detail in Chapter 12.

TABLE 7.5   *How Recovered Alcoholics Handle Pressure to Drink*

1. Just say no: "No thanks." "No, thank you."
2. Simply say, "I don't drink"; "I no longer drink"; "Thanks, I don't drink."
3. Explain that you have or had a drinking problem: "No, thanks. I'm a nonpracticing alcoholic"; "I had my quota years ago."
4. Blame it on a health problem: "I have an allergy—drinking makes me break out in spots";
5. "Drinking makes me sick."
6. Ask the person to stop pushing: "Why is it so important to you that I drink?" "Because when I drink, I tend to take off my clothes and dance on the tables, and my husband doesn't like it."

These quotes are by people who have successfully overcome drinking problems.

Source: Fletcher, 2001, p. 233.

Box 7.13

Health Psychology in the Real World—The Consequences of Drug Use and Abuse

The most commonly used illegal drug in the United States is marijuana (Centers for Disease Control, 2003). As shown in Figure 7.12, a sizeable minority of high school students has tried marijuana, and as with alcohol, its use is more common in males than females. Low doses of marijuana may lead to a number of positive effects, including a dreamy relaxation, vivid sensations, and even euphoria (Kelly, Foltin, Emurian, & Fischman, 1990). People who have smoked marijuana may also experience strong food cravings and distortions in their perceptions of time and space. In contrast, cocaine, a stimulant, has very different physiological effects. Cocaine stimulates the cardiovascular system; and hence, it can increase activity and alertness. Although people who use cocaine may initially feel self-confident, energetic, and optimistic, continued use can eventually lead to more negative effects, including nausea, insomnia, paranoia, and hallucinations (Lacayo, 1995).

Although some of the initial effects of these—and other—illegal drugs can seem positive, the use of such drugs can lead to dangerous, and even deadly, consequences over time. In fact, illegal drugs are estimated to cause about 20,000 deaths each year in the United States, and such deaths are particularly common in younger people (Centers for Disease Control, 2003). How does drug use lead to negative consequences? First, many of these drugs impact memory, thinking, perception, and muscle coordination, which in turn make people more susceptible to all sorts of accidents (car accidents, drownings, falls, etc.). One study found that pilots had difficulty landing an airplane (in a flight simulator) even a day after they had smoked just a single marijuana cigarette (Yesavage, Leirer, Denari, & Hollister, 1985). The use of illegal drugs can also have substantial direct effects on health. Someone who smokes marijuana regularly may develop many of the same symptoms as someone who smokes cigarettes, including frequent coughs, chronic bronchitis, and lung damage. Because the physiological effects of cocaine include increases in heart rate and blood pressure, after repeated use people can experience cardiovascular problems, including chest pain, disturbances in heart rhythm, and even heart attacks.

Lingering Issues

Is there a genetic link to smoking? Research indicates that about 60% of smoking behavior may be inherited—for example, twin studies indicate that identical twins are much more likely to be similar in their smoking behavior than fra-

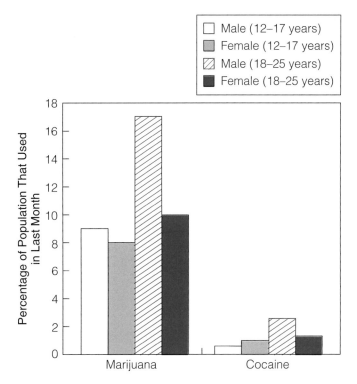

FIGURE 7.12 Rates of regular marijuana use are much higher than cocaine use, although men ages 18 to 25 years are the most likely to use both drugs (Centers for Disease Control, 2003).

ternal twins (Heath & Madden, 1995). Moreover, genetic factors contribute not only to whether a person smokes, but also influence the age at which smoking begins, the number of cigarettes smoked per day, and the persistence and intensity of smoking (Heath & Martin, 1993). One explanation of how genetic factors lead to smoking is that they cause personality traits (e.g., rebelliousness) that then lead to smoking. Heredity may also influence how pleasant or unpleasant someone finds tobacco. Finally, genetic factors may influence how easily and strongly someone becomes dependent on tobacco (Pomerleau, Collins, Shiffman, & Pomerleau, 1993).

Can alcoholics have controlled drinking? According to AA, loss of control occurs whenever an alcoholic consumes even a small amount of alcohol because the presence of alcohol in the bloodstream leads to an irresistible craving for more alcohol. Thus, controlled drinking would never be possible. However, other researchers believe that problem drinkers can eventually learn to drink in moderation after they have first abstained from alcohol for some period of time. The focus on the cause of drinking influences the treatment used: cognitive-behavioral programs may allow clients to choose their goals for modifying their drinking behavior (e.g., abstinence versus moderation), whereas other approaches (e.g., aversive treatment) do not.

Does successful treatment mean permanent abstinence from alcohol or just controlled drinking? Most research seems to support the view that controlled drinking is not usually possible—although some people may initially be able to drink in moderation, most people who have a history of alcohol abuse and who try to drink in a "controlled" way eventually return to problem drinking. However, there are some people who are able to drink in a controlled manner. People with the best odds of managing controlled drinking are young (under 40), are socially stable (married and/or employed), have a relatively brief history of alcohol abuse and dependence (less than 10 years), and have not suffered severe withdrawal symptoms (Miller & Hester, 1980). The controlled drinking approach has an advantage because it may be a more realistic goal—drinkers are often unwilling to even contemplate giving up alcohol completely. And, in fact, for people in this category, problem drinking relapses are more likely to occur following total abstinence. On the other hand, for people over 40 and with high levels of physical dependence, abstainers have lower relapse rates than those who attempt controlled drinking.

Thought Questions

1. Compare the affect-based and nicotine-based models that predict continued smoking.
2. Your friend Michael is trying to stop smoking and comes to you for advice. What are three different strategies you could suggest to him?
3. Describe two different psychological factors that can lead to alcohol abuse.
4. Describe how both aversive therapy and cognitive-behavioral therapy could be used to help people stop abusing alcohol.
5. You are a resident assistant in a dorm of first-year students and are trying to decrease your students' binge drinking. Describe two different approaches used to prevent alcohol abuse.

Answers to Questioning the Research

Answer 7.1: It is difficult to measure who is really a smoker and who is not. First, you must operationally define *smoking* : is it not having a cigarette in the last day/week/month/year? Would someone who has taken a puff or two from someone else's cigarettes but who has not smoked a whole cigarette be considered a smoker? Those of you who recall some of the issues with self-report survey data from Chapter 2 may also suggest—people can lie. In fact, smokers are quite likely to misreport how much they are smoking. Smoking prevention programs should therefore ideally include some type of physiological measure of smoking, such as a test for nicotine in saliva.

Answer 7.2: Although the study by Brian Borsari and Kate Carey (2000) shows that challenging students' beliefs about how common alcohol abuse is on campus can lead to less drinking, careful readers might wonder how representative their sample is of students in general. Who would be most interested in participating in an intervention on alcohol abuse? Many intervention studies, including those on alcohol use, tend to track highly interested and motivated participants. For example, participants might have been those concerned about the amount of drinking on campus (and are already uncomfortable with it) or students who have been personally affected by problems with alcohol (such as those who have a parent with a drinking problem). But it is possible that people who have the most severe problems with alcohol use are not at all interested in getting help with their drinking; hence, they would not participate in such a research project. We therefore must be careful about how we interpret the results of these research studies—the findings may not apply to all problem drinkers.

CHAPTER 8

Obesity and Eating Disorders

- Katie is 35 years old and is approximately 75 pounds over her ideal weight. Both of her parents are also overweight and she has always been somewhat heavy. However, after the birth of her two children, Katie's weight increased even more and she is now considered obese. Although she has tried several different diet plans, she finds it very hard to resist eating the tempting snack foods she keeps around for her children, including potato chips, Oreos, and ice cream.

- Elizabeth is a senior in college and is trying to lose 5 pounds before her planned spring break trip to Mazatlan. Although she is very focused on trying to lose weight, she tends to overeat when she is feeling nervous or stressed, which unfortunately is happening a lot now because she is in the middle of midterm exams and is also trying to apply for jobs. Moreover, when Elizabeth gives in and eats something that is not on her diet—such as pizza or brownies—she has trouble restraining herself and so she really overeats.

- Bill is 54 years old, overweight, and suffering from diabetes and high blood pressure. His doctor has told him that if he doesn't lose weight, he is very likely to experience a heart attack in the next 5 years. Bill has tried a number of different diets and sometimes even manages to lose some weight, but he always seems to regain the weight within a matter of months. Because Bill is desperate to lose weight, he just started a new weight-loss program at his office. He now exercises with a group of friends from work and has lost nearly 15 pounds in the last 3 months.

- Annie attends a private high school in New York City. Both her parents are attorneys, and they hope that she will attend a top college and perhaps even choose to go to law school one day. Although she has never been overweight, Annie has lost 15 pounds over the last few months and is hoping to lose perhaps 10 more pounds. Annie's grades in school have always been very high, but recently they have slipped some. Instead of working on her homework right after school, she now runs for 2 or 3 hours. Annie also has trouble concentrating during classes, in part because she is trying to remember exactly what she has eaten that day and about how many calories she has consumed.

- Rachel is a sophomore at college and has just started therapy to try to cope with her abnormal eating patterns. She usually eats normal meals, but whenever she is feeling anxious or depressed, she goes on huge eating binges—sometimes eating as much as a box of cookies, a bag of potato chips, a pizza, and a carton of ice cream all within just a few hours. Rachel then vomits immediately after eating to avoid gaining weight. Her therapist has asked her to keep a diary listing the times when she feels the need to binge, and together they are trying to identify some of the factors that lead to her negative feelings. Rachel has also just started taking Prozac, which is helping her feel more positive about herself.

Preview

This chapter examines how psychological factors influence eating. Obesity is very prevalent, at least in the United States, and is a significant cause of many health problems, such as cardiovascular disease and diabetes. Although eating disorders are much less common, these disorders are quite prevalent in the female college population and are associated with many negative health outcomes, including death. First, we examine the consequences of obesity and the role of biological/genetic factors in leading to eating. Next, we examine several different psychological factors that influence eating, as well as how psychological approaches can work to both prevent obesity in children and reduce obesity in adults. We then examine the consequences of eating disorders, such as anorexia and bulimia, and the impact of both biological/genetic and psychosocial factors in producing disordered eating. Finally, we examine strategies for preventing and treating eating disorders.

What Is Obesity?

For many years researchers relied on the use of tables that plot normal weight ranges for people of various heights (see Table 8.1). Unfortunately, because muscle tissue and bones weigh more than fat, relying on only weight as a measure of obesity can cause some highly fit people, such as muscular athletes, to test as obese. A more accurate way to assess obesity is by calculating percentage of body fat, which can be tested by measuring a pinch of skin in several places on a person's body or (ideally) using a water immersion technique. However, because the pinch test is not particularly accurate and the water immersion method is time-consuming and expensive, body fat measures are not widely used to determine obesity. The most common measure of obesity today is body mass index (BMI), which is calculated by dividing a person's weight (in kilograms) by the person's height (in meters) and squaring the sum (see Table 8.2). A BMI between 19 to 24 is considered ideal; 25 to 29 is

TABLE 8.1 *Height and Weight Tables for Women and Men*

Height and Weight Table for Women			
Height (in feet and inches)	Small Frame	Medium Frame	Large Frame
4'10"	102–111	109–121	118–131
4'11"	103–113	111–123	120–134
5'0"	104–115	113–126	122–137
5'1"	106–118	115–129	125–140
5'2"	108–121	118–132	128–143
5'3"	111–124	121–135	131–147
5'4"	114–127	124–138	134–151
5'5"	117–130	127–141	137–155
5'6"	120–133	130–144	140–159
5'7"	123–136	133–147	143–163
5'8"	126–139	136–150	146–167
5'9"	129–142	139–153	149–170
5'10"	132–145	142–156	152–173
5'11"	135–148	145–159	155–176
6'0"	138–151	148–162	158–179

These tables show the healthiest weights for men and women ages 25 to 59 years as a function of height.

Note: Weights at ages 25–59 years based on lowest mortality. Weight in pounds according to frame (in indoor clothing weighing 3 lbs.; shoes with 1-in. heels).

(continues)

TABLE 8.1   *(continued)*

Height and Weight Table for Men

Height (in feet and inches)	Small Frame	Medium Frame	Large Frame
5'2"	128–134	131–141	138–150
5'3"	130–136	133–143	140–153
5'4"	132–138	135–145	142–156
5'5"	134–140	137–148	144–160
5'6"	136–142	139–151	146–164
5'7"	138–145	142–154	149–168
5'8"	140–148	145–157	152–172
5'9"	142–151	148–160	155–176
5'10"	144–154	151–163	158–180
5'11"	146–157	154–166	161–184
6'0"	149–160	157–170	164–188
6'1"	152–164	160–174	168–192
6'2"	155–168	164–178	172–197
6'3"	158–172	167–182	176–202
6'4"	162–176	171–187	181–207

These tables show the healthiest weights for men and women ages 25 to 59 years as a function of height.

Note: Weights at ages 25–59 years based on lowest mortality. Weight in pounds according to frame (in indoor clothing weighing 5 lbs.; shoes with 1-in. heels).

TABLE 8.2   *Body Mass Index (BMI) Calculation Table*

BMI (kg/m^2)	19	20	21	22	23	24	25	26	27	28	29	30	35	40
Height (in.)							Weight (lb.)							
58	91	96	100	105	110	115	119	124	129	134	138	143	167	191
59	94	99	104	109	114	119	124	128	133	138	143	148	173	198
60	97	102	107	112	118	123	128	133	138	143	148	153	179	204
61	100	106	111	116	122	127	132	137	143	148	153	158	185	211
62	104	109	115	120	126	131	136	142	147	153	158	164	191	218
63	107	113	118	124	130	135	141	146	152	158	163	169	197	225

(continues)

TABLE 8.2   *(continued)*

BMI (kg/m²)	19	20	21	22	23	24	25	26	27	28	29	30	35	40
Height (in.)							Weight (lb.)							
64	110	116	122	128	134	140	145	151	157	163	169	174	204	232
65	114	120	126	132	138	144	150	156	162	168	174	180	210	240
66	118	124	130	136	142	148	155	161	167	173	179	186	216	247
67	121	127	134	140	146	153	159	166	172	178	185	191	223	255
68	125	131	138	144	151	158	164	171	177	184	190	197	230	262
69	128	135	142	149	155	162	169	176	182	189	196	203	236	270
70	132	139	146	153	160	167	174	181	188	195	202	207	243	278
71	136	143	150	157	165	172	179	186	193	200	208	215	250	286
72	140	147	154	162	169	177	184	191	199	206	213	221	258	294
73	144	151	159	166	174	182	189	197	204	212	219	227	265	302
74	148	155	163	171	179	186	194	202	210	218	225	233	272	311
75	152	160	168	176	184	192	200	208	216	224	232	240	279	319
76	156	164	172	180	189	197	205	213	221	230	238	246	287	328

Source: Adapted with permission from Bray, G. A. & Gray, D. S. (1988). Obesity, Part I, Pathogenesis. *Western Journal of Medicine, 149,* 429–441.

moderately overweight (about 15 to 30% over ideal weight), and people with indexes greater than 30 are considered obese (about 40% over ideal weight).

Regardless of how obesity is measured, it affects a substantial number of Americans: 65% of adults are overweight and 23% are obese (Centers for Disease Control, 2003). These rates are even higher in some subgroups, such as African American women (see Figure 8.1). Obesity in the United States has increased by one-third over the last 20 years (Williamson, 1995), and rates of obesity in many other countries, including Britain and Canada, have shown a similar climb (Taubes, 1998; see Figure 8.2). Moreover, 15% of the total school-age population is obese (Centers for Disease Control, 2003). Obesity is therefore a very common problem, particularly in the United States.

What Are the Consequences of Obesity?

Obesity is associated with a variety of negative physical consequences. People who are obese are at an increased risk of developing hypertension, kidney disease, gallbladder disease, diabetes, cardiovascular disease, and some types of

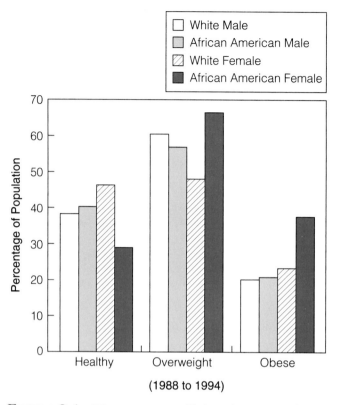

FIGURE 8.1 Women are more likely to be overweight and obese than men, and this trend is particularly true for African American women (Centers for Disease Control, 2003).

cancer (Bray, 1992). In 1976, one study collected data from 115,886 women who were registered nurses ages 30 to 55 years old (Manson et al., 1990). Researchers then collected follow-up data over 8 years to examine the predictors of illness. Women who had the lowest BMI had the lowest rates of coronary heart disease, whereas those who had the highest BMI had three times the rate of coronary disease (see Figure 8.3). Although women who were mildly to moderately overweight had an increased rate (80%) of coronary disease over the leanest women, even those of average weight had a rate that was approximately 30% higher. Both men and women who are overweight are at increased risk of death, and especially death caused by cardiovascular disease (Stevens et al., 1998). Being severely overweight is associated with even greater risks—in one study, death rates of very obese men and women (those with BMIs above 40) were twice as likely to die as those who were of normal weight (Bender, Trautner, Spraul, & Berger, 1998). According to a large study (over 750,000 subjects) by the American Cancer Society, people with a BMI between 18.6 and 23.0 (for women) and 19.9 to 22.6 (for men) had the lowest rates of coronary heart disease, diabetes, and mortality (Lew, 1985).

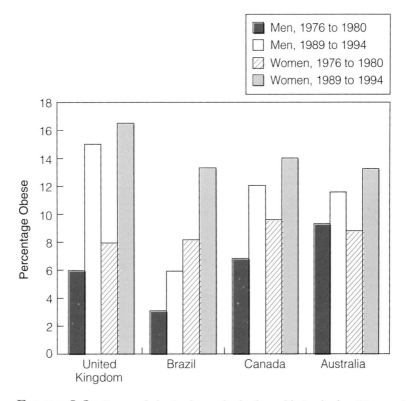

FIGURE 8.2 Rates of obesity have climbed steadily in the last 25 years in many countries (Taubes, 1998).

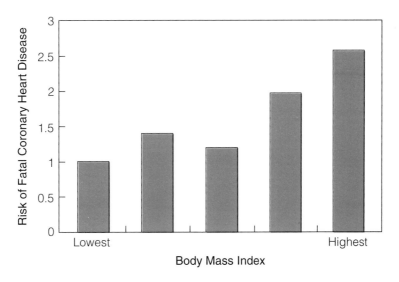

FIGURE 8.3 Women who are in the top 20% in terms of BMI are three and a half times more likely to die of coronary heart disease than those in the lowest 20% of BMI (data from Manson et al. 1990).

One of the most common health problems associated with obesity is diabetes, a chronic endocrine disorder in which the body is not able to produce or use the hormone insulin. Diabetes has increased dramatically in the United States over the last few decades and is now one of the most common chronic diseases as well as one of the leading causes of death. Type 2 diabetes (or non-insulin-dependent diabetes), which accounts for approximately 90% of diabetes cases, is most prevalent in older people and in those who are obese (Haffner, 1998). For example, 80% of people with Type 2 diabetes are obese, and a growing number of overweight children and adolescents are developing signs of diabetes (Sinha et al., 2002). In contrast, Type 1 diabetes (sometimes called insulin-dependent diabetes) typically arises in childhood or early adulthood. People with either type have high rates of cardiovascular disease and often experience other health problems, such as blindness, kidney failure, and nervous system damage that can lead to necessary amputation of various limbs.

Obese people also tend to suffer from social and psychological consequences. They tend to be rated as less likable, are at a disadvantage in dating people, get lower grades, earn less, and are generally the subject of negative social attitudes (Ryckman, Robbins, Kazcor, & Gold, 1989). One long-term study of obese women found that those who were obese made less money, completed fewer years of education, and were less likely to be married than their normal-weight peers (Gortmaker, Must, Perrin, Sobel, & Dietz, 1993). Even young children hold negative attitudes about people who are obese. In one study children were shown drawings of 5 children: one who was physically handicapped, one who had a facial disfigurement, one with crutches and a leg brace, one whose left arm had been amputated, and one who was obese (Richardson, Goodman, Hasdorf, & Dornbusch, 1961). All the children rated the obese child the one they liked the least.

One reason why there are such negative views about obese people is that obesity is often seen as something that is within a person's control—obese people are seen as slow, lazy, sloppy, and lacking in willpower (Ryckman et al., 1989). We often have the view that if they wanted to lose weight, they could just stop eating so much, so we blame obese people for their weight. In one study high school girls were shown a picture of a girl and read a short statement about her; they were then asked to rate how much they thought they would like her (DeJong, 1980). Some of the girls saw a picture of an overweight girl, and others saw a picture of a normal-weight girl. Of those who saw the picture of the overweight girl, some were told that her weight was a result of a medical problem with her thyroid. As predicted, the subjects who saw the normal-weight girl liked her more than those who saw the overweight girl, but those who saw the overweight girl and were told she had an acceptable reason for her weight (the thyroid condition) liked her just as much as those who saw the normal-weight girl liked the normal-weight girl. This study suggests that it is not just the weight that makes obese people seem unattractive, but the cause people attribute to the weight, such as laziness. But are obese people really different from others? No—the personality characteristics of obese and nonobese people are very similar (Poston et al., 1999).

How Do Genetic Factors Cause Obesity?

Considerable research indicates that genetic factors play a role in obesity. Obese people are more likely than nonobese people to have had obese parents and obese grandparents (Noble, 1997), and obese parents are more likely to have obese children. For example, about 7% of the children of normal-weight parents are obese, compared with 40% of the children in families with one obese parent, and 80% in families with two obese parents (Mayer, 1980). As described at the beginning of the chapter, Katie, who had struggled with her weight for many years, had two overweight parents. We cannot, however, attribute obesity solely to genetic factors, based upon this correlation alone. After all, parents who are obese might tend to buy and cook mostly high-fat foods or encourage their children to overeat, which may point to an environmental cause of obesity. Results from studies of adopted children provide some compelling evidence for the link between genetics and obesity, however. First, identical twins are very similar in terms of BMI regardless of whether they are raised together or apart, and identical twins are much more similar in BMI than are same-sex fraternal twins (see Figure 8.4; Grilo & Pogue-Geile, 1991). Second, there is a much

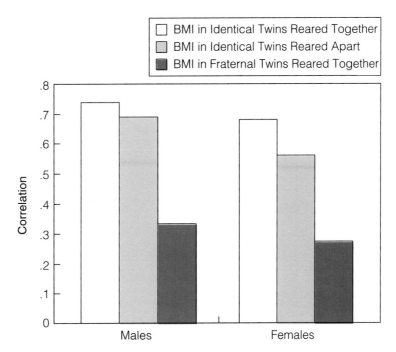

FIGURE 8.4 BMI is highly correlated in identical twins regardless of whether they are reared together, whereas BMI is much less correlated in fraternal twins, even when they are reared together (Grilo & Pogue-Guile, 1991).

stronger relationship between the adopted children's and their biological parents' weight than their adoptive parents' weight, and there is no significant correlation in weight between adopted siblings who are raised together (see Figure 8.5; Grilo & Pogue-Geile, 1991). Genetic factors appear to predict about 40 to 70% of the variation in BMI (Comuzzie & Allison, 1998).

Although research on the genetic factors predicting obesity is still relatively new, recent evidence suggests that genes may influence obesity in a variety of ways. First, genes may influence how much—and even what—people want to eat. Research with mice demonstrates that a gene is responsible for directing the fat cells to release leptin, a hormone that decreases appetite and increases energy expenditure (Wang et al., 1999). In turn, when we lose weight (and lose fat cells) less leptin is released into our bloodstream, which may lead us to feel hungrier. Obese people might also have a genetic preference for energy-dense fat-containing foods, such as chocolate, ice cream, pastries, and whipped cream (see Table 8.3; Drewnowski, 1996). Because dietary fats are the most concentrated source of energy, people who are obese might be particularly sensitive to these foods. One study found that young children's preference for fat foods was influenced not only by their own level of body fat but also their mother's level of body fat (Fisher & Birch, 1995).

Genes may also influence metabolism, the rate the body uses energy to carry out basic physiological processes, such as respiration, digestion, and blood pressure (Comuzzie & Allison, 1998). People who have a high metabolism are

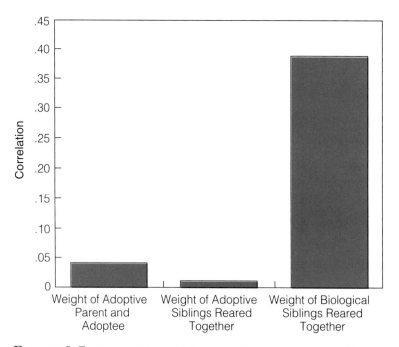

FIGURE 8.5   The weight of biological siblings is much more highly correlated than the weight of adoptive siblings or adoptive parents and children (Grilo & Pogue-Guile, 1991).

TABLE 8.3   *Food Preferences of Obese Men and Women*

Food	% Men	% Women
Meats	96.8	86.0
Carbohydrates and fats	92.5	91.5
Dairy products	50.5	49.2
Fats	16.1	23.8
Starches	44.1	49.2
Sugars	11.8	23.3
High-fat sweets	67.7	80.6
Vegetables	39.8	48.4
Fruits	29.0	38.9

Source: Drewnowski, 1996.

thought to use more energy to carry out these processes; hence, they burn off more calories. On the other hand, people with a lower metabolic rate gain more weight than people with higher metabolic rates, presumably because their bodies are not burning off as many calories (Ravussin et al., 1988). For example, in one study normal-weight people were asked to eat an extra 1000 calories a day for 8 weeks, and then researchers measured how much weight they gained (Levine, Eberhardt, & Jensen, 1999). Although some volunteers gained considerable amounts of weight (over 9 pounds), others gained only small amounts (less than 1 pound). The biggest predictor of low levels of weight gain was the incidental physical activity (not intentional exercise) people engaged in as part of daily life, such as fidgeting, sitting up straight, and flexing their muscles. People may vary in how easily they engage in activities that burn fat.

According to set-point theory, each person's body has a certain weight that it strives to maintain, much like a thermostat device (Keesey, 1995). When you eat fewer calories, your metabolism slows to keep your weight at the same level. Because people's set points may vary based on heredity, some will be heavier and some will be lighter. One way it may work is that the set point is determined by the number of fat cells a person has (Leibel, Berry, & Hirsch, 1983). Although there is little or no difference in the number of fat cells between people of normal weight and those who are slightly overweight, people who are severely obese have many more fat cells. Another possibility is that the hypothalamus influences fat stores and/or levels of glucose or insulin in the blood, which in turn influence feelings of hunger and fullness. In line with this view, research with animals demonstrates that damage to a certain part of the hypothalamus can lead to a change in weight, perhaps by allowing a new set point to be established (Keesey & Powley, 1975).

Although genes do play some role in obesity, it is clear that they do not totally predict a person's weight. First, rates of obesity in the United States have increased dramatically in recent years, which means genetics can't explain it all

(Hill & Peters, 1998; Katan, Grundy, & Willett, 1997). Second, people with the same genetic background who live in different parts of the world often have very different body weights (Hodge & Zimmet, 1994). For example, Japanese people who live in Japan are thinner than those who move to Hawaii, and Japanese people who live in Hawaii are thinner than those who move to the continental United States (Curb & Marcus, 1991). These differences in weight suggest that while genetics may play some role, cultural factors including diet and exercise also influence weight.

How Do Psychological Factors Influence Eating (and Overeating)?

Although genetic and biological factors do influence how much we eat, they aren't the whole story. There are probably many times you have eaten even when you are not hungry for instance. Maybe you eat when you are nervous; maybe you eat after you walk by a shop selling great-smelling cinnamon rolls in the mall; maybe you eat mindlessly while watching TV. All of these are examples of psychological factors that may lead to eating (and overeating).

Internal-External Hypothesis

One of the earliest hypotheses about why and when people eat is the internal-external hypothesis (Schachter, 1968). According to this view, people often fail to listen to their internal cues for eating (namely, hunger), and instead they pay attention to external cues, such as food taste, smell, and variety. Even when you are not hungry, tempting food smells and tastes can influence you to eat. For example, I gave up eating meat as a New Year's resolution when I was 14 years old, and I still almost never eat any type of meat (nearly 20 years later). However, whenever I am at a baseball park and smell hot dogs cooking on a grill, I crave a hot dog with mustard. We also eat more when we have a variety of different types of foods available (Rolls et al., 1981). Because people get tired of eating the same thing, having a diverse diet leads to more food consumption (just think about how much you eat at buffets). Similarly, rats who are given a wide variety of different foods show considerable weight gains, especially if these foods are high in fat and sugar (Sclafani & Springer, 1976). External cues can also lead us to avoid eating something we'd actually enjoy. A series of studies by Paul Rozin and his colleagues has shown that people will refuse to eat delicious chocolate fudge if it is formed into the shape of dog poop, for example (Rozin & Fallon, 1987).

Although we all sometimes eat in response to external cues, according to Schachter's (1968) internal-external theory, people who are trying to restrain how much they eat are particularly influenced by external prompts for eating, such as TV advertisements for food, sampling a particularly good-tasting food, and even believing that it is "time to eat" (see Box 8.1). For example, a normal-weight person who passes a bakery and sees tempting food will stop to buy something if he or she is hungry, but will walk by if he or she has just eaten and is full. However, an obese person will find the food irresistible even if he or she has just eaten. In other words, obese people don't really pay attention to what their bodies are telling them about whether they need to eat (see Figure 8.6).

In support of Schachter's externality theory, several studies have shown that obese people eat more when foods taste particularly good (Kauffman, Herman, & Polivy, 1995). In one study Richard Nisbett (1968) gave both normal-weight and obese subjects vanilla ice cream that was either very good

Box 8.1

Research Focus—Does Hunger Influence How Much You Eat? Not Always.

As a test of the internal-external theory, Stanley Schachter and his colleagues conducted a study examining whether normal-weight people are more responsive to internal cues for hunger than those who are overweight (Schachter, Goldman, & Gordon, 1968). Subjects were told to not eat a meal before coming in to the lab "to make sure all subjects are in the same physical state." Subjects then were randomly assigned to either the "full-stomach" condition, in which they were left in a room with a plate of sandwiches and told to eat until they were full, or the "empty-stomach" condition, in which they were not allowed to eat. Then, the subjects were brought into another room for a "cracker-rating test" in which they were asked to eat crackers from five unmarked boxes and to rate how much they liked each type of cracker. They were told to eat as many crackers of each type as necessary to accurately rate them on various dimensions, including saltiness, tastiness, and crunch. Researchers weighed the box of crackers before and after participants were given access to them as a way of determining how many crackers were consumed.

As predicted, the number of crackers eaten by normal-weight subjects was influenced by how hungry they were, whereas the number of crackers eaten by obese people was not influenced by whether they had just eaten a large meal. As shown in Figure 8.6, normal-weight people who were full (full-stomach group) ate an average of 15.32 crackers, whereas those who were hungry (empty-stomach group) ate an average of 21.89 crackers. However, the number of crackers eaten by obese people did not differ as a function of how full they were. Obese people ate an average of 18.65 crackers when they were full and 17.89 crackers when they were hungry. This study shows that normal-weight people pay attention to their internal cues for eating (namely, how hungry they are), whereas obese people eat the same amount regardless of how hungry they might be.

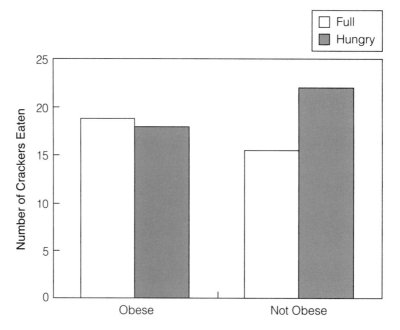

FIGURE 8.6 Normal-weight people eat more crackers when they are hungry than when they are full, but obese people eat the same number of crackers regardless of their hunger level (Schachter et al., 1968).

(think Haagen-Daaz or Ben and Jerry's) or really bad (made with cheap vanilla and having an acrid aftertaste). When the ice cream tasted pretty bad, no one ate very much, but when the ice cream was pretty good, obese subjects ate much more than normal-weight subjects. In another study on the influence of taste on eating, six grossly obese subjects and four normal-weight subjects were placed on a hospital diet—the only thing they could eat was a bland liquid diet shake; they could have as much of the unappealing shake as they wanted at any time (Hashim & Van Itallie, 1965). Normal-weight subjects basically took in the same number of calories on the liquid diet as they did in normal life; they ate to maintain their weight (and presumably they rely on their internal cue of hunger to guide their eating). On the other hand, obese subjects consumed significantly fewer calories on this diet than they normally did, presumably because the external cues of eating were weak. The real-world implications of this study may explain why diet drinks, such as those containing aspartame, do help people lose weight (at least in the short term): it is really unappetizing to get all of your calories through a bland-tasting, textureless diet drink. All of this research suggests that obese people show a close connection between the external circumstances of eating and amount eaten, whereas for normal-weight people, the close connection is between their physiological state and amount eaten.

More recent research, however, provides little support for the internal-external theory. First, even people of normal weight are not particularly good at interpreting internal signals for hunger, such as low blood sugar and stomach pains (Rodin, 1981). People are also not very good at surmising how many calories they have consumed or how many calories their bodies need to maintain weight. Second, people at varying weight levels, including those of average weight, can be very responsive to external cues for eating. There is some evidence, however, to suggest that people who are more responsive to external cues are particularly likely to overeat (and potentially gain weight). One study by Judith Rodin, for example, found that girls who were extremely responsive to external cues for eating gained the most weight at summer camp (presumably because of the frequent packages sent from home providing candy and baked goods, and their lack of focus on internal cues signifying fullness; Rodin & Slochower, 1976).

Mood Regulation

People often use food to regulate their moods—for example, you may constantly snack on junk foods while you are studying for exams. Specifically, people may eat to make themselves feel better when they experience stress, anxiety, or depression. For example, Charles Pine (1985) told subjects they would be participating in a study on how electrical stimulation influenced taste. He told some that the shock would be barely noticeable (low-anxiety condition) and others that the shocks would be painful, though not harmful (high-anxiety condition), and then he measured how many peanuts subjects ate while they waited for the shocks. As predicted, people who expected they would receive only mild shocks ate 9.02 grams of peanuts compared to 12.38 grams of peanuts for those who expected the painful shocks.

Interestingly, this tendency to eat more when nervous seems to be more common in women than men. One study with French high school students revealed that girls, but not boys, consumed more calories on examination days, and both boys and girls showed a tendency to eat more calories from fat on these stressful days (Michaud et al., 1990). Similarly, 62% of female college students, but only 29% of male students, report eating more when they are depressed (Rozin & Fallon, 1988). Experimental research demonstrates the same gender difference. In one study researchers showed men and women either a relaxing or a stressful video and then measured how much they ate (Grunberg & Straub, 1992). Men who were stressed ate about half as much as men who were not stressed, although there was no overall difference in amount eaten for women. However, women who were stressed ate more sweet foods.

There is rather mixed evidence, however, for the view that stress consistently leads to overeating. In fact, while some people seem to eat more when under stress, others eat less (Willenbring, Levine, & Morley, 1986). One study of female college students found that obese students ate nearly seven times as much during exam period than normal-weight students, whereas there was virtually no difference in how much obese and nonobese students ate during less stressful periods of the semester (Slochower, Kaplan, & Mann, 1981). Similarly, the study by Charles Pine (1985) described previously found that although people who expected severe shocks generally ate more than those who expected mild shocks, obese people who expected severe shocks ate about 15.4 grams of peanuts as compared to only 9.2 for nonobese people who expected severe shocks. Other research suggests that the tendency to eat more when stressed occurs only for those who are trying to lose weight (Friedman & Brownell, 1995). For example, Donald Baucom and Pamela Aiken (1981) found that stress leads to more eating for those who are dieting, but less eating among those who are not dieting. So, all of this research suggests that some people may indeed overeat when they are experiencing stress (such as those who are obese or who are trying to lose weight), but stress does not lead everyone to overeat.

Restraint Theory

Restraint theory was developed in part to explain the sometimes mixed findings that resulted from research based in the internal-external and mood-regulation theories of obesity. According to this theory, people are generally motivated to eat as a function of internal physiological signals that cue hunger (Herman & Polivy, 1984). However, when people are trying to lose weight they deliberately ignore these internal signals and instead use cognitive rules to

"I shouldn't, but I'm going to have the garbage."

CARTOON 8.1   Restrained eaters often divide foods into those things they are allowed to eat and those things they should not eat (©The New Yorker Collection 2001. Mike Twohy from cartoonbank.com. All Rights Reserved).

limit their caloric intake (see Cartoon 8.1). For example, dieters might develop rules about eating certain types of foods (e.g., celery, carrots, nonfat yogurt) and avoiding other types of foods (e.g., ice cream, brownies, meat).

This approach can be successful in helping people restrict their eating, but it can also backfire. Specifically, restrained eaters often develop an "all-or-nothing" mind-set about eating, which means that breaking the rules by eating small amounts of "forbidden food" can lead to overeating. For example, a person who is dieting but who gives in and eats a fattening first course at a dinner party may think, "Well, I've blown it now, so I may as well eat all I want." As described at the beginning of the chapter, Elizabeth's efforts to diet led her to overeat during times of stress. In a study by Peter Herman and Deborah Mack (1975) subjects were told the research focused on how tasting one flavor first influences the ability to judge another flavor. Some subjects were then given two milkshakes to drink (one chocolate, one vanilla) and others were given nothing to drink (the control condition). All participants were then asked to taste and rate three different flavors of ice cream—they were told they could eat as much ice cream as necessary to rate the flavors accurately. For nondieters, eating a high-calorie food decreased the amount of ice cream they ate, whereas for dieters, eating a high-calorie food led to even more eating (see Figure 8.7). Similarly, and as described in Box 8.2, when restrained eaters feel sad or stressed, they give up the cognitive rules and can then eat excessive amounts.

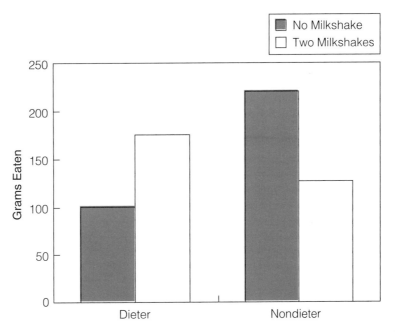

FIGURE 8.7 Nondieters who drank two milkshakes felt less hungry and hence ate less ice cream during the tasting task than those who did not have a milkshake, whereas dieters who drank two milkshakes ate significantly more ice cream than those who did not have a milkshake (data from Herman & Polivy, 1983).

Box 8.2

Research Focus—The Influence of Mood on Eating in Dieters and Nondieters

Todd Heatherton and colleagues examined the effects of feeling sad on eating in both dieters and nondieters (Heatherton, Striepe, & Wittenberg, 1998). Ninety college women were recruited to participate in a study on "personality and perceptual processes." They were randomly assigned to listen to either a very slow and depressing piece of music or a more neutral piece of music; prior research has shown that music influences people's moods. Participants were then asked to spend 10 minutes tasting and rating three different flavors of ice cream. The researchers weighed the ice cream bowls before and after subjects made their ratings so the amount of ice cream consumed could be measured.

As predicted, both dieting and listening to sad music influenced how much ice cream the women ate during their tasting task. First, and not surprisingly, dieters ate less than nondieters in the neutral-music condition. However, dieters ate significantly more ice cream than nondieters when they were in the sad-music condition (see Figure 8.8). In fact, dieters who heard the sad music ate more ice cream than dieters who were in the neutral condition and nondieters who were in either condition. Apparently, dieters use food as a way of regulating their mood; hence, they eat more ice cream when they are feeling sad.

However, some research by Michael Lowe and his colleagues suggests that restraint theory is not always a good predictor of eating behavior (Lowe, 1993). He believes that some people who are "restrained eaters" have developed cognitive rules that guide their eating, but they are not at the moment actively trying to lose weight (although they may have struggled with weight-loss issues in the past). In line with the predictions of restraint theory, these people should overeat under various conditions (when they are sad, when they are stressed, etc.). On the other hand, people who are actively trying to diet may also develop rules to guide their eating, but these people should not engage in the same type of "all-or-nothing" eating that nondieting restrained eaters show. In support of this view, restrained nondieters eat more after they have first had a milkshake (because they have already blown their diet anyway), whereas restrained dieters eat significantly less after having a milkshake (because they are actively trying to lose weight; Lowe, Whitlow & Bellwoar, 1991).

Lifestyle and Culture

Even subtle lifestyle and cultural factors can influence how much we eat. First, people eat more when they are with other people than when they are alone

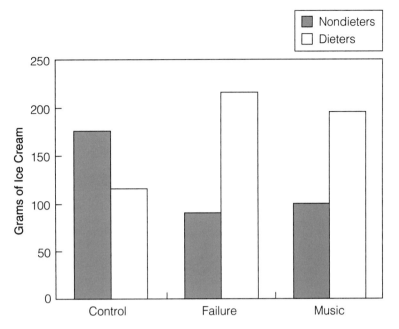

FIGURE 8.8   Restrained eaters who are depressed because they have heard sad music eat significantly more ice cream than both restrained eaters who have heard neutral music and nonrestrained eaters (data from Heatherton et al., 1998).

(Feunkes, De Graaf, & Van Staveren, 1995). In one study people were asked to keep a diary listing all the foods they ate for one week, noting how many other people were present while they were eating (DeCastro & DeCastro, 1989). The more people present, the more people ate, especially if they were with family and friends as in Photo 8.1 (DeCastro, 1994). Having other people around may lead to more eating in part because meals last longer. Another factor is that we are less sensitive to internal cues for hunger when we are with other people. For example, if you are eating alone, the amount you eat is influenced by how hungry you are (e.g., if you had a late or big lunch, you eat less for dinner), whereas if you are eating with other people, you eat the same amount regardless of when you have last had a meal.

Culture may also influence the types of foods and tastes people enjoy (Rozin, 1996). Most Americans, for example, find eating insects, snails, and dogs fairly repulsive, whereas these foods are considered delicacies in some cultures. Similarly, our food preferences are shaped by the types of flavors used in cooking, such as curry (common in India) and chili pepper (common in Mexico). Some very recent research suggests that these taste preferences are shaped even before we are born. Julie Mennella and her colleagues conducted a very clever study in which pregnant women who were planning to breast-feed were randomly assigned to one of three groups (Mennella, Jagnow, & Beauchamp, 2001). Women in one group drank carrot juice four times a week for 3 weeks during pregnancy, women in another group drank carrot juice

PHOTO 8.1   People eat more when they are with more people, especially if they are with family and friends.

four times a week for 3 weeks after the baby was born, and women in the third group did not drink carrot juice. The researchers then tested how babies reacted to the taste of carrots by asking mothers to rate their babies' facial reactions and measure how much of a carrot-flavored cereal the babies ate. Babies who were exposed to the taste of carrots either through amniotic fluid or breast milk liked the taste of carrots more than babies who had no exposure to this taste, and they tended to eat more flavored cereal. This study provides compelling evidence that our taste preferences may be established very early in life.

Finally, very subtle cultural factors such as the availability and amount of food may contribute to obesity (Wadden, Brownell, & Foster, 2002). The United States has the highest rates of obesity in the world, but also a great abundance of fast-food restaurants featuring inexpensive and very fatty foods. Many school cafeterias now feature fast foods and soda, despite the contribution of these products to obesity. As described by Kelly Brownell, a psychologist at Yale University, "If your task was to make the American child as unhealthy as possible, could you do much better than fast food and soft drinks in the cafeteria?" (*Time*, 2002). Food is not simply readily available, but is increasingly served in larger amounts. Portions at both high-end and low-end restaurants (think "Super Size" that) in the United States have become bigger over time, which encourages overeating (see Photo 8.2; Hill & Peters, 1998). Have you ever seen one of the original glass Coke bottles that was manufactured in the 1930s? It held 6 $\frac{1}{2}$ ounces. The current "single-size" plastic Coke bottle now holds 1 liter, which is five times as much.

PHOTO 8.2   One of the factors contributing to the high rate of obesity in the United States is the ready access to high-fat foods that are often served in supersized portions.

What Factors Help Prevent Obesity?

Preventing obesity must begin in childhood because obesity in childhood is very likely to lead to obesity in adulthood: One study examined the prevalence of adult obesity based on whether 6-month-old infants were above or below the 75th percentile for weight (Charney, Goodman, McBride, Lyon, & Pratt, 1976). Only 8% of nonobese infants became obese adults as compared to 14% of obese infants (nearly double the rate). The risk of adult obesity is even greater for children who are obese at older ages. For example, one study found that 40% of obese 7-year-olds became overweight adults as compared to only 10% of nonobese 7-year-olds (Stark, Atkins, Wolff, & Douglas, 1981). Fat cells develop in childhood and adolescence, and once they develop, they never disappear—they can get bigger or smaller, but they never disappear.

Efforts to prevent obesity can be relatively simple, such as encouraging children to exercise and eat healthy foods (and see Box 8.3 for a novel strategy for preventing obesity). Because I am an extremely clever psychologist, when my son Andrew was 2 years old I started calling wheat germ "treat" and would regularly ask him if he'd like "treat" on various food items, such as yogurt and cereal. It worked—he sometimes will eat the wheat germ off of his yogurt and then ask for more "treat." (My husband is concerned that he will later be ridiculed by other children, but I say at least he's eating healthy foods.) Parents also should model healthy behavior, such as using fruits as dessert, eating healthy snacks, and exercising.

Box 8.3

Health Psychology in the Real World—Breast-Fed Kids Are Thinner Kids

A recent study in the *Journal of the American Medical Association* suggests that breast-feeding is one important way to decrease obesity in children. Researchers at the National Institutes of Health examined data from 2,685 three- to five-year-old children (Hediger, Overpeck, Kuczmarski, & Ruan, 2001). Children who had been breast-fed for any length of time were 16% less likely to be overweight and 37% less likely to be obese than those who were never breast-fed. One reason why breast-feeding may be so beneficial is that babies who are breast-fed learn how to regulate how much they consume because mothers have no no way to gauge how much they are drinking. In contrast, bottle-fed babies are often fed a certain amount of formula periodically each day, and parents may therefore focus on getting the baby to eat the "right amount." However, there may also be other factors influencing the relationship between breast-feeding and obesity. For example, mothers with a higher income and more education are more likely to breast-feed and more likely to encourage their children to eat healthily. Moreover, overweight mothers are less likely to breast-feed than thin mothers, which suggests the association between breast-feeding and obesity could be due at least in part to genetic factors.

Parents should never use unhealthy food as a reward for good behavior even when it is really tempting to do so. One study of 427 parents of preschool children found that 56% reported promising children a special food, such as a dessert, for finishing their dinner and 48% reported promising children a special food for good behavior, such as cleaning their room (Stanek, Abbott, & Cramer, 1990). But what are the long-term effects of this approach? Children figure out very quickly that the "good foods" come after the "bad foods," and they in fact, show an increased desire for "forbidden" foods. In one study 3- to 6-year-old children were at one time allowed to eat a variety of different flavors of fruit cookie bars, and at other times they were specifically told they could eat any fruit cookie bar they wanted except for one particular flavor (Fisher & Birch, 1999). Researchers then measured how much children talked about each of the kinds of cookie bars, how much they tried to obtain them, and how much they asked for them. As shown in Figure 8.9, there were no real differences between their interest in the different types of fruit cookie bars when they had free access, but as soon as one type of cookie bar was forbidden, it became very desirable!

Another important factor in preventing obesity is limiting television watching (see Photo 8.3). First, watching television is a passive activity (particularly with the advent of the remote control). So, when children come home from

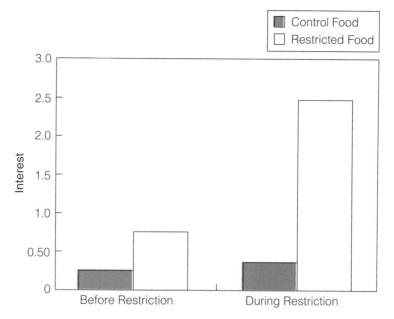

FIGURE 8.9 Children are much more interested in eating "forbidden food" (data from Mennella et al. 2001).

PHOTO 8.3 Children who watch considerable amounts of television are at increased risk of obesity, in part because they are exposed to many commercials for unhealthy foods and in part because they are less likely to participate in physical activity than children who watch less television.

school (or adults come home from work) and sit in front of the television, they aren't exercising. Studies with both adults (Ching et al., 1996) and children (Andersen, Crespo, Bartlett, Cheskin, & Pratt, 1998) have shown that people who watch a lot of television are more likely to be overweight than those who watch less television. Children from families in which the television is often on during meals also eat more salty snacks and sodas and less fruits, vegetables, and juices than those from families in which the television is rarely on (Coon, Goldberg, Rogers, & Tucker, 2001).

Watching television also encourages bad eating habits because the vast majority of food advertisements on TV promote unhealthy foods. Food and eating references are presented nearly five times in every 30 minutes of prime-time television (including programming and commercials), and 60% of these references are for low-nutrient beverages and sweets (Story & Faulkner, 1990). This type of influence can be particularly impactful for children. The average child sees more than 20,000 TV commercials in a year, and the two most common types of ads are for toys and food. One study of the types of food ads featured during Saturday morning cartoons revealed that two-thirds of the ads were promoting fats, oils, sweets, and high-sugar cereals (Kotz & Story, 1994). More than half of 9- to 10-year-old children believe that Ronald McDonald knows what is good for children to eat (Horgen, Choate, & Brownell, 2001).

How Is Obesity Treated?

It is no mystery that weight gain is at least partially a function of taking in more calories than the body burns off. There are, therefore, two major strategies used to treat obesity.

Eating Less

Many people try to lose weight by making changes in their diet—in fact, as many as 25 to 30% of the adult American population is dieting at any one time (Bouchard, 1991). A walk through any bookstore will show you hundreds and maybe even thousands of books describing diet plans to help people lose weight. You can eat based on your blood type or astrological sign, you can eat only protein or anything except carbohydrates, you can eat the Zone Diet. However, the amount of weight people lose on any of these diets tends to be small and temporary. These approaches don't focus on helping people make long-term changes in their dietary habits. It is may be so that eating only grapefruit for the rest of your life would allow you to maintain a very low body weight, but you would also suffer from various nutritional deficits. It is unrealistic to think that people could keep up maintain health on some dieting approaches.

A few strategies do help people consume fewer calories (see Photo 8.4). First, setting proximal or short-term goals is more effective than setting distal or longer-term goals (Bandura & Simon, 1977). For example, it is better to focus on cutting calories at each meal than on eliminating a certain number of calories each week. This short-term approach allows people to experience small successes in reaching their larger goals and thus can help them feel more confident in their ability to achieve their weight-loss goals. Similarly, the most effective techniques emphasize gradual weight loss (1 to 2 pounds a week), as opposed to more extreme approaches. The quick and extreme plans that are often featured on magazine covers just don't work—no one can safely lose 10 pounds in the week before spring break without having a limb amputated.

Second, monitoring exactly what, when, and where you eat can help you reduce calories (Wadden, 1993). People sometimes lack an understanding of precisely what they eat each day; therefore, they are confused when their dieting doesn't work. You may, for example, decrease the number of calories you eat at each meal, but if you consistently eat potato chips while you study or have a candybar as a quick between-classes snack, you may not remember to count those calories. In fact, dieters tend to both underreport how much food they eat and overestimate how much they exercise (Lichtman et al., 1992). Also, people often overeat in social situations because they aren't even aware of how much they are eating. (Sadly, calories consumed while standing up still count.) Once you have monitored the factors that lead to overeating, you can try to eliminate these triggers. Instead of stopping at Dunkin' Donuts for coffee and a doughnut on your way to class, you might try eating a bowl of cereal or fruit at home instead. If you eat while you watch TV, you might try eating when sitting at your dining room table with the TV off. The consequences of not self-monitoring can be very bad—one study found that weight-loss clients who failed to self-monitor their eating over a 3-week holiday period gained 57 times as much weight as those who continued to self-monitor (Fisher, Lowe, Jeffrey, Levenkron, & Newman, 1982).

PHOTO 8.4 Although many diet books claim to have "the answer" to weight loss, the best approach to dieting is to eat less and exercise more.

Other self-control approaches to weight loss focus on helping people make small changes in their behavior, or even in the way that they think about eating and weight loss (Wadden, 1993). Obese people might be encouraged to purchase healthy foods to snack on and to avoid keeping "problem foods" in the house, this way, if they overeat, they eat carrots as opposed to donuts. Similarly, people who are dieting may be advised to slow down their eating, perhaps by putting their fork down between each bite or chewing all of their food thoroughly. These methods focus on changing people's negative or unrealistic views about weight loss (e.g., "I will never be able to lose the weight," or "I should have lost the weight by now, this isn't working"). People who have struggled with obesity for some time may view their lack of weight-loss success as a sign of personal weakness and failure, which in turn can lead them to return to unhealthy eating patterns at the first sign of trouble.

Operant-conditioning approaches can be used so that people receive some type of reward for adhering to a diet or losing weight (Wadden, 1993). For example, you could give yourself some type of reward for successfully meeting your weight-loss goals—maybe a new CD or pair of sunglasses. (Obviously, it's better to not use food as a reward to motivate yourself!) In contingent-contracting approaches, people give a friend or therapist some money and then "earn it back" as they lose weight. In one study by Kelly Brownell and colleagues, people in different businesses participated in a 3-month weight-loss challenge in which each participant was given a weight-loss goal based on his or her actual and desired weight (Brownell, Cohen, Stunkard, Felix, & Cooley, 1984). The prize for the team that achieved the greatest percentage of weight loss was a pool of money to which each participant had previously contributed $5. The only help team members received in losing the weight was a series of weekly manuals that gave information about nutrition, exercise, self-monitoring, stimulus control, and reinforcement. The average weight lost was 12 pounds, and only one of the 213 participants dropped out of the contest. Most important, a 6-month follow-up revealed that people kept off 80% of the weight they lost.

Social influence techniques, including having the support of family members and friends as well as participating in formal weight-loss groups, can help people successfully make changes to their diet (Wadden, 1993). Individuals who have the support of their spouses in their weight-loss plans lose far more weight than those without such support (Brownell, Heckerman, Westlake, Hayes, & Monti, 1978). Group approaches are especially effective in helping people lose weight because they provide social support as well as healthy competition. For example, one study with 89 overweight men found that group contracts (receiving money based on the average group weight loss) were more effective at maintaining weight loss over 2 years than individual contracts (receiving money based on only one's own weight loss; Jeffery, Bjornson-Benson, Rosenthal, Lindquist, & Johnson, 1984).

Finally, in extreme cases, when obesity is a real threat to a person's health, surgical techniques can be used (Kral, 1992). One method is to wire shut a person's jaw for a certain amount of time so he or she only can drink fluids. Other surgical methods include stomach stapling (so that the person can eat only small amounts of food before feeling full) and removal of a portion of the small intestine (which prevents food from being absorbed into the body). Although these approaches often do lead to significant weight loss, they can have unpleasant side effects, including permanent diarrhea and long-term nutritional deficits. These methods are therefore used only in cases of severe obesity that have potentially life-threatening effects (see Photo 8.5).

Increasing Exercise

Efforts to lose weight can also focus on increasing the number of calories expended through exercise. Exercise helps with weight loss in a number of ways, including increasing metabolic rate (so calories are burned at a faster rate), increasing lean body mass (which requires more calories to maintain), and suppressing appetite (Gauvin, Rejeski, & Norris, 1996; Gauvin, Rejeski, & Reboussin, 2000; Grilo, Brownell, & Stunkard, 1993). Exercise also prevents people from eating, at least for some period of time—it is difficult, after all, to eat potato chips while jogging. In sum, increasing exercise is the single best predictor of long-term weight control (Wadden, 1993).

Many of the cognitive-behavioral strategies used to help people consume fewer calories can also work effectively to help people exercise (Marcus et al., 2000; Wadden, 1993). First, people are encouraged to set specific goals and work toward them to help their motivation stay high. For example, you might have a goal to exercise three times a week for 30 minutes each time or to jog 20 miles a week. Similarly, operant-conditioning approaches, in which people receive some type of reward for adhering to an exercise routine, are successful

PHOTO 8.5   Carnie Wilson, a singer with the band Wilson Phillips, lost a tremendous amount of weight after having her stomach stapled. However, the risks and side effects of this procedure are substantial.

as well (Jeffrey, Wing, Thorson, & Burton, 1998; Wadden, 1993). One study found that people who were given rewards (e.g., clothing, money, going to the movies) for engaging in regular exercise reported exercising an average of 2.29 times per week as compared to 1.36 for those who were not given such rewards (Noland, 1989). Social influence techniques, such as exercising with a friend, are often effective strategies for increasing physical activity (Duncan & McAuley, 1993; Wing & Jeffery, 1999). As described at the beginning of the chapter, Bill managed to lose 15 pounds after he started exercising with a group of friends from work.

Small, inexpensive efforts, such as reminders and prompts, can work to promote exercise (Andersen et al., 1998; Marcus et al., 2000). In one study signs saying, "Your heart needs exercise. Here's your chance" were posted at three locations in public areas (mall, train station, bus terminal) where escalators and stairs were both available (Brownell, Stunkard, & Albaum, 1980). As shown in Figure 8.10, the percentage of people choosing stairs increased when the sign appeared, then dropped when the sign was removed, and rose again when the sign was reinstated. One study that examined the effect of phone calls asking participants how their exercise routine was going revealed that women were more likely to follow through on their intentions to walk at least 20 minutes a day at least three times per week if they had a weekly prompt than if they received calls only every 3 weeks (Lombard, Lombard, & Winett, 1995). Similarly, print materials, such as mailings and brochures, can also be effective (Marcus et al., 1998).

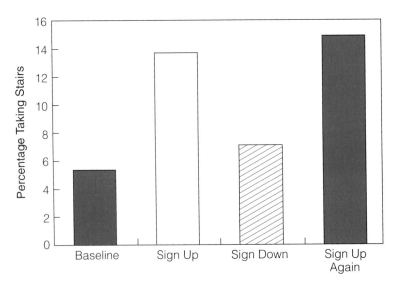

FIGURE 8.10 Helping people increase their amount of exercise can be as simple as reminding them to choose the stairs instead of the elevator (data from Brownell et al., 1980).

People are also more likely to follow through on their intentions to exercise when this behavior can easily fit in with their daily lives and schedules. For example, people are more likely to continue exercising when they are exercising at home as opposed to in a health club (Perri, Martin, Leermakers, Sears, & Notelovitz, 1997). Although formal exercise classes can provide social support and motivation, exercising at home is cheaper and more convenient. Similarly, people who commit to engaging in several short bouts of exercise each day (four 10-minute bouts of exercise such as climbing the stairs or walking briskly outside) are more successful at maintaining this behavior than those who attempt to engage in one longer period of exercise such as a 40-minute exercise class (Jakicic, Winters, Lang, & Wing, 1999). Even simple lifestyle changes, such as using stairs rather than escalators, walking rather than driving to work, and parking farther away from store entrances, can be as effective as more organized exercise activities in weight reduction (Andersen et al., 1999; Dunn et al., 1999; Kujala, Kaprio, Sarna, & Koskenvao, 1998; Wadden et al., 2002).

Engaging in regular exercise also leads to greater physical and psychological well-being (Blair et al., 1995; Kaplan, Strawbridge, et al., 1996; Kushi et al., 1997; Paffenbarger, Hyde, Wing, & Hsieh, 1986). Even moderate amounts of exercise can lead to major health benefits, including reduced risk of cardiovascular disease and diabetes (Blair et al., 1989; Helmrich, Ragland, Leung, & Paffenberger, 1991; Manson et al., 1992), lowered blood pressure (Kokkinos et al., 1995), and protection against osteoporosis (Greendale et al., 1995; Zhang, Feldblum, & Fortney, 1992) as well as cancer (Bernstein, Henderson, Hanisch, Sullivan-Halley, & Ross, 1994; Thune, Brenn, Lund, & Gaard, 1997; White, Jacobs & Dahling, 1996). Although some of these findings are based on correlational studies—which means that a third variable may be involved—experimental studies reveal similar findings. In one study, for example, women ages 50 to 70 years were randomly assigned to an exercise group or a control group (Nelson et al., 1994). Compared to those in the control group, women in the exercise group increased their muscle mass and muscle strength and maintained their bone mineral density, whereas those in the control group showed declines in bone density. Exercise also leads to lower levels of depression and anxiety (Camacho, Roberts, Lazarus, Kaplan, & Cohen, 1991; Norvell & Belles, 1993) and higher self-esteem (McAuley, Talbot, & Martinez, 1997; Stewart, 2001). For example, in one study 156 adults with clinical depression were randomly assigned to do aerobic exercise, receive drug treatment, or both (Babyak et al., 2000). Patients in all three conditions showed equivalent improvements at the 4-month and 6-month follow-up, suggesting that exercise can, at least in some cases, be as effective as drug treatment. Finally, one recent study revealed that exercise can lead to increased cognitive functioning: rats who were given the opportunity to run on an exercise wheel showed increased levels of brain-derived neurotrophic factor (BDNF), which leads to better cognitive functioning and memory (Cotman & Berchtold, 2002). Similarly, Arthur Kramer and colleagues (1999) found that older adults (ages 60 to 75) who were randomly assigned to participate in aerobic exercise showed improved performance on various cognitive and memory processes. Despite the numerous health benefits of exercise, only 25% of Americans report engaging in light to moderate physical activity at least 5 days per week, and approximately 25% of all adults report engaging in no leisure time physical activity (Centers for Disease Control, 2003).

Eating Disorders

I remember attending summer camp one year when I was in high school and hearing a close friend talk about consuming over a gallon of ice cream, and then vomiting it up. I remember watching a girl in high school jog around the school every day at lunch time, getting thinner almost literally before my eyes. I remember staying overnight with a friend during college and seeing cookie crumbs beside the toilet. As you read this section, you may recognize your friends, roommates, girlfriends, or even yourself. Eating disorders affect approximately 5 million Americans each year (Becker, Grinspoon, Klibanski, & Herzog, 1999).

Anorexia nervosa involves a drastic reduction in a persons food intake and an intentional loss of weight (maintaining a body weight 15% below one's normal weight based on height–weight tables, or a BMI of 17.5). This loss of weight eventually leads to amenorrhea, the absence of menstruation. People with anorexia often see themselves as heavy even when they are actually quite thin, and they have an excessive fear of gaining weight (see Table 8.4). They typically eat only very small amounts of food (e.g., a Cheerio for breakfast, a bite of an apple for lunch, lettuce for supper) and may have a variety of eating rituals that they engage in as a way of avoiding eating (e.g., cutting food into very small portions, eating very slowly). People with anorexia may also engage in strenuous exercise in an effort to lose weight. Anorexia is much more common in women than men, and tends to be most prevalent in upper-middle-class and upper-class white women (see Table 8.5). Women who participate in weight-conscious activities, including ballet, gymnastics, and cheerleading, are at greatest risk of developing anorexia (see Photo 8.6). Although the overall prevalence of anorexia nervosa in all women in the United States is approximately 0.5% (Becker et al.,

TABLE 8.4   *Diagnostic Criteria for Anorexia Nervosa*

1. Refusal to maintain body weight at or above a minimally normal weight for age and height (e.g., weight loss leading to maintenance of body weight less than 85% of that expected)
2. Intense fear of gaining weight or becoming fat, even though underweight
3. Disturbance in the way in which one's body weight or shape is experienced, undue influence of body weight or shape on self-evaluation, or denial of the seriousness of the current low body weight
4. Amenorrhea (the absence of at least three consecutive menstrual cycles)

These are a few criteria used to assess whether a person meets the clinical definition of anorexia nervosa.

Source: American Psychiatric Association, 1994.

TABLE 8.5   *Test Yourself: Sample Items from Drive for Thinness Scale*

1. I feel extremely guilty after overeating.
2. I am terrified of gaining weight.
3. I am preoccupied with the desire to be thinner.
4. If I gain a pound, I worry that I will keep gaining.
5. I think about dieting.

These items measure a person's focus on weight loss.

Source: Garner, Olmstead, & Polivy, 1983.

1999), 6 to 7% of women who attend professional schools for modeling and dance meet the criteria for having anorexia (Garner & Garfinkel, 1980).

Bulimia nervosa is characterized by recurrent episodes of binge eating followed by purging (see Tables 8.6 and 8.7). These episodes are typically triggered by some type of negative emotion, such as anxiety, tension, or even tiredness. During binges, bulimics rapidly consume enormous quantities of food. They typically select binge foods that are easy to swallow and vomit—fatty, sweet, high-energy foods. Bulimics then attempt to get rid of these calories, typically through vomiting or excessive exercise. This pattern of binge eating and purging occurs on a regular basis over some period of time. Bulimia is easier to hide than anorexia, in part because people with bulimia are typically normal weight. Although bulimia has a prevalence rate of 1 to 3% in North America, some surveys indicate that as many as 10% of women in college show symptoms of bulimia (Becker et al., 1999).

PHOTO 8.6   In 1992, Tracy Gold was forced to leave her role on the sitcom *Growing Pains* to seek treatment for anorexia nervosa.

Although the number of people who meet the diagnostic criteria for anorexia or bulimia is relatively few, many people, especially women, engage in some type of disordered eating. One study of 643 college women found that 82% engaged in some form of dieting behavior at least once daily (e.g., counting calories, eating low-calorie foods, skipping meals), 33% engaged in some form of destructive weight loss (e.g., taking laxatives, using appetite control pills, vomiting) at least once a month, and 38% had problems with binge-eating behavior (Mintz & Betz, 1988). Fully 61% were found to have some form of unhealthy eating behavior (e.g., chronic dieting, subclinical bulimia), and only 33% were considered "normal eaters." In the larger population, an estimated 2 million women are using unhealthy strategies to lose weight, including fasting, vomiting, using diet pills, and taking laxatives (Biener & Heaton, 1995).

Both anorexia and bulimia can lead to very serious, in some cases life-threatening, problems. Anorexia can cause low blood pressure, heart damage, and cardiac arrhythmia (Brownell & Fairburn, 1995). Women who recover from anorexia still may suffer with long-term problems, including bone loss (because of undernutrition and amenorrhea) and infertility (Becker et al., 1999); nearly 6% of all people with anorexia ultimately die from this disorder (Neumarker, 1997). Bulimia does not lead to starvation and hence is not typically fatal, but it can cause a variety of medical problems. Frequent vomiting may cause tearing

---

TABLE 8.6   *Diagnostic Criteria for Bulimia Nervosa*

1. Recurrent episodes of binge eating, namely, eating in a discrete period of time (e.g., within any 2-hour period) an amount of food that is definitely larger than most people would eat during a similar period of time and under similar circumstances, and feeling that one cannot stop eating or control what or how much one is eating.
2. Recurrent inappropriate compensatory behavior in order to prevent weight gain, such as self-induced vomiting; misuse of laxatives, diuretics, enemas, or other medications; fasting; or excessive exercise.
3. The binge eating and inappropriate compensatory behaviors both occur, on average, at least twice a week for 3 months.
4. Self-evaluation is unduly influenced by body shape and weight.

These are a few criteria used to assess whether a person meets the clinical definition of bulimia nervosa.

Source: American Psychiatric Association, 1994.

TABLE 8.7   *Test Yourself: Sample Items from the Bulimia Subscale*

1. I eat when I am upset.
2. I have gone on eating binges where I have felt that I could not stop.
3. I eat or drink in secrecy.
4. I eat moderately in front of others and stuff myself when they're gone.
5. I have the thought of trying to vomit in order to lose weight.

These items measure various symptoms of bulimia.

Source: Garner et al., 1983.

and bleeding in the esophagus, burning of throat and mouth by stomach acids, and damage to tooth enamel. Frequent purging can also lead to deficiencies in various nutrients, as well as anemia (an insufficient number of red blood cells), which both cause weakness and tiredness. Binge eating can cause damage to the stomach and intestines (Brownell & Fairburn, 1995) as well as hypoglycemia, which is a deficiency of sugar in the blood: following a binge of sweets, the pancreas releases excessive amounts of insulin, which drives down blood sugar levels and can leave a person feeling dizzy, tired, and depressed.

How Do Biological Factors Lead to Eating Disorders?

Some research suggests that biological factors may influence the development of eating disorders (Allison & Faith, 1997; Hewitt, 1997). First, women who have a close relative who suffers from an eating disorder are two to three times more likely to experience anorexia or bulimia than are women without this link. Second, twin studies have shown that these disorders are much more likely to appear in both twins of an identical pair than in fraternal twins. For example, one study examined rates of bulimia in over 2,000 female twins and found that genetic factors may predict bulimia in nearly 55% of cases.

Some evidence indicates that people with eating disorders have impairments in brain neurochemistry. For example, bulimics are less sensitive to serotonin, which cues feelings of fullness, than people with normal eating patterns (Sunday & Halmi, 1996). So, bulimics may eat huge amounts of food because they are unable to recognize feelings of fullness as quickly as others. On the other hand, anorexics show abnormally high levels of serotonin as well as leptin (which regulates eating; Walsh & Devlin, 1998). However, because these findings are correlational, it is not clear whether abnormal levels of serotonin produce disordered eating or perhaps are caused by disordered eating. One possibility is that these physiological changes are initially caused by irregular eating patterns, but then maintain these irregularities. For example, anorexics have low levels of leptin, which is secreted by fat cells, because they have such low levels of body fat. However, when anorexics increase how much they are eating, their leptin levels climb more quickly than their weight gain, making them feel full too early (hence less able to gain appropriate amounts of weight). Future research clearly must examine how biological and genetic factors can influence disordered eating.

What Psychological Factors Lead to Eating Disorders?

Most research indicates that psychological factors are heavily involved in the acquisition of eating disorders. This section therefore examines how cultural, social, family, and personality factors can lead to disordered eating.

Cultural Norms

Think quickly—who is the most attractive female movie star? I don't know who you named, but I bet she's very thin. Virtually all media images of women in the United States, including women in movies, on television shows, in music videos, and on the covers of magazines, show very thin women—some would say even dangerously thin: Miss America contestants have body weights 13 to 19% below the expected weight for women of their height (Wiseman, Gray, Mosimann, & Ahrens, 1992), which is one criterion for diagnosing anorexia.

The thinness norm portrayed in media is actually relatively new (see Box 8.4). Marilyn Monroe, the most revered sex symbol of the 1940s and 1950s, would be considered obese by our current standards (see Photo 8.7). Movie and magazine depictions of women have become consistently thinner in the past 20 years (Silverstein, Perdue, Peterson, & Kelly, 1986). For example, between 1959 and 1978, the weight of Miss America contestants and Playboy centerfolds decreased significantly (see Figure 8.11; Garner, Garfinkel, Schwartz, & Thompson, 1980). Similarly, over the last 20 years women's magazines have increased the number of articles on weight-loss techniques, presumably in an attempt to "help" women reach this increasingly thin ideal (Andersen & DiDomenico, 1992; Garner et al., 1980).

There are consequences of this focus on the thin ideal in the media (see Box 8.5). Not surprisingly, women of normal weight often feel too heavy. Nearly half of women of average weight are trying to lose weight (Biener & Heaton, 1995), as are 35% of normal-weight girls, and 12% of underweight girls

Photo 8.7 Although Marilyn Monroe was considered a major sex symbol in the 1950s, she would be considered obese by today's standards.

Box 8.4

Health Psychology in the Real World—"My, Look at How GI Joe Has Grown"

Although most research on social pressures leading to body image dissatisfaction has focused on the prevailing thin ideal for women, some recent research by Harrison Pope and colleagues suggests that men are also increasingly feeling pressure to conform to a similarly unrealistic body image norm (Pope, Olivardia, Gruber, & Borowiecki, 1999). However, the male ideal focuses on achieving a muscular ideal. To test the evolution of the "muscular male ideal" over time, researchers examined the measurements of the GI Joe action toy (the action toy with the longest continuous history) produced in 1973, 1975, and 1994. This review revealed a disturbing trend: The GI Joe action figure became much more muscular over time. For example, although there was no change in the height of the action figure, the biceps increased from 2.1 inches (1973) to 2.5 inches (1975) to 2.7 inches (1994). These may seem like small differences, but when translated into measurements for adult male bodies, bicep size would have increased from 12.2 inches to 16.4 inches. The latest GI Joe (the GI Joe Extreme, introduced in 1998) has biceps that translate to 26.8 inches—larger than any bodybuilder in history.

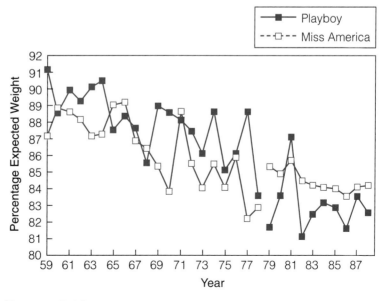

FIGURE 8.11 As this figure indicates, Miss America contestants have become increasingly thin over time (Wiseman et al., 1992).

(Schreiber et al., 1996). One study of teenage girls found that the "ideal girl" was perceived to be 5 feet, 7 inches tall and 100 pounds (translating into a BMI of less than 16, which is anorexic; Nichter & Nichter, 1991). Moreover, there is some evidence that repeated exposure to the extremely thin ideals presented by the media can lead some women to develop more negative attitudes about their own bodies. In one study at the University of South Florida 139 college women watched a 10-minute video of advertisements that featured either very thin women (such as those modeling weight-loss supplements, beer, and clothing) or average-weight women (such as those advertising pain relievers, household cleaning products, and insurance policies; Heinberg & Thompson, 1995). Women who already had negative views about their bodies (and hence were at greater risk of experiencing an eating disorder) increased in body dissatisfaction measures after watching the video featuring thin women (see Table 8.8).

Although in the United States the thin ideal has taken hold, this preference is by no means universal. In fact, in societies in which food is scarce, the ideal female body type is heavy (Anderson, Crawford, Nadeau, & Lindberg, 1992;

Box 8.5

Research Focus—Can Wearing a Swimsuit Hurt Your Math Performance?

Barbara Fredrickson and her colleagues hypothesized that the societal focus on thinness in women can lead to a variety of negative consequences (Frederickson, Roberts, Noll, Quinn, & Twenge, 1998). Both men and women at the University of Michigan were recruited to participate in a study on "emotions and consumer behavior" and were asked to try on either a swimsuit or a sweater and then rate how that item made them feel. They were then asked to complete a brief SAT-type math test, which was supposedly part of a separate experiment given by a researcher in the education department. It was hypothesized that trying on the swimsuit would lead many women to feel shame and disgust with their bodies, which in turn would disrupt their concentration on the math test and hence lead to lower scores. It was expected, however, that men would not show this type of disruption, regardless of what they had tried on.

The findings of this study were exactly as the researchers predicted. Specifically, women who tried on the bathing suit scored lower on the math test than those who tried a sweater (see Figure 8.12). There was no difference in math scores for men, regardless of whether they had tried on the sweater or the swimsuit. Apparently, women who wore a swimsuit felt shame about their bodies—presumably caused by societal pressures toward thinness in women—and this distraction lead them to perform more poorly on the math test.

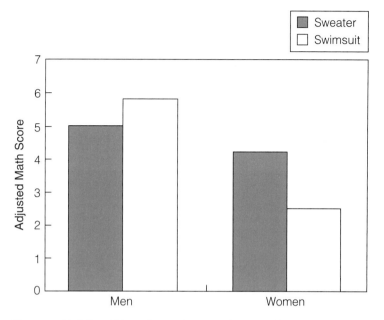

FIGURE 8.12 Although men's scores do not differ regardless of what they are wearing, women who wore a swimsuit had lower scores on a math test than those who wore sweaters (data from Fredrickson et al., 1998).

see Table 8.9): women who are heavier are perceived as healthy and more fertile, and heaviness can be a sign of wealth. Even within the United States ethnic groups vary on how much emphasis they place on the thin ideal (Halpern, Udry, Campbell, & Suchindran, 1999). As shown in Figure 8.13, studies of both high school and college girls show that African Americans have a heavier ideal weight than whites, are less preoccupied with weight and dieting, and are more satisfied with their weight (Desmond, Price, Hallinan, & Smith, 1989).

Questioning the Research 8.1

The Heinberg and Thompson (1995) study seems to indicate that exposure to media images of very thin women can lead women to increase in body dissatisfaction. However, what are some weaknesses of this study that may limit the conclusions we can draw?

Social Pressures

Because of the general focus on the thinness norm in our society, many women may feel pressure to conform to this ideal. Adolescent girls believe that being thinner makes them more successful in dating (Paxton et al., 1991)—and some data suggests that they are right. Although the average high school girl is 5 feet, 3 inches tall and 126 pounds, girls of this height who weigh 110 pounds are

TABLE 8.8   *Test Yourself: Sociocultural Attitudes toward Appearance Questionnaire*

Please read each of the following items and give the number that best reflects your agreement with the statement (1 = completely disagree, 3 = neither agree nor disagree, 5 = completely agree).

1. I tend to compare my body to TV and movie stars bodies.
2. I would like my body to look like the women/men who appear in TV shows and movies.
3. It's important for people to look attractive if they want to succeed in today's culture.
4. I often find myself comparing my physique to that of athletes pictured in magazines.
5. Music videos that show women who are in good shape make me wish that I were in better physical shape.
6. People with well-proportioned bodies look better in clothes.
7. Photographs of physically fit women/men make me wish that I had better muscle tone.
8. People find individuals who are in shape more attractive than individuals who are not in shape.
9. Attractiveness is very important if you want to get ahead in our culture.
10. I wish I looked like the women/men pictured in magazines who model underwear.

Women who compare themselves to media images of women are at increased risk of experiencing eating disorders.

Source: Cusumano & Thompson, 1997.

twice as likely to be dating, and girls who weigh 140 pounds are only half as likely to be dating (Halpern et al., 1999). Both men and women rate thin women as more feminine and attractive than normal-weight or overweight women (Silverstein et al., 1986). Box 8.6 describes a study showing how women often eat lightly to appear more attractive to desirable dating partners. Women may also engage in disordered eating in an attempt to be more popular with their friends. One study by Christian Crandall (1988) of women who lived in a sorority found that those who engaged in more frequent binge eating were more popular than those who engaged in less frequent binge eating.

There is some good news. Although the cultural norms in most Western societies seem to support a very thin ideal for women, these norms are not as extreme as people think. As shown in Figure 8.14, college women's ideal figure is significantly smaller than their current figure (Fallon & Rozin, 1985). In contrast, the gap between men's current and ideal figure is quite small! Women

TABLE 8.9   *Cultural Variations in Preference for a Thin Female Body*

| | **Reliability of Food Supply** | | | |
	Very Low	Fairly Low	Fairly High	Very High
Heavy	71%	50%	39%	40%
Medium	29%	33%	39%	20%
Light	0%	17%	22%	40%

People in cultures with a very reliable food supply, such as the United States, show a much stronger preference for a thin female body than cultures with a low reliability of food supply.

Source: Anderson et al., 1992.

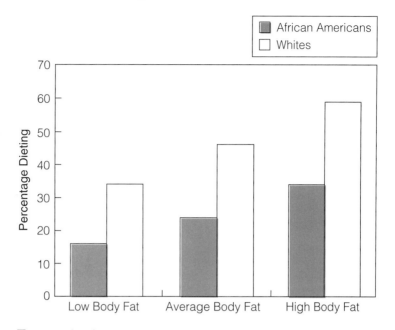

FIGURE 8.13 White girls in this scale at all levels of body fat are more likely to be dieting than African American girls. Note how many white and African American girls with low levels of body fat are dieting (data from Halpern et al., 1999).

also typically believe men prefer a female figure that is thinner than men actually do. Similarly, my own research has shown that women believe other women are more supportive of the thinness norm than these women actually are (Sanderson, Darley, & Messinger, 2002). For example, women have an average BMI of 22 but believe other women have a BMI of about 20.5; women exercise about 4 hours a week but believe other women exercise about 5.5 hours a week. Women who felt discrepant from the campus thinness norm had a greater frequency of symptoms of eating disorders, such as an extreme focus on thinness, binge eating, and purging.

Family Dynamics

Parents can influence their children's eating behaviors. First, families of women with eating disorders may also be particularly focused on weight and shape. In fact, girls who believe it is important to their parents that they are thin are more likely to be concerned about their weight and to diet than those who do not believe their parents have such preferences (Field et al., 2001). Women whose mothers are preoccupied with weight and dieting behaviors and who criticize their daughters' appearance also report more weight-loss behaviors themselves (Baker, Whisman, & Brownell, 2000; Sanftner, Crowther, Crawford, & Watts, 1996). For example, one study with 89 pairs of mothers and their teenage daughters found that girls who use extreme weight-loss methods (e.g.,

Box 8.6

Research Focus—"No, I'm Not Really Hungry"

One clever study by Mori, Chaiken, and Pliner (1987) examined whether women who wanted to appear particularly attractive to a desirable man would deliberately eat small amounts of food. To test this hypothesis, women were recruited to participate in a study that supposedly examined interpersonal interactions. They were told they would have a conversation with a student of the opposite sex and were given a background sheet to read before the conversation. The information on the background sheet in some cases made their partner seem particularly desirable as a dating partner (interested in travel, athletics, photography, wanted to go to law school, and single), and in other cases, made him seem not very desirable (no interests other than watching TV, no plans other than making money). The women were then asked to have a 20-minute conversation with the male student, and as the experimenter left the room, she gestured to a bowl of candy (M&Ms) and said, "Oh, these were left over from a party—help yourself." The dependent variable was how much the women ate.

As predicted, women ate significantly less when their conversation partner was desirable as opposed to undesirable. Specifically, women who were talking with an undesirable man ate an average of 25.24 grams of M&Ms, whereas women who were talking with a desirable man ate only 6.37 grams! This study shows that when women are trying to appear attractive to a potential dating partner, they don't eat much. (I always warn the male students in my classes, if their dates always eat well, they might need to get some better hobbies.)

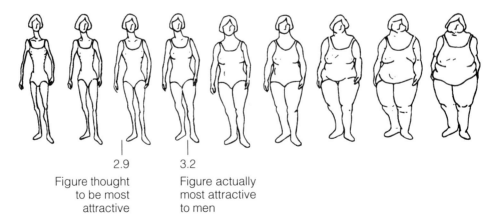

2.9
Figure thought
to be most
attractive

3.2
Figure actually
most attractive
to men

FIGURE 8.14 Although college women often believe that men prefer a very thin body, men actually prefer a somewhat larger figure than women assume; Fallon & Rozin, 1985; Stunkard, Sorenson, & Schuisinger, 1983).

fasting, crash dieting, skipping meals) are very likely to have mothers who also use such methods (Benedikt, Wertheim, & Love, 1998). Although they may not be directly encouraging their daughters to engage in such behaviors, these mothers are still modeling these attitudes and behaviors. Moreover, while only 14% of the girls in this sample were overweight, 51% of the mothers reported that they encouraged their daughters to lose weight and 39% of the mothers wanted their daughters to be thinner.

The families of anorexics often have some distinct, potentially dysfunctional, dynamics (Kog & Vandereycken, 1985). They may appear normal, and even high achieving, from the outside, but family members have problems with engaging in open communication and managing conflict. Parents also tend to be overinvolved in their daughters' lives, and may be demanding and controlling—they often do not encourage autonomy or assertiveness in their children. One study of anorexic patients found that they typically describe their parents as setting extremely high achievement standards and as often disapproving (Waller & Hartley, 1994). Similarly, at the beginning of the chapter I described Annie's struggle with anorexia and the pressure for high academic achievement she felt from her parents.

The families of bulimics also often show particular characteristics, including more conflict and hostility coupled with less nurturance and support within the family group (Wonderlich, Klein, & Council, 1996). Women with bulimia may binge and purge to cope with feelings of isolation and stress, in part because they are unlikely to have supportive interpersonal relationships in their families. In one study of 21 bulimic women and 21 women without symptoms of disordered eating, participants completed measures of social interactions and social support and were then videotaped while engaging in a conflict-resolution task with a partner for 5 minutes (Grissett & Norvell, 1992). Findings revealed that bulimics felt less socially competent in a variety of ways, including in their ability to form close relationships and function well socially. They were also rated by observers as less socially effective, including worse at problem solving, less likely to be a good friend, and less skilled in social interaction.

> **Questioning the Research 8.2**
>
> Although several studies suggest that families with certain types of unhealthy interaction patterns (e.g., lack of support,) can cause girls to develop bulimia, can you think of an alternative explanation for these findings? (Hint: Think about the difference between correlation and causation.)

Personality

Anorexics often have a distinct personality style—they are rigid, anxious, perfectionistic, and obsessed with order and cleanliness (Kaye, 1997). In fact, anorexics have high rates of diagnosis with obsessive-compulsive disorder. Anorexics hold themselves to particularly high standards; hence, they may seem like "the perfect child" to outside observers (Tiller, Schmidt, Ali, & Treasure, 1995). Often they have assimilated a very thin ideal. In one study anorexics and normal-weight women were asked to judge the weight at which their own bodies and other women's bodies would change from "thin" to "normal" to "fat" (Smeets, 1999). Compared to women of normal weight, anorexics gave lighter weights for each of the transition points, indicating that they were setting particularly strict standards for attractiveness. These personality characteristics may not be simply a result of their current eating disorder, and hence a reflection of malnutrition, because recovered anorexics who are of normal weight show similar traits.

Women who have bulimia have quite a different set of personality characteristics than those who develop anorexia. Bulimics are often depressed and anxious, leading some researchers to believe that they use food as a way of comforting themselves. Bulimics have often struggled with weight issues for some time and may have a history of binge eating, weight fluctuation, and frequent exercise or dieting (Kendler et al., 1991). Bulimics may lack a clear sense of self-identity or have very negative self-views (Humphrey, 1986, 1988). While anorexia involves extreme levels of control, bulimics typically report feeling out of control while they are binge eating, resulting in guilt and self-contempt following such episodes. Two studies suggest that 20 to 33% of bulimics who are in treatment have made at least one serious suicide attempt (Garfinkel & Garner, 1984). Women with bulimia report higher levels of other types of destructive behaviors, including alcohol use, substance abuse, and kleptomania (compulsive stealing), than women without an eating disorder (Holderness, Brooks-Gunn, & Warren, 1994). Bulimics are also more likely to have experienced sexual abuse during childhood (Wonderlich, Wilsnack, Wilsnack, & Harris, 1996).

What Approaches Help Prevent Eating Disorders?

Because eating disorders are so prevalent and so problematic, some high schools and most colleges and universities have programs designed to prevent such problems by giving students knowledge about the hazards of disordered eating in the hopes that having such information will help prevent serious disorders. Unfortunately, very little research suggests that interventions targeting large groups of women are effective. For example, in one study by Joel Killen and colleagues (1993) 967 sixth- and seventh-grade girls were randomly assigned to receive either 18 hour-long lessons on eating disorders or their regular health class (Killen et al., 1993). The lessons included information on normal growth and development, the dangers of unhealthy dieting strategies, the influence of media images, and strategies for healthy eating and exercise. Although girls who received this intense information did have higher scores on knowledge of eating behavior than those without this program, they did not show changes in their concern about weight.

On a more encouraging note, interventions specifically targeting women at greatest risk of developing eating disorders—those who have poor body image—can be beneficial (Kaminski & McNamara, 1996; Stice, Chase, Stormer, & Appel, 2001; Stice, Mazotti, Weibel, & Agras, 2000). Patricia Kaminski and Kathleen McNamara (1996) recruited women with poor body image to participate in an 8-week treatment consisting of educational information on realistic weights and healthy eating habits as well as cognitive strategies for enhancing self-esteem, improving body image, and combating social pressures for thinness. Women who were in the treatment group had greater self-esteem and body satisfaction and fewer destructive dieting behaviors than those in the control group even 5 months after participating in the intervention. Moreover, some recent research indicates that providing strategies for improving body image and reducing excessive concern with weight using the Internet can be effective in decreasing women's extreme focus on thinness (Winzelberg et al., 2000). We talk more about effective strategies for preventing eating disorders in Chapter 13.

What Is the Treatment for Eating Disorders?

Although eating disorders are obviously associated with serious health consequences, people with such disorders are often very reluctant to seek treatment (Pike & Striegel-Moore, 1997). They may feel ashamed and embarrassed to admit their behavior and may believe that the disorder will simply go away on its own at some point. While bulimics often feel out of control, depressed, and guilty about their eating habits, and hence are motivated to get better, anorexics typically feel in control and even proud of their highly restricted eating habits, and hence often resist treatment. People with anorexia may also be afraid that seeking treatment will lead them to gain weight. And in some cases, this is true—because people with anorexia often seek help (or, more often, are forced to seek help) only when they are on the verge of collapsing from starvation, tube or intravenous feeding may be used (in a hospital setting) to try to get their body weight and nutrition under control (Goldner & Birmingham, 1994).

A few approaches can help in treating eating disorders. First, because family interaction patterns are thought to influence the development of disordered eating, many therapists recommend some combination of individual and family therapy in treating eating disorders, especially for anorexia (Becker et al., 1999). Anorexics need help changing their social environment and, in particular, must understand that other people do not hold themselves up to the same high standards, which is why family therapy can be helpful (Garner, Garfinkel, & Bemis, 1982). One study of patients hospitalized for anorexia showed that family therapy was more effective than individual therapy in increasing weight gain as long as 5 years later (Dare & Eisler, 1995).

Cognitive-behavioral therapy is generally seen as the most effective treatment for bulimia; it can also be effective in treating anorexia (Walsh & Devlin, 1998). This type of therapy focuses on normalizing patients' eating patterns (by encouraging slow eating, regular meals), expanding their food choices (by eliminating "forbidden" foods), and changing their thoughts and attitudes about eating, food, and their bodies (by trying to avoid linking self-esteem with weight). Techniques can include monitoring the thoughts, feelings, and circumstances that lead to binge eating and purging and clarifying distorted views of eating, weight, and body shape. For example, therapists may use cognitive-behavioral therapy to attempt to change faulty beliefs, such as "If I gain one pound, I'll gain a hundred," and "Any sweet is instantly converted into fat." They teach patients that media images of women are often illusions (e.g., models often have their body flaws airbrushed away) as a way of helping them develop more realistic body ideals. Cognitive-behavioral therapy for bulimia is especially effective when coupled with antidepressant drugs, such as Prozac. As described at the beginning of the chapter, Rachel was able to stop bingeing after working with her therapist to identify the triggers of overeating and taking Prozac.

One study by David Garner and his colleagues (1993) compared the effectiveness on bulimia of two types of therapy. Sixty bulimic women, ages 18 to 35 years were randomly assigned to receive either cognitive-behavior or supportive-expressive therapy over 18 weeks, with one 45- to 60-minute session each week. The cognitive-behavior therapy consisted of self-monitoring of food intake, vomiting, and binge eating, as well as monitoring feelings and thoughts surrounding eating. Supportive-expressive therapy, which views eating disorders as a symptom of larger problems, had therapists listen to and help subjects identify feelings. Both treatments were equally effective in decreasing the frequency of binge eating, but cognitive-behavior therapy was somewhat better in decreasing the frequency of vomiting (82% reduction versus 64% reduction; see Figure 8.15). Although women in both groups gained some weight, those in the cognitive-behavior therapy group gained more weight (6.6 pounds versus 3.0 pounds respectively). Finally, patients who received the cognitive-behavior therapy also had lower rates of depression, higher rates of self-esteem, and greater satisfaction with their therapy than those in the supportive-expressive therapy.

Interpersonal therapy, which focuses on the interpersonal sources of stress that lead to disordered eating, can also be effective (Agras, 1993). This type of therapy can help disordered eaters identify interpersonal problems that cause stress, such as an obsession with perfectionism (in the case of anorexics) and negative self-image (in the case of bulimics).

Although some people with eating disorders do get better, there is a relatively high rate of relapse. About half of those with anorexia or bulimia had a full recovery, about 30% have a partial recovery, and about 20% have no real improvement (Becker et al., 1999). Many anorexics continue to be underweight and may require repeat hospitalizations. Similarly, about one third of bulimics who have fully recovered experience a relapse within 2 years (Olmsted, Kaplan & Rockert, 1994). These depressing statistics suggest that recovery from eating disorders is best viewed as a process; patients and their families should not expect instant results.

Lingering Issues

Is obesity really unhealthy? Although this chapter examined the negative physical effects of obesity, some research suggests that distribution of weight on a body may be a better predictor of health than amount of weight (Wickelgren,

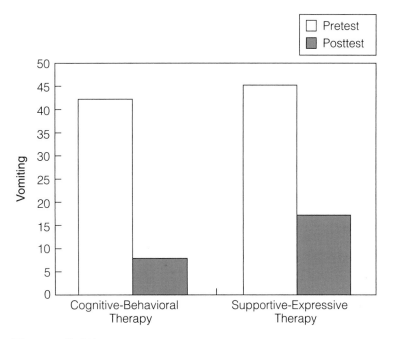

FIGURE 8.15 Although women who received either type of therapy showed considerably less frequent vomiting at the posttest, those who received the cognitive-behavioral therapy had less-frequent vomiting than those who received the supportive-expressive therapy (Garner et al., 1993).

1998). People who have upper-body fat (e.g., "apples") are at a greater risk of experiencing major health problems, such as diabetes, hypertension, and cardiovascular disease, than those who have lower-body fat (e.g., "pears"). Some studies even suggest that weight accumulated around one's waist may be a better predictor of mortality than overall obesity (Folsom et al., 1993). For example, one study found that women with a waist-to-hip ratio of 0.88 or higher (meaning their waists were nearly as large as their hips) were three times as likely to die of coronary heart disease than those with a ratio of less than 0.72 (meaning their waists were considerably smaller than their hips; Rexrode et al., 1998). Although men are more likely than women to carry fat in the abdominals as opposed to the lower body, both men and women who have higher amounts of abdominal fat suffer similar health risks. One reason why having upper-body fat is associated with such negative health consequences is that fat cells in the abdominals are much larger than fat cells in the legs and butt; hence, abdominal fat cells are more likely to form fatty acids. In turn, high levels of fatty acids in the blood lead to higher levels of glucose in the blood as well as higher blood pressure.

Can eating disorder prevention programs have dangerous effects? Some recent research suggests that providing eating disorder information can have detrimental effects. A study by Traci Mann and colleagues (1997) evaluated the effectiveness of an eating disorder prevention program that was presented to

788 first-year women attending Stanford University. Women who attended this program actually had more symptoms of disordered eating 1 month after than those who did not attend the program. The researchers suggest a few possible reasons for this unexpected finding. First, women who participated in the prevention program perceived eating disorders as much more common than they actually are; this suggests that receiving such information can inadvertently make disordered eating seem like relatively typical behavior. Second, because this program was presented by women who were recovering from eating disorders, yet who appeared attractive and articulate, it may have led women to see eating disorders as not particularly dangerous and potentially even desirable. This research suggests that eating disorder prevention programs must be very careful to avoid causing unintended harm to participants.

Thought Questions

1. Describe how psychological factors can influence both overeating (i.e., obesity) and undereating (i.e., anorexia).
2. Describe one physiological explanation for obesity and one psychological explanation.
3. Your roommate Jean is obese and is constantly trying, but failing, to lose weight. What two pieces of advice could you give him?
4. Describe how social, cultural, and personality factors can influence the acquisition of eating disorders.
5. Your friend Beth is a resident assistant in a dormitory of first-year students, and she thinks it would be a good idea to provide some type of eating disorder prevention program to her students. Because she knows you are in a health psychology course, she comes to you for advice on creating such a program. What would you tell her?

Answers to Questioning the Research

Answer 8.1: First, although this study suggests that exposure to media images of very thin women led some participants to increase in body dissatisfaction, remember that watching this video did not lead to greater dissatisfaction for all (or even most) women. Instead, only women who already had negative feelings about their bodies showed an increase in such feelings. This study therefore may indicate that women without such concerns are not really influenced by this type of exposure. Second, this study assessed women's body dissatisfaction only immediately after they viewed the tape; we cannot conclude whether seeing this video has any long-term effects.

Answer 8.2: Although this section describes the distinct features of the families of anorexics and bulimics, it is important to remember that these studies are correlational, not causational. Some of the patterning observed in these families may be a result—not a cause—of having a child with a chronic and even life-threatening illness. For example, perhaps having a daughter who is eating huge amounts of food and then vomiting or engaging in excessive exercise is very upsetting to parents, and they then distance themselves from their daughter as a way of coping with their feelings. Although this may not be a constructive approach, it may simply be too painful for them to remain close to their daughter while she is engaging in such destructive behavior. We must be very careful about how we interpret the results of correlational studies.

CHAPTER 9

The Experience and Management of Pain

- Billy is 7 years old and always seems to be sick. Sometimes he says his stomach hurts, sometimes he says his leg hurts, and sometimes he says his throat hurts. His mother becomes very concerned whenever Billy is sick and must miss school. She usually stays home from work with him, lets him watch videos, and prepares his favorite foods for him.

- Antonia is 25 years old and has always been very healthy. However, for the last 6 months she has experienced severe migraine headaches once or twice a week. Sometimes these headaches are so bad that she can't drive to work, and she is concerned that she will lose her job. Antonia doesn't know what causes her headaches, but finds that they are often worse after she's stayed up late taking care of her 3-month-old son or when she is feeling overwhelmed with her responsibilities at work.

- Melissa has just given birth to her first baby, a little boy named Matt. Although she had heard horror stories from several friends about the pain of labor,

Melissa found it not so bad. She and her husband attended childbirth preparation classes, in which they learned to engage in special types of breathing. They also chose an ultrasound picture of their baby as a "focal object" on which Melissa concentrated during the most painful contractions.

- Tom has suffered from back pain for over 10 years. He has tried many different approaches to treating his pain, including drugs, massage therapy, and even surgery. Although some of these treatments were effective for a few weeks or months, the pain always returned. However, his physician recently recommended he enter a pain clinic, in which Tom will receive training in relaxation, guided imagery, and hypnosis. His wife has also been asked to attend several sessions with other patients' family members to learn how to support Tom's therapy, in particular to understand that they must reinforce painfree behavior while ignoring pain-related behavior.

- Brian has had problems with his knees for nearly 20 years His doctor recently recommended a new type of drug, one he claims is the best drug he's seen developed for joint pain in some time from a company that makes many other well-performing drugs. Brian's doctor therefore strongly urged Brian to sample this new medicine. Although Brian has been taking the drug for only 3 weeks, he already feels less pain when he walks. He is thrilled with the new drug.

Preview

This chapter examines how psychological factors can influence the experience and management of pain. First, I describe different types of pain as well as different theories about how people experience pain. Then we examine different ways of measuring pain, including physiological, behavioral, and self-report methods. Next, we examine how various psychological factors, such as learning, cognition, personality, and experience of stress, can influence the experience of pain. We then review physical methods of controlling pain, including drugs, surgery, and acupuncture, and psychological methods of controlling pain, including hypnosis, relaxation, cognitive therapy, and behavior therapy. Finally, we examine the role of placebos in reducing pain.

Why Do We Care About Pain?

Pain is one of the most common health problems that causes people to seek medical care. Two to five percent of the adult American population experiences disabling lower-back pain at a given point in time, and 80% will experience some problems with lower-back pain during their lives (Garofalo & Polatin, 1999). One study of over 13,000 Americans found that 38.3% had experienced a tension-related headache in the last year (Schwartz, Stewart, Simon, & Lipton, 1998). And pain has major consequences for the individual and for society. Chronic low-back pain is the second most frequent cause of visits to doctors' offices (after the common cold), causes 12% of all sick leave, and costs $16 billion a year in direct medical costs (for surgery, disability, physician/hospital visits; Arena & Blanchard, 1996). Migraine headaches cost $6.5 billion to $17.2 billion annually in lost labor costs, when 8.3% of those who suffer from such headaches miss work and 43.6% report reduced effectiveness at work (Holroyd & Lipchik, 1999; Schwartz et al., 1998). In sum, pain is a common problem for many people and has major consequences.

Although no one likes to experience pain, feeling pain is actually beneficial to long-term health and survival (Vertosick, 2000). Pain is a warning signal that your body is experiencing a problem, and it thereby motivates you to change your behavior. For example, if you touch a hot stove and burn your finger, you learn to not touch the stove again. Similarly, if you hurt your ankle, you will try to avoid putting weight on that foot, and thereby prevent further damage. People who are born with an insensitivity to pain, and who therefore experience little or no sensation of pain, often suffer numerous health problems and die at a relatively young age (Manfredi et al., 1981). Because they don't experience pain, they do not have the opportunity to learn from small mistakes (e.g., they never learn that falling on pavement leads to abrasions and cuts and the potential development of infection), and hence they may suffer from constant bumps, bruises, and cuts. Their inability to feel pain also means they don't seek medical care when they should, so relatively small problems can become much larger ones (e.g., they don't see a doctor when they experience severe stomach pains, and therefore could develop a ruptured appendix). Although at times you may wish you'd never experience pain, as you can see, *not* feeling pain can have many negative consequences.

What Is Pain?

Although we all know what pain is, it can actually refer to many different sensations—a sharp pain when we step on a sliver of glass, the dull ache of a tension headache, the blistering of a sunburn, even the small but very irritating pain of a paper cut. The International Association for the Study of Pain (IASP) defines *pain* as "an unpleasant sensory and emotional experience associated with actual or potential tissue damage, or described in terms of such damage" (International Association for the Study of Pain, 1979).

Acute pain is intense but time-limited pain that is generally the result of tissue damage or disease, such as a broken bone, a cut or bruise, and the labor of childbirth (Turk, Meichenbaum, & Genest, 1983). This type of pain typically disappears over time (as the injury heals) and lasts less than 6 months. Because acute pain is intense, people suffering from it are highly motivated to seek out its causes and to treat it. Many of the pain-control techniques that we discuss later in this chapter are very effective at treating acute pain.

In contrast, *chronic pain* often begins as acute pain (in response to a specific injury or disease), but does not go away after a minimum of 6 months (Turk et al., 1983). Lower-back pain, headaches, and the pain associated with arthritis and cancer are all examples of chronic pain. Chronic pain can be divided into several different subcategories. *Recurrent acute pain* is caused by a benign, or harmless, condition and refers to pain that is sometimes intense but that also sometimes disappears. Migraine headaches are one example of this type of pain. *Intractable-benign pain* is, as its name suggests, benign but persistent. Although it may vary in intensity, it never really disappears. Lower-back pain is a particularly common type of intractable-benign pain. Finally, *progressive pain* is pain that originates from a malignant condition; hence, it is continuous and worsens over time. The pain caused by arthritis or cancer, for example, is a type of progressive pain.

Medical care professionals distinguish between acute and chronic pain because these different types of pain often have different causes and hence need to be treated in different ways. Acute pain generally is caused by physical damage to the body, which then gets improves time as body tissues, bones, and muscles heal. In contrast, most types of chronic pain are caused at least in part by behavioral factors (although this is not necessarily true, especially for progressive pain), and this type of pain lasts long after specific tissue damage has healed. This does not mean that chronic pain is "all in your head," but rather that psychological factors may contribute in some way to physical pain. Because chronic pain is extremely resistant to treatment, it lingers for some time, leading to a number of negative consequences (Melzack & Wall, 1982). People in constant pain may feel depressed and helpless, have difficulty sleeping, and experience weight loss or weight gain. Many people with chronic pain lose their jobs, lose friends, and have dysfunctional relationships with family (because they require or request constant assistance and attention and/or push people away completely). In some cases, chronic-pain patients become even more sensitive to pain over time, a condition known as *hyperalgesia* (Cervero, 2000).

How Do We Experience Pain?

One of the earliest theories of pain was *specificity theory* (Melzack & Wall, 1982), which posits that there are specific sensory receptors for different types of sensations, such as pain, warmth, touch, and pressure. The classic description of this theory was presented by René Descartes in 1664, which compared the experience of pain to a bell-ringing mechanism in a church—a person on th eground floor of the church pulls a rope, and this tug of the rope travels up to the bell in the belfry at the top of the tower, causing the bell to ring. Similarly, according to specificity theory, once a person experiences an injury, a direct chain carries these messages of pain to the brain, which then sets off an "alarm"; hence, the person experiences pain.

Another early theory was the *pattern theory* (Melzack & Wall, 1982), which describes pain as resulting from the type of stimulation received by the nerve endings and theorizes that the key determination of pain is the intensity of the stimulation. A small stimulation of the nerve endings could be interpreted as touch, whereas a more substantial stimulation could be interpreted as pain. This theory explains why touching a warm heating pad feels pleasant, but touching a very hot pan in the oven feels painful.

Although both specificity and pattern theory may have some components that are correct, current evidence suggests that both of these theories have limitations. First, people can experience pain without having tissue damage (Melzack & Wall, 1988). Phantom-limb pain, which is often experienced as a severe burning or cramping, is the experience of feeling pain in a limb that has been amputated. Because the limb is nonexistent, obviously this type of pain cannot have a purely physical basis. One study found that 72% of amputees experience pain in their phantom limb 8 days after surgery, 65% have pain 6 months later, and 60% continue to have pain 2 years later. Second, people can have tissue damage and feel no pain (Fordyce, 1988). Athletes who are in the

PHOTO 9.1 During the 1996 Olympics, U.S. gymnast Kerri Strug injured her ankle on the first of her two vault attempts. Although she initially had trouble standing up, Kerri managed to complete her second vault even with her sprained ankle—and her performance on this second vault led to a first-ever gold medal for the U.S. women's gymnastic team.

middle of a competition, for example, may experience a severe injury and yet report feeling no pain until later (see Photo 9.1). Emmitt Smith, a running back with the Dallas Cowboys in the 1990s, once dislocated his shoulder—a painful injury—in the middle of a game but kept playing. In sum, lots of evidence suggests that the link between physiological stimulation and the experience of physical symptoms is indirect. Both the specificity and pattern theories fail to account for the role of psychology in the experience of pain.

The *gate control theory* of pain, by Ronald Melzack and Patrick Wall (1965, 1982, 1988), attempts to correct for the limitations of prior theories by including the role of psychological factors in the experience of pain. According to this theory, when body tissues are injured, such as when you get cut or scraped, nerve endings, or *nociceptors*, in the damaged area transmit impulses to a particular part of the dorsal horn section of the spinal cord called the *substantia gelatinosa* (see Figure 9.1). Some nerve fibers, A-delta fibers, are small and myelinated (covered with a fatty substance that acts as insulation); and therefore, they carry information very rapidly. These fibers transmit sharp, localized, distinct pain sensations. Other nerve fibers, C-fibers, are unmyelinated (uncoated) and transmit the sensation of diffuse, dull, or aching pain much more slowly.

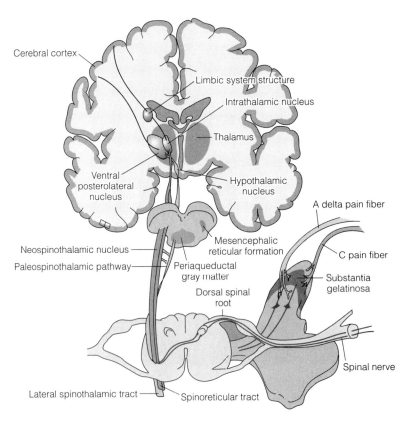

FIGURE 9.1   This figure shows how pain signals are normally transmitted by nerve fibers from the point of injury to the substantia gelatinosa in the dorsal section of the spinal cord, and then ultimately to the brain.

Once these nerve impulses reach the substantia gelatinosa, one of two things may happen. If the sensations are sufficiently intense, the nerve impulses are sent all the way up to the brain, where they are experienced as pain—the more signals that reach the brain, the more pain the person experiences. These signals also travel to the *somatosensory cortex* of the brain, which generally allows a person to figure out exactly where on the body he or she is experiencing pain. The pain from stubbing your toe is interpreted in one part of the somatosensory cortex, whereas the pain from a paper cut on your finger is interpreted by a different area. The size of the area in the somatosensory cortex devoted to a particular region of the body determines how sensitive we are to pain experienced in that region. The area corresponding to the fingers, which are particularly sensitive, is quite large. On the other hand, the area corresponding to the back, which is not very sensitive, is quite small.

However, according to the gate control theory, not all of the pain signals carried by the nerve fibers successfully reach the brain (see Figure 9.2). Specifically, this theory posits that there is a gate in the substantia gelatinosa that either lets pain impulses travel on to the brain or blocks their progress. Any competing sensation that increases stimulation to the site of potential pain could serve to block transmission of pain sensations, or close the gate. This is why rubbing a leg cramp, scratching an itch, and putting an ice pack on a sprained ankle may all reduce pain: this type of stimulation activates the large A-beta fibers, which are responsible for modulating pain sensations by closing the gate.

The brain can also control whether the gate is open or shut by sending signals down to the spinal cord. Specifically, the *central control mechanism* influences how much information is transmitted from the brain to the spinal cord. When a person feels anxious or scared, for example, the brain opens the gate and thereby increases the potential to experience pain. On the other hand, when a person is distracted or relaxed, the brain shuts the gate, thereby decreasing the potential to experience pain. This is why a person may experience something that should be very painful (e.g., an athlete who dislocates a shoulder during a game), but he or she doesn't consciously feel the pain immediately because the brain stopped the transmission of pain signals long enough for the person to "escape" (or at least finish the game). As we discuss later in the chapter, this is one of the explanations for the influence of hypnosis on pain relief—it may encourage the brain to close the gate.

Although the precise gating mechanism is not entirely understood, a portion of the midbrain, called the *periaqueductral gray*, seems to be involved in the experience of pain. Several studies, with both animals and humans, have shown that activating the periaqueductral gray area, such as through the use of mild electrical stimulation, can entirely block the experience of pain. For example, Dean Reynolds (1969) demonstrated that following electrical stimulation of this area of the brain, rats could withstand the pain of abdominal surgery without any other type of anesthetic.

Neurochemical processes are also involved in the experience of pain (Rabin, 1999). Specifically, the neurons release chemicals called *neurotransmitters* that can increase or decrease the amount of pain experienced (see Figure 9.3). Some neurotransmitters, such as *substance P* and *glutamate*, excite the neurons that send messages about pain, therefore increasing the experience of pain. Other chem-

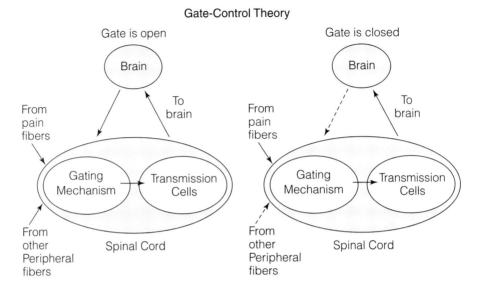

FIGURE 9.2   According to the gate control theory of pain, not all of the pain signals carried by the nerve fibers successfully reach the brain. Any competing sensation that increases stimulation to the site, such as pressure, heat, or cold, could shut the gate, thereby stopping the transmission of pain signals to the brain. Psychological factors, such as distraction and relaxation, can also send messages from the brain down to the spinal cord to shut the gate.

icals in the body, such as *bradykinin* and *prostaglandins*, are released by the body's cells when damage occurs; they, too, excite the neurons that carry information about pain as well as mobilize the body to repair the damage in a variety of ways, including causing inflammation at the site of the injury and increasing the immune system's functioning. Other neurotransmitters, such as *serotonin* and *endorphins*, work by slowing or blocking the transmission of any nerve impulses. Endorphins, for example, bind to receptors in the periaqueductal gray area of the midbrain, dramatically reducing pain. (Although endorphins are naturally produced in our bodies, opiate drugs, such as morphine, can serve a similar function in the brain, and therefore reduce pain.)

The gate control theory clearly differs from other theories in a number of ways. First, it describes pain as caused by a physiological stimulation as well as psychological factors. Specifically, it views pain as resulting partially from a person's perception or interpretation, not simply as a physiological sensation.

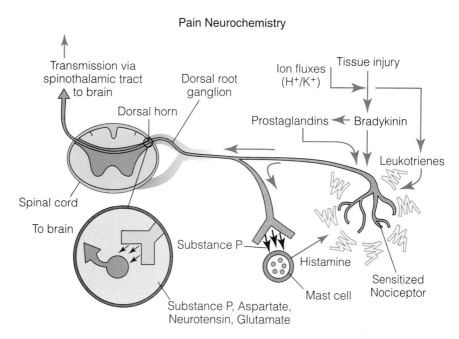

FIGURE 9.3 As shown in this figure, neurotransmitters such as *substance P* as well as other chemicals in the body, such as *bradykinin* and *prostaglandins*, excite the neurons that send messages about pain, thereby increasing the experience of pain. On the other hand, other neurotransmitters, such as *endorphins*, slow or block the transmission of nerve impulses and thereby reduce the experience of pain.

This theory explains why the same event can be interpreted by different people as more or less painful, and why sometimes pain is not experienced immediately. This theory also describes the person as having some control over the experience of pain. Specifically, people can take concrete steps to reduce their experience of pain, such as by distracting themselves, relaxing their muscles, or using an ice pack or heating pad.

Ronald Melzack (1993) has also proposed an extension to gate control theory that places an even stronger emphasis on the influence of the brain in the perception of pain. According to his *neuromatrix theory*, a network of neurons is distributed throughout the brain, which processes the information that flows through it. Although the neuromatrix typically acts to process sensory information transmitted from the body, the neuromatrix can process experiences even in the absence of sensations. Using brain-imaging technology, researchers have learned that people who have had a limb amputated show a reorganization of how the brain processes stimulation of various body parts

(Flor et al., 1995). For example, the parts of the brain that previously responded to the arm and hand may, in the case of a person who has lost that limb, now respond to facial stimulation. Moreover, the greater the reorganization, the more intense phantom limb pain is felt. This theory helps explain the phenomenon of phantom limb pain, in which the brain tells the body it is experiencing pain even in the absence of direct sensations.

How Is Pain Measured?

In order to assess (and hopefully ease) pain, it is important to know where it is and what it feels like. Researchers use a number of different strategies to assess pain.

Physiological Measures

Psychophysiological measures of pain are based on the assumption that the experience of pain should be associated in distinct ways with physiological responses, such as muscle tension, heart rate, and skin temperature (Nigl, 1984). Researchers have used a number of different physiological measures to determine whether pain is associated with such responses. For example, electromyography (EMG) can be used to measure muscle tension in patients with headaches and lower-back pain (see Photo 9.2; Chapman et al., 1985). Other

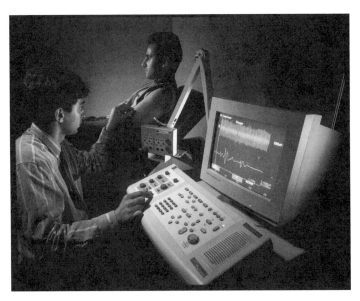

Photo 9.2 Electromyography (EMG) can measure muscle tension in patients with headaches and lower-back pain.

researchers, under the assumption that more substantial pain is associated with higher spikes in brain waves, have used electroencephalograms (EEGs) to measure electrical activity in the brain. Still other researchers have relied on autonomic nervous system responses, including increases in heart rate, blood pressure, and respiration, as a way of quantifying the amount of pain experienced.

However, most research using these measures has failed to demonstrate a consistent relationship between physiological responses and the experience of pain (Chapman et al., 1985). For example, EMG levels are sometimes higher in patients with low-back pain, but other times they are lower. People also adapt to painful stimuli over time—a person may initially show a very rapid heart rate in response to pain, but then over time, the heart rate decreases in response to the same stimulus. There is no consistent link between the experience of pain and physiological reactions; therefore, physiological measures of pain have limited use.

Behavioral Pain Measures

Behavioral pain measures assess the outward manifestations of pain, including physical symptoms (such as limping and rubbing), verbal expressions (such as sighing and groaning), and even facial expressions (such as grimacing and frowning; Craig, Prkachin, & Grunau, 1992; Keefe & Block, 1982). In some cases these observations are made by health care workers, and in other cases they are made by people familiar with the patient. For example, nurses may ask patients recovering from surgery to perform a variety of tasks, such as touching their toes, standing up, and sitting down. As an indirect measure of pain, the nurses may then rate how easily the patient performs each of these tasks.

Generally, behavioral pain measures are accurate in assessing pain. Different people seem to be able to rate pain behaviors in fairly similar ways (Keefe & Block, 1982), such as in five general clusters: guarding (abnormally stiff or rigid movement), bracing (a stationary position in which one part of the body maintains an abnormal distribution of weight), rubbing (touching, rubbing, or holding part of the body), grimacing (facial expressions such as clenching teeth and furrowing brow), and sighing (deep exhalations of breath). Behavioral approaches are an especially good way of measuring pain in children, who often are unable to accurately report on their experience of pain using self-report methods.

Although behavioral measures of pain can be very useful, patients may sometimes misrepresent their pain, either by pretending to feel more or less pain than they really are or by pretending to feel less pain than they really do (Block, Kerner, & Gaylor, 1980; Romano et al., 1992). People sometimes are motivated to show they are experiencing pain as a way of getting something (or getting out of something)—you might grab your knee and walk stiffly in an attempt to avoid playing a tennis match you fear you will lose. One study found that patients often report being unable to do various activities (e.g., walking, lifting, standing), but observations by unobtrusive staff reveal patients could do more than they admitted (Kremer, Block, & Gaylor, 1981). On the other hand, sometimes people go to some lengths to (falsely) show that they are not feeling pain, perhaps to avoid undergoing an unpleasant medical procedure or to avoid appearing weak to others. Athletes who are eager to get back into a game, for example, may demonstrate to their coach that they are able to perform, even though this action causes them substantial pain. Thus, simply relying on people's physical manifestations of pain may be problematic.

Self-Report Measures

Self-report measures of pain basically ask people to describe their pain (Turk et al., 1983). The advantage of this approach is that pain has many outward behavioral manifestations, but only the person experiencing it can tell how intense the feeling really is. In some cases professionals interview patients (and sometimes their family members) about issues related to the pain, such as when it began, the treatments they have tried, the impact it has had on the patients' professional and personal life, and how the patient typically handles it. In other cases patients report their experience of pain by responding to a written questionnaire. For example, the visual analog scale asks people to rate their experienced pain on a line, for which one end represents "no pain" and the other represents "pain as bad as it could be" (Feurestein, Labbe, & Kuczmierczyk, 1986). Another type of self-report pain inventory, the McGill-Melzack Pain Questionnaire, asks people to choose various words to describe their pain, the area of the body in which they feel pain, the timing of the pain, and the intensity or strength of the pain (see Figure 9.4; Melzack & Torgerson, 1971). This measure also assesses three different aspects of pain, including sensations (e.g., cramping, stabbing, aching), feelings (e.g., exhaustion, terror) and intensity (e.g., unbearable, intense, annoying). The West Haven–Yale Multidimensional Pain Inventory assesses the impact of pain on patients' lives, the response of others to patients' expression of pain, and the extent to which pain disrupts patients' daily lives (Kerns, Turk, & Rudy, 1985). See Table 9.1 for an example of a pain self-report measure.

Although self-rating scales are easy to use and at least in some cases can capture diverse types of pain, such measures clearly have limitations. First, self-report measures of pain often require fairly high levels of verbal skills (Chapman et al., 1985). Patients must have the ability to understand and make small distinctions between types of pain, such as the difference between lacerating versus cutting, pulsing versus throbbing, and scalding versus searing. Self-report measures are therefore less useful for children and people who are not fluent speakers of English (although see Figure 9.5 for a self-report measure of pain that requires few, if any, verbal skills). Most important, and as we discussed in the review of behavioral measures of pain, people sometimes misrepresent how much pain they are feeling. In some cases, people exaggerate to get sympathy or attention. For example, children learn quickly that expressing pain can lead to positive consequences (e.g., special adhesive strips, hugs and kisses, grape-flavored medicine). Similarly, professional athletes may express pain loudly immediately following a push or hit by another player in an effort to draw a foul or penalty. In other cases, people may attempt to downplay their

McGill-Melzack
PAIN QUESTIONNAIRE

Patient's name _____ Age _____
File No. _____ Date _____

Clinical category (eg. cardiac, neurological, etc.): _____

Diagnosis: _____
_____
_____

Analgesic (if already administered):
1. Type _____
2. Dosage _____
3. Time given in relation to this test _____

Patient's intelligence: circle number that represents best estimate
1 (low)   2   3   4   5 (high)
****

This questionnaire has been designed to tell us more about your pain. Four major questions we ask are:

1. Where is your pain?
2. What does it feel like?
3. How does it change with time?
4. How strong is it?

It is important that you tell us how your pain feels now. Please follow the instructions at the beginning of each part.

© R. Melzack, Oct. 1970

Part 1.   Where Is Your Pain?

Please mark, on the drawings below, the areas where you feel pain. Put E if external, or I if internal, near the areas which you mark. Put EI if both external and internal.

Part 2.   What Does Your Pain Feel Like?

Some of the words below describe your *present* pain. Circle ONLY these words that best describe it. Leave out any category that is not suitable. Use only a single word in each appropriate category—the one that applies best.

1	2	3	4
Flickering	Jumping	Pricking	Sharp
Quivering	Flashing	Boring	Cutting
Pulsing	Shooting	Drilling	Lacerating
Throbbing		Stabbing	
Beating		Lancinating	
Pounding			
5	**6**	**7**	**8**
Pinching	Tugging	Hot	Tingling
Pressing	Pulling	Burning	Itchy
Gnawing	Wrenching	Scalding	Smarting
Cramping		Searing	Stinging
Crushing			
9	**10**	**11**	**12**
Dull	Tender	Tiring	Sickening
Sore	Taut	Exhausting	Suffocating
Hurting	Rasping		
Aching	Splitting		
Heavy			
13	**14**	**15**	**16**
Fearful	Punishing	Wretched	Annoying
Frightful	Grueling	Blinding	Troublesome
Terrifying	Cruel		Miserable
	Vicious		Intense
	Killing		Unbearable
17	**18**	**19**	**20**
Spreading	Tight	Cool	Nagging
Radiating	Numb	Cold	Nauseating
Penetrating	Drawing	Freezing	Agonizing
Piercing	Squeezing		Dreadful
	Tearing		Torturing

Part 3.   How Does Your Pain Change With Time?

1. Which word or words would you use to describe the pattern of your pain?

1	2	3
Continuous	Rhythmic	Brief
Steady	Periodic	Momentary
Constant	Intermittent	Transient

2. What kind of things relieve your pain?

3. What kind of things increase your pain?

Part 4.   How Strong Is Your Pain?

People agree that the following 5 words represent pain of increasing intensity. They are:

1	2	3	4	5
Mild	Discomforting	Distressing	Horrible	Excruciating

To answer each question below, write the number of the most appropriate word in the space beside the question.

1. Which word describes your pain right now? _____
2. Which word describes it at its worst? _____
3. Which word describes it when it is least? _____
4. Which word describes the worst toothache you ever had? _____
5. Which word describes the worst headache you ever had? _____
6. Which word describes the worst stomach-ache you ever had? _____

FIGURE 9.4   Test Yourself: A Questionnaire for Measuring Pain

The McGill-Melzack Pain Questionnaire is a commonly used measure that assesses the location of pain, the type of pain, and the strength of the pain.

Source: Melzack & Torgerson, 1971.

experience of pain. One study found that male patients report experiencing less pain to females than they report to males (Levine & DeSimone, 1991)! So, self-report measures can be good, because they can provide information that is simply impossible to obtain through other measures, but these measures also have some weaknesses.

TABLE 9.1   *Test Yourself: The Pain Discomfort Scale*

1.	I am scared about the pain I feel.
2.	The pain I experience is unbearable.
3.	The pain I feel is torturing me.
4.	My pain does not stop me from enjoying life.
5.	I have learned to tolerate the pain I feel.
6.	I feel helpless about my pain.
7.	My pain is a minor annoyance to me.
8.	When I feel pain I am hurting, but I am not distressed.
9.	I never let the pain in my body affect my outlook on life.
10.	When I am in pain, I become almost a different person.

This scale assesses the intensity of pain and the level of distress pain causes.

Source: Jenson et al., 1991.

FIGURE 9.5   The Picture Scale is useful for assessing pain in children and people who have trouble with written language (Frank, Moll, & Hort, 1982).

How Do Psychosocial Factors Influence the Experience of Pain?

Although everyone has experienced pain, the amount of discomfort that people feel from a given injury or disease varies from person to person—one person may find that having a stomachache makes it impossible to get out of bed, whereas another person may find such pain a relatively small annoyance and continue with regular activities. In fact, people vary considerably in how much pain they can stand—some estimates are that some people can stand eight times as much pain as others (Rollman & Harris, 1987). Moreover, many pain complaints have no clear physical basis: it is estimated are that up to 85% of people seeing a doctor with a complaint of back pain have no apparent physical basis for the pain (White & Gordon, 1982). This lack of physical cause suggests that psychological factors have some role in producing such pain. This section examines several theories about how psychological factors influence the expression and/or experience of pain.

Learning

As we've discussed throughout this book, people acquire attitudes and behaviors by watching those around them. Children may learn how to respond to injury and disease by observing how their parents and other role models act (Bandura, 1986). As I described in Chapter 3, because my father always had cavities filled without novocaine, as a child I also refused this type of medication (insanely, in retrospect). One study by Kathryn Rickard (1988) found that teachers rated the children of chronic pain patients as displaying more illness-related behaviors, such as complaining and whining about pain, visiting the school nurse, and avoiding certain behaviors, than other children.

People may also learn to experience, or at least express, pain as a way of receiving some type of secondary gain or reinforcement (Turk, 1996). In some cases people experiencing pain are allowed to avoid doing things they really don't want to do—a type of negative reinforcement: perhaps you remember complaining of a stomachache on a morning you were supposed to take a test in school, hoping that your parents would let you stay home. In other cases experiencing pain leads to very desirable consequences, such as attention and expressions of concern from others—a type of positive reinforcement (see Photo 9.3). As I described at the beginning of the chapter, Billy was probably motivated to continue complaining about various illnesses because he enjoyed the tender care he received from his mother (as well as missing school). One study examined the amount of pain a person complained about as a function of whether the person was told his or her spouse or a hospital clerk was listening behind a one-way mirror (Block et al., 1980). Those with spouses who were generally caring and helpful complained more when they were told that their spouse was behind the mirror, whereas those with less helpful spouses complained more when they were told a clerk was behind the mirror. Similarly, children tend to show more anxiety during medical procedures when their parents are present than when their parents are not, presumably because children are more motivated to engage in behaviors, such as making noise and complaining, that will elicit their parents' attention when in their company (Gross, Stern, Levin, Dale, & Wojnilower, 1983; Shaw & Routh, 1982). One study found that children with chronic dermatitis (a painful, itchy skin condition) scratched more often when their parents paid attention to this behavior than when they ignored it (Gil et al., 1988).

Perhaps the most obvious benefit someone might receive from experiencing pain is financial, such as a disability payment. Considerable research shows

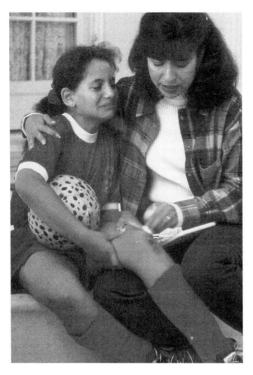

PHOTO 9.3   Children often show more pain when their parent is present than when they are alone or with other children, probably because parents reinforce crying with hugs, kisses, and special bandages.

that people who receive financial benefits for experiencing pain report having more pain and find pain treatments less effective (Block et al., 1980; Fordyce, 1988; Rohling, Binder, & Langhin-Richsen-Rohling, 1995). One study reported a case in which a disabled factoryworker had received $251 per week for his full-time work in a woolen mill, but began receiving $257 per week while on disability (Block et al., 1980). Can you imagine his incentive to stop feeling pain? This doesn't mean that all people who are experiencing pain—or receiving some type of benefit from the experience of such pain—are simply faking it, but it does mean that at times psychological factors can influence how much pain people feel (or how much they report feeling).

People also learn to avoid certain activities based on their fear that engaging in a particular behavior will lead to pain (Turk & Flor, 1999). For example, getting a cavity filled is typically somewhat painful, whereas simply getting your teeth cleaned is not. Someone who has had a cavity filled could then develop a general fear of going to the dentist, even if he or she is not scheduled to have painful dental work done. Similarly, if you once ate an entire bag of chips and then vomited shortly afterward (because of a stomach flu, not the snack consumption), you are quite likely to develop an association between chips and pain. Unfortunately, once a link between two behaviors is established (even in error), people's anxiety about experiencing pain again often leads them to avoid that activity completely—and they never learn that engaging in the activity would not cause the pain they anticipate. One study with low-back-pain patients found that 83% of them were unable to complete a series of exercises (e.g., leg lifts, bending at the waist) because of fear of pain, whereas only 5% of them were actually physically unable to complete the exercises (Council, Ahern, Follick, & Kline, 1988).

We also learn about pain from our culture, which have very different norms about what types of experiences are painful, as well as how much pain it is appropriate to express. Maryann Bates and her colleagues (1993) examined the expression of pain in 372 patients with chronic pain (typically back pain) from different ethnic backgrounds, including Hispanics, Italians, Polish, and "old Americans," or those whose families had lived in the United States for some time. Hispanics and Italians reported experiencing the most pain, worry, anger, and tension about their pain and also perceived their pain as interfering more with their work. In contrast, the old American and Polish patients felt they should suppress experiences of pain and were less expressive and emotional about their pain. Similarly, European Americans report experiencing less pain following dental surgery than African American and Latin patients (Faucett, Gordon, & Levine, 1994). Cross-cultural research shows that people in different countries vary in how much impairment low-back pain causes them. Specifically, Americans report experiencing greater work and social impairment than Italians and New Zealanders, who in turn report experiencing more problems than Japanese, Mexican, and Colombian individuals (Sanders et al., 1992). And, as you will discover in a later section Americans are much more likely to undergo back surgery than patients in other countries (Arena & Blanchard, 1996).

Cognition

One of the first people to demonstrate the power of cognition in the experience of pain was Dr. Henry Beecher, who treated injured soldiers during World War II. Although all of the soldiers had received surgery for severe wounds, only 49% reported experiencing "moderate" or "severe" pain, and only 32% accepted medication when it was offered (Beecher, 1959). In contrast, when Dr. Beecher later interviewed other patients in his office who had experienced similar types of surgery, 75% reported experiencing at least "moderate" pain, and 83% requested medication. According to Beecher, the cause of these differences is that the soldiers most likely compared their injuries to those of others around them who were dying; hence, they felt relatively good about their state of health, whereas those in civilian life probably compared their injuries to their own and others normal states of health, hence they felt much worse than

---

Questioning the Research 9.1

Why do Americans report more impairment from pain than people in other countries do? Is it nature, nurture, or both?

normal. Moreover, the soldiers may have also felt in some way rewarded by becoming injured, namely, getting to leave the war. The civilians, in contrast, were less likely to perceive such an obvious benefit from their surgery.

More recent research supports Dr. Beecher's findings on the impact of how people think about, or attribute the causes of, pain in how they experience pain (Keefe, Brown, Wallston, & Caldwell, 1989; Turk & Flor, 1999). Those who believe that their pain is caused by a very serious debilitating condition perceive pain as worse than those who believe the pain is caused by a more minor (and fixable) problem. For example, although chronic pain patients with cancer and chronic pain patients without cancer do not differ in self-reported pain severity, those whose pain is caused by cancer report feeling greater disability and engaging in fewer activities (Turk et al., 1998). People who blame themselves for their injury also experience more pain (Kiecolt-Glaser & Williams, 1987). On the other hand, people who perceive a clear benefit resulting from the experience of pain perceive such pain as less intense than those without such a "upside"; which may explain why people voluntarily undergo painful activities and procedures (e.g., having a navel pierced, getting a tattoo, climbing Mount Everest).

Moreover, people's beliefs about pain, and in particular their anxiety about pain, influence how much pain they report experiencing (see Box 9.1; Kent, 1985; Turk & Flor, 1999). People who focus their attention on the unpleasant aspects of a procedure, who anticipate negative outcomes, and who think negative thoughts may experience or report more pain (Gil et al., 1990; Keefe, Hauck, Egert, Rimer, & Kornguth, 1994). People who are very anxious about

Box 9.1

Research Focus—Is Premenstrual Syndrome All in the Mind?

Maria Marvan and Sandra Cortes-Iniestra (2001) examined whether women's beliefs about the experience of menstrual pain influenced how much pain they reported. Forty-nine undergraduate women in Mexico were recruited to participate in a study on the "interaction between psychological and physical states." To disguise the specific focus of the study, participants were told that researchers would compare responses from women to those of men. Participants completed a series of daily questionnaires that assessed their physical symptoms, such as headache, cramps, and nausea, as well as psychological symptoms, such as irritability, depression, and anxiety. Following completion of these daily measures, women then rated the severity of the symptoms they had experienced during their premenstrual period and rated how much they believed women in general experienced pre-

(continues)

menstrual syndrome (PMS). Researchers then calculated the difference between the intensity of the symptoms actually experienced during the premenstrual period versus the women's reports of these symptoms later.

As predicted, the more a woman believed in the phenomenon of menstrual pain, the more she exaggerated how severe her symptoms were during her last period. As shown in Figure 9.6, women who believed that most women experienced PMS showed a stronger bias in reporting their physical symptoms, including nausea, cramps, headaches, swelling, and painful breasts, than those who thought PMS was uncommon. Those who believed most women experienced PMS also exaggerated the number of psychological symptoms, including irritability, depression, anxiety, and difficulty concentrating, they experienced more than those without such beliefs about the frequency of PMS. In sum, women who believed PMS is common show a greater bias in the number of debilitating symptoms they report than those who thought PMS was rare.

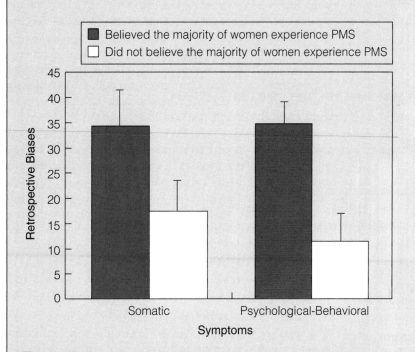

FIGURE 9.6 Women who believed the majority of women experience PMS show a stronger bias in their reports of physical and psychological symptoms than those who do not believe the majority of women experience PMS (Marvan & Cortes-Iniestra, 2001).

scheduled dental procedures, for example, 3 months after the procedure experiencing more pain than they actually felt (as reported by them immediately following the procedure). The power of individuals' expectations about pain in leading to the perception of pain has been demonstrated in women during childbirth (Green, 1993), children undergoing surgery (Palermo & Drotar, 1996), and people having harmless medical procedures done (Litt, 1996). When we experience a physical problem (e.g., migraine, broken leg), our anticipation about its consequences may make the pain seem that much greater. In fact, the *anticipation* of pain can in some cases be worse than the pain itself.

People's expectations about their ability to cope with pain also influence how much pain they experience (DeGood, 2000; Jensen, Karoly, & Harris, 1991; Turk & Flor, 1999). In fact, one study with surgery patients found that people's expected ability to cope with pain was the strongest predictor of both the intensity and duration of pain (Bachiocco, Scesi, Morselli, & Carli, 1993). Similarly, women's beliefs about their ability to go through childbirth without medication are a strong predictor of their success at doing so (Manning & Wright, 1983). Active strategies, such as thinking about pain as short term and manageable and distracting yourself from the pain, can be quite effective in reducing the experience of pain (DeGood, 2000). These approaches reduce people's physiological arousal and tension and can thereby have direct impact on pain intensity. On the other hand, passive strategies, such as self-criticism (blaming oneself for the pain), overgeneralizing (believing the pain will never end and will ruin other aspects of one's life), and catastrophizing (overestimating the insensity of the pain), are associated with greater pain (Holm, Holroyd, Hursey, & Penzien, 1986; Klapow, Slater, Patterson, & Atkinson, 1995; Mercado, Carroll, Cassidy, & Cote, 2000; Ukestad & Wittrock, 1996). For example, one study examined how frequent headache sufferers would handle submerging their hand of ice water for a period of time—a very painful task (Ukestad & Wittrock, 1996). Headache sufferers rated their discomfort as more severe and were more likely to rely on catastrophizing than nonheadache sufferers. Studies of patients with low-back pain and arthritis indicate that the use of passive strategies is a stronger predictor of pain than disease-related variables, such as severity of the disease and obesity (Flor & Turk, 1988; Keefe et al., 1987). See Table 9.2 to examine which coping strategies you use.

Personality

We have a common perception that people who experience chronic pain are of a certain personality type. For example, people who suffer from migraines are perceived as tense, driven, hostile, and perfectionistic (Holroyd & Lipchick, 1999). Some evidence suggests that this is true. People who experience chronic pain are more likely to have an anxiety or depressive disorder (Sullivan, Reesor, Mikail, & Fisher, 1992). For example, one study found that 33.7% of those in chronic pain were anxious or depressed, as compared to 10.1% of those who were not in chronic pain (Gurej, Von Korff, Simon, & Gater, 1998). Similarly, people with irritable bowel syndrome (IBS), a chronically painful disease, tend to have higher scores on measures of neuroticism (Blanchard & Scharff, 2002), and they and show higher rates of major depression, panic disorder, and agoraphobia (Walker, Katon, Jemelka, & Roy-Byrne, 1992). On the other hand, some evidence suggests that extraverted people are

TABLE 9.2 *Test Yourself: Coping Strategies Questionnaire*

1. I try to think of something pleasant.
2. I do something I enjoy, such as watching TV or listening to music.
3. It's terrible and I feel that it's never going to get any better.
4. I worry all the time about whether it will end.
5. I pretend it's not there.
6. I ignore it.
7. I imagine the pain is outside of my body.
8. I try not to think of it as my body, but rather as something separate from me.
9. I tell myself that I can overcome the pain.
10. I tell myself to be brave and carry on despite the pain.
11. I pray for the pain to stop.
12. I rely on my faith in God.

This scale assesses six different strategies that people can use for coping with pain: distraction (items 1 and 2), catastrophizing (items 3 and 4), ignoring pain (items 5 and 6), distancing themselves from the pain (items 7 and 8), coping self-statements (items 9 and 10), and praying (items 11 and 12).

Source: Riley & Robinson, 1997.

more tolerant of pain and have higher pain thresholds than introverts (Phillips & Gatchel, 2000). Another variable that influences the experience of pain is locus of control (see Table 9.3; Seville & Robinson, 2000). People with a strong internal locus of control believe they have control over their pain and can therefore cope with such pain more effectively than those with an external locus of control.

TABLE 9.3 *Test Yourself: The Pain Locus of Control Scale*

Please answer the following questions about your ability to manage your pain; use a 1 to indicate you strongly disagree with the item and a 5 if you strongly agree.

1. If my pain gets worse, it is my own behavior that determines how soon I will get relief.
2. I am in control of relieving my pain.
3. When my pain gets worse, I am to blame.
4. The main thing that affects relief of my pain is what I do.
5. If I take care of myself, I can relieve my pain.
6. If I take the right actions, I can relieve my pain.
7. If my pain gets worse, I have the power to relieve it.
8. I am directly responsible for the relief of my pain.
9. Whatever makes my pain worse is my own fault.
10. I can pretty much relieve my pain by taking good care of myself.

These items assess how much a person believes he or she is in control of pain. People with a high score on this scale are able to tolerate more pain than those who have a low score on this scale.

Source: Seville & Robinson, 2000.

> **Questioning the Research 9.2**
>
> Why might extraverts experience less pain than introverts? What factors may explain this relationship?

However, the bulk of evidence suggests that experiencing chronic pain tends to lead to depression, and not the reverse—in other words, people who live in chronic pain develop depression, anxiety, and anger (Magni, Moreschi, Rigatti-Luchini, & Merskey, 1994). People who suffer from chronic pain are exhausted because they have trouble sleeping, they engage in few social activities because they are preoccupied with their pain, and are irritable with family and friends (Sternbach, 1974). One study that examined college students over time found no initial differences in personality between those who would later develop inflammatory bowel disease as compared to those who would not (Siegler, Levenstein, Feaganes, & Brummett, 2000). Similarly, one study followed patients with chronic low-back pain for 6 months following treatment at an intensive rehabilitation clinic (Barnes, Gatchel, Mayer, & Barnett, 1990). Although patients with chronic pain had higher than normal scores on several measures of psychological well-being (hypochondria, neuroticism, depression) at the start of the program, these scores decreased to normal levels following treatment, which again suggests that pain is the cause of these psychological problems, not the result. Another study with 109 patients with chronic pain also found that pain led to increases over time in depression, anxiety, and anger (Feldman, Downey, & Schaffer-Neitz, 1999). However, it has also been found that depression also leads to pain over time, which suggests that pain may lead to depression as well as the reverse—the link between pain and depression may be bidirectional (see Figure 9.7).

Stress

Pain can also be influenced by stress, such as the stress caused by family or marital conflict, work pressures, and major life events (Sternbach, 1986). In fact, people who have low job satisfaction, poor relationships with coworkers, and stress at work are more likely to have chronic pain, as are those who perceive their work goals as conflicting with their nonwork goals (Karoly & Ruehlman, 1996). Conflicts with family members and coworkers highly stressful situations are also associated with the development of ulcers, a chronic and painful condition (Medalie, Stange, Zyzanski, & Goldbourt, 1992). Similarly, one study found that only 7% of those who experience low stress report experiencing frequent headache pain, as compared to 17% of those with moderate stress, and 25% of those with high stress (Sternbach, 1986). The experience of stress is also a predictor of increases in symptoms in patients with IBS (Levenstein et al., 2000) as well as recurrent abdominal pain (Walker, Garber, Smith, Van Slyke, & Claar, 2001). For example, children with recurrent abdominal pain (that has no clear physical cause) report more daily stressors, both in and out of school, than those without such pain (Walker et al., 2001); they also

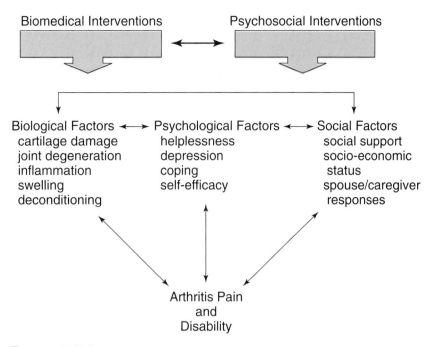

FIGURE 9.7 Biological, psychological, and social factors also influence the experience of pain (model from Keefe & Bonk 1999).

tend to describe their daily stress as more severe and report other symptoms (e.g., headache, fatigue) more often as compared to other children.

One way stress may influence the experience of pain is that experiencing stress leads people to engage in behaviors, such as tensing their muscles, that in turn cause pain. For example, while my husband, Bart, was studying for the bar exam, he developed a severe pain in his jaw. After undergoing a number of medical tests (e.g., for Lyme disease and others), a physician suggested that he might be grinding his teeth at night while he slept, which would lead to jaw pain. So, Bart was experiencing real pain, but the pain was caused by a behavior, which in turn was caused by stress. People who experience high levels of stress may stop taking care of themselves (they may engage overeat or exercise less) and distance themselves from their family and friends, all of which reduces their social support and thereby increases their experience of stress and pain. Finally, stress can lead directly to physiological problems, such as dilation of arteries surrounding the brain and tension in muscles in the head, neck, and shoulders, both of which may lead to headaches (Turner & Chapman, 1982a). As described at the beginning of the chapter, Antonia's stress at work and lack of sleep may have been creating considerable tension, which in turn contributed to her frequent migraines.

What Are Some Physical Methods of Controlling Pain?

Because the earliest theories of pain focused entirely on its physical causes, researchers concentrated on developing purely physical pain control techniques. This section reviews a number of different physical methods of controlling pain.

Medication

The most common way to control pain is with *analgesic drugs*, such as aspirin, acetaminophen, and ibuprofen, which reduce fever and inflammation at the site of wounds, and work to decrease pain by interfering with the transmission of pain signals (Whipple, 1987; Winters, 1985). Analgesics are very effective in reducing mild to moderate levels of pain, such as headache and arthritis pain. *Narcotics*, such as codeine and morphine, work by binding to the opiate receptors, thereby inhibiting the transmission of pain signals (Aronoff, Wagner, &

Box 9.2

Health Psychology in the Real World—The Case of OxyContin

In the late 1990s, Purdue Pharma, a major drug manufacturer, developed a narcotic painkiller called OxyContin to treat severe types of pain. This drug, which was designed to be taken orally, has a time-release component, so patients can take one pill and be painfree for some time. However, when these pills are crushed, and then injected or snorted, the time-release component is destroyed and creates a euphoric heroin-like high. This drug therefore leads to addiction very rapidly. OxyContin is blamed for more than 282 overdose deaths in 2000 and 2001, as well as a number of pharmacy robberies. In fact, in some cases thieves broke into drugstores and steal only OxyContin tablets. Experts believe part of the attraction of this drug is that it is often easier to come by through prescription than illegal drugs, such as cocaine and heroin, which produce similar effects. Some people who legitimately require this drug for pain relief may be willing to sell some of their pills to those who purely want to experience the high, and some doctors may be willing to write prescriptions for OxyContin based on little objective need; some doctors have been prosecuted and convicted of writing unnecessary prescriptions. This drug is now more strictly regulated, but it is difficult to simply ban it because it does provide some patients with much-needed relief for certain types of pain. The drug company is now exploring ways to make the drug less powerful when it is crushed in hopes of stemming its illegal use.

Spangler, 1986). These drugs are very effective in reducing severe pain. *Local anesthetics*, such as novocaine and lidocaine, can be applied directly to the site at which pain occurs; they work by blocking nerve cells in that region from generating impulses, which is why your mouth feels numb after a shot of novocaine. Other pharmacologic methods of pain control rely on blocking the transmission of pain impulses up the spinal cord. For example, during child-birth many women choose to have a spinal epidural, an injection of narcotics or local anesthetics in the spinal cord, which blocks the experience of pain from the point of injection down.

Although the use of drugs is quite effective in reducing pain, often doctors are reluctant to prescribe them (Fishman & Berger, 2000; Melzack & Wall, 1982). One reason may be that the topic of pain and pain relief typically receives little attention in medical school curricula, in part because pain is not viewed as a particularly serious problem—patients who complain of pain are often seen as "weak" or as desiring drugs because of addiction (see Box 9.2). This reluctance to prescribe medication for pain relief is also caused in part by physicians' concern that these drugs can produce dependence and addiction. In turn, even when pain-relieving drugs are prescribed, doctors often give smaller doses than is recommended by manufacturers, give medication less fre-quently, and stop medication earlier than is recommended. One study with cancer patients, who often experience severe pain, found that 42% were not receiving enough medication to ease their pain (Cleeland et al., 1994). Practi-tioners also tend to prescribe less pain relief for members of ethnic minority groups (Cleeland et al., 1994; Ng, Dimsdale, Shragg, & Deutsch, 1996).

The reluctance to prescribe drugs is especially common when patients are children, in part because both doctors and parents tend to believe that children feel less pain than adults. One study found that mothers underestimate the amount of pain their children experienced following tonsillectomy, which caused them to give their children less medication than the doctor ordered (Gedaly-Duff & Ziebarth, 1994). Similarly, for years, circumcision was prac-ticed on infant boys without any anesthesia, because of the belief that infants don't experience pain in the same way as adults (Anand & Craig, 1996). How-ever, recent research suggests that even very young infants do experience pain; hence, ethically they should be given some type of anesthesia during painful medical procedures. Moreover, infants who do not receive pain medication during circumcision show more distress during later injections than do those who receive anesthesia, presumably because early experiences with pain make people more sensitive to pain later in their lives (Taddio, Katz, Ilersich, & Koren, 1997).

When doctors do encourage the use of medication to reduce pain, they may encounter resistance from their patients (see Cartoon 9.1). Patients often believe they should accept the pain and save the medication for when the pain gets intense; they also may be concerned that they could become addicted to the drugs (Fishman & Berger, 2000; Ward et al., 1993). People may also refuse pain medication because of their concerns about its undesirable side effects, such as nausea, drowsiness, and mental confusion, and its high cost. In some cases patients may fail to ask for pain medication because they dislike the method of dispensing the medicine, such as swallowing pills and or getting a shot.

"We can give you enough medication to alleviate
the pain but not enough to make it fun."

CARTOON 9.1   Although medications can minimize the amount of pain people experience, their side effects can make people reluctant to take them. (©The New Yorker Collection 2000. Peter Steiner from cartoonbank.com. All Rights Reserved).

Surgery

In extreme cases, when other methods of pain control have failed, *surgical pain control* can be used to manage pain (Melzack & Wall, 1982). Surgical pain control typically involves severing or destroying the nerves by which pain signals are transmitted, thereby reducing the perception of pain. This technique is especially common in the treatment of chronic back pain. In the United States 115,000 laminectomies (in which pieces of a herniated disk are removed) and 34,000 other lumbar spine operations are performed each year (Arena & Blanchard, 1996). Surgery is much more common in the United States than in other industrialized countries: the rate of surgeries for herniated disks is four to nine times higher.

Surgical methods of pain control have very limited benefits, however. First, procedures can lead to other problems, including numbness, memory loss, and even paralysis in the region involved in the surgery. Even more problematic is that surgery sometimes provides only short-term pain relief: it may sever a particular pathway in the body that is transmitting pain signals, thereby initially eliminating or reducing pain, but because the nervous system can regenerate and pain messages can travel to the brain in different ways, patients may begin to experience pain again weeks or months following surgery (Melzack & Wall, 1982). Surgery should be considered a last resort when all other techniques have failed.

Physical Stimulation

Physical stimulation, or *counterirritation*, refers to irritating body tissue to ease pain. At first this seems counterintuitive—why, *increase* pain as a way to *reduce* it? However, the gate control theory of pain suggests that increasing pain by increasing stimulation of nerves in one region is a way to get the gate to close, thereby reducing the perception of pain (Melzack & Wall, 1982). This is why you put your finger in your mouth after you burn it on a hot stove and why you grab your foot after stubbing your toe. All of the physical stimulation methods of pain control are based on this general principle.

The *transcutaneous electrical nerve stimulation (TENS)* technique of pain reduction involves placing electrodes on the skin and administering continuous electrical stimulation (Melzack & Wall, 1982). Patients wear a small portable unit that attaches the electrodes to the skin; the degree of stimulation can be increased or decreased depending on need. This stimulation does not hurt and typically leads to a feeling of numbness in the area, which can be effective in reducing pain for some chronic conditions, such as phantom limb pain and arthritis, as well as pain following surgery.

Acupuncture, in which needles are inserted at specific points on the skin, is another type of physical stimulation technique that may help control pain (see Photo 9.4). This technique, is ancient and widely used in Asian medicine. It is based on the idea that the body's energy flows in 14 distinct channels (Richardson & Vincent, 1986; Vincent & Richardson, 1986) and a person's health is supposedly dependent on the balance of energy flowing through them. Imbalances can be corrected by inserting tiny needles into the skin and twirling them. Acupuncture is used to treat a variety of common health problems, including nausea caused by chemotherapy and pregnancy, pain following dental surgery, painful menstruation, tennis elbow, low-back and headache pain, and carpal tunnel syndrome (Brattberg, 1983; Helms, 1987; Richardson & Vincent, 1986). In some cases acupuncture can even be effective in reducing pain during surgery (Melzack & Wall, 1982).

Massage therapy, a technique in which people receive deep-tissue manipulation by a trained therapist has recently received considerable attention. Tiffany Field and her colleagues have conducted a number of studies showing that massage therapy can help reduce the experience of pain (Field, 1998). For example, in one study 24 adults with chronic lower-back pain were randomly assigned to receive either massage therapy for 30 minutes twice a week for 5 weeks or to practice progressive muscle relaxation. By the end of the sessions, people in the massage therapy group showed significantly less pain and anxiety, lower levels of depression, and even had greater range of motion in their

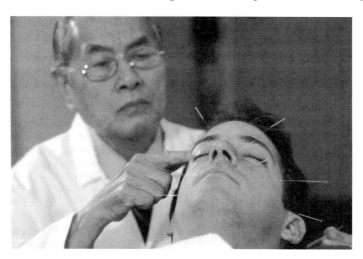

Photo 9.4   Have you ever had acupuncture? An estimated 1 million Americans seek this type of treatment each year (Verbseck, 2000).

backs compared to the other group. Another study with chronic migraine patients found that massage therapy led to less pain and more headache-free days as compared to those who received medication for migraines. Similar studies suggest that massage can be effective in reducing the pain of childbirth, postsurgery pain, and arthritis pain.

Like massage therapy, *chiropractic therapy* focuses on manipulating the bones, muscles, and joints to improve body alignment. Between 3 and 10% of Americans visit chiropractors each year, usually with complaints of back pain (Eisenberg et al., 1993). Although the medical community is skeptical about the benefits of this approach, spinal manipulation is as effective as more traditional medical treatments for back pain (Shekelle, Adams, & Chassin, 1992).

Physical stimulation methods, such as TENS, acupuncture, and massage therapy are not always effective in reducing pain, however, since in some cases their effects may be short-lived. Massage therapy, for example, is effective in reducing ongoing pain, but this approach has no long-term effectiveness once it is discontinued (Field, 1998). Similarly, although some evidence suggests that acupuncture can be effective in reducing pain, it is not consistently more effective than other types of treatments, such as medication (Taub, 1998). Moreover, physical stimulation techniques may work to reduce pain simply because they distract patients from their real pain, and not because of any true physical effects. For example, people who are undergoing acupuncture may focus intensely on the feeling of the needles going into their skin, and may stop concentrating on other pain. In fact, in some cases the effects of these methods seem to be based largely on patients' beliefs that they will work (a placebo effect). For example, one study randomly assigned patients with low-back pain to receive TENS or sham TENS (in which no actual stimulation was given) three times a day for 4 weeks (Deyo, Walsh, & Martin, 1990). Although following treatment 47% of patients who received TENS did report significant improvements in functioning as well as reduced pain, these benefits were reported by 42% of those who received sham TENS as well. Similarly, acupuncture is no more effective than a placebo control condition at reducing the pain associated with migraine headaches (Dowson, Lewith, & Machin, 1985).

But this is not to say that the power of physical stimulation methods is simply all in the mind. Some evidence suggests that physical stimulation methods of pain control do have some type of physical influences on pain because they work with animals, including monkeys and rats (Melzack & Wall, 1982). Moreover, in one study 53% of patients reported experiencing less pain following acupuncture as compared to only 33% of those in a placebo group (who received fake electrical nerve stimulation), which suggests that acupuncture may lead to some type of actual physical effect on the body that reduces pain (Dowson et al., 1985). As discussed later in this chapter, if people simply believe they have control over their pain, and that the pain will decrease, this can lead to physiological changes in the body, including the release of endorphins in the brain that do in fact inhibit the experience of pain (He, 1987).

Physical Therapy/Exercise

Because certain types of pain are exacerbated by weak muscles, a lack of flexibility, and muscle tension, physical therapy and exercise can help reduce pain (Davies, Gibson, & Tester, 1979). People with chronic low-back pain, for example, may experience this pain because their abdominal muscles are weak and they are overusing their back muscles to compensate. Similarly, patients with arthritis who engage in regular exercise may maintain the flexibility of their joints, and surgical patients who participate in physical therapy may restore muscle strength. This increased flexibility and muscle strength can in turn decrease the experience of pain.

Several studies indicate that people who engage in regular exercise show a reduction in disability, sometimes even as long as 2 years after participation in an intervention (Frost, Lamb, Moffett, Fairbank, & Moser, 1998). In some cases the exercise approach can be as effective as more traditional methods of therapy (e.g., behavior therapy). For example, one study of patients with lower-back pain assigned some to aerobic exercise treatment, others to behavior therapy, and a third group to aerobic exercise plus behavior therapy (Turner, Clancy, McQuade, & Cardenas, 1990). Patients in the behavior therapy condition received information about the power of social reinforcement in maintaining or reducing pain, and both they and their spouses were asked to keep track of pain behaviors and to try not to reward pain complaints but instead reward painfree behaviors. The combined group showed the greatest benefits initially, but all three treatments seemed to be effective in reducing pain at the 1-year follow-up. Exercise can also have psychological benefits, by decreasing rates of depression and anxiety, which in turn can lead to a reduction in the experience of pain (Blumenthal, Williams, Needels, & Wallace, 1982). Based on similar study results, physicians who previously prescribed bed rest for people with back pain, now urge patients with back pain to become active as soon as possible.

What Are Some Psychological Methods of Controlling Pain?

Given the considerable evidence suggesting that the experience of pain is influenced by psychological factors, as well as the limitations of some of the physical methods of pain management, researchers have also examined psychological methods of controlling pain. This section reviews several different psychological methods of managing pain.

Hypnosis

Hypnosis refers to an altered state of consciousness or trance state that individuals can experience under the guidance of a trained therapist (Chaves, 1994). People under hypnosis may be particularly responsive to statements made by the hypnotist. Some research suggests that hypnosis can be effective in controlling pain, including the pain associated with dental work, childbirth, back pain, headaches, and arthritis (Barber, 1998; Hilgard, 1975; Hilgard & Hilgard, 1983; Spanos & Katsanis, 1989). For example, one study with chronic headache patients randomly assigned people to a hypnosis therapy group or a control group and found that people receiving the hypnosis therapy reported less headache pain (ter Kuile et al., 1994). Similarly, and as shown in Figure 9.8, one study with 30 hospitalized burn patients found that those who were hypnotized had a significant reduction in pain compared to those who were told they were going to be hypnotized (but who weren't) and those in a no-treatment control group (Patterson, Everett, Burns, & Marvin, 1992). Interestingly, although people who are hypnotized report no discomfort while in the hypnotic state, their physiological characteristics, such as heart rate, breathing, and blood pressure, are consistent with measures of people experiencing pain (Orne, 1980). In fact, some highly hypnotizable subjects do not express or show signs of pain while hypnotized, but when they are asked whether any part of their body is experiencing pain (feedback from "a hidden observer"), some rate the pain as substantial (Hilgard & Hilgard, 1983). This suggests that hypnotized people may have awareness that the pain exists, but simply distract themselves from the sensation (e.g., they can separate mind and body). See Table 9.4 to determine how hypnotizable you are.

Although some researchers believe very strongly in the power of hypnosis in helping people cope with pain, others believe that hypnosis does not really represent a unique approach to pain relief (Spanos & Katsanis, 1989). Hypnosis may work to relieve pain simply because people believe it will work (e.g., the placebo effect) or because they want to please the experimenter (which is really a type of experimenter expectancy effect). In line with this view, people who are most susceptible to hypnosis may experience substantial pain relief, whereas those who are low in hypnotizability often show no benefits of hypnosis over a placebo (see Figure 9.9; Miller, Barabasz, & Barabasz, 1991; Smith, Barabasz, & Barabasz, 1996). Hypnosis may also work to decrease pain by distracting patients and helping them relax, which in turn reduces their awareness of pain. For example, one study found that there was no difference in pain

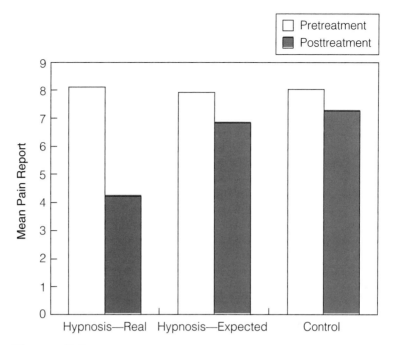

FIGURE 9.8 Burn patients who received hypnosis therapy showed a greater decrease in self-reported pain than those who expected they would receive hypnosis (but actually did not) and those in the control condition (data from Patterson et al. 1992).

TABLE 9.4 *Test Yourself: How Hypnotizable Are You?*

1. Close your eyes, put your feet together, imagine swaying.
2. Your arm, resting on the armrest of the chair, is heavy and limp, too heavy to lift. Just try to lift it.
3. Think about how it would feel to let your head fall forward.
4. Hold out your arm. Imagine it feels very heavy, as though you were holding a lead weight. Feel it pulled down.
5. Hold your hands out in front of you, tightly interlocking your fingers so that they cannot be separated. Now try to separate them.
6. Extend your arm and lock it into a straight position. Imagine it is an iron bar. Try to bend it.

These items test people's susceptibility to hypnosis. You can test yourself or your friends by having one person read these items, and then seeing whether the subject reacts. For example, if the person loses his or her balance while imagining swaying, you would give the person one point.

Source: Kelly & Kelly, 1985.

reduction between people who were hypnotized and those who were not when all participants were told that they were selected because they would be highly responsive to the pain reduction treatment they would receive (Spanos & Katsanis, 1989). The power of suggestion may therefore be a more important predictor of pain relief than the power of hypnosis. Other research suggests that while hypnotic treatment can be effective in reducing pain, it is no more effective than cognitive-behavioral therapy (Edelson & Fitzpatrick, 1989; Stam, McGrath, & Brooke, 1984). Although there are reports of people undergoing cardiac surgery, cesarean sections, and appendectomies with no anesthesia other than hypnosis, these cases are considered anecdotal because they were not conducted using controlled, scientific methods. In sum, hypnosis probably works for some people (namely those who are highly hypnotizable) better or as well as other psychological methods of pain control, but there is little evidence that hypnosis itself has unique pain-relieving qualities. Hypnosis is therefore not reliable enough to be used in place of other methods of pain control.

Biofeedback

In *biofeedback* people are trained, using electric monitors, to monitor and change selected physiological functions, such as their heart rate, finger tem-

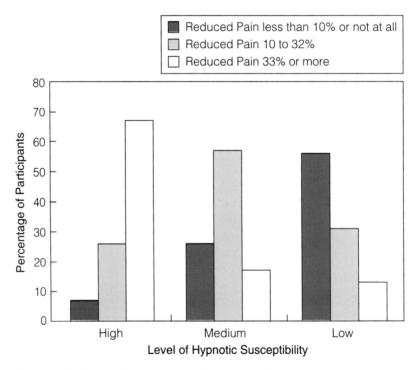

FIGURE 9.9 People who are highly hypnotizable experience much greater pain relief than those who are less susceptible to hypnosis (data from Hilgard, 1975).

perature, muscle activity, and brain wave patterns (Arena & Blanchard, 1996). How does this process work? First, a particular biological response, such as heart rate or muscle tension, is measured and the results are shown immediately to the patient. The patient is then asked to engage in different thoughts or behaviors in an attempt to influence that particular physiological response. They might be instructed, for example, to think relaxing thoughts or to tense their muscles, and then to see how these thoughts and behaviors influence their physiological responses. By providing constant feedback on how such thoughts and behaviors influence physiological reactions, over time patients can learn to change their physiological responses by changing their thoughts or behavior. Biofeedback is an effective way to control headache pain (Turner & Chapman, 1982a), back pain (Flor & Birbaumer, 1993), and hypertension (Nakao et al., 1997). For example, one study compared biofeedback to cognitive-behavioral therapy and medical treatment for chronic back pain, and found that biofeedback was superior to the other two approaches (see also Figure 9.10; Flor & Birbaumer, 1993).

Although biofeedback is an effective way of decreasing various types of pain, it has a number of drawbacks limiting its usefulness. Specifically, biofeedback is time-consuming and expensive, given the necessary equipment and time to learn the technique (Roberts, 1987). Patients must have considerable practice in order to learn how to influence their physiological responses, and this requires time on the part of a technician as well as access to very expensive

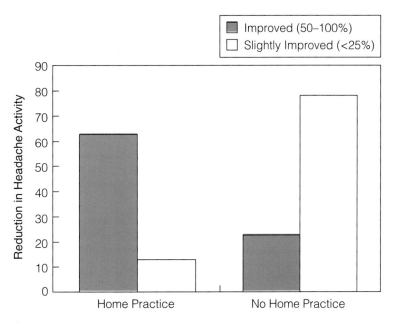

FIGURE 9.10 This study found that patients who received 5 weeks of training in biofeedback techniques and who were encouraged to practice these techniques at home reported a substantial decrease in headache activity compared to those who were not encouraged to do such home practice (data from Gauthier et al., 1994).

equipment. Moreover, while biofeedback can work to reduce pain, comparison studies suggest that it is often no better than more simplistic techniques, such as relaxation (Bush, Ditto, & Feurestein, 1985); therefore it is not widely used for managing pain.

Relaxation and Distraction

As its name implies, the relaxation approach to pain management works by helping people learn to relax, and thereby reduce their stress, anxiety, and pain (Blanchard, Appelbaum, Guarnieri, Morrill, & Dentinger, 1987). One relaxation method is called *progressive muscle relaxation*, in which patients focus on tensing and then releasing each part of their body (hands, shoulders, legs, etc.) one at a time (Jacobson, 1938). This process helps patients distinguish states of tension from states of relaxation, and therefore trains patients in ways to calm themselves in virtually any stressful situation. Other techniques that rely on some combination of relaxation and distraction include *guided imagery*, which pairs deep muscle relaxation with a specific pleasant image that serves to focus a patient's mind on something other than the pain (see Table 9.5), and *meditation*, in which patients relax their bodies and focus attention on a single

TABLE 9.5   *Tension-Reducing Imagery Practice (TRIP)*

1. Decide to take a mini-TRIP by stopping all other activities and thoughts. Decide where your trip will take you (e.g., the beach, the mountains, your backyard, an abstract location or experience).
2. Take a deep breath.
3. Purse your lips and slowly exhale your first deep breath through the small opening between your lips. As you slowly exhale, say the word *relax* to yourself.
4. After this first deep breath, let your jaw relax and go slack. Future deep breaths will be taken normally.
5. Relax your jaw and then allow the feeling of relaxation to travel downward from your jaw to the rest of your body. Allow the feeling of relaxation to wash like a wave over your entire body. As the wave travels down your body, make each breath you take a deep one.
6. Begin your imagery. Make the image as rich as possible by using all of your senses. For example, if you are imagining a beach, allow yourself to see the clouds, the water, the sand, and the sky. Hear the waves, the seagulls, and the wind. Feel the sand on your feet, the sea breeze on your face, and the waves wetting your ankles. Smell the ocean mist and the sweet coconut smell of suntan oil, and taste the salt on your lips. Bring this image into your mind quickly and intensely, so that your mind is highly distracted for a brief period of time.

The mini-TRIP can be a useful way of coping with pain during relatively short medical procedures, such as injections, spinal taps, and dental procedures.

Source: Williams, 1996.

thought, sometimes while verbalizing a single word or thought. Similarly, in the technique of *systematic desensitization*, a person is asked to describe the specific source of his or her anxiety, and then to create a hierarchy of different stimuli (which cause increasing levels of arousal) associated with that anxiety. The therapist then asks the patient to focus on the least-anxiety provoking image: the therapist changes the focus to a less-stressful stimulus whenever the patient experiences any anxiety during the technique. Gradually, when the patient is able to think about a low-level stimulus without feeling anxiety, the therapist continues to progressively higher-level, more-anxiety-provoking stimuli; over time, this enables people to build up their tolerance to specific stressful situations. Finally, some techniques simply focus on trying to distract the patient in order to get his or her mind off the pain (McCaul & Marlatt, 1984) based on the idea that patients will not be able to concentrate on the pain because they are focusing on something else. For chronic pain patients, even a simple activity such as reading a book, watching television, or listening to music can help distract them from their pain (see Figure 9.11). (This is why some dentist offices have televisions in the exam rooms.)

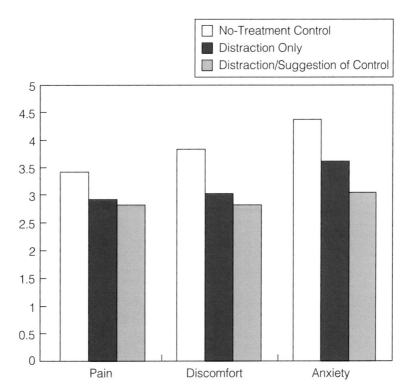

FIGURE 9.11 This study revealed that patients who listened to music while they had a cavity filled reported experiencing less pain and discomfort than those without the music. Moreover, dentists, who did not know which condition the patients were in, also reported that those who listened to music experienced less pain, discomfort, and anxiety (data from Anderson, Baron, & Logan, 1991).

Relaxation and distraction techniques can be quite effective in reducing a variety of different types of pain, including pain caused by chemotherapy (Lyles Burish, Krozely, & Oldham, 1982), migraine headaches (Illacqua, 1994), low-back problems (Carlson & Hoyle, 1993), dental procedures (Gatchel, 1980, 1986), and various medical procedures, including injections, lumbar punctures, and bone marrow aspirations (Blount et al., 1989). For example, one study found that people who listened to a tape narrating progressive muscle relaxation were able to withstand much more pain than those who did not have the help of the tape (Cogan, Cogan, Waltz, & McCue, 1987). Another study found that patients trained to meditate showed lower levels of pain and used fewer pain killers as compared to those who used traditional medical treatment (Kabat-Zinn, Lipworth, & Burney, 1985). Moreover, training in relaxation seems to provide relatively long-term relief—as long as 5 years according to some studies of chronic headache sufferers (Blanchard et al., 1987). As described in Box 9.3, distraction can even be an effective technique to reduce pain in very young infants and children, who may have trouble using other methods of pain control (Cohen, 2002; Cohen, Blount, Cohen, Schaen, & Zaff, 1999).

There are several possible explanations for how do these techniques work to decrease pain. First, they may give people power to cope with stress, which reduces pain. As discussed earlier, people who believe they can cope with pain actually feel less pain (DeGood, 2000; Jenson, Turner, Romano, & Karoly, 1991; Turk & Flor, 1999). Second, relaxation may reduce muscle tension, which can then decrease the experience of pain (for headaches, back pain, ulcers; Turner & Chapman, 1982a). Once again, all of these techniques may work to reduce pain primarily by giving patients the expectation that their pain will decrease, which in turn can lead to physiological changes in the body that can decrease the experience of pain. However, relaxation and distraction techniques are probably more effective with mild and moderate pain than with severe pain (McCaul & Marlott, 1984).

Cognitive Approaches

Cognitive methods focus on helping people understand of how their thoughts and feelings influence the experience of pain as well as helping people change their reactions to and perceptions of pain (Fernandez, 1986). For example, people may learn that feeling stress and anxiety could enhance pain; therefore, they might focus on reducing these feelings as a way of decreasing the experience of pain. As described previously, people who focus their attention on the unpleasant aspects of a medical procedure, who anticipate negative outcomes, and who think negative thoughts may experience more pain (Gil, Williams, Keefe, & Beckham, 1990; Keefe et al., 1994). In turn, helping patients see the consequences of maladaptive thoughts can therefore be effective in reducing pain. Giving people strategies for controlling pain is another way of helping to change their thoughts about pain. Patients could, for example, focus on believing pain is manageable and having confidence in their ability to cope with it (they might think "This really isn't so bad. I can get through this") Finally, cog-

Box 9.3

Research Focus—"I'll Take a Movie with My Shot"

A study by Laurie Cohen and her colleagues (1999) examined two different types of strategies for controlling children's pain while receiving a series of three hepatitis B vaccinations 1 month apart. Thirty-nine 4th-graders were randomly assigned to one of three treatment conditions during each of the vaccinations, so that all children experienced each of the treatment options. Children in the distraction condition watched a movie, such as *101 Dalmatians* or *Toy Story*, while they had their shot. Children in the anesthetic condition had an anesthetic cream, which numbs the skin applied to the site of the injection. Children in the typical care condition, the control condition, were simply comforted by the nurse. After receiving all three conditions (and all three injections), the children were asked which condition was the best at helping them cope with their fear and anxiety, and which condition they preferred the next time they needed a shot.

Findings from this study revealed that distraction was a very effective strategy for reducing pain and anxiety. Children showed less distress and more coping in the distraction condition, and both distraction and anesthetic were perceived by children as preferable to typical care. Specifically, 52% of the children said they would prefer distraction, whereas only 33% would select the cream, and 15% would prefer the nurse's presence. Moreover, the distraction care was significantly cheaper to implement than the anesthetic condition: researchers estimated that the distraction condition would cost $421 to implement (for costs of the television, VCR, and movies) and no additional expenses, whereas providing the cream would cost $750 as an annual expense. This study provides strong evidence that distraction can be an effective way of helping children cope with the pain of injections. However, the nurse—who interacted with children in all three conditions—was naturally aware of the difference between the conditions, although she did not know the study's specific hypotheses. The experiment therefore raises the possibility that experimenter expectancy effects may have influenced the findings.

nitive approaches to pain control can work by helping people think about pain in new ways, a technique called *cognitive redefinition*. For example, a woman might be trained to think about the pain of labor as her baby pushing its way into the world, which puts it in a more positive light.

Cognitive techniques are effective in helping people cope with various types of pain, including headaches and back pain (Compas, Haaga, Keefe, Leitenberg, & Williams, 1998; Sanders, Shepherd, Cleghorn, & Woolford, 1994; Turner & Jensen, 1993). For example, researchers in one study randomly

---

Box 9.4

Focus on Women—What Is Lamaze?

As one who has given birth to two children, I can assure you that the pain of childbirth is very, very real—within moments after delivering my first son, I turned to my husband in the delivery room and said, "I never, ever want to hear you complain about sports injuries again." My experience is not atypical—studies show that the pain of childbirth is among the most severe pain people experience (Melzack & Wall, 1982). As Joan Rivers eloquently suggested, people who want to learn what childbirth feels like should pull their bottom lip over their head. Given all this pain, how are some women able to go through childbirth without medication? According to Fernand Lamaze (1970), women can learn to manage this pain through the use of various psychological techniques. First, childbirth education classes can give couples some practical strategies for relieving pain, including positions to try during labor, massage techniques that a partner can do to help reduce pain, and special breathing exercises. These classes also provide training in relaxation and distraction. For example, couples are encouraged to choose a "focal object" to concentrate on during labor. This object, which could be a stuffed animal, special photo, or any personally meaningful object, is supposed to help distract women from the pain. Women are also taught to think about pain in a new way (a technique called *cognitive redefinition*)—to think about each (incredibly painful) contraction as working to bring the baby's arrival that much closer.

---

assigned patients with sickle cell anemia, a rare blood disease that causes severe pain, to receive either training in cognitive coping skills (relaxation, reinterpretation, calming self-statements) or a disease-education session (they were given information about the hereditary nature of the disease, its psychological consequences, and medical treatment; Gil et al., 1996). As predicted, patients who received coping skills training reported lower levels of negative thinking and pain than those who received education about sickle cell anemia. Another study randomly assigned 203 patients suffering from chronic tension headaches to receive either cognitive therapy, antidepressant medication, or placebo medication (Holroyd et al., 2001). Cognitive-behavioral therapy was more effective than the placebo and as effective as the antidepressant medication in reducing headache activity, medication use, and headache-related disability.

Cognitive therapy approaches might work to reduce pain for several reasons. First, these approaches give people practical strategies for reducing pain. Giving women information on helpful positions they can use during labor (e.g., standing as opposed to lying down), for example, can actually help reduce the pain of labor when employed (Melzack, 1993). Second, cognitive approaches give people information about what to expect, such as the types of sensations they may experience, which can decrease anxiety and thereby reduce pain. This may be why women who attend childbirth-training classes experience modest reductions in pain during labor as compared to those who don't attend classes (see Box 9.4 and Photo 9.5; Melzack, Taenzer, Feldman, & Kinch, 1981). Cognitive approaches to pain control may also work by increasing people's perceived control over the pain, which helps lessen its perceived severity (Zucker et al., 1998). As described at the beginning of the chapter, Melissa's training in cognitive techniques, such as breathing exercises and choosing a focal object, helped her to give birth without using pain medication. Similarly, one study of 141 patients with chronic pain who were enrolled in a pain program at the University of Washington found that increases in perceived control over pain were associated with decreases in depression, perceived disability, and pain intensity at the 6- and 12-month follow-ups (Jensen, Turner, & Romano, 2001). Moreover, patients who received cognitive therapy to cope with irritable bowel syndrome showed no decreases in the frequency of daily hassles following the therapy, but showed decreases in the distress such hassles caused them, suggesting that patients learned effective strategies for coping with these events (Payne & Blanchard, 1995). These findings suggest that changing patients' cognitions about pain can be an effective approach to changing perceived pain. Moreover, learning skills for managing pain may even lead to the release of pain-relieving endorphins (see Box 9.5; Bandura, O'Leary, Taylor, Gauthier, & Gossard, 1987).

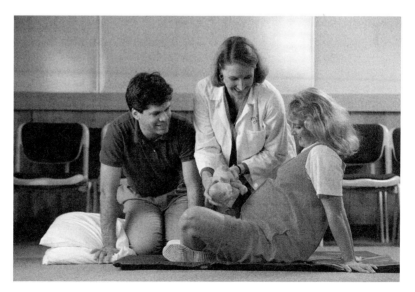

PHOTO 9.5 One of the reasons childbirth education classes may be effective in reducing the pain of labor and childbirth is that they provide couples with information about what to expect.

Box 9.5

Research Focus—The Power of Thinking "I Think I Can, I Think I Can"

Albert Bandura and his colleagues at Stanford University were interested in examining the effectiveness of training students in perceived self-efficacy for coping with pain (Bandura et al., 1987). Seventy-two students all first underwent a very painful procedure called the cold pressor test. This test involves submerging a hand in a bucket of very cold ice water for as long as a person can stand it, which virtually everyone finds very painful. Most students couldn't even keep their hand in the water as long as 1 minute. After completing this first test, the students were randomly assigned to one of three treatment conditions: a cognitive-coping group, a placebo-pill group, and a control group. Students in the cognitive-coping group were taught different ways to think about their pain, such as thinking about something other than the pain, thinking about the pain as completely separate from their bodies, and thinking encouraging thoughts about how well they were coping with the pain. The students in the placebo group were given an inert pill that they were told would prevent and/or alleviate their pain. All students then repeated the cold pressor test to see whether their pain tolerance had increased. Findings showed, as predicted, that those who were taught cognitive coping had a much higher pain tolerance than those in the other two conditions. Specifically, students in the cognitive-coping condition showed an increase in pain tolerance of nearly 60%, whereas those in the placebo and control conditions showed only very small increases (less than 10%).

The researchers were then interested in testing exactly how training someone in cognitive-coping skills for managing pain leads to such a remarkable increase in pain tolerance. Specifically, they were interested in examining whether this type of training increases the activation of endorphins in the body, which in turn leads to the reduction of pain. To test this part of their hypothesis, the researchers gave half of the subjects in each condition an injection of a drug called naloxone, which blocks the pain-reducing effects of endorphins, and the other half of the subjects received a saline injection, which should have had no influence on the activation of endorphins. As shown in Figure 9.12, these findings showed that there was no difference in pain tolerance as a function of whether students received the naloxone or saline for those who were in the control or placebo conditions. Apparently, people in these conditions did not experience the benefits of endorphins at reducing pain, and therefore it didn't matter whether the potential effects of endorphins were blocked (in the case of those receiving the naloxone injection) or not (in the case of those receiving the saline injection). However, students in the cognitive-control condition who received saline had a much higher pain tolerance than those in this condition

(continues)

who received the naloxone, suggesting that participants in this condition did have higher levels of endorphins—and hence were able to withstand much more pain when these endorphins were not blocked (in the case of the saline) than when they were blocked (in the case of the naloxone). Giving someone training in cognitive techniques for controlling pain actually increases the level of endorphins in the body, which in turn reduces the feeling of pain.

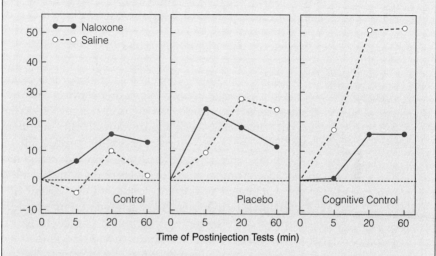

FIGURE 9.12   Although there is no difference in the change in pain tolerance as a function of whether the student received an injection of naloxone or saline for those in the control and placebo conditions, students in the cognitive-coping condition showed a much greater increase in pain tolerance if they received an injection of saline as opposed to naloxone (data from Bandura et al., 1987).

Behavior Therapy

As described previously, people who are in pain often receive certain relative benefits, such as attention from others, assistance with tasks, and avoidance of undesirable activities (Turk, 1996). Operant-conditioning approaches to the reduction of pain therefore focus on eliminating the "perks" of pain (Fordyce, Brockway, Bergman, & Spengler, 1986). This approach, developed by Wilbert Fordyce, focuses on reinforcing positive behaviors (e.g., increased activity) and ignoring negative behaviors (e.g., complaints of pain). One behavior therapy technique trains family members in how to respond to a patient's complaints of pain, namely by ignoring reports of pain and disability. Research by Joan Romano and her colleagues (1992) demonstrated that spouses of chronic pain patients were much more likely to discourage their partners from engaging in physical tasks than those whose spouses were not chronic pain patients. For example, they were much more likely to say, "I'll do that—you rest now," and

"Don't overdo it." Over time, family members are causing the patient to be dependent and may decrease patients' self-efficacy and self-esteem. Behavioral therapy programs often try to help family members understand the role they play in perpetuating pain behaviors. Behavior therapy programs also try to reduce patients' dependence on pain medication by providing drugs only at fixed intervals, as opposed to on demand, which also rewards complaints of pain. Moreover, the dose of pain medication given is gradually decreased over time without the patient knowing, so eventually he or she simply may be taking an inert substance. This approach helps reduce the patient's physical dependence on medication.

Behavioral approaches can work very well to decrease various types of chronic pain (Turner & Clancy, 1988; Roberts & Reinhardt, 1980). For example, one study examined chronic pain patients who spent 6 to 8 weeks in a hospital undergoing various types of behavior therapy (having their pain behaviors ignored, engaging in physical therapy, reducing pain-related medicines, participating in work opportunities; family members were also taught to not reinforce pain behaviors; Roberts & Reinhardt, 1980). At the end of treatment, patients were using fewer drugs, reported feeling less pain, and spent less time inactive. Another study of 148 patients with chronic back pain examined the effectiveness of an operant-conditioning program alone (they were given behavioral goals and spouses were trained to reinforce only healthy behaviors) as compared to an operant-conditioning plus cognitive coping skills program (patients received education about the role psychological factors play in the experience and management of pain; Kole-Snijders et al., 1999). Compared to the waiting-list control condition, both operant conditioning alone and operant conditioning plus cognitive coping skills led to less negative affect, less pain behavior, and higher pain coping and pain control. Although operant-conditioning techniques can be very effective in decreasing pain, they are most effective when they are supported by cooperative family members.

Conclusions

This section describes separately a number of psychological methods for controlling pain. However, many pain management programs use several techniques in combination. Pain management programs that include multiple approaches tend to be more effective than those that include only one (Flor, Fydrich, & Turk, 1992; Murphy, 1996). As described at the beginning of the chapter, Tom's back pain decreased substantially after he entered a pain clinic, which included training in relaxation, guided imagery, and cognitive redefinition as well as educated him and his wife about the consequences of rewarding pain behaviors. One study with chronic headache pain patients found that education, physical therapy, stress management, and pain management skills led to a substantial reduction in medication use (Scharff & Marcus, 1994). Patients who participate in combined programs are much more likely to return to work than those who receive no treatment or only a single-treatment approach (68% versus 36% respectively in one study; Flor et al., 1992).

Can Placebos Decrease Pain?

A placebo is a treatment that affects someone even though it contains no specific medical or physical properties relevant to the condition it is supposedly treating (Liberman, 1962). In other words, placebos are psychologically inert medicines or treatments that can produce very real and even lasting effects, effects that have been demonstrated on virtually every organ system in the body and many diseases, including chest pain, arthritis, hay fever, headaches, ulcers, hypertension, postoperative pain, seasickness, and pain from the common cold (Benedetti & Amanzio, 1997). In one review involving more than 1000 patients treated for a variety of conditions, Henry Beecher (1955) reported an average of 35% of patients benefited from placebo treatments, with the effectiveness of placebos ranging from 15 to 58%. For example, in one study 122 surgical patients were given either morphine or a placebo, but all were told they were getting morphine (Beecher, 1959). Of those given morphine, 67% reported some relief, but so did 42% of those given the placebo! Similarly, one recent study on the role of the placebo effect in influencing people's reactions to antidepressant medication found that 75% of the effectiveness of such drugs is caused by patients' expectations that they will work, as opposed to any psychological changes in brain chemistry (Kirsch & Sapirstein, 1999). These studies emphasize the power of placebos in leading to improvements in health; however, the expectation that a drug or treatment will have negative effects similarly can lead to adverse health effects (Turner, Deyo, Loeser, Von Korff, & Fordyce, 1994). This *nocebo effect* can, for example, lead people to experience unpleasant side effects from a medication—if they expect to feel such a reaction—even if the medication they are given is entirely inert. Although one recent study published in the *New England Journal of Medicine* suggests that the placebo effect is not quite as strong as it is often described (Hrobjartsson & Gotzche, 2001), most evidence suggests placebos can have a substantial impact on the experience of pain. In sum, placebos are often effective precisely because people *believe* that they will work to reduce pain.

But all placebo treatments are not equal in their effectiveness—some are more effective than others (Benedetti & Amanzio, 1997). Those administered through injection have greater effects than those taken orally; capsules are more effective than pills; and injections are better than capsules or pills. Even the brand name of the pill can influence its effectiveness: one study showed an increase of 10% in effectiveness through the use of a known name versus an unknown name (see Photo 9.6). The placebo effect is also stronger when a drug is administered by a doctor in a hospital setting than when given by a family member at home. In sum, having a placebo that looks, tastes, and feels like "real medicine" is likely to increase patient confidence, and thereby its effectiveness.

The behavior and attitudes of the practitioner can also influence the effectiveness of a placebo (Gracely, Dubner, Deeter, & Wolskee, 1985; Roberts, Kewman, Mercier, & Hovell, 1993). When a placebo is administered by an

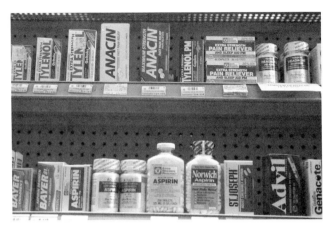

PHOTO 9.6   Which drug would you prefer? Although the chemical properties of namebrand and storebrand drugs are virtually identical, people often select the higher-priced namebrand drugs over cheaper alternatives.

enthusiastic and friendly practitioner who seems interested in and sympathetic to the patient, the placebo is more effective than when it is delivered by an angry or rejecting practitioner. For example, in one study with surgery patients, half were visited the night before their surgery,by the anesthesiologist, who told them in a brusque manner that everything would be fine (Talbot, 2000). The other patients were also visited by the same anesthesiologist, who this time sat on their beds, held their hands as he talked, and was very warm and friendly. As predicted, those who saw the kind and friendly practitioner required much less pain medication and were even discharged earlier from the hospital than those who had interacted with the brusque and cold practitioner. A practitioner's expectations about the effectiveness of the placebo can influence responsiveness rates as well: in one study rates ranged from 70 to 25% effective based on the attitude of the practitioner toward the placebo: one doctor always handled placebo tablets with forceps, to convey to patients that this type of drug was too powerful even to be touched by human hands. In one study doctors were told that they would be giving their patients either a painkiller or a placebo (see Figure 9.13; Gracely et al., 1985). Although all doctors were actually giving their patients a placebo, subjects treated by the doctors who believed they were administering a painkiller actually showed a reduction in their pain. Similarly, and as described at the beginning of the chapter, Brian's knee showed remarkable improvement after he started taking a drug that was strongly recommended by his physician—this effect could be caused by the physical properties of the drug, and/or Brian's expectations about the powerful effects as this drug as described by his trusted physician. The placebo effect as well as the practitioner expectancies effect are major reasons why clinical drug trials now use double-blind procedures in which neither the patient nor the practitioner know who is getting an active or a placebo drug.

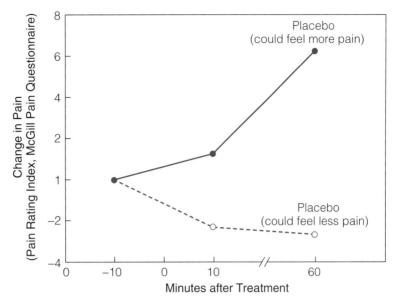

Note: Change in pain rating index between baseline (10 minutes before injection) and 10 and 60 minutes after administration of placebo.

FIGURE 9.13 All of the patients in this study received only a placebo—an injection of a saline solution. But those whose doctors thought they might get a pain-relieving drug reported feeling significantly less pain than those whose doctors thought they would receive a pain-enhancing drug (data from Gracely et al., 1985).

How Do Placebos Influence Pain?

One factor that influences the effectiveness of placebos is patients' expectations about the effects of the treatment (Skelton & Pennebaker, 1982). In other words, patients who expect a given reaction to a placebo may look for signs that show the treatment or drug is working. For example, in one study participants were told that they would be hearing some noise that might cause their skin temperature to change (Pennebaker & Skelton, 1981). Some subjects were told that their temperature might rise, whereas others were told it might fall although in reality the noise should have no psychological effect on temperature. As predicted, those who expected their skin temperature to rise reported feeling themselves get warmer, whereas those who expected their temperature to fall reported feeling cooler upon exposure to the stimulus. Expectations also influence other types of physiological reactions, including heart rate and amount of nasal congestion and stuffiness.

Placebos may also work as a result of broad principles in learning, such as classical conditioning (Benedetti & Amanzio, 1997). Many of the factors that increase the effectiveness of placebos are linked with environmental cues that suggest pain relief, such as sitting in a doctor's office, receiving a pill, or feeling an injection. Over time, people may learn to associate these types of stimuli with feeling better; therefore, placebos may work simply by triggering these associations. For example, if you always take an aspirin, which reduces the pain, when you have a headache, you may experience the same reduction in pain if you take a pill that you think is aspirin but which is actually just an inert sugar pill.

Another factor that may explain the placebo effect is patients' behavior (Benedetti & Amanzio, 1997). Specifically, when people are given a pain treatment they fully expect to work, they may change their behavior in ways that in turn lead to the desired reduction of pain. For example, if you have a bad headache and take an aspirin that you fully believe will alleviate the headache, you may relax because you know the pain will soon disappear; therefore, this conscious attempt to relax may lead to a decrease in your headache pain. In sum, just the belief that the treatment will work may lead to a decrease in anxiety, which may lead directly to a reduction in pain.

Finally, placebos may lead to physiological changes in the body, which in turn inhibit the experience of pain (Bandura et al., 1987; Benedetti & Amanzio, 1997; Levine, Gordon, & Fields, 1978). Some research suggests that the endorphin system is activated when people simply believe they are receiving a painkiller, even when they are receiving a placebo (Benedetti & Amanzio, 1997). For example, researchers in one study randomly assigned dental patients to receive an injection of naloxone (which is known to reduce the effect of endorphins in providing pain relief) followed by a placebo, a placebo followed by an injection of naloxone, or simply two placebos (Levine et al., 1978). As predicted, those who got a placebo first and then naloxone reported greater pain than those who got a placebo both times, presumably because naloxone reduced the effectiveness of the endorphins (created by the placebo). Similarly, in a study with patients having their wisdom teeth removed, half were given real ultrasound therapy (known to reduce pain) during their procedure, while the others thought they were receiving this therapy but in reality the machine was unplugged (Hashish, Hai, Harvey, Feinmann, & Harris, 1988). Patients in both cases showed a decrease in pain, jaw tightness, and swelling, indicating that all of these physical effects were caused simply by the expectation that they were receiving a pain-reducing therapy. All of this evidence suggests that placebos may have both psychological and physical effects.

Lingering Issues

Does the duration of pain matter? If people are asked to choose which they'd prefer, a shorter amount of pain or a longer amount of pain, virtually everyone says they'd prefer shorter amounts of pain to longer amounts of pain. However, some recent research from Princeton University suggests that what people really remember is the contrast between different amounts of pain; therefore, having less pain at the end of a procedure is preferable to having shorter amounts of consistently intense pain (even if that means prolonging the procedure; Kahneman, Fredrickson, Schreiber, & Redelmeier, 1993). For example, in one study subjects were exposed to two unpleasant experiences—in the short trial, they held their hand in cold water for 1 minute, and in the long trial, they held their hand in cold water for 1 minute and then in *slightly* less cold water for 30 seconds. They were then given the choice of which trial to repeat. Sixty-nine percent chose to repeat the longer treatments.

Although the cold-water test is perhaps not that painful (although most people really don't enjoy it), other studies reveal similar findings for more painful procedures. For example, another study by Danny Kahneman examined patients' experience of colonoscopy, a procedure in which a lighted, flexible, tubelike instrument is inserted into a person's anus and then up into their colon (Redelmeier & Kahneman, 1996). This procedure is quite painful for most people and is often carried out under conditions of mild sedation. Once again, it was shown that patients' memories of the pain were influenced not by how long the procedure lasted, but rather by the peak intensity of the pain they experienced and the amount of pain they experienced during the last 3 minutes of the procedure. The implications of this research are that perhaps gradual relief is better than abrupt relief; hence, medical practitioners should concentrate more on lowering the peak intensity of pain during a procedure or during the last few minutes of a procedure than on reducing the overall length of a procedure. It seems ironic that we can enhance someone's memory of a painful procedure by lengthening the procedure so that the last few minutes are more pleasant than earlier (even if they are still painful). In turn, improving people's memories of their painful experiences could increase their willingness to undergo the procedure in the future, and thereby may improve adherence to medical recommendations.

Can placebo surgery be effective? Although we commonly think of placebos as some type of medicine (a pill or an injection), placebos can also be treatments. To test the power of placebo treatments, in some cases patients have had "placebo surgery," in which they are cut open but nothing medical is done to them (Beecher, 1959; Diamond, Kittle, & Crockett, 1960). Amazingly enough, many patients show some benefits simply from having some type of surgery (see Photo 9.7). For example, Leonard Cobb, a cardiologist working in Seattle in the 1950s, performed fake surgery in which surgeons made incisions in people's chests, but did not tie off patients' arteries, as was typically done in surgery for angina at the time (Cobb, Thomas, Dillard, Merendino, & Bruce, 1959). However, this fake procedure was just as effective at decreasing chest pain as the actual procedure—which was quickly abandoned. Similarly, a recent study at the University of Toronto compared Parkinson's disease patients who simply had holes drilled in their skulls (the placebo sugery) to those who experienced a real procedure in which holes are drilled in their skulls and then fetal cells are implanted in the brain. Fetal-tissue transplantation is thought to re-activate some brain functions and thereby reverse motor problems associated with this disease. Patients who received the placebo surgery showed significant improvement in their motor functioning (although not as substantial as that shown by patients who actually received the cell implant; Talbot, 2000).

More recently, a surgeon named Bruce Moseley participated in an elaborate test of the placebo effect (Moseley et al., 2002). One hundred-eighty patients

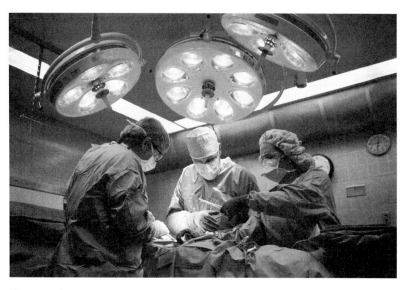

PHOTO 9.7   Surgery can clearly have a major impact on physical health—but is part of this effect merely caused by patients' belief in the power of surgery?

with osteoarthritis of the knee were scheduled for an operation that supposedly would relieve the arthritis pain they were experiencing in that joint. Most of them were middle aged, all were former military men (treated at a Veterans Hospital), and they were told exactly what could happen: some would have standard arthroscopic surgery, some would have their knee joint rinsed (but not scraped), and some would simply go to surgery and be anesthetized but have absolutely nothing medical done to their knees (they would simply be cut with the scalpel to create incisions and scars). To avoid experimenter expectancy effects, the study was double-blind—the surgeon went into the operating room and was then handed an envelope that told him which condition a subject was in. The patients were then assessed regularly over 2 years to determine whether "actual surgery" was indeed better than "placebo surgery" for reducing pain and increasing function (walking, climbing stairs, etc.). Results show that there were no differences in degree of pain or function among patients in the three groups at any point during the follow-up. This study was done to demonstrate, as we just discussed, that the placebo effect is most powerful when the subject really believes it, and patients strongly believe in the power of surgery. This study provides some evidence that at least in some cases, this belief alone can lead to positive results.

Thought Questions

1. Describe two psychological methods and two physical methods of controlling pain.

2. Your roommate is having her wisdom teeth extracted next week and is very concerned about the pain she expects to experience. What are three psychological techniques for controlling pain that you could recommend to her?

3. Describe two different ways of measuring pain; include in your answer the pros and cons of each.

4. Your 3-year-old nephew is going to the doctor next week for his annual checkup, which is includes a tetanus shot. What could you do to make sure this visit goes smoothly?

5. Describe three different explanations for the power of the placebo effect.

Answers to Questioning the Research

Answer 9.1: One reason Americans may experience more impairment resulting from pain is because they are less expressive about their emotions than people in other countries. They may, for example, feel that showing pain is a sign of weakness, and thereby try to "keep a stiff upper lip" and hide their pain, whereas people in other countries may feel more comfortable with the expression of pain. However, Americans may also experience more benefits from experiencing pain; thereby they are more willing to indicate their impairments caused by pain. Many employers in the United States provide a generous disability plan, allowing workers to benefit substantially in some cases from continued impairment resulting pain.

Answer 9.2: Extraverted people differ from introverted ones in a number of ways; therefore, it is difficult to explain why they may feel less pain. One possibility is that extraverts experience less stress because they probably have more social support. As discussed in Chapter 6, social support can buffer the effects of stress, and therefore extraverts overall may lead more pleasant lives. Another possibility is that extraverts are better at distracting themselves from pain than introverts. Extraverts may, for example, engage in more social activities or hobbies than introverts, which in turn may distract them from their pain.

CHAPTER 10

Chronic Illness

- Julie is 45 years old and has suffered from arthritis in her hands for nearly 20 years. Although she has experienced some mild joint pain for many years, the pain has increased significantly in the last few months. Julie also now has trouble managing many of her daily tasks, including using a can opener, buttoning shirts, and brushing her hair. Julie's difficulty with daily functioning has led to an increasing reliance on her husband, Mike, which has put a major strain on their relationship.

- Don is 15 years old and has diabetes. His parents are very concerned about his disease and are constantly reminding him to avoid eating junk foods and to monitor his blood sugar. Although Don knows he should not eat certain foods, when he is with his friends he finds it difficult to turn down junk food. Moreover, because Don finds it embarrassing to monitor blood and give himself shots in front of other people, he sometimes "forgets."

- Bill, who is 60 years old, has coronary heart disease. He has always been a little overweight and has smoked since he was 17 years old. However, after experiencing his first heart attack last year, Bill became very concerned about his health and made a number of lifestyle changes. He joined a gym and walks 2 miles a day on the treadmill, has stopped smoking, and is trying to eat healthier foods.

- Betty is 58 years old and had a cancerous lump removed from her breast 2 months ago. She is now undergoing several rounds of chemotherapy, to kill any cancer that possibly had spread to other parts of her body. Betty attends a weekly support group for women with breast cancer, which she thinks is very helpful. She often finds it hard to talk about her fears with her husband and children, but is able to share her concerns with the other women in the group. She believes it is very comforting to be around other women who truly understand what she is feeling.

- Leslie is 32 years old and is HIV-positive. She believes she contracted HIV during her early 20s, when she was living in Boston, although she still doesn't know which of her sexual partners infected her. Leslie learned she was HIV-positive 5 years ago, when she and a new boyfriend decided to get tested together. She was initially shocked about her diagnosis, particularly since she's never really had casual sex—almost all of her sexual partners were men she was dating, and she always made sure to use condoms with new partners.

Preview

This chapter examines psychosocial factors that can influence how individuals experience and manage chronic illness. First, I define chronic illness as well as its physical, social, and psychological consequences. Next, we examine factors that influence how people cope with having a chronic illness, including the extent to which the illness interferes with daily life, interaction with health care providers, type of coping used, and level of social support, as well as the role of different types of psychological interventions in helping people cope effectively with chronic illness. Finally, we examine how psychological factors influence the acquisition and management of three of the leading causes of death in the United States each year: cardiovascular disease, cancer, and AIDS.

What Are Chronic Diseases?

As we discussed in Chapter 1, in the early 1900s most people died from acute diseases—pneumonia, tuberculosis, and typhoid fever (Grob, 1983). Many of these diseases were caused by exposure to a specific virus, they are contagious, and they kill people rather quickly. In contrast, chronic conditions, which now cause 8 of 10 deaths in the United States, differ from acute conditions in several ways (Burish & Bradley, 1983). First, chronic conditions often have multiple causes, including people's behavioral choices or lifestyles. Perhaps as many as 85% of all cases of cancer, for example, are caused by people's behavior, such as smoking, drinking alcohol, and even tanning. Second, chronic conditions often have a slow onset, and the disease intensity increases over time. Many people with HIV infection do not even know when they were exposed to the disease, and often they are infected for months or years before they notice any symptoms. Third, whereas acute conditions often can be cured, with medication or some other intervention, chronic conditions only can be managed—people with chronic diseases sometimes get worse and sometimes stay the same, but they can't be cured.

An estimated 46% of all Americans (90 million people) have a chronic condition (Hoffman, Rice, & Sung, 1996). However, the frequency of chronic diseases varies substantially by age: 75% of children with serious health conditions have acute conditions, whereas 88% of those over age 65 years with serious health conditions have chronic conditions. The number of people living with chronic illness is likely to increase as life expectancy rates continue to rise. The type of chronic disease experienced also varies by age (see Figure 10.1). In children, Type 1 diabetes and paralysis caused by accident are the most common chronic health problems, whereas in adults, arthritis, Type 2 diabetes, and cardiovascular disease are the most prevalent (see Box 10.1).

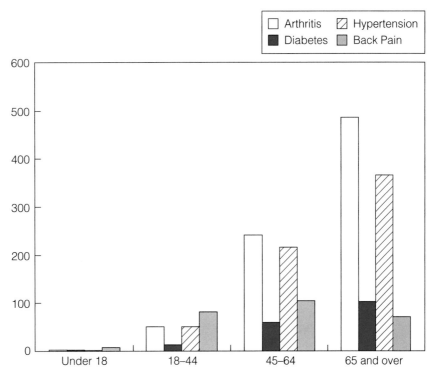

FIGURE 10.1   The number of people with chronic diseases increases dramatically as a function of age (Centers for Disease Control, 2003).

Box 10.1

Health Psychology in the Real World—Chronic Illness in Older Adulthood

Age 65 is commonly seen as the start of "older adulthood," in which those ages 65 to 74 represent the "young-old," those 75 to 84 years represent the "old-old," and people 85 years of age and older represent the "oldest-old." Although 100 years ago relatively few people lived to age 65, because of the increase in life expectancy that has occurred in the United States over the past century, approximately one in eight Americans is now over age 65, and estimates are that people in this age group will represent 20% of the population by 2030. The majority of these older Americans are women: although they are often seen as the "weaker sex," women show a distinct biological advantage over men in terms of life expectancy! Because overall health generally declines as people get older, they are more likely to develop chronic conditions: the majority of older adults suffer from at least one chronic condition. Older adults also experience changes in physiological functioning, which in turn increases their likelihood of developing an illness. For example, the responsiveness of the immune system decreases in older age, meaning that older individuals are more susceptible to mild illnesses that younger people may effectively fight off (Rabin, 2000). Older adults may also show decreases in cognitive functioning, including memory, attention, and concentration (Siegler, Bastian, Steffens, Bosworth, & Costa, 2002). Finally, virtually all older adults experience various social losses, as they retire and lose contact with colleagues and perhaps move to a new (warmer) area and of course, as friends and family members die.

Although older adults do experience a variety of losses, most research indicates that older people maintain overall high levels of psychological well-being. How do they manage to stay in such good spirits? First, successful aging involves making changes in one's priorities and emphasizing the domains in which fulfilling goals may be accomplished. A person who is coping with arthritis, for example, could choose to give up writing letters to friends, but instead make frequent telephone calls. Older people also compare themselves to other older people who are struggling with similar challenges, instead of using younger people—or themselves when they were younger—as comparison points. They may also accept that they have a chronic illness, but deny or minimize its negative consequences on their lives, and instead focus on its positive impact. For example, a person with cancer could ignore the pain or unpleasant side effects of treatment and instead concentrate on the new and valued friendships he or she has made with other people also struggling with this disease. All of these strategies help older adults maintain high self-esteem and an overall positive outlook on life—which, in turn, is associated with better physical health and well-being.

What Are the Consequences of Having Chronic Illnesses?

Because chronic diseases can be managed, but never cured, people with such a diagnosis face a lifetime of managing the symptoms and treatment of the disease. People diagnosed with a chronic illness therefore experience a number of consequences, including physical, social, and psychological problems (see Table 10.1).

Physical Problems

Many people with chronic diseases experience some type of physical debilitation (Devins & Binik, 1996). These vary depending on the illness, but can include highly distressing symptoms such as paralysis, disfigurement, incontinence, and pain. People with diabetes, for example, are at increased risk of developing heart disease, blindness, sexual dysfunction, kidney failure, and problems with circulation that can lead to amputation (Bishop, Roesler, Zimmerman, & Ballard, 1993). Patients with a chronic illness often have concerns about body image, particularly if their disease or its treatment causes significant physical changes in functioning (Taylor & Aspinwall, 1993). Symptoms of multiple sclerosis (MS), a neurological disorder, include impaired vision, weakness, tremors, incoordination, and bowel and bladder difficulties (Franklin & Nelson, 1993). Even non–life-threatening chronic diseases can lead to physical problems. For example, people with arthritis (a chronic, systemic, inflammatory condition causing pain and swelling of the joints) often experience constant pain from inflammation of the joints and have difficulty managing daily tasks, such as getting dressed, walking, or standing (Scott & Hochberg, 1993).

In other cases the disease itself is not debilitating, but the treatment for it is quite destructive to health (Jacobson, Bovbjerg, & Reid, 1993; Jacobsen et al., 1995). An individual with kidney failure, for example, may need to undergo hemodialysis, in which his or her blood is circulated through an artificial

TABLE 10.1 *Potential Threats of Chronic Illness*

Threats to life and physical well-being

Threats to body integrity and comfort (result of disease, treatment, or procedures)

Threats to independence, privacy, autonomy, and control

Threats to self-concept and fulfillment of customary roles

Threats to life goals and future plans

Threats to relationships with family, friends, colleagues

Threats to ability to remain in familiar surroundings

Threats to economic well-being

People who are diagnosed with a chronic disease face many potential challenges.

Source: Falvo, 1991.

kidney for several hours each week. Medications that are used to treat hypertension lead to a number of unpleasant side effects, such as impotence, weight gain, and drowsiness (Taylor & Aspinwall, 1993). Similarly, anticonvulsant drugs, which provide the main treatment for epilepsy, have several unpleasant side effects, such as drowsiness, nausea, mood change, and skin rash (Oles & Penry, 1987). Many of the treatments used to fight cancer, including chemotherapy—which involves administering toxic chemicals to the body in an attempt to kill the cancerous cells—and radiation—in which beams of radiation are used to destroy tissue in a particular area—have unpleasant side effects, including fatigue, diarrhea, vomiting, hair loss, loss of appetite, and nausea; even small physical problems, like hair loss from chemotherapy or radiation, can be very stressful to patients (see Photo 10.1). Although one of the most commonly used drugs to treat HIV is *zidovudine (AZT)*, its use is associated with numerous unpleasant side effects, including anemia, headaches, itching, and even mental confusion.

Surgery, one of the most common treatments for some types of cancer, can lead to various types of disability and disfigurement of the patient, including amputation of a limb (in the case of bone cancer), removal of part or all of one or both breasts (in the case of breast cancer), and removal of a testis (in the case of testicular cancer). Patients with colon cancer may require a colostomy, or surgical opening in the abdomen from which feces are evacuated from the body. Patients may experience feelings of shame as they are forced to handle their bodily wastes on a daily basis and may worry that others easily recognize their condition.

The physical changes caused by chronic illnesses and/or their treatment can also lead to sexual problems (Andersen, Woods, & Copeland, 1997; Druley,

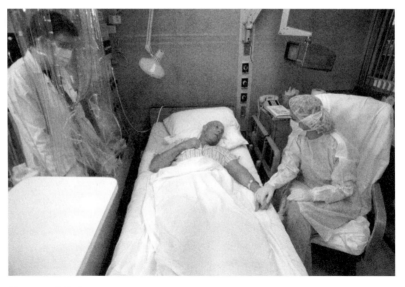

PHOTO 10.1   Many people find even relatively minor symptoms, such as hair loss, very upsetting.

Stephens, & Coyne, 1997; Moyer, 1997). Many different kinds of cancer treatment, including treatment for breast, prostate, urinary, and colorectal cancer, can lead to changes in sexual functioning (Moyer & Salovey, 1996). Women who are diagnosed with breast cancer, for example, must cope with their concerns about body image, particularly if their treatment involves removal of one or both breasts (Carver et al., 1998; Moyer, 1997; Spencer et al., 1999). These concerns are particularly salient for younger women. Women who undergo lumpectomies, in which only the cancerous tumor is removed from the breast, generally have fewer problems with marital and sexual adjustment than those who undergo mastectomies, in which one or both breasts are removed totally (Moyer, 1997; Taylor, Bandura, Ewart, Miller, & DeBusk, 1985). Similarly, many people with coronary heart disease report a decrease in sexual activity, which is often caused by the fear (on the part of the patient or his/her partner) that the physical exertion of sex could lead to a heart attack (Muller, Mittleman, Maclure, Sherwood, & Tofler, 1996). However, the risk of sex triggering a heart attack is actually quite low—less than 1%.

Social Problems

One of the most difficult aspects of coping with a chronic illness is the effect it can have on interpersonal relationships (Taylor & Aspinwall, 1993). People with chronic diseases sometimes choose to hide their conditions from others, in part because of concerns about being pitied and/or abandoned, and may thereby withdraw from many social relationships. This approach is taken particularly in cases when people have illnesses with high levels of stigma, such as epilepsy (a condition marked by recurrent, sudden seizures that result from electrical disturbances in the cerebral cortex) and AIDS (because there is the fear of contagion). For someone to admit that he or she has AIDS, for example, may mean admitting to other possibly shameful behaviors, such as homosexual sex or intravenous drug use. One study with 266 sexually active HIV-positive people found that 41% had not disclosed their HIV status even to their sexual partners (Kalichman & Nachimson, 1999). People with AIDS are often worried about rejection and abandonment (Marks, Richardson, Ruiz, & Maldonado, 1992; Simoni et al., 1995). And these fears are not unreasonable—one study found that one in five women who told her partner about her HIV-positive status was abandoned. In some cases this disclosure even leads to physical violence and abuse (Rothenberg & Paskey, 1995).

Although telling other people about a chronic illness has many advantages, including eliciting social support and avoiding having to deny the illness, even this approach has some potential problems. Friends may withdraw from the patient, either because of their own fears about acquiring the illness or because they cannot bear to face the physical changes in the patient. People often hold negative beliefs and biases about those with chronic illnesses, including perceiving them as helpless, depressed, and even deserving of their fate (Devins & Binik, 1996). Some people with chronic illnesses therefore report feeling shunned by others and experiencing a loss of social support—ironically, just at the time when they are most in need of such support. Wortman and

Box 10.2

Research Focus—How Does Having a Child with a Chronic Disease Impact Marital Satisfaction?

Alexandra Quittner and her colleagues (1998) examined how caring for a chronically ill child influenced marital satisfaction, intimacy, and daily mood. The researchers collected data from both husbands and wives who had a young child (ages 2 to 6 years) with cystic fibrosis, a common genetic disease that affects the lungs and pancreas and virtually always leads to death in childhood or early adulthood. The couples completed a number of questionnaires, including measures of parenting stress, division of household and child care tasks with their spouse, social and recreational time, depression, and marital satisfaction. Moreover, the researchers also collected the same types of data from a sample of 33 couples with a young child who was healthy in order to directly compare the impact of having a chronically ill child on marital interaction.

The findings revealed, not surprisingly, that having a child with a chronic illness had a major impact on marital interaction. First, compared to couples with a healthy child, couples with a child with cystic fibrosis reported having more conflict with their spouse on child-rearing practices, engaging in more child care tasks, and having fewer positive daily interactions with their spouse. This was particularly true for women, who seemed to feel the burden of having a chronically ill child more than their husbands did. Couples with a chronically ill child also spent less time engaging in recreational activities, such as watching TV and going to the movies, than those with a healthy child. For example, couples with a sick child spent about 23% of their time engaging in recreational activities as compared to 33% of the time for those with a healthy child. Although researchers expected that couples with a sick child would experience less marital satisfaction and more depression, there were no differences between the groups on these measures. Having a child with a chronic, and life-threatening, illness impacts marital functioning in several negative ways, including increasing conflict regarding child-rearing practices and decreasing positive daily interactions, but it does not seem to lead to decreased marital satifaction or depression.

Dunkel-Schetter (1979) have argued that patients with cancer are in a difficult situation in that they are likely to be in particular need of support, as they grapple with the emotional and physical aspects of the disease and its treatment, but may receive conflicting reactions from family members and friends, who are trying to cope with their own negative feelings about cancer and their uncertainty about how to help.

Even when family members and friends want to help, they simply may not have realistic conceptions of what the patient is going through. In some cases, people with a chronic illness have family and friends with unrealistically high expectations about how patients should cope with and manage their illnesses (Hatchett, Frierd, Symister, & Wadhwa, 1997). For example, family and friends may believe that the patient could do more tasks to help around the house or the patient's their feelings of depression and anxiety are too pessimistic. One study with patients with arthritis found that those whose spouses were impatient and critical of how they were coping with their illness used less-effective coping strategies and, in turn, experienced more anxiety and depression (Manne & Zautra, 1989). In other cases family members and friends have unrealistically low expectations about how people cope with having a chronic illness (Burish & Bradley, 1983; Hagedoorn et al., 2000; Mohr et al., 1999). They may be overly protective or indulgent, which in turn can cause patients to feel or become dependent. This pattern also interrupts the normal reciprocity in relationships, which can be a stressful disturbance. For example, family members might encourage the patient to simply "take it easy" and may try to discourage patients from talking about or thinking about the disease. Finally, family members can offer unhelpful advice or encouragement, such as "it will turn out all right"—these sentiments are typically well meant, but can raise false hopes and hence are inappropriate. So, social support is often, but not always, beneficial to patients with chronic illness.

Family members of people with chronic illnesses also may experience negative psychological reactions (see Box 10.3 for a humorous example; Andersen, 1993). One of the major problems that families experience is dealing with the increased dependency of the ill person (Burish & Bradley, 1983). The patient may need assistance with a variety of tasks, including personal hygiene, medical care, financial responsibilities, and household chores, which can be time-consuming and emotionally upsetting for family members to accomplish. These changes in family roles can lead to great imbalances in family relationships, which increases guilt on the part of the patient and adds resentment on the part of family members. As described at the beginning of the chapter, Julie's arthritis has made her extremely dependent on her husband, which has put a significant strain on their relationship. One study with the caregivers of patients with cancer and multiple sclerosis found that those who felt the relationship was inequitable experienced more emotional exhaustion and had more feelings of anger at and detachment from the patient (Ybema, Kuijer, Hagedoorn, & Buunk, 2001). Caregivers even may suffer health problems of their own, especially if they must take care of the ill person for a long time and that person is in very poor health (Wight, LeBlanc, & Aneshensel, 1998).

Family members also suffer their own losses when a loved one is diagnosed with a chronic illness; hence, they may experience negative psychological consequences, including depression and anxiety (see Box 10.2). These feelings are particularly likely when the patient has or will have a high level of functional impairment (Fang, Manne, & Pape, 2001). For example, spouses of patients with chronic disease may experience a decrease in social activities, such as spending time with family and friends, seeing movies, and engaging in athletic activities. They may also have to give up some of their own plans and dreams, to accommodate the ill person (Manne, Alfieri, Taylor, & Dougherty, 1999). Although most research has focused on the impact on marriage of chronic ill-

---

Box 10.3

A Humorous Look at the Impact of Chronic Disease on Marital Relationships

After her husband's checkup, a woman was called into the doctor's office. The doctor told her, "Your husband has a serious disease. There are several things you'll have to do for him, or he will surely die. Each morning fix him a healthy breakfast. Be pleasant to him. Make him a nutritious lunch for work, and an especially nice meal for his dinner at night. Don't give him chores, or that will increase his stress. Don't discuss your problems with him either. Try to relax him in the evenings by wearing lingerie and giving him backrubs. Let him watch his favorite sports on TV. And, most important, make love to him several times a week and satisfy his every whim. If you do these things for the next 10 months to a year, I think he'll pull through."

On the way home, the husband asked his wife what the doctor had told her. "You're going to die," she replied.

---

ness, other family members, including parents, children, and siblings, are also affected. One study on the effects of having a parent with cancer found that children experience a number of negative effects, including threat of losing the parent; the temporary loss of a parent because of hospitalization, side effects of treatments, or symptoms; and the disruption of normal family routines and roles (Compas et al., 1994).

People with chronic illnesses may also suffer financial problems when their symptoms or treatment affect their employment (Taylor & Aspinwall, 1993). In some cases the symptoms of chronic illness cause people to be unable to work, or at least to do certain tasks. Epileptics, for example, often have trouble holding a job because they are not allowed to drive. People who are chronically ill with life-threatening conditions, such as cancer, coronary heart disease, and AIDS, may find themselves offered less demanding positions or passed over for promotion because employers think investing time and resources in them is a waste. These economic problems can be particularly difficult because insurance companies often do not cover all of the costs associated with health problems.

Psychological Problems

People who are diagnosed with a chronic illness often experience an initial sense of shock and disbelief (see Box 10.4; Janoff-Bulman, 1992; Moos, 1977). Receiving such a diagnosis shatters people's core beliefs about a "just world," namely, that life is fair and just, and can be particularly difficult to deal with

> **Box 10.4**
>
> **Health Psychology in the Real World—How Do Children Cope with Having a Chronic Disease?**
>
> An estimated 30% of children in the United States have a chronic disease or disability that requires regular medical attention (Newacheck & Taylor, 1992). Of these chronic conditions, approximately 65% are mild, 30% are moderately severe and include some disability, and 5% are severe and include substantial disability. Although in some cases these diseases can be managed, such as diabetes, asthma, and arthritis, in other cases these illnesses may result in death during childhood. Cystic fibrosis and some types of cancers, for example, typically lead to death. Children with a chronic illness often have academic problems (Eiser, 1982). Potential causes include low parental/teacher expectations, missed school for medical reasons, and impairment with mental functioning caused by drugs. Social problems are also relatively common in children with severe chronic illnesses, who may become concerned about maintaining their friendships if they are frequently absent from school and worry about how other children might react if they look or act different in some way because of their illness or its treatment. The American Cancer Society and many cancer treatment centers have special programs that provide speakers for children's classes that describe why a child might look different following cancer treatment. These speakers can then let other children know what to expect when their classmate returns to school. Children with chronic illnesses are also likely to have various psychological problems, including high anxiety, negative self-concept, and feelings of interpersonal isolation. They may experience stress-related symptoms, such as bad dreams, nervousness, and depression.

because there is "no end in sight." People who learn they have a highly disabling chronic disease, such as Parkinson's disease, cancer, or Huntington's disease, may have to put aside some plans and dreams. They may, for example, decide not to have children or to pursue a new career. Disbelief, denial, and anger are therefore common immediate reactions to receiving a diagnosis of chronic illness (see Cartoon 10.1). These reactions are particularly common in younger people, perhaps because people expect greater disability with age and hence receiving such a diagnosis at a young age is more disturbing than when one is older.

Many people with chronic illnesses experience depression, which is caused at least in part by the major loss of control that comes with having a chronic disease (Epping-Jordan et al., 1999; Spiegel, 1996). In fact, estimates are that about 35% of individuals with disabilities suffer from depression, as compared with 12% in the nondisabled population. For example, one study of 50 patients

"What do you mean, I have an ulcer?
I give ulcers, I don't get them!"

CARTOON 10.1   People who are diagnosed with a chronic illness often experience intense disbelief, in part because this diagnosis challenges their worldview and thereby leads to considerable fear and uncertainty. (©The New Yorker Collection 2000. Joseph Farris from the cartoonbank.com. All Rights Reserved.)

with multiple sclerosis—a disease of the central nervous system that leads to loss of function in limbs, bowel, and bladder, pain, and a loss of cognitive functioning—found that many patients felt depressed and useless (Mohr et al., 1999). Depression is, not surprisingly, particularly common in cases of severe and life-threatening illnesses, such as cancer, AIDS, and Alzheimer's disease (Taylor & Aspinwall, 1993). One large study of HIV-positive men and women found that 40% were diagnosed with depression (Fleishman & Fogel, 1994). However, these high rates of depression are most common initially following diagnosis and tend to decrease over time. In fact, one study found that there were no differences in rates of depression between healthy people and those with various chronic illnesses (diabetes, arthritis, cancer, kidney disease) after the first 3 months following diagnosis (Cassileth et al., 1984).

Anxiety, which is caused in part by the great uncertainty caused by a diagnosis of chronic disease, is another common problem (Devins & Binik, 1996). Patients sometimes learn they have such a disease even before they are experiencing any symptoms; hence, they then wonder when the symptoms will begin and how the disease will progress. One study with 80 women newly diagnosed with breast cancer found that 40% reported high levels of anxiety, which is significantly greater than in the general population (Epping-Jordan et al., 1999). Anxiety may be heightened when people feel overwhelmed about controlling the disease and concerned about long-term problems. They also have no idea what to expect—when symptoms will start, what symptoms will be, when they can go back to work, how people will react. For example, upon learning of their status, HIV-positive individuals show considerable increases in anxiety, depression, and mood disturbances, which may persist for several weeks. One study asked patients with cancer to rate which aspects of their disease they found most stressful (Dunkel-Schetter, Feinstein, Taylor, & Falke, 1992). Forty-one percent rated fear and uncertainty about the future; 24% rated limitations in physical abilities, appearance, and lifestyle; and 12% rated managing pain as most stressful. In some cases experiencing the symptoms of a disease can cause great anxiety—patients with asthma, for example, often worry that they will die during an attack, which naturally heightens anxiety. Fortunately, this crisis period tends to be relatively short-lived— anxiety is high at the time of diagnosis, but then decreases over time as patients adjust to having such a disease (Cassileth et al., 1984).

Because many chronic diseases are influenced at least in part by lifestyle choices, such as smoking, exercise, tanning, and sexual activity, people often blame themselves for developing such diseases (see Photo 10.2 and Table 10.2; Burish & Bradley, 1983). For example, one study with patients with breast cancer found that 41% blamed themselves for getting the disease (Taylor, Lichtman, & Wood, 1984). And people who feel responsible for their illness often experience considerable guilt for the pain they are causing themselves as well as their loved ones. They may also have higher rates of depression and anxiety (Glinder & Compas, 1999).

Although the consequences of developing a chronic disease are primarily negative, people often experience some positive effects (see Figure 10.2; Collins et al., 2001; Cordova, Cunningham, Carlson, & Andrykowski, 2001; Mohr et al., 1999; Updegraff & Taylor, 2000; Updegraff, Taylor, Kemeny, & Wyatt, 2002). What possibly could be a benefit of having a chronic illness? People with chronic illnesses often report feeling closer and more in touch with family and friends, having a greater appreciation of life, feeling less inhibited and more compassionate, and experiencing positive changes in self-concept (e.g , feeling stronger, wiser, and better able to cope with other problems). In fact, in one study of patients with cancer, 90% reported experiencing at least one positive change as a result of the cancer (see Table 10.3). Another study compared women with breast cancer to other women and found that women with breast cancer showed a pattern of greater posttraumatic growth, including relating better with others, appreciating life, and spiritual growth (Cordova et al., 2001). Receiving a chronic illness diagnosis can even lead people to engage in health-promoting behavior. One study with nearly 3000 HIV-positive people found that many had made health-promoting changes since their diagnosis: 43% increased their exercise, 59% improved their diet, and 49%

PHOTO 10.2   People whose behavior contributed to their development of a chronic disease often blame themselves and experience higher rates of depression.

TABLE 10.2   *Sample Items from a Survey Assessing Health Outcomes*

1. In general, would you say your health is: excellent, very good, fair, or poor?
2. Compared to 1 year ago, how would you rate your health in general now?
3. During the past 4 weeks, to what extent has your physical health or emotional problems interfered with your normal social activities with family, friends, neighbors, or groups?
4. During the past 4 weeks, how much did pain interfere with your normal work (including both work outside and inside the home)?
5. How much bodily pain have you had during the past 4 weeks?
6. During the past 4 weeks, how much of your time has your physical health or emotional problems interfered with your social activities (visiting with friends, relatives, etc.)?

These items assess how much a person's chronic illness interferes with their physical and social activities.

Source: Ware & Sherbourne, 1992.

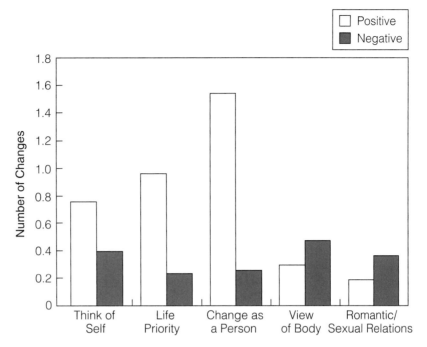

FIGURE 10.2   Although HIV-positive women view their illness as leading to more negative romantic/sexual relations and body image, having HIV also is associated with significant benefits in terms of self-views and life priorities. (data from Updegraff et al. 2002).

TABLE 10.3   *The Benefits of Having Cancer*

Having had breast cancer . . .

1. Has led me to be more accepting of things
2. Has brought my family closer together
3. Has led me to deal better with stress and problems
4. Has helped me realize who my real friends are
5. Has contributed to my overall emotional and spiritual growth
6. Has helped me take things as they come
7. Has taught me to be more patient
8. Has helped me become more aware of the love and support available from other people
9. Has helped me become more focused on priorities, with a deeper sense of purpose in life
10. Has made me realize the importance of planning for my family's future

This scale assesses the positive aspects of having breast cancer.

Source: Antoni et al., 2001.

of smokers decreased their smoking (Collins et al., 2001). Others report that contracting HIV infection led to changes in their priorities, greater closeness to family and friends, and a stronger focus on valued personal goals (Schwartzberg, 1993). Finally, receiving a diagnosis of chronic illness can encourage people to live life to the fullest and focus on achieving their dreams instead of delaying them. As writer Michael Kinsley (2001) notes, "It's like having a get-out-of-jail free card from the prison of delayed gratification. Skip the Democratic convention to go kayaking in Alaska? Absolutely. Do it now, in case you can't do it later."

How Do Illness Factors Influence How People Manage Having a Chronic Illness?

The extent of difficulty people have in coping with a chronic illness varies. This section examines three distinct factors that impact how well people cope with a chronic illness.

Illness Intrusiveness

In many cases people must make major changes in lifestyle in order to avoid exacerbating their conditions. These changes might include avoiding unhealthy foods, stopping smoking, and starting an exercise program. For example, patients with diabetes must limit the sugar in their diets, and patients with coronary heart disease (CHD) must eat healthier foods and give up cigarettes. In some cases people are even told to avoid certain locations and activities. People with asthma, for example, often must avoid spending time outside when pollen counts are high, and those who have experienced a heart attack may be asked to avoid stressful situations, strenuous activities, and heavy lifting. In turn, these changes can lead to anxiety, depression, and social withdrawal, particularly in cases in which managing the disease interferes with a person's daily life, including work, social, and recreational activities (Devins et al., 1990; Talbot, Nowven, Gingras, Belanger, & Audet, 1999).

People with chronic diseases must also engage in relatively complex behaviors to monitor their conditions and manage their treatment regimens (Devins & Binik, 1996). For example, diabetes is a metabolic disorder in which the body is unable to properly convert glucose (sugar) into usable energy. In normal metabolism, the body produces the hormone insulin. A person with diabetes has defective insulin production or use such that glucose cannot be readily used by the body cells, which in turn causes glucose to accumulate in the blood, leading to hyperglycemia. A person with diabetes therefore must monitor blood glucose levels to avoid both sugar shortage and insulin shock and must administer (by injection) appropriate amounts of insulin regularly. However, many people with diabetes find this constant maintenance tedious and fail to follow their treatment regimen (see Photo 10.3). As I described at the beginning of this chapter, Don had particular trouble monitoring his blood sugar, following dietary recommendations, and giving himself insulin when he was with friends.

Interaction with Health Care Providers

Individuals with chronic illnesses are often dependent on health care professionals and biomedical technology (Devins & Binik, 1996). Patients with severe kidney disease, for example, must undergo dialysis a procedure in which the blood is cleaned to remove excess salts, water, and waste products, three times a week for an average of 4 to 6 hours per session. Although they may experience frustration with their disease and treatment, which can influence their feelings toward health care workers, maintaining communication is an important part of managing their illness. Patients must also deal with medical professionals with great regularity and can experience difficulties in these relationships (e.g., understanding a physician's communications, expressing feelings, maintaining a sense of control over treatment options). One study with 97 patients with breast cancer found that 84% reported having trouble communicating with their medical team, including problems understanding physicians' instructions, expressing feelings, and asking questions (Lerman et al., 1993). Moreover, women who had more communications problems showed greater distress later. We examine some of these issues in patient–practitioner relationships in Chapter 12.

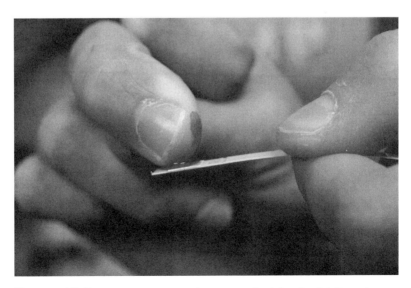

PHOTO 10.3   Chronic illnesses that require high levels of daily maintenance, such as diabetes, are particularly difficult to cope with.

Type of Coping Used

As discussed in Chapter 4, people cope with stressful situations in very different ways, which in turn lead to very different outcomes. What type of coping is helpful? Active *problem-focused coping* strategies, which focus on dealing directly with the source of the stress, are often helpful when people are able to change the stressor in some way (Carver et al., 1993; Felton & Revenson, 1984; Fleishman & Fogel, 1994; Macrodimitris & Endler, 2001; Patterson et al., 1996; Stanton & Snider, 1993). This type of coping can include *proactive,* or *preventive, coping,* in which people try to anticipate problems and then act to prevent their occurrence (Aspinwall & Taylor, 1997). For example, a person with diabetes could avoid experiencing a drop in blood sugar by reularly eating small meals to keep blood sugar at a consistent level. Another type of problem-focused coping is *combative coping,* which is used when a person must react to an unavoidable stressor. A variety of strategies are effective in reducing the effects of the stressor, including relaxation, social support, and exercise.

Emotion-focused coping strategies are also used in response to stressful situations, particularly in cases in which people believe they have little or no ability to directly reduce or avoid the stressor (Carver et al., 1993; Felton & Revenson, 1984; Fleishman & Fogel, 1994; Macrodimitris & Endler, 2001; Patterson et al., 1996; Stanton & Snider, 1993). This type of coping focuses on managing the reaction to stress, although not the cause of the stress itself. Emotion-focused coping can include escape–avoidance (trying to avoid the situation) and distancing (trying to stop thinking about the problem). Both of these types of emotion-focused coping rely on avoiding the stressor—either physically or psychologically. Emotion-focused coping can also include positive reappraisal (trying to think about a negative situation in a new way) or social support. For example, some people with cancer focus on the positive aspects of having this disease (e.g., discovering what is important in life, becoming closer to family and friends; Dunkel-Schetter et al., 1992; Stanton & Snider, 1993).

In one study, 42 patients with kidney disease were randomly assigned to either a problem-disclosure group (people described their difficulties in coping with the illness), a self-presentation group (people described the strategies they used to cope effectively with their disease), or a control group (people saw a videotape on effective coping with dialysis). At the 1-month follow-up, people in the self-presentation group had lower rates of depression and fewer physical symptoms than people in the control group or the problem disclosure group (see Figure 10.3). Apparently talking about how well you are coping, as opposed to focusing on how many problems you are having, may be an effective way of helping patients with chronic disease manage their illnesses, presumably because this approach helps patients generate their own coping strategies (Leake, Friend, & Wadhwa, 1999).

Although both problem-focused and emotion-focused coping can be effective strategies for managing the stress of a chronic illness, most research suggests that directly trying to reduce a stressor is generally a more effective approach (Macrodimitris & Endler, 2001; Pakenham, 1999). For example, one study of 122 patients with multiple sclerosis found that people who relied

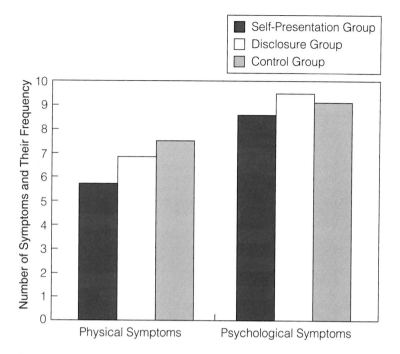

FIGURE 10.3   Being able to talk about their illnesses and describe their own coping strategies seems to help patients with chronic conditions (Leake et al., 1999).

more on problem-focused coping and less on emotion-focused coping were less depressed and felt better about their health (Pakenham, 1999). Similarly, a study of 115 adults with diabetes found that those who used more direct and problem-focused coping strategies experienced lower levels of anxiety and depression than those who engaged in wishful thinking (e.g., wishing the situation would go away or be over) and withdrawal (e.g., sleeping more than usual, avoiding being with people; Macrodimitris & Endler, 2001). However, some emotion-focused strategies, such as focusing on the positive and relying on social support, are also associated with better psychological adjustment (Dunkel-Schetter et al., 1992; Stanton & Snider, 1993). For example, one study with 603 cancer patients revealed that people who coped by seeking social support and focusing on the positive experienced less depression and anxiety than those who simply wished the situation would go away, avoided being with other people, or tried to make themselves feel better by smoking, eating, or drinking (Dunkel-Schetter et al., 1992).

The impact of denial on coping with chronic illness is an interesting one (Havik & Maeland, 1988). On the one hand, immediately after receiving a diagnosis of chronic illness denying this reality may help people cope with the very threatening and upsetting news (Taylor & Aspinwall, 1993). Pretending to not have the disease and attempting to let it affect daily life as little as possible reduces the threat of the illness and thereby decreases anxiety, which can help people cope with the devastating news diagnosis. However, people who continue to deny the existence of their illness over time can suffer severe consequences. Patients with spinal cord injuries, for example, show greater distress when they focus on wishful thinking (e.g., imagining the accident didn't happen) as opposed to a realistic acceptance of their condition (Buckelew, Baumstark, Frank, & Hewett, 1990). This type of unrealistic optimism, such as trying to mentally "undo" an event, inhibits the person from adapting to the condition and in turn adopting new, more realistic goals and expectations about the future. Denial may also decrease people's willingness to follow medical care advice or seek prompt treatment, and can therefore lead to very negative health outcomes.

Level of Social Support

Social support is a very important predictor of psychological and physical well-being in patients with chronic illness (see Chapter 6; Helgeson & Cohen, 1996; Taylor & Aspinwall, 1993). As discussed previously, receiving a diagnosis of a chronic illness is associated with various types of stress, and people who have high levels of social support are better able to buffer the effects of such stress (Alferi, Carver, Antoni, Weiss, & Duran, 2001; Brown, Wallston, & Nicassio, 1989; Dunkel-Schetter et al., 1992; Kulik & Mahler, 1989). Studies with patients with cancer and CHD indicate that those who receive higher levels of social support from their family and friends experience lower levels of anxiety, depression, and anger, recover more rapidly from surgery, and require less pain medication (Alferi et al., 2001; Kulik & Mahler, 1989). Similarly, HIV-positive men who are satisfied with their social support have less anxiety, depression, and anger, lower levels of pain, and better overall health (Namir, Alumbaugh, Fawzy, & Wolcott, 1989). Those men who have a large social network even live longer (Patterson et al., 1996).

Interestingly, some types of social support seem to be more effective than others (Helgeson & Cohen, 1996). Emotional support, such as the availability of people to listen, express concern, and encourage the patient to talk, consistently is found to be beneficial for people coping with a chronic illness. For example, people with cancer who feel they receive an adequate amount of emotional social support show lower distress over time. Instrumental support, such as help with chores, transportation, and assistance with child care, is helpful, especially if it is provided by family members (as opposed to friends). This type of support is also most beneficial for people with a poor prognosis for recovery, presumably because they have more trouble managing these practical tasks. Informational support, such as giving advice and answering questions, is helpful, but only if it

Questioning the Research 10.1

Although considerable research shows that greater social support leads to better coping with chronic disease, can you think of an alternative explanation for this association? (Hint: Is this association really causation, or just correlation?)

is given by a health care professional—advice from friends and family members is not generally perceived as valuable (Dunkel-Schetter, 1984).

How Can Psychological Interventions Help People Cope with Chronic Illness?

Given all the problems associated with having a chronic disease, how can people adjust effectively to such a diagnosis? Research suggests several different approaches that may have positive effects on patients' psychological adjustment as well as physical symptoms. These approaches include providing information and education, training in cognitive-behavioral techniques, and relying on social support groups (Meyer & Mark, 1995).

Education

One of the most common approaches to helping people adapt to a chronic disease is providing education (Taylor & Aspinwall, 1993). Patients and their families may benefit simply from learning about the disease and its treatment, in part because such knowledge enables them to feel more "in control" of the disease and its course (Helgeson & Cohen, 1996; Meyer & Mark, 1995). Education programs to help people cope with asthma, for example, teach patients about the physiology and mechanisms of breathing, as well as the common triggers for asthma attacks (Lehrer, Feldman, Giardino, Song, & Schmaling, 2002). People also are taught what occurs during an asthma attack and how medicine works to counteract the effects of an attack. Finally, they learn behavioral techniques for preventing and controlling asthma attacks. Providing this type of education decreases patients' anxiety about asthma and reduces use of medical services.

Most research suggests that education helps patients manage the psychological and physical symptoms of their disease. For example, patients with asthma who participate in an education program show fewer symptoms (Lehrer et al., 2002). Education can also be effective at reducing psychological and physical symptoms for those with cancer. Vicki Helgeson and her colleagues at Carnegie Mellon University (1999, 2001) randomly assigned 312 patients newly-diagnosed with breast cancer to either an education group, group-discussion group, education and group-discussion group, or a control condition. Women who received information about the disease benefited in terms of psychological and physical well-being even as long as 3 years after the intervention, whereas those who participated in the discussion groups showed no such improvement. Similarly, one study with patients with cancer found that those who received detailed information (including a tour of the oncology ward, a videotaped presentation about chemotherapy, and a take-home booklet) had lower levels of nausea and vomiting, were less depressed and hostile, and experienced less disruption in their daily lives while in chemotherapy treatment compared to those who received relaxation training as well as those who received only a brief (25-minute) information session (Burish, Snyder, & Jenkins, 1991). In sum, providing education about the disease, its symptoms, and its treatment may increase patients' sense of self-efficacy and control, and thereby improve psychological and physical functioning.

Cognitive-Behavioral Therapy

Cognitive-behavioral therapy focuses specifically on challenging individuals' irrational beliefs about their condition and giving them coping skills to handle their illness (Devins & Binik, 1996; Parker, 1995). For example, a therapist could challenge the belief held by a person with epilepsy that he or she will never get married. This type of therapy also provides training in various techniques to help people handle the stress of having a chronic illness, such as progressive relaxation, meditation, biofeedback, and guided imagery. For example, patients with cancer who engage in regular meditation (both on their own and as part of a group) show lower levels of anger, depression, and anxiety than those without such training (Speca, Carlson, Goodey, & Angen, 2000). Cognitive-behavioral training is especially effective for helping people cope with chronic diseases with symptoms that are brought on by stress, such as asthma attacks and epileptic seizures (Lehrer et al., 2002; Parker, 1995). People with these disorders can therefore learn effective ways of reducing their anxiety and tension, which in turn will decrease their likelihood of experiencing an attack.

Cognitive-behavioral training is effective at helping people cope with various problems caused by chronic illnesses, including reducing anxiety and nausea resulting from chemotherapy, decreasing pain, and lowering blood pressure (see Box 10.5; Agras, Taylor, Kraemer, Southam, & Schneider, 1987; Carey & Burish, 1988). For example, one study randomly assigned 67 patients with sickle cell disease to a pain coping skills intervention (e.g., relaxation, imagery, calming self-statements) or an education condition (Gil et al., 2000). At the 3-month follow-up those who had the pain coping skills intervention reported less pain and more efforts at coping than those in the other condition. Similarly, research with patients with cancer, who often experience nausea in anticipation of chemotherapy treatment, has shown that training in relaxation and specifically the use of *systematic desensitization* leads to a substantial decrease in nausea and vomiting (Morrow, Asbury, Hamman & Dobkin, 1992). And studies with both HIV-positive men as well as women with breast cancer indicate that people who receive training in stress management (including help on thinking through daily stressors in a new way, relying more on social support, and increasing assertiveness while decreasing anger) and relaxation (including progressive muscle relaxation, meditation, and guided imagery) show lower levels of anxiety, anger, and stress compared to those on a waiting list or in a brief-intervention control condition (Antoni et al., 2000; Antoni et al., 2001; Cruess et al., 2000). This type of training even leads to physiological changes 6 to 12 months later, including greater immune system functioning and higher levels of testosterone.

Box 10.5

Research Focus—Can Learning to Manage Stress Decrease Depression in Patients with Breast Cancer?

Michael Antoni and his colleagues at the University of Miami (2001) were interested in examining whether helping women with breast cancer manage stress would decrease rates of depression. One hundred women with early-stage breast cancer were recruited from local hospitals and medical practices. They were then randomly assigned to either a cognitive-behavioral stress management intervention program, which met for 2 hours each week for 10 weeks, or a control condition, which included a condensed version of the intervention program in the form of a 5- to 6-hour session given on a single day. The intervention program included training in relaxation techniques, expressing emotional reactions, and discussing practical strategies for coping with cancer and its treatment-related problems. All the women completed several different types of measures, including assessments of depression, anxiety, anger, optimism, and perceived benefits of cancer before and after their participation in these groups.

Participation in the lengthy intervention had a number of positive effects. First, women who attended the intervention group for 10 weeks showed a decrease in rates of depression. They also reported increases in general optimism as well as the benefits of having cancer, such as bringing their families closer together and making them stronger and more patient. Women who were least optimistic at the start of the intervention showed the greatest benefits from their participation: they showed the greatest increases in rates of optimism and perceived benefits of cancer. This research therefore suggests that gaining skills in managing the stress brought on by receiving a cancer diagnosis can be quite effective in reducing rates of depression and increasing rates of optimism, especially for women who are particularly devastated by their diagnosis. However, because this intervention included several distinct components, including training in expressing feelings, relaxation techniques, and practical advice, it is impossible to determine exactly which—or how many—of these components led to the positive changes.

Social Support Groups

Social support groups, which consist of other people suffering from the same illness, are another effective way of helping people cope with chronic diseases (Devins & Binik, 1996). This approach gives people an opportunity to compare coping strategies and solutions to daily problems and provide social support to each other. They can share emotions and discuss topics such as physical problems, communication with physicians, relationships with family members, finding meaning in life, and facing death. As described at the beginning of the chapter, Betty often felt more comfortable relying on her social support group for emotional support than on her family, in part because the women in the group understood exactly what she was experiencing. Self-help groups have beneficial effects on helping people cope with diabetes, cancer, herpes, scoliosis, and genetic diseases. One study by David Spiegel and his colleagues at Stanford University found that women with terminal breast cancer who participated in weekly group therapy sessions had lower levels of depression at the 1-year follow-up (Spiegel, Bloom, & Yalom, 1981). Most important, women who participated in the group therapy lived about twice as long as those in the control group (36.6 months versus 18.9 months, respectively; Spiegel, Bloom, Kraemer, & Gottheil, 1989). Some evidence suggests that participating in a social support group can improve patients' immunological response, which could help explain the longer life expectancy of those in the group therapy support group, previously mentioned (Fawzy et al., 1990). (However, and as I discuss at the end of this chapter, some very recent research suggests that benefits of social support groups are not always so clear.)

Support groups are especially useful for people who lack other types of social support (Helgeson et al., 2000). For example, one study with patients with cancer found that those who received low levels of emotional support from their partners benefited in terms of physical functioning from participation in a peer discussion group, but those who already had high levels of support at home showed no such change or decreases in physical funtioning following participation. Although this finding was unexpected, it may be that those who participated in the group talked about their problems more at home, which in turn led to more negative interactions. It could also be that they changed their expectations about the type of support they should receive at home, and that made them sad.

What Is Coronary Heart Disease?

Until the 20th century, coronary heart disease (CHD) was not a major health problem. However, there are now over 1 million new cases diagnosed a year, and it is the leading killer in the United States, causing 40% of deaths (Centers for Disease Control, 2003). Of healthy 40-year-olds, 40 to 50% of men and 25 to 35% of women will eventually develop coronary heart disease (Lloyd-Jones, Larson, Beiser, & Levy, 1999).

Under normal conditions, the heart contracts and releases, which pumps blood throughout the body (see Figure 10.4; Smith & Pratt, 1993). The blood carries necessary oxygen to all of the cells in the body and removes carbon dioxide and other waste material from the cells. However, over time because of diet or lifestyle the artery walls can become clogged with a buildup of fatty substances, such as, *low-density lipoprotein (LDL) cholesterol*, and other substances. (In contrast, *high-density lipoproteins, or HDLs,* remove LDL cholesterol from the bloodstream, and thereby reduce the risk of arterial clogging.) When this

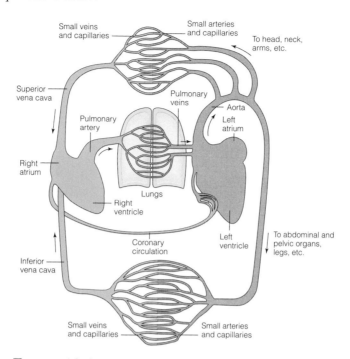

Small veins and capillaries — Small arteries and capillaries

To head, neck, arms, etc.

Superior vena cava

Pulmonary veins

Aorta

Left atrium

Pulmonary artery

Right atrium

Lungs

Right ventricle

Coronary circulation

Left ventricle

To abdominal and pelvic organs, legs, etc.

Inferior vena cava

Small veins and capillaries — Small arteries and capillaries

FIGURE 10.4　As the heart beats, blood is pumped through the body. The blood carries much-needed oxygen to all of the cells in the body and removes carbon dioxide and other waste material from the cells.

buildup occurs, the area through which blood can flow decreases and the likelihood of a blood clot increases (see Figure 10.5). This process, known as *atherosclerosis*, reduces the flow of blood and thereby deprives the heart of essential nutrients. Moreover, arteries can also lose their elasticity over time, which makes it difficult for them to expand and contract with the blood pressure. This process, known as *arteriosclerosis*, leads to a decrease in blood flow and an increase in the likelihood of a blood clot forming.

　　Although both atherosclerosis and arteriosclerosis can be present in the body without a person experiencing any symptoms for some time, they can eventually lead to very serious problems. First, a person may develop *angina*, a feeling of pain and tightness in the chest as the heart is deprived of oxygen. This type of attack may pass quickly, but is often a sign that future cardiovascular problems will develop. In more serious cases, in which there is a complete blockage of the coronary arteries, a person may experience a *myocardial infarction*, or heart attack. Heart attacks often occur because a blood clot formed around the built-up cholesterol blocks the passage of blood to the heart. This deprivation of oxygen causes permanent damage to the heart muscles. Atherosclerosis and arteriosclerosis can lead to *strokes*. The placque that forms on the artery wall may became detached, and then travel in the bloodstream. If one of these blood clots lodges in the circulatory system so that it deprives the brain of oxygen, the person experiences a stroke, which damages neurons in the brain that can never be replaced. People who have suffered a

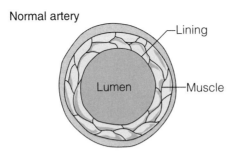

Normal artery

Lining

Lumen

Muscle

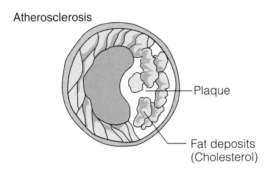

Atherosclerosis

Plaque

Fat deposits
(Cholesterol)

FIGURE 10.5   As cholesterol and fats build up in the arteries, the walls of the
arteries become thicker and thicker, leaving little room for blood to flow. Over time,
arteries can become completely blocked, which causes to a heart attack.

stroke may therefore experience some type of long-term damage, such as
speech impairment or difficulty in moving parts of their bodies.

How Do Psychological Factors Contribute to Coronary Heart Disease?

Some of the factors associated with CHD can't be changed (Smith & Pratt,
1993): the likelihood of developing CHD increases with age, for example, presumably because over time the arteries are more likely to become clogged or
hardened. People with a family history of CHD, such as a close relative who
experienced a heart attack, are also at greater risk of developing this disease.

Gender is another factor associated with cardiovascular disease: men are at
greater risk of experiencing CHD than women, which is one of the reasons
why men have a shorter life expectancy than women (Smith & Pratt, 1993).
One possible reason for this gender difference is that testosterone, which cir-
culates in higher levels in men than women, is associated with aggression and
competitiveness, and these behaviors may increase a person's risk of developing cardiovascular disease. However, men and women were relatively equally

likely to die of heart disease until the 1920s, suggesting that hormone levels alone are unlikely to explain this gender gap (Nikiforov & Mamaev, 1998). Another possibility is that men engage in more behaviors that lead to CHD than women, including smoking, drinking alcohol, and eating high-fat foods. However, even when men and women have the same level of risky behaviors, men are still more likely than women to die of CHD (Fried et al., 1998). Although research is clearly needed to show exactly why, it is important to recognize that cardiovascular problems are not just a "male problem." In fact, CHD is the leading cause of death in women as well as men—women simply develop such problems about 15 years later than men.

There are also clear differences in the frequency of CHD as a function of race and ethnicity, with Africans Americans showing more risk than white Americans, who in turn show more risk than Asian Americans and Hispanic Americans (Centers for Disease Control, 2003). For example, African American women are more than twice as likely to die of CHD than white women, and African American men are more than one and a half as likely to die of CHD than white men. What causes these racial differences in CHD? Most research points to the role of socioeconomic factors. Specifically, African Americans are more likely than whites to have low socioeconomic status (SES), and low-SES people tend to experience more risk factors for CHD, including eating a higher-fat diet, smoking, living under generally more stressful conditions, and having reduced access to health care (Stunkard & Sorensen, 1993). Other research suggests that African Americans may also experience more stress than whites because they must constantly cope with racial prejudice and discrimination (Krieger & Sidney, 1996; Krieger, Sidney, & Coakley, 1998). (We discuss the role of stress as a predictor of CHD in detail in the next section.) However, environmental factors are not the only cause of ethnic and racial differences in CHD: one recent study found that African American women were still at greater risk of experiencing a heart attack than white women even if they had similar levels of education and family income (Winkleby, Kraemer, Ahn, & Varady, 1998).

Demographic factors, including family history, age, gender, and race, contribute to CHD as do psychological factors (Smith & Pratt, 1993). This section examines the role of three psychosocial factors, namely, stress, behavioral choices, and personality, in contributing to CHD.

Stress

Stress, including pressure caused by work, interpersonal conflict, and financial concerns, is one factor that may contribute to CHD (see Box 10.6; Kop, Gottdiener, & Krantz, 2001). As discussed in Chapter 4, people who are under stress show an acceleration of the heartbeat, a strengthening of the heart's contractions, and higher blood pressure. Moreover, epinephrine is released during times of stress, which decreases the time needed for blood to coagulate and causes blood vessels to constrict. Chronic stress can therefore lead to excessive wear and tear on the cardiovascular system, which over time can lead to considerable damage to the heart and arteries (Sapolsky, 1994). For example, monkeys who

Box 10.6

Health Psychology in the Real-World—Is New York City Hazardous to Your Health?

Would you believe that living in—or even visiting—New York City could be hazardous to your health? That's exactly what some recent research by Nicholas Christenfeld and his colleagues at the University of California at San Diego suggests (Christenfeld, Glynn, Phillips, & Shrira, 1999). These researchers examined death certificates for a 10-year period, and specifically calculated the following rates of death caused by CHD: death rates for New York City residents who died in the city, New York City residents who died while traveling outside the city, and non–New York City residents who died while visiting the city. As predicted, people who lived in New York City had a very high death rate as a result of CHD while living in the city—in fact, their death rate from CHD was 55% higher than the national average. In contrast, New York City residents who were traveling outside of the city were 20% less likely to die from CHD than if they were in the city. Visitors to New York City experienced the same type of problems, with a death rate from CHD that is 34% higher than the national average. Is this pattern true in all cities? No. Researchers found no differences in CHD for people who lived in or visited other major cities, including Los Angeles, Chicago, Houston, Philadelphia, Dallas, San Diego, Phoenix, Detroit, San Antonio, and San Jose, as compared to the national average.

are at the bottom of the dominance hierarchy (hence, are continually under conditions of high stress) are very likely to develop high blood pressure as well as atherosclerosis. Similarly, people who work in jobs that have constant demands but low levels of control—such as working on an assembly line or waiting tables—are at greater risk of developing CHD than those who have less stressful jobs (Bosma, Stansfeld, & Marmot, 1998). Even relationship stress can lead to both CHD and cardiac events (Coyne et al., 2001; Matthews & Gump, 2002; Orth-Gomer et al., 2000). For example, women with CHD who experience high levels of marital conflict are three times as likely to experience a heart attack as those who are in low-conflict marriages (Orth-Gomer et al., 2000).

Some researchers have examined another type of stress that may lead to CHD—the stress of constant racial discrimination (Krieger & Sidney, 1996; Krieger et al., 1998). As described previously, African Americans have higher rates of CHD and hypertension than do Caucasian Americans, and some researchers believe that these differences are caused at least in part by the constant exposure to discrimination and racism that many African Americans encounter. In one study by Nancy Krieger and her colleagues, African American men and women who reported experiencing racial discrimination and accepting unfair treatment had significantly higher blood pressure than those who reported experiencing such discrimination but challenging unfair treatment. However, this association between accepting racial discrimination and high blood pressure was found in working-class African Americans, but not among African Americans business professionals (Krieger & Sidney, 1996; Krieger et al., 1998). This finding suggests that stress may be greatest among those who are trying to overcome adversity, but who have limited socioeconomic resources to do so. Racial discrimination may indeed influence rates of hypertension and CHD in African Americans, but this association is also influenced by gender and SES.

Behavioral Choices

Many behavioral choices also influence a person's risk of developing CHD. As discussed in Chapter 7, cigarette smoking influences CHD in a number of ways, including increasing the heart rate, increasing blood pressure, and constricting the blood vessels, which causes problems over time and particularly during times of stress (Smith & Pratt, 1993). Smoking also decreases the production of HDL cholesterol, which protects against heart attacks. Smoking basically increases wear and tear on the heart and accelerates atherosclerosis. In fact, a person who smokes is twice as likely to die from CHD than someone who doesn't smoke (Fried et al., 1998; Twisk, Kemper, Van Mechelen, & Post, 1997). Moreover, nonsmokers who live with smokers are about 20% more likely to develop CHD than nonsmokers who live with other nonsmokers (Werner & Pearson, 1998).

People who have *hypertension*, a condition in which their blood pressure is at a consistently high level, are at increased risk of developing CHD. Blood pressure represents the force of the blood against the artery walls, and when this pressure is too high, the artery walls can get damaged, which in turn leads to CHD. Because high blood pressure makes the heart beat more forcefully, this type of continuous wear and tear on the heart can weaken it, which also can contribute to CHD. In fact, people who have elevated blood pressure are two to four times as likely to develop CHD as those with normal blood pressure.

Although in many cases the exact cause of hypertension is unknown, considerable research suggests that diet may play a substantial role in leading to high blood pressure as well as CHD (Smith & Pratt, 1993). People who eat foods that are high in cholesterol, such as animal fats and some types of oils, are at greater risk of developing CHD than those who tend to eat foods that are low in cholesterol, such as fruits and vegetables (Stamler, Wentworth, & Neaton, 1986). Cholesterol, naturally occurring in the body as well as that introduced by diet, is transported in the bloodstream, and excessive amounts can lead to clogged or blocked arteries. A person's total cholesterol level at age 22 is a good predictor of his or her likelihood of experiencing CHD or stroke and age of death (Klag et al., 1993). People with cholesterol levels in the top 25% of the study participants are twice as likely to die of a heart attack than those with cholesterol levels in the bottom 25%. On the other hand, some types of food seem to protect people from developing CHD (see Photo 10.4; Stampfer, Rimm, & Walsh, 1993). For example, women who consume high levels of vitamin E are at reduced risk of CHD (Stampfer et al., 1993), as are people who have a diet high in fiber (Katan, Grundy, & Willett, 1997). Some recent research even suggests that people who eat deep-sea fish regularly have a lower likelihood of experiencing a heart attack (Albert et al., 1998).

Personality

How does personality impact development of CHD? As discussed in Chapter 5, the Type A personality trait is commonly thought to predict occurrence of CHD (Friedman & Rosenman, 1959; Rosenman & Friedman, 1961; Suinn, 1975). People who are Type A's, those who are competitive, time-urgent, and hostile, are more likely to experience a heart attack and to show signs of hypertension. One possibile reason for this is that Type A people show heightened levels of physiological arousal, including elevated heart rate, higher blood pressure, and increased catecholamines and corticosteroids, in stressful situations (Joregensen, Johnson, Kolodziej, & Schreer, 1996; Smith, 1992). While a Type B person might calmly sit in the car and listen to music during a traffic jam, a Type A person might experience this situation as very upsetting and arousing. Over time this constant physiological arousal can damage the heart

PHOTO 10.4   Do you know what you're consuming when you eat at McDonald's (or another fast-food restaurant)? A Big Mac has 34 grams of fat and 590 calories, an order of medium-size fries has 22 grams of fat and 450 calories, and a medium Coca-Cola Classic has 0 grams of fat and 220 calories. Remember, for someone eating 2000 calories per day (a rough average), today's nutritional guidelines recommend including 65 grams of fat per day.

and blood vessels and increase the formation of blood clots, which in turn can lead to cardiovascular disease as well as heart attacks.

Although Type A is the personality variable most often associated with CHD, recent research suggests that a specific component of the Type A personality, hostility, is a particularly strong predictor (Barefoot, Dodge, Peterson, Dahlstrom, & Williams, 1989; Matthews, Owens, Kuller, Sutton-Tyrrell, & Jansen-McWilliams, 1998; Miller, Smith, Turner, Guijarro, & Hallet, 1996; Smith, 1992; Williams et al., 1980). In fact, research by Richard Shekelle and his colleagues (1983) reveals that men's level of hostility, but not Type A behavior, predicts their likelihood of suffering a heart attack as well as experiencing other stress-related diseases. One prospective study assessed hostility in 200 healthy women and then followed these women over 10 years (Matthews et al., 1998). Even controlling for variables such as smoking, women who had higher hostility scores in the earlier test were more likely to show symptoms of cardiovascular disease 10 years later. Similarly, Redford Williams and his colleagues (1980) found that patients who were high in hostility had more severe heart disease than those who were low in hostility. Similarly, people who express high levels of anger, including raising their voice while arguing and yelling back when someone yells at them, are at greater risk of developing CHD (Siegman, 1993). In fact, people who frequently experience anger are three times as likely to suffer a heart attack as those who rarely experience anger (Williams et al., 2000). How does the expression of anger lead to CHD? When a person yells his or her heart rate probably increases, and, although the person may not be aware of it, blood pressure also increases. In turn, people who regularly experience this higher level of physiological arousal may be at greater risk of developing cardiovascular problems because they have so much wear and tear on their blood vessels and heart (Siegman et al., 1992). Physiological reactions may also explain why people who are high in hostility tend to have worse health: hostile people have consistently higher heart rates and blood pressure than those who are low in hostility, they show extreme cardiovascular reactions to stressful situations, and they take longer to have their bodies return to normal functioning following a stressful interaction (Raikkonen, Matthews, Flory, & Owens, 1999; Smith, 1992; Suarez, Schanberg, Williams, & Zimmermann, 1998).

Other personality traits, including anxiety, depression, pessimism, and neuroticism, are also associated with the development of CHD (Costa & McCrae, 1987; Everson, Goldberg, Kaplan, & Cohen, 1996; Kawachi et al., 1994; Markovitz et al., 1993). People who are high in anxiety are significantly more likely to develop and die from heart disease than those who are lower in anxiety (Kawachi et al., 1994; Markovitz, Matthews, Kannel, Cobb, & D'Agostino, 1993). For example, men who are high in anxiety are three times more likely to die from a heart attack than those who are low in anxiety. Similarly, men who are high in hopelessness are more than four times more likely to die from cardiovascular diseases as those who are low in hopelessness (Everson et al., 1996). Finally, one study of 347 women ages 18 to 94 years revealed that neuroticism was associated with reports of a number of physical symptoms, including frequency of illness, cardiovascular problems, digestive problems, and fatigue (Costa & McCrae, 1987). However, and as you may recall from Chapter 5, some evidence suggests that people who are high in neuroticism are more likely both to interpret minor health problems as more painful and problematic and complain about health symptoms, but do not actually experience more physical problems (Watson, 1988; Watson & Pennebaker, 1989).

How Can Psychological Interventions Help Reduce the Risk of Recurring Heart Attacks?

Because of the significant rate of CHD in the United States, many intervention programs have specifically targeted heart attack survivors in an effort to help them change their behavior. As described at the beginning of the chapter, following his first heart attack Bill became motivated to change his diet, stop smoking, and start exercising, all of which may decrease the likelihood of future heart problems. This is a type of secondary prevention approach to health, which focuses on reducing people's risk of experiencing another heart attack and dying of cardiovascular disease.

One type of treatment for CHD focuses on helping people change their health-related behavior (Dusseldorp, van Elderen, Maes, Meulman, & Kraaij, 1999; Smith & Pratt, 1993). Health education programs focus on changing people's behavior, including showing them how to reduce their sodium and fat intake, lower their weight, and stop smoking. Because smoking and high-fat diets can cause the heart to operate less efficiently, making changes in these behaviors reduces the risk of CHD. Health education programs also encourage people to start exercising, which decreases the risk of cardiovascular disease in several ways, including reducing weight and improving the efficiency of the heart (Rovario, Holmes, & Holmsten, 1984). Health education programs also provide patients with information about the medications they could take and encourage patients to follow prescribed medical regimens.

These programs can be quite effective in reducing CHD. People who make dietary changes show substantial reductions in cardiovascular risk factors (Brunner et al., 1997), and those who engage in regular exercise following a heart attack show lower blood pressure and lower heart rates (Rovario et al., 1984). Health-promotion programs are particularly effective at decreasing CHD risk when they also include cholesterol-lowering medication (Maher, Brown, Marcovina, Hillger, & Zhao, 1995). Lifestyle interventions can also lead to reductions in the rate of diabetes, which is often linked to CHD (Knowler et al., 2002).

The other common approach to reducing risk of CHD is through stress management programs (Dusseldorp et al., 1999). These programs focus on training patients in techniques for managing stress, such as relaxation training. One recent study by James Blumenthal and his colleagues at Duke University (2002) found that men who participated in a weekly stress management group for 4 months experienced fewer negative health events, including heart attacks, bypass surgery, and death, than those who simply received medicine for their condition and those who exercised. Other studies point to the availability of trained professionals as a resource in helping heart attack survivors manage stress. For example, Nancy Frasure-Smith and Raymond Prince (1989) assigned some patients to receive regular calls from a nurse for 1 year following their heart attack. The nurse asked them whether they were experiencing stress, and then either talked through the problems with the patient or referred them to another health care professional (therapist, physician, social worker). Patients who received such follow-up contact had lower rates of mortality over the 7-year follow-up as compared to those who received standard care.

Several studies have attempted to decrease individuals' risk of CHD by teaching them techniques and methods for changing Type A cognitions, behaviors, and emotions, such as by teaching people more adaptive ways to cope with stress (Friedman, Thoresen, & Gill et al., 1986). For example, patients might examine the triggers for their Type A behavior, and then learn cognitive and behavioral techniques to help them reduce their competitiveness, hostility, and cynicism. This type of program is very effective in reducing the risk of a second heart attack—in fact, rates of death caused by CHD were twice as high in the control group as compared to the treatment group. Similarly, other researchers have focused specifically on trying to modify anger and hostility. In one study 22 highly hostile men with CHD were randomly assigned to a control condition (information only) or a hostility-reduction intervention, which included training in listening, problem-focused coping, and enhancing self-awareness (Gidron, Davidson, & Bata, 1999). Findings at the 2-month follow-up revealed that those in the intervention group had lower blood pressure and rates of hostility, suggesting that this might be a good way to reduce CHD.

Finally, programs that combine health education and stress management techniques may be quite effective. For example, Dean Ornish and his colleagues (1990, 1998) created a very intensive program in an attempt to alter behavior that was putting people at risk of CHD. This program included severe dietary restrictions (such as allowing only 10% of their calories to come from fat), assistance in smoking cessation and reducing alcohol intake, and increasing exercise, as well as training in relaxation and other stress management techniques. Patients who participated in this program had significantly less blockage of their coronary arteries 1 year later compared to those in a control group. Moreover, findings from their 5-year follow-up indicated that patients who completed this program had fewer coronary problems. Although this approach is clearly successful in decreasing CHD, it is very costly in terms of time, energy, and expense and is therefore not likely to be a particularly useful approach in the general population.

What Is Cancer?

After heart disease, cancer is the leading cause of death in the United States, with more than 553,000 people dying from this disease each year (Centers for Disease Control, 2003). More than 1.2 million people in the United States alone are diagnosed with cancer each year (see Table 10.4). Although there are

TABLE **10.4**   *Ten Most Common Types of Cancer in Men and Women*

Type of Cancer in Men	Number of New Cases per 100,000 People
Prostate	135.7
Lung	70.0
Colon	34.9
Urinary and bladder	27.7
Non-Hodgkin's Lymphoma	19.2
Rectal	16.1
Oral cavity and pharyngeal	14.8
Leukemia	12.3
Pancreatic	10.0
Stomach	9.8

Type of Cancer in Women	Number of New Cases per 100,000 People
Breast	110.7
Lung	42.3
Colon	26.6
Uterine	21.1
Ovarian	12.1
Non-Hodgkin's lymphoma	12.2
Skin melanoma	11.4
Rectal	9.6
Cervicular	7.7
Pancreatic	7.4

Prostate and breast cancers are the most common types of cancer, and lung and colon cancer are the second and third most common types of cancer in both men and women.

Source: Centers for Disease Control, 2003.

more than 200 types of cancer, the majority of cases are one of four types: carcinomas (malignancies of tissure-cells and cells lining various body organs; e.g., breast cancer, lung cancer, and skin cancer), lymphomas (cancers of the lymphatic system, such as non-Hodgkin's lymphoma and Hodgkin's disease), sarcomas (cancers of the muscles or bones), and leukemias (cancers of the blood cells or bone marrow). The most common types of cancer are skin cancer (600,000 cases diagnosed each year), breast cancer (180,000 new cases each year), lung cancer (160,000 new cases each year), colorectal cancer (150,000 cases per year), prostate cancer (130,000 cases per year), and uterine/cervical cancer (45,000 cases per year).

Cancer is the uncontrollable growth and spread of abnormal cells, which form tumors (Brownson, Reif, Alavanja, & Bal, 1993). Benign tumors consist of cells that are similar to the nearby cells, and they grow relatively slowly and are mostly harmless. On the other hand, malignant tumors (commonly called cancers) consist of cells that are different from their surrounding cells and grow very rapidly. Malignant tumors often grow beyond their original location and invade other body organs (metastasize), spreading cancer throughout the body (see Figure 10.6). Tumors can cause intense pain when they put pressure on normal tissues and nerves and block the flow of fluids in the body (Melzack & Wall, 1982). If these tumors are not stopped (either by removing them with surgery or stopping their growth with radiation or chemotherapy or other therapies), they can obstruct vital organs (as in intestinal cancer), cause organs to fail (as in liver or kidney cancer), or lead to hemorrhaging or strokes.

Most cancers are caused by genetic mutations, which may gradually occur over time. Some of these mutations are simply a function of age—as cells continue to multiply, the chance of mutations occurring increases over time. This is why cancer is more common in older people than in younger people. Cancer can also be caused by *carcinogens*, any substance capable of converting normal cells into cancerous ones. Carcinogens change the cell's DNA, which in turn leads to cancer. For example, exposure to ultraviolet light while suntanning can cause a chemical reaction in cells that alters both the components

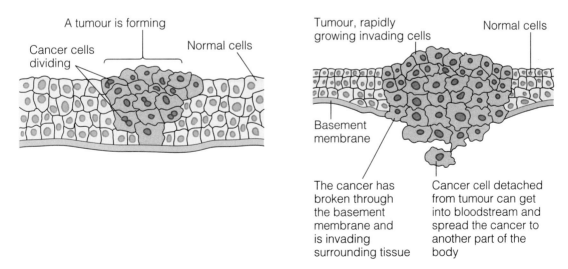

FIGURE 10.6 Cancer can be caused by random and naturally occurring mutations or by carcinogens, both of which lead to changes in cells' DNA. These changes disrupt the normal functioning of both the oncogenes, which work to control cell growth and reproduction, and the suppressor genes, which work to inhibit uncontrolled growth. In turn, cancer can spread out of control.

and the shape of the DNA molecule in cells. Although sometimes these changes are found and repaired by the cell, or the cell is killed before it can reproduce, other times these alterations go unnoticed and lead to cancer. In normal cells, two different types of genes act to regulate cell growth: *oncogenes* work to control cell growth and reproduction, and *suppressor genes* work to inhibit uncontrolled growth. However, when either of these types of genes is damaged by a mutation—either caused by random chance or exposure to a carcinogen—uncontrolled cell growth and reproduction can occur. For example, benzopyrene, a chemical in cigarette smoke, damages cancer suppressor genes, and may therefore lead to lung cancer (Denissenko, Pao, Tang, & Pfeifer, 1996). Similarly, mutations in two genes that are responsible for repairing damage to cell DNA, BRCA1 and BRCA2, are associated with an increased risk of developing breast cancer.

How Do Psychosocial Factors Influence the Development of Cancer?

Some of the factors associated with acquiring cancer are largely fixed and unchangeable. People who are older are at greater risk of developing cancer, perhaps in part because the genetic mutations that cause cancer are more likely to occur over time. However, cancer is the second leading cause of death in children ages 1 to 14 years (after accidents), so this is not simply a disease of the old. Ethnicity is also associated with the development of cancer, with African Americans at a greater risk of developing cancer than Caucasians (Meyerowitz, Richardson, Hudson, & Leedham, 1998). In fact, African Americans have the highest overall rate of cancer, a rate which is caused largely by the very high incidence of lung and prostate cancer among African American men. On the other hand, Latinos and Asian Americans in the United States have relatively low rates of cancer. African Americans probably do not have a genetic predisposition to cancer; most evidence suggests that these race differences in frequency of cancer are caused by nongenetic factors, such as knowledge, behavior, and access to health care. For example, as compared to African Americans, Caucasians know more about the risks and signs of cancer, have lower blood pressure, and eat less dietary fat (Meyerowitz et al., 1998; Winkleby, Robinson, Sundquist, & Kraemer, 1999). Genetic factors, however, clearly contribute to at least some types of cancer; a woman whose mother or sister has breast cancer is at nearly twice the risk of developing breast cancer as someone without such a genetic link (Claus, Risch, & Thompson, 1993; Colditz et al., 1993). However, only 2 to 5% of breast cancers are clearly linked to genetic factors, such as the presence of BRCA1 and BRCA2.

Although demographic variables such as age and race as well as genetic factors are associated with the likelihood of developing cancer, substantial evidence points to the link between psychosocial factors and the acquisition of cancer too. This section examines three such factors.

Behavioral Choices

Lifestyle factors are a strong predictor of the development of cancer, with some evidence suggesting that 85% of all cancers could be prevented by changing people's behavior (Brownson et al., 1993). What types of things do people do that lead to cancer? Smoking is an obvious one; as described earlier, benzopyrene, a chemical in cigarette smoke, leads to lung cancer by damaging a cancer suppressor gene. In fact, 87% of lung cancer cases are attributed to cigarette smoking. Smokers are also at increased risk of developing other types of cancer, including cancer of the mouth, cancer of the bladder and pancreas, leukemia, and lymphoma. One study even found that women who smoked were 25% more likely to die of breast cancer than those who never smoked (Calle, Miracle-McMahill, Thun, & Heath, 1994). Moreover, women who started smoking before age 16 are at a much greater risk of dying from breast cancer than those who start smoking after age 20, and women who smoke more cigarettes per day have a greater likelihood of acquiring breast cancer than lighter smokers. Simply being regularly exposed to second-hand cigarette smoke increases a person's risk of developing cancer (see also Photo 10.5; Fielding & Phenow, 1988).

PHOTO 10.5   It's not just cigarettes that cause cancer—chewing tobacco is strongly associated with oral cancer (Bolinder, Alfredsson, Englund, & deFaire, 1994; Winn et al., 1981).

After tobacco smoke, diet is the next leading cause of cancer (American Cancer Society, 1998). Although we don't know exactly how diet influences cancer risk, there is strong evidence that what you eat—and how much you eat—influences your likelihood of getting cancer. Women who eat more high-fat foods, such as milk, cheese, and butter, have an increased likelihood of developing breast cancer (Toniolo, Ribloi, Protta, Charrel, & Coppa, 1989), and men who eat diets that are high in dietary cholesterol have twice the risk of developing lung cancer than those who eat little excess cholesterol (Shekelle, Rossof, & Stamler, 1991). Similarly, people who eat large quantities of foods that are high in animal (saturated) fat, such as red meat, are at increased risk of developing several different types of cancers, including colon, rectum, and prostate cancers (Slattery, Boucher, Caan, Potter, & Ma, 1998). On the other hand, people who eat large quantities of fruits, vegetables, and foods high in fiber are much less likely to develop colon and rectal cancer (Slatttery et al., 1998; Zhang et al., 1999), perhaps in part because these foods work to quickly rid the body of cancer-causing fats. For example, one large-scale study found that women who consumed five or more servings of fruit and vegetables each day were 23% less likely to develop breast cancer than those who ate two or fewer servings per day. Similarly, people who have diets high in *antioxidants*, such as foods containing vitamin A and vitamin C, have lower rates of lung and stomach cancer, perhaps because these vitamins help block the work of carcinogens (Hunter et al, 1993; Yong et al., 1997).

Other lifestyles choices also influence peoples' risk of developing cancer. Sun exposure is clearly recognized as a major cause of skin cancer, yet many people who tan regularly do not use sunscreens at all (Brownson et al., 1993; Koh et al., 1997). And even people who do use sunscreen often use a lower-than-recommended level of protection. Some patterns of sexual behavior are also associated with cancer (Brownson et al., 1993). For example, women who have multiple sexual partners, a history of STDs, and begin having sex at an early age are at increased risk of developing cervical cancer (Brownson et al., 1993). Excessive alcohol use is associated with some types of cancer, including cancers of the pancreas, esophagus, and liver (Heuch, Kvale, Jacobsen, & Bjelke, 1983).

What's the good news? Engaging in regular exercise seems to offer some protection against various types of cancer, including breast cancer (Bernstein, Henderson, Hanisch, Sullivan-Halley, & Ross, 1994; Rockhill et al., 1999; Thune, Brenn, Lund, & Gaard, 1997), prostate cancer (Lee, Paffenbarger, & Hsieh, 1992), and colon cancer (Slattery, Schumacherm Smith, West, & Abd-Elghany, 1990; White, Jacobs, & Daling, 1996). For example, one study found that young women who engaged in regular physical exercise—at least four times a week—were half as likely to develop breast cancer as those who did not engage in regular exercise (Bernstein et al., 1994). Although this study was

---

Questioning the Research 10.2

Do these studies really show that specific types of diet can lead to cancer? Can you think of an alternative explanation for these findings?

conducted by matching women who exercised regularly to those who did not based on age, race, and whether they had children, and then comparing the rate of breast cancer in both groups, it does not definitively show that exercise descreases a woman's risk of cancer. Perhaps women who exercise regularly are generally healthier (e.g., less likely to smoke, more likely to eat healthy foods) and therefore less likely to develop cancer.

Stress

Stress, including a history of stressful life experiences as well as separation from or loss of a loved one, is associated with acquiring cancer (McKenna, Zevon, Corn, & Rounds, 1999). Studies comparing patients with cancer to those without cancer have found that those with cancer report significantly more negative life events, such as loss of loved ones and marital problems, than those without cancer. For example, children with cancer are quite likely to have experienced a number of life changes, such as personal injury and change in the health of a family member, in the year preceding their diagnosis (Jacobs & Charles, 1980). Although some of these studies are retrospective, and therefore it is difficult to tell whether patients' cancer diagnosis at one point leads them to look at the past in a more negative light, a recent review of many studies on the predictors of cancer demonstrated that both the experience of stressful life events and the loss of a loved one were associated with an increased likelihood of developing cancer (McKenna et al., 1999).

How exactly does stress lead to cancer? As discussed in Chapter 4, stress clearly weakens the immune system, which thereby decreases the body's ability to detect and kill abnormal cancer cells (Delahanty & Baum, 2001). Research with both humans and rats shows that stressful events, such as exams, divorce, and job loss (in humans) and rotation on a turntable, uncontrollable shocks, and flashing lights (in rats), reduces the number of immune cells in the blood. For example, people who were recently separated from their spouses have lower levels of natural killer (NK) cells and helper T cells (Kiecolt-Glaser & Glaser, 1989) as do people who are taking care of a terminally ill relative (Kiecolt-Glaser, Dura, Speicher, Trask, & Glaser, 1991). Stress may also reduce the body's ability to fix DNA errors, meaning that random errors that would normally be found and repaired by the body are allowed to remain instead in the body (Glaser, Thorn, Tarr, Kiecolt-Glaser, & D'Ambrosio, 1985).

Personality

Many people, including those with cancer, believe that this disease is caused at least in part by personality factors (Roberts, Newcomb, Trentham-Dietz, & Storer, 1996). A number of personality dimensions, including depression, extraversion, and difficulty expressing emotions, are often associated with the development of cancer (Dattore, Shontz, & Coyne, 1980; Perskey, Kempthorne-Rawson, & Shekelle, 1987; Shaffer, Graves, Swank, & Pearson, 1987; Shaffer, Duszynski, & Thomas, 1982). In fact, some researchers describe people with such traits, namely, those who present a pleasant and cheerful face to the world, show passivity in the face of stress, and tend to suppress negative emotions, as having a "Type C," or cancer-prone, personality (McKenna et al., 1999). Many of these studies, however, have used cross-sectional designs, in which they examine people with and without cancer at a single point in time, and therefore they cannot determine whether the presence of such traits caused the cancer or vice versa. After all, it is therefore not surprising that people with cancer would show distinct types of personality traits, including a tendency to try and suppress their difficult emotions about the disease as well as depression. However, other studies using longitudinal designs have often revealed similar results. For example, Shaffer and colleagues (1982) examined attitudes toward family by following a group of healthy medical students, and then followed these participants to measure illness over time for 30 years. Those with impaired self-awareness, a lack of emotional expression, and feelings of self-sacrifice and self-blame were 16 times more likely to develop cancer than the others. Similarly, another study revealed that men who were depressed at one point in time were twice as likely to die from cancer 20 years later than those who were not depressed (Shekelle et al., 1981).

A recent meta-analysis, a combination of various studies on the link between personality and cancer, provided only moderate evidence for the role of personality traits leading to cancer (McKenna et al., 1999). First, people who rely heavily on denial and repression as a way of coping with problems are at somewhat of a greater risk of developing cancer. This type of coping pattern is associated with an overall weakened immune system, which could be one explanation for this link between denial, repression, and cancer. Second, there is limited evidence that people with a conflict-avoidant personality style are more likely to develop cancer. This type of coping is similar to that of denial and repression and may also therefore impact the immune system. Finally, current research provides no evidence that other personality dimensions, including depression/anxiety, introversion/extraversion, and expression of anger, are associated with acquiring cancer.

What Factors Predict Effective Coping with Cancer?

People who are diagnosed with a chronic illness typically experience considerable fear and uncertainty about the future, in part because many such diseases are largely uncontrollable (Dunkel-Schetter et al., 1992). In turn, one predictor of effective coping with cancer is when a person believes he or she has some control over the disease, specifically whether it spreads or reoccurs (Taylor et al., 1984). One study with 78 patients with breast cancer revealed that women who had high levels of cognitive control, namely, believing that they and their doctors could control the cancer, experienced better adjustment (e.g., less anxiety, fear, depression, anger) to their disease. Although these beliefs are largely illusions (e.g., cancer is largely uncontrollable and unpredictable), they serve a valuable role in psychological adaptation and are therefore quite functional. In fact, women who believed that both they and their doctors had control over the cancer experienced the fewest psychological problems.

People who cope with cancer using an active and engaged approach also show better psychological adjustment (Carver, Pozo, Harris, Noriega, & Scheier, 1993; Epping-Jordan et al., 1999; Stanton & Snider, 1993). For example, Annette Stanton and Pamela Snider (1993) examined coping style in a sample of women who were just diagnosed with breast cancer. Those who simply wished the cancer would "go away" experienced more psychological distress than those who did not engage in such avoidant thinking. Similarly, people who cope with a cancer diagnosis by expecting positive outcomes show lower levels of anxiety and depression than those who try to avoid thinking

Box 10.7

Research Focus—Why You Feel Better By Comparing to Someone Who is Even Worse

Annette Stanton and her colleagues at the University of Kansas (1999) were interested in examining whether people with cancer who compared themselves to someone who was doing well would feel better than comparing themselves to someone who was doing poorly. To test this question, 94 women with breast cancer were randomly assigned to hear one of three audiotapes. In the "good adjustment" tape, the woman says, "I feel OK. In fact, I feel good most of the time. I have a lot of energy, and I keep a really hopeful outlook. I guess I'm coping well." In the "poor adjustment" tape, the woman says, "I feel bad and nervous most of the time . . . I don't have any energy and I just don't feel as hopeful as I used to. I'm constantly preoccupied. . . . I just can't stop worrying about it." In the third condition, the control condition, the woman on the videotape does not mention her adjustment. After listening to one of the tapes, the subjects rated the actor on likability and desire to interact with her, and then rated their own prognosis and psychological adjustment.

Women had very different reactions to hearing the different types of tapes. First, women saw the well-adjusted woman as more likeable and were more interested in receiving emotional support and information from her than from the poorly adjusted woman. However, women who compared themselves to the well-adjusted target felt worse about their own adjustment than those who compared their own condition to the woman who was doing poorly (see Figure 10.7). Women who compared themselves to a well-adjusted target also perceived their own prognosis for recovery as worse than those who compared themselves to the poorly adjusted target. So, while women may want to spend time with and interact with someone who is coping well with breast cancer, comparing themselves to this person can actually lead them to feel worse.

(continues)

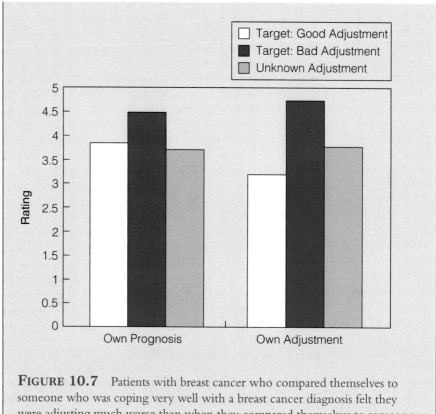

FIGURE 10.7 Patients with breast cancer who compared themselves to someone who was coping very well with a breast cancer diagnosis felt they were adjusting much worse than when they compared themselves to someone who was not coping well. There were no differences, however, on women's perceptions of their prognosis as a function of whom they compared themselves to (data from Stanton et al., 1999).

about the disease and those who focus on negative possibilities (Carver et al., 1993; Epping-Jordan et al., 1999). One study of 101 women with breast cancer found that those who were determined to beat the disease and who expressed their feelings of anger, anxiety, and depression showed a better adjustment, including lower levels of anxiety, depression, and hostility (Classen, Koopman, Angell, & Spiegel, 1996). These findings are in line with those described in Chapter 4—people who cope with stressful events with an optimistic and active style tend to experience fewer psychological problems (see Box 10.7).

People's style of coping with cancer can even influence survival (Greer, 1991; Pettingale, Morris, Greer, & Haybittle, 1985). Specifically, those who simply "give in" and stop fighting the disease, or deny its existence, often die more rapidly than those who maintain a more aggressive and active approach. For example, one study classified women based on their response to the cancer diagnosis: stoic acceptance, helplessness/hopelessness, optimistic spirit, and denial (Pettingale et al., 1985). These patients were then followed for 10 years.

Among those with stoic acceptance, 31% had died after 5 years and 75% had died after 10 years, and among those with helplessness, 80% had died after 5 years. In contrast, those with an optimistic spirit, 10% had died after 5 years and 30% after 10 years, and those who responded with denial had a 10% death rate after 5 years and a 50% death rate after 10 years. Although this study was based on a small sample of women, it certainly suggests that psychological factors may influence length of survival in patients with cancer.

Patients with cancer also benefit in terms of survival from having high levels of social support (Goodwin, Hunt, Key, & Samet, 1987). People who have strong social support, including a large social network, actually live longer than those without such support (Reynolds & Kaplan, 1990). In fact, married patients with cancer live longer following their diagnosis than patients who are single (Pistrang & Barker, 1995). Social support may work by giving people much-needed feelings of optimism, self-esteem, hope, and personal control (Helgeson, Cohen, & Fritz, 1998). Moreover, people with high levels of social support may have more access to information and may receive better medical care. For example, patients with cancer who have high levels of social support are likely to have people with whom they can share their fears and concerns about the disease. People who can express their emotions about having cancer report less stress than those who aren't able to express these emotions, and make they fewer appointments for cancer-related health problems (Stanton, Kirk, Camerson, & Danoff-Burg, 2000). These findings suggest one reason why people with cancer who attend social support groups show better psychological adjustment (Goodwin et al., 2001) and in some cases even longer survival (Spiegel et al., 1989).

What Is AIDS?

AIDS, which is caused by the human immunodeficiency virus (HIV), was first identified as a syndrome in 1981 (Foege, 1983). In the 1980s, in the early stages of the HIV epidemic, the vast majority of people with AIDS were men who had sex with men (as discussed in Chapter 2; Centers for Disease Control, 2003). Men having sex with men is still the largest route of transmission of HIV in the United States (but see Box 10.8). However, the rate of HIV transmission to heterosexual women is increasing dramatically, in part because women who have sex with an HIV-positive man are at much greater risk of acquiring the disease than men who have sex with an HIV-positive woman (Padian, Shiboski, Glass, & Vittinghoff, 1997). As of December 2000 women represented 47.3% of people with AIDS in the world, and 26% of people with AIDS in the United States. As shown in Table 10.5, about 40% of the women who develop HIV do so through sexual intercourse, and another 40% do so through injection drug use. There is a time lag between infection with HIV and development of full-blown AIDS, so an exact number of people with HIV is impossible to know. But it is estimated that there are over 42 million indi-

TABLE 10.5   *Common Routes of Transmission of HIV for Men and Women*

Men	Cases (%)
Sex with men	57.3
Injecting drug use	21.2
Sex with men and injecting drug use	7.6
Sex with women	4.3
Transfusion	0.8
Undetermined	8.0
Women	**Cases (%)**
Injecting drug use	41.5
Heterosexual contact	39.4
Transfusion	3.0
Undetermined	15.9

Although the majority of men who acquire HIV do so through sexual contact with another man, women are equally at risk from both injecting drug use and sexual contact with a man.

Source: Centers for Disease Control, 2003.

viduals worldwide with HIV, with 3.1 million deaths per year from AIDS (World Health Organization, 2003).

AIDS is much more prevalent in African Americans and Hispanics than in whites (Centers for Disease Control, 2003). In 2000, 47% of new AIDS cases occurred in African Americans, who make up only 12% of the U.S. population. Similarly, 19% of new AIDS cases occurred in Hispanics, who make up only 13% of the U.S. population. AIDS is now the leading cause of death for African American men and women between the ages of 25 and 44 years. This trend will likely continue for some time—72% of the new AIDS cases in women and 70% of the new AIDS cases in men are among African Americans and Hispanics. This greater rate of HIV infection is related to the greater likelihood of injection drug use in these populations than in the white population. African American women are also more likely to trade sex for drugs, which contributes to their likelihood of acquiring HIV both through sexual intercourse as well as injection, and they are less likely to insist on condom use (Amaro, 1995).

HIV, which causes AIDS, is a retrovirus. Retroviruses replicate by injecting themselves into host cells and literally taking over the genetic workings of these cells. They can then produce virus particles that infect new cells. After HIV enters the bloodstream, it invades the T cells, incorporates its genetic material into the cells, and then starts destroying cells' ability to function. As discussed in Chapter 4, T cells are responsible for recognizing harmful substances in the body and for attacking such cells, in part by releasing NK cells.

Box 10.8

HIV Transmission Through IV Drug Use: It's Not as Rare as You Might Think

Although the majority of HIV cases are caused by sexual activity, the second major route of HIV transmission is through intravenous (IV) drug use. Recent estimates suggest that approximately half of all new HIV infections in the United States occur through IV drug use (Holmberg, 1996). In some places, HIV has spread very rapidly this way because drug users often aren't aware of the risks of HIV infection and because people often share needles. Unless needles are cleaned carefully between users, one person with HIV can transmit the disease to others who use that needle. Although the ideal way of reducing this type of transmission would be to eliminate drug use, this is an extremely difficult goal. So other strategies must be used to help decrease the spread of HIV through injection drug use. Some programs have focused on teaching people not to share needles and to clean needles with bleach between uses (Des Jarlais & Friedman, 2001). Other programs have simply tried to supply people with clean needles, or allow users to exchange old, dirty needles for new clean ones. These syringe exchange programs, however, are somewhat controversial—opponents argue that these programs facilitate the continuation of drug use by providing clean needles. However, most studies show that these programs do not lead to increases in drug use, but do lead to a reduction in needle sharing as well as an overall leveling in HIV prevalence (Des Jarlais & Friedman, 1996; Watters, Estillo, Clark, & Lorvick, 1994).

Although HIV is able to stay in the body in a latent and dormant state, it gradually starts replicating itself, and in the process begins destroying the T cells.

The progression from HIV to AIDS varies in time, but follows a distinct pattern of four stages (McCutchan, 1990). During the first stage, which may last for a period of 1 to 8 weeks, people experience relatively mild symptoms, such as fever, headache, and sore throat. This initial stage is then followed by a latent period, in which people experience few, if any, symptoms; this stage can last as long as 10 years. During the third stage, people develop a specific group of symptoms, including night sweats, painful skin rash, swollen lymph nodes, and white spots in the mouth. Finally, as the patient's immune system begins to have trouble fighting off various infections, people may experience problems with the lungs, gastrointestinal tract, nervous system, bones, and the brain (see Figure 10.8). This stage is marked by a dramatic reduction in T-cell counts—which may be 200 or less per cubic millimeter of blood compared to a rate of 1000 in a healthy person. People infected with HIV may also experience more

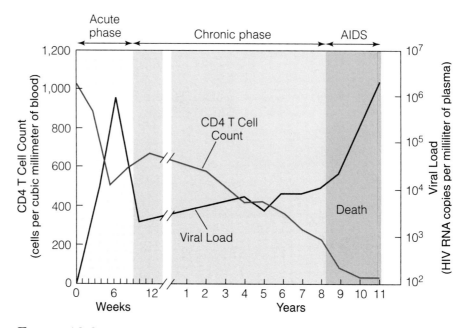

FIGURE 10.8   Although HIV may stay in its latent or dormant state for some time, eventually it spreads, which in turn leads to a dramatic decrease in the number of T cells. People with AIDS eventually die from a series of opportunistic infections because their immune systems are mostly destroyed.

severe symptoms, such as shortness of breath, substantial weight loss, personality shifts, and dementia (mental confusion and memory loss). Because HIV basically destroys the immune system, people with AIDS often die of *opportunistic infections*, such as pneumonia, tuberculosis, and a type of cancer called Kaposi's sarcoma.

How Do Psychological Factors Predict the Acquisition of HIV?

In the United States and other Western cultures, many routes of HIV transmission become available through behavioral choices, such as the choice to engage in unprotected sex and the choice to share needles for injecting drugs (Centers for Disease Control, 2003). Therefore, individuals who decide to protect themselves from HIV, and follow through on these intentions, are quite safe. In fact, researchers who examined condom use in an "expert population"—prostitutes at three brothels in Nevada—found that when used correctly, condoms virtually never break, hence can provide protection against

---

Box 10.9

Health Psychology in the Real World—The Often-Overlooked Danger of Sexually Transmitted Diseases

Although this section focuses on the role of psychological factors in leading to HIV infection, obviously the behaviors that put one at risk of HIV infection can also lead to other sexually transmitted diseases (STDs). College students are particularly at risk for several reasons. First, most college students are sexually active, and many engage in sexual activity with multiple sexual partners in a serial-monogamy pattern (Caron, Davis, Halteman, & Stickle, 1993; Goodwin & Roscoe, 1988; Reinisch, Sanders, Hill, & Ziemba-Davis, 1992). In one study of first-year students at a large northeastern university, 34% reported having two or more sexual partners since arriving at college, and 58% reported having engaged in sex in the last month (Caron et al., 1993). Another study found that the mean number of sexual partners for college students was 5.6 for women, and 11.2 for men (Reinisch et al., 1992). Similarly, other studies with college students have shown that approximately 22% of females and 25% of males report having more than seven lifetime sexual partners (Bishop & Lipsitz, 1991). Unfortunately, however, college students often fail to engage in safer sex. For example, studies on college campuses show that rates of consistent condom use, that is, using a condom during every act of intercourse, range from 8 to 42% (Boyd & Wandersman, 1991; Caron et al., 1993; DiClemente et al., 1990), with 37% of students never using condoms (Boyd & Wandersman, 1991). Given these campus behavioral norms, it is not surprising that there are high rates of STDs among college students. For example, about 40% of women seeking pregnancy tests at the University of Maryland student health center tested positive for an STD (American College Health Association, 1988), and another large-scale study of first-year college students revealed that 9% of those who were sexually active had been treated for an STD (Caron et al., 1993).

HIV transmission (Albert, Warner, Hatcher, Trussell, & Bennett, 1995). Moreover, one study with committed couples in which one partner was HIV-positive and the other was HIV-negative found that among those who consistently used condoms, none of the HIV-negative partners tested positive for HIV (de Vincenzi, 1994). So, what factors lead people to engage in unsafe sex?

According to the AIDS Risk Reduction Model (ARRM), people first must understand the threat of HIV infection and recognize that their behavior puts them at risk of acquiring this disease (Catania, Kegeles, & Coates, 1990). Information about HIV is widespread; hence, most people do understand how HIV is transmitted as well as strategies to for protecting themselves from this disease (Sheeran, Abraham, & Orbell, 1999). Most people also understand that HIV is a fatal disease and that acquiring this disease would have severe negative consequences. Despite these high levels of knowledge and perceived severity, many people do not see themselves as personally at risk of HIV infection (see Box 10.9). For example, college students tend to assume that risky people are those who dress provocatively, live in large cities, hang out in bars, and who are overly anxious for sex (Hammer, Fisher, Fitzgerald, & Fisher, 1996; Williams et al., 1992). In contrast, college students overwhelmingly believe that students they know and like are not risky. Similarly, one study with African American teenagers found that nearly one-third believed they could avoid HIV infection simply by not having sex with "people who look like they have AIDS" (St. Lawrence, 1993), and more than 84% of women in a drug treatment program saw themselves as unlikely to contract AIDS (Kline & Strickler, 1993). People who don't see themselves as at risk of acquiring AIDS, or don't view HIV as a very big threat, tend to engage in more risky sexual behavior (see Figure 10.9). Many young people have never known a world without AIDS, and therefore may have less concern about AIDS than those who are older. Young people may, for example, believe that people can manage HIV, and thereby prevent or drastically delay death, simply by taking medications (e.g., just like people "manage" diabetes).

People also must have a strong commitment to using condoms during sex, as well as strong confidence, or self-efficacy, in their ability to do so (Catania et al., 1990). Several factors influence whether someone makes such a commitment (see Table 10.6). Their attitudes toward condoms are one factor—people who hold a negative attitude toward condoms, such as believing that condoms reduce sexual pleasure and imply a lack of trust in their partner, are less likely to engage in protected sex (see Figure 10.10 and Table 10.7; Fisher, Fisher, & Rye, 1995; Kelley & Kalichman, 1998). For example, one recent large-scale survey of heterosexual adults found that people's beliefs about the influence of condom use on sexual pleasure were a strong predictor of whether they intended to use condoms as well as whether they actually used condoms (Albarracin et al., 2000). And even if people have positive attitudes about condoms, they still must feel confident in their ability to use them. For example, one recent study with 156 gay, lesbian, and bisexual adolescents found that those who weren't confident that they could suggest condom use as well as those who believed that suggesting condom use would make it seem as if they didn't trust their partner were the most likely to engage in unprotected sex (Rosario, Mahler, Hunter, & Gwadz, 1999).

People's attitudes toward condoms are also influenced by their beliefs about other people's attitudes toward condoms, including their friends and their partners (Catania et al., 1990; Fisher et al., 1995). People who believe that others in their social group are using condoms are more likely to use condoms themselves, whereas those who believe that few others use condoms are much less likely to choose to use protection. Similarly, those who feel social pressure to use condoms, namely, that other people who are important to them believe they should use condoms, are more likely to engage in safer sex. Because condom use is a behavior that involves two people, individuals' beliefs about their partner's attitudes toward condoms are a particular strong predictor of whether they use condoms. In line with this view, partner attitudes toward

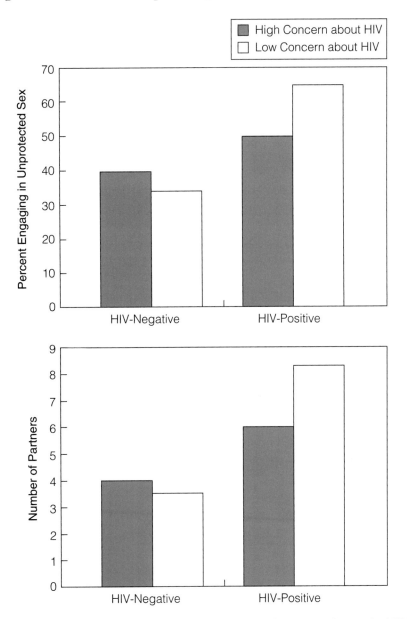

FIGURE 10.9 HIV-positive men who believe the recent advances in AIDS treatments mean they have relatively little risk of dying from HIV had the highest levels of unsafe behavior, including the most partners and the most frequent unprotected sex (data from Vanable, Ostrow, McKirnan, Taywaditep, & Hope, 2000).

condom use are a stronger predictor of condom use than more general social norms (Kashima, Gallois, & McCamish, 1993).

People also must be capable of actually using a condom at the critical moment, which is called the enactment stage (Catania et al., 1990). As discussed

TABLE 10.6   *Test Yourself: Would You Use a Condom?*

1. If I ask to use condoms, it might make my partner not want to have sex with me.
2. If I ask to use condoms, it will look like I don't trust my partner.
3. I would feel uncomfortable buying condoms.
4. I can make sex fun or sexy when using a condom with my partner.
5. Before I decide to have sex, I will make sure we have a condom.
6. I can stop to use a condom with my main partner even if I am very sexually aroused.
7. I don't know how to use a condom.
8. I don't know how to talk to my partner about safer sex.
9. It is embarrassing to talk about condoms with a sexual partner.
10. If my partner won't let us use a condom, I won't have sex.

These items measure people's beliefs about their partner's attitudes towards condoms, their own self-efficacy for condom use, and their ability to use condoms and negotiate condom use with their partner.

Source: Rosario et al., 1999.

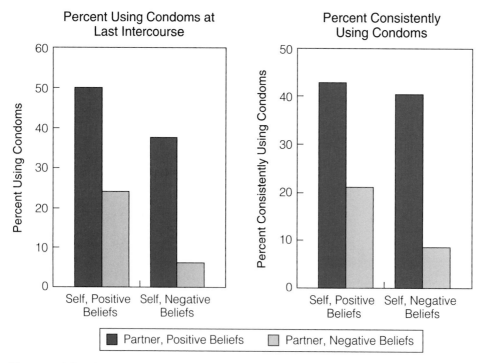

FIGURE 10.10   Although condom use is most likely to occur if individuals have positive beliefs about condoms and think their partners do too, people's perceptions of their partners' attitudes about condoms are actually a better predictor of whether condom use will occur than their own attitudes (data from Sanderson & Maibach, 1996).

TABLE **10.7**   *Countering Negative Attitudes Toward Condoms with Positive Ones*

Negative Attitudes	Positive Restatements
Condom use implies a lack of trust.	Using condoms is the best way to show someone that you care about them.
Using condoms is awkward and interrupts sex.	Condom use is fun when it becomes part of sex and lovemaking.
Condoms reduce pleasure.	Condoms increase pleasure by reducing worries about health and pregnancy.
Condoms decrease sensitivity.	Condoms can make sex last longer.
I'm not used to condoms.	Sex can be better when you try new things.

This table lists a few ways of thinking about condom use more positively.

Source: Kelly, 1995.

in Chapter 3, people's intentions do not always result in the desired behavior: people may strongly intend to use condoms but then fail to do so. A few factors influence whether people follow through on their condom-use intentions. One factor is very simple—having a condom available increases the odds that it will be used (see Photo 10.6). Carrying condoms is a simple way of increasing your likelihood of engaging in protected sex. Another factor that can influence whether a condom is used is level of sexual arousal. When people feel highly sexually attracted to their partners, they are less likely to use condoms (see Box 10.10). Sexual arousal may decrease the likelihood of condom use in part because people like feeling "swept away" and overcome by passion (Galligan & Terry, 1993), which somehow doesn't fit with making the rational decision to use condoms. Condoms are often seen as destroying the magic and ruining spontaneity, which in turn decreases their use. As discussed in Chapter 7, alcohol and drug use decreases the likelihood of condom use as well (Gordon, Carey, & Carey, 1997; Leigh & Stall, 1993; MacDonald, Zanna, & Fong, 1995). For example, one study with male college students found that after drinking about five vodka tonics, students had more negative attitudes about suggesting condom use and saw condom use as interfering more with sexual pleasure (Gordon & Carey, 1996).

Another factor that influences whether condoms are used is whether the couple is in a established and committed relationship (Katz, Fortenberry, Zimet, Blythe, & Orr, 2000; Misovich, Fisher, & Fisher, 1997; Morrill, Ickovics, Golubchikov, Beren, & Rodin, 1996). Considerable research indicates that individuals who are in steady dating relationships engage in higher levels of HIV risk-related behavior than do those who are in casual dating contexts. For example, a meta-analysis of a large number of studies found that, overall, 17% of people said they always use a condom with their steady partner as compared to 30% who always use a condom with their casual partners (Sheeran et al., 1999). As described at the beginning of this chapter, Leslie was shocked to

PHOTO 10.6   People are more likely to use condoms if they are available—this doesn't mean that having a condom means people will have safer sex, but it definitely increases the odds.

discover she was HIV-positive because she has had only a few sexual partners, and most of those were men with whom she was in a steady relationship. Similarly, an average of 52% of respondents report never using a condom with their steady partner as compared to 40% who never use a condom with casual partners. Women who are in casual sexual relationships are 11 times more likely than those in committed relationships to engage in safer sexual behaviors (Morrill et al., 1996).

Why do people in relationships tend to engage in more risky sexual behavior? One reason is that they perceive their partner as safer, and hence don't feel the need to protect themselves. As described previously, people generally think those they know well and who "look normal" couldn't possibly have a disease (Hammer et al., 1996; Williams et al., 1992). Moreover, people are concerned that by suggesting condom use, they will appear promiscuous, loose, or risky themselves (Afifi, 1999). For example, you might be concerned that if you suggest using a condom, your partner will think you have a disease that you don't want to pass on. Another factor is that individuals who are in steady dating relationships worry that suggesting condom use implies a lack of monogamy or trust (Galligan & Terry, 1993). This concern about disrupting the level of intimacy in a relationship is a major factor that inhibits people from suggesting condom use in an on-going relationship.

Box 10.10

Research Focus—Yet Another Way to Justify Your Lover

Hart Blanton and Meg Gerrard of Iowa State University (1997) conducted a very clever study to examine how men's interest in a sexual partner influences how they rate her risk of having a sexually transmitted disease. Male students read brief descriptions of nine hypothetical sexual partners and rated how likely each woman would be to have an STD. These descriptions included information about her number of previous sexual partners (one, three, or eight), and her consistency of condom use (extremely good, pretty good, not very good). They then saw on one of the trials a photograph of either a very attractive or very unattractive woman. The men were asked to imagine that they had met this woman at a bar and had returned with her to her apartment, at which point it became clear that she was interested in having sex. The men were then asked how they would respond to this temptation.

As the authors predicted, men's sexual attraction to the woman influenced how they rated her prior sexual behavior. Specifically, although men generally saw the woman who had had a number of previous partners and had rarely used a condom as quite likely to have an STD, when this woman was clearly very attractive, they actually saw her as quite unlikely to have such a disease! So, when men were highly motivated to see the woman as low risk because they were attracted to her, their sexual motivations may have overcome more rational thoughts. This finding suggests that college students might be very good at justifying their own risky behavior, especially in cases in which they are very attracted to their potential partner—they simply perceive such partners as lower in risk than they really are.

How Do Psychological Factors Predict the Progression of HIV?

People are now living for quite some time with HIV, and people vary considerably in the time between exposure to the virus and the development of symptoms. It is possible that psychological factors are partially responsible for these differences (Kemeny, 1994). For example, stress may increase the speed at which HIV is replicated, causing a quicker progression to AIDS. This section examines the role of several factors in influencing the progression of HIV, including coping strategies, social support, exercise, and adherence to drug regimens.

Not surprisingly, people who use active-coping strategies, such as taking control of the management of their disease and finding meaning in their illness, show better psychological adjustment as well as a slower rate of progression of the disease (Mulder, de Vroome, van Griensven, Antoni, & Sandfort, 1999; Reed, Kemeny, Taylor, Wang, & Visscher, 1994; Reed, Kemeny, Taylor, Visscher, 1999; Thompson, Nanni, & Levine, 1994). For example, a study by Karl Goodkin and colleagues (1992) with 62 HIV-positive gay men found that those who relied on active-coping strategies—including planning and seeking instrumental support from others—showed improved NK cell functioning. Similarly, among men who are HIV-positive, those who find some meaning in their condition, such as shifting their values and priorities, show slower declines in their T-cell levels and survive for longer periods of time (Bower, Kemeny, Taylor, & Fahey, 1998).

Although avoidance coping, such as trying to withdraw from the situation and focusing on other things, is often found to be a destructive coping technique, some recent research suggests that this approach can actually be quite beneficial for men with HIV. Specifically, HIV-positive men who use avoidance coping show a lower rate of decline of their CD4 cells and a longer progression to AIDS (Mulder et al., 1999). Similarly, HIV-positive men who refuse to accept their diagnosis actually survive 9 months longer than those who readily accept their dismal prognosis (Reed et al., 1994). This type of coping may be adaptive in the case of AIDS, especially early in illness, because there is nothing that can be done to cure it. Having an optimistic outlook may also motivate people to engage in health-promoting behaviors, such as following medical regimens and adapting a healthy lifestyle. In contrast, people who have negative expectations about their condition, such as a realistic acceptance of the disease, a belief that the disease will progress, and a belief that they have low control over its development, show a faster progression to AIDS and develop symptoms of HIV earlier than those without such beliefs (e.g., diarrhea, weight loss, high fever, night sweats; Reed et al., 1994; Reed et al., 1999). For example, one study with HIV-positive men found that those who attributed negative events to themselves had a faster rate of immune decline over the next 18 months than those without this type of attribution pattern (see Table 10.8; Segerstrom, Taylor, Kemeny, Reed, & Visscher, 1996). Similarly, women with a pessimistic outlook show lower NK-cell activity and T-cell levels and, hence, are less able to fight off their HIV progression (Byrnes et al., 1998).

Another factor that influences the progression of AIDS is social support (Hays, Turner, & Coates, 1992; Kalichman, Heckman, Kochman, Sikkema, & Bergholte, 2000; Kemeny et al., 1994; Leserman, Perkins, & Evans, 1992; Leserman et al., 1999; Patterson et al., 1996; Theorell et al., 1995). People with high levels of social support report less depression and anxiety, better social adjustment, fewer physical symptoms, and a slower rate of HIV progression, including a slower decline in T cells (Pakenham, Dadds, & Terry, 1994). As described previously, HIV-positive men with large social networks live longer (Patterson et al., 1996). Social support is likely to be especially important given the stigma of AIDS and of homosexuality in general—in fact, men who hide their sexual orientation experience negative health outcomes (Cole, Kemeny, Taylor,

TABLE 10.8   *Examples of Negative and Positive Attributions in HIV-Positive Men*

Negative

I lost a couple of friends because I am HIV-positive.

Sometimes at work I just feel isolated because I'm the only person that's gay there.

I would imagine that my T-cell count would get lower because over time that's the way it goes.

Positive

To actually die of AIDS or AIDS-related complications is less likely because I think effective therapies will continue to be developed.

I've never felt much isolation because I've always benefited from having other people there ... who share their feelings, support, and love with me.

I am less likely than other HIV-positive gay men to experience health problems related to AIDS. I think most gay men were promiscuous. . . . I just was not very promiscuous.

HIV-positive men who tend to make negative attributions show a faster decline in immune system functioning than those who tend to make positive attributions.

Source: Segerstrom et al., 1996.

Box 10.11

Health Psychology in the Real World—Coping with Life in a Wheelchair

Spinal cord injury is a lesion of the cord that causes permanent paralysis and loss of sensation below the level of the lesion (Zejdlik, 1983). The term *paraplegia* refers to paralysis of the lower part of the body, including the legs, whereas the term *quadriplegia* refers to paralysis of the upper and lower parts of the body, including the arms and hands. The damage is typically caused by an injury that compresses, severs, or tears the spinal cord. Motor vehicle accidents are responsible for nearly half of the cases of spinal cord injuries (46%), with falls and sports accidents each causing approximately 16% of the cases (see Photo 10.7). Most people who suffer a spinal cord injury are male (82%) and are between the ages of 16 and 30 (61%) when they suffer the injury (Hanak & Scott, 1993). More than 200,000 people in the United States today are living with spinal cord injuries.

People who experience a spinal cord injury face numerous physical and psychological challenges (Richards, Kewman, & Pierce, 2000; Zejdlik, 1983). First, they must focus on trying to regain as much physical functioning as possible,

(continues)

which can include redeveloping bladder and bowel control as well as maintaining a range of motion in their arms and legs. They may also work with physical therapists to strengthen the muscles they can control to partially compensate for their lack of control over other parts of their bodies. For example, quadriplegics may focus on improving respiration, whereas paraplegics may focus on exercises to strengthen the upper body. People with spinal cord injuries also experience significant psychological challenges and are likely to experience high levels of depression and anxiety, particularly early in their recovery. Many people report contemplating suicide or wishing that they had not survived their accident. They are often concerned about their social relationships, including whether their old friends will accept them, whether they will be a burden to their families, and whether they will be able to engage in romantic and sexual relationships. What predicts effective coping with this type of injury? People who see themselves as having meaningful social roles, including good relationships with family and friends, report better coping (Duggan & Dijkers, 2001). Financial stability and material resources are also strong predictors of adjustment, in part because people with this type of security are likely to be able to afford home health care, which can then reduce their reliance on friends and family members.

PHOTO 10.7   On Memorial Day in 1995, Christopher Reeve was thrown head-first from his horse during a riding competition. The accident broke his neck and left him unable to walk.

Visscher, & Fahey, 1996). One characteristic of social support that leads to better health and longer survival is clearly that people living with HIV or AIDS who have social support engage in more positive health behaviors, including practicing safer sex, than those without such support (Heckman, Kelly, & Somlai, 1998).

Finally, some evidence even suggests that engaging in regular exercise can help delay the progression of HIV infection (LePerriere et al., 1990; Lox, McAuley, & Tucker, 1996; Solomon, 1991). Several studies suggest that HIV-positive people who engage in aerobic exercise interventions show fewer declines in NK cells. They also show fewer symptoms of AIDS, such as substantial weight loss.

Length of survival with HIV infection is also, not surprisingly, associated with strict adherence to drug regimens (Ho, 1995, 1996). However, 80% of HIV care providers see treatment adherence as a major problem, and 43% of people with HIV report missing a dose of their medication in the past week (Gallant & Block, 1998). Unfortunately, even small rates of nonadherence to HIV drug regimens can lead to treatment failure (Catz, Kelly, Bogart, Benotsch, & McAuliffe, 2000). The role of psychological factors in influencing adherence to such regimens is discussed extensively in Chapter 12.

Lingering Issues

Should schools push abstinence or provide condoms? There are two major, and very different, approaches in government/school-based sex education programs. Some programs emphasize abstinence—which is obviously a very effective way of reducing people's risk of becoming infected with an STD or HIV. However, such programs fail to provide students with information that could help those who choose to become sexually active avoid unwanted consequences. Other programs push abstinence in conjunction with condom use and may even provide condoms. Although such programs have been criticized for "encouraging sex," providing information on contraception actually has no effect on rates of sexual activity. Moreover, one study compared rates of sexual activity and condom use in public high schools that do and do not distribute condoms (Guttmacher et al., 1997). Although rates of sexual activity were very similar in both schools—about 60% of the students were sexually active—those in schools that provided condoms were significantly more likely to be having safer sex (61% versus 56%). And the differences in rates of condom use were even more extreme among those who were at highest risk of acquiring HIV (those with three or more partners in the last 6 months, which represented 10% of the students).

Do social support groups really delay cancer deaths? The best-known work on the effect of group interventions on survival with cancer patients was conducted by David Spiegel and his colleagues at Stanford University (1989). In this study, 86 women with advanced breast cancer were randomly assigned to receive a weekly 90-minute group therapy session for 1 year or no therapy. The patients were then followed for 10 years. Those who received the group therapy lived nearly twice as long as those in the control condition (36.6 versus 18.9 months respectively). These results suggest that psychotherapy can help slow the progression of cancer, although it does not cure it. However, a very recent study by Canadian researchers refutes these findings (Goodwin et al., 2001). In this study 245 women with breast cancer were randomly assigned to either a weekly supportive-expressive group therapy group, or to a control group that received no group support. Although women in the therapy group reported less pain and fewer psychological symptoms, especially for those who were depressed at the start of the study, there was no difference in length of survival. Women in both conditions lived an average of 17.5 months.

One explanation for the differences in outcomes is that the studies were carried out approximately 20 years apart (Spiegel, 2001). Medical treatment for cancer as well as techniques for detecting cancer improved dramatically between the 1970s and 1990s, which in turn led to decreases in the rate of breast cancer deaths over time. Cancer has also become more understood and accepted during this period—patients with cancer experience lower levels of stigma and alienation, which may mean that social support groups are less beneficial. Finally, whereas now social support groups often are seen as a valued strategy for coping with chronic diseases, this acceptance was not abundant in the 1970s. Dr. David Spiegel, the author of the original study, recalls that in the 1970s it was difficult to convince patients to attend the (presumably worthless) group therapy sessions, whereas in the 1990s, patients not assigned to receive this type of treatment were disappointed. Future research is clearly needed to examine whether, when, and for whom group therapy can work to improve physical and psychological well-being.

Thought Questions

1. How might different psychological dimensions be associated with the experience of arthritis as compared to epilepsy?

2. Although psychological factors can clearly influence the acquisition of CHD and cancer as well as AIDS, people with AIDS are often seen as more responsible for their condition. Is this fair? Why or why not?

3. How can stress influence the acquisition and progression of two different chronic diseases?

4. Your aunt just was diagnosed with diabetes. What psychological, physical, and social consequences might she experience?

5. Describe three behaviors that people do that increase their risk of developing cancer.

Answers to Questioning the Research

Answer 10.1: The research in this section describes the role of social support in helping people adjust well to chronic disease. However, it is possible that this association is not exactly as it appears. One possibility is that people with a chronic disease who are coping well with it find that others like to spend time with them, whereas those with such a disease who are coping less well—such as feeling very depressed and anxious—may drive away people in their support network. Another possibility is that a third variable explains both social support and adjustment to disease. Perhaps optimistic people, for example, cope well (because they are optimistic, after all), and optimistic people receive more social support. Remember to carefully evaluate research you read about—many studies in health psychology report associations that may seem to indicate causation, but really only support correlation.

Answer 10.2: Although researchers have examined a number of different types of foods that may be associated with risk of developing cancer, it is not clear whether the major link between diet and cancer is a result of eating certain types of foods and avoiding others (e.g., eating fruits and vegetables, avoiding red meat), or simply maintaining a healthy body weight. People who eat foods that are high in fat and cholesterol, for example, may indeed be more likely to develop cancer, but this could be caused by their greater body weight resulting from this type of diet. Studies that show people with a particular diet are at greater risk of developing cancer may really just indicate that people who are obese are at greater risk.

CHAPTER 11

Terminal Illness and Bereavement

- Ramon is 24 years old and just found out he has an advanced stage of stomach cancer. The doctor has started him on a round of chemotherapy, but has warned Ramon that the cancer may not be curable. Ramon has always been very healthy and still can't really believe he may be dying. He is angry at the doctor who diagnosed him, the other patients in the hospital who have less serious illnesses, and his friends and family who tell him "it'll all be OK."

- Julia is 55 years old and is terminally ill with breast cancer. She has been through surgery, radiation, and chemotherapy, but the cancer has now spread throughout her body, and her physician has told her that more treatment would only cause additional pain and suffering. Julia made a decision to move from the hospital to a hospice, where she can wear her own clothes and have frequent visits from close family and friends. She is finding comfort in talking to other patients and the hospice staff.

- Sally is 28 years old and is a newlywed—she and her husband Paul would have celebrated their first wedding anniversary in May. Two weeks ago, Paul was in a severe car accident. Although he received almost immediate medical care, he fell into a coma shortly after reaching the hospital and never regained consciousness; he died after a few hours. Sally planned to spend her life with him and is now completely distraught over her loss. She dwells on the final words she said to him and simply cannot bring herself to contemplate life without him.

- Phillip is 72 years old and experienced the death of his wife to heart disease 6 months ago. He was constantly surrounded by friends and family members immediately after her death and received lots of help in making funeral arrangements and settling legal affairs. However, Phillip now finds himself largely alone—he retired 5 years ago and really isn't in touch with his old colleagues, and most of the couples he and his wife spent time with rarely call to include him in social events. He doesn't like going to the grocery store or cooking for himself, so mostly he eats fast food from drive-ins, even though his doctor has warned him to decrease the level of fat in his diet because he is at high risk of developing heart disease.

- Tiffany's brother just died from leukemia following a long illness. Tiffany grieves the loss of her only sibling, and although her friends keep inviting her to go places with them, she doesn't feel like she can relax and enjoy the same things she used to before her brother's death. Recently, her parents suggested she attend a support group for other teenagers who experienced the death of a sibling. Although she dreaded going to the meeting at first, Tiffany now finds the group very helpful. The other people in the group understand exactly what she is going through, and it feels good to be able to talk about her loss without worrying about upsetting her friends or parents.

Preview

This chapter examines how psychological issues influence the experience of dying as well as how survivors cope with death. First, we examine the leading causes of death and how the causes of death differ as a function of age, gender, and race. We then examine several different views about how terminally ill people cope with dying, including the stages of death and dying, task-based models, and the particular stages of dying in children. Next, we examine the different settings in which people die, including hospitals, nursing homes, hospice settings, and at home. We then examine how survivors cope with the loss of a loved one, including the factors that influence the intensity of people's grief, the stages of mourning, and the consequences of grief and bereavement, as well as how people react to different types of loss (e.g., loss of a spouse, parent, child, or sibling). Next, we examine how people cope with grief and bereavement. Finally, we examine children's views about death and dying.

When and How Do People Die?

As we discussed in Chapter 1, the leading causes of death in 1900 were acute diseases, such as pneumonia, tuberculosis, and influenza, and these diseases often killed people at very early ages. But given the technological advancements of the last 100 years, these diseases largely have been brought under control and people nowadays typically die from chronic conditions (see Table 11.1). Advancements have had a particularly dramatic impact on death rates for infants. As shown in Figure 11.1, the percentage of infants who die in the first week and first year of their lives has decreased substantially over the last 100 years. And this decrease in death rates in the first year of life has led to a sizeable increase in average life expectancy rates (Centers for Disease Control, 2003). At the start of the 20th century, people had a life expectancy of about 50 years, whereas a baby born in 2002 is quite likely to have a life expectancy of nearly 80 years. About 80% of the deaths in the United States today occur after age 60—once men reach age 75 they typically live nearly 10 more years and once women reach age 75 they typically live 12 more years (Kastenbaum, 1999).

At least in the United States, the vast majority of people die from heart disease and cancer (see Table 11.1; Centers for Disease Control, 2003). However, the leading causes of death vary considerably by age. Although we often associate high rates of mortality with senior citizens, the highest rate of death actually occurs in children in their first year of life. The majority of infant deaths are caused by congenital anomalies, disorders caused by premature birth and

TABLE 11.1   *Leading Causes of Death*

Cause of Death	Number of Deaths Each Year
Heart disease	724,859
Cancer	541,532
Stroke	158,448
Chronic obstructive pulmonary disease	112,584
Accidents	97,835
Pneumonia/influenza	91,871
Diabetes	64,751
Suicide	30,575
Nephritis, nephrotic syndrome, and nephrosis	26,182
Chronic liver disease and cirrhosis	25,192

As these numbers show, heart disease and cancer are responsible for the vast majority of deaths each year.

Source: Centers for Disease Control, 2003.

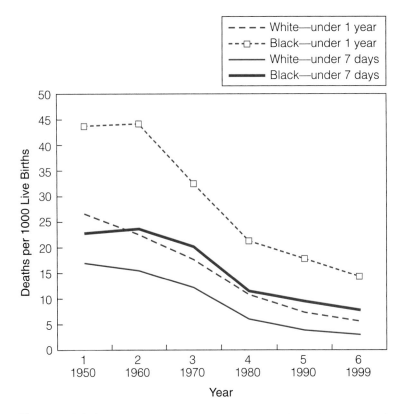

FIGURE 11.1 Although rates of infant mortality have dropped significantly in the last 50 years, African American infants are still at much greater risk of dying than white infants (Centers for Disease Control).

low birth weight, and sudden infant death syndrome (SIDS). Congenital anomalies are also responsible for a sizeable number of deaths in children ages 1 to 4 years, but the vast majority of deaths for children in this age group are caused by accidents (see Table 11.2). Accidents, including motor vehicle accidents, falls, drowning, suffocation, and fire/burns, are also the leading cause of death for children ages 5 to 14 years. Similarly, nearly half of all deaths of teenagers and young adults are caused by motor vehicle accidents, which are often the result of high-risk behavior such as drinking and driving (Baker, O'Neill, Ginsberg, & Li, 1992). Moreover, the three leading causes of death for teenagers and young adults all involve behavioral choices as opposed to diseases, infections, or other types of "natural causes."

Although technological advancements have led to an overall increase in life expectancy, women's life expectancy is significantly longer than men's (Centers for Disease Control, 2003). Women in the United States live an average of 7 years longer than men (79 versus 72 years, respectively), and dying before age 65 is twice as likely for American men as women. Moreover, this gender difference in life expectancy is true in most countries, suggesting that this is not just an American phenomenon (Waldron, 1983). One possible explanation for

Box 11.1

What Is Death?

Although defining death seems simple in this day and age, people have measured death in different ways at different times and in different places. Listening for a heartbeat, watching the chest for breathing, or holding a mirror to a person's nose or mouth to test for exhalation, for example, are all techniques for determining death. Obviously, the technology of a given society influences the types of tests available to it. Ironically, increasing technological advances have sometimes made it more difficult to determine when death occurs. If a person shows no signs of brain waves but the body is breathing on a respirator, is the person alive?

The current concept of death involves five guidelines that are accepted by medical professionals throughout the world (Ad Hoc Committee, 1968). First, the person is unreceptive and unresponsive to stimuli, such as touch, sound, light, and pain. Second, the person has no movement or breathing for at least 1 hour. (A person who has been on a respirator would be disconnected and then watched for 1 hour to see if he or she made any effort to breathe.) Third, the person has no reflexes, including blinking, yawning, vocalizing, and eye movements. Fourth, the person has a flat electroencephalogram (EEG) for at least 10 minutes, showing no activity in the upper brain. Fifth, the person has no circulation to or within the brain.

TABLE **11.2** *Leading Causes of Death by Age*

Ages 1 to 4 years: Accidents, congenital anomalies, homicide

Ages 5 to 14 years: Accidents, malignant neoplasms, homicide

Ages 15 to 24 years: Accidents, homicides, suicides

Ages 25 to 44 years: Accidents, malignant neoplasms, heart disease

Ages 45 to 64 years: Malignant neoplasms, heart disease, accidents

Ages 65 years and over: Heart disease, malignant neoplasms, cerebrovascular disease

Although heart disease and cancer are the overall leading causes of death, more people ages 1 to 44 years die from accidents than any other cause.

Source: Centers for Disease Control, 2003.

the gender differences in life expectancy is that men tend to engage in riskier behavior in general (e.g., drinking and driving) than women, and risky behavior, in turn, leads to more accidental deaths in men than women. In line with this view, men are much more likely than women to drown, accidentally get shot, and die in car accidents. Other theories suggest that these gender differences in life expectancy are a function of sex roles. For example, men tend to have more stressful jobs and feel more pressure to succeed at work, which may lead to excess wear and tear on the cardiovascular system (see Photo 11.1). On the other hand, women tend to get more social support, which could help them more effectively buffer the effects of stress. Third, and as we discussed in Chapter 4, men and women may differ in how they respond to stress. Men often show a greater physiological arousal than women in response to potentially stressful situations. Finally, some research indicates that sex differences in mortality are influenced by genetic factors. For example, women have two X chromosomes (which carry genes that influence the functioning of the immune system), whereas men have only one, which may explain why women seem to have greater resistance to infectious diseases than men.

There are also race differences in life expectancy as well as in the causes of death (Centers for Disease Control, 2003). While a white female born in 1998 has a mean life expectancy of 80 years, an African American female has a life expectancy of 74.8 years, and white males have a mean life expectancy of 74.5 years. In contrast, an African American male born in 1998 has a mean life expectancy of 67.6 years. While accidents are the leading cause of death for infants ages 1 to 4 years regardless of sex and race, homicide is the fourth leading cause of death for white infants but the second leading cause of death for African American infants. Similarly, suicide is one of the top three causes of death for white male and female teenagers and African American male teenagers, but it is only the sixth leading cause of death for African American females. HIV infection is the leading cause of death in African Americans ages

PHOTO 11.1   One of the explanations for the shorter life expectancy of men as opposed to women is that men are more likely to work in dangerous occupations.

25 to 44 years, but is only the sixth leading cause of death for white people of this age.

Socioeconomic factors are largely to blame for this dramatic difference in life expectancy among different races —African Americans are much more likely than whites to live in poverty and to have inadequate access to health care (see Box 11.2; Anderson, 1995; Bagley, Angel, Dilworth-Anderson, Liu, & Schinker, 1995; Flack et al., 1995). Also, African Americans are less likely to receive prenatal care (hence they have a higher rate of infant mortality), or to have regular vaccinations (hence they develop diseases), and they are more likely to live in dangerous situations. One study found that African American males who lived in Harlem were less likely to reach age 65 than men living in Bangladesh, one of the poorest countries in the world (McCord & Freeman, 1990).

Box 11.2

Health Psychology in the Real World—The Very Real Danger of Homicide in the African American Population

One of the leading causes of deaths, especially for young people, is homicide, and the prevalence of homicide is particularly high among African Americans (National Center for Health Statistics, 2003). In fact, one of the factors leading to the shorter life expectancy for African Americans as compared to whites is the substantially higher rate of deaths by homicide in the African American population. Homicide is the second leading cause of death (after accidents) in African Americans ages 1 to 4 years (boys and girls), the second leading cause of death in African American boys (ages 5 to 14 years), and the leading cause of death for African American males ages 15 to 24 years and the second leading cause of death for females in this age range. In fact, at every single age range African Americans are more likely than whites to die from homicide, and for all age groups, African Americans are eight times more likely than whites to be murdered. What accounts for this dramatic difference? One explanation is the rate of access to potentially lethal weapons in the inner cities, where African Americans are more likely than whites to live. For example, one study found that nearly half of 7th-and 8th-grade boys living in an inner city carried knives, and 25% carried guns (Webster, Gainer, & Champion, 1993). Firearms are the second leading cause of death in every age group from 10 years to young adulthood and are the leading cause of unintentional deaths in adolescents ages 15 to 19 years. Another factor is clearly poverty, which again is more likely to affect African Americans than whites and increases a person's likelihood of both committing and being victimized by violence (Greenberg & Schneider, 1994).

How Do People Cope with Dying?

Because chronic diseases are the leading causes of death today, terminally ill people are often aware that they are dying. For instance, a person may be ill for a long time, and death comes after a period of gradually declining health. Several different theories have been developed to describe the dying process. This section describes two distinct broad theories of dying and then describes the particular stages of dying as experienced by terminally ill children.

Stages of Death and Dying

The best-known model for explaining how people cope with dying was developed in the late 1960s by Dr. Elizabeth Kubler-Ross (1969). Based on interviews with 200 terminally ill patients, Dr. Kubler-Ross concluded that the process of dying involves a series of five stages that differ in content and emotional intensity. These stages are normal and predictable ways of coping with death, although people differ in how they experience them.

First, people go through a stage of *denial*. A very common initial reaction to receiving a diagnosis of a terminal illness is, "It can't be me—this must be a mistake." When people receive news that they have a terminal illness, it is stunning, and they may experience an initial state of numbness. They simply can't face the situation and believe the prognosis is a mistake or impossible. Although this period typically doesn't last very long, this initial denial may allow the person to come to terms with the situation psychologically.

After the initial stage of numbness and denial has worn off, a common reaction is *anger*. People feel that their prognosis is unfair and may search for reasons (e.g., "why me? what have I done?"). The person may express anger toward God, the medical staff, family members, or friends; as described at the start of this chapter, Ramon is clearly in the anger stage. Other feelings, such as rage, envy, and resentment, are also common. This stage can be hard for the family because the person's anger may be displaced, but it represents an attempt by the ill person to regain control of life.

Over time, anger transitions into *bargaining*, namely, an attempt to trade good behavior for good health. In this stage ill persons are trying to delay the inevitable. They may start attending church regularly, take their medicine without complaint, or give generously to charity in an attempt to make a pact for more time or bargain with God. For example, a person may try to bargain for time to reach a valued milestone, such as a child's wedding or graduation, or their own birthday or anniversary.

When bargaining fails to change the prognosis, people often experience a state of *depression*, a feeling of anticipatory grief in which the person grieves about the upcoming losses he or she will experience in death. This stage is about self-grieving, and it is important for family members and medical staff to accept the person's depression and share in the sadness. The dying person feels many losses, including that of body image, time, money, independence, social status, and relationships, and experiencing depression is a common and understandable response. This stage is often coupled with a growing realization, based on the individual's physical state, that he or she is really dying. In turn, the person may feel weak, fatigued, shameful, guilty, fearful, or many other anxieties. This is "the worst of the worst."

The final stage of dying is *acceptance*: people finally acknowledge that death is inevitable and believe they can face it calmly. During this stage people often cut off contact with all but a few close friends and family members in an attempt to disengage. Dr. Kubler-Ross believes that given enough time and help during the prior stages, patients can reach a stage in which they are no longer angry or depressed, but rather are accepting of their fate. This stage, which Kubler-Ross describes as "quiet expectation" should not, however, be perceived as a happy stage—in contrast, this stage is more appropriately described as a time of quiet resignation, as if the patient has given up his or her struggle and is resting prior to death.

Although this perspective has received a lot of attention, it has been criticized for several reasons (Feifel, 1990; Rainey, 1988). First, Dr. Kubler-Ross didn't demonstrate "actual" stages or an orderly progression. In other words, it is not clear that people go from one stage to the next in a particular order—maybe people jump around from one phase to another, or cycle, or maybe experience stages simultaneously. In fact, all people do not go through all the stages. Some patients struggle against death (or even deny it) until the very end, whereas others seem to face death with resignation. Second, other researchers suggest that this model excludes some stages, such as anxiety, and fails to adequately describe others. The stage of denial, for example, could include a range of different reactions (e.g., "I am not ill; I am not dying; I will get better"). Third, Kubler-Ross's work focuses on only one aspect of a person's response to dying and leaves out the totality of the person's life. The experience of dying is obviously influenced by other factors, such as gender, age, race, religion, socioeconomic status, coping strategies, and social support. Finally, although Kubler-Ross intended these stages to serve as a description of the process of dying, these stages are often seen as a prescription of how people "should" react to dying. Thus, caregivers or family members may draw the inference that terminally ill people should progress through these stages precisely and in proper order and may become concerned when the ill person is not "on schedule," which only adds unneeded stress to the situation. This model may also can lead caregivers to see these stages as "the right way to die" so they think they should encourage people to "move along" to the next stage.

Task Work Approach

According to Charles Corr's task-based model for coping with dying, people who are terminally ill focus on four distinct types of tasks (Corr, 1992). First, they must cope with physical tasks, such as managing their pain and physical symptoms, on satisfying the body's needs and reducing distress. Second, they must focus on psychological tasks, including maintaining independence, feeling secure in the support they receive from others, and even in managing day-to-day tasks that are rewarding (e.g., taking a bath, eating a favorite food); they often need to feel in control. Third, people who are dying are concerned with social tasks, such as enhancing their interpersonal relationships, which often become limited to just a few very close persons, or interacting with hospital workers, social workers, and physicians. Finally, dying people focus on spiritual tasks, including thinking through issues of meaningfulness, hope, connectedness, transcendence. For example, they may wonder what happens to their spirit following death and the contributions they have made in their life.

Kenneth Doka (1993) describes phase-specific tasks that people with life-threatening illnesses encounter. People in the prediagnostic phase experience symptoms of their illness or disease. They may, for example, notice a lump or feel an unusual pain. Once the condition is diagnosed, they are in the acute phase of the illness. In this stage they try to understand the disease and to cope with it. After this initial focus of coming to terms with the illness, people enter the chronic phase, in which they must manage the illness and its various effects. As discussed in Chapter 10, these effects could include carrying out medical regimens, coping with feelings regarding the illness, and managing the symptoms and side effects of the illness and its treatment. In cases in which the disease can be managed, people enter the recovery phase. During this stage, they deal with their anxiety about reoccurrence of the illness as well as any lingering physical effects. However, if the illness is incurable, the person eventually enters the terminal phase in which he or she copes with managing the often increasingly difficult symptoms, preparing for death, and finding meaning in life and death.

Both of these task-based approaches offer several valuable guidelines (Kastenbaum, 2000). They view dying as a normative event within the total lifespan as opposed to an event of a very different and distinct domain. They view dying people as continuing to strive to accomplish valued goals. These task-based approaches also focus attention on a broad range of problems that dying people may encounter, not simply on the physical process of dying. This should help people pay attention to the diverse sets of needs of terminally ill patients, not just on managing their pain and/or prolonging their lives.

Stages of Death and Dying in Children

Fatally ill children have specialized needs, including the normal developmental needs of healthy children, the special needs of children who are sick and hospitalized, and the particular needs of children who are dying (Stevens, 1997). The specific concerns of teminally ill children, however, vary by age. The youngest children, ages 3 to 5, worry primarily about separation from their parents, friends, and grandparents. They are worried that they will be left alone and are comforted by reassurance that their parents will never leave them. In contrast, children ages 5 to 9 are concerned about the ending of their life and what will happen to their body.

Adolescents have their own particular concerns about death and dying and, ironically seem to be more afraid of the process of dying than of death itself (Stevens & Dunsmore, 1996). Adolescents are very sensitive to body-image issues; hence, the physical side effects of a terminal illness can be especially upsetting at this age. Adolescents are also very focused on separating from their parents and establishing peer relationships, which can be disrupted if they are forced to spend time away from school seeking treatment and are unable to participate in many normal social activities because of their illness. They may be particularly concerned about their inability to attract a boyfriend or girlfriend, and they may worry that their peers will reject them.

Extensive observation of hospitalized children by Myra Bluebond-Langner (1977) describes five stages that children pass through as they attempt to understand their illness (see Photo 11.2). First, children are aware they have a serious illness and are concerned about feeling sick. They gradually become more sophisticated about the illness, learning names for medicines and side effects. In the second stage, they are still aware that they are ill, but are optimistic about the outcome (e.g., "I am sick, but I'll get better"). In the third stage, they learn more about the procedures and their purposes, and understand that this illness is long-term (e.g., "I'll always be sick, but I will get better"). This is followed by the fourth stage, which often comes after they have experienced several cycles of remissions and relapses. At this point they accept that they will never get better, that they will always have this illness. Finally, in the fifth state, their declining health and observation of other dying patients leads them to realize that they will die.

Although experts disagree about whether terminally ill children should be given honest information about their condition, most believe that parents, doctors, and nurses should encourage children to talk about their fears and should try to answer questions at an age-appropriate level (Stillion & Wass,

PHOTO 11.2   Children who are terminally ill go through several stages of understanding their illness and prognosis.

1984). Even if children are not told directly about the nature of their illness, terminally ill children are often aware of their condition, either based on observations of other children around them or based on conversations they've overheard of family members and medical personnel. Children can also sense from their parents' nonverbal behavior that their illness is more serious than they are being told. Not surprisingly, they tend to have very high levels of anxiety. In fact, anxiety levels of terminally ill children are twice as high as those of other hospitalized children and of chronically ill, but not fatally ill, children.

Where Do People Die?

Historically, most people have died in their own homes, but this trend has clearly changed during the last century—there is a growing shift from people dying at home to people dying in hospitals and nursing homes (Levy, 1983). This section describes the four main places people die.

Hospitals

Hospital settings clearly provide many advantages to terminally ill patients, including the availability of life-saving equipment, highly skilled personnel, and access to pain medication. The focus in hospitals is on curing patients, delivering technical skills and interventions, and thereby preventing death (MacLeod, 2001). However, hospitals often place relatively little emphasis on the care of terminally ill patients, which may represent a failure of medical techniques in curing their disease or injury (Benoliel, 1988; Rainey, 1988). In fact, one large-scale study of 9,105 adults hospitalized with a life-threatening diagnosis found that patients' care had a number of limitations, including shortcomings in communication, overuse of aggressive treatment, and insufficient pain relief (SUPPORT Principal Investigators, 1995). For example, one study found that only 47% of doctors knew when their terminally ill patients did not want to receive cardiopulmonary resuscitation (CPR).

People who are terminally ill are also viewed and treated in particular ways by medical professionals (Maguire, 1985). Nurses and doctors who interact with dying patients may use false reassurance and distancing techniques. For example, doctors and nurses may tell the person he or she will get better soon, even when they know that this is unlikely, as a way of avoiding giving negative news. They may also ignore patients' reports of psychological difficulties, such as depression and anxiety, and focus instead on patients' physical state, in part because providing intense psychological care is time-consuming and emotionally draining. In sum, hospitals are designed to diagnose and treat disease, which is good for people with curable conditions, but not as good for those who are dying of chronic, incurable diseases.

Nursing Homes/Long-Term Care Facilities

Nursing homes and other types of long-term care facilities were developed for people who require significant assistance in caring for themselves, but who do not have specific medical issues that require constant care by a physician. People with Alzheimer's disease, for example, experience memory loss and disorientation, and therefore require constant supervision, but do not necessarily have acute medical needs in the early stages of this disease. Nursing home patients are often elderly and chronically ill; therefore, they need the type of assistance that family members may be unable—or unwilling—to provide on a daily basis. Nursing home staff assist with routine activities of daily living, including dressing, eating, and bathing. Like hospitals, however, they are not specifically trained to help terminally ill patients cope with the process of death and dying. Nursing homes also do not generally provide intensive medical treatment—patients who need this type of care are typically transferred to a hospital.

Hospice Care

The hospice movement was developed by Dr. Cicely Saunders in London in the late 1960s and was specifically designed to provide better care for terminally ill patients and to provide an alternative to dying in an impersonal institution such as a hospital or nursing home (Feifel, 1990; Kastenbaum, 1999). This first hospice program in the United States was started in the mid-1970s, and such programs now care for approximately 25% of all deaths in this country (NHO.org, 2003). Although in some cases hospice care is provided in a designated building, this type of care can also be provided in a particular unit or floor in a hospital or even at the patient's home. In fact, most hospice care is now provided in people's homes.

Hospice care differs from hospital care in a number of ways (Kastenbaum, 1999). First, hospice care focuses primarily on treating the symptoms of terminal illness and minimizing the patient's discomfort and pain, never on helping patients recover or prolong their lives. Patients who choose hospice care often have a limited amount of time to live—typically less than 6 months—and have illnesses or diseases that cannot be cured. Second, hospice facilities allow people to personalize and control their surroundings much more than they could do in a hospital (see Photo 11.3). For example, patients can wear their own clothes, have visitors at any time, and even bring in special items from home, such as a quilt, family pictures, and special mementos. Finally, hospice staff try to provide a sense of comfort and support for the patient and his or her family. They also encourage engaging in open discussions on death and dying, and expressing feelings. Julia, described at the beginning of this chapter, made the decision to move from the hospital to a hospice care facility because she wanted the opportunity to spend more time with family and friends and to be able to openly discuss her concerns about dying. One study found that hospice patients experience less depression and anxiety, in part because they are encouraged to talk about the dying process (Hinton, 1979). In sum, hospice care focuses on providing for the patient's physical, social, psychological, and spiritual needs.

Many patients who have cancer, AIDS, or ALS (a progressive neurological condition often referred to as Lou Gehrig's disease; Kastenbaum, 1999) choose hospice care. When compared to hospital care, hospices can result in more peace of mind for patients and their families (see Box 11.3; Ganzini et al., 2002; Lynn, 2001; Kane, Wales, Bernstein, Leibowitz, & Kaplan, 1984; Viney, Walker, Robertson, Lilley, & Ewan, 1994). In one study patients who were terminally ill with cancer were randomly assigned to receive either conventional care or hospice care (Kane et al., 1984). Although there were no significant differences between hospice and hospital patients in measures of pain, symptoms, activities of daily living, or mood, hospice patients reported greater satisfaction with the care they received. Moreover, the family caregivers of hospice patients reported more satisfaction and less anxiety than did those of the controls. The hospice option may therefore be a very good one for patients who understand (and whose families understand) the terminal nature of their illness.

Home

Many people wish to die at home, surrounded by family—in fact, 100 years ago, most people died in their own beds. This can be more comfortable psychologically: patients are surrounded by familiar things and familiar people. They are not forced to cope with the rigid routines of hospital care, including constant monitoring by medical personnel, poor-quality meals on a set schedule, and limited visiting hours.

PHOTO 11.3   People who choose to die in a hospice care facility often receive little medical intervention and prefer to spend time in personal and comfortable surroundings.

Box 11.3

Research Focus—What Are the Advantages of Hospice Care?

Linda Viney and her colleagues examined quality of life in terminally ill cancer patients who were in a hospital versus hospice unit (Viney et al., 1994). One hundred and eighty-three patients who were dying of cancer participated in this study. Sixty-two of these patients were staying in a small hospice unit on a floor of a hospital, 60 were staying in a hospice care facility that was a separate building, and 61 were staying in a general hospital unit. Patients were interviewed by a trained therapist, and were asked about their overall mood, including anxiety, depression, and anger, and feelings of social support.

Patients in the hospice units had very different experiences than those who were in the general hospital unit. Specifically, patients in both the small and large hospice units reported better enjoyment of life and lower levels of anger than those in the general hospital unit. Although patients in the hospice units did have more anxiety about death than hospital patients, they had less general anxiety and worry. Moreover, hospice patients reported having more favorable interpersonal interactions and felt less lonely than hospital patients. In sum, terminally ill people have better overall psychological adjustment receiving care in hospice than in a general hospital unit.

However, dying at home has a number of disadvantages. Home deaths obviously have some drawbacks in terms of the quality of medical care. Insurance companies often will not cover home visits by doctors and, hence, terminally ill patients may not receive adequate medication to control their pain. It can also be very difficult to transport dying patients to doctors' offices or hospitals should they need to go. Some homes also may not be set up work well for dying people—there are issues of access for wheelchairs, appropriately equipped bathrooms, and more. Also, family members may find caring for a dying patient extremely stressful, both psychologically and physically. It can be very difficult to help that person with personal tasks, such as bathing and using a bedpan, and can be exhausting to help with virtually all of the person's needs, such as eating and dressing.

Providing home care for a terminally ill patient may be made easier if the caregivers are able to have some outside help to cope with the regular needs of the patient. In some cases hospice programs can provide assistance to a terminally ill person who wants to stay at home (Kastenbaum, 1999). These services include visits from nurses, social workers, and chaplains. Hospice professionals also offer assistance to caregivers, including staying with patients while family members are out, reading to and caring for the dying patient, and helping families to understand and cope with the dying process.

What Factors Influence the Experience and Consequences of Bereavement?

When people lose someone they care about, they experience a state of bereavement, which is accompanied by both grief, the feelings caused by this loss, and mourning, the expression of these feelings. Grief and mourning are not a sign of weakness or self-indulgence—they are a normal and natural human reaction to the loss of a significant person, which is intensified by our closeness to the person who has died (Berado, 1988; Feifel, 1990). This section examines factors that influence grief, the stages of mourning, and the psychological and physical consequences of bereavement.

Influences on Grief

Different paths to death are associated with very different reactions on the part of loved ones (Rainey, 1988). On the one hand, people who have a chronic disease such as cancer, Parkinson's disease, multiple sclerosis, or Alzheimer's disease, typically experience lingering trajectory deaths: the person is ill for a long time, and death comes after a period of gradually declining health. These are usually quiet deaths, in which efforts are made to help the person remain comfortable, and do not involve last-minute heroic attempts to save them. In the past, doctors and nurses often delayed informing family members of a patient's impending death, or they told families but not the patient, in fear that it would upset the patient and perhaps cause the person to give up hope (Glaser & Strauss, 1965). However, this conspiracy of silence is usually not helpful—patients generally want to know the truth about their condition and typically appreciate knowing what to expect, including various physical symptoms and strategies for coping with pain (Rainey, 1988). Moreover, patients can pick up both verbal and nonverbal cues from doctors and family members and are very likely to hear, directly or indirectly, statements made by physicians and other hospital personnel, family members, and friends, giving them information about their prognosis (Justin, 1988). This type of open awareness—on the part of the patient and his or her family members—means that patients can make realistic plans. They may, for example, prepare a will, say good-bye to important people, make arrangements for their funeral and the custody of their children, and prepare psychologically for death (Rainey, 1988).

Lingering-trajectory deaths are often the easier for survivors to cope with—they allow people to prepare themselves for the loss of their loved one and to say their good-byes. However, this type of progression toward death may also pose difficulties for survivors. First, loved ones may watch the patient go through long-term pain and suffering and experience the loss of physical bodily functions and of mental faculties. Friends and family members often engage in anticipatory grieving, namely, grieving small losses as they occur (e.g., loss of physical functioning, loss of ability to work); they are grieving the death, but also all that is lost in the process of dying. Lingering-trajectory deaths may be draining on the physical, emotional, and financial resources of family members. Interestingly, at least in some cases, people can show improvements in health habits, such as taking their medicine, resting, and exercising, following the death of their spouse (Schulz et al., 2001). One recent study found that people who were the primary caregivers for their spouses and reported feeling considerable physical, mental, and/or emotional strain from this role actually had better health habits following the death of their spouse, and they did not show an increase in depression. In contrast, people who were not caregivers, or those who were caregivers but who were not experiencing strain, showed no change in health habits and increases in depression following the death of their spouse.

In contrast, quick-trajectory deaths, especially if they are sudden, violent, and stigmatized (e.g., AIDS, suicide), are very hard on survivors (Berado, 1988; Bradach & Jordan, 1995). First, these deaths typically force survivors to cope with challenging practical issues. The deceased person typically has made no arrangements for his or her death, such as expressing wishes about funeral arrangements and burial preferences, writing a will, or taking care of financial issues (Becvar, 2001). Second, family members may feel a huge lack of closure—they've had no chance to say good-bye. As described at the beginning of the chapter, Sally felt completely unable to cope following the unexpected death of her husband, Paul. People may feel tremendous guilt about unresolved conflicts or things left unsaid and may dwell on the final words they said to the person, particularly if those words were unkind. Survivors of quick-trajectory deaths also don't have the opportunity to prepare themselves for a loss; hence, they can experience disbelief and intense anxiety for some time. Survivors of sudden, unexpected deaths often take considerable time to come to terms with the death and may report still actively trying to cope with it as long as 4 to 7 years later. This is why the families of victims of the 911 terrorist attacks have had such trouble coping with their losses—their loved ones simply went to work (or got on a routine airplane flight), and then never came home (see Photo 11.4).

Stages of Mourning

Bereavement begins as soon as one learns that a loved one died, and typically with an initial feeling of shock (Berado, 1988). During this *reaction stage,* survivors may feel numb and show little feeling. This period allows survivors to cope initially and to handle the necessary tasks, such as planning a funeral or memorial service, notifying friends and relatives, and handling legal arrangements. However, not all survivors will be able to handle such logistics and may therefore need considerable assistance from others. At this time, people may also try to make sense of the death, especially in cases in which the loss was unanticipated (e.g., a quick-trajectory death) and inappropriate (e.g., the death of a child). They may experience anger and frustration with the person who

PHOTO 11.4   Can anything positive come from a quick-trajectory death? Family members are often relieved that the person did not suffer or was in the midst of doing something he or she loved to do. Many family members of firefighters killed in the World Trade Center attack, for example, say that the firefighters died doing what they loved best. In some cases family members take pride knowing that their loved one died doing something courageous, such as when a soldier dies on a battlefield. Some of the survivors of people who died when Flight 93 crashed in Pennsylvania on September 11 took great pride in believing that their loved ones deliberately crashed the plane to avert deaths of others.

died and others who could be seen as responsible in some way (e.g., doctors, God), and those who encourage them to accept the loss when they just aren't ready to do so. This anger may also be self-directed: survivors may wonder what they could have done differently to prevent this death.

After this initial period of numbness, survivors enter a stage of *yearning and searching* (Berado, 1988). This stage represents a desire to return things to how they once were. Survivors may search crowds hoping to see the lost one, may expect to see the person coming up the driveway, and may wake up in the morning wondering if the person is really dead. One man whose mother was killed when he was a child recalls coming home after school and calling "Mom?" just hoping that she would answer. In this stage people are still hoping things will return to how they were before the death and are not acknowledging or accepting the extent and finality of their loss.

After reality sets in, the survivor enters the stage of *disorganization and reorganization* (Berado, 1988), in which he or she is disappointed that the loss cannot be undone and may experience despair and depression (see Box 11.4). Survivors may have trouble enjoying old activities and, hence, have difficulty making plans and engaging in new activities. They may also struggle with forming a new identity, especially if they've lost a spouse or child—these types of deaths cause major role changes since people have to give up their previous

---

Box 11.4

The Experience of Grief

Stop all the clocks, cut off the telephone,
Prevent the dog from barking with a juicy bone,
Silence the pianos and with muffled drum
Bring out the coffin, let the mourners come.

Let aeroplanes circle moaning overhead
Scribbling on the sky the message HE IS DEAD,
Put crepe bows round the white necks of the public doves,
Let the traffic policeman wear black cotton gloves.

He was my North, my South, my East and West,
My working week and my Sunday rest,
My noon, my midnight, my talk, my song;
I thought that love would last forever: I was wrong.

The stars are not wanted now: put out every one;
Pack up the moon and dismantle the sun;
Pour away the ocean and sweep up the wood;
For nothing now can ever come to any good.

As this poem by W. H. Auden (1940) clearly depicts, people who have lost a loved one often experience tremendous grief.

---

identity as wife, husband, or parent. The plans they had made are now ruined, and it can be difficult to know how to start a "new life." Survivors may become very dependent on those who provide care for them. Their feelings in this stage are often complicated and even conflicting—it can seem like a betrayal to the dead person to give up grieving and take joy in new activities.

Finally, people enter the *reorientation and recovery stage* (Berado, 1988), in which the bereaved person is able to take part in new activities and to "rejoin" the world. He or she has accepted the changes and is now able to get life back on track. Survivors in this stage may also give the deceased a new identity, such as a place in heaven. They are still sad, but are now able to move on with their own lives.

Although these stages of mourning are described as if they are a linear process, some bereaved people may experience *unresolved grief* and never return to a normal pattern of living (Berado, 1988). As described previously, people have greater difficulty adjusting to sudden and unexpected deaths; hence, in these cases adjustment may take longer (see Box 11.5). Adjustment may also take longer when coping with deaths caused by murder, especially if survivors are involved in the criminal justice system, which can prolong and even exacerbate the bereavement process (Wisocki & Skowron, 2000). People may also have difficulty resolving their grief in cases in which they had a highly conflictual relationship with the deceased person and in those in which they were excessively dependent on their relationship with that person.

Consequences of Bereavement

Psychological problems, including depression, sadness, anger, and anxiety, are very common following the loss of a loved one (Kastenbaum, 1999; Raphael & Dobson, 2000). Bereaved people may feel sad and empty and may have trouble contemplating continuing on with their lives without the deceased person. One study with HIV-positive gay men found that those whose close friends or lovers had died from AIDS in the last year were more depressed and likely to think about suicide and more likely to use sedatives, such as sleeping pills and tranquilizers, than those who were HIV-positive and had not experienced this type of loss (Martin & Dean, 1993).

Grief often leads to social problems, including loneliness and isolation (Berado, 1988; Harvey & Hansen, 2000). People who suffer the loss of a friend, spouse, or child often experience a decrease in available social networks. Widows may find that they are not invited to parties or other social gatherings at which other people are all part of a couple. Similarly, parents who've lost a child may lose the network of friends who had children of the same age. Older people, in particular, may feel socially isolated as they experience the loss of friends, spouses, and siblings. Interestingly, younger widows feel more isolated socially than older widows, presumably because this type of loss is less common for younger women. Similarly, women who have lost a spouse tend to cope better than do men who have lost a spouse, again because the social support for widows tends to be greater than such support for widowers (Wisocki & Skowron, 2000).

People who are bereaved have increased rates of minor and major illnesses and even death (Berado, 1988; Martikainen & Valkonen, 1996; Raphael & Dobson, 2000; Wisocki & Skowron, 2000). They may experience a number of physical symptoms, such as emptiness in the abdomen, a sense of physical weakness, choking and shortness of breath, and a tightness in the chest. Moreover, men in particular are at increased risk of dying following the death of their spouse, especially in the first year following the death. For example, one large-scale study in Finland examined death rates in the period immediately following the death of a spouse (Martikainen & Valkonen, 1996). Compared to others their age, men were 17% more likely to die in this period, whereas women were only 6% more likely to die. Similarly, another large-scale survey found that both men and women were significantly more likely to die in the year following the death of their spouse as compared to those who did not experience this type of loss (Schaefer, Quesenberry, & Wi, 995). And the impact of bereavement on mortality is not limited to those who lose a spouse,

Questioning the Research 11.1

What other factors might account for the finding that people who find meaning in a loved one's death experience better health?

Box 11.5

Health Psychology in the Real World—The Tragedy of Suicide

Suicide is the 11th overall leading cause of death in the United States, and the 3rd leading cause of death in people ages 15 to 24 years (National Center for Health Statistics, 2003). One large-scale survey of high school students revealed that 27% of girls and 15% of boys had seriously considered attempting suicide, and nearly 8% of all students had made at least one suicide attempt (Kann et al., 1998). Suicides cause many more deaths each year than homicides or HIV/AIDS: on an average day, 84 people in the United States die from suicide and close to 2000 make an unsuccessful suicide attempt (Fine, Rousculp, Tomasek, & Horn, 1999). Although more men than women die from suicide, women are much more likely to report attempting suicide. This gender difference is caused at least in part by the differences in methods used—men tend to use "more effective" methods, such as firearms, whereas women are more likely to use "less effective" methods, such as pill ingestion (see Figure 11.2; Fine et al., 1999). Although suicide is clearly influenced by multiple factors, including substance abuse, depression, and a history of family violence, one contributing factor is access to firearms (O'Donnell, 1995). In fact, 57% of all suicides are committed by firearms, making this by far the most common method of killing oneself (National Institute of Mental Health, 2002). People living in a house where a firearm is kept are almost five times as likely to die by suicide than people living in gunfree homes (Bailey et al., 1997; Kellerman et al., 1992; Resnick et al., 1997). Having a gun available also increases the likelihood that a suicide attempt will be successful.

A suicide has a major impact on other people in the victim's life. The common experiences people have in response to other types of loss, such as anger, guilty, and sadness, are often intensified in the case of suicides. First, because suicides are not caused by natural events, these deaths are seen by survivors as deaths that were avoidable. Suicide deaths are also sudden; hence, survivors have no chance to prepare themselves. Survivors are therefore especially likely to experience feelings of blame and guilt, a sense of rejection by the victim, and difficulty in coming to terms with the death (Silverman, Range, & Overholser, 1994). Moreover, because of the stigma of suicide, survivors may be less likely to receive much-needed assistance from others.

(continues)

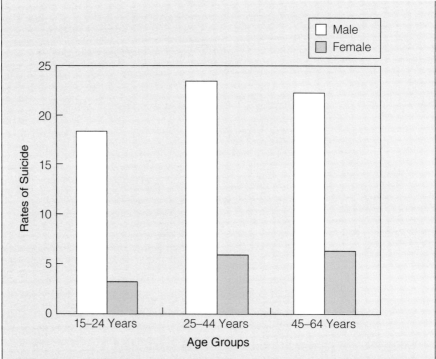

FIGURE 11.2 Although rates of suicide are significantly higher in males than females, females actually attempt suicide much more frequently than males—they are simply less likely to use an effective method. For example, males are more likely to use guns and hanging (which are very likely to work), whereas females are more likely to use poisoning (which is less likely to work; Centers for Disease Control, 2003).

but rather extends to those who lose any type of significant partner. For example, HIV-positive men who experience the loss of a partner to AIDS show signs of more rapid progression of their own AIDS illness (Kemeny et al., 1994).

One possible reason that may account for these increased rates of illness and death in bereaved people is that people who are bereaved are less likely to engage in health-promoting behavior, and are more likely to engage in health-damaging behavior (Berado, 1988). For example, following the loss of a spouse, people may use alcohol to try to dull their grief or may forget to eat healthy foods. Research with gay men who experienced the loss of their partner to AIDS demonstrated that rates of risky sexual behavior increased dramatically in the first 4 to 6 months following their loss, although it returned to normal levels later (Mayne, Acree, Chesney, & Folkman, 1998). Similarly, bereaved people may have trouble sleeping and eating, which in turn can wear down their bodies. This explanation may work especially well to explain why men who lose their wives, who in many cases may have done most of the grocery shopping and cooking, are at such great risk of showing health problems. As described at the beginning of the chapter, Phillip felt very isolated following the death of his wife, and he lapsed into several unhealthy habits.

Another factor that may explain the link between bereavement and illness is that bereavement-related stress impairs the immune system, which thereby leads to be more higher susceptibility to infection and disease (Kemeny et al., 1995; Raphael & Dobson, 2000; Zisook, Schuchter, Sledge, & Judd, 1994). For example, one study of former caregivers of patients with Alzheimer's disease revealed that they experienced a significant decline in their natural killer cell function (a measure of the immune system's ability to respond to health threats; Esterling, Kiecolt-Glaser, Bodnar, & Glaser, 1994). Interestingly, the negative effects of bereavement on health may be decreased if survivors can find some meaning in the loss (Bower, Kemeny, Taylor, & Fahey, 1998). For example, one study with 40 HIV-positive men who had recently experienced the death of a loved one to AIDS revealed that those who found meaning in the death, such as appreciating and become closer to their friends, shifting their priorities, and increasing their faith, had significantly better health than those who were not able to find such meaning. In fact, only 3 of the 16 men who found meaning died during the follow-up period, whereas 12 of the 24 who did not find meaning had died.

How Do People Cope with Bereavement?

Many bereaved people have a strong need to try to make sense of the loss and may seek out any information related to the death (Raphael & Dobson, 2000; Toth, Stockton, & Browne, 2000). For example, they may go over and over the details surrounding the person's death, including the precise cause of death, the timing of the death, and whether the person suffered. Even if these questions don't have answers, it can help the survivor recover to tell the story of their loss. Survivors have a particularly difficult time coping with deaths in which they don't have information, such as knowledge about how exactly the person died, and when they don't have the person's body. Many families of victims of the 911 tragedy, for example, report constantly thinking about whether their loved one was killed immediately, whether the person knew he or she was dying, and whether the person suffered.

This type of thinking about and trying to make sense of the death can be a valuable and even necessary component of working through the loss (Bower et al., 1998; Davis, Smith, & Nickels, 1998; Folkman, Chesney, Collette, Boccellari, & Cooke, 1996; Folkman, Chesney, Cooke, Boccellari, & Collette, 1994; McIntosh, Silver, & Wortman 1993; Stroebe & Stroebe, 1991). Some researchers even suggest that people who fail to engage in this type of "grief work" experience poorer psychological and physical well-being. For example, one study with parents who experienced the sudden loss of their child found that those who thought frequently about the death of their child experienced more grief in the short term (3 weeks following the death), but showed greater adjustment and less distress 18 months later than those who did not do this grief work (McIntosh et al., 1993). Similarly, gay men who experienced the death of their partner to AIDS but found meaning in this loss showed fewer signs of physical declines than those who were not able to find such "silver linings" (see Figure 11.3; Bower et al., 1998). As discussed in Chapter 4, people who try to avoid thinking about difficult thoughts show increased physiological arousal, which may in turn lead to more health problems. In line with this view, men who tried to avoid thinking about the loss of their spouse by suppressing their feelings and distracting themselves from their grief showed more maladjustment 2 years later than those who didn't use those strategies (Stroebe & Stroebe, 1991). This research suggests that confronting the loss can be a helpful coping strategy.

However, other research indicates that this type of direct confrontation and thinking about the loss is not particularly beneficial and can even have harmful effects on psychological and physical well-being (Bonanno, Keltner, Holen, & Horowitz, 1995; Stroebe & Stroebe, 1991; Schut, van den Bout, De Keijser, & Stroebe, 1996). Several studies indicate that the amount of grief work engaged in has no association with adjustment (Stroebe & Stroebe, 1991; Schut et al., 1996). For example, although men who avoided thinking about the death of their spouse showed more maladjustment, there was no associa-

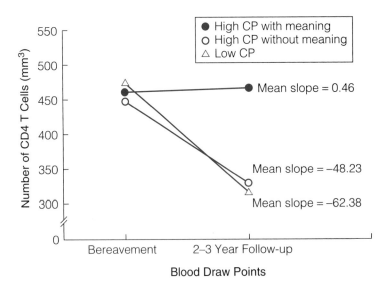

FIGURE 11.3 Men who thought frequently about the death of their partner (i.e., high cognitive processing or CP) but found meaning in the loss showed no decline in T cells (a marker of the immune system's effectiveness), whereas those who thought frequently about the death but did not find meaning as well as those who did not think frequently about the death showed substantial declines in the number of T cells (data from Bower et al., 1998).

tion between the amount of thinking about such a loss and psychological well-being in women (Stroebe & Stroebe, 1991). And some research even suggests that people who deliberately try to avoid thinking about the loss of their spouse and exposing themselves to reminders of the loss may experience better long-term adjustment. For example, George Bonnano and colleagues (1995) demonstrated that people who initially suppress or deny their sad feelings following the loss of a spouse actually show fewer symptoms of grief later on. Similarly, and as described in Box 11.6, persistently ruminating about or

Box 11.6

Research Focus—Why Rumination Is Not the Best Approach to Coping

Susan Nolen-Hoeksema of the University of Michigan has conducted a number of studies on how men and women cope following the loss of a loved one (Nolen-Hoeksema, Parker, & Larson, 1994). In one study she interviewed 253 people who had lost a loved one in the last month. All of the participants had lost someone very close to them, such as their spouse, child, or parent. These people were asked about the strategies they used to cope when they were feeling sad, blue, or depressed, and specifically whether they tended to rely on rumination (e.g., thinking about how hard they find concentrating, the negative consequences of their bad mood). They also completed measures of optimism, social support, depression, and major life events. The researchers then interviewed these people again 5 months later to see how their general coping styles influenced them over time.

This study revealed a number of interesting findings. First, compared to men, women showed higher levels of rumination; that is, thinking about the death and the impact of the problem on their mood, and showed higher levels of depression. People who tended to ruminate more about their problems also reported experiencing more stressors, having less social support, and feeling less optimistic about their expectations for the future. Although all of these findings describe data from the first interview, other results revealed that people who ruminated more, experienced more stressors, and had less social support 1 month following their loss had higher depression scores 5 months later. Moreover, people who were more depressed 1 month after their loss were more likely to report ruminating, suggesting that initially strong depressive reactions may contribute to the tendency to ruminate, which in turn leads to even more depression. However, even taking into account these initially higher levels of depression, people who rely on rumination to cope with the death of a loved one experience higher levels of depression later on.

obsessing about one's loss without taking action to relieve such emotions can also have detrimental effects.

What accounts for these differences? One explanation is that these discrepancies are caused by the type of thinking (or not thinking) people do in response to loss. Certain types of thinking, such as reflecting on the positive aspects of the deceased person's life and the meaning of his or her death, is likely to be beneficial. It may, for example, be reassuring to bereaved parents to talk about their child and to find meaning in the child's death (e.g., "This is part of God's plan"; "Our child's organs helped other babies survive"). On the other hand, ruminating and dwelling on the depression associated with the loss is likely to be detrminental (Stroebe & Schut, 2001). Similarly, people may find it helpful at times to distract themselves from thinking about the loss, but actively trying to not think about the loss (e.g., thought suppression) may have undesirable effects. The decision to not talk about the loss should also come from the bereaved person, and not from others: bereaved mothers who think frequently about their loss but believe their social environments would not be supportive of such disclosure experience high levels of depression (Lepore, Silver, Wortman, & Wayment, 1996). The most effective coping probably involves some moderate level of thinking about the loss, such as confronting memories when they arise but avoiding constant rumination about the deceased person.

Survivors also have a strong need to express their reactions to the death, including their feelings of anger, guilt, anxiety, helplessness, and depression, and, hence, can really benefit from the presence of social support (see Box 11.7; Kastenbaum, 1999; Raphael & Dobson, 2000; Toth et al., 2000). These feelings may be strange and intense—survivors may be angry at their loved one for getting killed, even if such a thought is totally irrational. People may feel they are going crazy, and they appreciate hearing that their reactions are normal. In fact, simply talking to other people about the loss has both psychological and physical benefits. One study of people who had lost a spouse to an accident or suicide found that those who talked to friends about the death had a smaller increase in number of illnesses following the death, whereas those who continued to ruminate about the death had more illnesses, including ulcers, headaches, and pneumonia (Pennebaker & O'Heeron, 1984). Bereaved people may also benefit from taking some type of action in response to the loss, such as planting a tree, starting a scholarship fund in the person's name, or creating a scrapbook of the person's life.

Survivors often find that friends and family are available to provide emotional and practical support immediately following the loss of a loved one, but this support typically declines over time. However, survivors often report experiencing intense pain for months, and even years, after the person's death. In fact, the intensity of a person's grief may not even be apparent immediately, when survivors often must cope with urgent matters, such as planning a funeral or memorial service, making plans for handling the body, and handling legal issues. Many survivors also experience an anniversary reaction, namely, a reaction to the death again at a later date that has some special significance (Dlin, 1985), such as an anniversary (in months or years) of the person's death, holidays, the loved one's birthday, or other special occasions.

Box 11.7

Information You Can Use—What Do You Say When Someone Dies?

People are often uncomfortable talking to people who are bereaved—they want to help, but just don't know what to say. In fact, one study of the remarks made to bereaved people found that 80% were nonhelpful! Let's start with what not to say. First, remember that the person is grieving, so try not to minimize the loss (Berado, 1988). It does not help to remind the bereaved person that "things could be worse." So, remarking that the loved one died quickly and without pain or that the person was old and had lived a full life is not helpful. Similarly, reminding bereaved persons of positive things, such as their ability to get married again (if they've lost a spouse) or their ability to have more children (if they've lost a child) only serves to downplay the very real grief they are experiencing. As one survivor said, "If I lost one leg, I'd still miss it." Second, remember that the bereaved person has experienced a substantial loss and needs the opportunity to grieve. Telling them to "keep a stiff upper lip" is simply asking them to deny showing what they are feeling. But bereaved people need to express their grief—this is an important part of the recovery period. On the other hand, don't assume that if someone isn't obviously showing grief, such as by crying, he or she isn't feeling very sad. People grieve in their own time and in their own way. Finally, unless you have suffered the same type of loss, do not say, "I know how you feel" because you really don't. And do not make comparisons between the loss of a person and the loss of an animal.

So, what can you say? You can offer some concrete and practical help, such as preparing food for the bereaved person, assisting with funeral arrangements, or running errands. Coping with the tasks of daily life are often overwhelming during times of intense grief; therefore, providing some assistance can be very helpful. Although people often avoid bringing up the person who has died—in fear that this will remind the bereaved person of the death—bringing up the loved one's name in natural ways is appreciated. People who have lost someone want the opportunity to talk about their memories of that person and often appreciate hearing stories about them. It's helpful to know that others are remembering the person. You can also signal your willingness to listen and help in any way, even if you don't know exactly what the bereaved person would prefer. Statements such as, "This must be very painful for you," "Tell me how you're feeling," and "How can I be of help?" are appreciated. Even something very simple, such as, "I'm so sorry," is helpful.

Professional help may aid survivors in coping with their loss (Neimeyer, 2000). Some people find guided imagery helpful as grief therapy (Aiken, 1985). In this technique, bereaved individuals are taken through exercises in which they relive aspects of their relationship with the deceased: they might recall their affection for the deceased person, and then replay receiving news of the death, attending the funeral, and watching the person be buried. The bereaved person is told to describe these events out loud as if they are occurring at that moment. They may also share imaginary dialogues with the deceased person, ask the person's permission to start new relationships, and ultimately say good-bye. This technique is supposed to help people come to terms with their grief and to finally make peace with the loss.

Many grief support groups have been formed to provide support for those who have experienced similar tragedies (see Table 11.3; Raphael & Dobson, 2000). These support groups are particularly helpful because they allow people to affiliate with others in the same situation. Survivors can gain information from others and learn whether their reactions and experiences are normal. They can share their experiences, obtain guidance on coping, and discuss big questions (e.g., is life fair? is there a God?). The Widow-to-Widow Program, for example, provides people with the opportunity to talk about the experience of losing a spouse with other people who have coped with this situation (Kastenbaum, 1999). Several support groups for survivors of the 911 attacks were formed, sometimes with very specific purposes (e.g., for women with

TABLE 11.3 *Survivor Support Groups*

Organization	Description
National SIDS Clearinghouse (www.circsol.com)	This group provides information for people affected by sudden infant death syndrome.
Parents of Murdered Children (www.pomc.com)	This group provides information for survivors of homicide.
Widowed Persons Service (www.aarp.org)	This group provides information for people who are widowed.
Mothers Against Drunk Driving (www.madd.org)	This group provides information for people who have lost someone to a drunk-driving accident.
American Association of Suicidology (www.suicidology.org)	This group provides information for survivors of suicide.
Compassionate Friends	This group provides information for those who have lost a child.
Hope for Youth	This group provides support for children whose parents have died.
Survivors of Loved Ones	This group provides support for those who lost a loved one to suicide.

Support groups are especially helpful when they bring together people who have all suffered the same type of loss.

children whose husbands were killed, children of firefighters who were killed); they allow people to spend time with others who really understand what they are going through. As described at the beginning of the chapter, Tiffany found the support group for children who have experienced the death of a sibling very beneficial.

How Do People React to Different Types of Deaths?

A death in the family virtually always changes the types of interactions occurring in the family, and the reactions people have to death can differ depending on their relationship to the person who has died (Berado, 1988). This section examines how survivors react to different types of deaths.

Death of a Spouse

Losing a spouse is particularly devastating for virtually any married person (Field, Nichols, Holen, & Horowitz, 1999) because it deprives people of the single relationship that they may have had for a lengthy period of time, which in turn means the loss of social support, plans and dreams, and even the identity as a spouse. Many people who experience the loss of a spouse feel lonely for sometime, even if they have a generally strong and supportive social network (Lichenstein, Gatz, Pederson, Berg, & McClearn, 1996). They may also experience a variety of physical symptoms, including believing they see, hear, or sense the presence of their spouse (Grimby, 1993; Lindstrom, 1995; LoConto, 1998). The loss of a spouse is particularly difficult for younger people, perhaps in part because this type of loss is less expected. Moreover, older people who have had to take care of their terminally ill spouse for some time may even feel some relief following the death (Schulz et al., 2001).

Interestingly, men and women react to and cope with the loss of their spouses in strikingly different ways (Lamme, Dykstra, & Broese Van Groenou, 1996; Stroebe, Stroebe, & Abakoumkin, 1999). Men are more likely than women to remarry, in part because women tend to outlive men and because men tend to prefer slightly younger partners than women do; hence, there are simply more eligible partners for older men than there are for older women. However, women are more likely than men to form new social relationships, such as with neighbors and other casual friends. Men also tend to suffer a greater loss of social support than do women following the death of a spouse. Men often rely on their wives for considerable social support and, therefore, are particularly devastated when she dies. Women, on the other hand, tend to rely on a broader network of people for support, including family members and friends as well as their spouse; hence, they suffer less of a decline in social support when they are widowed. This gender gap in social support is one explanation for the greater mortality risk men who have lost their spouse face as compared to women.

> **Questioning the Research 11.2**
>
> Although this research has focused on the impact of the death of a spouse, do you think the results would be the same if the study focused on people who lost long-term romantic partners who were not their spouses? Why or why not?

Death of a Parent

For adults, the death of a parent is the most common type of loss (Berado, 1988). Because these deaths are relatively common, and not so unexpected, they tend to be less traumatic than the loss of a spouse or a child. Adult children are generally able to continue with their own occupational and family responsibilities following the death of a parent, in part because there is typically some distance (emotional and physical) between adult parents and adult-children.

While adult children experience relatively little disruption following the death of a parent, the death of a parent is the most significant loss a young child can encounter (Stillion & Wass, 1984; Wass & Stillion, 1988). Children are likely to express the loss of a parent through actions, such as repeating play activities that they had engaged in with their parent, and may remember parents only in terms of a few salient images. They may blame themselves for the death, feel betrayed, and believe that if the parent had loved them enough, they would not have died. The loss of a parent may also trigger new worries for children, including a fear that they too will die, and anxiety about who will take care of them. Not surprisingly, bereaved children are quite likely to suffer from psychological problems and tend to be more submissive, dependent, and introverted. For example, one study with 105 children between the ages of 2 and 17 years found that those who lost a parent showed increases in depression, sadness, irritability, crying, and other difficulties (e.g., eating, bed-wetting, school performance, sleeping; Van Eerdewegh, Bieri, Parilla, & Clayton, 1982). Similarly, adults who lost parents as children are more likely to have problems with loneliness, depression, suicide, and physical disorders such as cardiovascular disease.

Death of a Child

Because parents expect that their children will outlive them, the death of a child is often seen as a particularly devastating type of loss—families literally can be torn apart dealing with this tragedy (Stillion & Wass, 1984). The intensity of grief following the death of a child is generally greater than that following the loss of a spouse or parent (Bass, Noelker, Townsend, & Deimling, 1990; Harvey & Hansen, 2000). Anger is a very common first reaction to learning that a child is dying. Parents may lash out at doctors, nurses, and even God. Parents may also feel anxious about the upcoming separation from their child, as well as their own eventual death (which is clearly brought home acutely in the case of a child's death). Guilt is another common reaction to learning that one's child is dying. Because parents see their role as protecting and nurturing their child, they can feel overwhelming guilt when they feel they have failed in this role. Parents often try to explain why the death happened and may feel that they are being punished (Downey, Silver, & Wortman, 1990). Parents often feel isolated and lonely. They are likely to find it difficult to continue to socialize with people who have healthy children, and they may not be able to cope with seeing other people's lives continuing normally while theirs is falling apart. All of these emotions are particularly strong when the child was initially healthy and when the death is unexpected, as in cases of an accident or suicide (see Box 11.8).

Parents can benefit from receiving particular types of support from the medical staff (Stillion & Wass, 1984). First, medical professionals must give parents clear and accurate information about the child's diagnosis, treatment, and prognosis, with a focus on relieving parents' guilt. If there is any hope that the condition will not be fatal, this possibility should be addressed in order to give parents some reason for optimism. They should also acknowledge the shock and despair the parents may be feeling and should encourage them to think through how they will tell others about the diagnosis (e.g., siblings, grandparents, friends). Finally, parents should be encouraged to treat the dying child as normally as possible, including maintaining consistent discipline. Parents often

Box 11.8

A Poem for a Child Who Died

Dear little child who never grew
Beyond the age of five,
I wish I could have died for you,
And you were still alive.

I loved you so and loved each day
When you and I were near.
I never thought that I would stay
And you would not be here.

But I survive and dream about
The times that used to be.
How hard it is to live without
Your sharing life with me.

The death of a child is a particularly difficult type of loss for parents, in part because such deaths are often so unexpected (Aiken, 1985).

456 Chapter 11. Terminal Illness and Bereavement

456 Chapter 11. Terminal Illness and Bereavement

Box 11.9

Health Psychology in the Real World—The Tragedy of Fetal Death

Many people experience the loss of a child in utero, during birth, or shortly after birth (Davis, 1991). These deaths, often called fetal deaths, include miscarriages, stillbirths, and perinatal deaths. It was assumed such deaths cause relatively little grief to parents because they happened at such an early point in the new life. Grieving parents are often told, "You can always have another child," or "Thank goodness it happened before you really got attached to the child." But in most cases parents start planning for and anticipating the birth of a child even at the very early stages of pregnancy. They may choose a name; buy furniture, clothes, and toys; and start imagining their lives with this baby. The death of a child, even during pregnancy, therefore typically leads to very real grieving and a sense of loss. In recent years programs have been developed in hospitals in which parents are encouraged to see and hold their dead baby. They may have the opportunity to take photographs of the child, to give it a name, and to take some type of momento (e.g., a lock of hair, a footprint, a hospital bracelet). These practices are thought to help parents acknowledge the depth of their loss and to validate their intense feelings of grief.

have a tendency, because of their guilt and grief, to indulge the terminally ill child, which can lead the child to feel confused and guilty.

Death of a Sibling

Although considerable research has examined the impact on parents of losing a child, relatively little research has examined the impact of losing a child on his or her siblings. However, the sibling relationship is a very important and unique one; hence, siblings experience many of the same emotions parents do following a child's death (Wass & Stillion, 1988), including shock, confusion, anxiety, depression, loneliness, and anger. Children may feel guilty for surviving, anxious that they will die, and responsible for their sibling's death (e.g., if the sibling had wished in a moment of anger that the child would die). The surviving child must also cope with a changed family situation, including neglect from their parents, who are focusing attention on the dying or dead child. Children often try to deny their own grief and sometimes even avoid mentioning their sibling's name, in an effort to avoid causing extreme pain to their parents. As one 12-year-old boy who recently lost a brother said, "My Dad doesn't talk about it, and my Mom cries a lot. I just stay in my room so I won't

Box 11.10

The Death of a Sister

At some point during Barbara's illness I began preparing myself for a different version of my old age. Without really thinking about it, I had always assumed we'd occupy adjacent rockers on some front porch, either literally or figuratively. Now one of these chairs would be empty. Intellectually, I understood that. But every time some new thing happens that she's not here for, emotionally it hits me all over again—that sense of charting new territories without the map of my older sister. And here's what I didn't expect at all—not only was I robbed of some part of my future, I was also deprived of my past. When a childhood memory needed checking, all my life I had simply run it by Barbara. Now there's no one to set me straight. There it is. For all the wonderful expressions of sisterhood from so many sources, for all the support I both receive and provide, for all of the friendships I cherish, it's not the same. I only had one sister.

This passage was written by Cokie Roberts (1998) to describe the loss of her sister, Barbara Sigmund, to breast cancer in 1991.

be a bother" (Wass & Stillion, 1988, p. 218). Finally, children can lose their own sense of identity if they lost their only sibling and are now no longer a sister or brother (see Box 11.10).

To help children cope with the death of a sibling try to make them feel included, if possible, during all stages of their sibling's illness (Stillion & Wass, 1984). They should be permitted to visit their sibling in the hospital and should be allowed to attend the funeral. Although parents may try to hide their grief in an effort to protect the surviving child, it is important for adults to acknowledge their own feelings as well as to encourage children to discuss their feelings. Sibling obviously should be reassured that their own thoughts were not responsible for their sibling's condition.

How Do Children Understand Death?

What did you learn about death from your parents? If you are like most college students, the answer is probably very little. Although it happens to us all, most people are very uncomfortable with the topic of death—because it causes anxiety, thoughts of death are usually pushed out of our minds whenever possible. The topic of death is often considered taboo in our society. For

Box 11.11

The Hidden Cost of Not Discussing Death with Loved Ones: The Issue of Donating Organs

One major medical advance of the 20th century was development of the ability of doctors to transplant organs, including kidneys, livers, lungs, and hearts, from one person to another (Dowie, 1988; Fox & Swazey, 1992). Although organ transplantation has allowed many people who have malfunctioning organs to live, the number of people who need organs is consistently much, much higher than the number of organs available for donation. As shown in Table 11.4, many people are waiting for organs. And 11 to 12 people who are on a waiting list die each day, before an organ becomes available. Although in some cases living people can donate an organ, such as a kidney (because we have two), or a portion of an organ, such as a piece of the liver, in most cases organ donations come from people who have died. However, many people who could donate organs choose not to, which is one reason why the waiting list for organ transplants is so long. Why would someone's family not choose to donate their loved one's organs? In many cases family members simply do not know the loved one's preferences and therefore choose not to donate. If you would like your organs to be donated at the time of your death, make your wishes known to people who are close to you—parents, siblings, and close friends.

TABLE 11.4   *Number of People on a Waiting List for Organ Transplants*

Age Range	Kidney	Liver	Heart	Lung
Age 0–5	92	384	134	16
Age 6–10	110	182	44	37
Age 11–17	446	288	89	144
Age 18–49	22,684	5,428	1,338	1,566
Age 50–64	15,132	4,867	2,283	1,333
Age 65+	3,900	907	297	69

Many people die each year while waiting for an organ transplant.

Source: www.organdonor.gov.

example, we use euphemisms for death (e.g., she passed away, he kicked the bucket, she bought the farm), delay making wills, and put off discussions of how we'd like to be buried. In fact, one study of high school seniors found that death was never talked about in 39% of the families, and only briefly and when "absolutely necessary" in another 26% (Stillion & Wass, 1984). However, children are naturally curious about virtually everything, and their questions about death simply represent a normal part of their development (even if these questions are difficult to answer).

Many children's earliest experience with death comes through the death of a pet. Although adults may be reluctant to discuss death with children, the death of a pet can serve as a valuable learning opportunity (Wass & Stillion, 1988). When my older son was 2½ years old, one of our cats died suddenly. After telling Andrew about the cat's death, we were barraged for months with questions about death—where is Huckleberry now? Will I die? Will you die? When will I die? Will I be scared? When will he feel better? When will he come back? Answering these questions was hard, but important because they let Andrew know that it was OK to talk about death—that death is not a "taboo topic."

Much of our knowledge about how children understand death comes from a series of studies conducted by Maria Nagy (1948) in Budapest, Hungary, in the 1930s. She interviewed 378 children (ages 3 to 10) and asked them write down their thoughts about death (for the older children) and to make drawings about death (for the younger children). She also held discussions with the children to get them to talk about their feelings and thoughts about death. This work revealed that children's understanding of death evolves as they reach greater maturity and are better able to use logical as well as abstract cognitive reasoning.

First, very young children (ages 3 to 5 years) think about death in terms of separation and as something gradual and temporary, like sleeping. They may believe that someone who is dead can return to life, or that a person who is dead is just living elsewhere, as if they've moved away. In turn, they may want to know where the person is and how he or she got there. Although they may be saddened by death, as they would be by any significant separation from a loved one, they do not yet understand its finality or that it happens to everyone.

During the second stage, which starts around 5 or 6 years and lasts through about age 8, children begin to understand that death is permanent, irreversible, and final (Nagy, 1948; Stillion & Wass, 1984). However, children at this stage may still believe that death can be eluded, if one is tricky or lucky—death only happens to some people, namely, those who are bad or unlucky. In this stage, death may also be perceived as a separate person (e.g., a skeleton, a ghost, the Grim Reaper), with the idea that you can avoid this person and thereby avoid dying. Death is therefore not viewed as universal, personal, or inevitable.

By around ages 9 and 10 years, children have a view of death that is similar to that of adults; they know that everyone will die and that death is permanent (Nagy, 1948; Stillion & Wass, 1984). Children of this age can think abstractly, and they understand that death is inevitable, final, and universal.

Although Nagy's research was the first to examine how children understand death, more recent research has replicated her general findings (Speece & Brent, 1996). Mark Speece and Sandor Brent (1996), for example, have conducted their own work on how children think about death, and their research suggests that by age 7, most children understand what they term the four key bioscientific components. These are universality (all living things die),

PHOTO 11.5   Parents should use naturally occurring events to talk to their children about death and should give accurate information at a level the child can understand. They should not tell children that a dead person is simply asleep.

irreversibility (things that are dead cannot be brought back to life), nonfunctionality (death involves the complete cessation of all functions and capabilities), and causality (external and internal forces can bring about death).

So, how should parents handle the topic of death with their children? First, parents must be sensitive to children's concerns about dying, and should be available to talk as the need arises (Stillion & Wass, 1984). Naturally occurring events, such as seeing a dead bird in the woods or a dead fish in an aquarium, can provide a good opportunity for parents to talk casually about death (see Photo 11.5). Parents also should be prepared to provide children with accurate information in a simple and direct way. Saying, "Grandpa has died" is better than saying, "Grandpa has gone to live with the angels" or "Grandpa is sleeping."

Lingering Issues

Should people be allowed to choose when to die? Proponents of assisted suicide believe that people who are in severe pain and who are terminally ill should have the right to end their suffering (see Box 11.12; Kastenbaum, 1999; Sears

& Stanton, 2001). They may fear losing physical and mental functioning and may fear living in an institution, particularly if they have suffered through the loss of a spouse or other caretaker. For example, in January 2002, Joan and Chester Nimitz Jr., a couple in their late 80s who lived outside Boston, chose to end their lives by taking pills (Quindlen, 2002). Chester Nimitz was suffering from congestive heart failure, constant back pain, and severe stomach problems, and Joan was blind, suffered repetitive broken bones because of severe osteoporosis, and needed round-the-clock care. They left a note in the apartment that said, "Do not dial 911 in the event we are discovered unconscious but still alive. We wish our friends and relatives to know we are leaving their company in a peaceful frame of mind." Over 60% of Americans believe people with a terminal illness should have the right to physician-assisted suicide (Blendon, Szalay, & Know, 1992). In 1994, Oregon became the first (and thus far, only) state to pass a law allowing physician-assisted suicide, meaning that physicians can, at a patient's request, provide a lethal dose of medicine. This type of suicide allows patients to die in a peaceful and nonviolent way and is a much less painful and faster way to die than simply refusing medical treatments (e.g., food, water, antibiotics).

Box 11.12

The Case of Dr. Kevorkian

Dr. Jack Kevorkian, a retired pathologist, received much media attention in the 1990s for his involvement in the deaths of over 100 people (see Photo 11.6). He believed that people should have the right to end their own lives, and he publicly announced his intention to help people do so. Dr. Kevorkian provided assistance to people, including creating a "suicide machine" that allowed severely disabled people to administer lethal drugs to themselves and giving people specific instructions on how to bring about their own deaths. Although he was brought to trial several times for these activities, prosecutors were consistently unable to convict Dr. Kevorkian of any crimes.

However, on September 17, 1998, Dr. Kevorkian videotaped his direct involvement in a death. A man, 52-year-old Thomas Youk, was suffering from Lou Gehrig's disease and actively sought Dr. Kevorkian's help in ending his life. The videotape, which clearly shows Dr. Kevorkian injecting Mr. Youk with two chemicals that caused his death, was shown on the television show *60 Minutes* in November 1998. Shortly thereafter, Dr. Kevorkian was charged with murder by a prosecutor in Michigan. He was found guilty of second-degree murder in March 1999 and is currently serving a 10 to 25 year jail term for murder. Dr. Kevorkian is, however, appealing these charges.

PHOTO 11.6   Jack Kevorkian, also known as "Dr. Death," was involved in the assisted-suicide deaths of over 100 people in the 1990s. He is currently in prison for these crimes, although he is appealing his sentence.

On the other hand, opponents of assisted suicide vehemently believe that this "solution" is wrong for several reasons (Kastenbaum, 1999). First, given the many errors in diagnosis and the advancement in medical treatment, some people may wrongly make the decision to end their lives. Opponents believe that the moral issues associated with assisted suicide, including violation of the physician's oath "first, do no harm" and the potential for this procedure to be used wrongly should make assisted suicide illegal. Also, terminally ill people who want to die often suffer from clinical depression and/or inadequate pain relief. For example, one recent study conducted in Canada found that 58.8% of patients who wanted to die were depressed, as compared to only 7.7% of those who did not want to die (Chocinov et al., 1995). Similarly, while 76.5% of those in moderate or greater pain wanted to die, only 46.2% of those who did not want to die were in such severe pain. In turn, treating depression and managing pain could be a more effective approach than helping people die.

How effective are "living wills"? Advance care directives, or living wills, allow people to specify their wishes about the type of care they would like to receive in the event they are incapacitated and therefore unable to make their own decisions (see Box 11.3; Kastenbaum, 1999). As shown in Figure 11.4, living wills provide very clear instructions to family members, friends, and medical personnel. For example, a person may request to not be tube-fed while in a coma if there is no chance of emerging from that state. The person also designates a particular person to make medical decisions for him or her, and in particular to make sure the wishes expressed in the living will are followed (although Box 11.14 describes some limits of this approach). The use of living wills therefore allows people to express their medical directives in advance of having an illness; thus, they are able to maintain control over their lives even when they have lost the ability to speak for themselves (see Cartoon 11.1).

Box 11.13

Health Psychology in the Real World—A Tattoo in Time

Seventy-one may seem an odd age at which to get your first tattoo, especially for a woman. Just about the only reason I haven't gone ahead and had it done is I haven't quite figured out the wording. It will read something like this: Do Not Resuscitate. And I'll have it written right across my chest.

I've always enjoyed good health, despite a mastectomy 15 years ago. But I do have a genuine fear of becoming incapacitated by a serious accident or illness. For me, the fear has not so much to do with dying but with remaining alive and dependent on others for my care. I've always been fiercely independent—my hair has never been touched by a hairdresser, for instance. My family knows that when I die, I want to be cremated. No one could ever apply my makeup the way I do, and I'm not about to be dolled up by some undertaker. My husband attributes my idiosyncrasies to a stubborn Swedish heritage.

Maybe I am a bit peculiar. And I do admit to a touch of crotchetiness. But as far "Do Not Resuscitate" goes, I'm deadly serious.

The legal and medical communities have several systems in place that recognize my right to refuse extreme measures to keep me alive, should it come to that. Still, I remain skeptical. What if I am treated by a doctor who believes it is a physician's responsibility to apply all the heroic efforts available, despite the patient's wishes? What if my paperwork gets lost? What if my paperwork is exactly where it is supposed to be, but no one stumbles across it until after I've been resuscitated, and my oblivious body is kept alive by life support?

I don't want my children to have to make the decision to "pull the plug" on Mom. I've lived a wonderful life. I'd prefer, when the time comes, to have a wonderful death, as well.

So what to do? It occurred to me that a tattoo right across my chest would be impossible to lose or ignore. (As an artist, I truly believe a visual display is worth a thousand words.) The idea, which at first was simply a flippant remark I tossed out to amuse my painting group, has merit. Think about it: The first thing they do to you in most emergency situations is rip your shirt open to attach monitors and other gizmos of the trade. Who could miss my message?

Determined I may be, but even I cringe at the thought of all those letters being pricked a dot at a time into my bony chest. Something shorter might work; the obvious abbreviation is DNR. But that could lead to other problems. Suppose something happens to me while we're visiting our daughter in Michigan, a state where DNR stands for the Department of Natural Resources. Might I be mistaken for property of the state, just another road kill that ended up in a hospital's emergency room?

(continues)

No, a shortened tattoo would leave too much to chance. As the notion continues to swirl in my mind, I envision a network much like Medic Alert. A tattoo, backed by the Do Not Resuscitate Society, should convince even the most reluctant rescue worker that I'm serious about this.

Seeing the letters, emergency-room personnel would know to contact the society at 1-800-HEYU-DNR. That call would confirm my membership and even elicit my degree of commitment:

Level 5: I really don't mean this, but I want to impress my friends with how urbane I am. Please do absolutely everything you can to revive me.

Level 4: If I probably won't die, but can be expected to live a compromised, dependent, yet relatively pain-free life, please do what you can to keep me around awhile longer.

Level 3: If it looks like I'm going to be dead by this time tomorrow, and that those next 24 hours will be extremely painful, go ahead and let me die peacefully right now.

Level 2: I mean it. If I'm going to be a vegetable, or what I define as a burden to my family, let's get this over with right now.

Level 1: Not only do I mean everything I said in Level 2, but while we're at it please help yourself to any of my usable organs so that others may enjoy a rich, full life.

"Yes, Ma'am, Mrs. Juhl is a DNR subscriber, Level 1. She asks that you please make every attempt to summon her family so they can say their goodbyes before you allow her to die with dignity."

Some people will no doublt be offended by this idea, and to them I say: Go soak your head. I don't care what you think. This is *my* life I'm talking about, and I'll decide how I want to live it.

It all boils down to mortality. If you have ever been diagnosed with a life-threatening disease, you know the issue of mortality looms large. If you're lucky, as I was, the outcome will be positive and you'll return to good health. But then, before you know it, you're 70. Suddenly, once again, you come face to face with mortality.

While I may feel decades younger, the fact is I'm in my "golden years." Although I certainly have no interest in seeing my life end any time soon, I need to be realistic. So this is far from a death wish. If anything, it's a *life* wish.

I've always been an idea person, and my family generally offers only a pat on the head ("good dog") when I try to work up some enthusiastic support for my latest brainstorm. I'm taken seriously much less often than I should be—and that's too bad, because I've had some darn good ideas. My friends, though, think I might be on to something with this one.

Yes, you say, but history is full of people who get tattoos and live to regret them. Wouldn't something like this be irrevocable? What if you change your mind? Easy enough. Society membership would include a coupon for a free, second tattoo. It would be the universal symbol for "Do Not"—a bright red circle with a slash mark across it. Have it applied right over the top of the old tattoo, and you're back among the living.

Living as well as I can is what I intend to do until it's time for me to go to my reward.

Source: Haglund Juhl, Marian. (1997, October 13). A tattoo in time. *Newsweek,* 19.

Values History Statement

Please use this section as a guide to my values when considering the likely result of treatment.

Circle the number on the scale of 1 to 5 that most closely indicates your feelings about each of the situations described.	Much Worse Than Death: I Would Definitely Not Want Life-Sustaining Treatment	Somewhat Worse Than Death: I Would Probably Not Want Life-Sustaining Treatment	Neither Better nor Worse Than Death: I'm Not Sure Whether I Want Life-Sustaining Treatment	Somewhat Better Than Death: I Would Probably Want Life-Sustaining Treatment	Much Better Than Death: I Would Definitely Want Life-Sustaining Treatment
(a) Permanently paralyzed. You are unable to walk but can move around in a wheelchair. You can talk and interact with other people.	1	2	3	4	5
(b) Permanently unable to speak meaningfully. You are unable to speak to others. You can walk on your own, feed yourself, and take care of daily needs such as bathing and dressing yourself.	1	2	3	4	5
(c) Permanently unable to care for yourself. You are bedridden, unable to wash, feed, or dress yourself. You are totally cared for by others.	1	2	3	4	5
(d) Permanently in pain. You are in severe bodily pain that cannot be totally controlled or completely eliminated by medications.	1	2	3	4	5
(e) Permanently mildly demented. You often cannot remember things, such as where you are, nor reason clearly. You are capable of speaking of speaking, but not capable of remembering the conversations; you are capable of washing, feeding, and dressing yourself and are in no pain.	1	2	3	4	5
(f) Being in a short-term coma. You have suffered brain damage and are not conscious and are not aware of your environment in any way. You cannot feel pain. You are cared for by others. These mental impairments may be reversed in about 1 week, leaving mild forgetfulness and loss of memory as a consequence.	1	2	3	4	5

SIGNATURE OF DECLARANT

Name (print clearly) . . . .   **Day/Month/Year** . . . .

Address . . . .

. . . .   **Date of Birth★** . . . .

★If you are under 18 years of age, you may still complete this document, though it may not have the same legal force.

WITNESS'S SIGNATURE: I declare that the above-named has signed this document in my presence. He/she has declared it to be his/her firm will, is in full capacity, and fully understands the meaning of it. I believe it to be a firm and competent statement of his/her wishes. As far as I am aware, no pressure has been brought to bear on him/her to sign such a document and I believe it to be his/her own free and considered wish. So far as I am aware, I do not stand to gain from his/her death.

Signed (Witness): . . . .   Name . . . .

Address . . . .

FIGURE 11.4   This is a sample living will. If you would like to register your own living will go to www.uslivingwillregistry.com.

"My goal is to die before there's a technology breakthrough
that forces me to live to a hundred and thirty."

CARTOON 11.1   Although this cartoon is humorous, it reflects a very real concern of some older adults, namely being kept alive by machines. (©The New Yorker Collection 2000. Barbara Smaller from cartoonbank.com. All Rights reserved.)

One problem with advance directives is that they cannot possibly provide guidance for all future medical possibilities. As an alternative, Peter Ditto at Kent State University suggests that people instead complete lists of "valued life activities," and then use these activities as a guide to determining whether or not to end someone's life (Ditto, Druley, Moore, Danks, & Smucker, 1996). For example, some people would choose to sustain their lives if they could still speak and think, even if they could not move (e.g., following a paralyzing physical injury); others might choose to end their lives if they could no longer recognize family and friends (e.g., following Alzheimer's disease). These decisions are obviously very personal. Studies with both college students and elderly adults reveal that people's beliefs about whether various health impairments, such as being unable to communicate, being blind and deaf, and being confined to bed, would interfere with their ability to engage in valued life activities influence their preference for death. In other words, the more each disability is seen as interfering with their engagement in their most valued life activities, the more they would prefer death.

Box 11.14

Research Focus—Would You Know What Your Loved One Wanted?

Angela Fagerlin and her colleagues (2001) conducted a series of studies to examine how good people were at predicting what type of end-of-life treatment their loved ones would prefer. People are often called upon to make treatment decisions when a person is severely incapacitated, such as when the person is in a coma or has Alzheimer's disease. However, we just don't know if people make the decisions that the patient would prefer. To examine this issue, students and one of their parents participated in a 15- to 30-minute discussion regarding the type of treatment they would prefer in various situations. Both parents and students then separately completed a questionnaire, which assessed the type of treatment they would want in various hypothetical situations. Students were also asked to predict what they thought their parents would want in each situation.

Students were not very effective at guessing the preferences of their parents. Students tended to predict their parents would want more treatment than the parents actually did prefer. Specifically, students often predicted that their parents would want a treatment, such as being placed on a respirator or given food and water even when in a coma, which their parents actually reported not wanting. This lack of accuracy is particularly interesting because the parents and students had very recently discussed the parents' preferences for end-of-life treatment! Moreover, students' predictions typically corresponded with their own preferences more than the actual preferences of their parents. Although this study was conducted entirely with a college student sample, in a follow-up study the researchers examined accuracy in making end-of-life treatment decisions in a sample of adults who were 65 years old or older and a person they specifically chose as the one they wanted to make medical decisions for them in case they were incapacitated. This study revealed very similar findings—people tended to assume the person would want more life-saving treatment than the person actually did and again projected their own treatment preferences onto those of their loved one.

Thought Questions

1. Your roommate's sister just died in a car accident. What are three things you could say to her that would be helpful during this difficult time?

2. Describe the five stages of death and dying, according to Dr. Elizabeth Kubler-Ross, and two critiques of this theory.

3. What are the psychological, social, and physical consequences of bereavement?

4. Your 9-year-old child asks you why her great-grandmother has died, and where she is now. What do you say?

5. What are the pros and cons of dying in a hospital versus dying in a hospice care facility? Which place of death would you prefer and why?

Answers to Questioning the Research

Answer 11.1: People who are able to find meaning in the death of a loved one may actually be different from those who cannot, and these differences may explain the different rates of longevity between these two groups. One possibility is that people who find meaning in such a death are generally more optimistic by nature, and in turn, research shows that optimism is associated with better physical health and a longer life expectancy. Another possibility is that people who find meaning in the death of a loved one have more social support. The presence of this support, in turn, may help them see the positive side even of such a tragedy.

Answer 11.2: Although most research has focused on the impact of the death of a spouse, it is likely that people would experience similar reactions to the death of any person with whom their were intimately involved, regardless of whether they were legally married. Anyone who experiences the death of a partner who is the most important person in his or her life clearly must cope with considerable grief and bereavement. In fact, grief can be greater when a person has lost someone who is not formally recognized by others as an important part of his or her life (Berado, 1988). This type of bereavement is called *disenfranchised grief*, and may be experienced by people who live together but who are not married.

CHAPTER **12**

Health Care Interaction: Screening, Utilization, Adherence, and Relapse

- Charlene was in the shower yesterday washing her hair when she felt a small lump in her neck. It was not painful and was quite small—just about the size of a pea. Charlene wondered what she should do about it and called her sister to ask for advice. Her sister recommended she see a doctor right away, but Charlene is really busy at work this week, so she decided to wait until things settle down at the office to then see a doctor.

- Peter is a 19-year-old college student and is concerned that he has an STD. He has developed a slight discharge from his penis and feels a strong burning sensation whenever he urinates. When he goes to see a doctor at the student health center, however, he is shocked to learn that the doctor is female. When she asks him to describe his problem, he suddenly loses his nerve and complains about a recurring backache.

- Bill is 62 years old and in very good health. He had his annual physical last week and passed with flying colors. His doctor did, however, suggest that he

469

make an appointment for a colonoscopy to check for signs of colon cancer. Although this procedure is recommended for all people over age 50 years, Bill just sees no need for it. He feels fine and generally eats a healthy diet—and he certainly has no interest in undergoing such an embarrassing and awkward procedure. However, his doctor seemed to feel strongly that having this test was important, and Bill therefore plans to have it done.

- Larry is 58 years old and has suffered from hypertension, or high blood pressure, for the last 10 years. He is supposed to take medication daily to lower his blood pressure, but he frequently forgets. Although Larry knows the medication is probably good for him, he really doesn't feel any different whether he takes it or not; hence, he wonders if it is doing anything to actually help him. Plus, the medication is relatively expensive, the cost is not covered by his health insurance, and many of the side effects, including dizziness, diarrhea, muscle weakness, and frequent urination, are irritating.

- Sarah is 25 years old and has had a problem with alcohol since high school. She often finds it just impossible to wake up to go to work on the mornings after she's passed out from drinking late the night before, and she has been warned by her boss that she will be fired if she is late again. To try to stop drinking, Sarah has started working with a therapist. The therapist has asked her to make a list of the situations that prompt her to drink and the alternative ways she could handle these situations.

Preview

This chapter examines how psychological factors influence individuals' willingness to seek and follow health care recommendations. First, we examine issues involved in screening for health care problems, including the predictors of screening, the benefits and costs of screening, and strategies for increasing screening. Next, we examine psychological factors that influence when people seek medical care, how they interact with their health care provider, and the experience of hospitalization. We then examine issues in adherence to health care regimens, including causes of nonadherence, measuring adherence, and increasing adherence. Finally, we examine issues in relapse, including theories of relapse, the influence of psychological factors on relapse, and strategies for preventing relapse.

What Is Screening?

Screening to detect illness, or even an increased likelihood of developing illness, at an early stage is an increasingly important part of health promotion (see Table 12.1). Screening behaviors, such as having your teeth cleaned to check

TABLE 12.1   *Screening Tests Available Today*

Diagnostic Testing: This type of testing shows whether a person has a given disease.

   Neurofibromatosis

   Marfan syndrome

   Achondroplasia

Presymptomatic Testing: This type of testing shows whether a person is going to develop a given disease.

   Huntington's disease

   Hypercholesterolemia

   Kidney disease

Predisposition Testing: This type of testing shows whether a person has a genetic predisposition to a given disease, but not whether he or she will definitely develop the disease.

   Breast cancer

   Colon cancer

   Alzheimer's disease

Carrier Status Testing: This type of testing shows whether a person carries a gene for a given disease and hence could pass it on to his or her children.

   Tay-Sachs disease

   Cystic fibrosis

   Sickle-cell anemia

   Duchenne muscular dystrophy

Prenatal Testing: This type of testing shows whether a fetus has a given disease

   Muscular dystrophy

   Down's syndrome

for cavities, getting your blood pressure checked during a physical exam, and checking your breasts or testicles for signs of cancer, are secondary prevention strategies. In other words, while they do not prevent health problems from developing, by detecting a treatable disease or abnormality in its early stages, screening may enable the individual's life to be prolonged or enhanced (Harris, 1992). For example, every 40,000 cervical smears saves one life (*Lancet*, 1985), and early detection of breast and colon cancer can reduce cancer mortality as much as 30% (Kerlikowske, Grady, Rubin, & Sardrock, 1995; Selby, Friedman, Quesenberry, & Weiss, 1992). (However, we will discuss a recent debate about the value of some types of breast cancer screening at the end of this chapter in the Lingering Issues section.) Similarly, testicular cancer is the leading cause of cancer deaths for men ages 20 to 34 years old, in part because many cases are not diagnosed until the cancer has spread to other areas of the body (Nicholson & Harland, 1995). Estimates are that if people followed screening recommendations, cancer deaths would drop by 25 to 40% (White, Urban, & Taylor, 1993).

Recent advances in molecular genetics, including the mapping of disorders onto particular genes, has led to the ability to test for over 200 inherited disorders (see Table 12.2; Croyle & Lerman, 1995; Lerman, 1997). In some cases this testing can determine whether a person is at risk of developing a disease. For example, genetic tests are now available for breast, ovarian, and some types of colorectal cancer, as well as Huntington's disease and Alzheimer's disease (Patenaude, Guttmacher, & Collins, 2002). In other cases genetic testing can determine whether a person carries a gene for a disorder, such as Tay-Sachs disease, cystic fibrosis, and sickle-cell anemia, which they could then transmit to their children. Couples may then use this information to determine whether they will have children or whether they might use in vitro fertilization with nongenetically related eggs or sperm to avoid passing this disease on to their children. In still other cases testing is used to evaluate whether a fetus has various genetic conditions. The vast majority of pregnant women in the United States undergo some kind of screening, such as blood tests, ultrasound, and amnioscentesis, to help evaluate the health of the fetus. Based on the results, couples can then decide to continue the pregnancy or to terminate it in cases in which the baby would not survive more than a few days or would suffer extreme, and possibly life-threatening, disability. Genetic screening will increase as more genetic tests are developed.

This section examines three topics involving screening. First, we examine the predictors of screening, including demographic factors and personality

TABLE 12.2   *When Should You Screen and for What?*

Early Cancer Detection for Men and Women

- Colorectal cancer: Yearly fecal occult blood test plus flexible sigmoidoscopy every 5 years starting at age 50; double contrast barium enema every 5 years starting at age 50; colonoscopy every 10 years starting at age 50

- Skin cancer: Skin exam every 3 years for those ages 20 to 40; skin exam every year for those over age 40

Early Cancer Detection for Men

- Prostate cancer: Yearly PSA blood test and digital rectal exam starting at age 50 or age 45 for those who are at high risk (African American, father or brother with prostate cancer at a young age)

Early Cancer Detection for Women

- Cervical cancer: Yearly pelvic exam with Pap test starting at age 18 or when sexually active (whichever is earlier)

- Breast cancer: Breast self-exam every month starting at age 20; clinical breast exam by a health care professional every 3 years for those ages 20 to 39; yearly clinical breast exam by a health care professional and yearly mammogram for those age 40 and over

These recommendations for screening were developed by the American Cancer Society—how many of them do you follow?

variables that influence screening as well as physician recommendations. We then examine the costs and benefits of screening, such as the ability to seek early treatment and make appropriate plans, as well as the creation of considerable anxiety and the potential for inaccurate results. Finally, we examine strategies for increasing screening, including educating people about its benefits, providing reminders, and removing barriers.

The Predictors of Screening

Demographic factors, including income and education, influence screening behavior (Jepson & Rimer, 1993; Manne et al., 2002). For example, one study found that 32% of those with only some high school education or less got screened for colorectal cancer, as compared to 78% of those with a graduate school degree (Manne et al., 2002). People who lack health insurance are, not surprisingly, less likely to have regular breast and cervical screening than those with such coverage (Rimer, Meissner, Breen, Legler, & Coyne, 2001).

Individual differences, such as self-efficacy, perceived vulnerability, and costs and benefits of screening, also influence who screens (see Table 12.3; Shiloh, Ben-Sinai, & Keinan, 1999). People who are conscientious and high in self-efficacy for carrying out screening behavior are more likely to have mammograms (Christensen & Smith, 1995; Siegler, Feaganes, & Rimer, 1995). People who see more benefits of screening (e.g., it can lead to longer life expectancy) as well as those who see fewer costs (e.g., saves money, saves time, increases safety) are more likely to screen (Aiken, West, Woodward, & Reno, 1994; Manne et al., 2002; McCaul, Branstetter, Schroeder, & Glasgow, 1996; Shepperd, Solomon,

TABLE 12.3 *Test Yourself: The Pros and Cons of Colorectal Cancer Screening*

1. Colon cancer tests can find growths that are not yet cancerous but that could become cancer.
2. Having colon cancer tests regularly would give me good peace of mind about my health.
3. Regular colon cancer tests will help me to live a long life.
4. Having colon cancer tests will help me avoid having a more serious cancer.
5. Colon cancer tests are a part of good health care.
6. Having a colon cancer test is very embarrassing.
7. I cannot afford to have a colon cancer test.
8. Tests for colon cancer take too much time.
9. Colon cancer tests are risky.
10. Too many things can go wrong with tests for colon cancer.

The first five items assess positive aspects of having a colon cancer test, and the next five items assess the costs or disadvantages of having a colon cancer test.

Source: Manne et al., 2002.

Atkins, Foster, & Frankowski, 1990). Some evidence suggests that women who are concerned about developing breast cancer are more likely to engage in screening behavior, such as mammograms and breast self-exam (BSE), than those with low concerns for developing the disease (Diefenbach, Miller, & Daly, 1999; McCaul, Branstetter et al., 1996; McCaul, Schroeder, & Reid, 1996). On the other hand, other research suggests that women who are at high risk for developing breast cancer, such as those with a relative who had breast cancer, are actually less likely to perform BSE and attend mammogram screenings when they are high in anxiety (Lerman, Rimer, Trock, Balshem, & Engstrom, 1990; Lerman et al., 1993). In sum, a curvilinear relationship may best predict screening:people with moderate levels of anxiety engage in more screening than those with low or high anxiety.

Practitioners' beliefs about the benefits of screening also influence screening behavior in their patients (Grady, Lemkau, McVay, & Reisine, 1992; Jepson & Rimer, 1993; Manne et al., 2002). For example, rates of HIV testing at prenatal clinics vary from 3 to 82%, and rates of mammography screening vary across communities from 22 to 70%, suggesting that practitioners' attitudes about the tests may influence how they present it as an option to patients (Bergner, Allison, Diehr, Ford, & Feigl, 1990; Meadows, Jenkinson, Catalan, & Gazzard, 1990). Women with physician referrals for screening are more likely to have both clinical breast exams and mammograms. Similarly, one study found that 89% of those with a doctor recommendation got screened for colorectal cancer, as compared to only 44% of those without such a recommendation (Manne et al., 2002). As I described at the beginning of this chapter, Bill's decision to have a colonoscopy was largely a result of his doctor's strong recommendation.

The Costs and Benefits of Screening

Proponents of screening argue that this type of knowledge may help a person seek early treatment and/or engage in health-promoting behaviors (Baum, Friedman, & Zakowski, 1997; Patenaude et al., 2002). Learning he or she has high blood pressure or elevated levels of cholesterol, for example, could motivate that person to make changes in diet or increase his or her rate of exercise in an attempt to prevent developing heart disease. Similarly, some women who find out they have a genetic predisposition to breast cancer make the decision to take the drug Tamoxifen to prevent breast cancer or they even undergo a mastectomy to avoid developing breast cancer completely (Hartmann et al., 1999; Meijers-Heijboer et al., 2001). One study found that 68% of women who learned they had the breast cancer gene had had a mammogram 1 year later as compared to 44% of those who learned they did not have this gene (Lerman et al., 2000). In line with this view, people who learn they are HIV-positive often engage in better physical and psychological care for themselves and appear motivated to not spread this disease to others (Coates, Morin, & McKuskick, 1987; Coates et al., 1988; Collins et al., 2001). Knowledge about one's genetic risk of developing a particular disease may also help people make realistic plans for their future. If they are aware that they are likely to develop Alzheimer's disease, for example, they may choose to not start a family or to start a family early. They could choose to forego a career that involves many years of education. Moreover, in the case of diseases that progress over time, patients could be more vigilant for symptoms of the disease and could seek more regular health care. For example, a woman with a genetic predisposition to breast cancer could perform BSE diligently and have very frequent mammograms in an effort to catch signs at a very early stage. Finally, knowing about genetic predisposition to a given disease can provide some peace of mind, especially for those who are already concerned they will develop such a disorder, perhaps based on family history, but who do not know for sure (Baum et al., 1997).

Despite the benefits of screening, this type of early detection also comes with significant potential costs. Individuals can experience psychological harm from a positive result (Marteau, Dundas, & Axworthy, 1997; Meissen et al., 1988; Tibben, Timman, Bannink, & Duivenvoorden, 1997). For example, people who test positive for Huntington's disease—a progressive inherited disease that involves motor disability; a disturbance of affect, behavior, and personality; cognitive impairment; and eventually death—typically experience considerable anxiety, fear, and even depression. One study found that 33% of subjects reported they would consider suicide if they learned they tested positive for this disease (Bloch, Fahy, Fox, & Hayden, 1989). Another study found that 48% of the men who were tested for HIV but then chose to not learn the results reported that getting a positive result would be too upsetting, and 31% believed they would be "unable to cope" with this information (Lyter, Valdiserri, Kingsley, Amoroso, & Rinaldo, 1987). Because most people who learn that they are at risk of developing a serious illness experience negative reactions at least initially, crisis intervention should be available immediately to help people deal with anxiety and fear and work through issues related to stigma, sexuality, and intimacy. These responses are particularly severe when the diagnosis is unexpected (see Figure 12.1; Croyle, Smith, Botkin, Baty, & Nash, 1997). These symptoms are generally high in the weeks immediately after a person learns the test results, but lessen or even disappear entirely over the next few years (Jemmott, Sanderson, & Miller, 1995; Wiggins et al., 1992). Another study revealed that 44% of people who learned they were carriers for cystic fibrosis reported having troubling thoughts even as long as 3 years after receiving the test results (Marteau et al., 1997). Moreover, people who don't know their risk status, either because their test results were inconclusive or they

---

Questioning the Research 12.1

Although all of these studies suggest that people who learn they have a positive result experience higher rates of depression initially, and then return to normal levels later on, can you think of a limitation of this research? (Hint: Who chooses to get tested?)

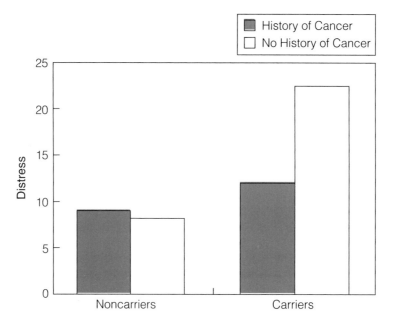

FIGURE 12.1   This study examined the psychological effects of getting tested for BRCA1, the test for breast and ovarian cancer. Carriers showed higher levels of distress, and this was particularly true for those who had never experienced cancer or cancer-related surgery, presumably because of the "surprise" element of the result (data from Croyle et al., 1997).

chose to not learn the results, experience more anxiety and depression than those who learn they have a positive result (Wiggins et al., 1992).

Although many people choose to undergo screening, especially for genetic disorders, in an attempt to reduce the anxiety of "not knowing," screening tests do not eliminate uncertainty (Lerman, 1997). The tests for breast, ovarian, and colon cancer, as well as Alzheimer's disease, all measure whether a person has an increased likelihood of developing the disease, but do not predict whether a person will definitely get the disease. For example, for women who have a known genetic mutation, such *BRCA1 (breast cancer gene 1)* and/or *BRAC2 (breast cancer gene 2)*, the risk of developing breast cancer is between 56 and 85%, and the risk of ovarian cancer is between 20 and 60% (Patenaude et al., 2002). In these cases additional genetic factors or environmental factors or both will determine whether the person develops the disease. Moreover, even in cases in which genetic testing reveals that the person will certainly develop the disease, it will not provide information about exactly when such symptoms will develop or about how the disease will progress. And because some types of diseases have no treatment (e.g., Huntington's disease), early detection only increases the amount of time the person knows about the problem before he or she begins to experience any symptoms (Wiggins et al., 1992).

When the results of a screening test indicate that a person does not have a particular disease, it can give a person peace of mind, a psychological benefit, but individuals can also experience psychological harm from a negative test result (Huggins et al., 1992; Lynch & Watson, 1992). A negative result may make people more comfortable with not getting screened again, perhaps because it decreases their feelings of vulnerability, or not taking adequate precautions (e.g., "I haven't gotten AIDS thus far, so why worry about condoms now?"). One study with patients at an urban STD clinic found that rates of gonorrhea decreased 29% six months after testing for those with a positive result, but increased 106% for those who tested negative (Otten, Zaidi, Wroten, Witte, & Peterman, 1993). In other cases people still feel susceptible to the disease, so receiving a negative test result does not even reduce uncertainty or distress (e.g., "I just haven't gotten AIDS yet"). Receiving a negative test result can also make people feel guilty, especially if others in their family have tested positive (Biesecker et al., 1993). They may wonder why they were spared and feel guilty about showing their relief.

One of the most significant problems with screening is the possibility of receiving an inaccurate result, which can lead to substantial psychological and even physical consequences (Lerman & Rimer, 1995). Even a test that is 99% accurate, such as the ELISA or Western Blot tests used to determine HIV, will produce 1% false positives, meaning that in 1 of every 100 cases, the test will indicate a person has the disease, but the person really does not (Sloand, Pitt, Chiarello, & Nemo, 1991). A false positive obviously can lead to psychological distress and anxiety, which in some cases may be maintained even after the patient receives accurate results (McCormick, 1989; Skrabanek, 1988). For example, one study found that 29% of women who received false-positive results from their mammogram continued to experience moderate anxiety even 18 months later as compared to 13% of those who received a negative result (Gram, Lund, & Slenker, 1990). A false positive can also lead to unwarranted medical procedures, including surgery. In some cases, receiving a false-positive result can lead to tragic consequences—a woman who is told her fetus has life-threatening abnormalities could choose to have an abortion, for instance. On the other hand, people who receive false-negative results, meaning the person has the disease but the test shows he or she doesn't, can experience a false sense of security (e.g., comfort with practicing unsafe sex). Receiving a false-negative test result also deprives the person of the opportunity to start treatment, a delay that can have devastating consequences in the case of illnesses such as cancer.

Finally, some of the techniques used to screen people for medical conditions can actually cause physical harm (Simon, 1977; Henifin, 1993). For example, the use of mammography to detect breast cancer exposes women to radiation, which is itself linked to cancer. Amniocentesis, a procedure in which fluid is drawn from the sack surrounding a fetus to test for abnormalities, causes miscarriage in between 1 and 200 and 1 and 400 cases (see Photos 12.1 and 12.2). Similarly, *chorionic villus sampling*, another type of prenatal testing, which can be done at 9 to 12 weeks of pregnancy, leads to miscarriage in 1 in 100 cases. Given these consequences, health professionals generally recommend that people undergo screening in only cases in which the risk of the disorder is greater than the risk of experiencing a negative outcome of the test. For example, it is recommended that women over age 35 years, who are at increased risk

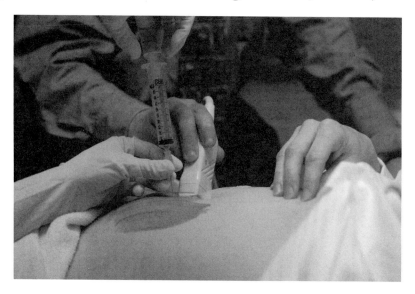

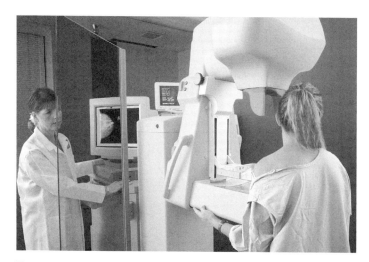

PHOTOS 12.1 AND 12.2   Although screening tests can save lives, they also can cause physical harm, including increasing the risk of miscarriage in the case of amniocentesis and exposing people to radiation in the case of mammograms and X rays.

of having a baby with Down's syndrome, undergo amniocentesis, but this procedure is not generally recommended for younger women (Henifen, 1993).

Strategies for Increasing Screening

Although screening can have significant benefits, many people do not follow screening recommendations (Kornguth, Keefe, & Conaway, 1996; National Center for Health Statistics, 2003; Newcomb et al., 1991; Shepperd et al.,

1990; Stevens, Hatcher, & Bruce, 1994). For example, the current guidelines from the American Cancer Society state that women should engage in a monthly breast self-exam, have a yearly clinical breast exam, and have a yearly mammogram starting at age 40. However, only 25 to 30% of women report performing BSE monthly, only one-third of women report having had a clinical breast exam in the last year, and only 63% report having had a clinical exam in the last 3 years (Newcomb et al., 1991; Shepperd et al., 1990). Similarly, only 38% of women ages 50 years or older have ever had a mammogram, and only 44% of American adults ages 50 and over have had a colon cancer screening (Centers for Disease Control, 2002; Kornguth et al., 1996). So, how can we increase screening?

First, some people simply are not aware of the need to screen; hence, one way of increasing screening is simply to provide education about its benefits (Jepson & Rimer, 1993; Rimer, 1994; Rimer et al., 2001). Various interventions, including mass mailings, brochures, and mass media campaigns, have been somewhat successful in increasing screening behaviors (Rimer, 1994; Rimer et al., 2001). For example, college men who read a brochure on testicular self-exam (TSE) develop more positive attitudes and greater intentions to perform TSE (Brubaker & Wickersham, 1990). Similarly, women who receive information about the benefits of mammograms are four times as likely to have a mammogram than those who do not receive such information (Champion, 1994). In cases in which the person must actually perform the screening behavior themselves, such as in the case of BSE and TSE, people also need training in exactly how to do it (Alagna & Reddy, 1984; Jones et al., 1993; Kegeles, 1985). The media can also be a powerful way of increasing awareness about the importance of screening (see Photo 12.3). For example, when Magic Johnson announced he was HIV-positive, calls to the AIDS Hotline at the Centers for Disease Control increased from 7,372 total calls in the previous 90 days to 28,000 calls the day after his announcement (Kalichman, Kelly, Hunter, Murphy, & Tyler, 1993).

In other cases, people are aware of the need to screen, but simply forget to do so; hence, providing reminders can be an effective way of increasing screening (Craun & Deffenbacher, 1987; Mayer & Frederiksen, 1986; Strauss, Solomon, Costanza, Worden, & Foster, 1987). For example, some college campuses put instructions for breast and testicular self-exams in shower stalls in college dormitories in an effort to increase rates of screening. One study compared the rates of screening for those who were randomly assigned to one of three conditions: an educational format (provided information about breast cancer and BSE), a demonstration format (showed a demonstration of correct BSE and allowed patients to practice), and a reminder-only format (women received a monthly postcard saying "remember to practice BSE this month"; Craun & Deffenbacher, 1987). The use of the reminder was the most effective in increasing BSE frequency.

Another strategy which helps people remember to screen is asking them to form their own specific plans about the how, where, and when they will engage in screening behavior (Orbell, Hodgkins, & Sheeran, 1997; Sheeran & Orbell, 2000). Setting this type of implementation intention increases the likelihood of screening by helping people to develop specific plans for following

PHOTO 12.3   After Michael J. Fox revealed that he had Parkinson's disease, knowledge about and interest in this disease increased dramatically. Similarly, significant increases in people engaging in BSE occurred after the news that Betty Ford (wife of the former president) and Happy Rockefeller (wife of the former vice president) had breast cancer, and a significant increase in screening for colorectal cancer occurred after the news of former president Ronald Reagan's cancer.

through on their intentions. For example, Sheina Orbell and colleagues (1997) asked 188 college women about their intentions to perform BSE, and of these, half were asked to write down where and when they would complete this exam. At the 1-month follow-up, all of the women who made an implementation intention reported completing the exam as compared to 53% of those who did not form such a specific plan. Another study found that 92% of those who formed an implementation intention attended a cervical cancer screening as compared to 69% of those who did not.

Because the actual or perceived costs of screening, such as convenience, embarrassment, expense, and anxiety about pain, deter screening, removing these barriers is another effective way of increasing this type of health-promoting behavior (Aiken et al., 1994; Jepson & Rimer, 1993; Rimer et al., 2001). One study by Barbara Rimer and colleagues found that using mobile vans, similar to bloodmobiles, led to higher rates of mammograms (Rimer et al., 1992). Similarly, interventions that decrease the costs of mammography are quite effective at increasing screening, particularly among low-income people and those who do not have health insurance (Kiefe, McKay, Halevy, & Brody,

1994). For example, in one study with female patients at a health clinic for migrant workers, women who received a voucher for a free mammogram were 47 times more likely to have a mammogram than women who did not have such a voucher (Skaer, Robinson, Sclar, & Harding, 1996). Finally, because some people do not engage in screening because of fear of what they might find, it is important to try to reassure people that catching disease early is the best approach to maintaining health.

How Do Psychological Factors Influence Health Care Utilization, Interaction, and Hospitalization?

Stanislav Kasl and Sidney Cobb (1966a, 1966b) distinguish between three types of health-related behaviors. First, *health behavior* refers to behavior that is designed to promote a person's good health and prevent illness. This type of behavior could include exercising regularly, wearing a seatbelt, and getting immunizations to prevent disease. Second, *symptom* or *illness behavior* describes behavior that is directed toward determining one's health status after experiencing symptoms. This could include talking to other people—family and friends as well as health professionals—monitoring symptoms yourself, and reading about your health problem. One of the most common illness behaviors is doing nothing and just waiting to see if the symptom will go away on its own! Third, *sick-role behavior* describes behavior that is directed at helping people who are ill return to good health (Parsons, 1951, 1975). The sick role has certain perks, including receiving sympathy and care from others and being exempt from daily responsibilities, such as chores, work, and classes. However, the person who is sick also has the responsibility to try to get better, which can include seeking medical attention and following medical recommendations. In this section, we examine two major issues in illness behavior, namely, health care utilization and patient–practitioner interaction, and then we discuss one major issue in sick-role behavior: the experience of hospitalization.

Health Care Utilization

In many cases, seeking urgent care for a medical problem is very important—sometimes even a matter of life or death. For example, seeking diagnosis of cancer can make a large difference in treatment success because cancers that are caught at an early stage can be treated directly and with less-invasive prodedures, whereas cancer that has metastasized (spread to other parts of the body) is much more difficult to treat. Women with breast cancer who delay seeking help less than 3 months have an 8-year survival rate of 50% as compared to 31% survival rate for those who delay treatment 6 months or more (Neale, Tilley, & Vernon, 1986). So, what factors lead people to delay seeking medical care?

First, people vary in how quickly they notice a physical experience. Some people pay more attention to their internal states than others and, hence, are more likely to notice symptoms (Pennebaker, 1982). For example, Suzanne Miller and her colleagues (1988) distinguish between monitors, who actively think about and focus on the physical sensations they are feeling, and blunters, who tend to deny or ignore these sensations. People who are high in neuroticism or negative affect may also notice symptoms faster (as discussed in Chapter 5; Gramling, Clawson, & McDonald, 1996). Similarly, research by Len Lecci and his colleagues at the University of North Carolina at Wilmington demonstrates that people with hypochondriacal tendencies, those who are preoccupied with illness, are particularly likely both to set health-related goals and pay attention to illness-related information (Lecci & Cohen, 2002; Lecci, Karoly, Ruehlman, & Lanyon, 1996).

Situational and social factors also influence how and even whether we perceive various symptoms (Pennebaker, 1982). In fact, people who are bored with their jobs and socially isolated tend to notice symptoms more quickly, possibly because they have fewer distractions. In contrast, sometimes athletes suffer an injury during a game, but do not notice the pain until the game is over. Similarly, the messages we get from friends, family members, and health professionals influence whether we notice as well as how we interpret health symptoms. You may have ignored an odd-shaped mole on your arm, for example, but may become concerned once a friend remarks that it could be a sign of cancer.

People's expectations about the symptoms they should experience may influence how intensely, and even whether, they feel various symptoms. For example, women who believe that most women experience severe physical symptoms prior to menstruation recall experiencing more symptoms themselves than they actually do (Marvan & Cortes-Iniestra, 2001). Similarly, medical students, who study the symptoms of many serious (but rare) diseases, often come to believe that any relatively minor symptoms are a sign of more serious disorders (Mechanic, 1972). These expectations can be created very easily. In one study people who were told that the inert substance they smelled was harmful reported experiencing more irritation and health symptoms than those who were told the odor was neutral or healthful (Dalton, 1999). In some cases these expectations can even cause various physical symptoms, such as rashes, nausea, and headaches. This phenomenon is called *mass psychogenic illness* (see Box 12.1).

Even after people notice a particular symptom, they do not necessarily decide that it requires medical attention. According to the self-regulatory model of illness behavior developed by Howard Leventhal and his colleagues at Rutgers University (1980), people form *commonsense illness representations* about their symptoms, and these representations determine the steps the person must take, if any, to manage that illness First, they try to *identify* the nature of their illness as well as its *cause*, based on the symptoms they are experiencing. If you are feeling pain in your stomach, you might interpret this as a stomach flu (a relatively mild condition) or appendicitis (a quite severe condition). But we often make wrong attributions; for example, older people often

Box 12.1

Health Psychology in the Real World—The Case of Mass Psychogenic Illness

When I teach the abnormal psychology section of my Introduction to Psychology course, an amazing thing happens each semester. As I describe the various clinical disorders (e.g., depression, schizophrenia), students all of a sudden recognize these relatively rare disorders in many of the people in their lives—their parents, siblings, friends, roommates, and sometimes even themselves all have abnormal psychological diseases. (This type of reaction is sometimes called "medical student's disease" because medical students, who learn about all sorts of rare and unusual symptoms, often start diagnosing themselves with multiple disorders!) This type of reaction, namely hearing about a symptom and then suddenly seeing that symptom in everyone you know, can also lead to the phenomenon of mass psychogenic illness, in which large numbers of people, typically in a relatively small and isolated group, report experiencing particular symptoms. For example, students in a school may hear about a specific virus that is going around or a suspected case of food poison, and suddenly many will report experiencing related symptoms. This is not—well, at least not usually—just a case of students trying to get a vacation! Instead, researchers believe that drawing people's attention to a particular type of symptom leads people to engage in careful (even too careful) monitoring of their bodies and to interpret various minor symptoms, such as a headache or nausea, as caused by the suspected problem.

attribute symptoms such as tiredness and memory loss to aging, when these could be signs of disease (Leventhal & Prochaska, 1986). Cameron and colleagues (1995) found that people who experience a new and ambiguous symptom typically seek help relatively quickly, unless they are under conditions of stress, in which case they attribute the symptom to stress and delay seeking medical care. Third, they try to figure out the *time line* of the illness, or how long it will last. People who believe their illness is acute, temporary and likely to disappear soon, are more likely to drop out of treatment than those who believe their illness is chronic, ongoing and likely to continue (Meyer, Leventhal, & Gutmann, 1985). Fourth, they think about the *consequences* of their illness, including physical consequences (e.g., pain), social consequences (e.g., ability to go out with friends, play sports), and emotional consequences (e.g., loneliness, boredom). People tend to ignore symptoms that disrupt their daily lives little, but are quite motivated to seek medical care for more disruptive symptoms. Finally, people think about whether the illness can be *treated and cured* and whether such treatment needs to be given by a doctor. If they believe that seeking a doctor won't help, they may not see a doctor or follow medical recommendations.

Martin Safer and his colleagues developed a model that describes the stages people go through when deciding to get help (see Figure 12.2; Anderson, Cacioppo, & Roberts, 1995; Safer, Tharps, Jackson, & Leventhal, 1979). First, even after people experience—and notice—some type of symptoms, they often show a delay in deciding whether they are ill. This type of delay is called an *appraisal delay*. For example, you might notice a small lump under your armpit, but decide it is just a clogged gland. Even after people decide they are sick, they may delay seeking professional help. *Illness delay* refers to the time between when people acknowledge they are sick and decide that help from a professional is required. People often believe that the symptoms will go away on their own and, hence, delay seeking medical care. For example, you may have a nagging sore throat for some time, but decide that you should see a doctor only when it lasts more than a week. Even after people decide to seek medical care, they may delay making an appointment and actually going to the a professional; this is called *utilization* or *behavioral delay*. Even after people decide help is needed, they may show two distinct types of *medical delay*: delay in making an appointment (*scheduling delay*) and delay in receiving medical recommendations (*treatment delay*).

What predicts when and how long people delay? The biggest predictor of length of delay during the appraisal phase is the nature of the symptoms—delay is short when people are experiencing very strong and clear signals that there is a problem, such as severe pain and bleeding (Eifert, Hodson, Tracey, Seville, & Gunawardan, 1996; Safer et al., 1979). For example, one study found that patients who were experiencing little or no severe pain waited an average of 7.5 days before seeking medical help, whereas those who were experiencing severe pain waited an average of 2.5 days. Similarly, patients who were bleeding delayed only 1.2 days compared to 4.8 days for those who were not bleeding. People also tend to seek help quickly for symptoms that involve a "vital organ," such as the heart (Eifert et al., 1996) and when they experience new, unexpected, visible, serious/disruptive, and continuous symptoms (Prochaska, Keller, Leventhal, & Leventhal, 1987; Safer et al., 1979). On the other hand, people tend to delay seeking help for symptoms that they have had for some time (Jemmott, Croyle, & Ditto, 1988), for symptoms that others they know have (Croyle & Hunt, 1991), and for symptoms that cause little pain and disruption (Safer et al., 1979). In fact, people often delay seeking help when they have a symptom of cancer, such as a change in the color and size of a mole or a small lump under the skin, in part because cancer is not initially painful (see Box 12.2; Timko, 1987). Finally, when people experience symptoms in private body parts, such as the genitals and anus, they are less likely to seek medical care (Klonoff & Landrine, 1993). As I described at the beginning of this chapter, Peter's embarrassment about the discharge from his penis and pain during urination inhibited him from getting help for these symptoms from a doctor.

People's concern about the impact of the symptom can also influence the length of delay (Safer et al., 1979). For example, people who imagine severe

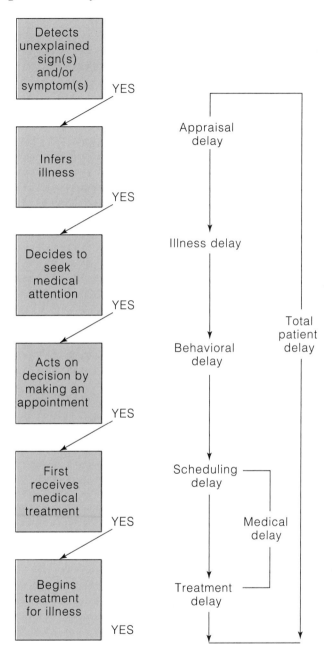

FIGURE 12.2 Even after people notice a physical symptom, they are likely to delay seeking medical attention (Anderson et al., 1995).

negative consequences of being ill (e.g., can imagine themselves on the operating room table) wait an average of 1.9 days, whereas those without such imagery delay 4.4 days. Because people don't like to experience pain, they

Box 12.2

Research Focus—What Would You Do If You Found a Lump?

Christine Timko (1987) of Yale University examined the factors that influenced whether women who noticed a lump in the breasts would promptly seek medical help. One hundred and thirty-four women between the ages of 35 and 65 years completed a questionnaire that included reading a specific medical scenario and several scales measuring attitudes and intentions about seeking medical advice. The scenario read as follows:

"One morning, Ann woke up and took a shower before getting dressed to leave the house. As Ann was showering, she happened to feel a hard, tiny thickening on the edge of her left nipple. The bump was quite small, smaller than the size of a pea. Ann wasn't sure there was anything unusual about the spot. Aside from this change, she hadn't noticed anything about her physical condition that was different from normal. Ann got out of the shower and thought about what she should do. She considered immediately calling a doctor for an appointment, but she thought that in this case it might be best to monitor the change herself for a while. The thickening was tiny and Ann was feeling as well as she usually did. Ann knew that women sometimes get lumps in their breast which soon disappear by themselves. She was not an alarmist, and she would closely watch the lump on her own. Ann decided she would call the doctor if the thickening persisted, grew, or changed. She felt that, for the time being, there was no risk in not calling the doctor."

Participants were then asked to imagine that what happened to Ann had just happened to them and to answer the rest of the questionnaire items as if they had just noticed a lump in their breast.

What factors predicted seeking prompt medical help? First, women who felt more emotions (e.g., anxiety, depression, concern) were the most likely to report intending to immediately call a doctor. Although some prior research suggests that feeling extreme emotions leads to denial, this study found that women who believed they would feel more upset about finding the lump were more likely to report seeking medical help. Similarly, women who saw the symptom as potentially life-threatening and a sign of breast cancer were more likely to intend to seek help. It is possible, however, that these findings showing that greater fear and concern led to greater intentions to immediately contact a physician are simply a reflection of what women report they would do following reading this hypothetical scenario, but may not represent their real-life behavior in this situation. Finally, this study found that women who were generally responsible in seeking regular health care were also more likely to report intending to seek help quickly.

tend to avoid—if at all possible—procedures and treatments that they believe will cause pain. For example, an estimated 12 to 15% of the U.S. population never visits a dentist, in part because of fear of pain (Sokol, Sokol, & Sokol, 1985), and one study found that 77% of women who indicated they would not undergo a future mammogram rated the experience of having a mammogram as "very uncomfortable" or "intolerable" (Jackson, Lex, & Smith, 1988). People also show longer delays if they don't think the disease can be cured.

Delay can also be caused by people's desire to seek information before resorting to the medical profession (Safer et al., 1979). People often rely on a lay referral network of friends and family to provide insight about health care symptoms and suggested treatment (Freidson, 1961). Similarly, people may choose to consult books or other information sources in an attempt to diagnose, and even treat, their health problem, and they turn to health care professionals only if they believe medical treatment is necessary (Matthews, Siegel, Kuller, Thompson, & Varat, 1983).

Demographic factors, also influence people's willingness and interest in seeking health care (Baum & Grunberg, 1991; Klonoff & Landrine, 1994). People who are very young, namely, infants and small children, often have very regular medical care: infants, for example, typically go to the doctor at 1 month, 2 months, 4 months, 6 months, 9 months, and 12 months of age!

"You know, Burkhart, if you're so damn afraid of the flu maybe you should just stay home."

CARTOON 12.1 While many people delay seeking medical care, hypochondriacs consistently seek such assistance even at the smallest sign of a potential health care problem (©The New Yorker Collection 2000 Robert Mankoff from cartoonbank.com. All Rights Reserved).

People who are very old also tend to seek medical care frequently, often because they have chronic conditions that require regular attention. Women are more likely than men to seek help, although the reasons for this are unclear. Pregnancy and childbirth, which typically involve frequent medical appointments, account for some of the difference, but not all. One possibility is that women are more focused on and aware of their physical states and, hence, are more likely than men to notice physical symptoms (Pennebaker, 1982). Another possibility is that women are simply more willing to admit they need help, whereas men may see expressing pain as a sign of weakness.

Not surprisingly, income also influences how often, and where, people seek health care (Adler, Boyce, Chesney, Folkman, & Syne, 1993; Flack et al., 1995; Kaplan & Kiel, 1993). Although people in higher socioeconomic classes have fewer health symptoms than those with lower incomes, they seek health care more often. In contrast, those in lower socioeconomic classes are less likely to seek regular preventive care (e.g., prenatal care, regular check-ups, and vaccinations), and therefore they are more likely to experience major illnesses that require care (including hospitalization). While 6.1% of those with moderate or high income report being in fair or poor health, 21.7% of those with low income report this these levels of health (National Center for Health Statistics, 2003). And when people in low socioeconomic classes seek help, it is more likely to come from emergency rooms than private doctors' offices. In some cases patients' concern about the monetary cost of the treatment can lead to delay. In fact, patients who are very concerned about cost delay an average of 9.7 days, whereas those without such concern delay only 2.0 days (Safer et al., 1979).

Race, ethnicity, and culture influence how likely people are to utilize medical services (Bates, Edwards, & Anderson, 1993; Landrine & Klonoff, 1994; Pennebaker, 1982; Sanders et al., 1992). First, people from different cultural and ethnic backgrounds vary in their awareness of and attention to physical symptoms, as well as in their willingness to express such symptoms (Burnam, Timbers, & Hough, 1984). For example, Americans tend to report much more pain and impairment from back pain than do people from other countries. Ethnic and cultural factors also influence people's willingness to rely on medical professionals as opposed to a "lay referral system" of family and friends. Finally, minorities are much less likely than whites to have access to regular health care, which in turn means that they are less likely to receive preventive treatment (e.g., immunizations) and more likely to receive treatment for medical conditions at later—and less treatable—stages (Adler et al., 1993; Adler et al., 1994; Gornick et al., 1996). Nearly twice as many African Americans as whites report they are in fair or poor health (National Center for Health Statistics, 2002). Religion, a particular aspect of culture, is another predictor of the utilization of health care. People who practice certain religions, including Christian Scientists and Jehovah's Witnesses, reject the use of some or all medical treatments completely, including blood transfusions and antibiotics.

Finally, although many people delay seeking medical help, others overuse medical care (Costa & McCrae, 1985, 1987; Larsen, 1992; Miranda, Perez-Stable, Munoz, Hargreaves, & Henke, 1991). People with *hypochondria* are very concerned about their health and interpret relatively benign symptoms as signs of more serious problems (see Cartoon 12.1). For example, a person with hypochondria might interpret a headache as a sign of a brain tumor. In turn, these "worried well" people seek medical attention for a variety of minor problems (Wagner & Curran, 1984). Similarly, *somaticizers* develop physical symptoms in response to psychological issues and, hence, seek medical treatment for problems that have no physical cause (Miranda et al., 1991). For example, people who are constantly anxious could develop stomach pains or other physical problems. Several large-scale studies have shown that people who are high in neuroticism (i.e., self-consciousness, have a vulnerability to stress, and have a tendency to experience negative emotions) report experiencing many health symptoms and exaggerate the severity of these symptoms (Ellington & Weibe, 1999). Some research suggests that many people who seek medical attention quite frequently may be suffering from psychological problems, including anxiety and depression (Malt et al., 1997; Simon, Gater, Kisely, & Piccinelli, 1996).

Patient–Practitioner Communication

Once a person has decided to see a doctor for help with a medical condition, a variety of factors regarding the patient–practitioner relationship can influence the nature of that interaction. Communication is a crucial aspect of interaction between practitioner and patient: 75% of any doctor's diagnosis is made on the basis of the patient's history (Leitzell, 1977), and hence patients need to be able to clearly express their symptoms (Mentzer & Snyder, 1982). Despite the importance of communication, health care providers and patients often have difficulty communicating effectively. First, patients can be reluctant to share certain types of highly personal information, such as sexual problems and embarrassing symptoms, (Mentzer & Snyder, 1982; Thompson, 1984). This concern is most common when there are differences between the doctor and patient in terms of age, gender, social class, and ethnicity (Reiff, Zakut, & Weingarten, 1999). For example, health professionals typically call patients by their first names, regardless of whether the age of the patient is greater than that of the practitioner, and this is a sign of disrespect in the African American community; hence, African American patients may be less willing to provide information as well as adhere to medical recommendations if so disresepected (Flack et al., 1995). Patients may also try to minimize how much pain they are experiencing—male patients, for example, report experiencing less pain to females than they do to males (Levine & DeSimone, 1991)! In other cases, patients may believe the doctor is able to discern their medical condition even without disclosing information. For example, they may believe that their symptoms will be evident throughout medical testing and that there is no need to describe them.

Second, doctors often fail to allow patients to provide information about their symptoms and give patients adequate information about their diagnosis, prognosis, and recommended treatment (Ley, 1982; Marvel, Epstein, Flowers, & Beckman, 1999; Waitzkin, 1985). For example, one study of 300 patient–practitioner interactions found that in 72% of cases physicians interrupted the patient's description of his or her symptoms, and that on average, this interruption occurred after just 23 seconds (Marvel et al., 1999)! Similarly, one recent study of over 1000 encounters between physicians and patients revealed that patients received complete information regarding important medical decisions in only 9% of the cases (Braddock, Edwards, Hasenberg, Laidley, & Levinson, 1999). Complete information includes specific details about different treatment options available, such as increasing the dose of one medicine or taking a new medicine, as well as the pros and cons of each option. In contrast, patients typically were told by their physician about the suggested choice (e.g., "I'd suggest you increase the dose of the atenolol you're already taking"). However, patients typically want as much information as possible about their illness (Faden, Becker, Lewis, Freeman, & Faden, 1981; Keown, Slovic, & Lichtenstein, 1984), and those who get more information are more satisfied (see Table 12.4; Hall, Roter, & Katz, 1988; Mentzer & Snyder, 1982).

What factors influence how much information is given to patients? Physicians who earn less money—and hence see fewer patients per day—tend to give more information and involve their patients more in making diagnostic and treatment decisions (Kaplan, Greenfield, Gandek, Rogers, & Ware, 1996; Waitzkin, 1985). Compared to male physicians, female physicians have longer appointments, give more information, and ask more questions (see Figure 12.3; Hall, Irish, Roter, Ehrlich, & Miller, 1994; Roter, Lipkin, & Korsgaard, 1991). Patient characteristics also influence the amount of information that is given: patients who are white, female, college-educated, and from an upper-middle-class background tend to get more information, ask more questions, and have longer appointments (Epstein, Taylor, & Seage, 1985; Hall et al., 1988; Waitzkin, 1985). One study revealed that high-socioeconomic-status patients received an average consultation of 7.3 minutes compared to 6.3 minutes for

TABLE 12.4   *How Much Information Would You Want? Would Your Doctor Agree?*

Type of Information	Percentage Who Think Patients Should Be Informed	
	Patients	Physicians
Name of drug	97	92
Common risks of normal use	89	85
Overdose information	86	76
Risks of using too little	80	52
Risks of not using at all	79	46
All possible risks of normal use	77	25
Other important uses	75	20

Patients generally want a lot of information, but physicians tend to underestimate this desire, which in turn leads to a gap between what patients want and what they get.

Source: Ley, 1982.

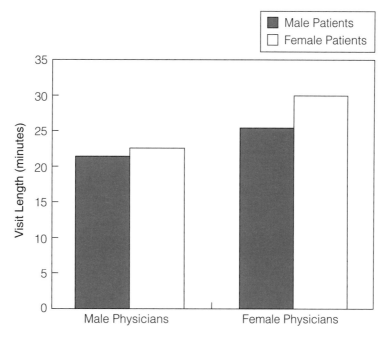

FIGURE 12.3   Female physicians spend more time with patients than do male physicians, and they have especially long appointments when they are seeing female patients (data from Hall et al., 1988).

those in the middle-status group and 5.8 minutes for those in the low-status group (Pendleton & Bochner, 1980). Finally, situational characteristics, including knowing the doctor for a longer period of time and having a serious illness, lead to getting more information.

Even when doctors do convey information to their patients, much of this information may be forgotten or misunderstood (Ley, 1982; Thompson, 1984). In fact, approximately 40% of what doctors say during a consultation is immediately forgotten. Patients who are anxious are particularly susceptible to forgetting information (Charles, Goldsmith, Chambers, & Haynes, 1996), as are those who receive results from a worried doctor (Shapiro, Boggs, Melamed, & Graham, 1992). Patients may also misinterpret the information they are given, especially if it includes complex medical jargon (Hadlow & Pitts, 1991). Patients may not understand a variety of terms commonly used by medical professionals, including *malignant, benign, void, sodium, migraine, stroke,* and *eating disorders.* Even telling a patient a test is positive or negative may be confusing to him or her—learning that the results of an HIV test is "positive" may seem like good news, but in reality it means the patient has contractd the disease. Although the use of medical jargon often is unintentional, in some cases physicians deliberately use confusing terms as a way of avoiding giving patients potentially upsetting information. For example, a physician may say "We're worried about adreno-CA" to avoid directly mentioning the risk of lung cancer, or "This is not an entirely benign procedure" to avoid describing the pain caused by a given procedure (Klass, 1987). Finally, people often misinterpret statistics they are given about the relative risks of various medical procedures and health risks. One recent study in the *Journal of the National Cancer Institute* suggests that physicians should convey health risks to patients by describing the risk in terms of individual people as opposed to an abstract risk estimate (Woloshin, Schwartz, & Welch, 2002). For example, patients think that a disease that kills 7 out of every 1000 people is more common than one that has a death rate of 0.7%, even those these numbers represent the same odds.

Many of these problems in patient–practitioner interaction are caused by old-fashioned models of these relationships. Thomas Szasz and Marc Hollender (1956) described three models of the patient–practitioner relationship: activity-passivity, guidance-cooperation, and mutual participation. The first model describes relationships in which the doctor is entirely in control and the patient is completely passive. This type of model is probably now best suited for describing situations in which the patient is unconscious (e.g., in surgery, in a coma), or when the patient is very young. However, this model was the common approach to medicine for much of the 1900s (Laine & Davidoff, 1996). The second model is probably still the most common model in medical practice today: the patient's thoughts and feelings are voiced, but the doctor still makes the major decisions. The third model, which is favored by those who prefer a more active involvement in their own medical care, describes a mutual interaction, in which both the patient and the practitioner share information and make decisions together. This might be the most appropriate model for describing how people manage a chronic illness, for example.

There are several techniques to improve patient–practitioner interaction? First, health care providers must pay attention not just to people's physical complaints, but also to their psychological concerns (Delbanco, 1992; Hall & Dornan, 1988). A man who is receiving treatment for prostate cancer, for example, may be more concerned about the potential side effect of impotence and its impact on his marriage than about his life expectancy. Basically, physicians must view patients as people, not just as a walking medical disease or condition! Second, health care providers must give straightforward explanations about the problem and its treatment, in terms that are at the appropriate level—not too complex and not too simplistic (Hall & Dornan, 1988; Mentzer & Snyder, 1982; Thompson, 1984; Waitzkin, 1984). Third, physicians must show better nonverbal behavior, such as maintaining eye contact, leaning toward the patient, and nodding their heads (Hall et al., 1988; LaCrosse, 1975). Physicians who engage in this type of verbal and nonverbal behavior are seen as warmer and friendlier, and in turn, their patients are more satisfied with their treatment—and are more likely to show up for future appointments (Feletti, Firman, & Sanson-Fisher, 1986; Yarnold, Michelson, Thompson, & Adams, 1998). For example, 86% of those who are pleased with their doctor's communication skills are satisfied with their medical care as compared to 25% of those who are not pleased with their doctor's communiction skills (Mentzer & Snyder, 1982). They are also less likely to switch doctors—one study found that, of physicians who engaged in high levels of interactive decision making with patients, only 15% of patients changed physicians within a year, as compared to 33% of those who were least interactive with their practitioners

Box 12.3

Focus on Gender and Ethnicity—Can Medical Treatment Be Separate But Equal?

Several studies have examined the frequency of use of various procedures and medical tests as a function of race and gender (Ayanian & Epstein, 1991; Chen, Rathore, Radford, Wang, & Krumholz, 2001; Fiscella, Franks, Gold, & Clancy, 2000; Schulman et al., 1999; Steingart et al., 1991). These studies rather consistently suggest that people are not all equally likely to get the same medical care. For example, in one study researchers examined all the cases of men and women hospitalized for coronary heart disease in Massachusetts and Maryland in a particular year (Ayanian & Epstein, 1991). They then examined the percentage undergoing various medical procedures as a function of sex. The results (at least from the point of view of women) were not encouraging: men were overall 15 to 45% more likely than women to receive these major diagnostic and therapeutic procedures. Although women experienced symptoms that were even more disabling and severe than men's symptoms, their chest pains were addressed using less-sophisticated medical procedures for diagnosis and treatment. For example, 27.3% of men underwent cardiac catheterization, compared to 15.4% of the women, and 12.7% of the men underwent coronary bypass surgery, compared to 5.9% of the women (Steingart et al., 1991). What causes these dramatic gender differences in receiving potentially life-saving procedures? In part physicians are less likely to see chest pain in women as a sign of coronary heart disease as they are in men. In contrast, physicians may be more likely to see women's physical symptoms as a sign of psychological problems, such as depression or anxiety. For example, in one study medical students were played an audiotape of a patient complaining of symptoms typical of depression (Hall et al., 1993). When the patient was a female, the students perceived her as less seriously ill, less in need of lab tests and follow-up care, and more likely to require psychiatric evaluation than when the patient was male.

Similarly, African Americans receive less-aggressive treatment for both diagnosing and treating serious illnesses, including coronary heart disease and cancer (Crawford, McGraw, Smith, McKinlay, & Pierson, 1994; Schulman et al., 1999; Whittle, Conigliaro, Good, & Lofgren, 1993). Specifically, as compared to whites, African Americans with heart symptoms are less likely to be referred to a cardiologist (Crawford et al., 1994). For example, a recent study published in the *New England Journal of Medicine* reported that 45.7% of white patients who were hospitalized for a heart attack received cardiac catheterization within 60 days of the attack as compared to 38.4% of African American patients (Chen et al., 2001). Catherization allows doctors to determine whether blood vessels are blocked and, hence, is an important step in determining whether patients require other treatments, such as heart bypass surgery. African Americans are also

(continues)

less likely than white patients to receive angioplasty (repair of blood vessels by surgery) as well as bypass surgery (Whittle et al., 1993). Similarly, Dr. Peter Bach and his colleagues (1999) found that 64% of African American patients with lung cancer received surgery, whereas 76.7% of white patients received surgery. And sadly, this difference in rate of surgery was associated with survival rates 5 years later: 34.1% of whites survived to this point as compared to 26.4% of African Americans.

(Kaplan et al., 1996). Patients also give more information to physicians who engage in this type of verbal and nonverbal behavior, which in turn can help doctors make more accurate diagnoses more quickly (Hall et al., 1994; Marvel et al., 1999). Given the tremendous value of effective patient–practitioner communication, some hospitals have developed training programs that specifically focus on encouraging these types of skills (Tosteson, 1990).

Patients also have a role in creating more effective doctor–patient interaction—those who take an active role in their medical care receive better care (Greenfield, Kaplan, Ware, Yano, & Frank, 1988; Greenfield & Kaplan, 1985; Thompson, Nanni, & Schwankovsky, 1990). One study revealed that patients who received a 20-minute session in "assertiveness training," which focused on how to convey honest and accurate information to their physician, asked specific questions regarding medical care and negotiate these decisions, get more information from their doctor (Greenfield & Kaplan, 1985). They also report fewer health symptoms and miss fewer days of work, even 4 months later. Even having patients list the questions they have for their physician increases doctor–patient communication and patient satisfaction (Thompson et al., 1990). Most important, the patients who benefit most from being assertive are those who are the least likely to receive aggressive treatment, namely, those who are African American, poor, and in generally bad health (Krupat et al., 1999).

The Experience of Hospitalization

Over 31 million people are admitted to the hospital each year, for an average stay of 5 days (Centers for Disease Control, 2002). The hospital is a very unique setting in that it is one of the only places (perhaps along with prison) in which a person gives up virtually every aspect of control, including normal control of one's body, the opportunity to engage in rewarding activities such as work and recreation, and the ability to predict what will happen (Lorber, 1975; Newman, 1984; Taylor, 1979).

People admitted to the hospital must live in an impersonal room (often with one or more roommates), are given typically bland food on a regimented schedule, and are subject to invasions of privacy when at virtually any moment hospital personnel enter the room (to clean, provide food, deliver medicines, check patient's vital statistics). Patients are often described by medical professionals based on their disease or illness (e.g., "the broken leg in Room 402," "the ulcer in Room 312"; Goffman, 1961), which enhances patients' feelings of depersonalization. Moreover, patients are asked a series of very personal questions ("when did you last have a bowel movement?"), forced to undergo a variety of unpleasant and sometimes painful tests, and must wear a backless gown without underwear! They may also be forced to be dependent on health care professionals for assistance with many personal care tasks, including eating, dressing and undressing, and even going to the bathroom (see Photo 12.4). Although many of the procedures and machines are likely to be unfamiliar and anxiety-provoking to patients (e.g., IV fluids, EKG machines), most patients don't get information about the procedures they are undergoing or why they are necessary (Newman, 1984). For example, one study of patients who had their chests X rayed revealed 92% were not told in advance that they were about to have an X ray and 82% were never provided with information about its results (Reynolds, 1978). All of this loss of control can lead to considerable stress and anxiety, which in turn can have negative immunological consequences and thereby inhibit recovery. One study found that 29% of pregnant women who had high blood pressure, an often dangerous condition during pregnancy, revealed an elevated blood pressure only when they were measured in their doctor's office (a potentially anxiety-provoking situation), a condition described as "white coat hypertension" (Bellomo et al., 1999). Moreover, women with white coat hypertension were just as likely to undergo cesarean sections (45%) as those with true high blood pressure (41%) and much more likely to undergo this procedure than those without high blood pressure (12%).

So, how do patients react to the extreme depersonalization that is common in many hospital settings? About 75% of the patients are classified as "good patients": they who make few demands on the staff, ask few questions, agree to

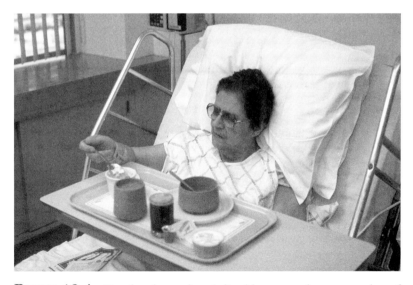

PHOTO 12.4 People who are hospitalized lose control over a number of aspects of their lives, including what they wear, what they eat, and who they see. In turn, this type of loss of control can enhance anxiety and thereby impede recovery.

whatever is suggested, and generally give up all desire for control (Lorber, 1975; Taylor, 1979). These people take up little time of the staff and are easy to manage. However, these patients may hesitate to question wrong orders, complain about an important symptom, or otherwise provide useful information about the symptoms they are experiencing out of fear about creating a problem. These patients may experience depression and learned helplessness, given the total lack of control, which in turn can ironically harm their recovery. As I discuss later in this section, some evidence even suggests that people who have less information and control over medical procedures experience more pain and take longer to recover.

On the other hand, about 25% of people are "bad patients" (Lorber, 1975; Taylor, 1979): they are younger and more educated and presumably score high in need for control; they may be demanding, questioning, and time-consuming. These patients may experience heightened anger, which leads to increased arousal. These patients may react to their loss of control by trying to regain some of it, which unfortunately can include engaging in destructive behaviors, such as smoking and not taking their medicine. Although bad patients do not experience the problems associated with giving up control, they may receive a lower quality of medical care. Specifically, medical professionals may respond less quickly to their needs, may keep them heavily sedated, and may even discharge them earlier!

One of the most threatening and anxiety-provoking aspects about hospitalization is the anticipation of surgery, in part because people often have little direct relevant experience with this situation (Contrada, Leventhal, & Anderson, 1994). Patients worry about the physical procedure (e.g., incision, anesthesia), the recovery (e.g., pain, ability to walk and eat), the resumption of normal activities (e.g., work, leisure activities), and the long-term management of their condition (e.g., the physical changes in their body, the need to diet or stop smoking following coronary heart surgery, the need to continue to take medications following an organ transplant). However, patients who are given information about what to expect during their surgery and recovery, as well as training in how to manage these experiences, require less pain medication and leave the hospital more rapidly (Contrada et al., 1994; Janis, 1958; Johnston & Vogele, 1993; Ludwick-Rosenthal & Neufeld, 1993). This information also decreases anxiety and pain (Anderson, 1987; Doering et al., 2000; Janis, 1958). For example, Stephan Doering and colleagues (2000) demonstrated that hip replacement surgery patients who saw a videotape of a patient who had been through that procedure showed less anxiety before surgery, lower blood pressure during surgery, and less use of pain medication after surgery (see Figure 12.4). In fact, in 11 studies in which the amount of information provided was examined to predict post-surgery drug use and length of hospital stay, 10 of the studies showed that more information led to a faster recovery, with a mean decrease of 2 days in the hospital (Ley, 1982).

In addition to giving patients knowledge about what to expect (i.e., informational control), other interventions focus on giving patients cognitive control (e.g., strategies for distracting/changing thoughts), or behavioral control (e.g., strategies for reducing discomfort, such as relaxation training; Egbert, Battit, Welch, & Bartlett, 1964; Leventhal, Leventhal, Shacham,, & Easterling,

Box 12.4

Health Psychology in the Real World—When Children Are Hospitalized

Of the over 41 million people who have surgery each year, more than 2 million are children under the age of 15 years (www.cdc.gov/nchs/fastats). All of the aspects of the hospital environment that are anxiety-producing for adults are especially upsetting for children. The procedures and treatments, particularly if they are painful or restrict patients' movement, are very difficult, and children often have no understanding of why they must undergo these procedures. They may, for example, view hospitalization as a punishment for being bad or unloved by their families. For very young children, such as those under the age of 5 years, one of the most difficult aspects of hospitalization is separation from their families. Although older children are likely to have a better understanding of why they are in the hospital, they face new issues, including concern with a loss of personal control, disruption of peer relationships, embarrassment about showing their body to others, and worry about the consequences of their illness (e.g., dying).

So, what can parents and health professionals do to help children cope with hospitalization? First, children, like adults, benefit from knowing what to expect, and hospitals should provide children and their families with information about various hospital procedures and routines (Koetting O'Byrne, Peterson, & Saldana, 1997; Pinto & Hollandsworth, 1989). This information could include pamphlets, tours, books, videos, and even puppet shows (for very young children). The staff at Children's Medical Center in Boston, for example, worked with children's books author Margaret Rey to write the story *Curious George Goes to the Hospital*, which describes the experience of George during a brief hospitalization (Rey & Rey, 1966). One study with children who were about to undergo surgery found that those who watched a video describing the surgery experienced less anxiety and arousal than did children who did not watch this video (Pinto & Hollandsworth, 1989). Second, parents should try to spend as much time with the child as possible—some hospitals now offer parents the chance to "room-in" with the child. Training parents in how to distract their children is also effective (Bush, Melamed, Sheras, & Greenbaum, 1986). Finally, children can be trained in how to cope with their anxiety about surgery (Jay, Elliott, Katz, & Siegel, 1987; Manne et al., 1992). For example, one study found that children who received training in how to reduce their own distress during hospitalization and surgery showed reduced anxiety as well as fewer maladaptive behaviors (Zastrowny , Kirschenbaum, & Meng, 1986). Hospitals are putting this information to good use—one study of 123 pediatric hospitals in the United States found that 75% reported increasing their use of research in health psychology to assist children in coping with medical procedures (Koetting et al., 1997).

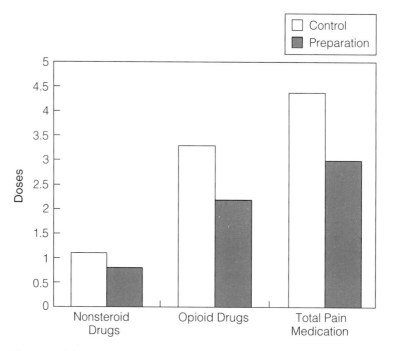

FIGURE 12.4   Hip replacement surgery patients who watch a videotape showing someone undergoing this surgery require significantly less pain medication after surgery than those who do not see this videotape (data from Doering et al., 2000).

1989; Manyande et al., 1995). In one early study, patients who were waiting for abdominal surgery were given information about the normality, duration, and severity of their postoperative pain and were trained in exercises to reduce the pain such as by relaxing their abdominal muscles and engaging in particular types of breathing (Egbert et al., 1964). Patients who received this type of information and training left the hospital an average of 2.7 days earlier and required roughly half as much morphine as those in the typical control condition. Interventions that give patients cognitive control demonstrate similar effects. For example, Anne Manyande and colleagues (1995) found that abdominal surgery patients who received training in guided imagery had lower heart rates following surgery, less pain, and requested less pain relief. All of these approaches share one very important feature; they give patients a much-needed sense of control in a generally stressful environment (see Box 12.4).

Even relatively small manipulations that increase control and positive experiences have important benefits in terms of recovery from surgery (see Box 12.5). One way to enhance control is by allowing patients to control the amount and timing of pain medication they receive, as opposed to making them call for a nurse to deliver the medication or administering the medication on a set schedule (e.g., every 4 hours). But does this type of control encourage patients to overmedicate themselves? No—in fact, it does just the opposite. For example, one study with patients who were recovering from a

---

Box 12.5

Research Focus—The Benefits of Having a Hospital Room with a View

Roger Ulrich (1984) at the University of Delaware conducted a study to test a very novel question—whether recovery from surgery was affected by the type of room patients were in. He reviewed the records of patients in a Pennsylvania hospital for a period of about 10 years who had gallbladder surgery. Specifically, he examined a number of factors listed in the hospital records, including length of hospital stay, amount of pain medication requested and given, and nurses' notes about the patients' recovery. He also noted what room the patients were in and whether that room overlooked a group of trees or a brick wall.

As predicted, patients whose hospital room had a view of trees recovered faster than those whose room looked out on a brick wall. First, patients in a room with a view stayed in the hospital for an average of 7.96 days, nearly one day shorter than those with a view of bricks (8.70 days). Patients who had a view of trees also requested less pain medication than those who had a view of bricks. Finally, the nurses' recordings on patient charts were more negative for those who had had a room with a view of bricks versus trees. An average of 3.96 negative notes per patient were made for those in a room with a view of bricks (e.g., "patient is upset and crying," "patient needs much encouragement") as compared to 1.13 comments per patient for those with the view of trees. In sum, patients with a view of trees had shorter hospital stays, needed less pain medicine, and received fewer negative evaluations from nurses than those without such a view.

---

bone marrow transplant revealed that those who received a device that directly provided pain relief intravenously, who were able to control the amount and timing of pain medication administration reported lower levels of pain (and gave themselves less medicine) than those who had to ask the hospital staff for medicine (Zucker et al., 1998).

What Predicts Adherence?

Although people invest a lot of time and energy in getting diagnosed, and doctors invest considerable time in making diagnoses, many patients fail to follow recommended medical regimens, such as taking antibiotics, making dietary changes, and having immunizations (Christensen & Ehlers, 2002; DiMatteo,

Box 12.6

Health Psychology in the Real World—The Very Real Problem of Burnout

How hard do you think doctors work? Many people see doctors as having a relatively easy job—they are typically well paid, respected by society, and can have very flexible schedules (e.g., play golf on Wednesday afternoons). However, doctors experience very high levels of stress (Maslach & Jackson, 1982) caused by several factors. First, dealing with patients can be emotionally demanding. These demands can be especially difficult when the patient is in severe pain, has unsightly injuries (e.g., defigurements, severe burns), and has little chance of recovery. Doctors may have to interact not only with the patients, but also their families. Family members may have many time-consuming questions and may be anxious, upset, and angry. Moreover, no matter how good a doctor is, he or she will experience failure on a relatively consistent basis—all doctors have patients who die or who cannot be helped. This type of loss is particularly difficult when they have tried very hard to save the patient. Another aspect of the job environment that leads to stress for doctors is their relative lack of control in a hectic and time-pressured environment. Doctors rarely get to choose exactly when they work, which patients they see, or how long they spend with a particular patient. Doctors are sometimes not even able to treat patients in their preferred way without seeking—and receiving—special permission from the patient's insurance company.

How do health professionals react to this type of pressure? Sadly, sometimes they depersonalize the patients as a way of maintaining emotional distance (Maslach & Jackson, 1982; Parker & Kulik, 1995; Shinn, Rosario, Morch, & Chestnut, 1984). They may, for example, start thinking of patients in terms of their problems (e.g., "the fractured leg," "the liver cancer") as opposed to thinking of them as people; hence, they may treat patients in a cynical and callous way. One physician noted that when a patient's cancer did not respond to chemotherapy, she was described as "failing chemotherapy" (Klass, 1987). Practitioners may also develop psychological and physical problems, including coronary heart disease, alcohol and drug abuse, and depression. For example, 12% of medical students show symptoms of depression, and these symptoms increase during the first 2 years of medical school (Clark & Zeldow, 1988). One recent study of 182 medical students found that 133 had cried at least once during their clinical rotations in the hospital, and another 30 reported being on the verge of crying (Angoff, 2001). Burnout in medical professionals can have a dramatic impact on patient care: one recent study found that nurses who care for too many patients at one time experience a 23% increase in rate of burnout, which is in turn associated with a 7% increase in the rate of patient death (Aiken, Clarke, Sloan, Sochalski, & Silber, 2002)!

(continues)

Although some of the causes of burnout are largely unavoidable given the stressful nature of the medical profession, giving people the opportunity to express their feelings is one way to help ameliorate the effects of this environment (Angoff, 2001). Some hospitals have developed support groups for hospital personnel, which can provide much-needed emotional support and give people the opportunity to express their feelings of frustration, exhaustion, and grief. These groups also allow medical professionals to learn they are not alone in their feelings, and to learn some strategies for coping with the difficult challenges of their profession. Moreover, physicians who are training medical students can encourage them to continue to express their feelings as opposed to denying them, as has often been the practice (Angoff, 2001). One medical student described how wonderfully a physician handled the first death of a patient for a group of students:

> "The whole team stayed outside the door while Doctor F and the intern went in to pronounce him. I was trying to fight back tears. Doctor F took us all into a room and handled it magnificently. He said let's take some time to talk about this, and said what a great guy the patient had been. He reminded us that when we had been in the patient's room, his mother looked out the window and said, "What a great day to go to God." I remember having a sense of peace."

Compare this experience to another report from a medical student:

> "It was my first surgical rotation and the first patient I found out had cancer. The patient went down for a scan. My job was to not inform the patient of the results, but as the person who knew the patient best, she kept asking me. I was avoiding her. The resident saw me cry. She gave me a lecture to not be so weak, patients die, bad things happen."

In sum, hospital environments that provide support to doctors, nurses, and medical students and acknowledge the sometimes difficult emotions that come with these jobs can help prevent some of the problems associated with burnout.

1994; DiNicola & DiMatteo, 1984; Dunbar-Jacob, Burke, & Puczynski, 1995; Kirscht & Rosenstock, 1979; Monane et al., 1996). Rates of nonadherence range from 15 to 93% (depending on the regimen), with a mean of 30%: About 50% of people do not take prescribed medications on the recommended schedule, 20 to 40% of people do not receive the recommended immunizations, and 20 to 50% of people miss scheduled appointments for medical treatment. For example, one early study on adherence revealed that only 12% of patients who were instructed to take penicillin for 10 days were actually still taking this antibiotic by the 10th day—50% had stopped by the 3rd day, 71% had stopped by the 6th day, and 82% had stopped by the 9th day (Bergman & Werner, 1963).

Nonadherence is associated with substantial costs to individuals and to society (Dunbar-Jabob et al., 1995; Kirscht & Rosenstock, 1979). Obviously, not taking one's medication, for instance, typically leads to a continuation of

> **Questioning the Research 12.2**
> Does adherence to medical regimens really lead to better health? Or could a third variable partially explain these findings?

symptoms. Moreover, not taking medication can cause the disease to persist or even get worse. Approximately 27,600 children developed measles in 1990 alone because their parents failed to have them immunized. Individuals who do not adhere to medical recommendations show poorer outcomes, including higher mortality (Gallagher, Viscoli, & Horwitz, 1993; Horwitz et al., 1990; Irvin, Bowers, Dunn, & Wanes, 1999). For example, hypertensive patients who fail to take their recommended medication are four times as likely to be hospitalized or die than those who adhere to the treatment (Psaty, Koepsell, Wagner, LoGerfo, & Inui, 1990). Nonadherence to medication regimens and the persistence of symptoms may then lead a health care professional to prescribe a larger dose of the drug—possibly causing an overdose—since he or she thinks the drug is having no effect at the lower dose. New diagnoses may be made based on patients' response to the treatment. Poor adherence also can lead to substantial societal costs, such as the development of drug-resistant strains of viruses (Catz, Kelly, Bogart, Benotsch, & McAuliffe, 2000; Dunbar-Jacob et al., 1995; Sumartojo, 1993) and widespread disease, with its attendant losses in productivity and quality of life.

Causes of Nonadherence

Nonadherence may take a variety of forms and be caused by a variety of reasons (DiNicola & DiMatteo, 1984; Epstein & Cluss, 1982). In cases of *intentional nonadherence*, patients understand the practitioner's directions, but modify the regimen in some way or ignore it completely because they are unwilling to follow the recommendations. Aspects of the treatment can affect whether someone adheres to physician recommendations (DiNicola & DiMatteo, 1984). People show high rates of adherence to medications and treatments that relieve painful and severe conditions (Brownlee-Duffeck et al., 1987). Most cancer patients, for example, undergo recommended chemotherapy and radiation treatments in the hope that these procedures will prolong their lives. People are also more likely to comply with short-term treatments than long-term treatments, particularly those that are complex, have unpleasant side effects, and provide few demonstrated rewards (Catz et al., 2000; Robie, 1987); at the beginning of the chapter I described how Larry often failed to take his medication to control hypertension, because of his lack of confidence in its effectiveness as well as its high cost and numerous side effects. Although the main treatment for HIV infection is *highly active antiretroviral therapy (HAART)*, this regimen involves a complicated drug-taking schedule—sometimes as many as 16 pills must be taken each day at precise times and under precise conditions (e.g., some on an empty stomach, some an hour before eating, some an hour after eating). The HAART regimen can also lead to a variety of side effects, including mental confusion, headaches, and anemia. Adherence to this regimen therefore is particularly challenging, despite its benefits in terms of reducing AIDS-related symptoms and potentially delaying death.

Individual differences including perceived vulnerability, self-efficacy, outcome expectancies, and locus of control, can influence whether a person complies with medical recommendations, as can the costs and benefits of complying (Bond, Aiken, & Somerville, 1992; Brownlee et al., 1987; DiNicola & DiMatteo, 1984; Dunbar-Jacob et al., 1995; Goldring, Taylor, Kemeny, & Anton, 2002; McCaul, Glasgow & Schafer, 1987; Christensen & Johnson, 2002; Krantz, Baum, & Wideman, 1980). People who see more benefits derived from following a regimen (e.g., feel better, experience less pain, live longer) are more likely to adhere to medical treatments, whereas those who think they'll be OK even if they don't follow medical recommendations tend to not adhere (Brock & Wartman, 1990; Sherbourne, Hays, Ordinay, DiMatteo, & Kravitz, 1992). Moreover, people who have negative beliefs about the value of medical recommendations, as well as those who are hostile, show low levels of adherence to medical regimens (see Table 12.5; Christensen, Moran, & Wiebe, 1999). In other cases people want to comply, and even believe complying is very important, but may lack the self-efficacy to successfully carry out the behavior (e.g., to resist tempting foods, avoid alcohol while taking medication; Catz et al., 2000; DiMatteo, 1994; Senecal, Nouwen, & White, 2000). People who are older tend to show higher rates of adherence than people who

TABLE 12.5 *Test Yourself: Irrational Health Beliefs*

1. During a routine physical examination, your doctor notices a mole on your hand and suggests that you see a specialist to have it examined further. You recall that a friend of yours had a similar mole for years and it never caused her any problems. You think, "I'm sure it won't ever cause me a problem either."

2. Your doctor prescribes a medication for an illness and instructs you to finish the entire bottle of pills. After taking half of the medication, you notice that your symptoms have cleared up. You find yourself thinking, "If I don't feel sick anymore, the medicine is unnecessary."

3. You have been taking a medication for 6 months and your medical problem has not improved. Your doctor has suggested a new drug. You think to yourself, "If the last medication didn't help, a new one won't do any good."

4. You smoke and are overweight but have never had a major health problem. At a recent checkup, your doctor tells you that these habits put you at risk for health problems down the road. Both of your parents have similar habits and have lived long, healthy lives. You find yourself thinking, "Smoking and eating too much just aren't a problem in my case."

People are asked to rate how similar the thought is to what they would think in a particular situation, with higher scores indicating more distorted and illogical beliefs.

Source: Christensen et al., 1999.

are younger, perhaps because younger people tend to feel more invulnerable (Lynch et al., 1992; Monane et al., 1996; Sherbourne et al., 1992; Thomas et al., 1995). There are few, if any, effects of gender on adherence.

Interestingly, adherence tends to be best when patients' characteristics or coping styles correspond with the particular demands of the medical treatment they are undergoing (Christensen & Ehlers, 2002). Specifically, and as shown in Figure 12.5, individuals with more active and internally focused coping styles tend to show higher levels of adherence when they are given treatments that emphasize self-control, whereas those with more avoidant styles of coping show higher levels of adherence when they are undergoing treatment administered by a therapist in a hospital or clinic setting. For example, one study of hemodialysis patients revealed that those who preferred active involvement in their health care showed better dietary control and adherence to fluid-intake recommendations when they were given patient-controlled dialysis at home, whereas those who preferred low levels of involvement in their own care showed better dietary control and adherence to medical recommendations when they were given staff-controlled dialysis at a hospital or clinic (Christensen, 2000). What accounts for these effects? Patients who have an active and monitoring coping style might feel out of control when given a provider-directed type of treatment, and in turn may respond to this type of situation by trying to reassert control—by deliberately disobeying medical recommendations. Similarly, patients who are high in self-efficacy and conscientiousness might be more responsive to treatments that require independence and self-reliance, because these treatments would utilize their preferred coping styles and strategies. On the other hand, patients who are low in self-efficacy and

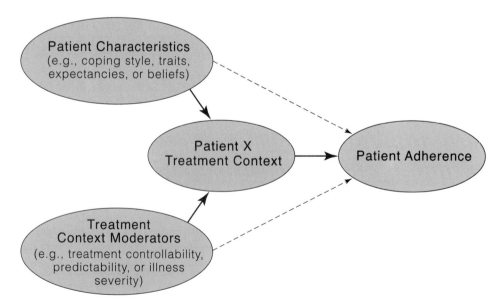

FIGURE 12.5 A model of patient X treatment interaction predicting adherence (Chrsitensen & Johnson, 2002).

high in agreeableness might prefer more passive, dependent, and possibly group-based treatments, which would encourage more (much-needed) reliance on others as well as social support (Rosenbaum & Ben-Ari Smira, 1986; Smith & Williams, 1992).

Some intriguing research by Nancy Bundek and her colleagues at the University of Southern California suggests that women's beliefs about their control over various health-related behaviors influence adherence to screening recommendations (Bundek, Marks, & Richardson, 1993). Specifically, women who believed they controlled their own health outcomes were more likely to engage in screening behaviors with a high degree of personal control, such as BSE. These women agreed with statements such as, "The main thing which affects my health is what I myself do," and "I am in control of my health." In contrast, women who believed that medical professionals have control over their health outcomes were more likely to engage in screening behaviors that medical professionals have control over, such as Pap smears and clinical breast exams. These women agreed with statements such as, "Having regular contact with my physician is the best way for me to avoid illness," and "Regarding my health, I can only do what my doctor tells me to do."

Social factors, such as support from family and friends, can influence adherence (Bovbjerg et al., 1995; Catz et al., 2000; DiNicola & DiMatteo, 1984; Kirscht & Rosenstock, 1979; Sherbourne et al., 1992; Stanton, 1987). Because making changes often requires social support, those who do not have the reinforcement of significant others may fail to comply. One study of patients with tuberculosis found that 56% of those who regularly took their medication felt their families were supportive of their taking medication as compared to 28% of those who did not regularly take their medication (Barnhoorn & Adriaanse, 1992). Similarly, people who have more supportive interpersonal relationships show more adherence to diabetic regimens (Sherbourne et al., 1992), and people who have more supportive spouses are more likely to adhere to dietary changes than those without such spousal support (Bovbjerg et al., 1995). However, family members and friends may interfere with recommended medical regimens if they see these behaviors as threatening to themselves in some way: a wife who is attempting to stop smoking, for example, may not receive support from her husband if he has decided to continue to smoke.

Cultural and demographic factors may also influence adherence (Bovbjerg et al., 1995; Catz et al., 2000; DiNicola & DiMatteo, 1984; Kirscht & Rosenstock, 1979; Sherbourne et al., 1992; Stanton, 1987). Few patients will comply with recommendations that go against their culture or religion, and cultural factors may also influence people's beliefs in the efficacy of medicine in general. For example, people from cultures that place a greater priority on using lay referral systems (e.g., family and friends) for advice about health problems may be reluctant to seek medical attention for such concerns. Finally, people with very low income may fail to comply simply because the recommended treatment is too costly (Robie, 1987). They may take medication less frequently than is recommended, skip follow-up appointments, or rely on nonprescription remedies as a way of saving money. For example, a study of mothers who did not keep their children's pediatric appointments found that the most common reasons were a lack of money, lack of transportation, or need to focus on more pressing problems (e.g., taking care of other children at home).

Another factor that is strongly related to patient cooperation is the quality of the relationship between the doctor and patient, because adherence depends largely on the patient's motivation to follow the doctor's recommendation (DiNicola & DiMatteo, 1984; Dunbar-Jacob et al., 1995). Practitioners who show warmth, encourage open communication, and address their patients' concerns have more-satisfied patients, who in turn are more likely to follow recommendations (see Table 12.6). One study examined over 800 interactions between pediatricians and mothers who had brought their children in for some type of disorder (Korsch, Gozzi, & Francis, 1968). Immediately after the mother and child left the office, they were questioned about their experience. Although the majority (76%) were satisfied with the doctor's performance, nearly 20% felt they did not receive a clear statement about their baby's problem, and almost 50% were left wondering what caused the baby's problem. They also felt the visit focused only on the technical disease aspects, not their emotional concerns. In turn, this lack of information was associated with overall poor adherence with medical instructions. In fact, only 42% complied with the doctor's orders, with 38% showing partial adherence and 11% showing no adherence. Those who were satisfied with their interaction with their doctor were three times as likely to comply as those who were unsatisfied (53% for the highly satisfied versus 17% for the highly dissatisfied).

In contrast, in the case of *unintentional nonadherence*, people intend to comply, and may even believe they are complying, but for some reason they are not following instructions. As described previously, physicians often give patients very little information about their diagnosis and treatment, which in

TABLE 12.6   *Test Yourself: Adherence Determination Questionnaire*

Please answer the following questions (1 = strongly disagree to 5 = strongly agree).

1. The doctors and other health professionals answer all my questions.
2. The doctors and other health professionals treat me in a very friendly and courteous manner.
3. The benefits of my treatment plan outweigh any difficulty I might have in following it.
4. Following my treatment plan will help me to be healthy.
5. The kind of cancer I have is a terrible disease.
6. The chances I might develop cancer again are pretty high.
7. Members of my immediate family think I should follow my treatment plan.
8. My close friends think I should follow my treatment plan.
9. I have made a commitment to follow my treatment plan.
10. I am able to deal with any problems in following my treatment plan.

This scale assesses an individual's likelihood of adhering to his or her treatment plan.

Source: DiMatteo et al., 1993.

turn can lead to nonadherence (Hall et al., 1988; Ley, 1982). As described previously, physicians may spend less than a minute and a half giving information to patients (Waitzkin, 1985). Even when patients are given information about their condition, they may forget or misunderstand the instructions they are given (DiNicola & DiMatteo, 1984). For example, one study found that patients failed to recall 56% of the instructions they had received and 48% of the treatment instructions even a short time after their appointments. Moreover, instructions for medical regimens are often vague; hence, patients may legitimately misunderstand exactly what they are supposed to do. In one study, patients were told to take a drug "with meals," by which the practitioner meant to imply patients should take the drug immediately after eating (Mazzullo, Cohn, Lasana, & Griner, 1974). However, 54% of the patients understood this to mean "take before meals," 33% thought it meant to "take during meals," and only 13% thought it meant to "take after meals." Although this type of misunderstanding is particularly common in patients from lower socioeconomic backgrounds, it can occur with patients from a variety of backgrounds. For example, when my son Andrew was an infant, he developed an ear infection, and I promptly took him to the doctor. I was already a professor at this time (and in fact was teaching health psychology). The doctor carefully explained that he needed medicine and to give it twice a day for 10 days, and as I was leaving, he asked if I had any questions. I didn't really have any questions, but on the way out the door, I said, "And I put the medication in his ear, right?" The doctor looked shocked, and quickly said, "No, the medication goes in his mouth!"

Measuring Adherence

The most common method of measuring adherence is simply to ask the patient whether he or she has taken the required amount of medicine (Epstein & Cluss, 1982). This approach is easy, inexpensive, and sometimes the only option. However, this method has problems because patients will rarely admit that they are not complying and, hence, typically will report adherence even if it is not so. One study with diabetic children found that 53.8% of the times they reported testing their blood, they fabricated glucose levels (Wilson & Endres, 1986). Patients may also forget whether they have complied, especially if they must report on their behavior over a long period of time, such as their diet and exercise behavior over the last month. Although some studies have tried using the reports of family members to judge adherence, as a way of avoiding problems of biased or forgetful reporting, family members often base their own estimates on what the patient reports to them! Similarly, although some studies suggest reports by doctors could be useful (Epstein & Cluss, 1982), doctors generally overestimate adherence because they believe patients cooperate perfectly with their treatment recommendations.

Given the significant likelihood of inaccurate findings using self-report measures, some studies have tried assessing adherence through pill or bottle counts (Epstein & Cluss, 1982). For example, a physician could ask patients to bring in their pill bottles and could then measure whether the right number of pills is missing. Although this approach may clarify whether the patient accurately understands the recommended dosage, obviously people can remove pills without actually ingesting them in order to appear compliant. Moreover, patients may have taken the right number of pills, but on the wrong schedule.

In some cases therapeutic outcomes, such as whether the patient is getting better, are used in many cases to judge adherence (DiNicola & DiMatteo, 1984; Epstein & Cluss, 1982). If the patient is showing signs of recovering, then he or she is assumed to be complying with medical recommendations. However, this method also poses problems simply because there is not necessarily a direct correspondence between adherence and recovery: in some cases people can show signs of recovery even when they are not complying, and in other cases, people show no signs of recovery even when they are complying (Hays et al., 1994). For example, in one study of people with hypertension, 12% controlled the disease without complying to the regimen, and 34% complied faithfully, but the regimen was ineffective in controlling the disease (Sackett, 1979).

Researchers have also tried to use more direct measures of testing adherence (Dunbar-Jacob et al., 1995; Epstein & Cluss, 1982), including using blood, serum, or urine assays to test the concentration of the drug in the patient's body. For example, if a patient is taking penicillin, a urine test could be used to determine whether the appropriate level of penicillin is in the body. Although physiological methods are quite accurate, and they avoid the problems associated with self-report and pill counts, patients who are warned about these tests may comply only immediately before the test. For example, some smoking cessation programs test for the presence of nicotine in saliva. But people who continue to smoke simply might not smoke in the hours before the test, and therefore appear to be not smoking, even if they usually are. Physiological measures are also relatively impractical—they are not available for all drugs, are relatively expensive, and, given individual differences in rates of metabolism, may not be entirely accurate.

Strategies for Increasing Adherence

Nonadherence is clearly irrational, a waste of time for patients and health care professionals, and potentially dangerous. Many of the strategies for decreasing unintentional nonadherence focus on giving the patient correct information (Dunbar-Jacob et al., 1995; Ley, 1982; Thompson, 1984). In fact, simply providing clear and understandable information about the medication, its purposes, and its dosage can be very effective in preventing this type of nonadherence. Practitioners should ask patients directly whether they have any questions. Moreover, because people sometimes forget or do not fully understand the information they receive from practitioners, providing easy-to-understand written materials, using illustrations to reinforce written materials, and even giving the patient a tape recording of the consultation can all be effective ways of increasing adherence (Ley, 1982). In fact, one study found that 91% of patients reported it was helpful to have a tape recording of their doctor visit, and patients claimed to have listened to the tape an average of 3.5 times (Butt, 1977).

Because unintentional nonadherence can also be caused by forgetting to adhere, other strategies for increasing adherence simply focus on reminding people to engage in a particular behavior, such as taking their medication or measuring their blood pressure (Dunbar-Jacobs et al., 1995; Ley, 1982; Macharia et, Leon, Rowe, Stephenson, & Haynes, 1992; Mayer & Frederiksen, 1986; Southam & Dunbar, 1986). In fact, one study found that giving patients special reminders (e.g., a sticker for their refrigerator) doubled rates of adherence to their medication regimen (see Photo 12.5; Lima, Nazarian, Charney, & Lahti, 1976). Reminder calls and postcards can also be very effective in improving attendance at follow-up appointments (Kirscht & Rosentstock, 1979). Reminder techniques and cues can be especially useful with the geriatric population. Asking patients to monitor their adherence behavior, such as by testing and recording their blood pressure (in the case of hypertensives) or blood glucose levels (in the case of diabetics), is another way of helping to remind them to adhere (Southam & Dunbar, 1986). This self-monitoring can also provide patients with increased understanding of their disease, and its management, and thereby enhance feelings of perceived control.

The strategies for decreasing intentional nonadherence are quite different, because in these cases, people understand the medical recommendations, but are simply unmotivated or unable to follow them (Dunbar-Jacobs et al., 1995;

PHOTO 12.5 Even simple reminders, such as telephone calls, postcards, and refrigerator magnets, can increase adherence to medication and treatment regimes.

Ley, 1982). In cases in which people fail to comply because they have little concern about having or developing a particular disease, the use of fear warnings can be effective in increasing adherence (Higbee, 1969; Janis, 1967). For example, smokers who see themselves as relatively unlikely to develop lung cancer could be brought to a hospital ward filled with people dying of lung cancer to increase their level of fear arousal and motivate them to take action. Similarly, people who engage in unsafe sex and have little fear of acquiring HIV could be asked to role-play how they would respond to learning they are HIV-positive, which could increase their feelings of perceived vulnerability. In one study mothers of obese children were randomly assigned to receive one of three communication messages—a control (no-information) message, a low-threat message, or a high-threat message (Becker, Maiman, Kirscht, Haefner, & Drachman, 1977). Children whose mothers had received either type of informational message had lost more weight than the controls at each of the four follow-up visits, and those whose mothers had received the high-threat message lost the most weight.

Another strategy for increasing adherence is to give patients some type of incentive or reward for following medical recommendations (DiNicola & DiMatteo, 1984; Hegel, Ayllon, Thiel, & Oulton, 1992; Macharia et al., 1992; Southam & Dunbar, 1986). This approach is particularly effective if patients agree to a written contract that describes specific goals they intend to meet as well as the reward they will receive if the contract is specifically carried out. These contracts are typically witnessed by others, such as physicians and family members. In some cases rewards alone, even in the absence of a specific contract, can be effective at increasing adherence. In fact, people who receive desirable—and self-chosen—rewards, such as attending a movie or purchasing a book, show better adherence to regimens for a variety of conditions, including arthritis, diabetes, asthma, and cardiovascular disease.

Intentional nonadherence can also be caused by patients' concern that following the medical recommendations will disrupt their lives in some way, such as taking too much time or interfering with relationships (Kirscht & Rosenstock, 1979). Increasing the convenience of engaging in the recommended behavior, such as simplifying the regimens (e.g., taking a pill twice a day instead of four times a day), making bottles easier to open (especially for older patients), lowering the cost, and improving the taste of medicine can increase adherence (Robie, 1987). For example, patients who have to take one to three pills a day show an adherence rate of 77% to 88% as compared to 39% for those who have to take four pills a day (Cramer, Mattson, Prevey, Scheyer, & Ouelette, 1989). Enlisting the support of family members or friends can increase adherence (Becker, 1985; DiNicola & DiMatteo, 1984; Kirscht, Kirscht, & Rosenstock, 1981; Morisky et al., 1983). For example, one program with hypertensive patients found that 53% of those who received an exit interview and family support complied with their medical regimen at 2-year follow-up as compared to only 40% off those in the control group (Morisky et al., 1983). Similarly, you can have buddy systems with pairs of patients. Some research suggests that patients who regularly attend group social support sessions with others who share their health issue show greater adherence (Kirscht & Rosenstock, 1979).

Finally, and as described previously, patients are more likely to adhere to treatment recommendations when they like their doctor and when their doctor emphasizes the importance of adherence (DiMatteo et al., 1993; Sherbourne et al., 1992). For example, one study with over 1000 chronic disease patients found that those who were satisfied with the interpersonal care they received from their physicians were more likely to adhere to medical recommendations (Sherbourne et al., 1992). Patients with physicians who make strong recommendations for adherence and provide realistic information about the importance of adherence also show higher rates of adherence (Goldring et al., 2002). Another important factor influencing patient satisfaction and adherence to medical recommendations is the physician's interactional style (Krantz et al., 1980; Laine & Davidoff, 1996). Specifically, physicians who use a patient-centered style encourage an interaction between the doctor and the patient to solve the problem and seek solutions, whereas those who use a doctor-centered style (the more traditional style) are more dominant and expect the patient largely to trust their expertise and defer to their judgment. Although most patients tend to prefer a more patient-centered style of interaction, others do prefer a more doctor-centered style, and, most important, patients are most satisfied when their physician uses the patients' preferred style. In one study by Edward Krupat and colleagues (2000), people read two doctor–patient scenarios and then rated how satisfied they would have been if they were the patient in each. In one scenario, the physician exhibited a controlling, doctor-centered style: the physician focused on the biomedical meaning of the symptoms, used closed-ended questions, gave relatively little information, and maintained an air of neutrality. In the other, the physician exhibited a more open, patient-centered style: the physician used open-ended questions and showed warmth and personal interest in the patient. Although patient-centered physicians overall generated more satisfaction, people who preferred a patient-centered style (e.g., those who agreed with such statements as "the patient and doctor share responsibility for making a diagnosis") were more satisfied with a patient-oriented doctor, whereas those who preferred a more physician-centered style (e.g., those who agreed with such statements as "if doctors are truly skilled at diagnosis and treatment, the way they interact with patients is relatively unimportant") were more satisfied with doctor-centered physicians. This research suggests that physicians may need to adopt a congruent style with patient preferences in order to lead to adherence and a good doctor–patient relationship. Training could focus on helping physicians recognize the orientations of their patients and being flexible in the interviewing style that they adopt.

What Is Relapse?

Even when people seek medical treatment and attempt to follow recommendations, maintaining health behavior change over time is a major problem. Have you ever made a change in your health-related behavior, such as stopping smoking, starting exercising, or adopting a healthier diet, but then returned to your old—less healthy—habits after a few weeks or months (or sometimes even days)? This pattern of relapse is very common. For example, most people (estimates range from 50 to 80%) who quit smoking start again within a year; and one study found that less than 10% of patients were able to maintain abstinence from alcohol over a period of 2 years following participation in a treatment plan (Marlatt, 1985a). As shown in Figure 12.6, the relapse curves for alcohol use, smoking, and heroin use are very similar, with about two-thirds of all relapse occurring in the first 90 days following treatment (Hunt, Barnett, & Branch, 1971; Ockene et al., 2000). This suggests that there is a common link to the process of relapse that may be similar across different types of addiction. This section examines the major theories of relapse, the influence of psychological factors on triggering relapse, and strategies for preventing relapse.

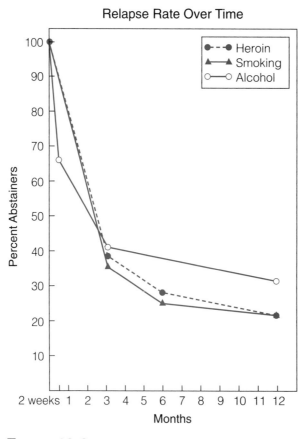

FIGURE 12.6   The relapse curves for various addictions, including heroin use, smoking, and alcohol abuse, are very similar, suggesting that the relapse process across different issues shares some common points (Hunt et al., 1971).

Theories of Addiction

The *moral* or *self-control theory* posits that people who engage in addictive behaviors, such as smoking, drinking, and gambling, have some type of moral weakness (Marlatt, 1985a). According to this theory, people who are lazy and undisciplined lack the "moral fiber" to stop engaging in these self-destructive behaviors. For example, the Temperance Movement during the 1940s and the ban of alcohol during Prohibition reflected this view advocating that people must be protected from themselves. Moreover, because any problem with addiction is a result of a lack of personal impulse control or willpower, people who engage in these behaviors in excess deserve whatever negative consequences befall them. This model holds people responsible for their own behavior and, thus, in one sense can be seen as empowering.

On the other hand, according to the *disease model*, addiction is caused primarily by internal physiological forces, such as cravings, urges, and compulsions; hence, the "addict" is unable to voluntarily control his or her behavior (Marlatt, 1985a). Alcoholics Anonymous is based on this model and posits that the alcoholic is completely powerless over the disease and that alcoholism can never be cured, only controlled. In this view, the only way for an alcoholic to stay in control is to not drink—after having one or two drinks, the alcoholic experiences a physiological addictive response that is triggered by the alcohol consumed, which leads the person to have an irresistible craving for more alcohol. The disease model of addiction has an "all or nothing" view, which means that only lifelong abstinence is effective, and hence relapse is failure. In turn, any slight deviation is seen as total failure, which of course then leads to more of the negative behavior. This can obviously lead to self-fulfilling prophecy ("I had one cigarette, I have no willpower, therefore I will return to smoking").

According to Bandura's *social learning theory*, people who engage in addictive behaviors have acquired these habits through learning, just like they learn other habits; hence, these behaviors can be examined and changed (Marlatt, 1985a). For example, people may learn to drink or smoke based on classical conditioning (the behavior of going to a pub leads to feeling relaxed, which leads to drinking, may turn into going to a pub leads to drinking), operant conditioning (I feel more confident when I drink), observational learning or modeling (others I respect drink), and cognitive factors (drinking helps me cope with stress). This model focuses on understanding the determinants of the behavior and the consequences of the behavior. For example, many addictive behaviors are performed to reduce stress and, hence, represent maladaptive coping mechanisms. Although there may be some source of the compulsion in internal body chemistry (a physical craving), this model emphasizes the importance of the individuals' expectation that the use of a particular drug or behavior will reduce stress in determining its use.

Relapse prevention programs are designed to teach people who are trying to make a long-term change in their behavior how to anticipate and cope with the very real problem of relapse (Marlatt, 1985b). These programs have two major goals: helping people identify high-risk situations, those that are likely triggers of relapse, and helping people learn new ways to cope with these situations (see Table 12.7). In sum, relapse prevention programs are like firedrills; people prepare for how they will act once a fire occurs so they can act this way easily and quickly when they are suddenly faced with a fire.

The Triggers of Relapse

Many people who are trying to give up an addictive behavior find that one of the most common triggers of relapse is experiencing a particular emotional state associated with engaging in the behavior (Grilo, Shiffman, & Wing, 1989; Hodgins, el-Guebaly, & Armstrong, 1995). Negative emotional states (which account for 35% of relapses) are situations in which the individual is experiencing anger or frustration, depression, helplessness, or boredom and are likely to lead to the first lapse. "Everything was going well until I failed my statistics exam. I was feeling low and decided a cigarette would cheer me up." These states are particularly likely to lead to relapse when individuals have made extensive use of the problem behavior in the past in a given situation (e.g., "every time I have a crunch at work, I have a drink to relax"), and thereby can feel helpless when faced with similar situations without the crutch of the negative behavior. Interpersonal conflict, which accounts for 16% of relapses, is another common high-risk situation. These situations often involve a conflict in a relationship, such as with a spouse, boss, friend, or family member. Finally, social pressure situations, which account for 20% of relapses, are those in which the individual is responding to the influence of another person or group of people exerting pressure to engage in the taboo behavior (see Figure 12.7). This can be direct (e.g., "you should have some champagne, this is a celebration") or indirect (e.g., all your friends are smoking while they play poker; see Photos 12.6 and 12.7). Other high-risk states can include positive emotional states (using the drug to enhance positive feelings, making "special exceptions"

TABLE 12.7   *What Would You Do?*

- You've just picked up your car from the mechanic and the bill is twice as much as you expected it to be. As you drive home you find that the very thing you took the car in for is still not fixed. The car stalls in rush-hour traffic. You feel angry and frustrated; you crave a cigarette.

- You're at a party with friends. People are smoking and drinking. You're having a glass of wine and intense conversation. You always used to have a cigarette with your drink. It looks good.

- While waiting at the market checkout stand, you find yourself next to the cigarette stand and you notice that the market carries your old brand of cigarettes. Boy, do those cigarettes look good—you can almost taste one.

Ex-smokers asked to read these situations and then quickly write down exactly what they would do as a way of testing how effective their coping strategy would be.

Source: Marlatt, 1985a.

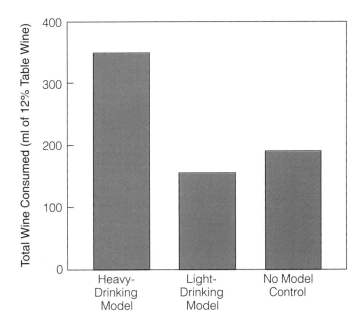

FIGURE 12.7 People drink more wine when they are taking part in a "tasting task" with a heavy-drinking model than with a light-drinking model or when alone (data from Caudill & Marlatt, 1975).

for using a drug during times of celebration) and testing personal control (to see if one really is no longer addicted).

Triggers of relapse can also include particular locations, people, times of day, and life stressors (Marlatt, 1985b; Marlatt & Gordon, 1980). For example, an alcoholic may need to be aware of hanging around with certain friends, being in certain places, or feeling particular moods. Specific triggers, however, vary for different people. People with an alcohol addiction, for example, are very likely to relapse while in a bar or tavern—in one study 63% of the relapses occurred in this type of location. On the other hand, smokers are more likely to relapse at their homes (44%) or at work (19%). Relatively few people relapse in the morning, presumably because willpower is still high, but people often have particular times of day that are most difficult for them. Having a tough day (or week or month) can lead people to say, "I deserve a break" and hence trigger relapse (Brandon, Copeland, & Saper, 1995; Shiffman et al., 1996). In fact, one study found that exercise adherence rates were 27% lower in those who experienced three or more life events in the last 6 months than in those who experienced none (Oman & King, 2000). The AA program uses the acronym HALT, which refers to avoiding being too hungry, angry, lonely, or tired, all of which are factors that can trigger a relapse (Fletcher, 2001).

Relapse can be precipitated by experiencing an unexpected situation with which people are unable to cope (Marlatt, 1985a). For example, a woman who is trying not to drink may deliberately go only to restaurants that do not serve alcohol. Then, a particular restaurant may be closed unexpectedly one day, so

PHOTOS 12.6 AND 12.7   Many of the triggers for relapse are situations in which the behavior has occurred previously and in the presence of particular people who are engaging in the behavior.

she and her friend go to the restaurant next door, which serves alcohol. When her friend orders a drink, it may be impossible for her not to also order a drink, because she has not thought through how to handle this situation. Smokers may relapse because they are offered a cigarette by someone or they find a cigarette.

Relapse can also be precipitated by making a series of very small, apparently irrelevant decisions that lead one closer and closer to temptation, and eventually to relapsing (Marlatt, 1985a). For example, an alcoholic may keep wine in the house "in case company stops by," but then finds himself unable to resist

extensive use of the problem behavior in the past in a given situation (e.g., "every time I have a crunch at work, I have a drink to relax"), and thereby can feel helpless when faced with similar situations without the crutch of the negative behavior. Interpersonal conflict, which accounts for 16% of relapses, is another common high-risk situation. These situations often involve a conflict in a relationship, such as with a spouse, boss, friend, or family member. Finally, social pressure situations, which account for 20% of relapses, are those in which the individual is responding to the influence of another person or group of people exerting pressure to engage in the taboo behavior (see Figure 12.7). This can be direct (e.g., "you should have some champagne, this is a celebration") or indirect (e.g., all your friends are smoking while they play poker; see Photos 12.6 and 12.7). Other high-risk states can include positive emotional states (using the drug to enhance positive feelings, making "special exceptions"

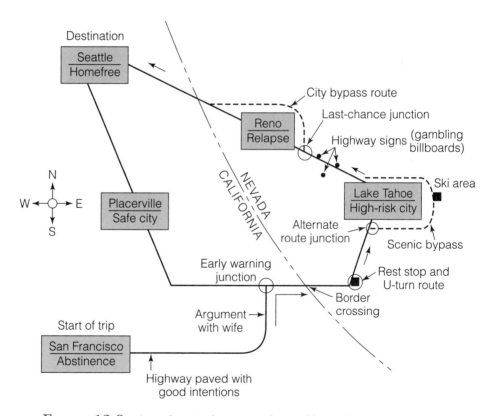

FIGURE 12.8 At each critical juncture, the gambling addict made a small decision that brought him one step closer to relapse. First, he chose to make a right and head to Lake Tahoe instead of a left heading to Placerville. Then, at the rest stop he opted to continue on toward Lake Tahoe instead of making a U-turn and heading back toward Placerville. Third, he drove right into Reno instead of taking the city bypass route. And this series of decisions ultimately lead to a weekend of gambling (Marlatt, 1985).

Strategies for Preventing Relapse

First, individuals need to identify high-risk situations that may lead them to experience a craving for a particular substance (Marlatt, 1985b). As one recovered alcoholic described it, "Look for the common thread in your relapses. Break that thread" (Fletcher, 2001). These situations can be identified through self-monitoring (recording exact amounts of alcohol consumed in each situation, including time of day, others present, location, mood, etc.), self-efficacy questionnaires, recall of past behaviors to determine their particular risk-prone situations, and/or direct observation. As I described at the beginning of this chapter, Sarah worked with a therapist to identify the situations that prompted her alcohol use. After these high-risk situations have been identified, in some cases people can simply remove themselves from the situation. They could, for example, avoid going to bars or being in other situations in which drinking is expected and could remove triggers for their behavior, such as ashtrays (for smokers), wine glasses, and junk food. One study with alcoholics in a hospital setting found that training in cue exposure techniques, in which as part of therapy they were allowed to see and smell their preferred alcoholic beverage while imagining situational pressures to drink, led to much lower rates of drinking over time—only 44% of the patients who received this therapy were drinking at the 6 month follow-up, as compared to 79% of those who received traditional therapy (Monti, Rohsenow, Rubonis, & Niura, 1993). People who participated in this type of cue exposure training learned coping skills that they could apply in real-life situations later on, which in turn likely increased their self-efficacy for refusing alcohol in tempting situations. People who are trying to make a change in their behavior should also be encouraged to choose the date carefully—dieters, for example, should not choose the week of Thanksgiving, nor should drinkers choose St. Patrick's Day!

In other cases people need training in ways to handle high-risk situations in a new way (Cohen & Lichtenstein, 1990; Marlatt, 1985b; Shadel & Mermelstein, 1993). For example, smokers could decide to drink coffee or chew gum during stressful times, and dieters could carry celery sticks or crackers to eat when they are bored. Because people often engage in addictive behaviors as a way of managing stress, relapse prevention programs often train people in various stress management techniques, such as relaxation and meditation. For example, instead of having a drink after a long day, people may learn to substitute other rewarding and positive behaviors, such as getting a massage, taking a long bath, or meditating. In this way, a negative addiction can be replaced by a positive addiction, or something else that the person enjoys and looks forward to. Similarly, because interpersonal conflict is often a trigger for relapse, people need to learn new skills for coping with these situations. One recovered alcoholic reports, "I share my feelings and get out anything that's on my mind, including old issues. Before, I always hid my feelings behind masks, and I drank to get away from all the emotional baggage. Now I make sure it doesn't pile up" (Fletcher, 2001). In one study, subjects received negative comments about their intelligence from another subject (really a confederate of the experimenters; Marlatt, Kosturn, & Lany, 1975). Subjects who had the opportunity to "retaliate" by giving electric shocks to the confederate then drank significantly less wine in a "wine-tasting test" than did those who did not get to express their anger.

Another strategy to prevent relapse is setting clear and attainable goals and creating an incentive for following through on them (Jason, Jayaraj, Blitz, Michaels, & Klett, 1990; Marlatt, 1985a). First, people should set attainable short-term goals so that they can experience quick feelings of success—a runner starts by jogging a mile or two or three, not by entering the Boston Marathon. In fact, the slogan of Alcoholics Anonymous is "One day at a time." The goals should also be reasonable—not smoking for a day can quickly (although not necessarily easily) be attained, whereas "never have another cigarette for the rest of my life" is not going to be quickly accomplished. Second, people should create an incentive program that rewards them for reaching their goals and/or punishes them for not reaching their goals (Petry, Martin, Cooney, & Kranzler, 2000). Ex-smokers could, for example, plan to use the money they've saved on cigarettes to take a trip or buy new clothes. One worksite-based smoking cessation program gave workers $10 for attending each of six group counseling sessions, and then $1 a day for the next 180 days if they continued to not smoke. It was highly successful; 42% of participants were not smoking at the end of the program compared to 13% of those in a control group (Jason et al., 1990). Some relapse prevention programs even ask people to set up a contract that specifies the costs of relapsing. One African American woman who was trying to stop smoking gave her therapist $50 and told her that if she smoked, the money should be donated to the Ku Klux Klan! These contracts could also specify that if a person is tempted to engage in the addictive behavior, they agree to wait at least 20 minutes before giving in. This will at least give them time to contemplate the behavior and not just act on the spur of the moment. They could also agree to only use a single "dose" at the time of relapse, for example, to have one beer, not a six-pack, or one cigarette, not a pack. This makes it easier to recover from a lapse.

Social support, either from friends and family members or therapists and support groups, can play an important role in helping people maintain a new behavior (Black, Gleser, & Kooyers, 1990; Marlatt, 1985a; McBride et al., 1998; Mermelstein, Cohen, Lichtenstein, Baer, & Kamarck, 1986; Nides et al., 1995; Tsoh et al., 1997). People who are trying to change their behavior should tell people they are close to as well as people they spend a lot of time with about their intentions. These other people can be asked to support the behavior change, such as by not smoking around them or offering them unhealthy foods and by expressing confidence in the person's ability to change the behavior (Cohen & Lichtenstein, 1990b; Sorensen, Pechacek, & Pallonen, 1986). For example, one study with pregnant smokers found that those who received high levels of support from their partner were much more likely to quit than those without such support (McBride et al., 1998). However, because relapse can be precipitated by a reaction against perceived imposition of rules or regulations governing the prohibited behavior, it is important that the person him- or herself makes the decision to change the behavior. For example, people can throw off this prohibition, particularly if they believe that others (family members, friends) are forcing them to abstain. Therapists and support groups are most effective at maintaining behavior change when they continue their interaction with the patient over time, in part because such contact helps people maintain their self-efficacy for behavior change even in the face of great temptation and occasional lapses (Curry & McBride, 1994; Irvin et al., 1999; Zhu et al., 1996). Ongoing social support, brief weekly phone calls from a therapist, and even mailings all lead to much greater sustained behavior change (Brandon, Collins, Juliano, & Lazev, 2000; Perri & Nezu, 1993). For example, one study found that 14.7% of smokers who received a self-help quit kit had stopped smoking at a 12-month follow-up as compared to 19.8% of those who received the kit plus one telephone counseling session and 26.7% of those who received the kit plus up to six counseling sessions (Zhu et al., 1996).

Another strategy for preventing relapse is helping people think about their old behaviors in new ways (Marlatt, 1985a). Relapse prevention programs try to help people focus on the short-term versus the long-term consequences of engaging in the behavior (PIG, or the Problem of Immediate Gratification). The immediate consequences of engaging in an addictive behavior may be particularly strong and positive (e.g., relaxation, feel good, fit in), whereas the long-term consequences may be less salient and largely negative (e.g., have trouble with work, develop serious health problems). So, people need to be trained to focus on the delayed effects of giving in to temptation. They also need to recognize that these responses arise and subside on their own (e.g., as opposed to thinking that these cravings will gain in intensity until they give in). Learning how to externalize and label their desires is one strategy for reducing the tendency to give in to the urge (e.g., "I am experiencing an urge to smoke" instead of "I really want a cigarette"). They may also need to be trained to reevaluate their expectancies for engaging in the behavior. As shown in Figure 12.9, people's expectancies are more powerful influences on drinking than the physiological effects of alcohol (Marlatt, Demming & Reid, 1973). However, physiological cravings do matter—one study found that only 7% of smokers who were highly dependent on nicotine were still not smoking 2 years after treatment, as compared to 19% of those without such a dependency (Killen, Fortmann, Kraemer, Varady, & Newman, 1992).

Finally, relapse prevention strategies include preparing people to see a lapse in behavior as a single, isolated incidence as opposed to a disaster that can never be undone (Marlatt, 1985a). According to the *abstinence violation effect*, if people expect they will never give in to temptation, when and if they do have a lapse in behavior, they are likely to blame it on themselves, which could lead to a total relapse (Curry, Marlatt, & Gordon, 1987; Marlatt & Gordon, 1980). For example, if I am dieting but choose to eat a piece of cheesecake, I will feel guilty. Then, how will I choose to reduce the guilt? Probably by relying on the same maladaptive coping mechanisms—eating more. Relapse prevention programs should include exposure to some such high-risk settings to give people a chance to cope with such challenges in a controlled environment—some programs even include a "scheduled lapse." These programs also point to one potential drawback of inpatient treatment for making behavior change; namely, that patients can make great strides in their behavior change when they are in a new environment and with new people, but have trouble maintaining this behavior once they return to their regular lives and the situations

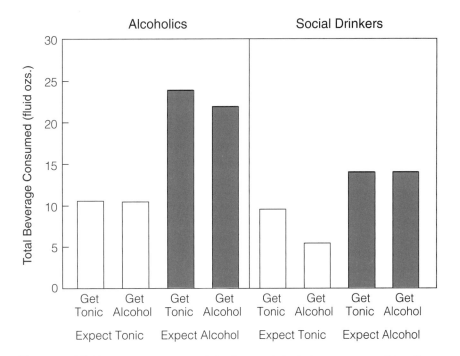

FIGURE 12.9   When both social drinkers and alcoholics participated in a "taste rating" of alcoholic or nonalcoholic beverages, the only significant predictor of amount of alcohol consumed was the *expectancy* of the tasters that they were drinking alcohol (data from Marlatt et al., 1973).

that triggered their old behaviors. Losing weight, for example, can be relatively easy in a special 1- or 2-week treatment program in which low-fat meals are attractively prepared and served, but much harder when you return to the rush of daily life and the temptation of fast food at every corner.

Lingering Issues

Do mammograms save lives? For a long time, mammograms have been seen as an important part of routine health care for women ages 50 years and over, with some experts believing mammograms should begin as early as age 40 (American Cancer Society, 2002). However, in early 2002 a National Cancer Institute Panel issued a startling statement: even for women over age 50, mammograms might make very little difference. Why? Some women have very slow-growing tumors, which are likely to be curable (by simply removing them) whenever a physician detects them during a manual exam. So, these women would not benefit from catching these tumors earlier than later. Other women have very fast-growing, aggressive tumors, and, unfortunately, these tumors are so fast-growing that even when they are caught at a relatively early point, it is typically too late to make a difference in terms of survival. Therefore, these women would also not benefit from having regular mammograms. Women who have tumors that grow at a moderate rate benefit from regular mammograms because catching these tumors early is important. These women, however, represent only about 15 to 20% of breast cancer cases, meaning that the majority of women shows no benefits from mammograms.

How should we measure relapse? One of the very tricky issues in measuring the effectiveness of different behavior change programs is defining exactly what *success* is. Many studies suggest that long-term behavior change is relatively rare (Brownell & Wadden, 1992; Hughes et al., 1992; Ockene et al., 2000; Wadden, 1993). About 97% of people who quit smoking on their own return to smoking within 6 months (Hughes et al., 1992), and even for those in formal smoking cessation programs, only about 20 to 30% achieve long-term quitting (Cohen et al., 1989). Similarly, Brownell and Wadden (1992) point out that some patients will maintain 60 to 70% of their weight loss as long as a year after participating in a treatment program, but that longer follow-up periods (of 3 to 5 years) reveal a return to baseline. However, to really measure the effectiveness of a program, you need to have some type of control or at least comparison group. After all, people on average gain about 1 to 2 pounds a year as they get older, so if people who attend a weight-loss program do return to their previous weight but do not gain weight, perhaps that is a mark of success. One study with hypertensive patients found that people in the treatment groups showed an average weight loss of 1.5 pounds after 5 years, whereas those in the control group showed an increase of nearly 7 pounds (Morisky et al., 1983). Similarly, even if smokers fail on multiple initial quitting attempts, these attempts at changing behavior may ultimately help them succeed later on. Another problem with measuring relapse is that different people define *relapse* in different ways. In the domain of smoking cessation, for example, Judith Ockene and colleagues (2000) suggest that researchers set specific criteria for assessing relapse (e.g., smoking five or more cigarettes per day for 3 consecutive days) as compared to lapse (e.g., taking even a puff), successful change (e.g., at least 7 days of not smoking), short-term change (e.g., 6 months or more of abstinence), and long-term change (e.g., 1 year or more of abstinence). In sum, researchers must be careful in exactly how they measure success and failure of a given behavior change program, including the length of time they track the participants, the measures used to assess behavior change, and the group to which the participants are compared—behavior change may be more possible than we believe!

Thought Questions

1. A close friend confides in you that she is thinking about getting tested for HIV. What four things would you advise her to consider prior to getting the test?

2. Describe two symptoms that lead people to seek help for a medical problem and two symptoms that lead people to delay getting help.

3. How can we increase patient–practitioner communication in a climate of HMOs and cost-saving measures?

4. Describe two strategies that could be useful in decreasing *unintentional* nonadherence and two strategies that could be useful in decreasing *intentional* nonadherence.

5. Your brother has smoked for nearly 5 years, but gave up smoking as his New Year's resolution 2 weeks ago. What four pieces of advice could you give him to help him stick with this goal?

Answers to Questioning the Research

Answer 12.1: It is important to remember that people are never randomly assigned to get tested for serious genetic disorders—estimates are that only between 5 and 20% of those at risk for Huntington's disease and HIV infection, for example, undergo testing (Marteau, 1995). People who do not choose to get tested may be more afraid of a positive test, or less prepared for the result. On the other hand, people who choose to get tested may already fear they are positive—especially if they have relatives with the disease, testing may reduce anxiety even if it provides bad news. In contrast, a person who has no expectation of getting a positive result may be shocked. In fact, younger women who learn that their baby has Down's syndrome show greater and more sustained anxiety than older women who are already aware of their higher risk. In sum, even if some people do show few signs of depression and anxiety following testing, others may experience negative psychological effects for some time.

Answer 12.2: Although it seems obvious that patients who adhere to medical recommendations would show better health than those who do not, research is quite mixed on whether adherence really benefits health (Gallagher et al., 1993; Haynes, McKibbon, & Kanani, 1996; Hays et al., 1994). In fact, while patients who took medicine had a lower mortality rate than those who did not, this association was true even for those who were in the placebo group; hence, they received no real physical benefits from adhering (Gallagher et al., 1993; Horwitz et al., 1990). For example, women in the placebo group who were poor adherers to the placebo medication were 2.8 times more likely to have died 2 to 3 years later than those who were good adherers. Similarly, men who were bad adherers were 2.6 times as likely to have died than those who took the placebo medication faithfully. It is likely that patients who adhere to medical recommendations differ in numerous ways from those who don't. They may, for example, be more optimistic, more conscientious, and have more social support, all of which could lead to better health. Future research clearly needs to examine exactly how—and indeed whether—adherence truly impacts health.

CHAPTER 13

Designing Persuasive Interventions

- Stephanie is 25 years old, and for as long as she can remember, she's spent most summer weekends at the beach. Although she's heard that tanning can lead to some types of cancer, Stephanie rarely uses sunscreen because she thinks she looks much more attractive when she has a tan. She's really not that concerned about cancer anyway—most of Stephanie's friends also don't use sunscreen, and she's heard that skin cancer can be treated quite easily.

- Damon is a sophomore in college and is a residential advisor in his dorm. As part of his training, he learns about the dangers of using illegal drugs, such as marijuana, cocaine, and Ecstasy, and then gives presentations to the students in his dorm to warn them away from these substances. Damon used to occasionally enjoy getting high when he was at a party, but now finds himself feeling more and more uncomfortable with that behavior.

- Bill is 45 years old and has been overweight since he was in this early 20s. He knows that his weight places him at risk of experiencing a heart attack, but he just doesn't see how he could find the time to exercise. However, Bill's doctor assures him that exercising would have substantial health benefits and suggests some specific approaches Bill could try, including using the stairs at work instead of the elevator and playing tennis with his kids on the weekend. This discussion gives Bill confidence that he could start exercising, and he decides to give it a try .

- Lucinda is 36 years old and desperately needs to have a cavity filled. Although she knows that she needs the filling, she is very anxious. Based on past experiences, Lucinda knows that she benefits from having lots of information about what to expect, and so she asks the dental hygienist to carefully describe each step of the procedure. Much to her surprise, the filling takes very little time and hardly hurts at all.

- Debbie has a summer job in a local Planned Parenthood clinic, and she has been asked to help create two different types of condom promotion workshops for teenagers—one for males and one for females. Debbie decides that the workshop designed for boys should focus on how condoms make sex last longer and how it can therefore feel even better for both partners. On the other hand, she believes the workshop designed for girls should emphasize how to put a condom on one's partner and how to assertively insist on condom use.

Preview

This chapter examines how psychological theories and principles can be used to design persuasive communications, such as television commercials, pamphlets, and interventions, that influence people's health-related behavior. First, we examine the use of rational and emotional appeals, with a particular focus on the effectiveness of threatening messages. Next, we examine how interventions based on psychological theories, including prospect theory, attribution theory, cognitive dissonance theory, social cognitive theory, and behavior theory, can influence health-related behaviors. Finally, we examine the benefits of receiving personally relevant messages in promoting various types of health-related behavior, including screening, managing pain, adhering to medical recommendations, and changing behavior.

Are Emotional Appeals Effective?

Many health-promotion messages simply provide the facts about a given behavior, with the hope that giving people the information will motivate change. According to this view, people who understand that smoking causes lung cancer or that unprotected sex can lead to pregnancy, for example, will be motivated to change their behavior to avoid these negative consequences. Early efforts at HIV prevention focused on providing people with straightforward information about the factors leading to the spread of HIV (e.g., unprotected sex, sharing needles). One study of 127 public service announcements on television about AIDS revealed that 51% simply presented factual information, such as how AIDS is transmitted and the safety of donating blood (Freimuth, Hammond, Edgar, & Monohan, 1990), and in the late 1980s the surgeon general of the United States even mailed a pamphlet containing this information to every U. S. household. Unfortunately, in most cases information is not a sufficient motivator of behavior change—most smokers, for example, are fully aware of the health consequences of their behavior, yet they continue to smoke. In fact, we all engage in behaviors (sometimes frequently) that we know are not great for our health (e.g., not wearing a seatbelt, failing to use sunscreen, eating high-fat foods). Research studies provide additional support for the view that information alone is rarely a sufficient motivator of behavior. In one early study on health-promotion messages, Howard Leventhal and colleagues (1965) found that none of the students who received information about the importance of having a tetanus shot actually went to the health center for the vaccination. In sum, although providing people with information about healthy behaviors does, not surprisingly, increase their knowledge about such behavior, it is rarely sufficient to lead to behavior change.

In contrast, other health-promotion messages provide emotional, as opposed to rational, messages about the consequences of engaging in a given behavior (Flora & Maibach, 1990; Reeves, Newhagen, Maibach, Basil, & Kurz, 1991). Because people tend to seek pleasant experiences, which help them maintain positive moods, some emotion-based messages have used positive stimuli, such as appealing music and attractive people. Positive emotion–based appeals could, for example, show people enjoying themselves at a party without drinking or smoking, or a couple becoming closer through discussing condom use. Emotion-based messages are more vivid and memorable than rational ones, especially if the person is not very involved in or concerned about the message.

Still other emotion-based appeals use negative stimuli in an attempt to create the threat of impending danger or harm caused by engaging in particular types of behavior (e.g., drug use, smoking) or failing to engage in other types of behavior (e.g., not using a condom, not wearing a seatbelt), and thereby attempt to motivate behavior (Higbee, 1969; Rogers, 1975). These messages sometimes use scary verbal statements and may show graphic, even disgusting, images. For example, one television ad promoting the use of seatbelts shows a young man backing his car out of the driveway on his way to pick up ice cream for his pregnant wife, but he wasn't wearing his seatbelt and then was hit by a speeding car. In some other countries, such as Australia and Canada, television ads may include even more graphic images, such as dead bodies and crash survivors learning how to walk again. Similarly, one public service poster promoting HIV prevention features only a woman's face and the words "I enjoy sex, but I don't want to die for it."One study of AIDS public

Box 13.1

Health Psychology in the Real World—The Pros and Cons of Different Mass-Media Approaches

One of the biggest challenges facing health professionals is how to effectively persuade people to change their health-related behavior. Many health-promotion campaigns rely at least in part on mass communication, including newpapers and magazines, billboards and posters, and radio and television ads. Each of these approaches has certain advantages and disadvantages. For example, brochures can provide detailed, factual information and can be read at a person's convenience. However, brochures can be hard to deliver to the people who need the information, and people may choose to not read them at all. On the other hand, television advertising easily reaches a large audience and can be very vivid and impactful. This type of advertising is, however, expensive to produce and often provides relatively little factual information. Public health professionals therefore must make complex decisions about the relative costs and benefits of each potential approach to delivering health-promotion information.

service announcements on television found that 26% used fear (Freimuth et al., 1990). Fear-based messages are designed to increase people's feelings of vulnerability to various health problems, and thereby motivate them to change their behavior (Janis, 1967; Leventhal, 1970). Moreover, as compared to positive messages, negative ones are thought to be more primary, easier to understand, more quickly processed, and more accurately remembered (see Table 13.1; Reeves, Lang, Thorson, & Rothschild, 1989).

But are fear appeals really effective in changing people's attitudes and behavior? Not often. In fact, although organizations and advertisers believe

TABLE 13.1   *What Type of Ad Do You Think Would Be Most Effective?*

- I enjoy sex but I don't want to die for it.
- Someone I respect has been urging me to use condoms. It's the surgeon general. Believe me, I'm listening.
- Introducing condoms that let you feel good before, during, and after.
- Men could use some protection from women—and vice versa.

The first two ads are designed to elicit high fear, whereas the second two are designed to elicit low fear.

Source: Struckman-Johnson et al., 1990.

that fear appeals work, and thereby continue to produce messages that emphasize the dire consequences of engaging (or not engaging) in particular behavior, most evidence suggests that this approach is not effective (Des Jarlais, Friedman, Casriel, & Kott, 1987; Evans, 1988). For example, one study of Project DARE (Drug Abuse Resistance Education), a commonly used fear-based drug prevention program for children, found that this program has little, if any, effect on preventing or reducing drug use, and it is often less effective than programs that focus simply on social skills (Ennett, Tobler, Ringwalt, & Flewelling, 1994). Similarly, a fear arousing mass-media campaign in Australia to promote condom use led to an increase in anxiety, but had little if any effect on knowledge or behavior (Rigby, Brown, Anagnostou, Ross, & Rosser, 1989; Sherr, 1990). Ironically, people who receive high-fear messages often *report* that they are very influenced, but in reality show lower levels of attitude and behavior change than those who receive positive approaches (Evans, Rozelle, Lasater, Dembroski, & Allen, 1970; Janis & Feshbach, 1953). But sometimes fear can work—one study found that 86% of those who saw a scary video on lung cancer reported trying to stop or cut down on smoking, as compared to 33% of those who saw a control video (Sutton & Eiser, 1984; Sutton & Hallett, 1988). Interestingly, high fear may be not so effective immediately, but could be very effective later on (see Box 13.2).

One of the problems with fear appeals is that they create considerable anxiety, which in turn can lead to a constriction of cognitive processing, resulting in marked interference with learning, attention, and comprehension (Janis, 1967). For example, smokers who receive a strong fear message show more tension and concern about lung cancer, but less attitude change (Janis & Terwilliger, 1962), and high schools students who receive a strong fear message about decayed teeth and gum disease remember fewer arguments from the message and show less attitude change than those who received a more mild argument (Janis & Fesbach, 1953). Moreover, because engaging in a behavior known to be risky makes people feel bad, people who receive threatening and personally relevant messages may ignore, deny, and minimize the threat (Kunda, 1990). Smokers, for example, see smoking as less risky and rate their own risk as even lower than the risk of the "typical smoker" (Halpern, 1994; McCoy et al., 1992; Strecher, Kreuter, & Kobrin, 1995). In fact, Halpern (1994) found that heavy smokers evaluate their health risks as lower than light smokers, and long-term smokers evaluate their health risks as lower than short-term smokers, presumably to justify their behavior. And when people are given messages about the realistic risks of their behavior, they are dismissive and critical of such information (Chaiken, 1987; Freeman, Hennessy, & Marzullo, 2001; Halpern, 1994; Kunda, 1990; Sherman, Nelson, & Steele, 2000). For example, heavy coffee drinkers were more critical of a study supposedly showing a link between caffeine consumption and disease than those who don't drink coffee, presumably because coffee drinkers really don't want to believe they are engaging in a health-damaging behavior (Liberman & Chaiken, 1992; Sherman et al., 2000).

Another way of reducing fear is by seeing the problem as more common—a strategy of "well, if everyone else is doing it, it must not be that bad" (Croyle,

Box 13.2

Research Focus—How Much Fear Is Too Much Fear?

Howard Leventhal and Jean Watts (1966) conducted one of the first studies on the effectiveness of fear appeals on smoking cessation. Visitors to a state fair were recruited to participate in a smoking cessation and were randomly assigned to receive one of three smoking cessation messages. The low-fear message consisted of a color film describing the threat of lung cancer using charts and diagrams; the medium-fear message consisted of the same film plus an additional segment documenting how a small-town newspaper editor discovered he had lung cancer; and the high-fear message consisted of the same film and additional segment plus a 10-minute color sequence showing an operation in which a lung is removed. Not surprisingly, people who watched the high-fear film showed many signs of distress, including looking away, groaning, and even crying. Researchers then gave participants the option to have a chest X ray at a nearby booth and also sent all participants a questionnaire 5 months later to examine long-term behavior change.

This study revealed that low- versus high-fear ads have a different impact on behavior at different times. First, those in the low-fear condition were the most likely to immediately get an X ray of their lungs at a nearby booth (53% in low fear versus 44% in medium fear, 6% in high fear). These findings clearly suggest that high-fear messages were much less effective than low or medium ones in influencing short-term behavior. However, the follow-up questionnaire revealed significant differences in the opposite direction: 57% of those in the low-fear and moderate-fear conditions reported cutting down on smoking compared to 79% of those in the high-fear condition. In sum, high-fear messages may be ineffective in the short term, as people react defensively to these upsetting and personally relevant messages, but may be quite effective over time.

Sun, & Louie, 1993; Gerrard, Gibbons, Benthin, & Hessling, 1996). For example, one study by Meg Gerrard and her colleagues at Iowa State University (1996) found that teenagers who engage in various risky behaviors, such as smoking, drinking, and reckless driving, convince themselves that other teenagers are engaging in similar levels of risky behavior. Similarly, as compared to students who are told their cholesterol is at a low level, students who receive information that their cholesterol is at a somewhat risky high level perceive high cholesterol as a less serious threat, view the test as less accurate, and see high cholesterol as more common (Croyle et al., 1993). All of this evidence suggests that fear-based appeals can have some unintended—and even dangerous—side effects.

Fear messages do work, but only in very specific situations. First, messages need to create a *moderate* level of fear (see Figure 13.1; Janis, 1967; Janis & Fesbach, 1953; Leventhal, 1970). At very low levels of fear, the danger is not seen as very important or very severe, and hence the average person will be relatively unmotivated to seek help. On the other hand, and as described previously, at high levels of fear people try to deny or minimize the threat to cope with their anxiety. However, at moderate levels of fear, people will be motivated to protect themselves, because the threat seems relatively likely and relatively severe, but they will not be paralyzed by anxiety and hence unable to act. For example, Janis and Fesbach (1953) found that messages that led to a moderate level of fear were the most effective in getting junior high school students to engage in better dental hygiene habits.

Second, because fear appeals create considerable anxiety, people must be given a specific strategy for handling the anxiety to avoid the motivation to minimize or deny the threat (Leventhal et al., 1965; Self & Rogers, 1990; Sturges & Rogers, 1996). Students who receive highly threatening messages but who are told that they can take some specific action to manage the threat

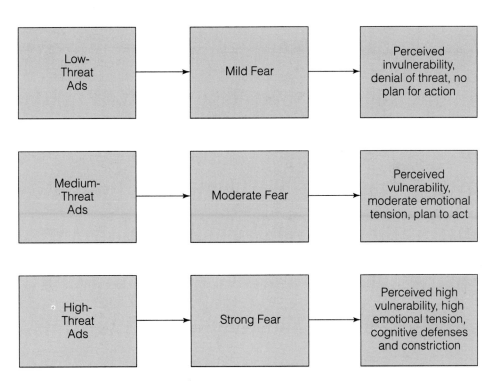

FIGURE 13.1 According to Janis (1967), medium-threat ads, which create moderate fear, are the most effective at creating attitude and behavior change. Low-threat ads don't motivate people to change, and high-threat ads lead to considerable anxiety, which in turn can reduce cognitive processing and paralyze behavior change.

show stronger intentions to change their behavior than those who receive messages that frighten them but don't give strategies for coping (Self & Rogers, 1990). Similarly, Leventhal and colleagues (1965) found that 27.6% of students who received a fear message coupled with specific instructions on how to get a tetanus shot did have the vaccination as compared to 3.3% of those with received a fear message without such detailed instructions. So, fear-based drug prevention campaigns are probably not an effective approach to attitude and behavior change, but programs that give teenagers specific techniques for managing peer pressure to use drugs without alienating friends may be quite effective. For example, the Midwestern Prevention Project, a moder-

Box 13.3

Health Psychology in the Real World—How Can Public Service Ads Work Best to Prevent Smoking?

Despite the challenges of trying to prevent smoking in teenagers, research suggests some important strategies for designing persuasive antismoking messages for this population (Pechmann, 1997). First, ads must focus on short-term and credible consequences, such as smelly breath and clothes, excessive expense, and the lack of social support among peers for smoking. Because even teenagers who understand that they are at risk of various health consequences from smoking may see the shorter-term benefits of smoking (e.g., looking "mature," feeling relaxed) as more important than the distant, long-term health consequences, ads must focus on the negative social and personal consequences of smoking behavior. Emphasizing the long-term consequences of smoking can backfire by making teenagers think there are no negative short-term effects—and teenagers often assume they'll smoke for a few years and then give it up.

Second, ads should present a conversational and casual approach, ideally using a self-confident attractive actor a couple of years older than the target audience. Because teenagers are strongly motivated to fit in with their crowd and they challenge authority, ads that are presented by other teenagers are much more effective than those presented by authority figures, including parents, doctors, and teachers.

Finally, teenagers must actually see the ads for them to work. Networks often run public service ads during adolescents' low viewing times (e.g., very late at night) because they are not paid for showing such service ads and have no economic justification for airing nonprofitable ads during prime time. Ads should ideally run on network television in the afternoons and evenings during television shows that teenagers watch. Ads on radio stations popular with teenagers can also be effective, especially if run anytime from 3 to 11 P.M.

ately successful drug prevention program for middle and junior high school students, provides students with information about drugs coupled with training in strategies for resisting social pressure, such as assertiveness training, modeling, and role play (MacKinnon et al., 1991). Participation in this program leads to more negative attitudes toward drugs and decreases in intentions to use drugs as well as decreased reported drug use.

Fear appeals are also effective when they focus on the short-term, as opposed to the long-term, consequences (Klohn & Rogers, 1991; Pechmann, 1997)—many people, especially teenagers, just aren't concerned about long-term consequences (see Box 13.3). I know many college students who say that having an unplanned pregnancy would be worse than getting HIV, presumably because pregnancy leads to an instant problem, whereas developing HIV is a much more distant problem. Similarly, people might learn that tanning can cause skin cancer, but still feel that they'd like to be tan because they look healthier and more attractive (Broadstock, Borland, & Garson, 1992; Leary & Jones, 1993). As I described at the beginning of the chapter, Stephanie's desire to tan—and thereby appear more attractive—was a much stronger motivator of her behavior (e.g., lack of sunscreen use) than her concern about skin cancer. In fact, Jones and Leary (1994) found that college students were more persuaded to use sunscreen after reading an essay describing the short-term negative effects of tanning on appearance (e.g., increasing wrinkles, scarring, aging) than an essay describing the long-term negative effects (e.g., the health risks of tanning, prevalence of different types of skin cancer). One study with 19 young drug sniffers (who often go on to use IV drugs) found that none gave concern about AIDS as a reason for not using IV drugs—they simply didn't want to lose control over their lives because of addiction (Des Jarlais et al., 1987).

Finally, fear appeals may also work when they force people to actually imagine having a particular disease or problem, and thereby lead to a heightened sense of vulnerability (Janis & Mann, 1965). One public service announcement designed to enhance people's perceived vulnerability to HIV featured an attractive Hispanic man saying the following: "Do I look like someone who has AIDS? Of course not. I am Alejandro Paredes. I finished school. I have a good job. I help support my family. My kind of guy doesn't get AIDS, right? Well, I have AIDS, and I don't mind telling you it's devastating. If I had a second chance, I'd be informed. Believe me" (Freimuth et al., 1990, p. 788). This appeal is clearly designed to increase people's vulnerability to HIV and to eliminate the use of various cognitive defenses against this information (e.g., only poor people get HIV, only people who look unhealthy have HIV). Similarly, in one study female smokers who had no intention to decrease smoking were asked to role-play five different scenes with the experimenter (Janis & Mann, 1965). These scenes were designed to heighten vulnerability to lung cancer and were highly emotionally arousing for the participants. For example, in one scene the experimenter—playing the part of the doctor and wearing a white lab coat to enhance realism—gave the participant the bad news that she had lung cancer and had only a few months to live. Women who participated in these role-plays had less-positive attitudes about smoking and greater intentions to stop smoking than those in the control condition, who simply listened to a tape of these role-plays.

How Effective Are Interventions Based in Psychological Theories?

Given the ineffectiveness of messages that simply provide information, and the potential dangers of messages that simply use scare tactics, researchers are increasingly developing health-related behavior change messages that are based on psychological theories. This section examines how various psychological theories, including prospect theory, attribution theory, cognitive dissonance theory, learning theories, and social cognitive theory, can be used to create persuasive health-related messages.

Prospect Theory

Prospect theory posits that people make very different choices when decisions are presented in different ways, such as in terms of their costs versus benefits (Tversky & Kahneman, 1981). For example, you might see condoms as more desirable when they are presented as "90% effective" than when they are presented as having a "10% failure rate." In fact, students rate a medical treatment with a 50% success rate as more effective and as one they are more likely to recommend it to members of their immediate family than a treatment with a 50% failure rate (Levin, Schnittjer, & Thee, 1988), and students feel more optimistic about a person with a 90% chance of survival than a 10% chance of dying. Prospect theory also specifically states that people are more willing to take risks when they are considering the losses or costs of a particular behavior than when they are considering the gains or benefits of engaging in a behavior. For example, in a classic study on this problem, people are presented with information about the outbreak of an epidemic that is expected to kill 600 people and are asked to select one of two programs (one offering a guaranteed outcome of lives saved and the other offering a risky outcome). When the program is phrased in terms of the number of lives that will be lost, people prefer a program that provides a 33% chance of no people dying and a 66% chance of everyone dying to a solution that is certain to lead to 400 people dying and 200 people living. On the other hand, when the program is phrased in terms of the number of lives that will be saved, people prefer a program in which 200 people will be saved (and 400 people killed) to one in which there is a 33% chance of saving all 600 patients and a 66% chance of saving no one. These different preferences are based in how people tend to see the relative costs of losing something versus the relative benefits of gaining something— and people seem to experience more pain from losses than they do joy from winning. As described by the former tennis star Jimmy Connors, "I hate to lose more than I love to win" (creativequotations. com, 2003).

In turn, message framing influences how persuaded people are to engage in certain health-promoting behaviors (Rothman & Salovey, 1997). According to prospect theory, people should be more persuaded to engage in behavior to detect a problem when it is framed negatively, namely, in terms of the costs of *not* engaging in a behavior (see Table 13.2). Engaging in detection behavior is somewhat risky, because the person must risk receiving a negative outcome (e.g., learning he or she has a disease); hence, messages that emphasize the immediate costs of engaging in this type of risky behavior should encourage risk seeking. To test this hypothesis, Beth Meyerowitz and Shelley Chaiken (1987) gave college women informational pamphlets on BSE that included either positively or negatively framed information (e.g., "Research shows that women who do BSE have an increased chance of finding a tumor in the early, more treatable stage of the disease" versus "Research shows that women who

TABLE 13.2   *Comparison of Sample Gain- versus Loss-Framed Persuasive Statements*

Gain Framed	Loss Framed
We will show that detecting breast cancer early can save your life.	We will show that failing to detect breast cancer early can cost you your life.
Although all women are at risk for breast cancer, there is something you can do to increase your chances of surviving it.	Although all women are at risk for breast cancer, there is something you can do that increases your risk of dying from it.
For this reason, when you get a mammogram, you are taking advantage of the best method for detecting breast cancer early.	For this reason, when you avoid getting a mammogram, you are failing to take advantage of the best method for detecting breast cancer early.
If a cancer has not spread, it is less likely to be fatal.	If a cancer has spread, it is more likely to be fatal.
Another advantage of finding a tumor early is that you are more likely to increase your treatment options and may need less radical procedures.	Another disadvantage of failing to find a tumor early is that you may have fewer treatment options and may need more radical procedures.
The bottom line is, when you get regular mammograms, you are doing your best to detect breast cancer in its early stages.	The bottom line is, when you fail to get regular mammograms, you are not doing your best to detect breast cancer in its early stages.

These statements provide examples of gain- versus loss-framed persuasive statements.

Source: Banks et al., 1995.

do not do BSE have a decreased chance of finding a tumor in the early, more treatable stage of the disease"). Women who were exposed to a negatively framed (loss-focused) message expressed the most positive attitudes and intentions about engaging in BSE and were more likely to report performing BSE at the 4-month follow-up. Similar results are found with use of mammograms (Banks et al., 1995; Schneider et al., 2001), amniocentesis (Marteau, 1989), skin cancer detection (Rothman, Salovey, Antone, et al., 1993), and HIV testing (Kalichman & Coley, 1995). For example, Sara Banks and colleagues (1995) found that 66.2% of women who received a loss-framed message about mammograms had obtained a mammogram 1 year later as compared to 51.5% of those who received a gain-framed message. Similarly, Kalichman and Coley (1995) found that 63% of women who received a negatively framed HIV video message had been tested 2 weeks later as compared to 23% of those who simply received information presented by an African American woman and 0% of those who received information presented by an Africa American man. In sum, loss-framed messages are more effective than gain-framed messages at encouraging people to engage in behaviors to detect a symptom of illness.

Prospect theory also states that gain-framed messages, those that emphasize the *benefits* of engaging in a behavior, should be more effective than loss-framed messages in promoting prevention behavior (e.g., use of sunscreen, condoms, and car seats; Rothman & Salovey, 1997). Because people should be more wary about taking a risk (e.g., they are risk averse) when considering gain information, they should be more willing to perform a prevention behavior after hearing a message emphasizing the benefits of engaging in a behavior than the consequences of not engaging in the behavior. Positive, gain-framed messages are indeed more effective than loss-framed ones at increasing intentions to use condoms (Linville, Fischer, & Fischhoff, 1993) as well as to wear sunscreen (Detweiler, Bedell, Salovey, Pronin, & Rothman, 1999; Rothman, Salovey, Antone et al., 1993). For example, 85% of students who are told that a particular brand of condoms has a 90% success rate intend to use this type of condom, whereas 63% of those who learn that this brand has a 10% failure rate intend to use that type (Linville et al., 1997). Another study found that 46% of those who got the loss-framed messages about skin cancer requested free sunscreen with a sun protection factor (SPF) level of 15 as compared to 71% who received the gain-framed messages (Rothman, Salovey, Antone, et al., 1993).

Similarly, the way health practitioners describe different treatment options influences patients' preferences (Levin et al., 1988; Marteau, 1989; McNeil, Pauker, Sox, & Tversky, 1982). The decision to undergo a surgical procedure, for example, is a risk-averse or safer option, because this operation should increase a person's life expectancy or relieve him or her of a given health problem (e.g., preventive behaviors). In turn, people should be more motivated to choose surgery when it is described in terms of its benefits to life expectancy as opposed to the costs in terms of life expectancy resulting from not undergoing the surgery. To test this hypothesis, physicians, patients, and medical students were given information that described the short- and long-term consequences of having surgery versus radiation to treat lung cancer (see Box 13.4). In the short term, surgery is a riskier option than radiation because some people die on the operating table. However, in the long term, surgery prevents various health

---

Box 13.4

Which Treatment Would You Choose?

Surgery for lung cancer involves an operation on the lungs. Most patients are in the hospital for 2 or 3 weeks and have some pain around their incisions; then they spend a month or so recuperating at home. After that, they generally feel fine.

Radiation therapy for lung cancer involves the use of radiation to kill the tumor and requires coming to the hospital about 4 times a week for 6 weeks. Each treatment takes a few minutes and during the treatment, patients lie on a table as if they were having an X ray. During the course of treatment, some patients develop nausea and vomiting, but by the end of the 6 weeks they also generally feel fine.

Loss-Framed Wording

Of 100 people having surgery, 10 will die during treatment, 32 will have died by 1 year, and 66 will have died by 5 years. Of 100 people having radiation therapy, none will die during treatment, 23 will die by 1 year, and 78 will die by 5 years. Which treatment would you prefer?

Gain-Framed Wording

Of 100 people having surgery, 90 will live during treatment, 68 will be alive at 1 year, and 34 will be alive at 5 years. Of 100 people having radiation therapy, all will live during treatment, 77 will be alive at 1 year, and 22 will be alive at 5 years. Which treatment would you prefer?

---

problems, and therefore it leads to longer life expectancy. As predicted, more people chose surgery when information was presented in terms of likelihood of living (a gain frame) than when information was presented in terms of likelihood of dying (a loss frame; see Figure 13.2).

Cognitive Dissonance Theory

According to Festinger's cognitive dissonance theory, people are highly motivated to have their attitudes, beliefs, and behaviors be in alignment, and when they engage in a behavior that is not consistent with their attitudes, they experience an unpleasant state of psychological arousal known as *dissonance* (Festinger, 1957). Imagine, for example, that you believe very strongly in the importance of recycling and regularly encourage others to recycle their papers, bottles, and cans. Then one day, perhaps because you are feeling lazy or rushed,

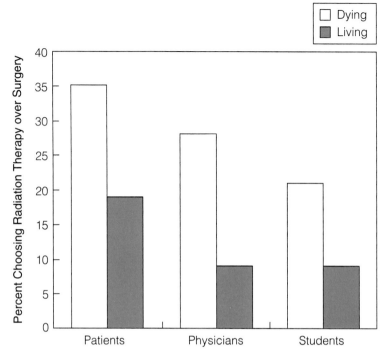

FIGURE 13.2   Patients, physicians, and medical students all preferred radiation therapy over surgery when it was presented in terms of probability of living as opposed to probability of dying. Even a subtle difference in wording influences people's preferences for different types of treatment (data from McNeil et al. 1982).

you toss an empty can in a trashcan instead of in a recycling bin. According to cognitive dissonance theory, you will then feel very uncomfortable, because you have done something that is not in line with your prorecycling attitude. You are now highly motivated to bring your attitudes and behavior back in line to reduce this unpleasant feeling. However, because it is very difficult, and sometimes impossible, to undo a behavior, people often try to resolve this uncomfortable feeling of arousal by changing their attitude to make it correspond with their behavior. So, perhaps after throwing the can in the trashcan you would become less a proponent of recycling and start to downplay its importance. Similarly, as I described at the beginning of the chapter, Damon's attitudes toward drug use became more negative over time as he continued to talk to students in his dorm about their dangers. Cognitive dissonance theory is one of the most famous theories in social psychology; hence, researchers have started using this theory to help people motivate behavior change.

One of the first studies to use cognitive dissonance theory to change people's health-related behavior was conducted by Jeff Stone and his colleagues at the University of California at Santa Cruz (Stone, Aronson, Crain, Winslow, & Fried, 1994). Seventy-two sexually active college students participated in a study on health and persuasion. All of the students were asked to

> **Questioning the Research 13.1**
>
> Does this study really show that creating cognitive dissonance increases condom use? (Hint: What exactly is the dependent variable?)

write a persuasive speech about the importance of safer sex as a way of preventing HIV, and half of these students were then videotaped giving this speech (which would supposedly be shown to high school students). Finally, half of the students in each of these two conditions were asked to make a list of the times they had failed to use condoms in the past, as a way of making them feel hypocritical about their past behavior. Students who were made to publicly advocate the importance of using condoms and who were reminded of their own past failures to use condoms (which should create a feeling of dissonance) bought more condoms than those in the other conditions—in fact, 83% of the students in this condition bought condoms, whereas 33 to 50% of students in the other conditions bought condoms.

More recent research has also used principles of cognitive dissonance theory to try to prevent eating disorders (Stice, Mazotti, Weibel, & Agras, 2000; Stice, Chase, Stormer, & Appel, 2001; Stice et al., 2002). In one study, 148 adolescent girls (ages 13 to 20 years) were recruited from local high schools and universities to participate in a study on helping women improve their body image (Stice et al., 2002). Participants were then randomly assigned to a dissonance intervention group, a healthy weight control intervention group, or a wait-list control condition. Those in the dissonance group were asked to discuss how to help other women avoid body image problems. The women therefore discussed (as a group) the nature of the thin ideal portrayed in the media, the perpetuation of this image, and the consequences of this image. They also role-played trying to convince someone not to adopt the thin ideal, and wrote an essay about the costs associated with the pursuit of the thin ideal (see Photo 13.1). Findings at the 3-month follow-up indicated that women who received either the dissonance-based intervention or the healthy weight control intervention reported fewer bulimic symptoms than those in the wait-list control condition.

Attribution Theory

Attribution theory posits that people try to explain the causes of their own and others' behavior; specifically, that people perceive behavior as caused by internal factors or external factors (Kelley, 1967). In turn, behavior that is motivated by internal factors, such as an individual's desire to engage in the behavior, is expected to continue over time. For example, if you brush your teeth because you like the feeling of having clean teeth and good-smelling breath, you will probably continue to regularly brush your teeth. In fact, internal attributions for the causes of behavior are associated with the adoption of various health-related behaviors, including use of fluoride mouthwash (Lund & Kegeles, 1984), smoking cessation (Coletti & Koppel, 1979), BSE (Bundek, Marks, & Richardson, 1993), and high blood pressure screening (King, 1982).

PHOTO 13.1   In one innovative approach to preventing eating disorders, female college students were asked to prepare messages for high school students about the dangers of the very thin idealized image of women presented in the media.

On the other hand, when people engage in behavior that they believe is the result of external pressures from others, they are unlikely to continue to engage in such behavior over time. So, if you brush your teeth because your parents give you a quarter each time you've brushed, you probably won't continue this teeth-cleaning routine over time. Correspondingly, external attributions for the causes of engaging in a particular behavior are associated with poorer adherence to recommendations and poorer maintenance of new behaviors.

In turn, one way to increase the persuasiveness of health messages is by trying to change the attributions people make for engaging in these behaviors (Rothman, Salovey, Turvey, & Fishkin, 1993). For example, in one study on this issue, 197 women were randomly assigned to receive one of three 20-minute tapes on mammography (Rothman, Salovey, Turvey, et al., 1993). The internal tape emphasized a woman's own responsibility to get a mammogram and detect breast cancer ("8 out of 10 lumps that you might find will not be breast cancer"; "while it is not known yet how to prevent breast cancer, the value and benefits of your finding it early are well known"). The external tape emphasized a doctor's responsibility for detecting breast cancer ("8 out of 10 lumps that a doctor might find will not be breast cancer"; "while it is not known yet how to prevent breast cancer, the value and benefits of a doctor finding it early are well known"). The information-only tape communicated information without making any particular types of attributions ("8 out of 10 lumps that are found will be breast cancer"). Subjects' reactions and amount of knowledge learned did not differ across conditions. However, when subjects were contacted 12 months later, 57% of those in the external condition and 55% of those in the information-only condition had obtained a mammogram compared to 66% of those in the internal condition.

Learning Theories

Learning theories are based on the assumption that behavior is influenced by basic learning processes, such as association, reinforcement, and modeling (Bandura, 1977; Pavlov, 1927; Skinner, 1938; Thorndike, 1905). In turn, health-promotion interventions use a variety of techniques developed by learning theoriests to help people change their behavior. For example, in the technique of *operant conditioning,* desired behaviors are positively reinforced through rewards, whereas undesired behaviors are punished in some way. Reinforcement should lead to the continuation of positive behaviors and the avoidance of negative behaviors. As discussed in Chapter 12, many relapse prevention programs encourage people to give themselves rewards for maintaining a change in behavior. Programs based on operant-conditioning principles can be very effective in leading to behavior change. For example, in one study participants were asked to set rewards for themselves for accomplishing their exercise goals (e.g., "will get my morning cup of coffee after I've finished my 2 mile walk"; Atkins, Kaplan, Timms, Reinsch, & Lofback, 1984). Participants with these self-rewards were much more likely to continue exercising over time than those without this incentive. Similarly, in one creative health-promotion plan based on the behavioral perspective, campus police officers at a large university were asked to record the license plate numbers of vehicles with drivers wearing seatbelts (Rudd & Geller, 1985). These numbers were then entered into a raffle, and 10 winners every 3 weeks were given a gift certificate to local stores. Although faculty and staff increased their seatbelt use significantly during this "seatbelt sweepstakes" time, students' seatbelt use increased only slightly. The preceeding examples describe rewarding positive behavior, but conditioning techniques can also be used to punish negative behavior. For example, and as discussed in Chapters 7 and 12, aversion therapy is designed to eliminate unhealthy behaviors by pairing a given action, such as smoking or drinking alcohol, with a negative consequence, such as an electric shock or negative visual images (Kamarck & Lichtenstein, 1985). Over time, it is thought that this pairing should work to eliminate the undesired behavior.

Moreover, according to Bandura's social learning theory, people do not need to directly experience the rewards or costs of engaging in a particular behavior

---

Questioning the Research 13.2

This study reveals that providing rewards for seatbelt use increases use among faculty and staff, but not students. Why do you think this program had a relatively small effect on students' behavior?

to learn about its outcomes; he believed that people could learn about such consequences through modeling (ie. , vicarious learning through observation; Bandura, 1977, 1986). As described previously, people often form their beliefs about various health-related behaviors from watching their parents' and older siblings' behavior. They can even form such beliefs from observing the behavior of someone they do not personally know, such as a famous athlete, model, or actor. In turn, many health-promotion messages portray desirable role models promoting a particular behavior. Public service announcements on television, for example, often feature an actor urging people to avoid drug use, driving under the influence, and cigarettes. Similarly, many smoking prevention programs for teenagers present adolescents with role models—including older students as well as media figures—describing the hazards of smoking and the benefits of refusing cigarettes (and see Box 13.5; Evans et al., 1981).

Social Cognitive Theory

Bandura's social cognitive theory extends social learning theory by including the role of both self-efficacy and outcome expectancies in predicting behavior (Bandura, 1986). According to this theory, an individual's *self-efficacy*, the extent to which a person believes he or she can engage in a particular behavior, is a powerful predictor of whether that person actually engages in the behavior (Bandura, 1977, 1986). For example, a person's beliefs about his or her ability to exercise every day would be a strong predictor of whether the person successfully maintains a new fitness program. Although social cognitive theory was the first to include this concept of self-efficacy, many more recent theories of health behavior (e.g., theory of planned behavior, protection motivation theory) include similar constructs.

Given the important role that self-efficacy plays in predicting behavior, many health-promotion intervention programs have focused on increasing people's confidence in engaging in a given behavior. For example, Edward McAuley and his colleagues at the University of Illinois gave some college women positive feedback on their fitness (e.g., told them that they were in the top 20 percentile of fitness for college-age women), whereas other women were given negative feedback (e.g., that they were in the bottom 20 percentile for fitness; McAuley, Talbot, & Martinenz, 1999). When the women later participated in a 20-minute stair-climbing-machine exercise, those who received high-self-efficacy feedback reported having more positive affect, less negative affect, and less fatigue than those who received the negative feedback. Similarly, and as I described at the start of this chapter, Bill decided to start an exercise program after his doctor gave him confidence that he could be successful in this pursuit. Other research suggests that increasing people's self-efficacy for quitting smoking leads to higher rates of smoking cessation (Blittner, Goldberg, & Merbaum, 1978).

One of the most common uses of social cognitive theory is in designing HIV-prevention programs; because one major reason for failure to use a condom is lack of confidence in discussing or implementing condom use, many HIV-prevention interventions use various techniques to increase condom use self-efficacy (Bryan, Aiken, & West, 1996; Kelly, St. Lawrence, Hood, & Brasfield, 1989). For example, Angela Bryan and her colleagues at Arizona State University (Bryan et al., 1996) tried to increase condom use in 100 undergraduate women by showing them a videotape of a woman purchasing condoms at a drugstore, demonstrating the proper way to put a condom on a man, and giving each participant a condom to carry in her purse or backpack. As shown in Figure 13.3, women who saw this tape were more likely to report carrying condoms, discussing condoms, and using condoms than those who instead received training in stress management. Similar findings about the benefits of receiving training to increase self-efficacy for condom use are found with male and female college students (Fisher, Fisher, Misovich, Kimble, & Malloy, 1996), gay men (Kelly et al., 1989), low-income adult STD patients (National Institute of Mental Health Multisite HIV Prevention Trial Group, 2001), African American male adolescents (Jemmott, Jemmott, & Fong, 1992), inner-city high school students (Fisher, Fisher, Bryan, & Misovich, 2002), inner-city women (Hobfoll, Jackson, Lavin, et al., 1994), and African American adult women (Carey et al., 2000).

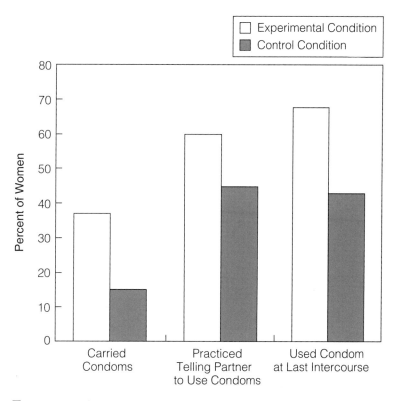

FIGURE 13.3 Women who saw a videotape of a woman modeling condom-related behaviors (e.g., buying condoms, discussing condom use) were more likely to carry condoms, practice telling their partner to use condoms, and use condoms the last time they had sex than women in the control condition (data from Bryan et al. 1996).

Box 13.5

Research Focus—It's Not How Many Use Condoms, It's Who Uses Condoms

Jeff Kelly and his colleagues at the Medical College of Wisconsin (1997) created a very novel approach to HIV prevention. They asked bartenders at gay bars to identify men who seemed to be popular—those who socialized and were greeted positively by others. These men (called "opinion leaders") were then asked to participate in five weekly 2-hour group sessions in which they learned information about HIV, strategies for preventing HIV transmission, and how to talk about HIV-prevention methods. The researchers then displayed posters throughout the gay clubs that featured a traffic light logo (red, yellow, and green circles) and asked the opinion leaders to wear small lapel buttons featuring this logo whenever they were in the club. These logo buttons would then prompt discussion with these men, and in turn lead to conversations about HIV-prevention strategies. Researchers then gave surveys to all male club patrons 1 year later to measure changes in sexual behavior.

The results from this study revealed that this intervention had several positive changes on patterns of sexual behavior. First, while 32% of the participants reported they had engaged in unprotected sex in the 2 months before the intervention, only 20% reported engaging in this type of behavior at the follow-up. Moreover, rates of condom use increased from 44.7% before the intervention to 66.8% at the follow-up. The researchers also collected data from men in a similar city during this time period and found no changes in their sexual behavior. For example, 27% of the participants in the other city reported engaging in unprotected sex at the first survey time, and 29% reported engaging in this behavior 1 year later. Similarly, rates of condom use remained unchanged (62 to 59%). The inclusion of data from this control city makes us more confident that the results obtained in this study were caused by the intervention and not by other factors, such as national media coverage of AIDS. This study provides evidence that social influences play an important role in health-related behavior.

Are Personally Relevant Messages the Most Effective?

Although traditional health education messages have used a "one size fits all" approach, namely, by giving the same information to everyone, recent research suggests that different people respond in different ways to different types of information: as poet William Blake (Gilchrist, 1942) noted, "To generalize is to be an idiot" (Kreuter & Holt, 2001; Kreuter & Skinner, 2000; Kreuter,

Strecher, & Glassman, 1999; Skinner, Campbell, Rimer, Curry, & Prochaska, 1999; Skinner, Strecher, & Hospers, 1994). According to the interactionist or "aptitude-treatment interaction" perspective, people are much more responsive to personally relevant information. Specifically, people are more likely to read, remember, comprehend, and discuss personally relevant messages, and they perceive these messages as more interesting, likeable, and in line with their attitudes (Brug, Steenhuis, van Assena, & de Vries, 1996; Campbell et al., 1994; Kreuter, Bull, Clark, & Oswald, 1999; Skinner et al., 1994). They also have more positive thoughts about the material, make more personal connections to the material, develop stronger intentions to change their behavior, and, most important, are more likely to be successful in their behavior change efforts. Given these findings, researchers have created messages that are tailored to an individual's particular needs and goals, as well as messages that are targeted to specific characteristics of a group of people (Schneider et al., 2001). A message that is created to address a specific woman's concerns about mammography (e.g., fear of pain, anxiety about learning she has cancer) is a *tailored* message; a message that is created to promote mammography in women in general (e.g., emphasis on the effectiveness of mammograms in locating early-stage cancer) is a *targeted* message. This section examines the benefits of receiving both types of personally relevant materials on a number of health-related behaviors.

Screening

Several studies have examined whether individuals who receive a tailored message are more likely to engage in screening behaviors (Kreuter & Strecher, 1996; Rakowski et al., 1998; Skinner et al., 1994; Skinner et al., 1999). Much of this research is based in the transtheoretical, or stages of change, model of behavior change, and hence it measures not simply whether people engaged in the given screening behavior, but rather whether they moved further along in the stages leading to engaging in this behavior. For example, Celette Skinner and her colleagues at the University of North Carolina at Chapel Hill (1994) compared whether women who received letters from their physicians encouraging BSE that were tailored to a person's particular risk factors (e.g., age, family history) were more effective in increasing screening than standardized letters. Follow-up interviews 3 months after the letters were sent indicated that both African American and low-income women (who are at particular risk of not getting screened) were more influenced by the tailored letter than the standardized letter. For example, 27% of Black women who received tailored letters compared to 8% of those who received standardized letters showed stage movement, as did 28% of those who were low-income that received tailored letters (compared to 17% of those who were-low income and received standardized letters). Personally tailored intervention messages are also more effective than standard interventions at increasing mammography (Rakowski et al., 1998).

Messages that specifically target a given population are also more effective at increasing screening than standard messages (Kreuter & Skinner, 2000). These messages often rely on the use of particular narrators, language, or music, and a more cost-effective approach than personally tailoring messages. Personally relevant messages are more effective, for instance, at motivating people to get tested for HIV. In one study, Seth Kalichman and his colleagues at the Medical College of Wisconsin (1993) randomly assigned 106 African American women to watch one of three videotapes on HIV risk reduction. One tape simply presented information about the importance of risk reduction delivered by a white broadcaster; another gave the same information presented by an African American woman; and a third gave the same information presented by an African American woman and included culturally relevant themes, including cultural pride, community concern, and family responsibility. Two weeks later women who had seen either of the videos featuring African American women were more likely to have discussed AIDS with friends, request condoms at the follow-up, and have been tested for AIDS. Fifty percent of the women who received the standard video requested condoms as compared to 88% and 91% of those in the other two conditions.

Pain Management

Another contribution of research on patient–treatment matching is in managing pain—a topic that is very important to most people at one time or another. Personality researchers have shown that people vary considerably on the type of information they want to receive about medical procedures to manage their pain (see Table 13.3; Carpenter, Gatchel, & Hasegawa, 1994; Litt, Nye, & Shafer, 1995; Ludwick-Rosenthal & Neufeld, 1993). Specifically, some people prefer to manage pain by seeking detailed information about the pro-

TABLE 13.3 *Test Yourself: How Much Information Would You Want?*

1. I usually don't ask the doctor or nurse many questions about what he or she is doing during a medical exam.
2. I'd rather have doctors and nurses make the decisions about what's best than for them to give me a whole lot of choices.
3. Instead of waiting for them to tell me, I usually ask the doctor or nurse immediately after an exam about my health.
4. I usually ask the doctor or nurse lots of questions about the procedures during a medical exam.
5. It is better to trust the doctor or nurse in charge of a medical procedure than to question what he or she is doing.
6. I usually wait for the doctor or nurse to tell me the results of a medical exam rather than asking for the results immediately.
7. I'd rather be given many choices about what's best for my health than to have the doctor make the decisions for me.

This questionnaire measures people's desire to ask questions and desire to get information regarding medical decisions.

Source: Krantz, Baum, & Wideman, 1980.

posed management procedure and to learn as much as possible about what to expect. Other people strongly prefer simply to not think about the procedure and to adopt an "ignorance is bliss" approach. Neither of these styles seems to be "better." What appears to be important is that people get the type of information that they want.

Many research studies provide support for the importance of matching people to treatment preferences in the management of pain and specifically suggest that different people benefit from receiving different amounts of information (Auerbach, Martelli, & Mercuri, 1976; Law, Logan, & Baron, 1994; Ludwick-Rosenthal & Neufeld, 1993; Miller & Mangan, 1983; Shipley, Buff, Horwitz, & Farbry, 1978). Specifically, people who desire high levels of control and information about their upcoming surgical procedure show lower levels of arousal, stress, and anxiety when they receive such information than when they receive little information, whereas those who prefer to know as little as possible show the reverse pattern (Ludwick-Rosenthal & Neufeld, 1993; Miller & Mangan, 1983; Shipley et al., 1978). For example, Alan Law and his colleagues at the University of Iowa (1994) found that people who desired high levels of control experienced less pain when they first saw a video of a woman seeking dental treatment and received training in coping and relaxing as compared to when they saw a neutral film (on local areas of interest) and engaged in a neutral conversation (see Cartoon 13.1 and Photo 13.2). Similarly, Lucinda, as described at the beginning of the chapter, who wanted to receive lots of information, was much less anxious about having a cavity filled after receiving a detailed description of the procedure that would be used.

People also show lower levels of arousal and anxiety when they are given the *type* of information they prefer. For example, in another study dental patients were randomly assigned to receive either general information (information about the dental clinic's history and finances) or specific information (detailed information about the exact procedures used to extract a tooth; see Box 13.6; Auerbach et al., 1976). Patients with an internal locus of control (those who wanted to actively control and manipulate their environment) showed better adjustment when they received the specific information, whereas those with an external locus of control (those who were less comfortable with navigating their own environment) showed better adjustment after receiving general information. This research all provides strong support for the importance of giving people what they need as a way of improving adjustment to medical procedures.

People benefit not only from receiving different amounts of information prior to medical procedures, but also from receiving different types of information (Litt, Kalinowski, & Shafer, 1999; Martelli, Auerbach, Alexander, & Mercuri, 1987). For example, Mark Litt and his colleagues at the University of Connecticut (1999) examined the effectiveness of different types of interventions to reduce anxiety in dental patients. Patients who were highly fearful of dental procedures in general benefited most in terms of distress (e.g., tension, nervousness, edginess) from distraction, whereas those who were fearful only in response to specific cues (e.g., sound of drill, sight of dentist) benefited most

"We have adult teeth now, Debbie, and, as such, they demand adult pain."

CARTOON 13.1   Although some people find visits to the dentist quite anxiety-provoking, having information can reduce the pain associated with various dental procedures. Different people, however, benefit from receiving different types of information. (©The New Yorker Collection 2001. Jack Ziegler from cartoonbank.com. All Rights Reserved.)

from receiving desensitization training. Another study examined how 46 patients about to undergo oral surgery handled different types of stress management interventions (Martelli et al., 1987). Some of the patients were randomly assigned to a problem-focused intervention, which provided information about the surgery, including instruments used, sequence of steps, sensations produced by the anesthesia, and instruction in the use of strategies to cognitively reanalyze information about the procedure. Others received an emotion-focused intervention, which was designed to reduce the emotion or distress associated with the surgery and which included instruction on deep relaxation, distraction, and the use of calming emotion-focused statements, such as "it will soon be over." Finally, others received a mixed message, which included both types of coping strategies. The problem-focused intervention led to the lowest levels of pain and anxiety for those who wanted lots of information, whereas the emotion-focused intervention led to similarly low levels of arousal for those who wanted little information. This study shows that effectiveness in reducing stress is enhanced when treatment conditions or interventions are congruent with people's individual coping tendencies.

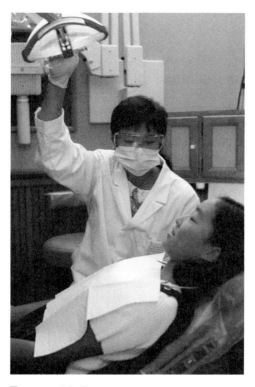

PHOTO 13.2 How could this person best control her anxiety during this dental procedure? It is hard to say—some people experience lower anxiety and pain when they receive considerable information about what to expect, whereas others benefit from receiving virtually no information.

Health Promotion

Finally, different people should find different types of health promotion information most convincing, and specifically they should show greater behavior change in response to personally relevant messages (see Figure 13.4; Amaro, 1995; Jemmott & Jones, 1993; Kalichman, Carey, & Johnson, 1996; Mays & Cochran, 1988; Peterson & Marin, 1988). For example, teenagers might be most convinced by information about the negative effects of smoking on appearance (e.g., smelly clothes, yellow teeth, bad breath), whereas women who smoke may be most convinced by information about preventing weight gain (see Box 13.7 for another example of how different people respond to different types of smoking cessation programs). Similarly, women and men often have different concerns about using condoms; hence, condom promotion ads may be more effective when they present different types of information to men as opposed to women (Amaro, 1995; Mays & Cochran, 1988; Marin & Marin, 1992). For example, at the beginning of the chapter I described Debbie's decision to design distinct condom promotion ads for men and women. Specifically, condom promotion ads for women might be most

Box 13.6

What Type of Information Would You Want Before Dental Surgery?

General Information

This clinic was opened in 1970. At that time, 100 or more junior or senior dental students were able to provide service to the Washington, D.C., community. At present, because of continuing expansion of our facilities, there are 260 students providing services to over 5000 patients a year. Present clinical facilities include six departments that can provide for all your dental needs. These six departments, oral diagnosis and treatment planning, periodontics, endodontics, oral surgery, fixed and removable prosthodontics, and operative denistry, cannot be maintained without your financial support. Your financial support is matched and exceeded by the federal government through the Health Professions and Loan Act. The quality of any clinic depends not only on the availability of all the needed facilities but also on the excellence of its staff. The Georgetown Dental School maintains an esteemed faculty, people who are consultants for other hospitals, participants in scientific meetings and other educational organizations, and active in their respective communities.

Specific Information

Upon your arrival in the surgery department, your diagnosis will be reviewed. Before removal, an anesthetic will be administered. This anesthetic will numb the tooth and the surrounding tissues, thus removing all pain sensations from the immediate area. After the anesthetic has taken effect, the surgical procedure will begin. The first procedure is the removal of the attachment apparatus with a multcurette. This helps to loosen the tooth. A forcep will then be placed on the tooth, and a front-to-back rocking motion will be initiated by the surgeon. This motion further helps loosen the tooth and will continue until the tooth is removed. During this procedure, you may feel considerable pressure on your tooth tissues, but you should not feel any pain. If you do feel pain, more anesthetic will be given. In some impaction cases, it will be necessary to use a mallet and a chisel. These instruments help the surgeon remove the bone surrounding the tooth. This procedure produces very little trauma and enables the surgeon to quickly remove the tooth.

effective if they portrayed condom use in romantic, committed relationships, in part because women are often concerned that buying and carrying condoms makes them appear promiscuous or "loose" (Struckman-Johnson, Gilliand, Struckman-Johnson, & North, 1990). In contrast, condom promotion ads for men, who are generally more concerned about condom use reducing

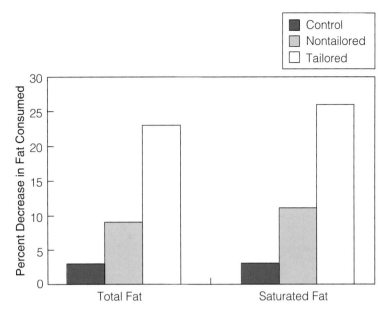

FIGURE 13.4 As compared to patients who received general information on dietary and nutrition guidelines, those who received an individually tailored letter (e.g., based on their beliefs about the benefits of changing their diet and their susceptibility to diet-related diseases) were more likely to remember receiving the letter, were more likely to have read all of the message, and reported eating less total fat 4 months later (data from Campbell et al. 1994).

their own sexual pleasure, might be more effective if they used sexually arousing content and emphasized that condoms can lengthen sex and thereby enhance both partners' experiences (Struckman-Johnson et al., 1990). In sum, health-promotion messages should be most effective when they provide people with personally relevant information.

In line with this view, considerable research on smoking cessation programs suggests that these programs are more effective when they provide personally relevant information than when they provide generic information (Strecher et al., 1994). For example, in one study smokers were given either a generic letter about the reasons for stopping smoking (e.g., the general benefits of and barriers to quitting) or a personally tailored letter that addressed the specific benefits and barriers that the person had revealed during an interview in the waiting room of their doctor's office (see Box 13.8; Strecher et al., 1994). Four months later 7.4% of those who received a generic letter had stopped smoking as compared to 20.8% of those who received the personally tailored letter. The results were even more dramatic for light to moderate smokers (those smoking fewer than 20 cigarettes a day); 30.7% quit as compared to 7.1% of those who received the generic letter. Prochaska and colleagues (1993) found that smokers who received individualized manuals matched to their stage of change at the start of a smoking cessation intervention program were more likely to have stopped smoking at the 18-month follow-up than those who

Box 13.7

Research Focus—Nicotine Gum Works for Some, but Rapid Smoking Works for Others

A study by Diane Zelman and her colleagues at the University of Wisconsin (1992) examined the effectiveness of different types of smoking cessation interventions (rapid smoking versus nicotine gum) for different people. One hundred twenty-six smokers were randomly assigned to one of two interventions, which each met six times over a 2-week period. The rapid-smoking intervention required subjects to inhale from cigarettes every 6 seconds for a 60-minute period, during which time they consumed an average of 4.7 cigarettes, they were to refrain from smoking outside of the sessions. Those in the nicotine-gum intervention were given prescriptions for gum, and they were encouraged to use the gum whenever they wanted to. Participants were then contacted several times over a 1-year period to assess their smoking behavior. These assessments included blood testing for nicotine at the 6-month follow-up and contact with a friend or family member of the participant at the 6-month and 12-month follow-ups to verify the self-reports.

Findings from this study revealed no long-term overall differences between the effectiveness of the nicotine gum and rapid-smoking conditions, with approximately 30 to 40% of smokers in each condition abstaining from smoking at the 12-month follow-up. However, these researchers were also interested in examining whether different people responded to these interventions in different ways. Specifically, the researchers predicted that for low-craving subjects, rapid smoking would be the most effective in increasing abstinence from smoking because this type of procedure would produce disgust, whereas for those with high cravings for cigarettes, nicotine gum would be the most effective. This hypothesis was indeed confirmed: the nicotine-gum intervention was most effective when used with people who were high on physical dependence, whereas the rapid-smoking intervention was most effective when used with people who were low on physical dependence. This study provides further evidence that treatments must be matched to people's preferences and individual needs to maximize their effectiveness.

simply received standardized self-help manuals. Similar results were found in a sample of 349 low-income pregnant women who smoked (Solomon, Secker-Walker, Skelly, & Flynn, 1996).

People are also more responsive to personally relevant health-related messages about alcohol use, nutrition, and condom use (Jaffe et al., 1996; Kadden, Cooney, Getter, & Litt, 1989; Sanderson & Cantor, 1995). For example, an alcohol treatment program found that people who experience strong cravings

Box 13.8

Samples of Tailored Smoking Cessation Messages

Letter A

In the survey you filled out, you told us you'd like to quit smoking to take more control of your life. We think that's great! Many smokers feel "controlled" by their smoking habit. Quitting smoking is an important step toward regaining that control.

Relax without lighting up. . . . Like others, you told us that "stress" would keep you from quitting smoking. Many people smoke to relieve stress. But if you're going to quit smoking, you'll need to find other ways to cope with stress. The following simple breathing exercise has been used by psychologists to help thousands of smokers cope with stressful situations. The next time you're feeling stressed at home or at work, try this exercise instead of reaching for a cigarette.

- Find a comfortable place to sit down.
- Relax your arms and legs completely.
- Close your eyes. Inhale slowly and deeply.
- Exhale very slowly.
- Repeat this three to five times.

With practice, you'll find this exercise can help you relax without ever lighting up. If you can cope with the stresses of life without having a cigarette, you're well on your way to becoming a nonsmoker.

Since you smoke more than 20 cigarettes a day and you smoke your first cigarette within 30 minutes of waking up, you're probably addicted to cigarettes. If you're addicted to cigarettes, you may get headaches and feel stressed or anxious when you try to quit. Nicotine gum or the new nicotine skin patch can help. Addicted smokers who use the nicotine patch or gum do twice as well at quitting as those who don't. If you think a nicotine patch or nicotine gum might work for you, call your doctor for more information.

Letter B

In the survey you filled out, you told us you'd like to quit smoking to feel better about yourself. We think that's great! Quitting smoking can improve your mental health as well as your physical health. You'll feel a great sense of accomplishment after quitting, and you'll feel more in control of your life, too.

Weigh the benefits. . . . You told us you're worried about gaining weight if you quit smoking. Some people do gain weight after quitting, but many do not. The average weight gain after quitting is just 5 pounds—that's about as much as most of us gain each year during the holidays!

Nicotine, a chemical found in all cigarettes, makes your body burn calories faster than normal. So, during the first few months after quitting smoking, you'll

(continues)

need to find other ways to burn those calories. For most people, 15 minutes of brisk walking each day will be more than enough to keep the extra weight off. Walking not only keeps your weight down, but also helps you relieve stress and gives you more energy.

Many smokers crave sweets right after quitting. You can satisfy your cravings without gaining weight by having plenty of sugarless candy and gum nearby after you quit. Carry a package of small breath mints with you everywhere—they have only about one calorie each, and they keep your hands and mouth busy with something other than cigarettes.

Letter A is designed to help a person who is addicted to nicotine stop smoking, whereas Letter B is designed to help a person who is concerned about weight gain to stop smoking (Strecher et al., 1994).

for alcohol benefit from receiving medication that reduces the cravings, whereas those who are high in verbal skills really benefit from relapse prevention training (e.g., training in self-monitoring, stress management, modeling, role-plays; Jaffe et al., 1996). Similarly, Kadden and colleagues (1989) found that patients who scored high in measures of psychopathology and sociopathy benefited much more from training in coping skills related to alcohol use than group-based, interactional therapy, presumably because they lack the social skills to benefit from the group experience. Similar findings emerge from studies employing computer-tailored letters about nutrition changes (Brug et al., 1996). Finally, a study I conducted examined whether different college students like and learn from different types of messages regarding condom use (Sanderson & Cantor, 1995). Specifically, we believed that some college students would prefer to receive information about condom use that focused on the technical skills related to condom use, such as how to put on a condom and how to eroticize condoms, and that others would prefer to receive information that focused on the communication skills related to condom use, such as how to discuss condom use with a sexual partner and how to insist a partner use a condom. We randomly assigned 100 college students to receive either a technical-skills or a communication-skills small-group interventions, which included videos, activities, and discussion, and then measured their attitudes and intentions to use condoms 3 months and 12 months later. As predicted, students who were strongly focused on intimacy in their dating relationships and received the communication-skills intervention (e.g., the one that "matched" their interests) had stronger attitudes toward, self-efficacy for, and intentions regarding condom use, whereas those with identity goals were more responsive to interventions stressing skills in technical and hedonistic use of condoms (see Figure 13.5). Students who received a "matching" condom use intervention also reported engaging in lower levels of risky sexual behavior as long as 1 year later.

I have also conducted two studies showing that the most effective eating disorder prevention interventions match women's distinct needs (Mutterperl & Sanderson, 2002; Sanderson & Holloway, 2003). Jenny Mutterperl and I

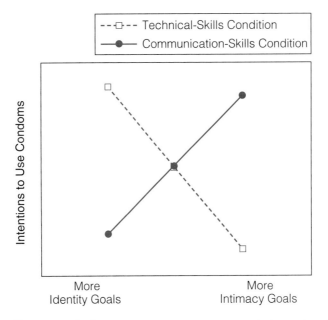

FIGURE 13.5   Participants who were strongly focused on intimacy goals in their dating relationships benefited from receiving training in the communication skills necessary for condom use, whereas those who were strongly focused on independence goals in romantic relationships benefited from receiving training in the technical skills necessary for condom use (data from Sanderson & Cantor (1995).

(2002) found that college women who tend to compare their own weight and body size to that of other women on campus benefit from learning that other women on campus actually eat more and weigh more than women often believe, as described in Chapter 8. These women reported higher actual and ideal body weights as well as lower frequencies of disordered eating 5 months later than those who simply received information on "healthy eating." However, women who tend to compare themselves to more idealized images of women in the media (e.g., the cover model on *Cosmopolitan* magazine) report lower actual and ideal weights and more frequent disordered eating when they receive this information than when they receive the healthy-behaviors brochure. In turn, such information may have led these women to feel alienated from their peers, and they may have reacted to such information by redoubling their efforts to achieve the thin ideal typically portrayed in the media (hence, they showed decreases in self-reported actual and ideal weight coupled with increases in frequency of disordered eating). In another study I found that women who already showed symptoms of eating disorders and who received messages regarding the signs, symptoms, and dangers of eating disorders presented by women who have recovered from such disorders develop an even stronger focus on achieving a very thin body (Sanderson & Holloway, 2003). Apparently, women who are struggling with eating disorders may view recovered women as role models in terms of attaining the thin ideal, and correspondingly they increase their own motivation to exercise as a way of achieving such a body. These findings provide some important information about how best to target eating disorders on college campuses—and strongly suggest that different women will benefit from receiving different types of health-promotion messages.

Finally, interventions for women who already have an eating disorder are also more effective when they take into account individuals' stage of change. Rachel Levy (1997), for example, demonstrated that women with bulimia preferred treatment that matched their current readiness for change. Specifically, women who were at the stage of precontemplation preferred a treatment group that provided only general listening support, whereas those who were in the stage of preparation preferred a group that worked on setting specific goals for decreasing the frequency of binging and purging; those who were in the stage of maintenance preferred a group that focused on how to prevent relapse. Once again, people particularly benefit from receiving health-promotion information that matches their specific needs: "one size" clearly does not "fit all."

Lingering Issues

1. *Do people know what they need?* Although many research studies on different topics have shown that different people benefit from receiving different types of information, we don't know whether people know what type of information is best for them. This question obviously has great practical importance—if people know what type of information would be best for them, health-promotion programs could simply offer a choice of messages and media (e.g., brochures, videos, intervention groups) and then ask people to choose which they prefer. If this view is correct, it would be easy to give people the "matching," and most effective, message. On the other hand, in some cases people may not really know what type of information they would find most beneficial. A smoker, for example, may not know whether her cigarette use is triggered more by psychological factors (e.g., stress reduction) or physiological factors (e.g., nicotine cravings). In turn, if people don't know what they need, health-promotion programs would have to develop a quick way to sort people into different groups, such as through a brief questionnaire or interview. Future research is clearly needed to examine whether people do in fact know what they need or, alternatively, to develop appropriate strategies for sorting people into their "matching" group.

2. *Can personal relevance backfire?* Although much of the information in this chapter describes how personally relevant messages can be more effective than generic ones, in some cases this type of information can lead people to react in a negative and defensive way. For example, obese people who feel that their weight is outside of their control (e.g., influenced by luck, genetics) actually respond more negatively to tailored than generic infor-

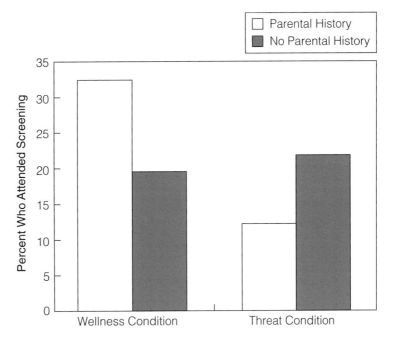

FIGURE 13.6 Students who had a parental history of hypertension and, hence, already felt vulnerable to this disease were most likely to seek screening after receiving the wellness information, whereas those without a family history of hypertension were more likely to receive screening after they received threatening information (data from Gintner et al., 1987).

mation: they counterargue the messages that provide personally relevant strategies for taking control of their eating and exercise behavior (Holt, Clark, Kreuter, & Scharff, 2000). In contrast, obese people who believe they are in control of their weight respond more favorably to messages that provide personally relevant strategies for weight loss than to generic information. Similarly, a study by Gintner and his colleagues (1987), for example, found that people who had a parent with hypertension and, who, hence, already see themselves as vulnerable to this problem were more than twice as likely to attend a blood pressure screening if they read a message about the benefits of acting to maintain well-being than a message that emphasized the dire consequences of hypertension (see Figure 13.6). This research suggests that *personally irrelevant* messages may at times be more effective (and less detrimental) than personally relevant ones.

Thought Questions

1. What are the problems with using fear-based appeals? Can this approach ever work? When?

2. You have a summer job with your city's health department, and you are asked to design a program to reduce drug use in teenagers. Describe one potential program based on attribution theory and another one based on cognitive dissonance theory. Which one do you think would be more effective and why?

3. What is the difference between a tailored message and a targeted message?

4. As part of your community psychology class, you are asked to create two different types of television messages promoting responsible drinking in college students. What are two different approaches you could use?

5. Your younger brother is having his appendix removed and is very nervous about the procedure. You know that your brother generally reacts to stressful situations by adopting an "ignorance is bliss" attitude. What types of things will you do to help him cope before the surgery?

Answers to Questioning the Research

Answer 13.1: Although this study seems to provide convincing evidence that students who experience cognitive dissonance change their behavior—and thereby increase their condom use—remember that the researchers measured only how many condoms students took—not whether they used them! It is possible that students who took more condoms were indeed more likely to use condoms during their next sexual encounter, but it is also possible that the effects on intentions to use condoms of creating this dissonance wore off by the time the students were next in a sexually intimate situation. Remember, intending to do a behavior sometimes but not always leads to actually doing the behavior.

Answer 13.2: One explanation for the slight improvement in frequency of seatbelt use in students is their overall feelings of invulnerability. As previously noted, adolescents often feel invulnerable to various types of health problems, and therefore they may be much less responsive to health-promotion interventions than children or adults. Another factor that may inhibit seatbelt use in adolescents is the desire to appear daring and rebellious (e.g., deliberately not following the law in terms of seatbelt use). In turn, if this type of self-presentation motive is more valued than the possibility of winning an award, behavioral intervention programs may have little impact on this population.

CHAPTER 14

Future Directions for Health Psychology

- Betsy is 56 years old and in excellent health. Although Betsy smoked for 5 years in her late teens and early 20s, after receiving a strong warning from her doctor about the dangers of smoking, she quit. Quitting was indeed very difficult, but Betsy had a strong belief that she could accomplish this goal if she just set her mind to it. She also received high levels of social support: her husband bought gum and candy for Betsy to use whenever she felt a craving for a cigarette, and her friends promised to treat her to a weekend at a spa once she'd gone 6 months without smoking. Betsy has not had a cigarette in nearly 30 years.

- Dylan is 83 years old and in good health. He walks a mile or two each day for exercise, takes medication to control his arthritis, and eats a balanced and healthy diet. Although Dylan is in good health right now, he has already talked to his children about his desire to have minimal medical intervention if he were to become very ill. He has seen several friends spend the last years of their lives in considerable pain and with very limited mobility, and Dylan feels strongly that he would not want to be kept alive under those conditions. He has also spoken with his doctor about his preferences and hopes that his wishes to focus on quality of life, not just quantity of life, will be honored.

- Kelly is a junior in college and has a summer job working in a local day care center. She has noticed that while most of the children are very healthy, a few children always seem to be suffering from a lingering cold or ear infection. Kelly suggested to one such child's mothers that her son see a doctor, but the mother said she had only recently started a new job and hence had no health insurance for the next month. Another mother reported that she had indeed taken the child to the doctor, but that the antibiotic prescribed was very expensive, and therefore she was giving the child only half of the recommended dose because that's all she could afford.

- Dr. Yellen is a pediatrician in a city and is on the budget committee of the local hospital. The committee is currently deciding how to spend its infant care budget and must choose between two main projects: expanding its prenatal care program to reach more low-income pregnant women, or upgrading its neonatal care unit to treat premature infants. Dr. Yellen has read several studies on the importance of evaluating the relative costs and benefits of different medical treatment options and therefore votes to expand the prenatal care program, which would in turn decrease the number of premature births.

- Mark is a psychology major and, because of his interest in health, he has always intended to go to medical school. However, after taking a course in health psychology last semester, he realized that while he is still interested in health-related issues, he would be more interested in working on preventing health problems than treating already-existing ones. Mark is therefore trying to find a summer job with a social service agency and is planning to apply to graduate programs in public health.

Preview

This chapter describes how the field of health psychology has made significant contributions to the promotion of psychological and physical well-being, as well as the major challenges this field faces in the future. First, we review the major contributions of the field of health psychology, including how psychological factors influence health-compromising and health-enhancing behaviors, how people cope with and manage pain as well as chronic and terminal illnesses, and how people interact with and respond to medical regimens and persuasive messages. Next, we examine how health psychology can contribute to health in various ways, such as by enhancing quality of life, reducing ethnic and racial differences in health, and preventing health problems. The following section addresses some of the "hot topics" that the field of health psychology is currently facing. These include making ethical decisions, reducing health care costs, addressing women's unique health needs, and focusing on cross-cultural health issues. Finally, we will examine career options in health psychology as well as the pathways to such careers.

What Are the Contributions of Health Psychology?

Research in health psychology has provided a number of major contributions to the prevention and treatment of illness and disease. First, research in health psychology demonstrates that psychological factors, including how we experience and cope with stressful situations, our distinct personality traits, and the amount of social support we receive from others, influence physical health. Chapter 4 describes the role of environmental pressures in creating stress, psychological appraisal in influencing our physiological reactions to stress, and the impact of coping strategies on the experience of stress. As you read in Chapter 5, people who are optimistic and generally expect good outcomes experience better health and even live longer, whereas people who are generally hostile and expect the worst experience a number of health problems. Chapter 6 discusses the influence of social factors on health, including the various ways that social support can benefit health (e.g., by buffering the effects of stress) and the ways that social support can sometimes damage health (e.g., by encouraging unhealthy behaviors). As described at the beginning of this chapter, the considerable social support Betsy received from her friends and husband helped her to quit smoking. Research in health psychology has also made important contributions in the prevention of disease. Virtually all of the leading causes of death are now influenced at least in part by behavior that people choose to engage in, and in Chapters 7 and 8, we discuss how psychological factors influence health-related behaviors, such as smoking, drinking excessive amounts of alcohol, and eating a high-fat diet.

Research in health psychology has also provided important information about how to help people cope with pain and illness. As described in Chapter 9, considerable evidence suggests that the experience of pain is influenced at least in part by psychological factors, including observational learning (e.g., "How does my mother react when she must have an injection?") and reinforcement (e.g., "Do I get attention if I fall on the playground?"), and many pain management treatments, such as acupuncture, meditation, and relaxation, work at least in part through psychological factors. Psychological factors also influence how people react to and cope with chronic and terminal diseases. For example, Chapter 10 discusses the influence of psychological factors on acquiring CHD, cancer, and AIDS, as well as the effectivenss of psychological therapies in managing these diseases. Chapter 11 extends this topic by focusing specifically on the role of psychological factors in influencing how a person copes with a terminal disease diagnosis as well as the nature of bereavement.

Finally, research in health psychology has examined when people seek medical treatment, whether they follow medical recommendations, and how they respond to health-promotion messages and interventions. Chapter 12 describes research showing that psychological factors influence whether people get screened for various disorders and how they react to test results, when they seek health care and how they interact with their health care provider, how they adjust to surgery, whether they adhere to medical recommendations, and whether they relapse to old patterns of behavior. Chapter 13 discusses persuasive communications and interventions based on psychological theories and principles that have already played a valuable role in changing people's health-related behavior, including encouraging screening behavior, decreasing pain, improving doctor–patient relationships, and reducing detrimental health behaviors.

How Can Health Psychology Contribute to Improved Health?

In 1990, the U.S. Department of Health and Human Services set forth a number of health goals for the ensuing 10 years in a report entitled *Healthy People 2000* (McGinnis & Lee, 1995). This report focused on three main goals: increasing the span of healthy life, reducing disparities in health among people in different ethnic groups, and providing access to preventive services. (Although the revised goals for *Healthy People 2010* include only the first two goals, increasing access to preventive services would clearly lead to both an increase in healthy lifespan as well as a decrease in health disparities across different groups.) Accomplishing these goals would go a long way toward improving the overall health of Americans; hence, many health psychologists are working on these issues. This section examines each of these topics in turn.

Enhancing the Quality of Life

One major goal of health psychology is to help people live higher-quality lives, lives that are free from pain and major disability. One aspect of this goal is increasing life expectancy—which is indeed significantly higher now than it was 100 years ago. However, the increase in life expectancy has led to an increase in the number of people suffering from chronic, disabling conditions. Many diseases, such as cancer, CHD, and Alzheimer's disease, are much more prevalent with age; hence, as people live longer, they are more likely to develop such problems. Other diseases are not life-threatening but also increase in incidence with age and can decrease people's overall quality of life. For example, osteoporosis, arthritis, hearing loss, and vision problems caused by glaucoma and cataracts are all more prevalent in older people and can severely hamper a person's ability to engage in various activities (see Photo 14.1).

This focus on quality of life, not just quantity of life, has led researchers to measure people's disability-adjusted life expectancy (Kaplan & Bush, 1982). This measure calculates the number of years a person can spend free from disease and disability—their well years or health expectancy. Some researchers

PHOTO 14.1 Chronic health problems, such as Alzheimer's disease, osteoporosis, and arthritis, can severely decrease a person's overall quality of life.

even propose that people should rate the quality of their overall life, based on the symptoms they are experiencing, as well as the length of time they will spend experiencing these symptoms to determine their quality-adjusted life years, (QALY; Kaplan, 1991). The quality is determined both by the severity of the symptoms (e.g., being confined to a wheelchair or experiencing considerable pain is more severe than experiencing a mild headache or spraining an ankle) and their duration (e.g., even a very painful bout of food poisoning lasts a few days at most, whereas severe cancer pain could last for years). People's rating of their QALYs can have a substantial impact on their decisions regarding health care. For example, many people would choose to have surgery to remove a cancerous tumor, in part because this surgery can lengthen life expectancy dramatically and is associated only with a relatively brief period of low life quality during the recovery from surgery. However, many people might choose to not undergo a treatment that provides only a small increase in life expectancy and puts one in a very dependent state (e.g., being tube-fed and on a respirator). As described at the beginning of the chapter, Dylan has already discussed with his children, the types of medical procedures he would and would not want and has emphasized his desire to not be kept alive under conditions of high pain, low cognitive clarity, and poor prognosis for recovery. The ultimate goal is to allow people to maintain very good psychological and physical well-being for a long time, and then experience a relatively short period of pain and disability immediately prior to death (a compression of mortality).

One way to increase the quality of life is through primary prevention, preventing health problems from ever developing (see Table 14.1). Some of the most important types of primary prevention strategies are avoiding smoking, eating a healthy diet, and engaging in regular exercise. Another way to increase quality of life is to help people catch and treat health symptoms at an early point in a disease's progression, a type of secondary prevention. Cancer rates

TABLE 14.1 *Timing of Prevention*

Level	Primary	Secondary	Tertiary
	Timing		
Individual	Self-instruction guide on HIV prevention for noninfected lower-risk individuals[a]	Screening and early intervention for hypertension[c]	Designing a very low-fat vegetarian diet for an individual with heart disease[c]
Group	Parents group to gain skills to communicate better with teens about risk behaviors[a]	Supervised exercise program for lower-SES individuals with higher risk of heart disease[c]	Cardiac rehabilitation program for groups of heart disease patients[c]
Organization	Worksite dietary change program focusing on altering vending machine and cafeteria offerings[b]	Worksite incentive program to eliminate employee smoking[a]	Extending leave benefits so employees can care for elderly/ill parent[b]
Community	Focused media campaign to promote exercise in minority population segments[a]	Developing support networks for recently widowed individuals[c]	Providing better access for disabled individuals to all recreational facilities[b]
Institution	Enforcing laws banning the sale of cigarettes to minors[b]	Substantially increasing insurance premiums for smokers[b]	Mandating a course of treatment to facilitate recovery of stroke victims[b]

Prevention of health problems can occur at three different stages, and can be provided at many different levels.

Source: Winett, 1995.
Note: SES = socioeconomic status.

[a]Health promotion.
[b]Health protection.
[c]Preventive services.

dropped an average of 0.8% per year throughout the 1990s, which is probably a result of increases in detection as well as lifestyle changes (Ries et al., 2000). Finally, the most common—and expensive—approach to prevention is tertiary prevention, in which steps are taken to manage or control the effects of an already-developed illness or disease. Chemotherapy, social support groups, and surgery are all types of tertiary prevention approaches for people with cancer.

Decreasing Racial-Ethnic Health Differences

Although overall life expectancy has climbed dramatically in the United States over the last 100 years, the average life span differs considerably for people in different ethnic groups: White females live an average of 5 years longer than African American females (80 versus to 74.8 years), and White males live an average of 8 years longer than African American males (74.5 years versus 67.6 years). In fact, compared to whites, African Americans have higher rates of death caused by homicide, cancer, and cardiovascular disease and a higher mortality rate at every age category (Flack et al., 1995; Geronimus, Bound, Waidmann, Hillemeier, & Burns, 1996; National Center for Health Statistics, 2003). African Americans are also more likely than whites to suffer from chronic health conditions, including renal disease, stroke, and AIDS. For example, although African Americans make up only 12% of the U.S. population, they account for 47.1% of AIDS cases (www.cdc.gov). African Americans are even more likely than whites to experience fatal job-related injuries, primarily because they are more likely to work in hazardous industries, such as construction, manufacturing, agriculture, and transportation (Loomis & Richardson, 1998). Although most studies of ethnic differences in health have focused on differences between whites and African Americans, studies with both Hispanics/Latinos and Native Americans generally reveal similar findings (Bagley, Angel, Dilworth-Anderson, Liu, & Schinke, 1995; Flack et al., 1995; Grossman, Krieger, Sugarman, & Forquera, 1994; Johnson et al., 1995). For example, compared to whites, both Hispanics and Native Americans show higher rates of many diseases, including tuberculosis, diabetes, cancer, cardiovascular disease, and AIDS. Relatively little research has examined health in Asian Americans, and the existing data on health in this population suffer from several major limitations (Flack et al., 1995). However, some evidence suggests that compared to whites, Asian Americans have higher rates of some diseases (e.g., hepatitis, tuberculosis), but lower rates of others (e.g., CHD; Johnson et al., 1995).

What leads to these dramatic differences in health and longevity? One factor is health behaviors (Johnson et al., 1995; Myers, Kagawa-Singer, Kumanika, Lex, & Markides, 1995; Yee et al., 1995). As compared to whites, African Americans eat more high-fat foods, such as bacon, sausage, and fried foods, and eat fewer high-fiber cereals and fruits, in part because African Americans are more likely to live near fast-food restaurants but less likely to live near supermarkets (where healthier foods could be purchased; Morland, Wing, & Diez, 2002). In turn, African Americans—especially women—are more likely to be obese than whites, and are less likely to engage in regular exercise. African Americans are also more likely to be infected with AIDS as well as other STDs than are people in other ethnic groups (Laumann & Youm, 1999; Maxwell, Bastani, & Warda, 1999). Although alcohol use and smoking rates are similar for African American and white women, African American men are more likely to engage in both of these behaviors than white men are, perhaps because of a desire to use alcohol as a means of "escaping" negative working and living conditions. It is not an accident that there are more stores selling alcoholic beverages, as well as outdoor billboard advertisements for alcohol and tobacco products, in African American and low-income neighborhoods than in more affluent ones (Moore, Williams, & Qualls, 1996; Rabow & Watts, 1984). Similarly, rates of smoking and alcohol use are higher in Native Americans than in whites. Rates of injuries, such as those caused by drownings and fires, are significantly more common in African Americans and Native Americans than in whites. Finally, deaths caused by homicides are much more likely in African American, Hispanic, and Native American groups than in white populations.

Minorities are also much less likely than whites to engage in regular, preventive health care, in part because they have higher rates of unemployment and are more likely to hold low-paying jobs that do not provide health insurance (Fiscella, Franks, Gold, & Clancy, 2000; Flack et al., 1995; Johnson et al., 1995). In turn, this lack of regular health care increases people's risk of developing major health problems, because they do not use preventive measures or catch health problems at earlier, treatable—stages (Adler et al., 1993; Adler, Boyce, Chesney, Folkman, & Syme, 1994; Gornick et al., 1996). Whites, for example, are much more likely to have regular immunizations than African Americans (see Table 14.2). Similarly, although white women are 20% more likely to get breast cancer than African American women, the survival rate of African American women is 17% lower than that of white women (see Figure 14.1; National Center for Health Statistics, 2003; White, Urban, & Taylor, 1993). Moreover, members of minority groups may be less likely than whites to rely on medical professionals for health care even when they have health insurance (Fiscella et al., 2000). Both Hispanics and Asians sometimes avoid seeking health care because of a lack of comfort with speaking English, as well as a cultural preference for both relying primarily on family members and friends for advice about physical symptoms and using alternative medical treatments (e.g., acupuncture, herbs). Ethnic minorities may also have a general distrust of the medical community, based in part on prior experiments in which minority group members were used—without their knowledge or consent—in medical experiments (Jemmott & Jones, 1993; Marin & Marin, 1991). For example, and as described in Chapter 2, in the 1930s some African American men with syphilis were left untreated so that researchers could measure the long-term effects of the disease. Finally, and as described in Chapter 12, even when minorities seek health care, they receive fewer diagnostic and treatment procedures than do whites (see Figure 14.1).

Still another factor leading to ethnic differences in health is income—minorities are more likely than whites to be poor, which in turn is associated with worse health for several reasons (see Figure 14.2; Adler & Matthews, 1994; Geronimus et al., 1996). For example, in 1991, 32.7% of African Americans

TABLE 14.2 *Rates of Vaccinations of Children by Race*

Vaccination	White	African American	American Indian/ Alaska Native	Asian/Pacific Islander	Hispanic
Diphtheria/tetanus	84	76	75	85	79
Polio	91	87	90	93	88
Measles	92	88	87	90	90
Hepatitis	91	89	91	91	88

Although vaccinations are one of the best ways to prevent many childhood diseases, white and Asian children are much more likely to receive most types of vaccinations than African Americans, American Indian/Alaska Natives, and Hispanics.

Source: Centers for Disease Control, 2003.

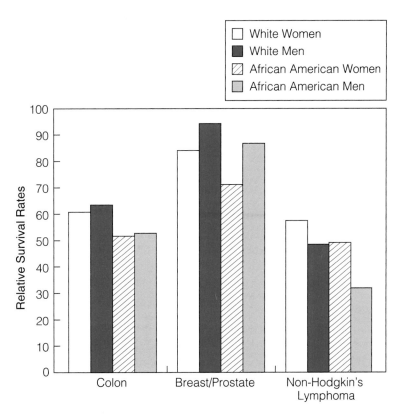

FIGURE 14.1 White men and women are less likely than African American men and women to die within 5 years of receiving a cancer diagnosis (data from www.cdc.gov).

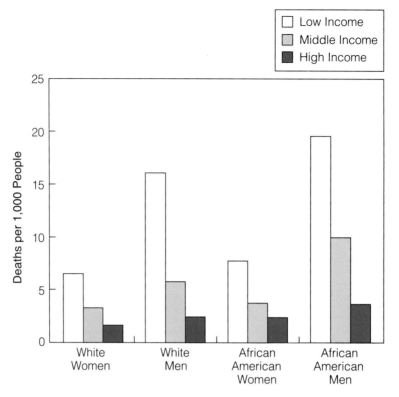

FIGURE 14.2   Although men in general have higher death rates than women, both men and women in the lowest income group have significantly higher death rates than those in the middle or highest income groups (data from Pappas et al., 1993).

were living in poverty as compared to 11.3% of whites (Flack et al., 1995). People who are poor are less likely to have access to regular health care (Anderson & Armstead, 1995; Johnson et al., 1995). People in the lowest income groups have much lower rates of immunization (26% lower among whites, 39% lower among African Americans) than those in the highest income groups, which in turn means they have a higher risk of acquiring many preventable diseases (Gornick et al., 1996). They are also less likely to catch diseases in an early, and more treatable, stage. One study of women with annual household incomes below $15,000 found that 90% did not obtain regular mammograms and more than 33% had never even heard of mammography (Mickey, Durski, Worden, & Danigelis, 1995). Although people who have extremely low incomes qualify for Medicaid (health coverage paid for by the government), because Medicaid reimburses health care providers much less than they charge other patients, patients with this type of health coverage often have trouble locating a physician who will accept this low level of reimbursement. Moreover, many people who make just enough so that they don't qualify for Medicaid often have no health insurance at all, typically because the cost of this coverage simply would be too much. In fact, an estimated 38.5 million Americans under the age of 65 years, or 16.1% of the population, do not have health insurance (National Center for Health Statistics, 2002). And even when they do seek medical attention, people with Medicaid or no insurance receive less comprehensive medical care than those with private insurance (see Cartoon 14.1). One study found that privately insured patients were 80% more likely to get an angiography, 40% more likely to receive bypass grafting, and 28% more likely to receive angioplasty compared to those with no insurance or those on Medicaid (Wenneker, Weissman, & Epstein, 1990).

Although lack of access to regular health care is one explanation for the link between low income and poor health, even in countries with universal free health care, people with low income are less healthy than those with more income (Adler et al., 1993). This finding indicates that factors other than the ability to pay for health care must influence the link between low income and poor health. One explanation is that poor people tend to engage in more destructive health-related behaviors, including smoking, alcohol consumption, failure to exercise, and obesity (Adler et al., 1993; Adler et al., 1994; Anderson & Armstead, 1995; Stunkard & Sorensen, 1993; Wardle, Waller, & Jarvis, 2002). For example, 41% of men and 36% of women with only a high school education or less smoke as compared to 18% of men and 17% of women with some post-college education (Winkleby, Fortmann, & Barrett, 1990). Another

CARTOON 14.1 Although this cartoon is supposed to be funny, it describes a very real situation—people with health insurance receive more diagnostic and treatment procedures than do those without such coverage (Mike Keefe, The Denver Post).

explanation is that people in low socioeconomic groups experience higher levels of stress than those with greater income (see Photo 14.2). These stressors include overcrowded housing, homelessness, pollution, and neighborhood crime (Anderson & Armstead, 1995; Myers et al., 1995; Yee et al., 1995). Relatedly, people with low socioeconomic resources may have limited ability to cope with stressful life events, which in turn further heightens feelings of stress. A family with little disposable income, for example, may experience a variety of negative life events as more stressful, such as needing to have a car repaired, losing a job, or having a child with a chronic medical condition.

Eliminating racial and ethnic differences in health is a difficult task, but is a feasible goal. One step toward accomplishing this goal would be providing some type of universal health care, which would help increase access to health care services for members of minority groups (Johnson et al., 1995). This type of coverage would lead to the prevention of health problems caused by a lack of prenatal care and immunizations. As described at the beginning of the chapter, Kelly noted that some of the children in the day care center where she worked did not have access to regular health care or low-cost prescriptions and, hence, experienced many lingering illnesses. Focusing on prevention is another strategy for decreasing these differences, particularly because members of minority groups often engage in high rates of health-compromising behaviors. Strategies for this type of prevention could include emphasizing the importance of eating a healthy diet and engaging in regular exercise, as well as avoiding smoking. Most important, reducing the drastic rate of poverty in some parts of the United States, especially in inner cities, is probably the most important means of improving health in members of minority groups.

PHOTO 14.2   Low-income families face a variety of stressors, including overcrowded housing, pollution, and neighborhood crime, all of which can have negative effects on health.

Improving the overall standard of living, by encouraging people to continue their education, providing low-cost housing and job training, and decreasing poverty, would go a long way toward reducing many of the ethnic and racial differences in health.

Preventing Health Problems

Another major goal of health psychology is preventing the development of health problems, which is a much easier and cheaper way of increasing life expectancy and life quality than treating already-established medical problems (Sullivan, 1990). This is why many people take their car in for an oil change every 3000 to 5000 miles—they choose to pursue regular, brief, and inexpensive care for their car as a way of preventing the development of severe and costly problems. The difference between prevention and treatment is well illustrated by this example from physician John McKinlay (1975):

> You know, sometimes it feels like this. There I am standing by the shore of a swiftly flowing river, and I hear the cry of a drowning man. So I jump into the river, put my arms around him, pull him to shore, and apply artificial respiration. Just as he begins to breathe, someone else cries for help. So I jump into the river again, reach him, pull him to shore, apply artificial respiration, and then, as he begins to breathe, there's another cry for help. So back into the river again, reaching, pulling, applying breathing, and then another yell. I'm so busy jumping in and pulling them to shore that I have no time to see who the [heck] . . . upstream is pushing them in. (McKinlay, 1975, p. 7).

How we can we prevent the development of health problems? First, we can try to motivate people to take an active role in the prevention of health problems. Because motor vehicle–related injuries are one of the leading causes of death, one very effective way to prevent health problems—and mortality—is to protect people from serious injuries while in motor vehicles (Christophersen, 1989; Williams & Lund, 1992). Requiring people to wear seatbelts and children to sit in car seats are both very effective ways of decreasing injuries and fatalities. Estimates are that requiring seatbelts in New York State alone saved an estimated 220 lives in the first 6 months of the program and prevented over 7000 injuries (Latimer & Lave, 1987). Similarly, more than 1300 people die each year from injuries sustained while riding a bicycle, often because of collisions with cars, and 90% of those people may have lived if they had worn a helmet (Sacks, Holigreen, Smith, & Sosin, 1991). Helmet use also reduces the number of injuries to the face, head, and brain (Thompson, Rivara, & Thompson, 1996; Thompson, Nunn, Thompson, & Rivara, 1996), saving an average of $6,000 per patient in hospitalization costs alone (Brandt, Ahrens, Corpron, Franklin, & Wahl, 2002). However, one recent survey found that 20% of high school students rarely or never use seatbelts when they are passengers in a car, and of those who have ridden a bicycle, 88% rarely or never used a helmet (Kann et al., 1998). The use of a helmet is particularly important for motorcycle riders (a common emergency room saying: "What do you call motorcycle riders without helmets? Organ donors"). Using seatbelts, wearing helmets, and putting children in car seats are all examples of active strategies, those that require engaging in some type of repeated action to prevent health problems, to prevent injuries from occurring, or to decrease the harm resulting from such injuries.

Other approaches to injury prevention are passive—they do not require people to change their behavior or take any action, but rather change people's environment. Many accidents leading to death in children, such as drownings, falls, fires, shootings, and poisonings, could be prevented through relatively simple measures, such as putting locks and window guards on windows; installing smoke detectors; keeping chemicals, firearms, and matches in high and locked cabinets; buying medication with childproof caps. These strategies are often particularly effective in preventing injuries because they do not require continuing effort. For example, airbags are more effective than seatbelts in reducing serious injury and death in motor vehicle accidents, and require no active effort on the part of the passengers. Risk of death is reduced 19% for drivers (Zador & Ciccone, 1993), and 11% overall for passengers in the front seat (Braver, Ferguson, Greene, & Lund, 1997). Similarly, making cars with headlights that automatically turn on when the car is started is very inexpensive, yet leads to a reduction in crashes (Williams & Lancaster, 1995). Even simple and relatively low-cost efforts, such as putting woodchips under playground equipment, can reduce the likelihood of injuries.

Another strategy for preventing health problems is instituting societal changes, such as restricting advertisements, reducing speed limits, requiring warning labels, and mandating behaviors by law (Dannenberg, Gielen, Beilenson, Wilson, & Joffe, 1993; Heishman, Kozlowski, & Henningfield, 1997; Jacobson, Wasserman, & Anderson, 1997; Kaplan, Orleans, Perkins, & Pierce, 1995). Both tobacco and alcohol companies, for example, are restricted in where and how they can advertise their products. Cigarettes cannot be advertised on television, or in magazines that are often read by teenagers, and when alcohol is advertised, these ads cannot show people actually drinking. Similarly, the use of the Joe Camel character in advertisements for Camel cigarettes was banned by the Federal Trade Commission in 1997 because of concerns that this character increased the appeal of cigarettes to teenagers. Cigarette packages are required to have warning labels describing the risks of smoking, and signs in establishments that provide alcohol must warn people about the dangers of drinking while pregnant. Smoking is now banned in numerous places, including restaurants, public buildings, and public transportation. In 1989, Congress voted to ban smoking on airline flights of less than 2 hours, which was later extended to flights under 6 hours. Given the concerns about driving accidents caused by "driving while calling," some communities have now banned the use of handheld cell phones while driving. Laws requiring the use of bicycle helmets, car seats, and seatbelts, for example, are common and are quite effective in reducing injuries and deaths (see Figure 14.3; Dannenberg et al., 1993). And other bans focus not on *where* a person can engage in a given behavior, but rather *when*. Alcohol use, for example, is allowed on for people over the ages of 18 or 21 (depending on the state), and riding in the front seat of a car is allowed only at age 12.

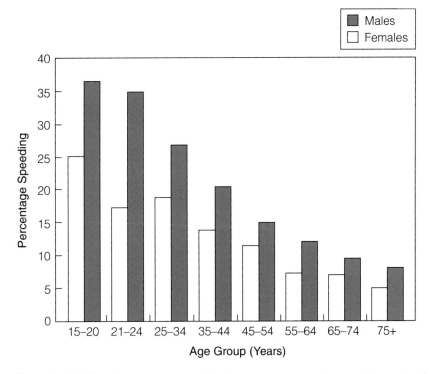

FIGURE 14.3   The percentage of fatal car crashes caused by speeding is significantly higher in people in adolescence and early adulthood than in older adults (data from Nell 2002).

The most effective types of prevention programs are multifaceted and community based. An example of a widespread and quite successful health-promotion program occurred in San Francisco in the 1980s in response to the AIDS epidemic (Coates, 1990). This community-level HIV risk reduction program included giving out information about risky behavior, increasing feelings of vulnerability, and modeling skills to prevent such behavior (e.g., using condoms, saying "no") and was presented through multiple organizations, including schools, churches, worksites, the health care system, and community agencies as well as the media. This program was very successful—although before the program 60% of the gay and bisexual men in the sample engaged in high-risk behavior, only 30% reported such behavior 3 to 4 years later. A similar community-wide approach to fighting the problem of unplanned teenage pregnancy was implemented in South Carolina (Vincent, Clearie, & Schluchter, 1987). This program included school-based sex education for children in all grades with participation of parents and church leaders in various educational programs and community-wide events as well as media coverage to raise awareness of the problem. Once again, this approach was highly successful: the pregnancy rate among teenage girls ages 14 to 17 years dropped from 5.4% to 2.5%—a 23.3% decrease in pregnancy rate—over the course of this intervention while it remained unchanged in surrounding communities that did not use this type of widespread prevention technique. Finally, the Safe Kids/Healthy Neighborhood Injury Prevention Program in Harlem, New York, targeted numerous aspects of the community, including renovating playgrounds, involving children in safe and fun activities (e.g., dance, arts, sports), offering classes on injury and violence prevention, and providing safety equipment (e.g., bicycle helmets; see Photo 14.3; Davidson et al., 1994). Rates of injuries declined 44% following the intervention, once again demonstrating the power of primary prevention programs in improving physical health.

PHOTO 14.3   Although wearing a helmet while biking is a very important strategy for reducing serious injuries, children are often reluctant to wear them. One Seattle campaign to promote helmet use employed widespread educational messages to raise parents' awareness about the importance of helmet use, provided a subsidy to reduce the cost of purchasing helmets, and recruited prominent sports figures from the Seattle Seahawks, Seattle Mariners, and the University of Washington Huskies football team to describe how helmets are just a standard part of the sports uniform. Helmet use increased from 5 to 23% following this campaign (Bergman, Rivara, Richards, & Rogers, 1990; Rivara, Thompson, & Thompson, 1994).

What Are the Hot Topics in Health Psychology?

Each chapter in this book has ended with a description of two "hot topics," lingering issues that are currently under debate among researchers in the field of health psychology and often among the general public. This section addresses four relatively new issues in the field of health psychology: making ethical medical decisions, reducing health care costs, examining the distinct predictors of women's health, and extending research in health psychology to other countries.

Making Ethical Medical Decisions

One of the major advances in health care over the last 20 years is clearly the development of new medical technology, such as organ transplantation, chemotherapy, and artificial hearts. Although the growing number of technological advances in health and medicine have had a major impact on life expectancy by allowing some people to live who would certainly have died, these advances lead to some tricky ethical decisions (see Box 14.1). For example, researchers are now able, at least in some cases, to extract an egg from a woman and sperm from a man and to combine the egg and sperm, and then implant the resulting embryo into the woman's uterus, thereby allowing many couples to have children who were previously considered infertile. However, physicians can screen the embryos prior to implantation, and then choose to implant only those that meet some specified set of criteria. In some cases this poses few, if any, ethical dilemmas. A couple who is at risk of having a child with cystic fibrosis, for example, might want to implant only those embryos that do not carry this gene, and most people would probably think this selection is morally appropriate. But how about if a couple wanted to implant only those embryos that would produce babies with perfect eyesight (poor vision is another type of genetic defect—just ask my husband), or who would be right-handed, or heterosexual. Already some couples have used this technique to have a child of their preferred sex. Experts are concerned that advancing reproductive technology will lead to an unending quest for "better babies." And even when the couple is choosing to implant embryos only on the basis of their physical health, ethical issues can still emerge. For example, in one case a woman with a rare genetic mutation that would almost certainly lead her to develop Alzheimer's disease by age 40 sought help from fertility experts in creating a child who would not share her dismal fate. Doctors extracted eggs from the woman, fertilized those without the mutation, and then replanted these eggs into the woman's uterus. Although this child will not develop early-onset Alzheimer's, she will suffer from the loss of her mother at a relatively early age.

The increasing use of genetic screening is another example of a technological advance that leads to challenging ethical issues (Moum, 1995). Researchers with the Human Genome Project are now working to map the location and precise role of every gene in the human body (Watson, 1990). This

> **Box 14.1**
>
> **Health Psychology in the Real-World—That Will Be $5,000 for My Kidney**
>
> Although we now have the capacity to transplant organs, many more people need organs each year than organs are available. Some medical ethicists have proposed that family members should receive some type of incentive for donating a loved one's organs in order to increase the number of organs available for transplantation. If the person had expressed his or her intention to donate organs and the family chooses to follow the person's wishes, family members would receive a $10,000 federal income tax credit to apply to the deceased person's estate. This type of program would also bring publicity to the organ donation program and thereby encourage discussion of people's wishes.
>
> Others are firmly opposed to this proposal for a variety of reasons. First, the majority of people who could successfully donate viable organs die in relatively unusual situations, namely accidents while they are relatively young. These people are unlikely to have thought about or expressed their wishes about organ donation; hence, this incentive program would be unsuccessful in reaching them. Second, some people believe this type of incentive could encourage family members to hasten deaths, and potentially make people less willing to sign an organ donor card or express their wishes to family members. Finally, some people believe this type of incentive would devalue the altruism demonstrated by the person and his or her family in donating an organ, thereby making it less likely that people would choose to donate.

information will provide health professionals with new ways to prevent, diagnosis, and treat illness and disease, but will also raise numerous complex ethical, moral, and legal issues. Some types of screening, such as for HIV infection and cholesterol levels, are already commonly used by insurance companies to set premium rates, and genetic screening could be next. Genetic screening could also determine whether a person has a "preexisting condition," which is typically excluded from insurance. Screening can lead to discrimination in hiring and in securing health insurance. Employers obviously want healthy workers, who are absent less, more productive, less likely to quit work and/or need disability (Faden & Kass, 1993). Employers also pay less for health insurance if they hire healthy workers; hence, they are motivated to hire people who don't use a lot of health care. Would a company want to hire a worker who was certain to develop Huntington's disease within a few years? Would an insurance company charge higher rates to women with the "breast cancer gene"? How about a worker who is a carrier for a life-threatening disease, such as cystic fibrosis, and who may then have a child who needs expensive medical care (which would be covered by the employer)? Would you want to hire a diabetic or someone with a genetic predisposition for alcoholism?

Finally, technology is expensive, and therefore when money is spent on technology, it takes money away from other types of health care (Butter, 1993). Health professionals must therefore decide when to use technology. For example, in 1987 the legislature of the state of Oregon had to make a decision about how to use its limited health care budget, and specifically to choose between funding organ transplantation surgery and prenatal care. This choice is really between providing a very large effect for a small number of people (only about 30 people each year in Oregon will need an organ transplant, but for those who do, this surgery literally saves their lives) versus providing a relatively small effect for a large number of people (over 1500 women in Oregon become pregnant and need prenatal care each year, and providing such care decreases infant mortality and birth defects). As described at the start of this chapter, Dr. Yellen's hospital committee faced the difficult decision of funding either an expanded prenatal program or upgrading its neonatal care unit—both laudable health-promotion goals, but they address very different types of health care needs. Similarly, and as discussed in Chapter 11, because we now have the capacity to keep people alive using technological means, medical professionals are forced to examine when such technology should be used and when individuals and/or their families should have the right to refuse this type of treatment. Very expensive technologies are often used to keep people alive for very short periods of time—hours or days—and sometimes in an unconscious state (Kaplan, 1991). One researcher describes this phenomenon as turning "inexpensive dying into prolonged living, usually through expensive means" (McGregor, 1989, p. 119).

And even when technological advances are used, because they are expensive and have limited availability, health professionals must decide who gets this type of treatment (Jennings, 1993). For example, the growth of organ transplantation procedures, coupled with a limited supply of usable organs, means that decisions must be made about who receives each available organ. These decisions are made in part based on the patient's ability to cope with the stress of such a major procedure and their ability to follow the complex medical procedures necessary to help their body accept the new organ (Olbrisch, 1996). These criteria mean that very old people, who are likely to already have shorter life expectancies, and adolescents, who may have trouble following demanding medical recommendations, often are seen as poor candidates for donor organs (Olbrisch, Benedict, Ashe, & Levenson, 2002). Ethical considerations such as fairness and justice may also influence how organs are allocated. When baseball great Mickey Mantle received a liver transplant in 1995, following the destruction of his own liver through years of alcohol abuse, some people questioned whether he was "deserving" of this organ and whether his celebrity status had shortened his waiting time. In line with these concerns, a recent study found that people were much more likely to offer heart transplant to someone who has never smoked than to someone who is either a current or former smoker (Sears, Marhefka, Rodrigue, & Campbell, 2000).

Reducing Health Care Costs

One of the hottest topics in health psychology is the rapidly increasing costs of health care in the United States and how these costs can be controlled (see Figure 14.4). Thirteen percent of the gross domestic product was spent on health care in 1999, with a total cost of $1,210.7 billion (National Center for Health Statistics, 2002). In contrast, other similar countries, such as Germany, Canada, and Japan, spent about 7% of their gross domestic product on health care (see Box 14.2). Overall health care costs are about 40% more in the United States than in other countries, yet we are not a healthier country, as measured in terms of life expectancy or infant mortality (Bingamon, Frank, & Billy, 1993).

One obvious factor contributing to the high costs of health care is that people are living longer, so they develop more chronic, long-term diseases that require ongoing care, possibly for years. AIDS, Alzheimer's disease, coronary heart disease, and cancer are all examples of very common diseases that people

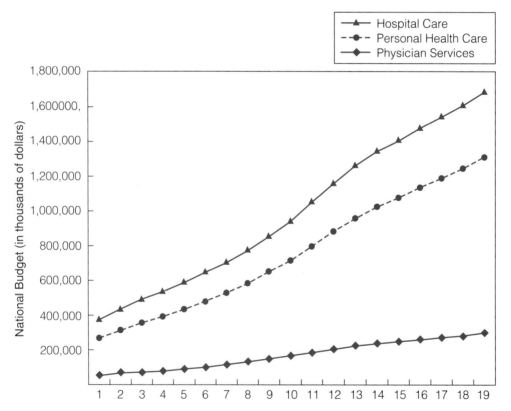

FIGURE 14.4   Costs of personal health care, hospital health care, and physician services have all increased dramatically over the last 20 years (Centers for Disease Control, 2003).

Box 14.2

Health Psychology in the Real World—How Do Other Countries Handle Health Care?

Many countries, including Canada and most European countries, view health care as a guaranteed consumer good or service; hence, health care is funded at least in part by the government. Patients can typically choose any doctor they want, and all citizens medical bills are covered by taxes. Many countries also include prescription drug benefits and mental health services. These benfits are not based on consumer ability to pay, as is often true in the United States. In Canada, for example, all citizens have universal health insurance, regardless of age, health status, employment—health insurance doesn't come with a job, as in the United States. These benefits are comprehensive, so people don't pay doctor or hospital bills. This system is usually complicated less with bureaucratic hurdles. The per-person expenditure on health care in the United States is $347 per year, compared to $202 in Canada (Fuchs & Hahn, 1990).

One reason costs are so much higher in the United States than in other similar countries is that physicians and hospitals in the United States spend much more on administrative costs, including advertising to recruit patients, filing for reimbursement from insurance companies, and obtaining permission to do various procedures. A 1987 comparison of the health care costs in the United States versus Canada revealed that in the United States 19.3 to 24.1% of total health care spending was for administrative costs, versus 0.4 to 11.1% of costs in Canada (see Table 14.3; Woolhandler & Himmelstein, 1990). For example, the average U.S. physician's office spent about 1 hour on each insurance claim (private or Medicare), which is 20 times as long as time spent in Canada. Given the litigious nature of U.S. society, physicians in the United States often pay much more for malpractice insurance than do doctors in other countries. Physicians in the United States also spend more money than do Canadian physicians on "amenities" for their offices, including renting desirable office space, buying attractive furniture, and paying for interior decorating perhaps as a way of attracting patients. In contrast, Canadian physicians are more likely to attract patients by offering lower fees. U.S. physicians also rely more on technology and use more medically advanced procedures (Kaplan, 1989). Finally, as compared to Canadian doctors, U.S. doctors work shorter hours, see fewer patients, perform fewer procedures, and receive higher salaries (Fuchs & Hahn, 1990)! The Canadian government keeps a tight control on fees given to physicians and on hospital budgets; hence, the fees charged for procedures as well as the income paid to physicians are lower. However, the wait for nonemergency medical procedures is often much longer in Canada than in the United States.

may live with for many years—sometimes requiring expensive treatment (e.g., bypass surgery, drug regimens, chemotherapy, and radiation). Another factor contributing to high costs is the administrative costs built into the current health care system in the United States (Woolhandler & Himmelstein, 1991). As shown in Table 14.3, as compared to Canada, health care in the United States includes significantly more administrative costs, caused in part by our complicated system of insurance payment systems as opposed to Canada's national health care insurance. Similarly, because of the high rate of malpractice suits in the United States, physicians must carry expensive malpractice insurance (the cost naturally is passed on to patients) and often practice "defensive medicine" in which they order every test and do every procedure to protect themselves from lawsuits (Butter, 1993).

Another factor contributing to the high cost of health care is the increasing reliance on medical technology. State-of-the-art treatment is often seen as superior to low-tech options (Butter, 1993). Technology use is also profitable for hospitals (who can charge for the equipment) and physicians (who can charge for their specialized services). In fact, rates of cesarean section are lower among women who are uninsured or are covered by Medicaid (a government program that pays health care costs for poor people) than those who are using private insurance (Gould, Davey, & Stafford, 1989; Placek, Taffel, & Moien, 1988). Unfortunately, this infatuation with technology has led to an overreliance on it in some cases. Some surgeries, such as coronary bypass surgery and cesarean section, are clearly beneficial to some patients, but are often overused for patients that might benefit the same or more from other less-expensive procedures. In fact, one study suggested that about 20% of the pacemakers implanted in people in 1988 were unwarranted (Greenspan et al., 1988). Similarly, childbirth is usually straightforward and certainly can occur with relatively little technology intervention: for many years women gave birth at home, often with only the assistance of a midwife. Now childbirth often includes the use of many different types of technology, including ultrasounds, epidural pain relief, and electronic fetal monitoring (Butter, 1993). This means

TABLE 14.3   *Per Capita Cost of Health Care Administration in the United States versus Canada*

Cost Category	United States	Canada
Insurance administration	106	17
Hospital administration	162	50
Nursing home administration	26	9
Physician billing expenses caused by hiring personnel	106	41

The administrative structure of the U.S. health care system is significantly less efficient—and therefore significantly more expensive—than the Canadian health care system.

Source: Woodlhandler & Himmelstein, 1991.

that women today typically have a more "technologically advanced" birth, but not necessarily "better" births.

As a step toward controlling the high cost of health care, a growing number of people are now enrolled in some type of managed care system (Miller & Luft, 1994). In fact, estimates are that over 78 million Americans now receive medical care through a health maintenance organization (HMO). In this arrangement, an employer or an employee pays a set fee every month and in turn has unlimited access to medical care (at either no cost or a greatly reduced cost). In some cases HMOs require patients to see their own staff, whereas in other systems patients can choose from among a group of medical professionals who have agreed to accept a specified payment for their services (preferred provider organizations). HMOs assign people to a primary care physician, who manages their care and must refer patients to specialists. For a long time, most Americans received health care from a physician they paid each time they had an appointment; this is called fee-for-service care; HMOs are different from this care methodology.

One way HMOs help to decrease health care costs is by classifying all health problems into "diagnostic-related groups" (DRGs), and then giving practitioners and hospitals a set fee for treatment of a given problem. This means that all physicians working for a given HMO have agreed to accept a set fee for their services (which is often lower than they would receive in a typical fee-for-service arrangement). HMOs also require that all of a patient's care be approved by their doctor as well as the HMO organization. Patients even need approval from their physician and/or HMO before being admitted to the hospital (another way to save HMOs money). When I went into labor during my first pregnancy, I forgot to call for approval from my insurance company before I checked in to the hospital, and was therefore charged a very expensive hospital bill for my "unauthorized admission." My insurance company eventually agreed to pay the bill, but seeking this "exception to the rule" required many phone calls!

Unfortunately, many patients find this system less satisfying than a more traditional fee-for-service approach for several reasons (Miller & Luft, 1994). First, because HMOs have agreements with only certain specified doctors (who are willing to accept a given—often lower—payment for their services), people must choose a doctor who participates with their HMO. This means that patients may not necessarily be able to see their preferred doctor. Moreover, because all care must be approved by their physician as well as the HMO organization, patients sometimes face major obstacles in getting approval for the treatment they need. They are also less likely to be admitted to the hospital than patients on a more traditional plan, and when they are hospitalized, they are discharged faster than other patients with comparable conditions (Rogers et al., 1990). One study with a sample of 14,012 Medicare patients found that the introduction of a DRG-based payment system led to a 24% drop in length of hospital stays, although there were no differences in health outcomes or mortality (Kahn et al., 1990). After I gave birth to my second son, my HMO plan offered me a "bonus" for leaving the hospital within 24 hours (although state law allowed me to stay up to 48 hours)—women who leave within 24 hours after giving birth are giving 10 hours of household and child care help free of charge from a doula, a trained companion who provides support and assistance during childbirth and afterward. Finally, and most important, some evidence suggests that HMOs lead to worse health outcomes, especially for the chronically ill and poor people (Miller & Luft, 1994). For example, researchers in Seattle, Washington, found that for elderly patients, 54% of those in an HMO showed declines in health as compared to 28% of those in a traditional fee-for-service plan, (Ware, Bayliss, Rogers, & Kosinski, 1996). Despite these problems, it is important to remember that there is little evidence overall that HMOs lead to lower quality of health care, and in fact, people in HMOs are very pleased with some aspects of their care, including waiting times for appointments and costs (Rossiter, Langwell, Wann, & Rivnyak, 1989). And while Americans want free choice of providers, complete access to medical services, no waiting, and lots of technology, they don't want to pay more for health care (Jennings, 1993; Kerrey & Hofschire, 1993).

Given the skyrocketing costs of health care, health psychologists are increasingly asked about the costs of health-promotion interventions, specifically whether these costs justify the programs (Friedman, Sobel, Myers, Caudill, & Benson, 1995; Kaplan, 1989; Kaplan & Groessl, 2002). In many cases, the costs of health-promotion programs are quite low, given their potential benefits. For example, the Stanford Five City Project (described in Chapter 7) provided 5 years of intensive education and training, including television and radio spots, brochures, classes, and contests, to two small cities in northern California in an effort to decrease coronary heart disease (Farquhar et al., 1990). Although the overall effects of this intervention were relatively small, the cost was only about $4 per person per year. In this case, the benefits (even if small) would probably outweigh the costs (also quite small). Similarly, David Holtgrave and Jeff Kelly (1996) found that a 12-session, small-group HIV-prevention intervention for gay men cost about $470 per person, yet the medical costs savings of this program were substantial. Other studies indicate that giving people information about detrimental health behavior (e.g., problem drinking, smoking) and providing advice about home remedies for common health problems are quite inexpensive and lead to a substantial overall savings (Fries et al., 1993; Windsor et al., 1993). Even relatively expensive lifestyle interventions can be effective, if they reduce costly medical procedures (e.g., Ornish et al., 1990). For example, insurance companies may prefer to pay the considerable costs of a lifestyle-change program that includes diet, exercise, meditation, and so on than the cost of a coronary artery bypass surgery. However, and as shown in Figure 14.5, the most cost-effective methods of health promotion are primary prevention strategies, such as requiring daylight-running lights on cars, using seatbelts, and prohibiting teenagers from smoking (Kaplan, 2000). For example, in one ambitious program to increase seatbelt use, Florida state employees were required to read and sign a sheet describing the state rules requiring seatbelt use (Rogers et al., 1988). They were then given stickers for their dashboards to remind them to "buckle up." Although only about 10% of workers were using their seatbelts initially, this rate climbed to 52%! Moreover, this program led to

---

Box 14.3

Health Psychology in the Real World—The Use of Unconventional Therapy

Unconventional, or *alternative, therapies* are medical practices that are not widely taught or recommended by U.S. medical schools or practiced at U.S. hospitals (Astin, 1998; Eisenberg et al., 1993, 1998). These types of therapies include, among others, acupuncture, massage therapy, herbal medicine, aromatherapy, megavitamins, meditation, and chiropractic therapy. Although these treatments generally have not been proved effective through scientific testing and are not available in doctor offices or hospitals, many people choose such treatment for various health-related conditions, including cancer pain, back pain, arthritis, and AIDS. In fact, one survey found that 34% of people reported using at least one type of unconventional therapy to treat a medical problem in the past year and that one-third of them had seen a practitioner for this care. People who are well educated and those who are in poor health are more likely to use alternative approaches. Alternative therapies are sought most commonly for back pain (by 36% of people), anxiety (28%), headaches (27%), chronic pain (26%), and cancer (24%). Between 3 and 10% of Americans see a chiropractor each year. People often believe that alternative approaches will help them achieve pain relief faster (and perhaps more safely) than just using traditional medicine. Although most people who sought unconventional care also saw a medical doctor for the same condition, only 28% told their medical doctor about their use of alternative treatment.

Seeking alternative care can be very expensive, particularly because this type of treatment often is not covered by insurance plans. One estimate suggests that Americans pay 60% of the cost for alternative treatment themselves, at a cost of $12.2 billion a year (Eisenberg et al., 1998). Although it can be tempting to believe stories told by friends and in the media about the effectiveness of alternative approaches, remember to think critically about what you are reading and hearing. Very few of these treatments have been shown to be effective in rigorous scientific testing, and even if improvement does occur, it could be placebo effect or patient selection bias.

---

a substantial decrease in the cost of accident claims, from a little over $2,000 to just under $1,000.

However, in other cases the benefits of a program in terms of health may not justify its costs (White et al., 1993). Screening programs, for example, are often found not to be as cost-effective because they involve testing many people who would never develop the disease (Moum, 1995). For example,

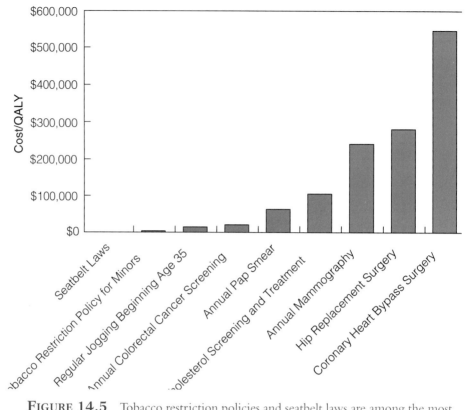

FIGURE 14.5   Tobacco restriction policies and seatbelt laws are among the most cost-effective health-promotion programs, whereas surgical procedures are among the least cost-effective (data from Kaplan, 1989, 2000).

requiring yearly mammograms is more expensive (in general and per cancer prevented) than biannual or even screenings once every 5 years, yet is more effective in reducing cancer deaths. Screening programs are also more cost-effective when they focus on those at greatest risk for the disease (Kaplan, 2000). Mammograms cost about $21,400 to produce a single year of life when used with women ages 50 to 64 years, but $105,000 per quality year lived when used in women ages 40 to 49 years. Similarly, a mass prenatal screening for cystic fibrosis could detect whether children would have this disease. However, given the tremendous costs associated with this screening, including genetic counseling, public education, and the tests themselves, it is estimated that more than $1 million would be spent to avoid a single cystic fibrosis birth (Wilfond & Fost, 1990). Because this is five times the cost of caring for a person with cystic fibrosis, this type of screening is clearly cost-ineffective. Finally, screening is especially cost-inefficient when it is used for relatively old people, who will not benefit from increased life expectancy as dramatically as younger people, and in cases in which the treatment for the condition detected leads to lower quality of life (Kaplan, 2000). For example, screening

70-year-old men for prostate cancer extends life expectancy less than 5 hours, and the treatment for prostate cancer often significantly reduces their overall enjoyment of life (Krahn et al., 1994). Once again, screening is not always the right approach to enhancing health.

Concern about high costs of health care has led to increasing acceptance of psychologists and their research by physicians and other health care professionals for several reasons. First, principles in health psychology can be used to prevent health problems from developing, which is much more cost-effective than diagnosing and treating illness and disease (Fries, 1998; Winett, 1995). For example, preventing premature birth by ensuring pregnant women have prenatal care reduces medical costs considerably (Brown, 1985)—babies who weigh as little as 1 pound at birth can be saved, but it costs about $350,000 per baby for 4 months of care in the neonatal intensive care unit, and these babies often have ongoing struggles and disabilities. In contrast, it would cost about $600 per pregnant woman to provide prenatal care to 583 women, which substantially reduces the likelihood of premature birth (Butter, 1993). Although this type of prevention program would reduce the demand for medical services, and thereby reduce health care costs, the vast majority of funds devoted to researching health issues each year are devoted to treating illness, not preventing it (DeLeon, 2002).

Second, in many cases psychological treatments may help people cope with and recover from medical problems, but at a lower cost. Many interventions for hospitalized patients are extremely cost-effective because they help patients use less pain medication and be discharged earlier (see Chapter 12; Devine, 1992). For example, of women who are supported during labor, only 8% have a Cesarean section, compared to 18% of those in the control group (Kennell, Klaus, McGrath, Robertson, & Hinkley, 1991). Patients who had a "doula" (a trained supportive companion to assist with labor and delivery) also had shorter labors, less use of epidural anesthesia, and were less likely to have babies that require neonatal hospitalization. This is a big cost savings. Although the medical community has often resisted collaborating with psychologists (or other nonmedically trained personnel), as of July 1, 2001, the Accreditation Council for Graduate Medical Education (ACGME) requires that residency programs teach skills in such collaboration, and residency programs must now demonstrate that residents have these skills prior to graduation.

Focusing on the Predictors of Women's Health

For many years, research in psychology in general and health psychology in particular was based largely on samples of men (and typically samples of young, white, upperclass men who were in college; Matthews et al., 1997). This focus was caused in part by the easy access of this type of population—many researchers work in college and university settings (and many prestigious schools did not even admit women until relatively recently) and, hence, often used students who were readily available. Women may also be excluded from medical studies because of concern about the influence of hormonal changes across the menstrual cycle as well as the potential dangers to fetuses

(Wenger, Speroff, & Packard, 1993). However, this exclusion of women severely limits our knowledge about the factors that influence women's health and how women respond to various psychological and medical treatments. In fact, women are even excluded from many studies of drugs that are primarily used by women, such as weight-loss pills and antidepressants (Rodin & Ickovics, 1990).

One explanation for the greater focus on men's health is that women typically have a much longer life expectancy than men; therefore they must be healthier. However, this gender gap in life expectancy is narrowing, in part because women are increasingly engaging in health-compromising behaviors at higher rates (Rodin & Ickovics, 1990). For example, the rate of lung cancer used to be much higher in men than women, but between 1979 and 1986 the rate of lung cancer deaths climbed 44% in women and only 7% in men. In fact, lung cancer—not breast cancer—is the leading cause of cancer death for U.S. women. Moreover, women who smoke and use the birth control pill experience a greater risk of stroke and cardiovascular disease. Women are also at a greater risk than men of acquiring HIV (Rodin & Ickovics, 1990). Although men still represent the majority of AIDS cases in the United States, the rate of new HIV infection in women is increasing dramatically, in part because women are at much greater risk of acquiring the disease during sex (Padian, Shiboski, Glass, & Vittinghoff, 1997).

Women also have unique health issues and concerns (Rodin & Ickovics, 1990; Stanton, Lobel, Sears, & DeLuca, 2002). First, reproductive issues and technology, including pregnancy, infertility, abortion, contraception, prenatal screening, cesarean sections, and in vitro fertilization, impact women more directly than they do men. The experience of postpartum depression, for example, has recently received considerable attention because of well-

PHOTO 14.4   After Andrea Yates drowned her five children in 2001, the tragic consequences of postpartum depression received considerable attention in the media.

publicized tragedies (see Photo 14.4). Women also face unique challenges related to the experience of menstruation and menopause. Many women take the hormone estrogen, often as part of oral contraceptives prior to menopause and as hormone replacement therapy following menopause. Although for some time researchers have thought that taking these hormones was an effective way of preventing some of the side effects of menopause, a very recent study by the National Institutes of Health revealed that women who take estrogen and progestin to minimize the effects of menopause are at risk of experiencing major health problems. Specifically, as compared to women in the control group who received a placebo, those who took these hormones experienced a 41% increase in strokes, a 29% increase in heart attacks, and a 26% increase in breast cancer. Finally, other diseases, such as osteoporosis and Alzheimer's disease, can occur in men and women, but are much more common in women, in part because they tend to live longer. In sum, women face particular health issues and challenges, and research must focus on examining how best to promote women's health. As described by Andrew Baum and Neil Grunberg (1991):

> Research on health and behavior should consider men and women—not because it is discriminatory not to do so—but because it is good science. The study of women and men, of young and old, of African Americans and Caucasians, Asians, Latinos, and American Indians will all help to reveal psychosocial and biological mechanisms that are critical to understanding mortality, morbidity, and quality of life (p. 84).

Some evidence also suggests that women consistently receive lower-quality health care than men (Ayanian & Epstein, 1991; Chen, Rathore, Radford, Wang, & Krumholz, 2001; Fiscella et al., 2000; Schulman et al., 1999; Steingart et al., 1991). As described in Chapter 12, women are less likely than men to receive a number of major diagnostic and therapeutic procedures, even when they are experiencing symptoms that are as severe as men's, in part because physicians are more likely to see women's physical symptoms as signs of psychological problems. Women are also less likely than men to have health insurance, primarily because they tend to have lower-paying jobs, which are less likely to provide benefits. And even when women do have health insurance, the coverage provided to men and women differs in some subtle but important ways. For example, many health insurance plans pay for Viagra (which aids men in having sex), but not for birth control pills (which aid women in preventing pregnancy)!

Broadening the Focus to Other Cultures

Much of the research that you've read about in this book was conducted in the United States and other Western, industrialized countries. A major focus of the future in health psychology must be on conducting research in other countries, particularly because many of these countries are in desperate need of improved health care. Infectious diseases, lack of nutrition, and lack of sanitary living conditions are major causes of death in other countries, and poor countries in particular could benefit from some of the principles of health psychology. Although major technological advances are expensive and unlikely to be of great practical help in many very poor countries, improved prenatal care, access to contraceptives, regular immunizations, and better nutrition could all lead to great increases in life expectancy (see Table 14.4). The United Nations International Children's Education Fund (UNICEF, 1991) identifies the key targets for improving international public health as birth timing and safe motherhood, breast-feeding and child growth, diarrhea and the management of respiratory infections, immunizations, home hygiene, mosquito control, and AIDS (see Photo 14.5). In fact, one of the easiest ways to promote health in many developing countries is to promote breast-feeding, which leads to significantly lower rates of diarrhea, malnutrition, and infant mortality (Elder, 2001).

TABLE **14.4**   *UNICEF's Key Messages for Improving International Health*

Family Planning and Reproductive Health

Birth spacing of less than 2 years increases mortality risk for young children by 50%.

Regular checkups during pregnancy reduce risks related to childbirth.

Having more than four children in total increases the health risks of pregnancy and childbirth.

Breast-Feeding and Nutrition

Breast milk alone in the best possible baby food during the first 4 to 6 months of life.

Babies should begin breast-feeding as soon as possible after birth.

Children between the ages of 6 months and 3 years should be weighed every month for growth monitoring.

Diarrhea and Acute Respiratory Infections

Diarrhea can kill children through dehydration. Therefore, children with diarrhea need plenty of liquids to drink.

If diarrhea becomes serious, trained medical attention is necessary.

Children with coughs or colds should be kept warm and should not be exposed to smoke.

Immunization, Hygiene, and HIV

Children not immunized are far more likely to become malnourished, suffer from disability, or die.

Illnesses can be prevented by washing hands with soap and water.

Any use of an unsterilized needle or syringe is dangerous.

These messages were designed by UNICEF to promote health-improving practices in many developing countries.

Source: United Nations International Children's Fund, 1991.

PHOTO 14.5   Many children in developing countries die each year from malnutrition, diarrhea, and starvation.

Some of the problems caused by malnutrition and starvation could be eliminated by reducing family size through use of contraceptives. An estimated 500,000 women die each year from pregnancy-related causes, and many others suffer serious health problems caused by (often unplanned) pregnancies (World Health Organization, 2002). Unintended pregnancies are relatively common given the high cost of and limited access to contraceptives, as well as the cultural and religious beliefs that may discourage their use. However, research in the field of family planning suggests that the media can be very helpful. In Tanzania, a country with a birthrate of six children per woman, a radio-based soap opera was created that featured popular characters communicating about the importance of using contraceptives and planning for small families (Rogers et al., 1999). This show was broadcast twice a week for 2 years, and then researchers compared the rate of contraceptive use in those who listened to the soap opera to those who did not. Although 19% of the nonlisteners used contraceptives, 64% of those who listened used contraceptives. This show also led to increased conversations between spouses about family planning—33% among nonlisteners versus 85% in listeners.

One international problem that health psychologists could help with is the public health crisis in Central and Eastern Europe (Little, 1998). After the dissolution of the Soviet Union in 1989 and the shifting economic base, numerous countries, including Bulgaria, Poland, and Romania, experienced huge socioeconomic changes. Rates of unemployment, poverty, and crime increased, and the quality and availability of health services decreased. In turn, while life expectancy increased throughout much of the world during this time, death rates increased dramatically in these countries. For example, the death rate in Russia alone increased 35% from 1989 to 1993. What led to such a high death rate? Behavior choices, such as smoking and alcohol abuse (see Table 14.5), are clearly one contributor, and poor medical care—including

TABLE 14.5   *Prevalence of Smoking around the World*

	% Men	% Women
North America		
USA (ages 18+)	27.6	22.1
Canada (ages 15+)	27	23
Mexico (ages 18+)	51.2	18.4
Western Europe		
France (ages 18+)	39	27
Germany (ages 18–59)	43.2	30
United Kingdom (ages 16+)	29	28
Asia and the Mediterranean		
China (ages 15–69)	63	3.8
India (ages 25–64)	45	7
Egypt (ages 18+)	43.6	4.8
Saudi Arabia (ages 15+)	40	8.2
Africa		
Kenya (ages 20+)	66.8	31.9
Nigeria (ages 15+)	15.4	1.7

Although about a quarter of American adults smoke, the smoking rates are considerably higher in other countries, especially among men.

Source: www.who.int/tobacco.

shortage of common vaccinations and underpaid, undertrained physicians—are another. A very important problem, yet a difficult one to solve, is the presence of high levels of pollution in the air, soil, and water. Principles in health psychology can assist with many of these problems, including the prevention of health harming-behaviors and the regulation of pollution by industries, thereby improving health for many people in other countries.

Another substantial international problem is the continuing spread of HIV infection. Although the rate of new cases of HIV each year in the United States is declining, 90% of new HIV infections occur in developing countries (Coates et al., 1996). In fact, while the rate of new infections seems to be relatively stable in the United States, Canada, and Western Europe, evidence suggests rates of HIV infection are still climbing, in some cases at dramatic rates, in Africa, Asia, Latin America, and Eastern Europe (see Table 14.6). As shown in Table 14.7, heterosexual transmission is the major cause of the spread of HIV in most developing countries, yet less is known about how to successfully prevent this type of transmission than preventing sexual transmission between men. Research in health psychology is clearly needed to examine how to help decrease the spread of HIV in developing countries.

TABLE 14.6 *Prevalence of AIDS around the World*

	Cumulative Deaths	AIDS Cases
North America	420,000	690,000
Western Europe	190,000	230,000
Australia/New Zealand	7,000	<10,000
North Africa/Middle East	42,000	49,000
Eastern Europe/Central Asia	5,400	<10,000
East Asia/Pacific	11,000	14,000
Southeast Asia	730,000	850,000
Sub-Saharan Africa	9,600,000	10,500,000
Caribbean	110,000	120,000

Although the initial cases of HIV infection were discovered in North America, AIDS is now most prevalent in Africa and Southeast Asia.

TABLE 14.7 *Routes of HIV Transmission around the World*

	%Heterosexual Intercourse	%Homosexual Intercourse	%Intravenous Drug Use	%Blood Transfusion	%Mother–Child
United States	13	52	33	2	0
Canada	13	71	13	2	1
France	19	48	16	5	1
United Kingdom	15	70	8	5	2
Germany	19	48	26	5	1
China	17	5	59	20	0
Japan	39	27	1	33	1
Egypt	67	14	6	14	0
Saudi Arabia	69	2	2	21	5
Ethiopia	97	0	0	2	2
Nigeria	95	0	0	4	1
Pakistan	92	0	0	0	8
Australia	5	89	3	4	0

Although homosexual intercourse is still the predominant route of HIV transmission in the United States, Canada, Australia, and many western European countries, heterosexual transmission accounts for the vast majority of HIV infection in many Middle Eastern and African countries.

What Can You Do with a Degree in Health Psychology?

Health psychologists work on a variety of topics in a variety of settings (Belar, 1997; Enright, Resnick, DeLeon, Sciava, & Tanney, 1990). During the 1980s, the number of psychologists working in health-related fields more than doubled (Enright et al., 1990; Frank, Gluck, & Buckelew, 1990), and this trend will continue (Kaplan, 2000). Some health psychologists conduct research in academic settings, and may also teach courses to undergraduate and/or graduate students. They might also do research and teach in medical, dental, and nursing schools. Other health psychologists work directly with patients to prevent and/or improve psychological and physical well-being, such as by providing diagnostic and counseling services, preparing patients for surgery and other medical procedures, and designing programs to help patients adhere to medical recommendations and cope with chronic pain. These positions often involve working in a hospital, medical school, HMO, pain and rehabilitation clinic, or independent practice. Still other health psychologists work on forming health policies and finding funding research on health-related issues, often in a government agency such as the National Institutes of Health or the Centers for Disease Control and Prevention.

What should you do if you are interested in a career in health psychology? First, you should enroll in a range of courses in psychology. The field of health psychology draws on a number of parts of the field of psychology; hence, students who are interested in this field should try to get a broad background. Taking courses in anatomy and physiology may also be beneficial, as would courses in statistics and research methods (which are required for some graduate programs). Second, many students find that getting hands-on experience in health psychology is a great way of learning more about the field, as well as a good résumé builder! You might be able to assist one of your professors with his or her research in health psychology, find a summer internship in a hospital, or volunteer with a social service agency.

After receiving an undergraduate degree in psychology, training in health psychology can involve a number of different programs. The majority of health psychologists obtain a Ph.D. (a doctorate degree) in some type of psychology. Graduate programs in health psychology typically provide training in biology (e.g., anatomy, physiology, psychopharmacology, epidemiology, neuropsychology), the broad domains of psychology (e.g., social, developmental, personality, cognitive, neuroscience), and social factors (e.g., family, ethnicity, culture, race). They also include training in statistics and research methods. The field of *clinical health psychology* focuses on using knowledge gained in the discipline of psychology to promote and maintain physical health, including preventing and treating injury and disease, identifying causes of health problems, and improving health policy and the health care system (Belar, 1997). Other people receive a Ph.D. in a subfield of psychology, such as developmental, social, physiological, or clinical, but focus their coursework and research on health-related issues. My Ph.D., for example, is in social-personality psychology, and my research during graduate school focused on HIV prevention. Graduate school consists of coursework as well as training in research, which culminates in the completion of a dissertation (an original research project). Many health psychologists also choose to do postdoctoral training or an internship, often in a hospital, clinic, or university setting, for a year or two after graduate school to gain additional experience and skills (see Photo 14.6).

Other people who are interested in the broad topic of health psychology choose a different training path, which could include enrolling in medical or nursing school; obtaining a master's or doctorate degree in public health; pursuing a degree in physical therapy, occupational therapy, or nutrition, or social work (see Boxes 14.4 and 14.5). The specific training route you choose is determined by your major interest and career goal. Do you really like working directly with people and personally helping people make changes in their behavior or manage their pain? If so, you may want to pursue a degree in counseling or clinical psychology, social work, or nursing and work in an applied setting. Do you really like working on research projects and forming and testing different hypotheses to find the answer to a particular question? If so, you may want to pursue a degree in psychology or public health and work in a research setting. Are you primarily interested in people's physical and physiological responses and in exploring how their bodies work? In this case, you should consider pursuing a degree in medicine, physical therapy, or occupational therapy. As described at the beginning of the chapter, Mark ultimately decided to pursue a degree in public health because he realized that his primary interest was preventing large-scale public health problems.

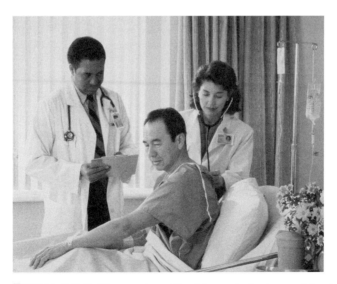

PHOTO 14.6 The number of health psychologists working in hospital settings is rapidly increasing, partly because of a greater understanding of how psychological factors influence physical health.

Box 14.4

Health Psychology in the Real World—Careers in Health-Related Fields

When you think of people working as health professionals, what types of jobs come to mind? Probably doctors, nurses, and perhaps dentists. But there are many types of careers in health-related fields, and virtually all of them involve and use principles and research of health psychology in some way. Most of these careers require an undergraduate degree in the field and often some type of additional training or education for a year or two after college.

Physical therapists help people with diseases of or injuries to muscles, joints, nerves, or bones. They evaluate a patient's capabilities, including muscle strength, coordination, endurance, and range of motion, and then design a treatment to address the person's limitations. For example, a person who has experienced a major accident may need to learn how to walk again. Physical therapists may also work to increase people's mobility and decrease their pain. They may also provide training in using adaptive devices, such as crutches, canes or walkers, or a prostheses (artificial limbs). They work in hospitals, nursing homes, and rehabilitation clinics.

Occupational therapists work with patients who have physical, mental, or emotional disabilities and try to help them learn the skills they need to function in a productive way. For example, they might help people learn to dress themselves, write, and prepare meals. They often work in a school, work, or community setting and may specialize in treating patients with a particular type of disability (e.g., the elderly, children, patients with spinal cord injuries). They also may evaluate a patient's capabilities and then design a treatment program.

Dietitians and nutritionists work on helping people create and manage healthy diets. Some people in this field work in hospitals, clinics, or nursing homes to design appealing and balanced meals. They may also work with patients and their families on making and adhering to dietary changes, especially in cases in which a person's health is seriously at risk if their diet does not change (e.g., diabetics, CHD patients).

Social workers, who work in hospitals, community agencies, clinics, nursing homes, help individuals and their families cope with psychological and social issues. In some cases social workers serve as therapists, such as by helping people talk about their feelings after receiving a chronic disease diagnosis. This therapy might include the patient as well as his or her family members as well. Social workers also provide important assistance with connecting people with various community services. For example, they could help a family receive temporary assistance with cooking and cleaning if the person who has provided this type of household care becomes disabled, or could refer a chronically or terminally ill patient as well as his or her family to a local support group.

(continues)

Public health researchers, who may work in academic settings, government agencies, hospitals, social service agencies, and clinics, work in a direct way to improve the health of people in a given community. They may develop and implement interventions to prevent health problems or may evaluate programs that are currently in use. For example, a public health researcher could work in a Planned Parenthood clinic to test whether its teen pregnancy prevention program is effective.

Box 14.5

Health Psychology in the Real World—Occupational Health Psychology in Action

Occupational health psychology is an emerging area of health psychology that focuses specifically on healthy workplaces, namely, ones in which people produce high-quality work and achieve great personal satisfaction (Quick, 1999). This field blends issues in public health, clinical psychology, organizational behavior, and industrial/organizational psychology. For example, research results of occupational health psychologists suggest that people who are able to have some control and flexibility in their jobs experience better health and satisfaction, that workers benefit from having effective ways of reducing stress (e.g., exercise, social support), and that workers can be more effective when they are not concerned about family issues. These psychologists could work directly with a business and in this capacity advise employers on ways to improve employee health (e.g., smoking cessation interventions, exercise facilities, stress management), as described in the following two examples.

U.S. Air Force

In 1993, Joyce Adkins of the U.S. Air Force Biomedical Sciences Corps started an organizational health center at the McClellan Air Force Base in Sacramento, California (Quick, 1999). The goals of this center included improving working conditions; monitoring psychological disorders and risk factors; providing information, training, and education; and providing psychological health services to all employees. Within the first year of the project, several substantial changes were noted. First, the total cost of worker's compensation payments (given to employees who were injured) decreased 3.9%, leading to a savings of $289,099. Second, medical visits and health care utilization for job-related injury and illness decreased by 12%, again leading to a cost savings of $150,918. Finally, there was a decrease in death rates, suggesting that perhaps 10 deaths caused by behavioral-related events were avoided. In turn, this decrease in premature mortality

(continues)

was associated with a tremendous savings in terms of productive years gained (e.g., recruiting, hiring, training new employees).

Johnson & Johnson

In 1978, Johnson & Johnson developed a comprehensive health-promotion program entitled Live for Life (Quick, 1999). This program included health assessments, materials promoting health behavior change, and the development of a physical fitness program. In turn, the addition of this program led to improvements in workers' psychological and physical well-being (Bly, Jones, & Richardson, 1986). First, employees showed an increase in attitudes toward commitment, supervision, working conditions, job competence, pay and benefits, and job security. These increases should lead to lower turnover and, thereby, reduce the considerable costs associated with hiring and training new employees. The company also experienced lower health care costs, partly because of to lower rates of hospital admissions and fewer hospitalized days. Specifically, inpatient health care costs for workers in this program were only $42 to $43 per employee as compared to $76 for those without this program.

What's the "Take Home" Point?

Now that you are at the end of this book—and perhaps at the end of your health psychology course—you should be asking yourself, "What exactly have I learned?" I hope that most of all, you will have a clear understanding of the diverse ways in which psychological factors influence physical well-being: our thoughts about various daily life situations influence whether we experience arousal; our amount and type of social support influences how long we live; our feelings of vulnerability influence our health-promoting behavior; and our need for information can influence how we respond to surgical procedures, to name a few instances. I also hope that you've learned some things in this book that you will use in your everyday life, regardless of whether your career path takes you to a health-related field. Perhaps information you've learned in this book will motivate you to always wear your seatbelt, start an exercise program, or even teach your children healthy eating behaviors. One of the reasons I love teaching health psychology—why I've enjoyed writing this book—is because this is a field that truly matters to us all. Good health also matters to our society. As Marc Lalonde (1974), the Canadian minister of national health and welfare in the 1970s, describes:

> Good health is the bedrock on which social progress is built. A nation of healthy people can do those things that make life worthwhile, and as the level of health increases so does the potential for happiness. The Governments of the Provinces and of Canada have long recognized that good physical and mental health are necessary for the quality of life to which everyone aspires. (p. 5)

I hope this book helps you to have a life that is long in quantity and high in quality, including physical, mental, and psychological health.

Thought Questions

1. Tina has a summer job with the organization MADD (Mothers Against Drunk Driving), and she has been asked to help design three different strategies for preventing injuries and deaths caused by drunk drivers. What are three distinct types of approaches to such prevention?

2. What are four explanations for the link between low socioeconomic status and poor health? Which factor do you think is the biggest contributor to this association and why?

3. Your local hospital can fund only one of the following three programs: developing technology that will allow animal organs to be used for critically ill patients in need of organ transplants, training all surgical patients in coping and behavioral strategies for managing pain, and creating a healthy eating and exercise program that will be used in gym classes at local schools. In your opinion, which of these programs should be funded and why?

4. Describe two advantages of the HMO health care system and two disadvantages.

5. Your roommate, Mark, is taking a health psychology course right now and is really enjoying it. He comes to you for advice about what he should do if he thinks he wants a career in health psychology, and he also wants to know what a person can do with a degree in health psychology. What do you tell him?

GLOSSARY

abstinence violation effect—if a person expects they will never give in to temptation, when and if they do have a lapse in behavior, they are likely to blame it on themselves, which could lead to a total relapse.

acupuncture—a technique in which needles are inserted in specific points on the skin in an attempt to control pain.

acute pain—an intense but time-limited pain that is generally the result of tissue damage or disease, such as breaking a bone, receiving a cut or bruise, and giving birth. Acute pain typically disappears over time (as the injury heals) and lasts less than six months.

A-delta fibers—small and myelinated (covered with a fatty substance that acts as insulation) nerve fibers that carry information very rapidly. These fibers transmit sharp, localized, distinct pain, such as the pain caused by cutting your finger with a knife.

addiction—the condition in which a person has a physical and psychological dependence on a given substance, such as cigarettes, alcohol, or caffeine. Addiction is caused by repeatedly consuming the substance, which over time leads the body to adjust to the substance and incorporate it into the "normal" functioning of the body's tissues.

adherence—the extent to which a person follows recommended treatments and health behaviors.

adrenocorticotropic hormone (ACTH)—a hormone released by the pituitary gland which in turn leads the adrenal gland to produce glucocorticoids, such as cortisol.

affect-regulation model—a model proposing that people smoke to attain positive affect or to avoid (or reduce) negative affect. Positive affect smokers may smoke as a way of enhancing the pleasure associated with other events, such as eating a great meal or having sex, whereas negative affect smokers smoke as a way of coping with negative affect, such as reducing anxiety, tension, and frustration.

AIDS—a disease caused by the human immunodeficiency virus (HIV) in which the body's natural defense system is disabled, leaving the body unable to fight off even mild infections. Although there is no cure for AIDS, some drug regimens (such as AZT and HAART regimens) can help prolong survival and improve the quality of life.

AIDS Risk Reduction Model (ARRM)—a model predicting whether people engage in HIV prevention behavior. According to this model, people first must understand the threat of HIV infection and recognize that their behavior puts them at risk of acquiring this disease. People also must have a strong commitment to using a condom during sex, as well as a strong confidence, or self-efficacy, in their ability to do so. Finally, people also need to be capable of actually using a condom at the critical moment, which is the enactment stage.

alcohol myopia—the state in which individuals under the influence of alcohol make decisions based on salient short-term concerns while ignoring longer-term consequences of their behavior. This state occurs because individuals are unable to engage in the complex cognitive processing required to consider the more distant consequences, and instead base decisions primarily on the most salient and immediate cues. Alcohol myopia theory also describes the effects of alcohol on a person's self-evaluation. Specifically, people who are intoxicated often experience "drunken self-inflation," meaning that people who are drinking see themselves in an idealized way.

Alcoholics Anonymous (AA)—the most widely known self-help program for alcohol abuse, which is attended more often than any other alcohol program. The general AA philosophy is based on two principal views. First, people who abuse alcohol are alcoholics and will remain that way for life, even if they never drink. Second, taking even a single drink after being abstinent can set off an alcoholic binge, and therefore the goal is total abstinence from alcohol.

alcoholism—alcohol consumption that is compulsive and uncontrollable, physically addictive, or habitual, and results in serious threats to a person's health and well-being. Alcoholics have a very high tolerance for alcohol, suffer blackouts or memory losses, and experience withdrawal symptoms such as delirium tremens (e.g., hallucinations, impaired motor coordination,

cognitive disruption) when they stop drinking.

allostatic load—the body's attempt to adapt to a stressful situation. This physiological response involves a number of systems in the body and is shut off as soon as the challenge ends.

ammenorrhea—the absence of menstruation, which is often a symptom of anorexia nervosa.

amniocentesis—a procedure in which fluid is drawn from the amniotic sac surrounding a fetus to test for abnormalities; causes miscarriage in between 1 and 200 and 1 and 400 cases.

analgesic drugs—drugs, such as aspirin, acetaminophen, and ibuprofen, that reduce fever and inflammation at the site of a wound and work to decrease pain by interfering with the transmission of pain signals. Analgesics are very effective in reducing mild to moderate levels of pain, such as headache and arthritis pain.

angina—a feeling of pain and tightness in the chest as the heart is deprived of oxygen. This type of attack may pass quickly but is often a sign that future cardiovascular problems will develop.

anorexia nervosa—an eating disorder that involves a drastic reduction in people's food intake and an intentional loss of weight (maintaining a body weight 15% below one's normal weight based on height-weight tables or a BMI of 17.5).

appraisal delay—the delay from when people experience—and notice—some type of symptoms to when they decide that they are ill.

approach-approach conflict—a type of conflict in which a person is torn between wanting to do two desirable things that are incompatible (e.g., take a spring break trip with friends and earn money from spending that week working).

approach-avoidance conflict—a type of conflict in which a person is torn between wanting to do one thing and wanting to avoid another thing (e.g., eat chocolate but avoid gaining weight).

archival research—a type of research that uses already recorded behavior, such as divorce rates, disease rates, and death rates.

arteriosclerosis—a condition in which the arteries have lost their elasticity, making it difficult for them to expand and contract. This process leads to a decrease in blood flow and an increase in the likelihood of a blood clot.

assisted suicide—helping a person to kill himself or herself, such as by providing the means to accomplish this task.

atherosclerosis—a condition which occurs when fatty substances build up in the artery walls, thereby decreasing blood flow and increasing the likelihood of a blood clot. Because the flow of blood is reduced, it can deprive the heart of essential nutrients.

attribution theory—a theory which posits that people try to explain the causes of their own and others' behavior, and specifically that people can see behavior as caused by internal factors or external factors. In turn, behavior that is motivated by internal factors, such as an individual's desire to engage in the behavior, is expected to continue over time, whereas behavior that is the result of external pressures from others is unlikely to continue.

autonomic nervous system—one of the two parts of the peripheral nervous system. The autonomic nervous system, which consists of the sympathetic and parasympathetic divisions, carries information that is directly related to survival (e.g., organs that are not under voluntary control).

aversion strategies—strategies for behavior change that are based on principles of classical conditioning—these approaches try to reduce a behavior by pairing it with some type of unpleasant stimuli.

avoidance-avoidance conflict—a type of conflict in which a person is torn between two undesirable things that are incompatible. For example, a person with cancer might have to choose between chemotherapy and radiation.

AZT (zidovudine)—a type of medication commonly used to treat HIV infection. However, its use is associated with numerous unpleasant side effects, including anemia, headaches, itches, and mental confusion.

behavior therapy—therapy that is designed to decrease people's experience of pain by changing their behavior. For example, a person with chronic back pain might receive physical therapy to increase flexibility and/or be taught how to strengthened their abdominal muscles to put less strain on their back.

behavioral medicine—the development and application of behavioral techniques for treatment, management, and rehabilitation of patients. These techniques are used widely to help people overcome various types of health-damaging behaviors, including overeating, smoking, and alcohol abuse.

belongingness support—this type of support refers to the availability of social companionship, such as having others with whom to engage in social activities (e.g., going out to dinner, seeing a movie, attending a party).

binge drinking—having five or more drinks on the same occasion.

biobehavioral model—a model suggesting that both psychological and physiological factors lead people to continue to smoke over time. This model proposes that nicotine has a number of physiological effects that make people feel good (e.g., improves memory and concentration, reduces anxiety and tension), which leads people to readily become dependent on smoking. Smokers then become dependent (both physically and psychologically) on using nicotine to experience these positive effects.

biofeedback—a technique in which people are trained, using electric monitors, to monitor and change selected physiological functions, such as their heart rate, finger temperature, muscle activity, and brain wave patterns. Biofeedback is an effective way of controlling headache pain, back pain, and hypertension.

biomedical model—a model, which was formed in the 19th and 20th century, which proposes that illnesses are caused by physical problems, such as viruses and bacteria, injuries, and biochemical imbalances. According to this perspective, physical health is completely separate from psychological health—the body is a physical entity and the mind is a psychology/mental/spiritual entity, and that these operate completely separately.

biopsychosocial model—a model which views health as determined by individual, social, and cultural factors. It acknowledges that biological factors can and do influence health and illness, but at the same time maintains that social, cultural, and psychological factors also exert an effect. This model is holistic, in that it sees the mind and body as inherently connected, and sees health as an interactive system in which biological factors (e.g., genetics, physiology) interact with psychological factors (e.g., personality, cognition) and social factors (e.g., community, family, media).

blind/double-blind—a blind study is one in which the participants do not know the hypotheses of the study nor the particular conditions that are being tested. A double-blind study is one in which neither the participants nor the experimenter conducting the study know which participant is receiving which treatment.

Body Mass Index (BMI)—the most commonly used measure of obesity today. BMI is calculated by dividing a person's weight (in kilograms) by their height (in meters) squared. A BMI between 19 to 24 is seen as ideal, with 25 to 29 seen as moderately overweight (about 15 to 30% over ideal weight) and greater than 30 seen as obese (about 40% over ideal weight).

bradykinin—a neurotransmitter that is released by the body's cells when damage occurs, and excites the neurons that carry information about pain. These chemicals mobilize the body to repair the damage in a variety of ways, including causing inflammation at the site of the injury and increasing the immune system's functioning.

BRCA1/BRCA2—two genes (breast cancer gene 1 and breast cancer gene 2) that are associated with an increased risk of breast cancer.

BSE (breast self-exam)—an important screening behavior to help detect breast cancer at an early stage.

buffering hypothesis—a hypothesis which suggests that social support leads to better health by protecting people from the negative effects of high stress, and hence social support is particularly beneficial during stressful times.

bulimia nervosa—an eating disorder that is characterized by recurrent episodes of binge eating followed by purging. These episodes are typically triggered by some type of negative emotion, such as anxiety, tension, or even being tired. During these binges, bulimics rapidly consume enormous quantities of food and then attempt to get rid of these calories, typically through either vomiting or excessive exercise. This pattern of binge eating and purging occurs on a regular basis over some period of time.

C fibers—unmyelinated (uncoated) fibers that transmit pain very slowly. These fibers transmit more diffuse, dull, or aching pain, such as the pain caused by chronic back pain.

cancer—an uncontrollable growth and spread of abnormal cells, which form tumors. Benign tumors consist of cells that are relatively typical of the nearby cells and grow relatively slowly. On the other hand, malignant tumors (which are commonly called cancers) consist of cells that are different from their surrounding cells and grow very rapidly. Malignant tumors often grow beyond their original location and invade other body organs (metastasize), spreading cancer throughout the body.

carcinogen—any substance capable of converting normal cells into cancerous ones. Carcinogens change the cell's DNA, which in turn leads to cancer.

cardiovascular system—a network of body systems that work to transport oxygen to and remove carbon dioxide from each cell and organ in the body. This work is accomplished through the beating of the heart, which generates the necessary force in the bloodstream.

case study/case report—a research technique that relies on studying one or more individuals in great depth to determine the causes of their behavior and to predict behavior in others.

catecholamines—neurotransmitters, such as epinephrine and norepinephrine, that are released by the adrenal glands during stress.

cell-mediated immune response system—an immune response in which the T cells, which originate in the thymus, bind to foreign cells in order to kill them.

central control mechanism—a portion of the brain that influences how much information is transmitted from the brain to the spinal cord.

central nervous system—a system within the body, consisting of the brain and spinal cord, where information processing occurs.

chiropractic therapy—a therapy that focuses on manipulating the bones, muscles, and joints to improve body alignment.

chronic disease—a condition which often has multiple causes, including people's behavioral choices or lifestyles, and a slow onset and increase over time. Chronic conditions can only be managed—although people with a chronic disease sometimes get worse and sometimes stay the same, they can't be cured.

chronic pain—a type of pain that may begin as acute pain (in response to a specific injury or disease), but just doesn't go away after a minimum of six months. Lower back pain, headaches, and the pain associated with arthritis and cancer are all examples of chronic pain.

classical conditioning—learning that occurs when a previously neutral stimulus comes to evoke the same response as another stimulus with which it is paired.

clinical health psychology—a new field that focuses on using knowledge gained in the discipline of psychology to promote and maintain physical health, including preventing and treating injury and disease, identifying causes of health problems, and improving health policy and the health care system

clinical studies—a type of research that is very similar to experiments in many ways, in that they use random assignment to condition and are often blind or even double-blind. However, because these studies often involve patients who have actively sought help for a given disorder, the practical and ethical issues involved in conducting this type of research, such as who is eligible to participate and whether they have multiple disorders, can be complex.

cognitive dissonance theory—a theory which states that people are highly motivated to have their attitudes, beliefs, and behaviors all be in line, and when they engage in a behavior that is not consistent with their attitudes, they experience an unpleasant state of psychological arousal known as dissonance. However, because it is very difficult, and sometimes impossible, to undo a behavior, people often try to resolve this uncomfortable feeling of arousal by changing their attitude to make it correspond with their behavior.

cognitive redefinition—a cognitive technique which works to help people think about pain in a new way. For example, a woman might be trained to think about the pain of labor as her baby pushing its way into the world.

cognitive-behavioral strategies—strategies for coping with pain and chronic illness that include physical, cognitive, and emotional techniques. For example, cognitive-behavior strategies for regulating weight could include thinking about food in a new way and having smaller portions of food.

cognitive theory—a theory which describes alcohol use as a function of its physiological effects and their impact on information processing.

combative coping—a problem-focused coping strategy in which a person attempts to avoid a stressor that cannot be avoided.

commonsense illness representations—people's beliefs about the nature and cause of their health symptoms.

conscientiousness—a personality trait describing people who are hardworking, motivated, and persistent. They show high levels of self-restraint and an intense focus on their goals.

contingency contracting—a behavior change technique used to give people additional motivation to change their behavior. In this technique, people who wish to change their behavior give some money to a friend (or therapist), with the understanding that if they are not smoking six months later, they get the money back. This technique therefore uses the promise of a reward to encourage behavior change (an operant conditioning approach).

controlled drinking—one view of managing alcoholism, namely by teaching people with serious drinking problems to engage in moderate amounts of drinking.

coronary heart disease—a chronic disease in which the arteries become narrowed or clogged, due to atherosclerosis or arteriosclerosis. Coronary heart disease is the leading cause of death in the United States.

corticosteroids—hormones that are produced by the adrenal cortex and work to fight inflammation and promote healing.

cortisol—a hormone that increases the production of energy from glucose and inhibits the swelling around injuries and infections.

counterirritation—irritating one type of body tissue to ease pain in another type of body tissue (e.g., putting your finger in your mouth after you burn it on a hot stove, rubbing your calf muscle to reduce a painful cramp). This is a type of physical stimulation.

chorionic villus sampling (CVS)—a type of prenatal testing which can be done at 9 to 12 weeks of pregnancy. This procedure leads to miscarriage in 1 in 100 cases.

cystic fibrosis—a hereditary disease characterized by abnormal secretions in various body parts, particularly the lungs, pancreas, and intestines. These secretions can block breathing and digestion, and hence this condition often leads to death by adolescence or early adulthood.

debriefing—a disclosure made to subjects after research procedures are completed in which the researcher explains the purpose of the study, answers any questions, attempts to resolve any negative feelings, and emphasizes the contributions to science of the research. This is especially important in cases in which deception has been used.

deception—giving research participants incomplete, or sometimes false, information about the study they are participating in.

dependent variable—a variable that is measured as the outcome of the study.

Dependent variables may be influenced by one or more independent variables.

detoxification—the drying out process in which an alcoholic withdraws from alcohol completely. This process takes about a month and can include severe symptoms, such as intense anxiety, tremors, and hallucinations.

direct effects hypothesis—a hypothesis that posits that social support can help people at both low and high levels of stress, and hence having high levels of social support is always advantageous to health.

disease model—a theory of behavior that describes addiction as caused primarily by internal physiological forces, such as cravings, urges, and compulsions, and hence the "addict" is unable to voluntarily control his/her behavior.

drunken invincibility—the situation in which people who have been drinking believe they are invulnerable to the dangers they might normally experience.

emotion-based appeals—a type of persuasive message designed to elicit an emotional reaction, such as fear or happiness.

emotion-focused coping—a type of coping that focuses on managing the emotional effects of a stressful situation. This strategy could include a number of different approaches, including simply not thinking about the problem (e.g., denial or avoidance) as well as venting about the problem to others (e.g., seeking social support).

emotional support—the expression of caring, concern, and empathy toward a person as well as the provision of comfort, reassurance, and love.

endocrine system—a body system which regulates a number of different physiological processes in the body, including physical growth, sexual arousal, metabolism, and stress response. The endocrine system works by releasing hormones from an endocrine gland, such as the pituitary, thyroid, and pancreas, into the blood stream.

endorphins—neurotransmitters that work by slowing or blocking the transmission of any nerve impulses. Endorphins bind to receptors in the periaqueductral gray area of the midbrain, which dramatically reduce pain.

epinephrine—a hormone (also called adrenaline) which is released when the sympathetic nervous system and endocrine system are stimulated in response to stress. High levels of epinephrine in the bloodstream leads to a number of other physiological responses, including increases in heart rate, blood pressure, and breathing, a widening of the pupils, and the movement of blood towards the muscles.

esteem/validational support—affirmation of self-worth, including feedback that one is valued and respected by others.

eustress—the beneficial, as opposed to harmful, stresses.

euthanasia—ending the life of a person who has a painful terminal illness as a way of reducing their suffering.

exhaustion stage—a stage at which the body's resources are depleted and thus it becomes very susceptible to physiological damage and disease.

experimental/psychological realism—the degree to which experimental procedures are involving to subjects and lead them to behave naturally and spontaneously.

experimental research—a type of study in which researchers manipulate one or more independent variables and then measure the effect of the independent variable on one or more dependent variables. Experiments include random assignment to condition and high levels of control over the participants' environment.

ex-post facto research—a type of quasi-experimental study in which researchers cannot randomly assign people to various conditions or treatments, but instead they select people who differ on a particular variable of interest.

external validity—the degree to which there can be reasonable confidence that the same results would be obtained for other people and in other situations.

extraversion—a personality trait describing people who are outgoing, social, and assertive—they have many friends, show high levels of energy, and often take on leadership roles. People who are extraverted also tend to seek a high level of stimulation—they get bored easily, enjoy new challenges, and like to take risks.

false positive—an inaccurate test result showing people have a disease or condition, when they really don't. A false positive can obviously lead to psychological distress and anxiety, which in some cases may be maintained even after the patient receives accurate results.

false negative—an inaccurate test result showing people don't have a disease or condition, when they actually do. False negative results can lead people to experience a false sense of security and deprive them of the opportunity to start treatment.

fear appeals—a type of persuasive message designed to elicit fear and anxiety, which in turn may lead to attitude and behavior change.

framing—the way information is presented, which can have a significant impact on decisions.

gate control theory—a theory describing the experience of pain which states that when body tissues are injured, nerve endings, or nociceptors, in the area that is damaged transmit impulses to a particular area of the dorsal horn section of the spinal cord called the substantia gelatinosa. Once these nerve impulses reach the substantia gelatinosa, one of two things can happen. If these sensations are sufficiently intense, then these signals are sent all the way up to the brain, where they are experienced as pain—the more signals that reach the brain, the more pain you experience. However, according to the gate control theory, not all of the pain signals carried by the nerve fibers will successfully reach the brain. Specifically, this theory posits that there is a gate in the substantia gelatinosa that either lets pain impulses travel to the brain, or blocks their progress, and any competing sensation that increases stimulation to the site could serve to block transmission.

General Adaptation Syndrome (GAS)—a model describing how stress can lead to negative health consequences over time.

glucocorticoids—a hormone produced by the adrenal gland which hinders the formation of some white blood cells, including NK cells, and kills other white blood cells.

glutamate—a neurotransmitter that excites the neurons that send messages about pain, and therefore increase the experience of pain.

guided imagery—a type of relaxation method for coping with pain which pairs deep muscle relaxation with a specific type of pleasant image that serves to focus a patient's mind on something other than the pain.

hardiness—a personality variable that is associated with how a person reacts in challenging and potentially stressful situations. People who are hardy have a strong commitment to what they are doing, possess a sense of control over what is happening to them, and see stressful events as challenging rather than threatening. Hardiness is associated with better health outcomes.

highly active antiretroviral therapy (HAART)—a regimen used for the treatment of HIV infection which involves a complicated drug-taking schedule—sometimes as many as 16 pills must be taken each day at precise times and under precise conditions. The HAART regimen can also lead to a variety of side effects, including mental confusion, headaches, and anemia.

health behavior—behaviors designed to promote a person's good health and prevent illness. This type of behavior could include exercising regularly, wearing a seatbelt, and getting immunizations to prevent disease.

health belief model—one of the oldest and widely used theories to explain people's health-related behavior. According to this model, the likelihood that individuals will take preventive action is a function of four types of factors: susceptibility to the disease, severity of the disease, and the benefits and costs of taking action.

high-density lipoproteins, or HDL, cholesterol—a type of cholesterol that removes LDL (low-density lipoproteins) cholesterol from the bloodstream, and thereby reduces the risk of blood clots.

HIV (human immunodeficiency virus)—a retrovirus that causes AIDS. Retroviruses replicate by injecting themselves into host cells and literally taking over the genetic workings of these cells. They can then produce virus particles that infect new cells.

HMO—a very common type of health care plan in which an employer or an employee pays a set fee every month and in turn has unlimited access to medical care (at either no or a greatly reduced cost). In some cases, HMOs require patients to see their own staff, whereas in other systems patients can choose from among a group of medical professionals who have all agreed to accept a specified payment for their services (preferred provider organizations). HMOs assign people to a primary care physician, who manages their care and must refer to specialists.

homeostasis—a state of internal physiological equilibrium or balance in which people are normally in.

hospice—an alternative care choice for terminally ill patients which is designed to provide personal comfort and open discussion. Hospice care may be delivered within one's home, a hospital, or a separate facility.

hostility/disagreeableness—a personality trait in which people believe that others are motivated by selfish concerns and expect that other people will deliberately try to hurt them. In turn, because of their general mistrust and cynicism about other people's motivations, hostile people don't hesitate to express these feelings—they are often uncooperative, rude, argumentative, condescending, and aggressive.

humoral immune response system—an immune system response in which proteins called antibodies are produced that bind to foreign toxins and inactivate or destroy them. This response is controlled by the B cells, which originate in the bone marrow.

Huntington's disease—an inherited nerve disorder that leads, typically in early middle age, to disorganized body movements and mental deterioration. Although there is no way to prevent this disease, some of the physical symptoms can be somewhat managed with drugs.

hypertension—a condition in which blood pressure is at a consistently high level. Patients are at increased risk of developing CHD.

hypnosis—an altered state of consciousness or trance state that individuals can enter under the guidance of a trained therapist. Hypnosis can be effective in controlling pain, including the pain associated with dental work, childbirth, back pain, headaches, and arthritis.

hypochondria—an excessive concern about one's health, which can include interpreting relatively benign symptoms as signs of more serious problems.

hypothesis—a testable prediction about the conditions under which an event will occur.

hypothalamic-pituitary adrenal (HPA) system—part of the endocrine system that responds during times of stress. This response starts by secreting corticotropin-releasing hormone (CRH), which in turn triggers the anterior pituitary gland to release adrenocorticotropic hormone (ACTH). Finally, the presence of ACTH leads the adrenal gland to release glucocorticoids, including cortisol.

illness (or symptom) behavior—behavior that is directed towards determining one's health status after experiencing symptoms. This could include talking to other people—family and friends as well as health professionals, monitoring symptoms yourself, and reading about your health problem.

illness delay—the time required for a person to decide that help from a professional is required after he/she realizes he/she is ill. People often believe that the symptoms will go away on their own, and hence delay seeking medical care.

immune system—a body system which is the major line of defense against infection, illness, and disease. The immune system works to eliminate foreign, "nonself" materials, such as bacteria, viruses, and parasites, which contact or enter the body.

incidence—the frequency of new cases of a disease.

independent variable—a variable that is measured or manipulated to determine its effect on one or more dependent variables.

informational/appraisal support—advice and guidance about how to cope with a particular problem.

informed consent—an individual's deliberate, voluntary decision to participate in research, based on the researcher's description of what such participation will involve.

instrumental/tangible support—the provision of concrete assistance, such as financial aid, material resources, or needed services.

intentional nonadherence—the condition in which patients understand the practitioner's directions, but modify the regimen in some way, or ignore it completely because they are not willing to follow the recommendations.

internal validity—the likelihood that the effects on the dependent variable were caused by the independent variable.

internal–external hypothesis—one of the earliest hypotheses about why and when people eat, which posits that people often fail to listen to their internal cues for eating (namely hunger) and instead pay attention to external cues, such as food taste, smell, and variety.

intractable-benign pain—a type of benign but persistent pain. Although it may vary in intensity, it never really disappears. Lower back pain is a particularly common type of intractable-benign pain.

leptin—a hormone released by the fat cells which decreases appetite and increases energy expenditure.

life skills training programs—a smoking prevention program based on the assumption that adolescents who lack self-esteem and self-confidence are at greater risk of smoking. These programs may include some of the same components as social influence programs, such as information about the negative short-term consequences of smoking and the impact of media on smoking, but they also provide adolescents with general assistance in enhancing self-esteem and social competence.

living will—a document which provides very clear instructions to family members, friends, and medical personnel about the type of treatment and procedures that a person does—or does not—want to have. The person also designates a particular person to make medical decisions for them, and in particular, to make sure the wishes expressed in the living will are followed. The use of living wills therefore allows people to express their medical directives in advance of having an illness, and thus maintain the ability to exercise control over their lives even when they have lost the ability to speak for themselves. This allows people to specify their own wishes about the type of care they would like to receive in the event that they are incapacitated in some way and are therefore unable to make their own decisions.

local anesthetics—drugs, such as novocaine and lidocaine, which can be applied directly to the site at which pain will occur (e.g., having a shot of novocaine before having a cavity filled). These drugs work by blocking nerve cells in that region from generating impulses.

locus of control—a generalized belief people have about the extent to which events are under their own (internal) control or outside of their control (external). People who have an internal locus of control generally experience better health.

low-density lipoproteins (LDL) cholesterol—a type of fatty cholesterol which over time can lead to clogging in the artery walls.

macrophages—a type of immune cell which engulf and digest foreign cells, such as bacteria.

mammogram—a procedure for detecting early stage breast cancer. Mammograms are an important screening test and are recommended for women ages 50 and over.

mass psychogenic illness—a phenomenon in which people's expectations about the symptoms they should experience may influence how intensely, and even whether, they feel various symptoms. In some cases, these expectations can even cause various physical symptoms, such as rashes, nausea, and headaches.

massage therapy—a technique in which people receive deep tissue manipulation by a trained therapist. Massage can be effective in reducing various types of pain, including pain caused by childbirth, recovery from surgery, and arthritis.

matching hypothesis—a hypothesis stating that individuals benefit from receiving the type of social support that fits what they need to cope with a particular problem

medical anthropology—a field which examines differences in how health and illness are viewed by people in different cultures. Cultures in fact vary tremendously in how they define health, how they see disease, and in turn, how they treat illness.

medical delay—a delay that may occur after a person decides that he or she is ill. Medical delay consists of both delay in making an appointment (**scheduling delay**) and delay in receiving medical recommendations (**treatment delay**).

medical psychology—a field which focuses on teaching physicians how to consider the role of the person in interacting with patients. Researchers in this tradition might examine how to handle patients who are moody or those who are reluctant to seek or follow medical care.

medical sociology—a field which examines how social relationships influence illness, cultural and societal reactions to illness, and the organization of health care services. For example, researchers in the field of medical sociology might examine the effects of social stress on health and illness, how attitudes and behaviors influence health and illness, and the negative consequences of labeling someone a "patient."

meditation—a type of relaxation technique for coping with pain in which patients relax their bodies and focus attention on a single thought, sometimes while verbalizing a single syllabus.

modeling—learning gained by watching someone else engage in a behavior.

mood regulation theory—a theory that people often use food to regulate their moods. People may eat to make themselves feel better when they experience stress, anxiety, or depression.

moral/self-control theory—a theory which posits that people who engage in addictive behaviors, such as smoking, drinking, and gambling, have some type of moral weakness. According to this model, people who are lazy and undisciplined lack the "moral fiber" to stop engaging in these self-destructive behaviors.

multiple regulation model—a theory predicting smoking which states that the combination of physiological and psychological factors leads to addiction. This model predicts that smoking is initially used to regulate emotions, like the affect-regulation model, but over time how you feel becomes linked with how much nicotine you have in your blood.

mundane realism—the extent to which a study resembles places and events that exist in the real world. Experiments that are high in mundane realism are more likely to be able to apply their findings to the real world.

myocardial infarction—a heart attack, which is caused by the complete blockage of the coronary artery. Heart attacks often occur because a blood clot formed around the built-up cholesterol blocks the passage of blood to the heart. This deprivation of oxygen causes permanent damage to the heart.

narcotics—medications, such as codeine and morphine, that work by binding to the opiate receptors and thereby inhibiting the transmission of pain signals. These drugs are very effective in reducing severe pain and can help patients cope with pain following surgery.

natural experiments—a type of quasi-experiment in which researchers take advantage of a naturally occurring event, such as an earthquake or an incident of terrorism, to study its impact on physical and/or psychological health.

natural killer (NK) cell—cells that work to detect and then destroy damaged cells, such as precancerous cells, before they develop into tumors, and macrophages.

naturalistic observation—a research technique in which people's behavior in everyday situations is observed and then rated or categorized in some way.

nervous system—the body system which is responsible for transmitting information from the brain throughout the body as well as from the body back to the brain. The nervous system consists of the central nervous system and the peripheral nervous system.

neuromatrix theory—a theory that a network of neurons is distributed throughout the brain, which in turn processes the information that flows through it. Although the neuromatrix typically acts to process sensory information from the body, such as pain, the neuromatrix can process experiences even in the absence of sensations. This theory, which was developed by Ronald Melzack, helps explain the phenomenon of phantom limb pain in which the brain tells the body it is experiencing pain even in the absence of direct sensations.

neuroticism/negative affect—a personality trait that refers to the tendency to experience negative emotions, such as distress, anxiety, nervousness, fear, shame, anger, and guilt. They are likely to worry about upcoming events, dwell on failures and shortcomings, and have a less favorable view of themselves and others.

neurotransmitters—chemicals released by the brain that can increase or decrease the amount of pain experienced.

nicotine-fixed effects model—a theory of smoking which states that nicotine stimulates reward-inducing centers in the nervous system. It increases the levels of neuroregulators, such as dopamine, norepinephrine, and endogenous opiods, which in turn lead to better memory and concentration and reduced feelings of anxiety and tension. Nicotine has a number of reinforcing physiological effects, including speeding up the heart and relaxing the skeletal muscles. These physiological effects lead to simultaneous mental alertness and relaxation. These positive effects are reinforcing, so people are motivated to continue smoking in order to experience these physiological benefits. This model is very simple—it basically proposes that smoking feels good, so people are motivated to continue the behavior.

nicotine regulation model—a theory of smoking which states that smoking is rewarding only when the level of nicotine is above a certain "set point" in the body. In other words, individuals need to smoke enough cigarettes to maintain a certain amount of nicotine or they do not experience the physiological benefits of smoking.

nicotine-replacement strategies—substances that provide nicotine in some form other than cigarettes (e.g., the patch, nicotine gum) in an attempt to ease withdrawal symptoms in smokers who are trying to stop. They do not end smokers' cravings for cigarettes but may reduce such cravings.

nocebo effect—the phenomenon in which having an expectation that a drug or treatment will have negative effects leads to adverse health effects. This nocebo effect can, for example, lead people to experience unpleasant side effects from a medication—if they expect to feel such a reaction—even if the medication they are given is entirely inert.

nociceptors—nerve endings that transmit pain signals to a particular area of the dorsal horn section of the spinal cord called the substantia gelatinosa.

norepinephrine—a hormone (also called noradrenaline) which is released when the sympathetic nervous system and endocrine system are stimulated in response to stress. High levels of norepinephrine in the bloodstream leads to a number of other physiological responses, including increases in heart rate, blood pressure, and breathing, a widening of the pupils, and the movement of blood toward the muscles.

obesity—the state of being 40% or more over one's ideal weight. The most commonly used measure of obesity is body mass index (BMI), which is calculated by dividing a person's weight (in kilograms) by their height (in meters) squared. A BMI between 19 to 24 is seen as ideal, with 25 to 29 seen as moderately overweight (about 15 to 30% over ideal weight) and greater than 30 seen as obese (about 40% over ideal weight).

observational learning—learning gained by watching someone else engage in a behavior.

observational/naturalistic methods—a type of research used to describe and measure people's and/or animals' behavior in everyday situations. In this approach, researchers observe behavior and record some type of systematic measurement of that behavior

oncogene—genes that work to control cell growth and reproduction.

operant conditioning—the theory that behaviors can be increased or decreased as a function of the positive as well as negative consequences of engaging in them.

operational definition—a precise definition of a variable in terms of its specific measurement.

optimism—a personality trait which refers to the expectation that good things will happen in the future whereas bad things will not. This personality trait is associated with better health outcomes.

outcome expectancies—an individuals' beliefs about whether engaging in a particular behavior will have a desired outcome.

parasympathetic division—a part of the autonomic nervous system which works to demobilize the body to conserve energy during times of stress. This process includes increasing digestion; decreasing heart rate, respiration, and pulse; and constricting pupils.

Parkinson's disease—a progressive disorder that is most common in people over 60 years old. This disease is not usually fatal, but leads to uncontrollable tremors in the limbs, muscle rigidity, and a shuffling gait. Drug treatment can ease some of the symptoms, although this medication has several undesirable side effects.

pattern theory—a theory which describes pain as resulting from the type of stimulation received by the nerve endings and states that the key determination of pain is the intensity of the stimulation. A small stimulation of the nerve endings could be interpreted as touch, whereas a more substantial stimulation could be interpreted as pain. This theory explains why touching a warm heating pad feels pleasant, but touching a very hot pan in the oven feels painful.

perceived behavioral control—the extent to which one believes one can successfully enact a behavior. This concept is similar to self-efficacy and is one of the components of the theory of planned behavior.

periaqueductal gray—a portion of the midbrain that seems to be involved in the experience of pain. Several studies, with both animals and humans, have shown that activating the periaqueductal gray area, such as through the use of mild electrical stimulation, can entirely block the experience of pain.

phantom limb pain—the experience of feeling pain in a limb that is no longer there. Phantom limb pain is often described as a severe burning or cramping.

physical stimulation—the irritation of one type of body tissue to ease pain in another type of body tissue (e.g., putting your finger in your mouth after you burn it on a hot stove, rubbing your calf muscle to reduce a painful cramp).

placebo—a treatment that affects someone even though it contains no specific medical or physical properties relevant to the condition it is supposedly treating. In other words, placebos are psychologically inert medicines or treatments that can produce very real, and even lasting effects. The effects of placebos have been demonstrated on virtually every organ system in the body and many diseases, including chest pain, arthritis, hay fever, headaches, ulcers, hypertension, postoperative pain, seasickness, and pain from the common cold.

positive psychology—a newly developed field within psychology that examines how to help people achieve healthy physical and psychological well-being, including the predictors of life satisfaction, altruism, forgiveness, and hope.

post-traumatic stress disorder (PTSD)—a particular type of anxiety disorder caused by experiencing extreme stressors, such as war, natural disasters, and assault.

precaution adoption process model—a model of behavior change that proposes that when individuals consider engaging in new health-related behaviors they go through a series of seven stages.

prevalence—the proportion of a population that has a particular disease.

primary appraisal—an appraisal in which people assess the situation. In this stage, people are interpreting the situation and what it will mean for them (e.g., "am I in danger?").

primary prevention—the prevention of illnesses and diseases either by increasing health-promoting behavior (e.g., wearing seatbelts, engaging in regular exercise, using sunscreen) and/or by decreasing health-damaging behavior (e.g., smoking, drinking and driving, eating a fatty diet).

proactive/preventive coping—a type of active, problem-focused coping in which people try to anticipate problems and then act to prevent their occurrence.

problem-drinking—a condition in which people drink alcohol heavily on a regular basis, are psychologically dependent on alcohol, experience loss of memory while drinking, and suffer social and occupational impairments from their drinking. They may drink often, frequently alone, drink during the day (including while going to work), and drive under the influence.

problem-focused coping—a common strategy for managing challenging situations by trying to confront and change the stressor, which can include seeking assistance from others, taking direct action, and planning.

progressive muscle relaxation—a technique in which people focus on tensing and then releasing each part of their body (e.g., hands, shoulders, legs, etc.) one at a time. This process helps patients distinguish states of tension from states of relaxation, and therefore trains patients in ways to calm themselves down in virtually any stressful situation.

progressive pain—a type of pain which originates from a malignant condition, and hence is continuous and worsens over time. The pain caused by arthritis and cancer, for example, are types of progressive pain.

prospect theory—a theory which posits that people make very different choices when decisions are presented in different ways, such as in terms of their costs versus benefits. Moreover, according to this theory, people are more willing to take risks when they are considering the losses or costs of a particular behavior than when they are considering the gains or benefits of engaging in a behavior.

prostaglandins—neurotransmitters that are released by the body's cells when damage occurs and excite the neurons that carry information about pain. These chemicals mobilize the body to repair the damage in a variety of ways, including causing inflammation at the site of the injury and increasing the immune system's functioning.

psychoneuroimmunology—a field that examines the complex connection between psychosocial factors, such as stress, and the nervous, cardiovascular, endocrine, and immune systems.

psychosomatic medicine—a field which examines how emotional, social, and psychological factors influence the development and progression of illness. For example, researchers might study how psychological factors, such as anxiety, depression, and stress, might lead to physical problems, such as ulcers, migraine headaches, arthritis, and asthma.

quality-adjusted life years (QALY)—a measure of the number of years a person would likely live following the treatment times the quality of each of those years. The quality is determined both by the severity of the symptoms (e.g., being confined to a wheelchair or experiencing considerable pain is more severe than experiencing a mild headache or spraining your ankle), and their duration (e.g., even a very painful bout of food poisoning lasts a few days at most, whereas severe cancer pain could last for years

quasi-experiments—a type of research study in which there are distinct groups of people, and these groups serve as the independent variable, but unlike in true experiments, the people were not randomly assigned to the groups.

random assignment—a procedure used in experiments to make sure that every person has an equal chance of being in any of the conditions. Random assignment improves the quality of research studies.

recurrent acute pain—a type of pain caused by a benign, or harmless, condition, which is sometimes intense but also sometimes disappears. Migraine

headaches are one example of this type of pain.

relapse—a return to an old pattern of behavior after beginning to change it.

restraint theory—a theory of eating stating that people are generally motivated to eat as a function of internal physiological signals that cue hunger. However, when people are trying to lose weight, they deliberately ignore these internal signals and instead use cognitive rules to limit their caloric intake.

scheduling delay—a type of delay which occurs when people fail to make an appointment for medical care once they have decided they are in need of assistance.

screening—behaviors designed to detect an illness or disease at an early stage.

secondary appraisal—a type of appraisal in which people assess the resources available for coping with the situation. In this stage, people examine their ability to cope with the event based on their resources (e.g., "what can I do about this?").

secondary prevention—the detection of illness at an early stage, as a way of reducing its effects, such as checking cholesterol, performing a breast self-exam, and following insulin-taking regimens (in the case of a diabetic). Secondary prevention is very important because in many cases, people have more treatment options and a better likelihood of curing their problem if it is caught early.

self-efficacy—one's confidence that he or she can effectively engage in a given behavior. Self-efficacy is one of the components of the theory of planned behavior.

serotonin—a neurotransmitter that works by slowing or blocking the transmission of any nerve impulses.

set-point theory—a theory stating that each person's body has a certain weight that it strives to maintain, much like a thermostat device. When you eat fewer calories, your metabolism slows to keep your weight at the same level. Because people's set points may vary, based on heredity, some will be heavier and some will be lighter.

sick role behavior—behavior that is directed at helping people who are ill

return to good health. The sick role has certain perks, including receiving sympathy and care from others and being exempt from daily responsibilities, such as chores, work, and classes. However, the person who is sick also has the responsibility for trying to get better, which can include seeking medical attention and following medical recommendations.

social cognitive theory—a theory which posits that people's behavior is a result of their beliefs, expectancies, and confidence. According to this view, behavior is routed in people's thoughts, which can include their beliefs about their own ability to engage (or not engage) in a particular behavior as well as their beliefs about the consequences of engaging (or not engaging) in a particular behavior.

social influence programs—programs that are designed to prevent adolescents from smoking. First, these programs tell teenagers about the immediate physiological and social consequences of smoking, such as the financial cost of smoking, rejection by potential dating partners who don't like the smell of smoke, and having stained teeth and bad breath. These programs also appeal to adolescents' desire for independence by pointing out the manipulative nature of cigarette ads. Third, because peers play a major role in the initiation and maintenance of smoking, these programs often emphasize that many adolescents are against smoking. Finally, social influence programs are typically presented by desirable role models, namely slightly older students (e.g., high school students leading groups for junior high school students). These peer leaders demonstrate strategies for resisting peer pressure to smoke and allow participants to role play various situations to practice their responses.

social learning theory—a theory stating that people do not need to directly experience the rewards or costs of engaging in a particular behavior to learn about their outcomes, but rather could learn about such consequences through observational learning or modeling.

somatic nervous system—a part of the nervous system which transmits messages regarding sensation, such as touch, pressure, temperature, and pain, as well as messages regarding the voluntary movement of the body.

somaticizers—people who develop physical symptoms in response to psychological issues, and hence seek medical treatment for problems that have no physical cause. For example, people who are constantly anxious could develop stomach pains or other physical problems.

specificity theory—a theory of pain which states that there are specific sensory receptors for different types of sensations, such as pain, warmth, touch, and pressure. Once a person experienced an injury, a direct chain carried these messages of pain to the brain, which then sets off an "alarm," and hence the person experiences pain.

stimulus control—a self-management strategy for behavior change which focuses on identifying those situations that lead people to engage in a given behavior (e.g., smoking, drinking, over-eating, etc.) and then avoiding these situations.

stomach stapling—a surgical procedure in which the size of the stomach is reduced so that the person can only eat small amounts of food before feeling full. This procedure is used only in cases of severe obesity.

stress—a state of challenge or threat that disrupts the normal rhythm and balance of a person's life.

stroke—a condition in which a blood clot lodges in the circulatory system and deprives the brain of oxygen. Strokes occur when the plaque that forms on the artery wall becomes detached, travels in the blood, and lodges in the circulatory system.

subjective norms—individuals' beliefs about whether other people would support them in engaging in a new behavior and whether they are motivated to follow the beliefs of these salient others, including family members, friends, and romantic partners. Subjective norms are one of the components of the theory of reasoned action and the theory of planned behavior.

substance P—a neurotransmitter that excites the neurons that send messages about pain and therefore increase the experience of pain.

substantia gelatinosa—a particular area of the dorsal horn section of the spinal cord through which pain fibers travel to the brain.

suppressor gene—a gene that works to inhibit uncontrolled growth. However, when these genes are damaged by a mutation—either caused by random chance or exposure to a carcinogen—uncontrolled cell growth and reproduction can occur.

survey research—a type of study which relies on asking people questions about their thoughts, feelings, desires, and action. These questions could be asked directly by the experimenter in an interview either in person or on the phone, or participants could complete written surveys.

sympathetic system—a part of the nervous system that works to mobilize the body to react in the face of a threat, much like the response that occurs in Cannon's "fight-or-flight" response. This response includes increases in respiration, heart rate, and pulse; decreases in digestion and reproduction; dilating pupils (for far vision); and moving of blood to the muscles to prepare for action.

sympathetic-adrenal medullary (SAM) system—a part of the endocrine system that responds during times of stress. When this system is activated, the hypothalamus triggers the adrenal glands to release epinephrine and norepinephrine. These hormones act very quickly and lead to a number of physiological effects, including increased heart rate, increased blood flow, and increased sweating.

symptom behavior—behavior that is directed toward determining one's health status after experiencing symptoms. This could include talking to other people—family and friends as well as health professionals, monitoring symptoms yourself, and reading about your health problem.

systematic desensitization—a technique in which a person is asked to describe the specific source of their anxiety, and then to create a hierarchy of different stimuli (that cause increasing levels of arousal) associated with that anxiety. The therapist then asks the patient to focus on the least anxiety-provoking image and changes the focus to a less stressful stimuli whenever the patient experiences any anxiety. Gradually, as the patient is able to think about a low-level stimuli without feeling anxiety, the therapist continues to higher level (e.g., more anxiety-provoking) stimuli, which, over time, enables people to build up their tolerance to the stressful situation.

T cells—immune cells which originate in the thymus and control the cell-mediated immune response system, in which they bind to foreign cells in order to kill them.

tangible support—the provision of concrete assistance, such as financial aid, material resources, or needed services.

transcutaneous electrical nerve stimulation (TENS)—a technique of pain reduction which involves placing electrodes on the skin and giving small electrical stimulation to the skin. This system consists of a small portable unit that attaches electrodes to the skin and gives continuous electrical stimulation. This stimulation does not hurt, and the degree of stimulation can be increased or decreased depending on a patients' needs. This technique can be effective in reducing pain for some chronic conditions, such as phantom limb pain and arthritis, as well as pain following surgery.

tension reduction theory—a theory of alcohol use which posits that people drink to cope with or regulate negative moods, including tension, anxiety, and nervousness.

terminal disease—a disease with no known cure that will eventually cause a person's death.

tertiary prevention—actions taken to minimize or slow the damage caused by an illness or disease, such as taking medicine, engaging in regular physical therapy, and following a recommended diet.

theory—an organized set of principles used to explain observed phenomena.

theory of planned behavior—a theory of health behavior which extends the theory of reasoned action by adding the component of perceived behavioral control. This theory describes behavior as a result of intentions and perceived behavior control, and sees intentions as determined by people's attitudes toward the behavior, subjective norms for the behavior, and perceived behavioral control over the behavior.

theory of reasoned action—a theory of health behavior which posits that the key determinant of people's behavior is their intention to engage in that behavior, and that intentions are determined by people's attitudes toward the behavior as well as their subjective norms for the behavior.

tolerance—the situation in which people's bodies no longer respond at the same level to a particular dose of a given substance (e.g., alcohol, tobacco), but rather need larger and larger doses to experience the same effects. They also experience unpleasant withdrawal symptoms, such as irritability, difficulty concentrating, fatigue, nausea, and weight gain, when they discontinue using the substance.

transactional/relational model—a model which posits that the meaning a particular event has for a person is a more important predictor of the experience of stress than the actual event.

transtheoretical/stages of change theory—a continuum model of health behavior change which describes making changes in health-related behavior as a complex process in which individuals make such changes only gradually, and not necessarily in a linear order. Instead people move from one stage to another in a spiral fashion, which can include movement to new stages as well as movement back to previous stages, until they have finally completed the process of behavior change. The five stages of this model are: precontemplation, contemplation, preparation, action, and maintenance.

treatment delay—a type of medical delay that occurs when people delay in receiving medical recommendations.

testicular self-exam (TSE)—an important screening behavior to help detect testicular cancer at an early stage.

Type A behavior—a personality trait that refers to three distinct types of behavior, namely time urgency, competitive drive, and anger/hostility. Type A people experience high levels of time urgency—they are irritated by and impatient with time delays and constantly try to do more than one thing at a time. Second, Type A's have a strong competitive drive and are focused on doing better than other

people in all sorts of situations (work and play). Finally, Type A's are prone to experiencing anger and hostility (e.g., more irritable when frustrated in their goal pursuit, easily aroused to anger). Like people who are high in hostility, Type A people are quick to experience anger and may lash out at others in frustration.

Type C personality—a type of personality trait describing those who represent a pleasant and cheerful face to the world, show passivity in the face of stress, and tend to suppress negative emotions. Although Type C personality was originally thought to predict the development of cancer, more recent research provides little support for this theory.

unintentional nonadherence—the condition in which a person intends to comply, and may even believe he or she is complying, but for some reason is not following instructions.

utilization/behavioral delay—a delay to the time it takes people to decide to actually get help from a professional once they realize they are ill and in need of medical help.

withdrawal—the unpleasant physical and psychological symptoms that people experience when they stop using a particular substance (e.g., tobacco, alcohol) on which they are dependent.

REFERENCES

Abernethy, A. D., Chang, H. T., Seidlitz, L., Evinger, J. S., & Duberstein, P. R. (2002). Religious coping and depression among spouses of people with lung cancer. *Psychosomatics, 43*, 456–463.

Abramson, L. Y., Metalsky, G. I., & Alloy, L. B. (1989). Hopelessness and depression: A theory-based subtype of depression. *Psychological Review, 96*, 358–372.

Adams, P. R., & Adams, G. R. (1984). Mount Saint Helen's ashfall: Evidence for a disaster stress reaction. *American Psychologist, 39*, 252–260.

Ader, R., & Cohen, N. (1975). Behaviorally conditioned immunosuppression. *Psychosomatic Medicine, 37*, 333–340.

Ader, R., & Cohen, N. (1985). CNS-immune system interactions: Conditioning phenomena. *Behavioral and Brain Sciences, 8*, 379–394.

Ad Hoc Committee of the Harvard Medical School to Examine the Definition of Brain Death. (1968). A definition of irreversible coma. *Journal of the American Medical Association, 205*, 337–340.

Adler, N., & Matthews, K. (1994). Health psychology: Why do some people get sick and some stay well? *Annual Review of Psychology, 45*, 229–259.

Adler, N. E., Boyce, T., Chesney, M. A., Cohen, S., Folkman, S., Kahn, R. L., & Syme, S. L. (1994). Socioeconomic status and health: The challenge of the gradient. *American Psychologist, 49*, 15–24.

Adler, N. E., Boyce W. T., Chesney M. A., Folkman S., & Syme S.L. (1993). Socioeconomic inequalities in health: No easy solution. *Journal of the American Medical Association, 269*, 3140–3145.

Adler, N. E., & Stone, G. C. (1979). Social science perspectives on the health system. In G. C. Stone, F. Cohen, & N. E. Adler (Eds.), *Health psychology—A handbook: Theories,* *applications, and challenges of a psychological approach to the health care system* (pp. 19–46). San Francisco: Jossey-Bass.

Adler, R. (2001). Psychoneuroimmunology. *Current Directions in Psychological Science, 10*, 94–98.

Affleck, G., Tennen, H., Urrows, S., & Higgins, P. (1992). Neuroticism and the pain-mood relation in rheumatoid arthristis: Insights from a prospective daily study. *Journal of Consulting and Clinical Psychology, 60*, 119–126.

Afifi, W. A. (1999). Harming the ones we love: Relational attachment and perceived consequences as predictors of safe-sex behavior. *Journal of Sex Research, 36*, 198–206.

Agras, W. S. (1993). Short-term psychological treatments for binge eating. In C. G. Fairburn & G. T. Wilson (Eds.), *Binge eating: Nature, assessment, and treatment* (pp. 270–286). New York: Guilford Press.

Agras, W. S., Taylor, C. B., Kraemer, H. C., Southam, M. A., & Schneider, J. A. (1987). Relaxation training for essential hypertension at the worksite: II. The poorly controlled hypertensive. *Psychosomatic Medicine, 49*, 264–273.

Aiken, L. H., Clarke, S. P., Sloane, D. M., Sochalski, J., & Silber, J. H. (2002). Hospital nurse staffing and patient mortality, nurse burnout, and job dissatisfaction. *Journal of the American Medical Association, 288*, 1987–1993.

Aiken, L. R. (1985). Dying, death, and bereavement. Boston: Allyn and Bacon.

Aiken, L. S., West, S. G., Woodward, C. K., & Reno, R. R. (1994). Health beliefs and compliance with mammography-screening recommendations in asymptomatic women. *Health Psychology, 13*, 122–129.

Ajzen, I. (1985). From intentions to actions: A theory of planned behavior. In J. Kuhl & J. Beckman (Eds.), *Action control: From cognition to behavior* (pp. 11–39). Berlin: Springer.

Alagna, S. W., & Reddy, D. M. (1984). Predictors of proficient technique and successful lesion detection in breast self-examination. *Health Psychology, 3*, 113–127.

Albarracin, D., McNatt, P. S., Williams, W. R., Hoxworth, J., Zenlumer, J., Ho, R. M., Rhode, F., Nalotte, C. K., Bolan, G. A., & Iatesta, M. (2000). Structure of outcome beliefs in condom use. *Health Psychology, 19*, 458–468.

Albert, C. M., et al. (1998). Fish consumption and risk of sudden cardiac death. *Journal of the American Medical Association, 279*, 23–28.

Alcoholics Anonymous World Services. (1977). Alcoholics Anonymous: The twelve steps and twelve traditions (3rd ed.). New York: Author.

Aldwin, C., & Revenson, T. A. (1987). Does coping help? A reexamination of the relation between coping and mental health. *Journal of Personality and Social Psychology, 53*, 337–348.

Aldwin, C. M., Levenson, M. R., Spiro, A., III., & Bosse, R. (1989). Does emotionality predict stress? Findings from the Normative Aging Study. *Journal of Personality and Social Psychology, 56*, 618–624.

Alferi, S. M., Carver, C. S., Antoni, M. H., Weiss, S., & Duran, R. E. (2001). An exploratory study of social support, distress, and life disruption among low-income Hispanic women under treatment for early stage breast cancer. *Health Psychology, 20*, 41–46.

Allen, K., Blasovich, J., & Mendes, W. B. (2002). Cardiovascular reactivity and the presence of pets, friends, and spouses: The truth about cats and dogs. *Psychosomatic Medicine, 64*, 727–739.

Allison, D. B., & Faith, M. S. (1997). Issues in mapping genes for eating disorders. *Psychopharmacology Bulletin, 33*, 359–368.

Alloy, L. B., Abramson, L. Y., & Francis, E. L. (1999). Do negative cognitive styles confer vulnerability to depression? *Current Directions in Psychological Science, 8*, 128–132.

Aloise-Young, P. A., Hennigan, K. M., & Graham, J. W. (1996). Role of the self-image and smoker stereotype in smoking onset during early adolescence: A longitudinal study. *Health Psychology, 15*, 494–497.

Alpert, A. E., Warner, D. L., Hatcher, R. A., Trussell, J., & Bennett, C. (1995). Condom use among female commercial sex workers in Nevada's legal brothels. *American Journal of Public Health, 85*, 1514–1520.

Amaro, H. (1995). Love, sex, and power: Considering women's realities in HIV prevention. *American Psychologist, 50*, 437–447.

American Cancer Society. (1998). Cancer facts & figures—1998. Atlanta: Author.

American Psychiatric Association. (1994). Diagnostic and statistical manual of mental disorders (4th ed.). Washington, DC: Author.

American Psychological Association. (1992). Ethical principles of psychologists and code of conduct. *American Psychologist, 47*, 1597–1611.

American Psychological Association (APA). Task Force on Health Research. (1976). Contributions of psychology to health research: Patterns, problems, and potentials. *American Psychologist, 31*, 263–274.

Amick, B. C., McDonough, P., Chang, H., Rogers, W. H., Pioper, C. F., & Duncan, G. et al. (2002). Relationship between all-cause mortality and cumulative working life course psychosocial and physical exposures in the United States labor market from 1968 to 1992. *Psychosomatic Medicine, 64*, 370–381.

Anand, K. J., & Craig, K. D. (1996). New perspectives on the definition of pain. *Pain, 67*, 3–6.

Anda, R. F., Williamson, D. R., Escobedo, L. G., Mast, E. E., Giovino, G. A., & Remington, P. L. (1990). Depression and the dynamics of smoking. *Journal of the American Medical Association, 264*, 1541–1545.

Andersen, A. E., & DiDomenico, L. (1992). Diet vs. shape content of popular male and female magazines: A dose-response relationship to the incidence of eating disorders? *International Journal of Eating Disorders, 11*, 283–287.

Andersen, B. L. (1993). Cancer. In C. Niven & D. Carroll (Eds.), *The health psychology of women* (pp. 75–89). Chur, Switzerland: Harwood Academic.

Andersen, B. L., Cacioppo, J. T., & Roberts, D. C. (1995). Delay in seeking a cancer diagnosis: Delay stages and psychophysiological comparison processes. *British Journal of Social Psychology, 34*, 33–52.

Andersen, B. L., Woods, X. A., & Copeland, L. J. (1997). Sexual self-schema and sexual morbidity among gynecologic cancer survivors. *Journal of Consulting and Clinical Psychology, 65*, 1–9.

Andersen, R. E., Crespo, C. J., Bartlett, S. J., Cheskin, L. J., & Pratt, M. (1998). Relationship of physical activity and television watching with body weight and level of fatness among children: Results from the third National Health and Nutrition Examination Survey. *Journal of the American Medical Association, 279*, 938–942.

Andersen, R. E., Wadden T. A., Bartlett S. J., Zemel B., Verde T. J., & Franckowiak S. C. (1999). Effects of lifestyle activity vs. structured aerobic exercise in obese women: A randomized trial. *Journal of the American Medical Association, 281*, 335–340.

Anderson, C. R. (1977). Locus of control, coping behaviors and performance in a stress setting: A longitudinal study. *Journal of Applied Psychology, 62*, 446–451.

Anderson, E. A. (1987). Preoperative preparation for cardiac surgery facilitates recovery, reduces psychological distress, and reduces the incidence of acute postoperative hypertension. *Journal of Consulting and Clinical Psychology, 55*, 513–520.

Anderson, J. L., Crawford, C. B., Nadeau, J., & Lindberg, T. (1992). Was the Duchess of Windsor right? A cross-cultural review of the socioecology of ideals of female body shape. *Ethology and Sociobiology, 13*, 197–227.

Anderson, N. B. (1995). Behavioral and sociocultural perspectives on ethnicity and health. *Health Psychology, 14*, 589–591.

Anderson, N. B., & Armstead, C. A. (1995). Toward understanding the association of socioeconomic status and health: A new challenge for the biopsychosocial approach. *Psychosomatic Medicine, 57*, 213–225.

Anderson, R. A., Baron, R. S., & Logan, H. (1991). Distraction, control, and dental stress. *Journal of Applied Social Psychology, 21*, 156–171.

Angoff, N. R. (2001). Crying in the curriculum. *Journal of the American Medical Association, 286*, 1017–1018.

Antoni, M. H., Cruess, D. G., Cruess, S., Lutgendorf, S., Kumas, M., Ironson, G., Klimas, N., Fletcher, M., & Schneidermann, N. (2000). Cognitive-behavioral stress management intervention effects on anxiety, 24-hour urinary norepinephrine output, and T-cytotoxic/suppressor cells over time among symptomatic HIV-infection gay men. *Journal of Consulting and Clinical Psychology, 68*, 31–45.

Antoni, M. H., Lehman, J. M., Kilbourn, K. M., Boyers, A. E., Culver, J. L., Alferi, S. M., Yount, S. E., McGregor, B. A., Arena, P. L., Harris, S. D., Price, A. A., & Carver, C. S. (2001). Cognitive-behavioral stress management intervention decreases the prevalence of depression and enhances benefit finding among women under treatment for early-stage breast cancer. *Health Psychology, 20*, 20–32.

Antonosky, A. (1987). Unraveling the mystery of health: How people manage stress and stay well. San Francisco: Jossey-Bass.

Antonucci, T. C. (1990). Social support and social relationships. In R. H. Binstock & L. K. George (Eds.), *Handbook of aging and the social sciences* (3rd ed., pp. 205–226). Orlando, FL: Academic Press.

Antonucci, T. C., & Akiyama, H. (1987). An examination of sex differences in social support among older men and women. *Sex Roles, 17*, 737–749.

Arena, J. G., & Blanchard, E. B. (1996). Biofeedback and relaxation therapy for chronic pain disorders. In R. J. Gatchel & D. C. Turk (Eds.), *Psychological approaches to pain management: A practitioner's handbook* (pp. 179–230). New York: Guilford.

Aronoff, G. M., Wagner, J. M., & Spangler, A. S. (1986). Chemical interventions for pain. *Journal of Consulting and Clinical Psychology, 54*, 769–775.

Ary, D. V., & Biglan, A. (1988). Longitudinal changes in adolescent smoking behavior: Onset and cessation. *Journal of Behavioral Medicine, 11*, 361–382.

Ashley, M. J., & Rankin, J. G. (1988). A public health approach to the prevention of alcohol-related problems. *Annual Review of Public Health, 9*, 233–271.

Aspinwall, L. G., Kemeny, M. E., Taylor, S. E., Schneider, S. G., & Dudley, J. P. (1991). Psychosocial predictors of gay men's AIDS risk-reduction behavior. *Health Psychology, 10*, 432–444.

Aspinwall, L. G., & Taylor, S. E. (1997). A stitch in time: Self-regulation and proactive coping. *Psychological Bulletin, 21*, 417–436.

Astin, J. A. (1998). Why patients use alternative medicine: Results of a national study. *Journal of the American Medical Association, 279*, 1548–1553.

Atkins, C. J., Kaplan, R. M., Timms, R. M., Reinsch, S., & Lofback, K. (1984). Behavioral exercise programs in the management of chronic obstructive pulmonary disease. *Journal of Consulting and Clinical Psychology, 52*, 591–603.

Auden, W. H. (1940). Collected poems. New York: Random House.

Auerbach, S., Martelli, M., & Mercuri, L. (1976). Anxiety, information, interpersonal impacts, and adjustment to a stressful health care situation. *Journal of Personality and Social Psychology, 44*, 1284–1296.

Ayanian, J. Z., & Epstein, A. M. (1991). Differences in the use of procedures between women and men hospitalized for coronary heart disease. *New England Journal of Medicine, 325*, 221–225.

Babyak, M., Blumenthal, J. A., Herman, S., Rhatri, P., Doraiswamy, M., Moore, K., Craighead, W. E., Baldewicz, T. T., & Krishnan, K. R. (2000). Exercise treatment for major depression: Maintenance of therapeutic benefit at 10 months. *Psychosomatic Medicine, 62*, 633–638.

Bach, P. B., Cramer, L. D., Warren, J. L., & Begg, C. B. (1999). Racial differences in the treatment of early-stage lung cancer. *New England Journal of Medicine, 341*, 1198–1205.

Bachiocco, V., Scesi, M., Morselli, A. M., & Carli, G. (1993). Individual pain history and familial pain tolerance models: Relationships to post-surgical pain. *Clinical Journal of Pain, 9*, 266–271.

Baer, J. S., & Carney, M. M. (1993). Biases in the perceptions of the consequences of alcohol use among college students. *Journal of Studies on Alcohol, 54*, 54–60.

Baer, J. S., Stacy, A., & Larimer, M. (1991). Biases in the perception of drinking norms among college students. *Journal of Studies on Alcohol, 52*, 580–586.

Bagley, S. P., Angel, R., Dilworth-Anderson, P., Liu, W., & Schinke, S. (1995). Adaptive health behaviors among ethnic minorities. *Health Psychology, 14*, 632–640.

Bailey, D. S., Leonard, K. E., Cranston, J. W., & Taylor, S. P. (1983). Effects of alcohol and self-awareness on human physical aggression. *Personality and Social Psychology Bulletin, 9*, 289–295.

Bailey, J. E., Kellermann, A. L., Somes, G. W., Banton, J. G., Rivara, F. P., & Rushforth, N. P. (1997). Risk factors for violent death of women in the home. *Archives of Internal Medicine, 157*, 777–782.

Baker, C. W., Whisman, M. A., & Brownell, K. D. (2000). Studying intergenerational transmission of eating attitudes and behaviors: Methodological and conceptual questions. *Health Psychology, 19*, 376–381.

Baker, S. P., O'Neill, B., Ginsburg, M. J., & Li, G. (1992). The injury fact book. New York: Oxford University Press.

Banaji, M. R., & Steele, C. M. (1989). The social cognition of alcohol use. *Social Cognition, 7*, 137–151.

Bandura, A. (1977). Self-efficacy: Toward a unifying theory of behavioral change. *Psychological Review, 84*, 191–215.

Bandura, A. (1986). Social foundations of thought and action: A social cognitive theory. Englewood Cliffs, NJ: Prentice Hall.

Bandura, A. (1997). Self-efficacy: The exercise of control. New York: Freeman.

Bandura, A., O'Leary, A., Taylor, C. B., Gauthier, J., & Gossard, D. (1987). Perceived self-efficacy and pain control: Opioid and non-opioid mechanisms. *Journal of Personality and Social Psychology, 53*, 563–571.

Bandura, A., & Simon, K. M. (1977). The role of proximal intentions in self-regulation of refractory behavior. *Cognitive Therapy and Research, 1*, 177–193.

Bandura, A., Taylor, C. B., Williams, S. L., Mefford, I. N., & Barchas, J. D. (1985). Catcholamine secretion as a function of perceived coping self-efficacy. *Journal of Consulting and Clinical Psychology, 53*, 406–414.

Banks, S. M., Salovey P., Greener S., Rothman A. J., Moyer A., Beauvais J., & Epel E. (1995). The effects of message framing on mammography utilization. *Health Psychology, 14*, 178–184.

Barber, J. (1998). When hypnosis causes trouble. *International Journal of Clinical & Experimental Hypnosis, 46*, 157–170.

Barefoot, J. C., Dahlstrom, W. G., & Williams, R. B. (1983). Hostility, CHD incidence, and total mortality: A 25-year follow-up study of 255 physicians. *Psychosomatic Medicine, 45*, 59–63.

Barefoot, J. C., Dodge, K., Peterson, B., Dahlstrom, W. G., & Williams, R. (1989). The Cook-Medley Hostility Scale: Item content and the ability to predict survival. *Psychosomatic Medicine, 51*, 46–57.

Barnes, D., Gatchel, R. J., Mayer, T. G., & Barnett, J. (1990). Changes in MMPI profiles of chronic low back pain patients following successful treatment. *Journal of Spinal Disorders, 3*, 353–355.

Barnes, V. A., Treiber, F., & Davis, H. (2001). Impact of Transcendental Meditation® on cardiovascular function at rest and during acute stress in adolescents with high normal blood pressure. *Journal of Psychosomatic Research, 51*, 597–605.

Barnett, R. C., Gareis, K., & Brennan, R. T. (1999). Fit as a mediator of the relationship between work hours and burnout. *Journal of Occupational Health Psychology, 4*, 307–317.

Barnett, R. C., & Hyde, J. S. (2001). Women, men, work, and family: An expansionist theory. *American Psychologist, 56*, 781–796.

Barnhoorn, F., & Adriaanse, H. (1992). In search of factors responsible for noncompliance among tuberculosis patients in Wardha District, India. *Social Science & Medicine, 34*, 291–306.

Baron, R. S., Cutrona, C. E., Hicklin, D., Russell, D. W., & Lubaroff, D. (1990). Social support and immune function among spouses of cancer patients. *Journal of Personality and Social Psychology, 59*, 344–352.

Barrerra, M., Chassin, L., & Rogosch, F. (1993). Effects of social support and conflict on adolescent children of alcoholic and nonalcoholic fathers. *Journal of Personality and Social Psychology, 64*, 602–612.

Barrerra, M., Jr., Sandler, I., & Ramsey, T. (1981). Preliminary development of a scale of social support: Studies on college students. *American Journal of Community Psychology, 9*, 435–447.

Bass, D. M., Noelker, L. S., Townsend, A. L., & Deimling, G. T. (1990). Losing an aged relative: Perceptual differences between spouses and adult children. *Omega, 21*, 21–40.

Bates, M. E., & Labouvie, E. W. (1995). Personality-environment constellations and alcohol use: A process-oriented study of intraindividual change during adolescence. *Psychology of Addictive Behaviors, 9*, 23–35.

Bates, M. S., Edwards, W. T., & Anderson, K. O. (1993). Ethnocultural influences on variation in chronic pain perception. *Pain, 52*, 101–112.

Baucom, D. H., & Aiken, P. A. (1981). Effect of depressed mood on eating among obese and nonobese dieting and nondieting persons. *Journal of Personality and Social Psychology, 47*, 577–585.

Baum, A., Friedman, A. L., & Zakowski, S. G. (1997). Stress and genetic testing for disease risk. *Health Psychology, 16*, 8–19.

Baum, A., & Gatchel, R. J. (1981). Cognitive determinants of reaction to uncontrollable events: Development of reactance and learned helplessness. *Journal of Personality and Social Psychology, 40*, 1078–1089.

Baum, A., & Grunberg, N. E. (1991). Gender, stress, and health. *Health Psychology, 10*, 80–85.

Baum, A., Grunberg, N. E., & Singer, J. E. (1982). The use of psychological and neuroendocrinological measurements in the study of stress. *Health Psychology, 1*, 217–236.

Beck, K. H., & Lund, A. K. (1981). The effects of health threat seriousness and personal efficacy upon intentions and behavior. *Journal of Applied Social Psychology, 11*, 401–415.

Becker, A. E., Grinspoon, S. K., Klibanski, A., & Herzog, D. B. (1999). Current concepts: Eating disorders. *New England Journal of Medicine, 340*, 1092–1098.

Becker, D. M. (2001). Public health and religion. In N. Schneiderman et al. (Eds.), *Integrating behavioral and social sciences with public health* (pp. 351–368). Washington, DC: American Psychological Association.

Becker, M. H., Maiman, L. A., Kirscht, J. P., Haefner, D. P., & Drachman, R. H. (1977). The health belief model and prediction of dietary compliance: A field experiment. *Journal of Health and Social Behavior, 18*, 348–366.

Becvar, D. S. (2001). *In the presence of grief: Helping family members resolve death, dying, and bereavement issues.* New York: Guilford.

Beecher, H. K. (1955). The powerful placebo. *Journal of the American Medical Association, 159*, 1602–1606.

Beecher, H. K. (1956). Relationship of significance of wound to pain experience. *Journal of the American Medical Association, 161*, 1609–1613.

Beecher, H. K. (1959). Measurement of subjective responses. New York: Oxford University Press.

Belar, C. D. (1997). Clinical health psychology: A specialty for the 21st century. *Health Psychology, 16*, 411–416.

Bellomo, G., Narducci, P. L., Rondoni, F., Pastorelli G., Stangoni G., Angeli G., Verdecchia, P. (1999). Prognostic value of 24-hour blood pressure in pregnancy. *Journal of the American Medical Association, 282*, 1447–1452.

Bender, R., Trautner, C., Spraul, M., & Berger, M. (1998). Assessment of excess mortality in obesity. *American Journal of Epidemiology, 147*, 42–48.

Benedetti, F., & Amanzio, M. (1997). The neurobiology of placebo analgesia: From endoge-nous opioids to cholecystokini. *Progress in Neurobiology, 52*, 109–125.

Benedikt, R., Wertheim, E., & Love, A. (1998). Eating attitudes and weight-loss attempts in female adolescents and their mothers. *Journal of Youth and Adolescence, 27*, 43–57.

Ben-Eliyahu, S., Yirmiya, R., Liebeskind, J. C., Taylor, A. N., & Gale, R. P. (1991). Stress increases metastatic spread of a mammary tumor in rats: Evidence for mediation by the immune system. *Brain, Behavior, and Immunity, 5*, 193–205.

Benoliel, J. Q. (1988). Institutional dying: A convergence of cultural values, technology, and social organization. In H. Wass, F. M. Berado, & R. A. Neimeyer (Eds.), *Dying: Facing the facts* (2nd ed., pp. 159–184). New York: Hemisphere.

Berado, D. H. (1988). Bereavement and mourning. In H. Wass, F. M., Berado, & R. A. Neimeyer (Eds.), *Dying: Facing the facts* (2nd ed., pp. 279–300). New York: Hemisphere.

Bergin, A. E., Masters, K. S., & Richards, P. S. (1987). Religiousness and mental health reconsidered: A study of an intrinsically religious sample. *Journal of Counseling Psychology, 34*, 197–204.

Bergman, A. B., Rivara, F. P., Richards, D. D., & Rogers, L. W. (1990). The Seattle Children's Bicycle Helmet Campaign. *American Journal of Diseases of Children, 144*, 727–731.

Bergman, A. B., & Werner, R. J. (1963). Failure of children to receive penicillin by mouth. *New England Journal of Medicine, 268*, 1334–1338.

Bergner, M., Allison, C. J., Diehr, P., Ford, L. G., & Feigl, P. (1990). Early detection and control of cancer in clinical practice. *Archives of Internal Medicine, 150*, 431–436.

Berkman, L. F. (1985). The relationship of social networks and social support to morbidity and mortality In S. Cohen & L. Syme (Eds.), *Social support and health* (pp. 243–262). New York: Academic Press.

Berkman, L. F. (1986). Social networks, support, and health: Taking the next step forward. *American Journal of Epidemiology, 123*, 559–562.

Berkman, L. F., Leo-Summers, L., & Horowitz, R. I. (1992). Emotional support and survival after myocardial infarction. *Annals of Internal Medicine, 17*, 1003–1009.

Berkman, L. F., & Syme, S. L. (1979). Social networks, host resistance, and mortality: A nine-year follow-up study of Alameda County residents. *American Journal of Epidemiology, 109*, 186–204.

Bernstein, L., Henderson, B. E., Hanisch, R., Sullivan-Halley, J., & Ross, R. K. (1994). Physical exercise and reduced risk of breast cancer in young women. *Journal of the National Cancer Institute, 86,* 1403–1408.

Best, J. A., Flay, B. R., Towson, S. M. J., Ryan, K. B., Perry, C. L., Brown, K. S., Kersell, M. W., & d'Avernas, J. R. (1984). Smoking prevention and the concept of risk. *Journal of Applied Social Psychology, 14,* 257–273.

Biener, L., & Heaton, A. (1995). Women dieters of normal weight: Their motives, goals, and risks. *American Journal of Public Health, 85,* 714–717.

Biesecker, B. B., Boehnke M, Calzone K, Markel D. S., Garber J. E., Collins F. S., & Weber B. L. (1993). Genetic counseling for families with inherited susceptibility to breast and ovarian cancer. *Journal of the American Medical Association, 269,* 1970–1974.

Billings, A. G., & Moos, R. H. (1985). Life stressors and social resources affect posttreatment outcomes among depressed patients. *Journal of Abnormal Psychology, 94,* 140–153.

Bingamon, J., Frank, R. G., & Billy, C. L. (1993). Combining a global health budget with a market-driven delivery system: Can it be done? *American Psychologist, 48,* 270–276.

Bishop, D. B., Roesler, J. S., Zimmerman, B. R., & Ballard, D. J. (1993). Diabetes. In R. C. Brownson, P. L., Remington, & J. R. Davis (Eds.), *Chronic disease epidemiology and control* (pp. 221–240). Washington, DC: American Public Health Association.

Bishop, P. D., & Lipsitz, A. (1991). Sexual behavior among college students in the AIDS era: A comparative study. *Journal of Psychology and Human Sexuality, 4,* 135–148.

Black, D. R., Gleser, L. J., & Kooyers, K. J. (1990). A meta-analytic evaluation of couples weight-loss programs. *Health Psychology, 9,* 330–347.

Blair, S. N., Kohl H. W. 3rd, Barlow C. E., Paffenbarger R. S., Jr., Gibbons L. W., Macera C. A. (1995). Changes in physical fitness and all-cause mortality: A prospective study of healthy and unhealthy men. *Journal of the American Medical Association, 273,* 1093–1098.

Blair, S. N., Kohl H. W. III, Paffenbarger, R. S., Jr., Clark D. G., Cooper K. H., & Gibbons L. W. (1989). Physical fitness and all-cause mortality: A prospective study of healthy men and women. *Journal of the American Medical Association, 262,* 2395–2401.

Blalock, S. J., DeVellis, R. F., Giorgino, K. B., DeVellis, B. M., Gold, D. T., Dooley, M. A.,

Anderson, J. J. B., & Smith, S. L. (1996). Osteoporosis prevention in premenopausal women: Using a stage model approach to examine the predictors of behavior. *Health Psychology, 15,* 84–93.

Blanchard, E. B., Appelbaum, K. A., Guarnieri, P., Morrill, B., & Dentinger, M. P. (1987). Five year prospective follow-up on the treatment of chronic headache with biofeedback and/or relaxation. *Headache, 27,* 580–583.

Blanchard, E. B., & Scharff, L. (2000). Psychosocial aspects of assessment and treatment of irritable bowel syndrome in adults and recurrent abdominal pain in children. *Journal of Consulting and Clinical Psychology, 70,* 725–38.

Blanchard, E. B., Andrasik, F., Neff, D. F., Arena, J. G., Ahles, T. A., Jurish, S. E., Pallmeyer, T. P., Saundear, N. L., Tedens, S. J., Barron, K. D., & Rodichok, L. D. (1982). Biofeedback and relaxation training with three kinds of headache: Treatment effects and their prediction. *Journal of Consulting and Clinical Psychology, 50,* 562–575.

Bland, S. H., Krogh, V., Winkelstein, W., & Trevisan, M. (1991). Social network and blood pressure: A population study. *Psychosomatic Medicine, 53,* 598–607.

Blanton, H., & Gerrard, M. (1997). Effect of sexual motivation on men's risk perception for sexually transmitted disease: There must be 50 ways to justify a lover. *Health Psychology, 16,* 374–379.

Blazer, D. (1982). Social support and mortality in an elderly community population. *American Journal of Epidemiology, 116,* 684–694.

Blendon, R. J., Szalay, U. S., & Knox, R. A. (1992). Should physicians aid their patients in dying? The public perspective. *Journal of the American Medical Association, 267,* 2658–2662.

Blittner, M., Goldberg, J., & Merbaum, M. (1978). Cognitive self-control factors in the reduction of smoking behavior. *Behavior Therapy, 9,* 553–561.

Bloch, M., Fahy, M., Fox, S., & Hayden, M. R. (1989). Predictive testing for Huntington disease: II. Demographic characteristics, lifestyle patterns, attitudes, and psychosocial assessments of the first fifty-one test candidates. *Journal of Medical Genetics, 32,* 217–224.

Block, A. R., Kremer, E. F., & Gaylor, M. (1980). Behavioral treatment of chronic pain: The spouse as a discriminative cue for pain behavior. *Pain, 9,* 243–252.

Blount, R. L., Corbin, S. M., Sturges, J. W., Wolfe, V. V., Prater, J. M., & James, L. D. (1989). The relationship between adults' behavior and child coping and distress during BMA/LP procedures: A sequential analysis. *Behavior Therapy, 20,* 585–601.

Bluebond-Langner, M. (1977). Meanings of death to children. In H. Feifel (Ed.), *New meanings of death* (pp. 47–66). New York: McGraw-Hill.

Blumenthal, J. A., Burg, M., Barefoot, J., Williams, R. B., Haney, T., & Zimet, G. (1987). Social support, Type A behavior, and coronary artery disease. *Psychosomatic Medicine, 49,* 331–340.

Blumenthal, J. A., Sanders, W., Wallace, A. G., Williams, R. B., & Needles, T. L. (1982). Physiological and psychological variables predict compliance to prescribed exercise therapy in patients recovering from myocardial infarction. *Psychosomatic Medicine, 44,* 519–527.

Blumenthal, J. A., Williams, R. S., Needels, T. L., & Wallace, A. G. (1982). Psychological changes accompany aerobic exercise in healthy middle-aged adults. *Psychosomatic Medicine, 44,* 529–535.

Blumenthal, J. A., Babyak, M., Wei, J., O'Connor, C., Waugh, R., Eisenstein, E., Mark, D., Sherwood, A., Woodley, P. S., Irwin, R. J., & Reed, G. (2002). Usefulness of psychosocial treatment of mental stress-induced myocardial ischemia in men. *American Journal of Cardiology, 89,* 164–168.

Bly, J. L., Jones, R. C., & Richardson, J. E. (1986). Impact of worksite health promotion on health care costs and utlization. *Journal of the American Medical Association, 256,* 3235–3240.

Bolger, N., DeLongis, A., Kessler, R. C., & Schilling, E. A. (1989). Effects of daily stress on negative mood. *Journal of Personality and Social Psychology, 57,* 808–818.

Bolinder, G., Alfredsson, L., Englund, A., & deFaire, U. (1994). Smokeless tobacco use and increased cardiovascular mortality among Swedish construction workers. *American Journal of Public Health, 84,* 399–404.

Bonanno, G. A., Keltner, D., Holen, A., & Horowitz, M. J. (1995). When avoiding unpleasant emotions might not be such a bad thing: Verbal-autonomic response dissociation and midlife conjugal bereavement. *Journal of Personality and Social Psychology, 69,* 975–989.

Bond, G. G., Aiken, L. S., & Somerville, S. C. (1992). The health belief model and adolescents with insulin-dependent diabetes mellitus. *Health Psychology, 11,* 190–198.

Bond, M. H. (1991). Chinese values and health: A cultural-level examination. *Psychology and Health, 5*, 137–152.

Boney McCoy, S., Gibbons, F. X., Reis, T. J., Gerrard, M., Luus, C. A. E., & Von Wald Sufka, A. (1992). Perceptions of smoking risk as a function of smoking status. *Journal of Behavioral Medicine, 15*, 469–488.

Booth-Kewley, S., & Vickers, R. R., Jr. (1994). Associations between major domains of personality and health behavior. *Journal of Personality, 62*, 281–298.

Borrelli, B., & Mermelstein, R. (1994). Goal setting and behavior change in a smoking cessation program. *Cognitive Therapy and Research, 18*, 69–82.

Bosari, B., & Carey, K. B. (2000). Effects of a brief motivational intervention with college students. *Journal of Consulting and Clinical Psychology, 68*, 728–733.

Bosma, H., Stansfeld, S. A., & Marmot, M. G. (1998). Job control, personal characteristics, and heart disease. *Journal of Occupational Health Psychology, 3*, 402–409.

Botvin, G. J., Baker, E., Renick, N., Filazzola, A. D., & Botvin, E. M. (1984). A cognitive-behavioral approach to substance abuse prevention. *Addictive Behaviors, 9*, 137–147.

Bouchard, C. (1991). Is weight fluctuation a risk factor? *New England Journal of Medicine, 324*, 1887–1889.

Bovbjerg, V. E., McCann, B. S., Brief, D. J., Follette, W. C., Retzlaff, B. H., Dowdy, A. A., Walden, C. E., & Knopp, R. H. (1995). Spouse support and long-term adherence to lipid-lowering diets. *American Journal of Epidemiology, 141*, 451–460.

Bower, J. E., Kemeny, M. E., Taylor, S. E., & Fahey, J. L. (1998). Cognitive processing, discovery of meaning, CD4 decline, and AIDS-related mortality among bereaved HIV-seropositive men. *Journal of Consulting and Clinical Psychology, 66*, 979–986.

Boyd, B., & Wandersman, A. (1991). Predicting undergraduate condom use with the Fishbein and Ajzen and the Triandis attitude-behavior models: Implications for public health interventions. *Journal of Applied Social Psychology, 21*, 1810–1830.

Bradach, K. M., & Jordan, J. R. (1995). Long-term effects of a family history of traumatic death on adolescent individuation. *Death Studies, 19*, 315–336.

Bradburn, N. M., & Sudman, S. (1988). Polls and surveys: Understanding what they tell us. San Francisco: Jossey-Bass.

Braddock, C. H., III, Edwards, K. A., Hasenberg, N. M., Laidley, T. L., & Levinson, W. (1999). Informed decision making in outpatient practice: Time to get back to basics. *Journal of the American Medical Association, 282*, 2313–2320.

Brafford, L. J., & Beck, K. H. (1991). Development and validation of a condom self-efficacy scale for college students. *Journal of American College Health, 29*, 219–225.

Brandon, T. H., Collins, B. N., Juliano, L. M., & Lazev, A. B. (2000). Preventing relapse among former smokers: A comparison of minimal interventions through telephone and mail. *Journal of Consulting and Clinical Psychology, 68*, 103–113.

Brandon, T. H., Copeland, A. L., & Saper, Z. L. (1995). Programmed therapeutic messages as a smoking treatment adjunct: Reducing the impact of negative affect. *Health Psychology, 14*, 41–47.

Brandt, M. M., Ahrens, K. S., Corpron, C. A., Franklin, G. A., & Wahl, W. L. (2002). Hospital cost is reduced by motorcycle helmet use. *Journal of Trauma, 53*, 69–71.

Brattberg, G. (1983). Acupuncture therapy for tennis elbow. *Pain, 16*, 285–288.

Braver, E. R., Ferguson, S. A., Greene, M. A., & Lund, A. K. (1997). Reductions in deaths in frontal crashes among right front passengers in vehicles equipped with passenger air bags. *Journal of the American Medical Association, 278*, 1437–1439.

Bray, G. A. (1992). Pathophysiology of obesity. *American Journal of Clinical Nutrition, 55*, 488S–494S.

Broadstock, M., Borland, R., & Gason, R. (1992). Effects of suntan on judgements of healthiness and attractiveness by adolescents. *Journal of Applied Social Psychology, 22*, 157–172.

Brock, D. W., & Wartman, S. A. (1990). When competent patients make irrational choices. *New England Journal of Medicine, 322*, 1595–1599.

Brown, G. K., Wallston, K. A., & Nicassio, P. M. (1989). Social support and depression in rheumatoid arthritis: A one year prospective study. *Journal of Applied Social Psychology, 19*, 1164–1181.

Brown, J. D. (1991). Staying fit and staying well: Physical fitness as a moderator of life stress. *Journal of Personality and Social Psychology, 60*, 555–561.

Brown, S. S. (1985). Can low birth-weight be prevented? *Family Planning Perspectives, 17*, 112–118.

Brownell, K. D., Cohen, R. Y., Stunkard, A. J., Felix, M. R. J., & Cooley, N. B. (1984). Weight loss competitions at the work site: Impact on weight, morale and cost-effec-tiveness. *American Journal of Public Health, 74*, 1283–1285.

Brownell, K. D., & Fairburn, C. G. (1995). Eating disorders and obesity: A comprehensive handbook. New York: Guilford.

Brownell, K. D., Heckerman, C. L., Westlake, R. J., Hayes, S. C., & Monti, P. M. (1978). The effects of couples training and partner cooperativeness in the behavioral treatment of obesity. *Behavior Research Therapy, 16*, 323–333.

Brownell, K. D., Stunkard, A. J., & Albaum, J. M. (1980). Evaluation and modification of exercise patterns in the natural environment. *American Journal of Psychiatry, 137*, 1540–1545.

Brownell, K. D., & Wadden, T. A. (1992). Etiology and treatment of obesity: Understanding a serious, prevalent, and refractory disorder. *Journal of Consulting and Clinical Psychology, 60*, 505–517.

Brownlee-Duffeck, M., Peterson, L., Simonds, J. F., Goldstein, D., Kilo, C., & Hoette, S. (1987). The role of health beliefs in the regimen adherence and metabolic control of adolescents and adults with diabetes mellitus. *Journal of Consulting and Clinical Psychology, 55*, 139–144.

Brownson, R. C., Reif, J. S., Alavanja, M. C. R., & Bal, D. G. (1993). Cancer. In R. C. Brownson, P. L., Remington, & J. R. Davis (Eds.), *Chronic disease epidemiology and control* (pp. 137–167). Washington, DC: American Public Health Association.

Brubaker, R. G., & Wickersham, D. (1990). Encouraging the practice of testicular self-examination: A field application of the theory of reasoned action. *Health Psychology, 9*, 154–163.

Brug, J., Steenhuis, I., van Assema, P., & de Vries, H. (1996). The impact of computer-tailored nutrition information. *Preventive Medicine, 25*, 236–242.

Brunner, E., White, I., Thorogood, M., Bristow, A., Curle, D., & Marmot, M. (1997). Can dietary interventions change diet and cardiovascular risk factors? A meta-analysis of randomized controlled trials. *American Journal of Public Health, 87*, 1415–1422.

Bryan, A. D., Aiken, L. S., & West, S. G. (1996). Increasing condom use: Evaluation of a theory-based intervention to prevent sexually transmitted diseases in young women. *Health Psychology, 15*, 371–382.

Buckelew, S. P., Baumstark, K. E., Frank, R. G., & Hewett, J. E. (1990). Adjustment following spinal cord injury. *Rehabilitation Psychology, 35*, 101–109.

Budd, R. J., North, D., & Spencer, C. P. (1984). Understanding seat-belt use: A test of Bentler and Speckart's extension of the theory of reasoned action. *European Journal of Social Psychology, 14,* 69–78.

Bundek, N. I., Marks, G., & Richardson, J. L. (1993). Role of health locus of control beliefs in cancer screening of elderly Hispanic women. *Health Psychology, 12,* 193–199.

Burish, T. G., & Bradley, L. A. (1983). Coping with chronic disease: Definitions and issues. In T. G. Burish & L. A. Bradley (Eds.), *Coping with chronic disease: Research and applications* (pp. 3–12). New York: Academic Press.

Burish, T. G., Snyder, S. L., & Jenkins, R. A. (1991). Preparing patients for cancer chemotherapy: Effect of coping preparation and relaxation interventions. *Journal of Consulting and Clinical Psychology, 59,* 518–525.

Burke, R. J., Weir, T., & DuWors, R. E. (1979). Type A behavior of administrators and wives' reports of marital satisfaction and well-being. *Journal of Applied Psychology, 64,* 57–65.

Burke, R. J., Weir, T., & DuWors, R. E. (1980). Perceived Type A behavior of husbands and wives' satisfaction and well-being. *Journal of Occupational Behavior, 1,* 139–150.

Burnam, M. A., Timbers, D. M., & Hough, R. L. (1984). Two measures of psychological distress among Mexican Americans, Mexicans, and Anglos. *Journal of Health and Social Behavior, 25,* 24–33.

Burt, R. D., Dinh, K. T., Peterson, A. V., & Sarason, I. G. (2000). Predicting adolescent smoking: A prospective study of personality variables. *Preventive Medicine, 30,* 115–125.

Bush, C., Ditto, B., & Feuerstein, M. (1985). A controlled evaluation of paraspinal EMG biofeedback in the treatment of chronic low back pain. *Health Psychology, 4,* 307–321.

Bush, J. P., Melamed, B. G., Sheras, P. L., & Greenbaum, P. E. (1986). Mother–child patterns of coping with anticipatory medical stress. *Health Psychology, 5,* 137–157.

Buss, A. H., & Durkee, A. (1957). An inventory for assessing different kinds of hostility. *Journal of Consulting Psychology, 21,* 343–349.

Butt, H. R. (1977). A method for better physician–patient communication. *Annals of Internal Medicine, 86,* 478–480.

Butter, I. H. (1993). Premature adoption and routinization of medical technology: Illustrations from childbirth technology. *Journal of Social Issues, 49,* 11–34.

Byrnes, D. M., Antoni, M. H., Goodhin, K., Efanto-Potter, J., Asthane, A., Simon, T., Munajj, J., Ironson, g., & Fletcher, M. (1998). Stressful events, pessimism, natural kill cell cytotoxicity, and cytotoxic/suppressor T cells in HIV+ black women at risk for cervical cancer. *Psychosomatic Medicine, 60,* 714–722.

Calle, E. E., Miracle-McMahill, H. L., Thun, M. J., & Health, C. W. (1994). Cigarette smoking and risk of fatal breast cancer. *American Journal of Epidemiology, 139,* 1001–1007.

Camacho, T. C., Roberts, R. E., Lazarus, N. B., Kaplan, G. A., & Cohen, R. D. (1991). Physical activity and depression: Evidence from the Alameda County study. *American Journal of Epidemiology, 134,* 220–231.

Cameron, C. L., Cella, D., Herndon, J. E., III, Kornblith, A. B., Zuckerman, E., Henderson, E., Weiss, R. B., Cooper, M. R., Silver, R. T., Leone, L., Canellos, G. P., Peterson, B. A., & Holland, J. C. (2001). Persistent symptoms among survivors of Hodgkin's disease: An explanatory model based on classical conditioning. *Health Psychology, 20,* 71–75.

Cameron, L., Leventhal, E. A., & Leventhal, H. (1995). Seeking medical care in response to symptoms and life stress. *Psychosomatic Medicine, 57,* 37–47.

Campbell, M. K., DeVellis, B. M., Strecher, V. J., Ammerman, A. S., DeVellis, R. F., & Sandler, R. S. (1994). Improving dietary behavior: The effectiveness of tailored messages in primary care settings. *American Journal of Public Health, 84,* 783–787.

Lancet. (1985). Cancer of the cervix—Death by incompetence. *Lancet, ii,* 363–364.

Cannon, W. B. (1932). The wisdom of the body. New York: Norton.

Carey, M. P., Braaten, L. S., Maisto, S. A., Gleason, J. R., Forsyth, A. D., Durant, L. E., & Jaworski, B. C. (2000). Using information, motivational enhancement, and skills training to reduce the risk of HIV infection for low-income urban women: A second randomized clinical trial. *Health Psychology, 19,* 3–11.

Carey, M. P., & Burish, T. G. (1988). Etiology and treatment of the psychological side effects associated with cancer chemotherapy: A critical review and discussion. *Psychological Bulletin, 104,* 307–325.

Carlson, C. R., & Hoyle, R. H. (1993). Efficacy of abbreviated muscle relaxation training: A quantitative review of behavior medicine research. *Journal of Consulting and Clinical Psychology, 61,* 1059–1067.

Carney, M. A., Armeli, S., Tennen, H., Affleck, G., & O'Neil, T. P. (2000). Positive and negative daily events, perceived stress, and alcohol use: A diary study. *Journal of Consulting and Clinical Psychology, 68,* 788–798.

Caron, S. L., Davis, C. M., Halteman, W. A., & Stickle, M. (1993). Predictors of condom-related behaviors among first-year college students. *Journal of Sex Research, 30,* 252–259.

Carpenter, D. J., Gatchel, R. J., & Hasegawa, T. (1994). Effectiveness of a videotaped behavioral intervention for dental anxiety: The role of gender and need for information. *Behavioral Medicine, 20,* 123–132.

Carver, C. S., Coleman, A. E., & Glass, D. C. (1976). The coronary-prone behavior pattern and the suppression of fatigue on a treadmill test. *Journal of Personality and Social Psychology, 33,* 460–466.

Carver, C. S., & Gaines, J. G. (1987). Optimism, pessimism, and postpartum depression. *Cognitive Therapy and Research, 11,* 449–462.

Carver, C. S., Pozo, C., Harris, S. D., Noriega, V., Scheier, M. F., Robinson, D. S., Ketcham, A. S., Moffat, F. L., Jr., & Clark, K. S. (1993). How coping mediates the effect of optimism on distress: A study of women with early stage breast cancer. *Journal of Personality and Social Psychology, 65,* 375–390.

Carver, C. S., Pozo-Kaderman, C., Price, A. A., Noriega, V., Harris, S. D., Dehagopion, R. P., Robinson, D. S., & Moffatt, F. L., Jr. (1998). Concern about aspects of body image and adjustment to early stage breast cancer. *Psychosomatic Medicine, 60,* 168–174.

Carver, C. S., Scheier, M. F., & Weintraub, J. K. (1989). Assessing coping strategies: A theoretically based approach. *Journal of Personality and Social Psychology, 56,* 267–283.

Caspi, A., Begg, D., Dickson, N., Harrington, H., Langley, J., Moffitt, T. E., Silva, P. A. (1997). Personality differences predict health-risk behaviors in young adulthood: Evidence from a longitudinal study. *Journal of Personality and Social Psychology, 73,* 1052–1063.

Cassileth, B. R., Lusk, E. J., Strouse, T. B., Miller, D. S., Brown, L. L., Cross, P. A., & Tenaglia, A. N. (1984). Psychosocial status in chronic illness: A comparative analysis of six diagnostic groups. *New England Journal of Medicine, 311,* 506–511.

Catania, J. A., Kegeles, S. M., & Coates, T. J. (1990). Towards an understanding of risk behavior: An AIDS reduction model (ARRM). *Health Education Quarterly, 17,* 53–72.

Catz, S. L., Kelly, J. A., Bogart, L. M., Benotsch, E. G., & McAuliffe, T. L. (2000). Patterns, correlates, and barriers to medication adherence among persons prescribed new treatments for HIV disease. *Health Psychology, 19,* 124–133.

Caudill, B. D., & Marlatt, G. A. (1975). Modeling influences in social drinking: An experimental analogue. *Journal of Consulting and Clinical Psychology, 143,* 405–415.

Cervero, F. (2000). Visceral hyperalgesia revisited. *Lancet, 9236,* 1127–1135.

Cha, K. Y., Wirth, D. P., & Lobo, R. A. (2001). Does prayer influence the success of an in vitro fertilization-embryo transfer?: Report of a masked, randomized trial. *Journal of Reproductive Health, 46,* 781–787.

Chaiken, S. (1987). The heuristic model of persuasion. In M. P. Zanna, J. M. Olson, & C. P. Herman (Eds.), *Social influence: The Ontario symposium* (Vol. 5, pp. 3–39). Hillsdale, NJ: Erlbaum.

Champion, V. L. (1994). Strategies to increase mammography utilization. *Medical Care, 32,* 118–129.

Chapman, C. R., Casey, K. L., Dubner, R., Foley, K. M., Gracely, R. H., & Reading, A. E. (1985). Pain measurement: An overview. *Pain, 22,* 1–31.

Chapman, H. A., Hobfoll, S. E., & Ritter, C. (1997). Partners' stress underestimation lead to woman's distress: A study of pregnant inner-city women. *Journal of Personality and Social Psychology, 73,* 418–425.

Charles, C., Goldsmith, L. J., Chambers, L., & Haynes, R. B. (1996). Provider-patient communication among elderly and nonelderly patients in Canadian hospitals: A national survey. *Health Communication, 8,* 281–302.

Charney, E., Goodman, H. C., McBride, M., Lyon, B., & Pratt, R. (1976). Childhood antecedents of adult obesity: Do chubby infants become obese adults? *New England Journal of Medicine, 295,* 6–9.

Chassin, L., Presson, C. C., Rose, J. S., & Sherman, S. J. (1996). The natural history of cigarette smoking from adolescence to adulthood: Demographic predictors of continuity and change. *Health Psychology, 15,* 478–484.

Chassin, L., Presson, C. C., Sherman, S. J., Corty, E., & Olshavsky, R. W. (1981). Self-images and cigarette smoking in adolescence. *Personality and Social Psychology Bulletin, 7,* 670–676.

Chassin, L., Presson, C. C., Todd, M., Rose, J. S., & Sherman, S. J. (1998). Maternal socialization of adolescent smoking: The intergenerational transmission of parenting and smoking. *Developmental Psychology, 34,* 1189–1201.

Chatters, L. M., & Taylor, R. J. (1993). Intergenerational support: The provision of assistance to parents by adult children. In J. S. Jackson, L. M. Chatters, & R. J. Taylor (Eds.), *Aging in Black America* (pp. 69–83). Newbury Park, CA: Sage.

Chaves, J. F. (1994). Recent advances in the application of hypnosis to pain management. *American Journal of Clinical Hypnosis, 37,* 117–129.

Chen, J., Rathore, S. S., Radford, M. J., Wang, Y., & Krumholz, H. M. (2001). Racial differences in the use of cardiac catheterization after acute myocardial infarction. *New England Journal of Medicine, 344,* 1443–1449.

Chen, K., & Kandel, D. B. (1995). The natural history of drug use from adolescence to the mid-thirties in a general population sample. *American Journal of Public Health, 85,* 41–47.

Chesney, M., & Darbes, L. (1998). Social support and heart disease in women: Implications for intervention. In K. Orth-Gomer, M. Chesney, & N. K. Wenger (Eds.), *Women, stress, and heart disease* (pp. 165–182). Mahwah, NJ: Erlbaum.

Chesney, M. A., Eagleston, J. R., & Rosenman, R. H. (1980). The Type A structured interview: A behavioral assessment in the rough. *Journal of Behavioral Assessment, 2,* 252–272.

Ching, P. L. Y. H., Willett, W. C., Rimm, E. B., Colditz, G. A., Gortmaker, S. L., & Stampfer, M. J. (1996). Activity level and risk of overweight in male health professionals. *American Journal of Public Health, 86,* 25–30.

Chochinov, H. M., Wilson, K. G., Enns, M., Mowchun, N., Lander, S., Levitt, M., & Clinch, J. J. (1995). Desire for death in the terminally ill. *American Journal of Psychiatry, 152,* 1185–1191.

Christenfeld, N., Glynn, L. M., Phillips, D. P., & Shrira, I. (1999). Exposure to New York City as a risk factor for heart attack mortality. *Psychosomatic Medicine, 61,* 740–743.

Christensen, A. J. (2000). Patient-by-treatment context interaction in chronic disease: A conceptual framework for the study of patient adherence. *Psychosomatic Medicine, 62,* 435–443.

Christensen, A. J., & Ehlers, S. L. (2002). Psychological factors in end-stage renal disease: An emerging context for behavioral medicine research. *Journal of Consulting and Clinical Psychology, 70,* 712–724.

Christensen, A. J., & Johnson, J. A. (2002). Patient adherence with medical treatment regimens: An interactive approach. *Current Directions in Psychological Science, 11,* 94–97.

Christensen, A. J., Moran, P. J., & Wiebe, J. S. (1999). Assessment of irrational health beliefs: Relation to health practices and medical regimen adherence. *Health Psychology, 18,* 169–176.

Christensen, A. J., & Smith, T. W. (1995). Personality and patient adherence: Correlates of the five-factor model in renal dialysis. *Journal of Behavioral Medicine, 18,* 305–313.

Christensen, A. J., Smith, T. W., Turner, C. W., Holman, J. M., Jr., Gregory, M. C., & Rich, M. A. (1992). Family support, physical impairment, and adherence in hemodialysis: An investigation of main and buffering effects. *Journal of Behavioral Medicine, 15,* 313–326.

Christophersen, E. R. (1989). Injury control. *American Psychologist, 44,* 237–241.

Chrousos, G. P. (1998). Stressors, stress, and neuroendocrine intregration of the adaptive response. *Annals of the New York Academy of Sciences, 851,* 311–335.

Chrousos, G. P., & Gold, P. W. (1992). The concepts of stress and stress system disorders. Overview of physical and behavioral homeostasis. *Journal of the American Medical Association, 267,* 1244–1252.

Cinciripini, P. M., Lapitsky, L., Seay, S., Wallfisch, A., Kitchens, K., & VanVunakis, H. (1995). The effects of smoking schedules on cessation outcome: Can we improve on common methods of gradual and abrupt nicotine withdrawal? *Journal of Consulting and Clinical Psychology, 63,* 388–399.

Clark, D. C., & Zeldow, P. B. (1988). Vicissitudes of depressed mood during four years of medical school. *Journal of the American Medical Association, 260,* 2521–2528.

Clark, P. A. (2000). The ethics of medical marijuana: Govenment restriction vs. medical necessity. *Journal of Public Health Policy, 21,* 40–60.

Classen, C., Koopman, C., Angell, K., & Speigel, D. (1996). Coping styles associated with psychological adjustment to advanced breast cancer. *Health Psychology, 15,* 434–437.

Claus, E. B., Risch, N., & Thompson, W. D. (1993). Autosomal dominant inheritance of early onset breast cancer: Implications for risk prediction. *Cancer, 73,* 643–651.

Cleeland, C. S., Gonin, R., Hatfield, A. K., Edmonson, J. H., Blum, R. H., Stewart, J. A., & Pandya, K. J. (1994). Pain and its treatment in outpatients with metastatic cancer. *New England Journal of Medicine, 330,* 592–596.

Clemow, L., Costanza, M. E., Haddad, W. P., Luckmann, R., White, M. J., Klaus, D., & Stoddard, A. M. (2000). Underutilizers of mammography screening today: Characteristics of women planning, undecided about, and not planning a mammogram. *Annals of Behavioral Medicine, 22*, 80–88.

Cloninger, C. R. (1991). D2 dopamine receptor gene is associated but not linked with alcoholism. *Journal of the American Medical Association, 266*, 1833–1834.

Coates, T. (1990). Strategies for modifying sexual behavior for primary and secondary prevention of HIV disease. *Journal of Consulting and Clinical Psychology, 58*, 57–69.

Coates, T. J., Aggleton, P., Gutzorller, F., Des Jarlais, D., Kihara, M., Kippax, S., Schechter M., & van der Hoek, J. A. (1996). HIV prevention in developed countries. *Lancet, 348*, 1143–1148.

Coates, T. J., Stall, R. D., Kegeles, S. M., Lo, B., Morin, S. F., & McKusick, L. (1988). AIDS antibody testing. Will it stop the AIDS epidemic? Will it help people infected with HIV? *American Psychologist, 43*, 859–864.

Coates, T. J., Morin, S. F., & McKusick, L. (1987). Behavioral conseqeunces of AIDS antibody testing among gay men. *Journal of the American Medical Association, 258*, 1989.

Cobb, L. A., Thomas, G. I., Dillard, D. H., Merendino, K. A., & Bruce, R. A. (1959). An evaluation of internal mammary artery ligation by double blind technique. *New England Journal of Medicine, 260*, 1115–1118.

Cochran, S. D., & Mays, V. M. (1993). Applying social psychological models to predicting HIV-related sexual risk behaviors among African Americans. *Journal of Black Psychology, 19*, 142–154.

Coe, C. L., Wiener, S. G., Rosenberg, L. T., & Levine, S. (1985). Endocrine and immune responses to separation and maternal loss in nonhuman primates. In M. Reite & T. Field (Eds.), *The psychobiology of attachment and separation* (pp. 163–199). Orlando, FL: Academic Press.

Cogan, R., Cogan, D., Waltz, W., & McCue, M. (1987). Effects of laughter and relaxation on discomfort thresholds. *Journal of Behavioral Medicine, 10*, 139–144.

Cohen, L. (2002). Reducing infant immunization distress through distraction. *Health Psychology, 21*, 207–211.

Cohen, L., Blount, R. L., Cohen, R. J., Schaen, E. R., & Zaff, J. F. (1999). Comparative study of distraction versus topical anesthesia for pediatric pain management during immunizations. *Health Psychology, 18*, 591–598.

Cohen, L. H., McGowan, J., Fooskas, S., & Rose, S. (1984). Positive life events and social support and the relationship between life stress and psychological disorder. *American Journal of Community Psychology, 12*, 567–587.

Cohen, S. (1988). Psychosocial models of the role of social support in the etiology of physical disease. *Health Psychology, 7*, 269–297.

Cohen, S., Doyle, W. J., Skoner, D. P., Rabin, B. S., & Gwaltney, J. M. (1997). Social ties and susceptibility to the common cold. *Journal of the American Medical Association, 277*, 1940–1944.

Cohen, S., & Herbert, T. B. (1996). Health psychology: Psychological factors and physical disease from the perspective of human psychoneuroimmunology. *Annual Review of Psychology, 47*, 113–132.

Cohen, S., Kamarck, T., & Mermelstein, R. (1983). A global measure of perceived stress. *Journal of Health and Social Behavior, 24*, 385–396.

Cohen, S., & Lichtenstein, E. (1990a). Partner behaviors that support quitting smoking. *Journal of Consulting and Clinical Psychology, 58*, 304–309.

Cohen, S., & Lichtenstein, E. (1990b). Perceived stress, quitting smoking, and smoking relapse. *Health Psychology, 9*, 466–478.

Cohen, S., Mermelstein, R., Karmarck, T., & Hoberman, H. M. (1985). Measuring the functional components of social support. In I. G. Sarason & B. R. Sarason (Eds.), *Social support: Theory, research, and applications* (pp. 73–94). The Hague: Martinus Nijhoff.

Cohen, S., Sherrod, D. R., & Clark, M. S. (1986). Social skills and the stress-protective role of social support. *Journal of Personality and Social Psychology, 50*, 963–973.

Cohen, S., & Spacapan, S. (1978). The aftereffects of stress: An attentional interpretation. *Environmental Psychology and Nonverbal Behavior, 3*, 43–57.

Cohen, S., Tyrell, D. A. J., Russell, M. A. H., Jarvis, M. J., & Smith, A. P. (1993). Smoking, alcohol consumption, and susceptibility to the common cold. *American Journal of Public Health, 83*, 1277–1283.

Cohen, S., Tyrrell, D. A. J., & Smith, A. P. (1991). Psychological stress in humans and susceptibility to the common cold. *New England Journal of Medicine, 325*, 606–612.

Cohen, S., & Wills, T. A. (1985). Stress, social support, and the buffering hypothesis. *Psychological Bulletin, 98*, 310–357.

Cohen, S., et al. (1989). Debunking myths about self-quitting: Evidence from 10 prospective studies of persons who attempt to quit smoking by themselves. *American Psychologist, 44*, 1355–1365.

Cohen, S., et al. (1995). State and trait negative affect as predictors of objective and subjective symptoms of respiratory viral infections. *Journal of Personality and Social Psychology, 68*, 159–169.

Colditz, G. A., Willett, W. C., Hunter, D. J., Stampfer, M. J., Manson, J. E., Hennekens, C. H., & Rosner, B. A. (1993). Family history, age, and risk of breast cancer: Prospective data from the Nurses' Health Study. *Journal of the American Medical Association, 270*, 338–343.

Cole, S. W., Kemeny, M. E., Taylor, S. E., Visscher, B. R., & Fahey, J. L. (1996). Accelerated course of human immunodeficiency virus infection in gay men who conceal their homosexual identity. *Psychosomatic Medicine, 58*, 219–231.

Colerick, E. J. (1985). Stamina in later life. *Social Science and Medicine, 21*, 997–1006.

Colletti, G., & Kopel, S. A. (1979). Maintaining behavior changes: An investigation of three maintenance strategies and the relationship of self-attribution to the long-term reduction of cigarette smoking. *Journal of Consulting and Clinical Psychology, 11*, 25–33.

Collins, N. L., Dunkel-Schetter, C., Lobel, M., & Scrimshaw, S. C. M. (1993). Social support in pregnancy: Psychosocial correlates of birth outcomes and postpartum depression. *Journal of Personality and Social Psychology, 65*, 1243–1258.

Collins, R. L., Kanouse, D. E., Gifford, A. L., Senterfitt, J. W., Schuster, M. A., McCaffrey, D. F., Shapiro, M. F., & Wenger, N. S. (2001). Changes in health-promoting behavior following diagnosis with HIV: Prevalence and correlates in a national probability sample. *Health Psychology, 20*, 351–360.

Compas, B. E., Haaga, D. A., Keefe, F. J., Leitenberg, H., & Williams, D. A. (1998). Sampling of empirically supported psychological treatments from health psychology: Smoking, chronic pain, cancer, and bulimia nervosa. *Journal of Consulting and Clinical Psychology, 66*, 89–112.

Compas, B. E., Worsham, N. L., Epping-Jordan, J. E., Grant, K. E., Mireault, G., Howell, D. C., & Malcarne, V. L. (1994). When mom or dad has cancer: Markers of psychological distress in cancer patients, spouses, and children. *Health Psychology, 13*, 507–515.

Comuzzie, A. G., & Allison, D. B. (1998). The search for human obesity genes. *Science, 280*, 1374–1377.

Connell, C. M., & D'Augelli, A. R. (1990). The contribution of personality characteristics to the relationship between social support and perceived physical health. *Health Psychology, 9,* 192–207.

Contrada, R. (1989). Type A behavior, personality hardiness, and cardiovascular responses to stress. *Journal of Personality and Social Psychology, 57,* 895–903.

Contrada, R. J., Leventhal, E. A., & Anderson, J. R. (1994). Psychological preparation for surgery: Marshalling individual and social resources to optimize self-regulation. In S. Maes, H. Leventhal, & M. Johnston (Eds.), *International Review of Health Psychology* (Vol. 3, pp. 219–266). New York: Wiley.

Conway, T. L., Vickers, R. R., Ward, H. D., & Rahe, R. H. (1981). Occupational stress and variation in cigarette, coffee, and alcohol consumption. *Journal of Health and Social Behavior, 22,* 155–165.

Cook, W. W., & Medley, D. M. (1954). Proposed hostility and pharisaic-virtue scales for the MMPI. *Journal of Applied Psychology, 38,* 414–418.

Coon, K. A., Goldberg, J., Rogers, B. L., & Tucker, K. L. (2001). Relationships between use of television during meals and children's food consumption patterns. *Pediatrics, 107,* E7.

Cooper, M. L., Frone, M. R., Russell, M., & Mudar, P. (1995). Drinking to regulate positive and negative emotions: A motivational model of alcohol use. *Journal of Personality and Social Psychology, 69,* 960–1005.

Cooper, M. L., Russell, M., Skinner, J. B., Frone, M. R., & Mudar, P. (1992). Stress and alcohol use: Moderating effects of gender, coping, and alcohol expectancies. *Journal of Abnormal Psychology, 101,* 139–152.

Corah, W. L., & Boffa, J. (1970). Perceived control, self observation and responses to aversive stimulation. *Journal of Personality and Social Psychology, 16,* 1–4.

Cordova, M. J., Cunningham, L. L. C., Carlson, C. R., & Andrykowski, M. A. (2001). Posttraumatic growth following breast cancer: A controlled comparison study. *Health Psychology, 20,* 176–185.

Corr, C. A. (1992). A task-based approach to coping with dying. *Omega, 24,* 81–94.

Costa, P. T., Jr., & McCrae, R. R. (1980). Influence of extraversion and neuroticism on subjective well-being: Happy and unhappy people. *Journal of Personality and Social Psychology, 38,* 668–678.

Costa, P. T., Jr. & McCrae, R. R. (1985). Hypochondriasis, neuroticism, and aging.

When are somatic complaints unfounded? *American Psychologist, 40,* 19–28.

Costa, P. T., Jr., & McCrae, R. R. (1987). Neuroticism, somatic complaints, and disease: Is the bark worse than the bite? *Journal of Personality, 55,* 299–316.

Costa, P. T., Jr., & McCrae, R. R. (1990). Personality: Another "hidden factor" in stress research. *Psychological Inquiry, 1,* 22–24.

Costa, P. T., Jr., & McCrae, R. R. (1992). Four ways five factors are basic. *Personality and Individual Differences, 13,* 653–665.

Cotman, C. W., & Berchtold, N. C. (2002). Exercise: A behavioral intervention to enhance brain health and plasticity. *Trends in Neuroscience, 5,* 295–301.

Council, J. R., Ahern, D. K., Follick, M. J., & Kline, C. L. (1988). Expectancies and functional impairment in chronic low back pain. *Pain, 33,* 323–331.

Coyne, J. C., Rohrbaugh, M. J., Shoham, V., Sonnega, J. S., Nicklas, J. M., Cranford, J. A. (2001). Prognostic importance of marital quality for survival of congestive heart failure. *American Journal of Cardiology, 88,* 526–529.

Craig, K. D., Prkachin, K. M., & Grunau, R. V. E. (1992). The facial expression of pain. In D. C. Turk & R. Melzack (Eds.), *Handbook of pain assessment* (pp. 257–276). New York: Guilford.

Cramer, J. A., Mattson, R. H., Prevey, M. L., Scheyer, R. D., & Ouellette, V. L. (1989). How often is medication taken as prescribed? *Journal of the American Medical Association, 261,* 3273–3277.

Crandall, C. S. (1988). Social contagion of binge eating. *Journal of Personality and Social Psychology, 55,* 588–598.

Craun, A. M., & Deffenbacher, J. L. (1987). The effects of information, behavioral rehearsal, and prompting on breast self-exam. *Journal of Behavioral Medicine, 10,* 351–366.

Crawford, S. L., McGraw, S. A., Smith, K. W., McKinlay, J. B., & Pierson, J. E. (1994). Do blacks and whites differ in their use of health care for symptoms of coronary heart disease? *American Journal of Public Health, 84,* 957–964.

Creer, T. L., & Winder, J. A. (1986). The self-management of asthma. In K. A. Holroyd & T. L. Creer (Eds.), *Handbook of self-management in health psychology and behavioral medicine* (pp. 269–303). New York: Academic Press.

Critelli, J. W., & Neumann, K. F. (1984). The placebo: Conceptual analysis of a construct in transition. *American Psychologist, 39,* 32–39.

Cronk, C. E., & Sarvela, P. D. (1997). Alcohol, tobacco, and other drug use among rural/small town and urban youth: A secondary analysis of the monitoring the future data set. *American Journal of Public Health, 87,* 760–764.

Croyle, R. T., & Hunt, J. R. (1991). Coping with health threat: Social influence processes in reactions to medical test results. *Journal of Personality and Social Psychology, 60,* 382–389.

Croyle, R. T., & Lerman, C. (1995). Psychological impact of genetic testing. In R. T. Croyle (Ed.), *Psychosocial effects of screening for disease prevention and detection* (pp. 11–38). New York: Oxford University Press.

Croyle, R. T., Smith, K. R., Botkin, J. R., Baty, B., & Nash, J. (1997). Psychological responses to BRCA1 mutation testing: Preliminary findings. *Health Psychology, 16,* 63–72.

Croyle, R. T., Sun, Y., & Louie, D. H. (1993). Psychological minimization of cholesterol test results: Moderators of appraisal in college students and community residents. *Health Psychology, 12,* 503–507.

Cruess, D. G., Antoni, M. H., Schneiderman, N., Ironson, G., McCabe, P., Fernandez, J. B., Cruess, S. E., Klimas, N., & Kumas, M. (2000). Cognitive-behavioral stress management increases free testosterone and decreases psychological distress in HIV-seropositive men. *Health Psychology, 19,* 12–20.

Cunningham, M. R., & Barbee, A. P. (2000). Social support. In C. Hendrick & S. S. Hendrick (Eds.), *Close relationships: A sourcebook* (pp. 273–285). Thousand Oaks, CA: Sage.

Curb, J. D., & Marcus, E. B. (1991). Body fat and obesity in Japanese Americans. *American Journal of Clinical Nutrition, 53 (Suppl. 1),* 1552S–1555S.

Curran, P. J., Stice, E., & Chassin, L. (1997). The relation between adolescent alcohol use and peer alcohol use: A longitudinal random coefficients model. *Journal of Consulting and Clinical Psychology, 65,* 130–140.

Curry, S., Marlatt, G. A., & Gordon, J. R. (1987). Abstinence violation effect: Validation of an attributional construct with smoking cessation. *Journal of Consulting and Clinical Psychology, 55,* 145–149.

Curry, S. J., & McBride, C. M. (1994). Relapse prevention for smoking cessation: Review and evaluation of concepts and interventions. *Annual Review of Public Health, 15,* 345–366.

Cusumano, D. L., & Thompson, J. K. (1997). Body image and body shape ideals in magazines: Exposure, awareness and internalization. *Sex Roles, 37,* 701–721.

Cutrona, C. E., & Russell, D. W. (1990). Type of social support and specific stress: Toward a theory of optimal matching. In B. R. Sarason, I. G. Sarason, & G. R. Pierce (Eds.), *Social support: An interactional view* (pp. 319–366). New York: Wiley.

Dakof, G. A., & Taylor, S. E. (1990). Victims' perceptions of social support: What is helpful from whom? *Journal of Personality and Social Psychology, 58,* 80–89.

Dalton, P. (1999). Cognitive influences on health symptoms from acute chemical exposure. *Health Psychology, 18,* 579–590.

D'Amico, E. J., & Fromme, K. (1997). Health risk behaviors of adolescent and young adult siblings. *Health Psychology, 16,* 426–432.

Dannenberg, A. L., Gielen, A. C., Beilenson, P. L., Wilson, D. H., & Joffe, A. (1993). Bicycle helmet laws and educational campaigns: An evaluation of strategies to increase children's helmet use. *American Journal of Public Health, 83,* 667–674.

Danner, D. D., Snowden, D. A., & Friesen, W. V. (2001). Positive emotions in early life and longevity: Findings from the nun study. *Journal of Personality and Social Psychology, 80,* 804–813.

Dare, C., & Eisler, I. (1995). Family therapy and eating disorders. In K. D. Brownell & C. G. Fairburn (Eds.), *Eating disorders and obesity: A comprehensive handbook* (pp. 318–323). New York: Guilford.

Darkes, J., & Goldman, M. S. (1993). Expectancy challenge and drinking reduction: Experimental evidence for a mediational process. *Journal of Consulting and Clinical Psychology, 61,* 344–353.

Dattore, P. J., Shontz, F. C., & Coyne, L. (1980). Premorbid personality differentiation of cancer and non-cancer groups: A list of the hypotheses of cancer proneness. *Journal of Consulting and Clinical Psychology, 48,* 388–394.

Davidson, L. L., Durkin, M. S., Kuhn, L., O'Connor, P., Barlow, B., Heagarty, M. C. (1994). The impact of the Safe Kids/Healthy Neighborhoods Injury Prevention Program in Harlem, 1988–1991. *American Journal of Public Health, 84,* 580–586.

Davidson, R. S. (1985). Behavioral medicine and alcoholism. In N. Schneiderman & J. T. Tapp (Eds.), *Behavioral medicine: The biopsychosocial approach* (pp. 379–404). Hillsdale, NJ: Erlbaum.

Davies, J. E., Gibson, T., & Tester, L. (1979). The value of exercises in the treatment of low back pain. *Rheumatology and Rehabilitation, 18,* 243–247.

Davis, D. L. (1991). Empty cradle, broken heart: Surviving the death of your baby. Golden, CO: Fulcrum.

Davis, M. C., & Swan, P. D. (1999). Association of negative and positive social ties with fibrinogen levels in young women. *Health Psychology, 18,* 121–139.

Davis, R. C., Smith, B. E., & Nickles, L. B. (1998). The deterrent effect of prosecuting domestic violence misdemeanors. *Crime and Delinquency, 44,* 434–443.

Dawson, D. A., Grant, B. F., & Harford, T. C. (1995). Variation in the association of alcohol consumption with five DSM-IV alcohol problem domains. *Alcoholism: Clinical and Experimental Research, 19,* 66–74.

De Castro, J. M. (1994). Family and friends produce greater social facilitation of food intake than other companions. *Physiology & Behavior, 56,* 445–455.

De Castro, J. M., & De Castro, E. S. (1989). Spontaneous meal patterns of humans: Influence of the presence of other people. *American Journal of Clinical Nutrition, 50,* 237–247.

DeGood, D. E. (2000). Relationship of pain-coping strategies to adjustment and functioning. In R. J. Gatchel & J. N. Weisberg (Eds.), *Personality characteristics of patients with pain* (pp. 129–164). Washington, DC: American Psychological Association.

DeJong, W. (1980). The stigma of obesity: The consequences of naive assumptions concerning the causes of physical deviance. *Journal of Health and Social Behavior, 21,* 75–87.

Delahanty, D. L., & Baum, A. (2001). Stress and breast cancer. In A. Baum, T. A. Revenson, & J. E. Singer (Eds.), *Handbook of health psychology* (pp. 747–756). Mahwah, NJ: Erlbaum.

Delbanco, T. L. (1992). Enriching the doctor–patient relationship by inviting the patient's perspective. *Annals of Internal Medicine, 116,* 414–418.

DeLeon, P. H. (2002). Presidential reflections: Past and future. *American Psychologist, 57,* 425–430.

Delin, C. R., & Lee, T. H. (1992). Drinking and the brain: Current evidence. *Alcohol & Alcoholism, 27,* 117–126.

Denissenko, M. F., Pao, A., Tang, M., & Pfeifer, G. P. (1996). Preferential formation of benzoapyrene adducts at lung cancer muta-

tional hotspots in P53. *Science, 274,* 430–432.

Depner, C., & Ingersoll, B. (1982). Employment status and social support: The experience of mature women. In M. Szinovacz (Ed.), *Women's retirement: Policy implications of recent research* (pp. 61–76). Beverly Hills, CA: Sage.

Des Jarlais, D. C., & Friedman, S. R. (1996). HIV epidemiology and interventions among injecting drug users. *International Journal of STD and AIDS, 7* (Suppl. 2), 57–61.

Des Jarlais, D. C., & Friedman, S. R. (2001). Strategies for preventing HIV infection among injecting drug users: Taking interventions to the people. In N. Schneiderman, M. A. Speers, J. M. Silva, N. Tomes, & J. H. Gentry (Eds.), *Integrating behavioral and social sciences with public health* (pp. 141–158). Washington, DC: American Psychological Association.

Des Jarlais, D. C., Friedman, S. R., Casriel, C., & Kott, A. (1987). AIDS and preventing initiation into intravenous (IV) drug use. *Psychology and Health, 1,* 179–194.

Desmond, S. M., Price, J. H., Hallinan, C., & Smith, D. (1989). Black and white adolescents' perceptions of their ideal weight. *Journal of School Health, 59,* 353–358.

Detweiler, J. B., Bedell, B. T., Salovey, P., Pronin, E., & Rothman, A. J. (1999). Message framing and sunscreen use: Gain-framed messages motivate beach-goers. *Health Psychology, 18,* 189–196.

DeVellis, B. M., Blalock, S. J., & Sandler, R. S. (1990). Predicting participation in cancer screening: The role of perceived behavioral control. *Journal of Applied Social Psychology, 20,* 639–660.

de Vincenzi, I. (1994). A longitudinal study of human immunodeficiency virus transmission by heterosexual partners. *New England Journal of Medicine, 331,* 341–346.

Devine, E. C. (1992). Effects of psychoeducational care for adult surgical patients: A meta-analysis of 191 studies. *Patient Education and Counseling, 19,* 129–142.

Devins, G. M., & Binik, Y. M. (1996). Faciliating coping with chronic physical illness. In M. Zeidner & N. S. Endler (Eds.), *Handbook of coping: Theory, research, applications* (pp. 640–696). New York: Wiley.

Devins, G. M., Mandin, H., Hons, R. B., Burgess, E. D., Klassen, J., Taub, K., Schorr, S., Letourneau, R. K., & Buchle, S. (1990). Illness intrusiveness and quality of life in end-stage renal disease: Comparison and stability across treatment modalities. *Health Psychology, 9,* 117–142.

Deyo, R. A. (1991). Fads in the treatment of low back pain. *New England Journal of Medicine, 325,* 1039–1040.

Deyo, R. A., Walsh, N. E., & Martin, D. (1990). A controlled trial of transcutaneous electrical nerve stimulation (TENS) and exercise for chronic low back pain. *New England Journal of Medicine, 322,* 1627–1634.

Diamond, E. G., Kittle, C. F., & Crockett, J. F. (1960). Comparision of internal mammary artery ligation and sham operation for angina pectoris. *American Journal of Cardiology, 5,* 483–486.

DiClemente, R. J., Durbin, M., Siegel, D., Krasnovsky, F., Lazarus, N., & Comacho, T. (1992). Determinants of condom use among junior high school students in a minority, inner-city school district. *Pediatrics, 89,* 197–202.

DiClemente, R. J., Forrest, K. A., Mickler, S., & Principal site investigators (1990). College students' knowledge and attitudes about AIDS and changes in HIV-preventative behaviors. *AIDS Education and Prevention, 2,* 201–212.

DiClemente, C. C., Prochaska, J. O., Fairhurst, S. K., Velicer, W. F., Velasquez, M. M., & Rossi, J. S. (1991). The process of smoking cessation: An analysis of precontemplation, contemplation, and preparation stages of change. *Journal of Consulting and Clinical Psychology, 59,* 295–304.

Diefenbach, M. A., Miller, S. M., & Daly, M. B. (1999). Specific worry about breast cancer predicts mammography use in women at risk for breast and ovarian cancer. *Health Psychology, 18,* 532–536.

Diener, E. (2000). Subjective well-being: The science of happiness and a proposal for a national index. *American Psychologist, 55,* 34–43.

DiMatteo, M. R. (1994). Enhancing patient adherence to medical recommendations. *Journal of the American Medical Association, 271,* 79–83.

DiMatteo, M. R., Hays, R. D., Gritz, E. R., Bartoni, R., Crane, L., Elashoff, R., Gunz, R., Heber, A., McCarthy, W., & Marcus, A. (1993). Patient adherence to cancer control regimens: Scale development and initial validation. *Psychological Assessment, 5,* 102–112.

Dimond, M. (1979). Social support and adaptation to chronic illness: The case of maintenance hemodialysis. *Research in Nursing and Health, 2,* 101–108.

Dinh, K. T., Sarason, I. G., Peterson, A. V., & Onstad, L. E. (1995). Children's perception of smokers and nonsmokers: A longitudinal study. *Health Psychology, 14,* 32–40.

DiNicola, D. D., & DeMatteo, M. R. (1984). Practitioners, patients, and compliance with medical regimens: A social psychological perspective. In A. Baum, S. E. Taylor, & J. E. Singer (Eds.), *Handbook of psychology and health: Vol. 4. Social psychological aspects of health* (pp. 55–84). Hillsdale, NJ: Erlbaum.

Ditto, P. H., Druley, J. A., Moore, K. A., Danks, H. J., & Smucker, W. D. (1996). Fates worse than death: The role of valued life activities in health-state evaluations. *Health Psychology, 15,* 332–343.

Dlin, B. (1985). Psychobiology and treatment of anniversary reactions. *Psychosomatics, 26,* 505–520.

Doering, S., Katzlberger, F., Rumpold, G., Roessler, S., Hofstoetter, B., Schatz, D. S., Behenshy, H., Krismer, M., Luz, G., Immerhofer, P., Benzer, H., Saria, A., & Schuessler, G. (2000). Videotape preparation of patients before hip replacement surgery reduces stress. *Psychosomatic Medicine, 62,* 365–373.

Doka, K. J. (1993). Living with life-threatening illness. Lexington, MA: Lexington Books.

Donahue, M. J., & Benson, P. L. (1995). Religion and the well-being of adolescents. *Journal of Social Issues, 51,* 145–160.

Dowie, M. (1988). "We have a donor": The bold new world of organ transplanting. New York: St. Martin's Press.

Downey, G., Silver, R. C., & Wortman, C. B. (1990). Reconsidering the attribution-adjustment relationship following a major negative event: Coping with the loss of a child. *Journal of Personality and Social Psychology, 59,* 925–940.

Dowson, D. I., Lewith, G. T., & Machin, C. (1985). The effects of acupuncture versus placebo in the treatment of headache. *Pain, 21,* 35–42.

Drach-Zahavy, A., & Somech, A. (2002). Coping with health problems: The distinctive relationships of Hope sub-scales with constructive thinking and resource allocation. *Personality & Individual Differences, 33,* 103–117.

Dressler, W. (1985). Extended family relationships, social support, and mental health in a southern Black community. *Journal of Health and Social Behavior, 26,* 39–48.

Drewnowski, A. (1996). The behavioral phenotype in human obesity. In E.D. Capaldi (Ed.), *Why we eat what we eat: The psychology of eating* (pp. 291–308). Washington, DC: American Psychological Association.

Drinka, T., & Smith, J. (1983). Depression in caregivers of demented patients. *Gerontologist, 23,* 116.

Druley, J. A., Stephens, M. A., & Coyne, J. C. (1997). Emotional and physical intimacy in coping with lupus: Women's dilemmas of disclosure and approach. *Health Psychology, 16,* 506–514.

Drummond, D. C., & Glautier, S. (1994). A controlled trial of cue exposure treatment in alcohol dependence. *Journal of Consulting and Clinical Psychology, 62,* 809–817.

Dubus, R. (1959). The mirage of health. New York: Harper.

Duggan, C. H., & Dijkers, M. (2001). Quality of life after spinal cord injury: A qualitative study. *Rehabilitation Psychology, 46,* 3–27.

Dunbar-Jabob, J., Burke, L. E., & Puczynski, S. (1995). Clinical assessment and management of adherence to medical regimens. In P. M. Nicassio & T. M. Smith (Eds.), *Managing chronic illness: A biopsychosocial perspective* (pp. 313–349). Washington, DC: American Psychological Association.

Duncan, T. E., & McAuley, E. (1993). Social support and efficacy cognitions in exercise adherence: A latent growth curve analysis. *Journal of Behavioral Medicine, 16,* 199–218.

Dunkel-Schetter, C. (1984). Social support and cancer: Findings based on patient interviews and their implications. *Journal of Social Issues, 40,* 77–98.

Dunkel-Schetter, C., Feinstein, L. G., Taylor, S. E., & Falke, R. L. (1992). Patterns of coping with cancer. *Health Psychology, 11,* 79–87.

Dunkel-Schetter, C., & Wortman, C. (1982). The interpersonal dynamics of cancer: Problems in social relationships and their impact on the patient. In H. S. Friedman & M. R. DiMatteo (Eds.), *Interpersonal issues in health care* (pp. 69–100). New York: Academic Press.

Dunn, A. L., Marcus, B. H., Kampert, J. B., Garcia, M. E., Kohl, H. W., III, Blair, S. N. (1999). Comparison of lifestyle and structured interventions to increase physical activity and cardiorespiratory fitness. *Journal of the American Medical Association, 281,* 327–334.

Durkheim, E. (1951). *Suicide.* New York: Free Press.

Dusseldorp, E., van Elderen, T., Maes, S., Meulman, J., & Kraaij, V. (1999). A meta-analysis of psychoeducational programs for coronary heart disease patients. *Health Psychology, 18,* 506–519.

Eckhardt, M. J., Harford, T. C., Kaelber, C. T., Parker, E. S., Rosenthal, L. S., Ryback, R. S.,

Salmoiraghi, G. C., Vanderveen, E., & Warren, K. R. (1981). Health hazards associated with alcohol consumption. *Journal of the American Medical Association, 246*, 648–666.

Edelson, J., & Fitzpatrick, J. L. (1989). A comparison of cognitive-behavioral and hypnotic treatments of chronic pain. *Journal of Clinical Psychology, 45*, 316–323.

Egbert, L. D., Battit, C. E., Welch, C. E., & Bartlett, M. K. (1964). Reduction of postoperative pain by encouragement and instruction of patients: A study of doctor-patient rapport. *New England Journal of Medicine, 75*, 1008–1023.

Ehrenwald, J. (1976). The history of psychotherapy: From healing magic to encounter. New York: Aronson.

Eifert, G. H., Hodson, S. E., Tracey, D. R., Seville, J. L., & Gunawardane, K. (1996). Heart-focused anxiety, illness beliefs, and behavioral impairment: Comparing healthy heart-anxious patients with cardiac and surgical inpatients. *Journal of Behavioral Medicine, 19*, 385–399.

Eisenberg, D. M., Davis, R. B., Ettner, S. L., Appel, S., Wilkey, S., Van Rompay, M., Kessler, R. C. (1998). Trends in alternative medicine use in the United States, 1990–1997: Results of a follow-up national survey. *Journal of the American Medical Association, 280*, 1569–1575.

Eisenberg, D. M., Kessler, R. C., Foster, C., Norlock, F. E., Calkins, D. R., Delbanco, T. L. (1993). Unconventional medicine in the United States: Prevalence, costs, and patterns of use. *New England Journal of Medicine, 328*, 246–252.

Eisenberg, N., & Lennon, R. (1983). Sex differences in empathy and related capacities. *Psychological Bulletin, 94*, 100–131.

Eiser, C. (1982). The effects of chronic illness on children and their families. In J. R. Eiser (Ed.), *Social psychology and behavioral medicine* (pp. 459–481). New York: Wiley.

Elder, J. P. (2001). Behavior change and public health in the developing world. Thousand Oaks, CA: Sage.

Ellington, L., & Wiebe, D. J. (1999). Neuroticism, symptom presentation, and medical decision making. *Health Psychology, 18*, 634–643.

Emmett, C., & Ferguson, E. (1999). Oral contraceptive pill use, decisional balance, risk perception and knowledge: An exploratory study. *Journal of Reproductive and Infant Psychology, 17*, 327–343.

Emmons, K. M., Wechsler, H., Dowdall, G., & Abraham, M. (1998). Predictors of smoking among U.S. college students. *American Journal of Public Health, 88*, 104–107.

Emmons, R. A., & King, L. A. (1988). Conflict among personal strivings: Immediate and long-term implications for psychological and physical well-being. *Journal of Personality and Social Psychology, 54*, 1040–1048.

Emrick, C. D., & Hansen, J. (1983). Assertions regarding effectiveness of treatment for alcoholism: Fact or fantasy? *American Psychologist, 38*, 1078–1088.

Engel, G. L. (1977). The need for a new medical model: A challenge for biomedicine. *Science, 196*, 129–136.

Engel, G. L. (1980). The clinical application of the biopsychosocial model. *American Journal of Psychiatry, 137*, 535–544.

Ennett, S. T., Tobler, N. S., Ringwalt, C. L., & Flewelling, R. L. (1994). How effective is drug resistance education? A meta-analysis of Project DARE outcome evaluations. *American Journal of Public Health, 84*, 1394–1401.

Enright, M. F., Resnick, R., DeLeon, P. H., Sciara, A. D., & Tanney, F. (1990). The practice of psychology in hospital settings. *American Psychologist, 45*, 1059–1065.

Epping-Jordan, J. E., Compas, B. E., Osowiecki, D. M., Oppedisano, G., Gerhardt, C., Prine, K., & Krag, D. N. (1999). Psychological adjustment in breast cancer: Processes of emotional distress. *Health Psychology, 18*, 315–326.

Epstein, A. M., Taylor, W. C., & Seage, G. R. (1985). Effects of patients' socioeconomic status and physicians' training and practice on patient–doctor communication. *American Journal of Medicine, 78*, 101–106.

Epstein, L. H., & Cluss, P. A. (1982). A behavioral medicine perspective on adherence to long-term medical regimens. *Journal of Consulting and Clinical Psychology, 50*, 950–971.

Esterling, B. A., Kiecolt-Glaser, J. K., Bodnar, J. C., & Glaser, R. (1994). Chronic stress, social support, and persistent alterations in the natural kill cell response to cytokines in older adults. *Health Psychology, 13*, 291–298.

Evans, R. I. (1988). Health promotion—science or ideology? *Health Psychology, 7*, 203–219.

Evans, R. I., Rozelle, R. M., Lasater, T. M., Dembroski, T. M., & Allen, B. P. (1970). Fear arousal, persuasion, and actual versus implied behavior change: New perspective utilizing a real-life dental hygiene program. *Journal of Personality and Social Psychology, 16*, 220–227.

Evans, R .I., Rozelle, R. M., Maxwell, S. E., Raines, B. E., Dill, C. A., Guthrie, T. J., Henderson, A. H., & Hill, P. C. (1981). Social modeling films to deter smoking in adolescents: Results of a three year field investigation. *Journal of Applied Psychology, 66*, 399–414.

Evans, G. W., Bullinger, M., & Hygge, S. (1998). Chronic noise exposure and physiological response: A prospective study of children living under environmental stress. *Psychological Science, 9*, 75–77.

Everson, S. A., Goldberg, D. E., Kaplan, G. A., & Cohen, R. D. (1996). Hopelessness and risk of mortality and incidence of myocardial infarction and cancer. *Psychosomatic Medicine, 58*, 103–121.

Ewart, C. K., Harris, W. L., Iwata, M. M., Coates, T. J., Bullock, R., & Simon, B. (1987). Feasibility and effectiveness of school-based relaxation in lowering blood pressure. *Health Psychology, 6*, 399–416.

Eysenck, H. J. (1967). The biological basis of personality. Springfield, IL: Thomas.

Eysenck, H. J. (1990). Biological dimensions of personality. In L. A. Pervin (Ed.), *Handbook of personality theory and research* (pp. 244–276). New York: Guilford.

Eysenck, H. J., & Eysenck, S. B. G. (1964). Eysenck personality inventory. San Diego, CA: Education and Industry Testing Service.

Faden, R .R., & Beauchamp, T. L. (1986). A history and theory of informed consent. New York: Oxford University Press.

Faden, R. R., Becker, C., Lewis, C., Freeman, J., & Faden, A. I. (1981). Disclosure of information to patients in medical care. *Medical Care, 19*, 718–733.

Faden, R. R., & Kass, N. E. (1993). Genetic screening techonology: Ethical issues in access to tests by employers and health insurance companies. *Journal of Social Issues, 49*, 75–88.

Fagerlin, A., Ditto, P. H., Danks, J. H., Houts, R. M., & Smucker, W. D. (2001). Projection in surrogate decisions about life-sustaining medical treatment. *Health Psychology, 20*, 166–175.

Fallon, A. E., & Rozin, P. (1985). Sex differences in perception of desirable body shape. *Journal of Abnormal Psychology, 94*, 102–105.

Falvo, D. R. (1991). Medical and psychosocial aspects of chronic illness and disability. Gaithersburg, MD: Aspen.

Fang, C. Y., Manne, S. L., & Pape, S. J. (2001). Functional impairment, marital quality, and patient psychological distress as predictors of psychological distress among cancer patients' spouses. *Health Psychology, 20*, 452–457.

Farquhar, J. W., Fortmann, S. P., Flora, J. A., Taylor, C. B., Haskell, W. L., Williams, P. T., Maccoby, N., & Wood, P. D. (1990). Effects of community-wide education on cardiovascular disease risk factors: The Stanford Five-City Project. *Journal of the American Medical Association, 264,* 359–364.

Faucett, J., Gordon, N., & Levine, J. (1994). Differences in postoperative pain severity among four ethnic groups. *Journal of Pain and Symptom Management, 9,* 383–389.

Fawzy, F. I., Cousins, N., Fawzy, N. W., Kemeny, M. E., Elashoff, R., & Morton, D. (1990). A structured psychiatric intervention for cancer patients: I. Changes over time in methods of coping and affective disturbance. *Archives of General Psychiatry, 47,* 720–725.

Feifel, H. (1990). Psychology and death: Meaningful rediscovery. *American Psychologist, 45,* 537–543.

Feldman, S. I., Downey, G., & Schaffer-Neitz, R. (1999). Pain, negative mood, and perceived support in chronic pain patients: A daily diary study of people with reflex sympathetic dystrophy syndrome. *Journal of Consulting and Clinical Psychology, 67,* 776–785.

Feletti, G., Firman, D., & Sanson-Fisher, R. (1986). Patient satisfaction with primary-care consultations. *Journal of Behavioral Medicine, 9,* 389–399.

Felson, D. T., Zhang, Y., Hannan, M. T., Kannel, W. B., & Kiel, D. P. (1995). Alcohol intake and bone mineral density in elderly men and women: The Framingham Study. *American Journal of Epidemiology, 142,* 485–492.

Felton, B. J., & Revenson, T. A. (1984). Coping with chronic illness: A study of illness controllability and the influence of coping strategies on psychological adjustment. *Journal of Consulting and Clinical Psychology, 52,* 343–353.

Fernandez, E. (1986). A classification system of cognitive coping strategies for pain. *Pain, 26,* 141–151.

Fernandez, E., & Turk, D. C. (1992). Sensory and affective components of pain: Separation and synthesis. *Psychological Bulletin, 112,* 205–217.

Festinger, L. (1957). *A theory of cognitive dissonance.* Stanford, CA: Stanford University Press.

Feunkes, G. I. J., De Graaf, C., & Van Staveren, W. A. (1995). Social facilitation of food intake is mediated by meal duration. *Physiology and Behavior, 58,* 551–558.

Feurestein, M., Labbe, E. E., & Kuczmierczyk, A. R. (1986). *Health psychology: A psychobiological perspective.* New York: Plenum.

Field, A. E., Camargo, C. A. Jr., Taylor, C. B., Berkey, C. S., Roberts, S. B., & Colditz, G. A (2001). Peer, parent, and media influences on the development of weight concerns and frequent dieting among preadolescent and adolescent girls and boys. *Pediatrics, 107,* 54–60.

Field, N. P., Nichols, C., Holen, A., & Horowitz, M. J. (1999). The relation of continuing attachment to adjustment in conjugal bereavement. *Journal of Consulting and Clinical Psychology, 67,* 212–218.

Field, T. M. (1998). Massage therapy effects. *American Psychologist, 53,* 1270–1281.

Fielding, J. E., & Phenow, K. J. (1988). Health effects of involuntary smoking. *New England Journal of Medicine, 319,* 1452–1460.

Fine, P. R., Rousculp, M. D., Tomasek, A. D., & Horn, W. S. (1999). Intentional injury. In J. M. Raczynski & R. J. DiClemente (Eds.), *Handbook of health promotion and disease prevention* (pp. 287–308). New York: Plenum.

Fiore, M. C., Novotny, T. E., Pierce, J. P., Giovino, G. A., Hatziandreu, E. J., Newcomb, P. A., Surawicz, T. S., & Davis, R. M. (1990). Methods used to quit smoking in the United States: Do cessation programs help? *Journal of the American Medical Association, 263,* 2760–2765.

Fiscella, K., Franks, P., Gold, M. R., & Clancy, C. M. (2000). Inequality in quality: Addressing socioeconomic, racial, and ethnic disparities in health care. *Journal of the American Medical Association, 283,* 2579–2584.

Fishbein, M., & Ajzen, I. (1975). Belief, attitude, intention, and behavior. Reading, MA: Addison-Wesley.

Fishbein, M., & Middlestadt, S. E. (1989). Using the theory of reasoned action as a framework for understanding and changing AIDS-related behaviors. In V. M. Mays, G. W. Albee, & S. Schneider (Eds.), *Primary prevention of AIDS: Psychological approaches* (pp. 93–110). Newbury Park, CA: Sage.

Fisher, E. B., Lowe, M. R., Jeffrey, C., Levenkron, J. C., & Newman, A. (1982). Reinforcement and structural support of maintained risk reduction. In E.B. Stuart (Ed.), *Adherence, compliance, and generalization in behavioral medicine* (pp. 145–168). New York: Brunner/Mazel.

Fisher, J. O., & Birch, L. L. (1995). Fat preferences and fat consumption of 3- to 5-year-old children are related to parental adiposity. *Journal of the American Dietetic Association, 95,* 759–764.

Fisher, J. O., & Birch, L. L. (1999). Restricting access to palatable foods affects children's behavioral response, food selection, and intake. *American Journal of Clinical Nutrition, 69,* 1264–1272.

Fisher, J. D., & Fisher, W. A. (1992). Changing AIDS-risk behavior. *Psychological Bulletin, 111,* 455–474.

Fisher, J. D., Fisher, W. A., Bryan, A. D., & Misovich, S. J. (2002). Information-motivation-behavioral skills model-based HIV risk behavior change intervention for inner-city high school youth. *Health Psychology, 21,* 177–186.

Fisher, J. D., Fisher, W. A., Misovich, S. J., Kimble, D. L., & Malloy, T. E. (1996). Changing AIDS risk behavior: Effects of an intervention emphasizing AIDS risk reduction information, motivation, and behavioral skills in a college student population. *Health Psychology, 15,* 114–123.

Fisher, W. A., Fisher, J. D., & Rye, B. J. (1995). Understanding and promoting AIDS-preventive behavior: Insights from the theory of reasoned action. *Health Psychology, 14,* 255–264.

Fishman, S., & Berger, L. (2000). *The war on pain: How breakthroughs in the new field of pain medicine are turning the tide against suffering.* New York: HarperCollins.

Flack, J. M., Amaro, H., Jenkins, W., Kunitz, S., Levy, J., Mixon, M., & Yu, E. (1995). Epidemiology of minority health. *Health Psychology, 14,* 592–600.

Flaherty, J., & Richman, J. (1989). Gender differences in the perception and utilization of social support: Theoretical perspectives and an empirical test. *Social Science and Medicine, 28,* 1221–1228.

Flay, B. R. (1987). Social psychological approaches to smoking prevention: Review and recommendations. In W. B. Ward (Ed.), *Advances in health education and promotion, Vol. 2* (pp. 121–180). Greenwich, CT: JAI Press.

Flay, B. R., Koepke, D., Thomson, S. J., Santi, S., Best, A., & Brown, S. (1989). Six-year follow-up of the first Waterloo school smoking cessation trait. *American Journal of Public Health, 79,* 1371–1376.

Flegal, K. M., Carrol, M. D., Kuczmaraki, R. J., & Johnson, C. L. (1998). Overweight and obesity in the United States: Prevalence and trends, 1960–1994. *International Journal of Obesity Related Metabolic Disorders, 22,* 39–47.

Fleishman, J. A., & Fogel, B. (1994). Coping and depressive symptoms among people with AIDS. *Health Psychology, 13,* 156–169.

Fleming, R., Baum, A., Gisriel, M. M., & Gatchel, R. J. (1982). Mediating influences of social support on stress at Three Mile Island. *Journal of Human Stress, 8,* 14–22.

Fletcher, A. M. (2001). *Sober for good.* New York: Houghton-Mifflin.

Flor, H., & Birbaumer, N. (1993). Comparison of the efficacy of electromyographic biofeedback, cognitive-behavioral therapy, and conservative medical interventions in the treatment of chronic musculoskeletal pain. *Journal of Consulting and Clinical Psychology, 61,* 653–658.

Flor, H., Elbert, T., Knecht, S., Wienbruch, C., Pantev, C., Birbaumer, N., Larbig, W., Taub, E. (1995). Phantom-limb pain as a perceptual correlate of cortical reorganization following arm amputation. *Nature, 375,* 482–484.

Flor, H., Fydrich, T., & Turk, D. C. (1992). Efficacy of multidisciplinary pain treatment centers: A meta-analytic review. *Pain, 49,* 221–230.

Flor, H., & Turk, C. D. (1988). Chronic back pain and rheumatoid arthritis: Predicting pain and disability from cognitive variables. *Journal of Behavioral Medicine, 11,* 251–265.

Flora, J. A., & Maibach, E. W. (1990). Cognitive responses to AIDS information: The effects of issue involvement and message appeal. *Communication Research, 17,* 759–774.

Florian, V., Mikulincer, M., & Taubman, O. (1995). Does hardiness contribute to mental health during a stressful real-life situation? The roles of appraisal and coping. *Journal of Personality and Social Psychology, 68,* 687–695.

Flynn, B. S., Worden, J. K., Secker-Walker, R. H., Badger, G. J., Geller, B. M., & Costanza, M. C. (1992). Prevention of cigarette smoking through mass media intervention and school programs. *American Journal of Public Health, 82,* 827–834.

Foege, W. (1983). The national pattern of AIDS. In K. M. Cahill (Ed.), *The AIDS epidemic* (pp. 1–17). New York: St. Martin's Press.

Folkman, S., Chesney, M., Collette, L., Boccellari, A., Cooke, M. (1996). Post-bereavement depressive mood and its prebereavement predictors in HIV+ and HIV– gay men. *Journal of Personality and Social Psychology, 70,* 336–348.

Folkman, S., Chesney, M. A., Cooke, M., Boccellari, A., & Collette, L. (1994). Caregiver burden in HIV-positive and HIV-negative partners of men with AIDS. *Journal of Consulting and Clinical Psychology, 62,* 746–756.

Folkman, S., & Lazarus, R. S. (1980). An analysis of coping in a middle-aged community sample. *Journal of Health and Social Behavior, 21,* 219–239.

Folkman, S., & Lazarus, R. S. (1985). If it changes it must be a process: Study of emotion and coping during three stages of a college examination. *Journal of Personality and Social Psychology, 48,* 150–170.

Folkman, S., Lazarus, R. S., Dunkel-Schetter, C., DeLongis, A., & Gruen, R. J. (1986). Dynamics of a stressful encounter: Cognitive appraisal, coping, and encounter outcomes. *Journal of Personality and Social Psychology, 50,* 992–1003.

Folsom, A. R., Hughes, J. R., Buehler, J., Mittlemark, M. B., Jacobs, D. R., Jr., & Grimm, R. H., Jr. (1985). Do Type A men drink more frequently than Type B men? Findings in the Multiple Risk Factor Intervention Trial (MRFIT) *Journal of Behavioral Medicine, 8,* 227–236.

Folsom, A. R., Kaye, S. A., Sellers, T. A., Hong, C. P., Cerhan, J. D., Potter, J. D., & Prineas, R. J. (1993). Body fat distribution and 5-year risk of death in older women. *Journal of the American Medical Association, 269,* 483–487.

Fordyce, W. E. (1988). Pain and suffering: A reappraisal. *American Psychologist, 43,* 276–283.

Fordyce, W. E., Brockway, J. A., Bergman, J. A., & Spengler, D. (1986). Acute back pain: A control-group comparison of behavioral vs. traditional management methods. *Journal of Behavioral Medicine, 9,* 127–140.

Forsythe, C. J., & Compas, B. E. (1987). Interaction of coping appraisals of stressful events and coping: Testing the goodness of fit hypothesis. *Cognitive Therapy and Research, 11,* 473–485.

Fox, R. C., & Swazey, J. P. (1992). *Spare parts: Organ replacement in American society.* New York: Oxford University Press.

Frank, A. J. M., Moll, J. M. H., & Hort, J. F. (1982). A comparison of three ways of measuring pain. *Rheumatology and Rehabilitation, 21,* 211–217.

Frank, R. G., Gluck, J. P., & Buckelew, S. P. (1990). Rehabilitation: Psychology's greatest opportunity. *American Psychologist, 45,* 757–761.

Frankenhaeuser, M. (1975). Sympathetic-adrenomedullary activity behavior and the psychosocial environment. In P. H. Venables & M. J. Christie (Eds.), *Research in psychophysiology* (pp. 71–94). New York: Wiley.

Frankenhaeuser, M. (1978). Psychoneuroendocrine approaches to the study of emotion as related to stress and coping. *Nebraska Symposium on Motivation, 26,* 123–162.

Franklin, G. M., & Nelson, L. M. (1993). Chronic neurologic disorders. In R. C. Brownson, P. L., Remington, & J. R. Davis (Eds.), *Chronic disease epidemiology and control* (pp. 307–335). Washington, DC: American Public Health Association.

Frasure-Smith, N., & Prince, R. (1989). Long-term follow-up of the Ischemic Heart Disease Life Stress Monitoring Program. *Psychosomatic Medicine, 51,* 485–513.

Frederickson, B. L., Roberts, T.-A., Noll, S. M., Quinn, D. M., & Twenge, J. M. (1998). That swimsuit becomes you: Sex differences in objectification, restrained eating, and math performance. *Journal of Personality and Social Psychology, 75,* 269–284.

Freeman, M. A., Hennessy, E. V., & Marzullo, D. M. (2001). Defensive evaluation of anti-smoking messages among college-age smokers: The role of possible selves. *Health Psychology, 20,* 424–433.

Freidson, E. (1961). Patients' views of medical practice. New York: Russell Sage.

Freimuth, V. S., Hammond, S. L., Edgar, T., & Monohan, J. L. (1990). Reaching those at risk: A content-analytic study of AIDS PSAs. *Communication Research, 17,* 775–791.

French, S. A., Perry, C. L., Leon, G. R., & Fulkerson, J. A. (1994). Weight concerns, dieting behavior and smoking initiation among adolescent: A prospective study. *American Journal of Public Health, 84,* 1818–1820.

Freud, S. (1963). Dora: An analysis of a case of hysteria. New York: Macmillan.

Fried, L. P., Kronmal, R. A., Newman, A. B., Bild, D. E., Mittelmark, M. B., Polak, J. F., Robbins, J. A., & Gardin, J. M. (1998). Risk factors for 5-year mortality in older adults: The Cardiovascular Health Study. *Journal of the American Medical Association, 279,* 585–592.

Friedman, H. S. (1992). Hostility, coping, and health. Washington, DC: American Psychological Association.

Friedman, H. S., & Booth-Kewley, S. (1987a). The "disease-prone personality": A meta-analytic view of the construct. *American Psychologist, 42,* 539–555.

Friedman, H. S., & Booth-Kewley, S. (1987b). Personality, Type A behavior, and coronary heart disease: The role of emotional expression. *Journal of Personality and Social Psychology, 53,* 783–792.

Friedman, H. S., Hall, J. A., & Harris, M. J. (1985). Type A behavior, nonverbal expressive style, and health. *Journal of Personality and Social Psychology, 48,* 1299–1315.

Friedman, H. S., Tucker, J. S., Tomlinson-Keasey, C., Schwartz, J. E., Wingard, D. L., & Criqui, M. H. (1993). Does childhood personality predict longevity? *Journal of Personality and Social Psychology, 65,* 176–185.

Friedman, M., & Rosenman, R. H. (1959). Association of specific overt pattern with blood and cardiovascular findings. *Journal of the American Medical Association, 169,* 1286–1296.

Friedman, M., Thoresen, C., Gill, J., et al. (1986). Alteration of Type A behavior and its effects on cardiac recurrences in post myocardial infarction patients: Summary results of the recurrent coronary prevention project. *American Heart Journal, 112,* 653–665.

Friedman, M. A., & Brownell, K. D. (1995). Psychological correlates of obesity: Moving to the next research generation. *Psychological Bulletin, 117,* 3–20.

Friedman, R., Sobel, D., Myers, P., Caudill, M., & Benson, H. (1995). Behavioral medicine, clinical health psychology, and cost offset. *Health Psychology, 14,* 509–518.

Friedrich, M. J. (2000). More healthy people in the 21st century? *Journal of the American Medical Association, 283,* 37–38.

Fries, J. F. (1998). Reducing the need and demand for medical services. *Psychosomatic Medicine, 60,* 140–142.

Fries, J. F., Koop, C. E., Beadle, C. E., Cooper, T. P., England, M. J., Greaves, R. F., Sokolov, J. J., & Wright, D. (1993). Reducing health care costs by reducing the need and demand for medical services. The Health Project Consortium. *New England Journal of Medicine, 329,* 321–325.

Frost, H., Lamb, S., Moffett, J., Fairbank, J., & Moser, J. (1998). A fitness programme for patients with chronic low-back pain: 2 year follow-up of a randomized controlled trial. *Pain, 75,* 273–279.

Fuchs, C. S., Stampfer, M. J., Colditz, C. A., Giovannucci, E. L., Manson, J. E., Kawachi, I., Hunter, D. J., Hankinson, S. E., Hennekens, D. H., & Rosner, B. (1995). Alcohol consumption and mortality among women. *New England Journal of Medicine, 332,* 1245–1250.

Fuchs, V. R., & Hahn, J. S. (1990). How does Canada do it? A comparison of expenditures for physicians' services in the United States and Canada. *New England Journal of Medicine, 323,* 884–890.

Funk, S. C., & Houston, B. K. (1987). A critical analysis of the Hardiness scale's validity and utility. *Journal of Personality and Social Psychology, 53,* 572–578.

Gallagher, E. J., Viscoli, C. M., & Horwitz, R. I. (1993). The relationship of treatment adherence to the risk of death after myocardial infarction in women. *Journal of the American Medical Association, 270,* 742–743.

Gallant, J. E., & Block, D. S. (1998). Adherence to antiretroviral regimens in HIV-infected patients: Results of a survey among physicians and patients. *Journal of the International Association of Physicians in AIDS Care, 4,* 32–35.

Galligan, R. F., & Terry, D. J. (1993). Romantic ideals, fear of negative implications, and the practice of safe sex. *Journal of Applied Social Psychology, 23,* 1685–1711.

Gallup, G. G., & Suarez , S. D. (1985). Animal research versus the care and maintenance of pets: The names have been changed but the results remain the same. *American Psychologist, 45,* 1104–1111.

Ganzini, L., Harvath, T. A., Jackson, A., Goy, E. R., Miller, L. L., & Delorit, M. (2002). Experiences of Oregon nurses and social workers with hospice patients who requested assistance with suicide. *New England Journal of Medicine, 347,* 582–588.

Garfinkel, P. E., & Garner, D. M. (1984). Bulimia in anorexia nervosa. In R. C. Hawkins, W. J. Fremouw, & P. F. Clement (Eds.), *The binge–purge syndrome: Diagnosis, treatment and research* (pp. 27–46). New York: Springer.

Garner, D. M., & Garfinkel, P. E. (1980). Sociocultural factors in the development of anorexia nervosa. *Psychological Medicine, 10,* 647–656.

Garner, D. M., Garfinkel, P. E., & Bemis, K. M. (1982). A multidimensional psychotherapy for anorexia nervosa. *International Journal of Eating Disorders, 1,* 3–46.

Garner, D. M., Garfinkel, P. E., Schwartz, D., & Thompson, M. (1980). Cultural expectations of thinness in women. *Psychological Reports, 47,* 483–491.

Garner, D. M., Olmstead, M. A., & Polivy, J. (1983). Development and validation of a multidimensional eating disorder inventory for anorexia nervosa and bulimia. *International Journal of Eating Disorders, 2,* 12–34.

Garner, D. M., Rockert, W., Davis, R., Garner, M.V., Olmsted, M. P., & Eagle, M. (1993). A comparison between cognitive-behavioral and supportive-expressive therapy for bulimia nervosa. *American Journal of Psychiatry, 150,* 37–46.

Garofalo, J. P., & Polatin, P. (1999). Low back pain: An epidemic in industrialized countries. In R. J. Gatchel & D. C. Turk (Eds.), *Psychosocial factors in pain: Critical perspectives* (pp. 164–174). New York: Guilford.

Garrity, T. F. (1973). Vocational adjustment after first myocardial infarction: Comparative assessment of several variables suggested in the literature. *Social Science and Medicine, 7,* 705–717.

Gatchel, R. J. (1980). Effectiveness of procedures for reducing dental fear: Group-administered desensitization and group education and discussion. *Journal of the American Dental Association, 101,* 634–637.

Gatchel, R. J. (1986). Impact of a video taped fear reduction program on people who avoid dental treatment. *Journal of the American Dental Association, 123,* 37–41.

Gauthier, J., Cote, G., & French, D. (1994). The role of home practice in the thermal biofeedback treatment of migraine headache. *Journal of Consulting and Clinical Psychology, 62,* 180–184.

Gauvin, L., Rejeski, W. J., & Norris, J. L. (1996). The impact of acute physical activity on feeling states and affect of women in a naturalistic setting. *Health Psychology, 15,* 391–397.

Gauvin, L., Rejeski, W. J., & Reboussin, B. A. (2000). Contributions of acute bouts of vigorous physical activity to explaining diurnal variations in feeling states in active, middle-aged women. *Health Psychology, 19,* 365–375.

Gaziano, J. M., Buring, J. E., Breslow, J. L., Goldhaber, S. Z., Rosner, B., Van-Denburgh, M., Willett, W., & Hennekens, C. H. (1993). Moderate alcohol intake, increased levels of high-density lipoprotein and its subfractions, and decreased risk of myocardial infarction. *New England Journal of Medicine, 329,* 1829–1834.

Gedaly-Duff, V., & Ziebarth, D. (1994). Mothers' management of adenoid-tonsillectomy pain in 4- to 8-year-olds: A preliminary study. *Pain, 57,* 293–299.

Gentry, W. D. (1984). Behavioral medicine: A new research paradigm. In W. D. Gentry (Ed.), *Handbook of behavioral medicine* (pp. 1–13). New York: Guilford.

George, L. K., Larson, D. B., Koenig, H. G., & McCullough, M. E. (2000). Spirituality and health: What we know, what we need to know. *Journal of Social and Clinical Psychology, 19,* 102–116.

Gerin, W., Pieper, C., Levy, R., & Pickering, T. G. (1992). Social support in social interaction: A moderator of cardiovascular reactivity. *Psychosomatic Medicine, 54,* 324–336.

Geronimus, A. T., Bound, J., Waidmann, T. A., Hillemeier, M. M., & Burns, P. B. (1996). Excess mortality among blacks and whites in the United States. *New England Journal of Medicine, 335,* 1552–1558.

Gerrard, M., Gibbons, F. X., Benthin, A. C., & Hessling, R. M. (1996). A longitudinal study of the reciprocal nature of risk behaviors and cognitions in adolescents: What you do shapes what you think, and vice versa. *Health Psychology, 15,* 344–354.

Gidron, Y., Davidson, K., & Bata, I. (1999). The short-term effects of a hostility-reduction intervention on male coronary heart disease patients. *Health Psychology, 18,* 416–420.

Gil, K. M., Carson, J. W., Sedway, J. A., Porter, L. S., Schaeffer, J. J. W., & Orringer, E. (2000). Follow-up of coping skills training in adults with sickle cell disease: Analysis of daily pain and coping practice diaries. *Health Psychology, 19,* 85–90.

Gil, K. M., Keefe, F. J., Sampson, H. A., McCaskill, C. C., Rodin, J., & Crisson, J. E. (1988). Direct observation of scratching behavior in children with atopic dermatitis. *Behavior Therapy, 19,* 213–227.

Gil, K. M., Williams, D. A., Keefe, F. J., & Beckham, J. C. (1990). The relationship of negative thoughts to pain and psychological distress. *Behavior Therapy, 21,* 349–362.

Gil, K. M., Wilson, J. J., Edens, J. L., Webster, A. A., Abrams, M. A., Orringer, E., Grant, M., Clark, W. C., & Janal, M. N. (1996). Effects of cognitive coping skills training on coping strategies and experimental pain sensitivity in African American adults with sickle cell disease. *Health Psychology, 15,* 3–10.

Gilchrist, A. (1942). *Life of William Blake.* London: JM Dent.

Gilligan, C. (1982). *In a different voice.* Cambridge, MA: Harvard University Press.

Ginsberg, R. J., Kris, M. G., & Armstrong, J. G. (1993). Cancer of the lung. In V. T. DeVita, Jr., S. Hellman, & S. A. Rosenberg (Eds.), *Cancer: Principles and practice of oncology* (pp. 673–758). Philadelphia: Lippincott.

Gintner, G., Rectanus, E., Accord, K., & Parker, B. (1987). Parental history of hypertension and screening attendance: Effects of wellness appeal versus threat appeal. *Health Psychology, 6,* 431–444.

Glaser, B., & Strauss, A. (1965). Awareness of dying. Chicago: Aldine.

Glaser, R., & Kiecolt-Glaser, J. K. (1994). Handbook of stress and immunity. San Diego, CA: Academic Press.

Glaser, R., Thorne, B. E., Tarr, K. L., Kiecolt-

Glaser, J. K., & D'Ambrosio, S. M. (1985). Effects of stress on methyltransferase synthesis: An important DNA repair enzyme. *Health Psychology, 4,* 403–412.

Glass, D. C., Krakoff, L. R., Contrada, R., Hilton, W. F., Kehoe, K., Mannucci, E. G., Collins, C., Snow, B., & Elting, E. (1980). Effect of harassment and competition upon cardiovascular and plasma catecholamine responses in Type A and Type B individuals. *Psychophysiology, 17,* 453–463.

Glenn, S. W., Parsons, O. A., & Stevens, L. (1989). Effects of alcohol abuse and familial alcoholism on physical health in men and women. *Health Psychology, 8,* 325–341.

Glinder, J. G., & Compas, B. E. (1999). Self-blame attributions in women with newly diagnosed breast cancer: A prospective study of psychological adjustment. *Health Psychology, 18,* 475–481.

Goffman, E. (1961). *Asylums.* Garden City, NY: Doubleday.

Goldman, M. S., Del Boca, F. K., & Darkes, J. (1999). Alcohol expectancy theory: The application of cognitive neuroscience. In K. E. Leonard & H. T. Blane (Eds.), *Psychological theories of drinking and alcoholism* (2nd ed., pp. 203–246). New York: Guilford.

Goldner, E. M., & Birmingham, C. L. (1994). Anorexia nervosa: Methods of treatment. In L. Alexander-Mott & D. B. Lumsden (Eds.), *Understanding eating disorders: Anorexia nervosa, bulimia nervosa, and obesity* (pp. 135–157). Washington, DC: Taylor & Francis.

Goldring, A. B., Taylor, S. E., Kemeny, M. E., & Anton, P. A. (2002). Impact of health beliefs, quality of life, and the physician–patient relationship on the treatment intentions of inflammatory bowel disease patients. *Health Psychology, 21,* 219–228.

Goldstein, A. O., Sobel, R. A., & Newman, G. R. (1999). Tobacco and alcohol use in G-rated children's animated films. *Journal of the American Medical Association, 281,* 1131–1136.

Gomel, M., Oldenburg, B., Lemon, J., Owen, N., & Westbrook, F. (1993). Pilot study of the effects of a workplace smoking ban on indices of smoking, cigarette craving, stress and other health behaviours. *Psychology and Health, 8,* 223–229.

Goodkin, K., Blaney, N. T., Feaster, D., Fletcher, M. A., Baun, M. K., Montero-Atienza, E., Klimas, N. G., Millon, C., Szapocznik, J., & Eisdorfer, C. (1992). Active coping style is associated with natural killer cell cytotoxicity in asymptomatic HIV-1 seropositive

homosexual men. *Journal of Psychosomatic Research, 36,* 635–650.

Goodwin, C. J. (1998). Research in psychology: Methods and design (2nd ed.). New York: Wiley.

Goodwin, J. S., Hunt, W. C., Key, C. R., & Samet, J. M. (1987). The effect of marital status on stage, treatment, and survival of cancer patients. *Journal of the American Medical Association, 258,* 3125–3130.

Goodwin, M. P., & Roscoe, B. (1988). AIDS: Students' knowledge and attitudes at a Midwestern university. *Journal of American College Health, 36,* 214–222.

Goodwin, P. J., Leszcz, M., Ennis, M., Koopmans, J., Vincent, L., Guther, H., Drysdale, E., Hundleby, M., Chocinou, H. M., Navaro, M., Speca, M., & Hunter, J. (2001). The effect of group psychosocial support on survival in metastatic breast cancer. *New England Journal of Medicine, 345,* 1719–1726.

Gordon, C. M., & Carey, M. P. (1996). Alcohol's effects on requisites for sexual risk reduction in men: An initial experimental investigation. *Health Psychology, 15,* 56–60.

Gordon, C. M., Carey, M. P., & Carey, K. B. (1997). Effects of a drinking event on behavioral skills and condom attitudes in men: Implications for HIV risk from a controlled experiment. *Health Psychology, 16,* 490–495.

Gornick, M. E., Eggers, P. W., Reilly, T. W., Mentnech, R. M., Fitterman, L. K., Kucken, L. E., Vladeck, B. .C. (1996). Effects of race and income on mortality and use of services among medicare beneficiaries. *New England Journal of Medicine, 335,* 791–799.

Gorsuch, R. L. (1995). Religious aspects of substance abuse and recovery. *Journal of Social Issues, 51,* 65–83.

Gortmaker, S. L., Must, A., Perrin, J. M., Sobol, A. M., & Dietz, W. H. (1993). Social and economic consequences of overweight in adolescence and young adulthood. *New England Journal of Medicine, 329,* 1008–1012.

Gottlieb, B. H. (1985). Social support and community mental health. In S. Cohen & S. L. Syme (Eds.), *Social support and health* (pp. 303–326). Orlando, FL: Academic Press.

Gould, J. B., Davey, B., & Stafford, R. (1989). Socioeconomic differences in rates of cesearean section. *New England Journal of Medicine, 321,* 233–239.

Gracely, R. H., Dubner, R., Deeter, W. R., & Wolskee, P. J. (1985). Clinicians' expectations influence placebo analgesia. *Lancet, 1,* 43.

Grady, K. E., Lemkau, J. P., McVay, J. M., & Reisine, S. T. (1992). The importance of physician encouragement in breast cancer screening of older women. *Preventive Medicine, 21,* 766–780.

Graham, J. W., Marks, G., & Hansen, W. B. (1991). Social influence processes affecting adolescent substance use. *Journal of Applied Psychology, 76,* 291–298.

Gram, I. T., Lund, E., & Slenker, S. E. (1990). Quality of life following a false positive mammogram. *British Journal of Cancer, 62,* 1018–1022.

Gramling, S. E., Clawson, E. P., & McDonald, M. K. (1996). Perceptual and cognitive abnormality model of hyopchondriasis: Amplification and physiological reactivity in women. *Psychosomatic Medicine, 58,* 423–431.

Greeley, J., & Oei, T. (1999). Alcohol and tension reduction. In K. E. Leonard & H. T. Blane (Eds.), *Psychological theories of drinking and alcoholism* (2nd ed., pp. 14–53). New York: Guilford.

Green, J. M. (1993). "Who is unhappy after childbirth?": Antenatal and intrapartum correlates from a prospective study. *Journal of Reproductive and Infant Psychology, 8,* 175–183.

Greenberg, M. R., & Schneider, D. (1994). Violence in American cities: Young Black males is the answer, but what was the question? *Social Science and Medicine, 39,* 179–187.

Greendale, G. A., et al. (1995). Lifetime leisure exercise and osteoporosis: The Rancho Bernardo Study. *American Journal of Epidemiology, 141,* 951–959.

Greenfield, S., & Kaplan, S. (1985). Expanding patient involvment in care: Effects on patient outcomes. *Annals of Internal Medicine, 102,* 520–528.

Greenfield, S., Kaplan, S. H., Ware, J. E., Jr., Yano, E. M., & Frank, H. J. (1988). Patients' participation in medical care: Effects on blood sugar control and quality of life in diabetes. *Journal of General Internal Medicine, 3,* 448–457.

Greenspan, A. M, Kay, H. R., Berger, B. C., Greenberg, R. M., Greenspon, A. J., & Gaughan M. J. (1988). Incidence of unwarranted implementation of permanent cardiac pacemakers in a large medical population. *New England Journal of Medicine, 318,* 158–163.

Greer, S. (1991). Psychological response to cancer and survival. *Psychological Medicine, 21,* 43–49.

Grilo, C. M., Brownell, K. D., & Stunkard, A. J. (1993). The metabolic and psychological importance of exercise in weight control. In

A. J. Stunkard & T. A. Wadden (Eds.), *Obesity: Theory and therapy* (2nd ed., pp. 253–273). New York: Raven.

Grilo, C. M., & Pogue-Geile, M. (1991). The nature of environmental influences in weight and obesity: A behavior genetic analysis. *Psychological Bulletin, 110,* 520–537.

Grilo, C. M., Shiffman, S., & Wing, R. R. (1989). Relapse crises and coping among dieters. *Journal of Consulting and Clinical Psychology, 57,* 488–495.

Grimby, A. (1993). Bereavement among elderly people: Grief reactions, post-bereavement hallucinations and quality of life. *Acta Psychiatrica Scandinavica, 87,* 72–80.

Grimley, D. M., Riley, G. E., Bellis, J. M., & Prochaska, J. O. (1993). Assessing the stages of change and decision-making for contraceptive use for the prevention of pregnancy, sexually transmitted diseases, and acquired immunodeficiency syndrome. *Health Education Quarterly, 20,* 455–470.

Grissett, N. I., & Norvell, N. K. (1992). Perceived social support, social skills, and quality of relationships in bulimic women. *Journal of Consulting and Clinical Psychology, 60,* 293–299.

Grob, G. N. (1983). Disease and environment in American history. In D. Mechanic (Ed.), *Handbook of health, health care, and the health professions* (pp. 3–22). New York: Free Press.

Gross, A. M., Stern, R. M., Levin, R. B., Dale, J., & Wojnilower, D. A. (1983). The effect of mother–child separation on the behavior of children experiencing a diagnostic procedure. *Journal of Consulting and Clinical Psychology, 51,* 783–785.

Gross, J. J., & Levenson, R. W. (1997). Hiding feelings: The acute effects of inhibiting negative and positive emotion. *Journal of Abnormal Psychology, 106,* 95–103.

Grossman, D. C., Krieger, J W., Sugarman, J. R., & Forquera, R. A. (1994). Health status of urban American Indians and Alaska Natives: A population-based study. *Journal of the American Medical Association, 271,* 845–850.

Grube, J. W., & Wallack, L. (1994). Television beer advertising and drinking knowledge, beliefs, and intentions among schoolchildren. *American Journal of Public Health, 84,* 254–259.

Grunberg, N. E., Brown, K. J., & Klein, L. C. (1997). Tobacco smoking. In A. Baum, S. Newman, J. Weinman, R. West, & C. McManus (Eds.), *Cambridge handbook of psychology, health and medicine* (pp. 606–611). Cambridge, England: Cambridge University Press.

Grunberg, N. E., & Straub, R. O. (1992). The role of gender and taste class in the effects of stress on eating. *Health Psychology, 11,* 97–100.

Grunberg, N. E., Winders, S. E., & Wewers, M. E. (1991). Gender differences in tobacco use. *Health Psychology, 10,* 143–153.

Gureje, O., Von Korff, M., Simon, G. E., & Gater, R. (1998). Persistent pain and well-being: A World Health Organization study in primary care. *Journal of the American Medical Association, 280,* 147–151.

Guttmacher, S., Lieberman, L., Wards, D., Freudenberg, N., Radosh, A., & Des Jarlais, D. (1997). Condom availability in New York City public high schools: Relationships to condom use and sexual behavior. *American Journal of Public Health, 87,* 1427–1433.

Hadlow, J., & Pitts, M. (1991). The understanding of common health terms by doctors, nurses, and patients. *Social Science and Medicine, 32,* 193–196.

Haffner, S. M. (1998). Epidemiology of type 2 diabetes: Risk factors. *Diabetes Care, 21,* C3–6.

Hagedoorn, M., Kuijer, R. G., Buunk, B. P., DeJong, G. M., Wobbes, T., & Sanderman, R. (2000). Marital satisfaction in patients with cancer: Does support from intimate partners benefit those who need it the most? *Health Psychology, 19,* 274–382.

Hall, J. A., & Dornan, M. C. (1988a). Meta-analysis of satisfaction with medical care: Description of research done in and analysis of overall satisafction levels. *Social Science and Medicine, 26,* 637–644.

Hall, J. A., & Dornan, M. C. (1988b). What patients like about their medical care and how often they are asked: A meta-analysis of the satisfaction literature. *Social Science and Medicine, 27,* 935–939.

Hall, J. A., Epstein, A. M., DeCiantis, M. L., & McNeil, B. J. (1993). Physicians' liking for their patients: More evidence for the role of affect in medical care. *Health Psychology, 12,* 140–146.

Hall, J. A., Irish, J. T., Roter, D. L., Ehrlich, C. M., & Miller, L. H. (1994). Gender in medical encounters: An analysis of physician and patient communication in a primary care setting. *Health Psychology, 13,* 384–392.

Hall, J. A., Roter, D. L., & Katz, N. R. (1988). Meta-analysis of correlates of provider behavior in medical encounters. *Medical Care, 26,* 657–675.

Halpern, C. T., Udry, J. R., Campbell, B., & Suchindran, C. (1999). Effects of body fat on weight concerns, dieting, and sexual activity: A longitudinal analysis of Black and White adolescent girls. *Developmental Psychology, 35,* 721–736.

Halpern, M. (1994). Effect of smoking characteristics on cognitive dissonance in current and former smokers. *Addictive Behaviors, 19,* 209–217.

Hammer, J. C., Fisher, J. D., Fitzgerald, J. F., & Fisher, W. A. (1996). When two heads aren't better than one: AIDS risk behavior in college-age couples. *Journal of Applied Social Psychology, 26,* 375–397.

Hanak, M., & Scott, A. (1993). Spinal cord injury: An illustrated guide for health care professionals (2nd ed.). New York: Springer.

Hansen, W. B., Raynor, A. E., & Wolkenstein, B. H. (1991). Perceived personal immunity to the consequences of drinking alcohol: The relationship between behavior and perception. *Journal of Behavioral Medicine, 14,* 205–224.

Harrell, E. H., Kelly, K., & Stutts, W. A. (1996). Situational determinants of correlations between serum cortisol and self-reported stress measures. *Psychology: A Journal of Human Behavior, 33,* 22–25.

Harris, J. R. (1992). Breast cancer (First of three parts). *New England Journal of Medicine, 327,* 319–328.

Hartmann, L. C., Schaid, D. J., Woods, J. E., Crotty, T. P., Myers, J. L., Arnold, P. G., Petty, P. M., Sellers, T. A., Johnson, J. L., Mcdonnell, S. K., Frost, M. H., & Jenkins, R. B. (1999). Efficacy of bilateral prophylactic mastectomy in women with a family history of breast cancer. *New England Journal of Medicine, 340,* 77–84.

Harvey, J. H., & Hansen, A. M. (2000). Loss and bereavement in close romantic relationships. In J. H. Harvey and A. M. Hansen (Eds.), *Close Relationships* (pp. 359–370). Thousand Oaks, CA: Sage.

Hashim, S., & Van Itallie, T. (1965). Studies in normal and obese subjects with a monitored food dispensing device. *Annals of the New York Academy of Science, 131,* 654–661.

Hasish, I., Hai, H. K., Harvey, W., Feinmann, C., & Harris, M. (1988). Reduction of postoperative pain and swelling by ultrasound treatment: A placebo effect. *Pain, 33,* 303–311.

Hatchett, L., Friend, R., Symister, P., & Wadhwa, N. (1997). Interpersonal expectations, social support, and adjustment to chronic illness. *Journal of Personality and Social Psychology, 73,* 560–573.

Havik, O. E., & Maeland, J. G. (1988). Verbal denial and outcome in myocardial infarction patients. *Journal of Psychosomatic Research, 32,* 145–157.

Haynes, G. S., Levine, S., Scotch, N., Feinleib, M., & Kanner, W. B. (1978). The relationship of psychosocial factors to coronary heart disease in the Framingham study. *American Journal of Epidemiology, 107,* 362–383.

Haynes, R. B., McKibbon, K. A., & Kanani, R. (1996). Systematic review of randomized trials of interventions to assist patients to follow prescriptions for medications. *Lancet, 348,* 383–386.

Hays, R. B., Turner, H., & Coates, T. J. (1992). Social support, AIDS-related symptoms, and depression among gay men. *Journal of Consulting and Clinical Psychology, 60,* 463–469.

Hays, R. D., Kravitz, R. L., Mazel, R. M., Sherbourne, C. D., DiMatteo, M. R., Rogers, W. H., & Greenfield, S. (1994). The impact of patient adherence on health outcomes for patients with chronic disease in the Medical Outcomes Study. *Journal of Behavioral Medicine, 17,* 347–360.

He, L. F. (1987). Involvement of endogenous opiod peptides in acupuncture analgesia. *Pain, 31,* 99–121.

Heath, A. C., & Madden, P. G. (1995). Genetic influences on smoking behavior. In J. R. Turner, L. R. Cardon, & J. K. Hewitt (Eds.), *Behavior genetic approaches in behavioral medicine* (pp. 37–48). New York: Plenum.

Heath, A. C., & Martin, N. G. (1993). Genetic models for the natural history of smoking: Evidence for a genetic influence on smoking persistence. *Addictive Behaviors, 18,* 19–34.

Heatherton, T. F., Striepe, M., & Wittenberg, L. (1998). Emotional distress and disinhibited eating: The role of stress. *Personality and Social Psychology Bulletin, 24,* 301–313.

Heckman, T. D., Kelly, J. A., & Somlai, A. M. (1998). Predictors of continued high-risk sexual behavior in a community sample of persons living with HIV/AIDS. *AIDS and Behavior, 2,* 127–135.

Hediger, M. L., Overpeck, M. D., Kuczmarski, R. J., & Ruan, W. J. (2001). Association between infant breastfeeding and overweight in young children. *Journal of the American Medical Association, 285,* 2453–2460.

Hegel, M. T., Ayllon, T., Thiel, G., & Oulton, B. (1992). Improving adherence to fluid restrictions in male hemodialysis patients: A comparison of cognitive and behavioral approaches. *Health Psychology, 11,* 324–330.

Heinberg, L. J., & Thompson, J. K. (1995). Body image and televised images of thinness and attractiveness: A controlled laboratory experiment. *Journal of Social and Clinical Psychology, 14,* 325–338.

Heishman, S. J., Kozlowski, L. T., & Henningfield, J. E. (1997). Nicotine addiction: Implications for public health policy. *Journal of Social Issues, 53,* 13–33.

Helgeson, V. S. (1991). The effects of masculinity and social support on recovery from myocardial infarction. *Psychosomatic Medicine, 53,* 621–633.

Helgeson, V. S. (1992). Moderators of the relation between perceived control and adjustment to chronic illness. *Journal of Personality and Social Psychology, 63,* 652–666.

Helgeson, V. S., & Cohen, S. (1996). Social support and adjustment to cancer: Reconciling descriptive, correlational, and intervention research. *Health Psychology, 15,* 135–148.

Helgeson, V. S., Cohen, S., & Fritz, H. L. (1998). Social ties and cancer. In J. C. Holland (Ed.), *Psychooncology* (pp. 99–109). New York: Oxford University Press.

Helgeson, V. S., Cohen, S., Schulz, R., & Yasko, J. (1999). Education and peer discussion group interventions and adjustment to breast cancer. *Archives of General Psychiatry, 56,* 340–347.

Helgeson, V. S., Cohen, S., Schulz, R., & Yasko, J. (2000). Group support interventions for women with breast cancer: Who benefits from what? *Health Psychology, 19,* 107–114.

Helgeson, V. S., Cohen, S., Schulz, R., & Yasko, J. (2001). Long-term effects of educational and peer discussion group interventions on adjustment to breast cancer. *Health Psychology, 20,* 387–392.

Helmrich, S. P., Ragland, D. R., Leung, R. W., & Paffenbarger, R. S. (1991). Physical activity and reduced occurrence of non-insulin-dependent diabetes mellitus. *New England Journal of Medicine, 325,* 147–152.

Helms, J. M. (1987). Acupuncture for the management of primary dysmenorrhea. *Obstetrics and Gynecology, 69,* 51–56.

Helsing, K., & Szklo, M. (1981). Mortality after bereavement. *American Journal of Epidemiology, 114,* 41–52.

Hemenover, S. H. (2001). Self-reported processing bias and naturally occurring mood: Mediators between personality and stress appraisals. *Personality and Social Psychology Bulletin, 27,* 387–394.

Hemenover, S. H., & Dienstbier, R. A. (1996). Prediction of stress appraisals from mastery, extraversion, neuroticism, and general appraisal tendencies. *Motivation and Emotion, 20,* 299–318.

Henifin, M. S. (1993). New reproductive technologies: Equity and access to reproductive health care. *Journal of Social Issues, 49,* 62–74.

Henry, J. P. (1990). The arousal of emotions: Hormones, behavior, and health. *Advances, 6,* 59–62.

Herman, C. P., & Mack, D. (1975). Restrained and unrestrained eating. *Journal of Personality, 43,* 647–660.

Herman, C. P., & Polivy, J. (1983). A boundary model for the regulation of eating. *Psychiatric Annals, 13,* 918–927.

Herman, C. P., & Polivy, J. (1984). A boundary model for the regulation of eating. In A. J. Stunkard & E. Stellar (Eds.), *Eating and its disorders* (pp. 141–156). New York: Raven.

Herzog, T. A., Abrams, D. B., Emmons, K. M., Linnan, L. A., & Shadel, W. G. (1999). Do processes of change predict smoking stage movements? A prospective analysis of the transtheoretical model. *Health Psychology, 18,* 369–375.

Heuch, I., Kvale, G., Jacobsen, B. K., & Bjelke, E. (1983). Use of alcohol, tobacco and coffee, and risk of pancreatic cancer. *British Journal of Cancer, 48,* 637–643.

Hewitt, J. K. (1997). Behavior genetics and eating disorders. *Psychopharmacology, 33,* 355–358.

Hewitt, J. L., & Flett, G. L. (1996). Personality traits and the coping process. In M. Zeidner & N. S. Endler (Eds.), *Handbook of coping: Theory, research, applications* (pp. 410–433). New York: Wiley.

Hewitt, P. L., Flett, G. L., & Mosher, S. W. (1992). The Perceived Stress Scale: Factor structure and relation to depression symptoms in a psychiatric sample. *Journal of Psychopathology and Behavioral Assessment, 14,* 247–257.

Higbee, K. L. (1969). Fifteen years of fear arousal: Research on threat appeals: 1953–1966. *Psychological Bulletin, 72,* 426–444.

Hilgard, E. R. (1975). The alleviation of pain by hypnosis. *Pain, 1,* 213–231.

Hilgard, E. R., & Hilgard, J. R. (1983). Hypnosis in the relief of pain. Los Altos, CA: Kaufman.

Hill, A. J., Boudreau, F., Amyot, E., Dery, D., & Godin, G. (1997). Predicting the stages of smoking acquisition according to the theory of planned behavior. *Journal of Adolescent Health, 21,* 107–115.

Hill, J., & Peters, J. (1998). Environmental contributions to the obesity epidemic. *Science, 280,* 1371–1374.

Hillhouse, J. J., Stair, A. W., III, & Adler, C. M. (1996). Predictors of sunbathing and sunscreen use in college undergraduates. *Journal of Behavioral Medicine, 19,* 543–562.

Hinton, J. (1979). Comparison of places and policies for terminal care. *Lancet, 1,* 29–32.

Ho, D. D. (1995). Time to hit HIV, early and hard. *New England Journal of Medicine, 333,* 450–451.

Ho, D. D. (1996). Therapy of HIV infections: Problems and prospects. *Bulletin of the New York Academy of Medicine, 73,* 37–45.

Hobfoll, S. E., Jackson, A. P., Lavin, J., Britton, P. J., & Shepherd, J. B. (1994). Reducing inner-city women's AIDS risk activities: A study of single, pregnant women. *Health Psychology, 13,* 397–405.

Hodge, A. M., & Zimmet, P. Z. (1994). The epidemiology of obesity. In I.D. Caterson (Ed.), *Bailliere's clinical endocrinology and metabolism: International practice and research* (pp. 577–599). London: Bailliere Tindall.

Hodgins, D. C., El-Guebaly, N., & Armstrong, S. (1995). Propsective and retrospective reports of mood states before relapse to substance abuse. *Journal of Consulting and Clinical Psychology, 63,* 400–407.

Hoffman, C., Rice, D., & Sung, H.-Y. (1996). Persons with chronic conditions: Their prevalence and costs. *Journal of the American Medical Association, 276,* 1437–1479.

Holahan, C. J., Moos, R. H., Holahan, C. K., & Brennan, P. L. (1997). Social context, coping strategies, and depressive symptoms: An expanded model with cardiac patients. *Journal of Personality and Social Psychology, 72,* 918–928.

Holderness, C. C., Brooks-Gunn, J., & Warren, M. P. (1994). Co-morbidity of eating disorders and substance abuse: Review of the literature. *International Journal of Eating Disorders, 16,* 1–34.

Holm, J., Holroyd, K., Hursey, K., & Penzien, D. (1986). The role of stress in recurrent tension headache. *Headache, 26,* 160–167.

Holmberg, S. (1996). The estimated prevalence and incidence of HIV in 96 large U.S. metropolitan areas. *American Journal of Public Health, 86,* 642–654.

Holmes, J. A., & Stevenson, C. A. Z. (1990). Differential effects of avoidant and attentional coping strategies on adaptation to chronic and recent-onset pain. *Health Psychology, 9,* 577–584.

Holmes, T. H., & Masuda, M. (1974). Life change and illness susceptibility. In B. S. Dohrenwend & B. P. Dohrenwend (Eds.), *Stressful*

life events: Their nature and effects (pp. 45–72). New York: Wiley.

Holmes, T. H., & Rahe, R. H. (1967). The Social Readjustment Rating Scale. *Journal of Psychosomatic Research, 11,* 213–218.

Holroyd, K. A., & Andrasik, F. (1982). Do the effects of cognitive therapy endure? A two-year follow-up of tension headache sufferers treated wtih cognitive therapy or biofeedback. *Cognitive Therapy and Research, 6,* 325–334.

Holroyd, K. A., & Lipchik, G. L. (1999). Psychological management of recurrent headache disorders: Progress and prospects. In R. J. Gatchel & D. C. Turk (Eds.), *Psychological factors in pain: Critical perspectives* (pp. 193–212). New York: Guilford.

Holroyd, K. A., Nash, J. M., Pingel, J. D., Cordingley, G. E., & Jerome, A. (1991). A comparison of pharmacological (amitriptyline HCL) and nonpharmacological (cognitive-behavioral) therapies for chronic tension headaches. *Journal of Consulting and Clinical Psychology, 59,* 387–393.

Holroyd, K. A., O'Donnell, F. J., Stensland, M., Lipchik, G. L., Cordingley, G. E., & Carlson, B. W. (2001). Management of chronic tension-type headache with tricyclic antidepressant medication, stress management therapy, and their combination: A randomized controlled trial. *Journal of the American Medical Association, 285,* 2208–2215.

Holt, C. L., Clark, E. M., Kreuter, M. W., & Scharff, D. P. (2000). Does locus of control moderate the effects of tailored health education materials? *Health Education Research, 15,* 393–403.

Holtgrave, D. R., & Kelly, J. A. (1996). Preventing HIV/AIDS among high risk urban women: The cost-effectiveness of a behavioral group intervention. *American Journal of Public Health, 86,* 1442–1445.

Horgen, K. B., Choate, M., & Brownell, K. D. (2001). Television food advertising: Targeting children in a toxic environment. In D. G. Singer & J. L. Singer (Eds.), *Handbook of children and the media* (pp. 447–461). Thousand Oaks, CA: Sage.

Horwitz, R. I., Viscoli, C. M., Berkman, L., Donaldson, R. M., Horwitz, S. M., Murray, C. J., Ransohoff, D. F., & Sindelar, J. (1990). Treatment adherence and risk of death after myocardial infarction. *Lancet, 336,* 542–545.

House, J. S. (1981). Work stress and social support. Reading, MA: Addison-Wesley.

House, J. S., & Kahn, R. L. (1985). Measures and concepts of social support. In S. Cohen & S.

L. Syme (Eds.), *Social support and health* (pp. 83–108). New York: Academic Press.

House, J. S., Landis, K. R., & Umberson, D. (1988). Social relationships and health. *Science, 241,* 540–545.

House, J. S., Robbins, C., & Metzner, H. L. (1982). The association of social relationships and activities with mortality: Prospective evidence from the Tecumseh Community Health Study. *American Journal of Epidemiology, 116,* 123–140.

Houston, B., & Vavak, C. (1991). Cynical hostility: Developmental factors, psychosocial correlates and health behaviors. *Health Psychology, 10,* 9–17.

Howard, J. H., Cunningham, D. A., & Rechnitzer, P. A. (1976). Health patterns associated with Type A behavior: A managerial population. *Journal of Human Stress, 2,* 24–31.

Hrobjartsson, A., & Gotzche, P. C. (2001). Is the placebo effect powerless? An analysis of clinical trials comparing placebo with no treatment. *New England Journal of Medicine, 344,* 1594–1602.

Huggins, M., Bloch, M., Wiggins, S., Adam, S., Suchowersky, O., Trew, M., Klimek, M., Greenberg, C. R., Eleff, M., Thompson, L. P. (1992). Predictive testing for Huntington's disease in Canada: Adverse effects and unexpected results in those receiving a decreased risk. *American Journal of Medical Genetics, 42,* 508–515.

Hughes, J. R., Gulliver, S. B., Fenwick, J. W., Valliere, W. A., Cruser, K., Pepper, S., Shea, P., Solomon, L. J., & Flynn, B. S. (1992). Smoking cessation among self-quitters. *Health Psychology, 11,* 331–334.

Hughes, J. R., & Hatsukami, N. D. (1986). Signs and symptoms of tobacco withdrawal. *Archives of General Psychiatry, 43,* 289–294.

Hughes, L. (2001). The collected works of Langston Hughes. Columbia, MO: University of Missouri Press.

Hull, J. G., Van Treuren, R. R., & Virnelli, S. (1987). Hardiness and health: A critique and alternative approach. *Journal of Personality and Social Psychology, 53,* 518–530.

Hull, J. G., & Young, R. D. (1983). Self-consciousness, self-esteem, and success–failure as determinants of alcohol consumption in male social drinkers. *Journal of Personality and Social Psychology, 44,* 1097–1109.

Humphrey, L. L. (1986). Structural analysis of parent–child relationships in eating disorders. *Journal of Abnormal Psychology, 95,* 395–402.

Humphrey, L. L. (1988). Relationships within subtypes of anorexic, bulimic, and normal families. *Journal of the American Academy of Child and Adolescent Psychiatry, 27,* 544–551.

Hunt, W. A., Barnett, L. W., & Branch, L. G. (1971). Relapse rates in addiction programs. *Journal of Clinical Psychology, 27,* 455–456.

Hunter, D. J., Manson, J. E., Colditz, G. A., Stampfer, M. J., Rosner, B., Hennekens, c. H., Sprizer, F. E., & Willett, W. C. (1993). A prospective study of the intake of vitamins C, E, and A and the risk of breast cancer. *New England Journal of Medicine, 329,* 234–40.

Hygge, S., Evans, G. W., & Bullinger, M. (2002). A prospective study of some effects of aircraft noise on cognitive performance in schoolchildren. *Psychological Science, 13,* 469–474.

Ikard, F. F., & Tomkins, S. (1973). The experience of affect as a determinant of smoking behavior: A series of validity studies. *Journal of Abnormal Psychology, 81,* 172–181.

Illacqua, G. E. (1994). Migraine headaches: Coping efficacy of guided imagery training. *Headache, 34,* 99–102.

International Association for the Study of Pain. (1979). Pain terms: A list with definitions and a note on usage. *Pain, 6,* 249–252.

Iribarren, C., Sidney, S., Bild, D. E., Liu, K., Markovitz, J. H., Roseman, J. M., & Matthews, K. (2000). Association of hostility with coronary artery calcification in young adults: The CARDIA Study. *Journal of the American Medical Association, 283,* 2546–2551.

Ironson, G., Wynings, C., Schneiderman, N., Baum, A., Rodriguez, M., Greenwood, D., Benight, C., Antoni, M., LaPerriere, A., Huang, H. B. S., Klimas, N., & Fletcher, M. A. (1997). Posttraumatic stress symptoms, intrusive thoughts, loss, and immune function after Hurricane Andrew. *Psychosomatic Medicine, 59,* 128–141.

Irvin, J. E., Bowers, C. A., Dunn, M. E., & Wang, M. C. (1999). Efficacy of relapse prevention: A meta-analytic review. *Journal of Consulting and Clinical Psychology, 67,* 563–570.

Irwin, M., Mascovich, M., Gillin, C., Willoughby, R., Pike, J., & Smith, T. L. (1994). Partial sleep deprivation reduces natural killer cell activity in humans. *Psychosomatic Medicine, 56,* 493–498.

Izard, C. E., Libero, D. Z., Putnam, P., & Haynes, O. M. (1993). Stability of emotion experiences and their relations to traits of personality. *Journal of Personality and Social Psychology, 64,* 847–860.

Jackson, J. S., & Inglehart, M. R. (1995). Reverberation theory: Stress and racism in hierarchically structured communities. In S. E. Hobfoff & M. W. De Vries (Eds.), *Extreme stress and communities: Impact and intervention* (pp. 353–373). Dordrecht, Netherlands: Kluwer Academic Publishers.

Jackson, K. M., & Aiken, L. S. (2000). A psychosocial model of sun protection and sunbathing in young women: The impact of health beliefs, attitudes, norms, and self-efficacy for sun protection. *Health Psychology, 19,* 469–478.

Jackson, V. P., Lex, A. M., & Smith, D. J. (1988). Patient discomfort during screen-film mammography. *Radiation, 168,* 421–423.

Jacobs, T. J., & Charles, E. (1980). Life events and the occurrence of cancer in children. *Psychosomatic Medicine, 42,* 11–24.

Jacobsen, P. B., Bovbjerg, D. H., & Redd, W. H. (1993). Anticipatory anxiety in women receiving chemotherapy for breast cancer. *Health Psychology, 12,* 469–475.

Jacobsen, P. B., Bovbjerg, D. H., Schwartz, M. D., Hudis, C. A., Gilewski, T. A., & Norton, L. (1995). Conditioned emotional distress in women receiving chemotherapy for breast cancer. *Journal of Consulting and Clinical Psychology, 63,* 108–114.

Jacobson, E. (1938). *Progressive relaxation: A physiological and clnical investigation of muscle states and their significance in psychology and medical practice* (2nd ed.). Chicago: University of Chicago Press.

Jacobson, P. D., Wasserman, J., & Anderson, J. R. (1997). Historical overview of tobacco legislation and regulation. *Journal of Social Issues, 53,* 75–95.

Jaffe, A. J., Rounsaville, B., Chang, G., Schottenfeld, R. S., Meyer, R. E., & O'Malley, S. S. (1996). Naltrexone, relapse prevention, and supportive therapy with alcoholics: An analysis of patient treatment matching. *Journal of Consulting and Clinical Psychology, 64,* 1044–1053.

Jakicic, J. M., Winters, C., Lang, W., & Wing, R. R. (1999). Effects of intermittent exercise and use of home exercise equipment on adherence, weight loss, and fitness in overweight women: A randomized trial. *Journal of the American Medical Association, 282,* 1554–1560.

Janis, I. L. (1958). *Psychological stress.* New York: Wiley.

Janis, I. L. (1967). Effects of fear arousal on attitude change: Recent developments in theory and experimental research. In L.

Berkowitz (Ed.), *Advances in experimental social psychology* (Vol. 3, pp. 166–224). San Diego, CA: Academic Press.

Janis, I. L., & Fesbach, S. (1953). Effects of fear-arousing communications. *Journal of Abnormal and Social Psychology, 48,* 78–92.

Janis, I. L., & Mann, L. (1965). Effectiveness of emotional role-playing in modifying smoking habits and attitudes. *Journal of Experimental Research in Personality, 1,* 84–90.

Janis, I. L., & Terwilliger, R. (1962). An experimental study of psychological resistance to fear-arousing communications. *Journal of Abnormal and Social Psychology, 65,* 403–410.

Janoff-Bulman, R. (1992). *Shattered assumptions: Towards a new psychology of trauma.* New York: Free Press.

Janz, N. K., & Becker, M. H. (1984). The health belief model: A decade later. *Health Education Quarterly, 11,* 1–47.

Jason, L. A., Jayaraj, S., Blitz, C. C., Michaels, M. H., Klett, L. E. (1990). Incentives and competition at a worksite smoking cessation intervention. *American Journal of Public Health, 80,* 205–206.

Jay, S. M., Elliott, C. H., Katz, E., Siegel, S. E. (1987). Cognitive-behavioral and pharmacologic interventions for childrens' distress during painful medical procedures. *Journal of Consulting and Clinical Psychology, 55,* 860–865.

Jeffery, R. W., Bjornson-Benson, W. M., Rosenthal, B. W., Lindquist, R. A., & Johnson, S. L. (1984). Behavioral treatment of obesity with monetary contracting: Two-year follow-up. *Addictive Behaviors, 9,* 311–313.

Jeffery, R. W., Hennrikus, D. J., Lando, H. A., Murray, D. M., & Liu, J. W. (2000). Reconciling conflicting findings regarding postcessation weight concerns and success in smoking cessation. *Health Psychology, 19,* 242–246.

Jeffery, R. W., Wing, R. R., Thorson, C., & Burton, L. R. (1998). Use of personal trainers and financial incentives to increase exercise in a behavioral weight-loss program. Journal of *Consulting and Clinical Psychology, 66,* 777–783.

Jemmott, J. B., Croyle, R. T., & Ditto, P. H. (1988). Commonsense epidemiology: Self-based judgments from laypersons and physicians. *Health Psychology, 7,* 55–73.

Jemmott, J. B., Sanderson, C. A., & Miller, S. M. (1995). Changes in psychological distress and HIV risk-associated behavior: Consequences of HIV antibody testing. In R. T. Croyle (Ed.), *Psychosocial effects of screening for*

disease prevention and detection (pp. 82–125). New York: Oxford University Press.

Jemmott, J. B., III, Jemmott, L. S., & Fong, G. T. (1992). Reductions in HIV risk-associated behaviors among Black male adolescents: Effects of an AIDS prevention intervention. *American Journal of Public Health, 82,* 372–377.

Jemmott, J. B., III, & Jones, J. M. (1993). Social psychology and AIDS among ethnic minority individuals: Risk behaviors and strategies for changing them. In J. B. Pryor & G. D. Reeder (Eds.), *The social psychology of HIV infection* (pp. 183–224). Hillsdale, NJ: Erlbaum.

Jemmott, J. B., III, & Locke, S. E. (1984). Psychosocial factors, immunologic mediation, and human susceptibility to infectious disease: How much do we know? *Psychological Bulletin, 95,* 78–108.

Jemmott, J. B., III, & Magliore, K. (1988). Academic stress, social support, and secretory immunoglobulin A. *Journal of Personality and Social Psychology, 55,* 803–810.

Jennings, B. (1993). Health policy in a new key: Setting democratic priorities. *Journal of Social Issues, 49,* 169–184.

Jensen, M. P., Karoly, P., & Harris, P. (1991). Assessing the affective component of chronic pain: Development of the Pain Discomfort Scale. *Journal of Psychosomatic Research, 35,* 149–154.

Jensen, M. P., Turner, J. A., & Romano, J. M. (2001). Change in beliefs, catastrophizing, and coping are associated with improvement in multidisciplinary pain treatment. *Journal of Consulting and Clinical Psychology, 69,* 655–662.

Jenson, M. P., Turner, J. A., Romano, J. M., & Karoly, P. (1991). Coping with chronic pain: A critical review of the literature. *Pain, 47,* 249–283.

Jepson, C., & Rimer, B. K. (1993). Determinants of mammography intentions among prior screenees and nonscreenees. *Journal of Applied Social Psychology, 23,* 40–51.

Johnson, K. W., Anderson, N. B., Bastida, E., Kramer, B. J., Williams, D., Wong, M. (1995). Macrosocial and environmental influences on minority health. *Health Psychology, 14,* 601–612.

Johnston, L. D., O'Malley, P. M., & Bachman, J. G. (1998). *National survey results of drug use from the Monitoring the Future Study, 1975–1997: Vol. 1. Secondary School Students.* National Institute on Drug Abuse No. 98–4345. Rockville, MD: National Institute on Drug Abuse.

Johnston, M., & Vogele, C. (1993). Benefits of psychological preparation for surgery: A meta-analysis. *Annals of Behavioral Medicine, 15,* 245–256.

Jones, J. A., Eckhardt, L. E., Mayer, J. A., Bartholomew, S., Malcarne, V. L., Hovell, M. .F., & Elder, J. P. (1993). The effects of an instructional audiotape on breast self-examination proficiency. *Journal of Behavioral Medicine, 16,* 225–235.

Jones, J. L., & Leary, M. R. (1994). Effects of appearance-based admonitions against sun exposure on tanning intentions in young adults. *Health Psychology, 13,* 86–90.

Jorgensen, R. S., Johnson, B. T., Kolodziej, M. E., & Schreer, G. E. (1996). Elevated blood pressure and personality: A meta-analytic review. *Psychological Bulletin, 120,* 293–320.

Justin, R. G. (1988). Adult and adolescent attitudes toward death. *Adolescence, 23,* 429–435.

Kabat-Zinn, J., Lipworth, L., & Burney, R. (1985). The clinical use of mindfulness meditation for the self-regulation of chronic pain. *Journal of Behavioral Medicine, 8,* 163–190.

Kadden, R. M., Cooney, N. L., Getter, H., & Litt, M. D. (1989). Matching alcoholics to coping skills or interactional therapies: Post-treatment results. *Journal of Consulting and Clinical Psychology, 57,* 698–704.

Kahn, K. L., Keeler, E. B., Sherwood, M. J., Rogers, W. H., Draper, D., Bentow, S. S., Reinisch, E. J., Rubenstein, L. U., Kosecoff, J., & Brook, R. H. (1990). Comparing outcomes of care before and after implementation of the DRG-based prospective payment system. *Journal of the American Medical Association, 264,* 1984–1988.

Kahneman, D., Fredrickson, B. L., Schreiber, C. A., & Redelmeier, D. A. (1993). When more pain is preferred to less: Adding a better end. *Psychological Science, 4,* 401–405.

Kalichman, S. C., Carey, M. P., & Johnson, B. T. (1996). Prevention of sexually transmitted HIV infection: A meta-analytic review of the behavioral outcome literature. *Annals of Behavioral Medicine, 18,* 6–15.

Kalichman, S. C., & Coley, B. (1995). Context framing to enhance HIV-antibody-testing messages targeted to African American women. *Health Psychology, 14,* 247–254.

Kalichman, S. C., Kelly, J. A., Hunter, T. L., Murphy, D. A., & Tyler, R. (1993). Culturally tailored HIV-AIDS risk-reduction messages targeted to African American urban women: Impact on risk sensitization and risk reduction. *Journal of Consulting and Clinical Psychology, 61,* 291–295.

Kalichman, S. C., Heckman, T., Kochman, A., Sikkema, K., & Bergholte, J. (2000). Depression and thoughts of suicide among middle-aged and older persons living with HIV-AIDS. *Psychiatric Services, 51,* 903–907.

Kalichman, S. C., & Nachimson, D. (1999). Self-efficacy and disclosure of HIV-positive serostatus to sex partners. *Health Psychology, 18,* 281–287.

Kalichman, S. C., Russell, R. L., Hunter, T. L., & Sarwer, D. B. (1993). Earvin "Magic" Johnson's HIV serostatus disclosure: Effects on men's perceptions of AIDS. *Journal of Consulting and Clinical Psychology, 61,* 887–891.

Kamarck, T. W., & Lichtenstein, E. (1985). Currents trends in clinic-based smoking control. *Annals of Behavioral Medicine, 7,* 19–23.

Kamarck, T. W., Manuck, S. B., & Jennings, J. R. (1996). Social support reduces cardiovascular reactivity to psychological challenge: A laboratory model. *Psychosomatic Medicine, 52,* 42–58.

Kamen-Siegel, L., Rodin, J., Seligman, M. E. P., & Dwyer, J. (1991). Explanatory style and cell-mediated immunity in elderly men and women. *Health Psychology, 10,* 229–235.

Kaminski, P. L., & McNamara, K. (1996). A treatment for college women at risk of bulimia: A controlled evaluation. *Journal of Counseling and Development, 74,* 288–294.

Kane, R. I., Wales, J., Bernstein, L., Leibowtiz, A., & Kaplan, S. (1984). A randomized controlled trial of hospice care. *Lancet, 1,* 890–894.

Kaniasty, K., & Norris, F. (1993). A test of the support deterioration model in the context of natural disaster. *Journal of Personality and Social Psychology, 64,* 395–408.

Kaniasty, K., & Norris, F. H. (1995). Mobilization and deterioration of social support following natural disasters. *Current Directions in Psychological Science, 4,* 94–98.

Kann, L., Kincher, S. A., Williams, B. I., Ross, J. G., Lowry, R., Hill, C. V., Grunbaum, J. A., Blumson, P. S., Collons, J. L., & Kolbe, L. J. (1998). Youth Risk Behaviora Surveillance-United States, 1997. *Morbidity and Morality Weekly Report, 47,* No. SS-3.

Kanner, A. D., Coyne, J. C., Schaeffer, C., & Lazarus, R. S. (1981). Comparison of two modes of stress measurement: Daily hassles and uplifts versus major life events. *Journal of Behavioral Medicine, 4,* 1–39.

Kaplan, G. A., & Kiel, J. E. (1993). Socioeconomic factors and cardiovascular disease: A

review of the literature. *Circulation, 88,* 1973–1998.

Kaplan, G. A., Salonen, J. T., Cohen, R. D., Brand, R. J., Syme, S. L., & Puska, P. (1988). Social connections and mortality from all causes and from cardiovascular disease: Prospective evidence from Eastern Finland. *American Journal of Epidemiology, 128,* 370–380.

Kaplan, G. A., Strawbridge, W. J., Cohen, R. D., & Hungerford, L. R. (1996). Natural history of leisure-time physical activity and its correlates: Association with mortality from all causes and cardiovascular disease over 28 years. *American Journal of Epidemiology, 144,* 793–797.

Kaplan, R. M. (1989). Health outcome models for policy analysis. *Health Psychology, 9,* 723–735.

Kaplan, R. M. (1991). Health-related quality of life in patient decision making. *Journal of Social Issues, 47,* 69–90.

Kaplan, R. M. (2000). Two pathways to prevention. *American Psychologist, 55,* 382–396.

Kaplan, R. M., & Bush, J. W. (1982). Health-related quality of life measurement for evaluation research and policy analysis. *Health Psychology, 1,* 61–80.

Kaplan, R. M., & Groesll, E. J. (2002). Applications of cost-effectiveness methodologies in behavioral medicine. *Journal of Consulting and Clinical Psychology, 70,* 482–493.

Kaplan, R. M., Orleans, C. T., Perkins, K. A., & Pierce, J. P. (1995). Marshaling the evidence for greater regulation and control of tobacco products: A call for action. *Annals of Behavioral Medicine, 17,* 3–14.

Kaplan, S. H., Greenfield, S., Gandek, B., Rogers, W. H., & Ware, J. E., Jr. (1996). Characteristics of physicans with participatory decision-making styles. *Annals of Internal Medicine, 124,* 497–504.

Karoly, P., & Ruehlman, L. S. (1996). Motivational implications of pain: Chronicity, psychological distress, and work goal construal in a national sample of adults. *Health Psychology, 15,* 383–390.

Kashima, Y., Gallois, C., & McCamish, M. (1993). The theory of reasoned action and cooperative behaviour: It takes two to use a condom. *British Journal of Social Psychology, 32,* 227–239.

Kasl, S. V., & Cobb, S. (1966a). Health behavior, illness behavior, and sick role behavior I. Health and illness behavior. *Archives of Environmental Health, 12,* 246–266.

Kasl, S. V., & Cobb, S. (1966b). Health behavior, illness behavior, and sick role beahvior II.

Sick role behavior. *Archives of Environmental Health, 12,* 531–541.

Kastenbaum, R. (1999). Dying and bereavement. In J. C. Cavanaugh & S. K. Whitbourne (Eds.), *Gerontology: An interdisciplinary perspective* (pp. 155–185). New York: Oxford University Press.

Kastenbaum, R. (2000). The psychology of death (3rd ed.). New York: Springer.

Katan, M. B., Grundy, S. M., & Willett, W. C. (1997). Beyond low fat diets. *New England Journal of Medicine, 337,* 563–567.

Katz, B. P., Fortenberry, J. D., Zimet, G. D., Blythe, M., & Orr, D. P. (2000). Partner-specific relationship characteristics and condom use among young people with sexually transmitted diseases. *Journal of Sex Research, 37,* 69–75.

Kauffman, N. A., Herman, C. P., & Polivy, J. (1995). Hunger-induced finickiness in humans. *Appetite, 24,* 203–218.

Kawachi, I., Colditz, G. A., Stampfer, M. J., Willett, W. C., Manson, J. E., Rosner, B., Speizer, F. E., & Hennekens, C. H. (1994). Smoking cessation and time course of decreased risks of coronary heart disease in middle-aged women. *Archives of Internal Medicine, 154,* 169–175.

Kaye, W. H. (1997). Anorexia nervosa, obsessional behavior, and serotonin. *Psychopharmacology Bulletin, 33,* 335–344.

Keefe, F. J., & Block, A. R. (1982). Development of an observation method for assessing pain behavior in chronic low back pain patients. *Behavior Therapy, 13,* 363–375.

Keefe, F. J., & Bonk, V. (1999). Psychosocial assessment of pain in patients having rheumatic diseases. *Rheumatic Disease Clinics of North America, 25,* X–Y.

Keefe, F. J., Brown, G. K., Wallston, K. A., & Caldwell, D. S. (1989). Coping with rheumatoid arthritis pain: Catastrophizing as a maladaptive strategy. *Pain, 37,* 51–56.

Keefe, F. J., Caldwell, D. S., Queen, K. T., Gil, K. M., Martinez, S., Crissor, J. E., Ogden, W., & Nunley, J. (1987). Pain coping strategies in osteoarthritis patients. *Journal of Consulting and Clinical Psychology, 55,* 208–212.

Keefe, F. J., Hauck, E. R., Egert, J., Rimer, B., & Kornguth, P. (1994). Mammography pain and discomfort: A cognitive-behavioral perspective. *Pain, 56,* 247–260.

Keesey, R. E. (1995). A set-point model of weight regulation. In K. D. Brownell & C. G. Fairburn (Eds.), *Eating disorders and obesity* (pp. 46–50). New York: Guilford.

Keesey, R. E., & Powley, T. L. (1975). Hypothalamic regulation of body weight. *American Scientist, 63,* 558–565.

Kegeles, S. S. (1985). Education for breast self-examination: Why, who, what, and how? *Preventive Medicine, 14*, 702–720.

Keinan, G., Friedland, N., & Ben-Porath, Y. (1987). Decision making under stress: Scanning of alternatives under physical threat. *Acta Psychologica, 64*, 219–228.

Kellermann, A. L., et al. (1992). Suicide in the home in relation to gun ownership. *New England Journal of Medicine, 327*, 467–472.

Kelley, H. H. (1967). Attribution theory in social psychology. In D. Levine (Ed.), *Nebraska Symposium on Motivation* (pp. 192–238). Lincoln: University of Nebraska Press.

Kelley, J. A., & Kalichman, S. C. (1998). Reinforcement value of unsafe sex as a predictor of condom use and continued HIV/AIDS risk behavior among gay and bisexual men. *Health Psychology, 17*, 328–335.

Kelley, J. E., Lumley, M. A., & Leisen, J. C. C. (1997). Health effects of emotional disclosure in rheumatoid arthritis patients. *Health Psychology, 16*, 331–340.

Kelly, J. A. (1995). *Changing HIV risk behavior: Practical strategies.* New York: Guilford.

Kelly, J. A., , Murphy, D. A., Sikkem, K. J., McAuliffe, T. L., Roffman, R. A., Solomon, L. J., Winett, R. A., & Kalichman, S. C. (1997). Randomized, controlled, community-level HIV-prevention intervention for sexual-risk behaviour among homosexual men in U.S. cities. *Lancet, 350*, 1500–1505.

Kelly, J. A., St. Lawrence, J. S., Diaz, Y. E., Stevenson, L. Y., Hauth, A. C., Brasfield, T. L., Kalichman, S. C., Smith, J. E., & Andrew, M. E. (1991). HIV risk behavior reduction following intervention with key opinion leaders of population: An experimental analysis. *American Journal of Public Health, 81*, 168–171.

Kelly, J. A., St. Lawrence, J. S., Hood, H. V., & Brasfield, T. L. (1989). Behavioral intention to reduce AIDS risk activities. *Journal of Consulting and Clinical Psychology, 57*, 60–67.

Kelly, K. E., & Houston, B. K. (1985). Type A behavior in employed women: Relation to work, marital, and leisure variables, social support, stress, tension, and health. *Journal of Personality and Social Psychology, 48*, 1067–1079.

Kelly, S. F., & Kelly, R. J. (1985). *Hypnosis: Understanding how it can work for you.* Reading, MA: Addison-Wesley.

Kelly, T. H., Foltin, R. W., Emurian, C. S., & Fischman, M. W. (1990). Multidimensional behavioral effects of marijuana. *Progress in Neuro-Psychopharmacology and Biological Psychiatry, 14*, 885–902.

Kemeny, M. E. (1994). Stressful events, psychological responses, and progression of HIV infection. In R. Glaser & J. Kiecolt-Glaser (Eds.), *Handbook of human stress and immunity* (pp. 245–266). New York: Academic Press.

Kemeny, M. E., Weiner, H., Duran, R., Taylor, S. E., Visscher, B., Fahey, J. L. (1995). Immune system changes following the death of a partner in HIV positive gay men. *Psychosomatic Medicine, 57*, 549–554.

Kemeny, M. E., Weiner, H., Taylor, S. E., Schneider, S., Visscher, B., & Fahey, J. L. (1994). Repeated bereavement, depressed mood, and immune parameters in HIV seropositive and seronegative gay men. *Health Psychology, 13*, 14–24.

Kendler, K. S., MacClean, C., Neale, M. C., Kessler, R., Heath, A. C., & Eaves, L. (1991). The genetic epidemiology of bulimia nervosa. *American Journal of Psychiatry, 148*, 1627–1637.

Kennedy, S., Kiecolt-Glaser, J. K., & Glaser, R. (1990). Social support, stress, and the immune system. In B. R. Sarason, I. G. Sarason, & G. R. Pierce (Eds.), *Social support: An interactional view* (pp. 253–266). New York: Wiley.

Kennell, J., Klaus, M., McGrath, S., Robertson, S., & Hinkley, C. (1991). Continous emotional support during labor in a U.S. hospital. *Journal of the American Medical Association, 265*, 2197–2201.

Kent, G. (1985). Memory of dental pain. *Pain, 21*, 187–194.

Keown, C., Slovic, P., & Lichtenstein, S. (1984). Attitudes of physicians, pharmacists, and laypersons toward seriousness and need for disclosure of prescription drug side effects. *Health Psychology, 3*, 1–12.

Kerlikowske, K., Grady, D., Rubin, S. M., Sandrock, C., & Ernster, V. L. 1995). Efficacy of screening mammography: A meta-analysis. *Journal of the American Medical Association, 273*, 149–154.

Kerns, R. D., Turk, D. C., & Rudy, T. E. (1985). The West Haven–Yale Multidimensional Pain Inventory. *Pain, 23*, 345–356.

Kerrey, B., & Hofschire, P. J. (1993). Hidden problems in current health-care financing and potential changes. *American Psychologist, 48*, 261–264.

Kessler, R., McLeod, J., & Wethington, E. (1985). The costs of caring: A perspective on the relationship between sex and psychological distress. In I. G. Sarason & B. R. Sarason (Eds.), *Social support: Theory, research, and applications* (pp. 4951–506). The Hague: Martinus Nijhoff.

Kessler, R. C., Crum, R. M., Warner, L. A., Nelson, C. B., Schulenberg, J., & Anthony, J. C. (1997). Lifetime co-occurrence of DSM-III-R alcohol abuse and dependence with other psychiatric disorders in the National Comorbidity Survey. *Archives of General Psychiatry, 54*, 313–321.

Kessler, R. C., Sonnega, A., Bromet, E., Hughes, M., & Nelson, C. B. (1995). Post-traumatic stress disorder in the National Comorbidity Survey. *Archives of General Psychiatry, 52*, 1048–1060.

Kiecolt-Glaser, J. K., Dura, J. R., Speicher, C. E., Trask, O. J., & Glaser, R. (1991). Spousal caregivers of dementia victims: Longitudinal changes in immunity and health. *Psychosomatic Medicine, 53*, 345–362.

Kiecolt-Glaser, J. K., Fisher, L., Ogrocki, P., Stout, J. C., Speicher, C. E., & Glaser, R. (1987). Marital quality, marital disruption, and immune function. *Psychosomatic Medicine, 49*, 13–34.

Kiecolt-Glaser, J. K., Garner, W., Speicher, C., Penn, G. M., Holliday, J., Glaser, R. (1984). Psychosocial modifiers of immunocompetence in medical students. *Psychosomatic Medicine, 46*, 7–14.

Kiecolt-Glaser, J. K., & Glaser, R. (1986). Psychological influences on immunity. *Psychosomatics, 27*, 621–624.

Kiecolt-Glaser, J. K., & Glaser, R. (1988). Methodological issues in behavioral immunology research with humans. *Brain, Behavior, and Immunity, 2*, 67–78.

Kiecolt-Glaser, J. K., & Glaser, R. (1989). Psychoneuroimmunology: Past, present, and future. *Health Psychology, 8*, 677–682.

Kiecolt-Glaser, J. K., & Glaser, R. (1995). Psychoneuroimmunology and health consequences: Data and shared mechanisms. *Psychosomatic Medicine, 57*, 269–274.

Kiecolt-Glaser, J. K., Glaser, R., Cacioppo, J. T., MacCallum, R. C., Snydersmith, M., Kim, C., Malarkey, W. B. (1997). Marital conflict in older adults: Endocrinological and immunological correlates. *Psychosomatic Medicine, 59*, 339–349.

Kiecolt-Glaser, J. K., Glaser, R., Shuttleworth, E. C., Dyer, C. S., Ogrocki, P., & Speicher, C. E. (1987). Chronic stress and immunity in family caregivers of Alzheimer's disease victims. *Psychosomatic Medicine, 49*, 523–535.

Kiecolt-Glaser, J. K., Glaser, R., Strain, E. C., Stout, J. C., Tarr, K. K., Holiday, J. E., & Speicher, C. E. (1986). Modulation of cellular immunity in medical students. *Journal of Behavioral Medicine, 9*, 311–320.

Kiecolt-Glaser, J. K., Glaser, R., Williger, D., Stout, J., Messick, G., Sheppard, S., Ricker, D., Romisher, S. C., Briner, W., Bonnell, G., & Donnerberg, R. (1985). Psychosocial enhancement of immunocompetence in a geriatric population. *Health Psychology, 4,* 25–41.

Kiecolt-Glaser, J. K., Kennedy, S., Malkoff, S., Fisher, L., Speicher, C. E., & Glaser, R. (1988). Marital discord and immunity in males. *Psychosomatic Medicine, 50,* 213–229.

Kiecolt-Glaser, J. K., Malarkey, W. B., Chee, M., Newton, T., Cacioppo, J. T., Mao, H. Y., Glaser, R. (1993). Negative behavior during marital conflict is associated with immunological down-regulation. *Psychosomatic Medicine, 55,* 395–409.

Kiecolt-Glaser, J. K., Marucha, P. T., Malarky, W. B., Mercado, A. M., & Glaser, R. (1995). Slowing of wound healing by psychological stress. *Lancet, 346,* 1194–1196.

Kiecolt-Glaser, J. K., & Williams, D. A. (1987). Self-blame, compliance, and distress among burn patients. *Journal of Personality and Social Psychology, 53,* 187–193.

Kiefe, C. L., McKay, S. V., Halevy, A., & Brody, B. A. (1994). Is cost a barrier to screening mammography for low-income women receiving Medicare benefits? A randomized trial. *Archives of Internal Medicine, 154,* 1217–1224.

Kilbey, M. M., Downey, K., & Breslau, N. (1998). Predicting the emergence and persistence of alcohol dependence in young adults: The role of expectancy and other risk factors. *Experimental and Clinical Psychopathology, 5,* 149–156.

Killen, J. D., Fortmann, S. P., Kraemer, H. C., Varady, A., Newman, B. (1992). Who will relapse? Symptoms of nicotine dependence predict long-term relapse after smoking cessation. *Journal of Consulting and Clinical Psychology, 60,* 797–801.

Killen, J. D., Taylor, C. B., Hammer, L. D., Litt, I., Wilson, D. M., Rich, T., Hayward, C., Simmonds, B., Kraemer, H., & Varady, A. (1993). An attempt to modify unhealthful eating attitudes and weight regulation practices of young adolescent girls. *International Journal of Eating Disorders, 13,* 369–384.

Kimzey, S. L. (1975). The effects of extended spaceflight on hematologic and immunologic systems. *Journal of the American Medical Women's Association, 30,* 218–232.

King, J. B. (1982). The impact of patients' perceptions of high blood pressure on attendance at screening: An extension of the health belief model. *Social Science and Medicine, 16,* 1079–1992.

King, K. B., Reis, H. T., Porter, L. A., & Norsen, L. H. (1993). Social support and long-term recovery from coronary artery surgery: Effects on patients and spouses. *Health Psychology, 12,* 56–63.

King, L. A., & Miner, K. N. (2000). Writing about the perceived benefits of traumatic events: Implications for physical health. *Personality and Social Psychology Bulletin, 26,* 220–230.

Kinsley, M. (2001). A defense of denial. *Time.* December 17th, 2001.

Kirsch, I., & Sapirstein, G. (1999). Listening to Prozac but hearing placebo: A meta-analysis of antidepressant medications. In I. Kirsch (Ed.), *How expectancies shape experience* (pp. 303–320). Washington, DC: American Psychological Asssociation.

Kirschbaum, C., Klauer, T., Filipp, S., & Hellhammer, D. H. (1995). Sex-specific effects of social support on cortisol and subjective responses to acute psychological stress. *Psychosomatic Medicine, 57,* 23–31.

Kirscht, J. P. (1988). The health belief model and predictions of health actions. In D. S. Gochman (Ed.), *Health behavior: Emerging research perspectives* (pp. 27–42). New York: Plenum.

Kirscht, J. P., Kirscht, J. L., & Rosenstock, I. M. (1981). A test of interventions to increase adherence to hypertensive medical regimens. *Health Education Quarterly, 8,* 261–272.

Kirscht, J. P. & Rosenstock, I. M. (1979). Patients' problems in following recommendations of health experts. In G. C. Stone, F. Cohen, & N. E. Adler (Eds.), *Health psychology: A handbook* (pp. 198–215). San Francisco: Jossey-Bass.

Kivilan, D. R., Marlatt, G. A., Fromme, K., Coppel, D. B., & Williams, E. (1990). Secondary prevention with college drinkers: Evaluation of an alcohol skills training program. *Journal of Consulting and Clinical Psychology, 58,* 805–810.

Klag, M. J., Ford, D. E., Mead, L. A., He, J., Whelton, P. K., Liang, K. Y., & Levine, D. M. (1993). Serum cholesterol in young men and subsequent cardiovascular disease. *New England Journal of Medicine, 328,* 313–318.

Klapow, J., Slater, M., Patterson, T., & Atkinson, J. (1995). Psychological factors discriminate multidimensional clinical groups of chronic low back-pain patients. *Pain, 62,* 349–355.

Klass, P. (1987). *A not entirely benign procedure: Four years as a medical student.* New York: Putnam.

Klatsky, A. L., Friedman, G. D., & Sigelaub, A. B. (1981). Alcohol and mortality: A ten-year Kaiser-Permanente experience. *Annals of Internal Medicine, 94,* 139–145.

Kleiwer, W., Lepore, S. J., & Evans, G. W. (1990). The costs of Type B behavior: Females at risk in achievement situations. *Journal of Applied Social Psychology, 20,* 1369–1382.

Kline, A., & Strickler, J. (1993). Perceptions of risk for AIDS among women in drug treatment. *Health Psychology, 12,* 313–323.

Klohn, L. S., & Rogers, R. W. (1991). Dimensions of the severity of a health threat: The persuasive effects of visibility, time of onset, and rate of onset on young women's intentions to prevent osteoporosis. *Health Psychology, 10,* 323–329.

Klonoff, E. A., & Landrine, H. (1993). Cognitive representations of bodily parts and products: Implications for health behavior. *Journal of Behavioral Medicine, 16,* 497–508.

Klonoff, E. A., & Landrine, H. (1994). Culture and gender diversity in commonsense beliefs about the causes of six illnesses. *Journal of Behavioral Medicine, 17,* 407–418.

Knowler, W. C., Barrett-Conner, E., Fowler, S. E., Hammon, R. F., Lachin, J. M., Walker, E. A., & Nathan, D. M. (2002). Reduction in the incidence of type 2 diabetes with lifestyle intervention or metformin. *New England Journal of Medicine, 346,* 393–403.

Knowles, J. H. (1977). The responsibility of the individual. In J. H. Knowles (Ed.), *Doing better and feeling worse: Health in the United States* (pp. 57–80). New York: Norton.

Kobasa, S. C., Maddi, S. R., & Kahn, S. (1982). Hardiness and health: A prospective study. *Journal of Personality and Social Psychology, 42,* 168–177.

Kobasa, S. C., & Puccetti, M. C. (1983). Personality and social resources in stress resistance. *Journal of Personality and Social Psychology, 45,* 839–850.

Koenig, H. G., McCullough, M. E., & Larson, D. B. (2001). *Handbook of religion and health.* New York: Oxford University Press.

Koetting-O'Byrne, K., Peterson, L., & Saldana, L. (1997). Survey of pediatric hospitals' preparation programs: Evidence of the impact of health psychology research. *Health Psychology, 16,* 147–154.

Kog, E., & Vandereycken, W. (1985). Family characteristics of anorexia nervosa and bulimia: A review of the research literature. *Clinical Psychology Review, 5,* 159–180.

Koh, H. K., et al. (1997). Sunbathing habits and sunscreen use among White adults: Results of a national survey. *American Journal of Public Health, 87*, 1214–1217.

Kohen, J. A. (1983). Old but not alone: Informal social supports among the elderly by marital status and sex. *Gerontologist, 23*, 57–63.

Kokkinos, P. F., Narayan, P., Colleran, J. A., Pittaras, A., Notargiacomo, A., Reda, D., & Papademetriou, V. (1995). Effects of regular exercise on blood pressure and left ventricular hypertrophy in African-American men with severe hypertension. *New England Journal of Medicine, 333*, 1462–1467.

Kole-Snijders, A. M. J., Vlaeyen, J. W., Goossens, M. E., Rutten-van Molken, M. P., Heuts, P. H., van Breukelen, G., & van Eek, H. (1999). Chronic low-back pain: What does cognitive coping skills training add to operant behavioral treatment? Results of a randomized clinical trial. *Journal of Consulting and Clinical Psychology, 67*, 931–944.

Kop, W. J., Gottdiener, J. S., & Krantz, D. S. (2001). Stress and silent ischemia. In A. Baum, T. A. Revenson, & J. E. Singer (Eds.), *Handbook of health psychology* (pp. 669–682). Mahwah, NJ: Erlbaum.

Kornguth, P. J., Keefe, F. J., & Conaway, M. R. (1996). Pain during mammography: Characteristics and relationship to demographic and medical variables. *Pain, 66*, 187–194.

Korsch, B. M., Gozzi, E. K., & Francis, V. (1968). Gaps in doctor–patient communications: 1. Doctor–patient interaction and patient satisfaction. *Paediatrics, 42*, 855–871.

Kosmin, B. A., & Lachman, S. P. (1993). *One nation under God: Religion in contemporary American society*. New York: Harmony Books.

Kotz, K., & Story, M. (1994). Food advertisements during children's Saturday morning television programming: Are they consistent with dietary recommendations? *Journal of the American Dietetic Association, 94*, 1296–1300.

Krahn, M. D., Mahoney, J. E., Eckman, M. H., Trachtenberg, J., Pauker, S. G., Detsky, A. S. (1994). Screening for prostate cancer: A decision analytic view. *Journal of the American Medical Association, 272*, 773–780.

Kral, J. G. (1992). Overview of surgical techniques for treating obesity. *American Journal of Clinical Nutrition, 55*, 552S–555S.

Kramer, A. F., Hahn, S., Cohen, N. J., Banich, M. T., McAuley, E., Harrison, G. R., Chason, J., Vakil, E., Bardell, L., Boileau, R. A., & Colcombe, A. (1999). Ageing, fitness, and neurocognitive function. *Nature, 400*, 418–419.

Krantz, D. S., Baum, A., & Wideman, M. V. (1980). Assessment for preferences for self-treatment and information in health care. *Journal of Personality and Social Psychology, 39*, 977–990.

Kremer, E. F., Block, A., & Gaylor, M. S. (1981). Behavioral approaches to treatment of chronic pain: The inaccuracy of patient self-report measures. *Archives of Physical Medicine and Rehabilitation, 62*, 188–191.

Kreuter, M. W., Bull, F. C., Clark, E. M., & Oswald, D. L. (1999). Understanding how people process health information: A comparison of tailored and nontailored weight-loss materials. *Health Psychology, 18*, 487–494.

Kreuter, M. W., & Holt, C. L. (2001). How do people process health information? Applications in an age of individualized communication. *Current Directions in Psychological Science, 10*, 206–209.

Kreuter, M. W., & Skinner, C. S. (2000). Tailoring: What's in a name? *Health Education Research, 15*, 1–3.

Kreuter, M. W., & Strecher, V. J. (1996). Do tailored behavior change messages enhance the effectivenss of health risk appraisal? Results from a randomized trial. *Health Education Research: Theory and Practice, 11*, 97–105.

Kreuter, M. W., Strecher, V. J., & Glassman, B. (1999). One size does not fit all: The case for tailoring print materials. *Annals of Behavioral Medicine, 21*, 276–283.

Krieger, N., & Sidney, S. (1996). Racial discrimation and blood pressure: The CARDIA study of young Black and White adults. *American Journal of Public Health, 86*, 1370–1378.

Krieger, N., Sidney, S., & Coakley, E. (1998). Racial discrimination and skin color in the CARDIA study: Implications for public health research. *American Journal of Public Health, 88*, 1308–1313.

Kruger, L. (Ed.). (1996). *Pain and touch*. San Diego, CA: Academic Press.

Krupat, E., Irish, J. T., Kasten, L. E., Freund, K. M., Burns, R. B., Moskowitz, M. A., McKinlay, J. B. (1999). Patient assertiveness and physician decision-making among older breast cancer patients. *Social Science & Medicine, 49*, 449–457.

Krupat, E., Rosenkranz, S. L., Yeager, C. M., Barnard, K., Putnam, S. M., & Inui, T. S. (2000). The practice orientations of physicians and patients: The effect of doctor-patient congruence on satisfaction. *Patient Education and Counseling, 39*, 49–59.

Kubler-Ross, E. (1969). *On death and dying*. London: MacMillan.

Kujala, U. M., Kaprio, J., Sarna, S., & Koskenvuo, M. (1998). Relationship of leisure-time physical activity and mortality: The Finnish Twin Cohort. *Journal of the American Medical Association, 279*, 440–444.

Kulik, J. A., & Mahler, H. I. M. (1989). Social support and recovery from surgery. *Health Psychology, 8*, 221–238.

Kulik, J. A., Mahler, H. I. M., & Moore, P. J. (1996). Social comparison and affiliation under threat: Effects on recovery from major surgery. *Journal of Personality and Social Psychology, 71*, 967–979.

Kunda, Z. (1990). The case for motivated reasoning. *Psychological Bulletin, 108*, 480–498.

Kushi, L. H., Fee, R. M., Folsom, A. R., Mink, P. J., Anderson, K. E., Sellers, T. A. (1997). Physical activity and mortality in postmenopausal women. *Journal of the American Medical Association, 227*, 1287–1292.

Kushner, M. G., Mackenzie, T. B., Fiszdon, J., Valentiner, D. P., Foa, E., et al. (1996). The effects of alcohol consumption on laboratory-induced pain and state anxiety. *Archives of General Psychiatry, 53*, 264–270.

Lacayo, R. (1995). Neurologic and psychiatric complications of cocaine abuse. *Neuropsychiatry, Neuropsychology, and Behavioral Neurology, 8*, 53–60.

LaCrosse, M. B. (1975). Nonverbal behaviour and perceived counsellor attractiveness and persuasiveness. *Journal of Counseling Psychology, 22*, 563–566.

Lai, J. Y., & Linden, W. (1992). Gender, anger expression style, and opportunity for anger release determine cardiovascular reaction to and recovery from anger provocation. *Psychosomatic Medicine, 54*, 297–310.

Laine, C., & Davidoff, F. (1996). Patient-centered medicine: A professional evolution. *Journal of the American Medical Association, 275*, 152–156.

Lakey, B. (1988). Self-esteem, control beliefs and cognitive problem solving as risk factors in the development of subsequent dysphoria. *Cognitive Therapy and Research, 12*, 409–412.

Lakey, B., & Heller, K. (1988). Social support from a friend, perceived support, and social problem solving. *American Journal of Community Psychology, 16*, 811–824.

Lalonde, M. (1974). *A new perspective on the health of Canadians*. Ottawa: Government of Canada.

Lamaze, F. (1970). *Painless childbirth: Psychoprophylactic method*. Chicago: Regnery.

Lamme, S., Dykstra, P. A., & Brose Van Groenou, M. I. (1996). Rebuilding the network: New relationships in widowhood. *Personal Relationships, 3,* 337–349.

Landrine, H., & Klonoff, E. A. (1994). Cultural diversity in causal attributions for illness: The role of the supernatural. *Journal of Behavioral Medicine, 17,* 181–193.

Lang, A. R, Goeckner, D. J., Adesso, V. J., & Marlatt, G. A. (1975). Effects of alcohol on aggression in male social drinkers. *Journal of Abnormal Psychology, 84,* 508–518.

Lang, A. R., & Marlatt, G. A. (1982). Problem drinking: A social learning perspective. In R. J. Gatchel, A. Baum, & J. E. Singer (Eds.), *Handbook of psychology and health* (pp. 121–169). Hillsdale, NJ: Erlbaum.

Langer, E. J., & Rodin, J. (1976). The effects of choice and enhanced personal responsibility for the aged: A field experiment in an institutional setting. *Journal of Personality and Social Psychology, 34,* 191–198.

Lannin, D. R., Mathews, H. F., Mitchell, J., Swanson, M. S., Swanson, F. H., Edwards, M. S. (1998). Influence of socioeconomic and cultural factors on racial differences in late-stage presentation of breast cancer. *Journal of the American Medical Association, 279,* 1801–1807.

LaPerriere, A. R., Antoni, M. H., Schneiderman, N., Ironson, A., Klimas, N., Caralis, P., & Fletcher, M. A. *Archives of General Psychiatry, 53.* (1990). Exercise intervention attenuates emotional distress and natural killer cell decrements following notification of positive serologic status for HIV-1. *Biofeedback and Self-Regulation, 15,* 229–242.

Larroque, B., Kaminski, M., Dehaene, P., Subtil, D., Delfosse, M.-J., & Querleu, D. (1995). Moderate prenatal alcohol exposure and psychomotor development at preschool age. *American Journal of Public Health, 85,* 1654–1661.

Larsen, R. J. (1992). Neuroticism and selective encoding and recall of symptoms: Evidence from a combined concurrent-retrospective study. *Journal of Personality and Social Psychology, 62,* 480–488.

Latimer, E. A., & Lave, L. B. (1987). Initial effects of the New York State auto safety belt law. *American Journal of Public Health, 77,* 183–186.

Laumann, E. O., & Youm, Y. (1999). Racial/ethnic group differences in the prevalence of sexually transmitted diseases in the United States: A network explanation. *Sexually Transmitted Diseases, 26,* 250–261.

Law, A., Logan, H., & Baron, R. S. (1994). Desire for control, felt control, and stress inoculation training during dental treatment. *Journal of Personality and Social Psychology, 67,* 929–936.

Lazarus, R. S., & Folkman, S. (1984). Stress, appraisal, and coping. New York: Guilford.

Lazarus, R. S., Kanner, A., & Folkman, S. (1980). Emotions: A cognitive-phenomenological analysis. In R. Plutchik & H. Hellerman (Eds.), *Theories of emotion* (pp. 189–217). New York: Academic Press.

Leake, R., Friend, R., & Wadhwa, N. (1999). Improving adjustment to chronic illness through strategic self-presentation: An experimental study on a renal dialysis unit. *Health Psychology, 18,* 54–62

Leary, M. R., & Jones, J. L. (1993). The social psychology of tanning and sunscreen use: Self-presentational motives as a predictor of health risk. *Journal of Applied Social Psychology, 23,* 1390–1406.

Lecci, L., & Cohen, D. J. (2002). Perceptual consequences of an illness—Concern induction and its relation to hypochondriacal tendencies. *Health Psychology, 21,* 147–156.

Lecci, L., Karoly, P., Ruehlman, L. S., & Lanyon, R. I. (1996). Goal-relevant dimensions of hypochondriacal tendencies and their relation to symptom manifestation and psychological distress. *Journal of Abnormal Psychology, 105,* 42–52.

Lee, D., Mendes de Leon, C., Jenkins, C., Croog, S., Levine, S., & Sudilovsky, A. (1992). Relation of hostility to medical adherence, symptom complaints, and blood pressure reduction in a clinical field trial of antihypertensive medication. *Journal of Psychosomatic Research, 36,* 181–190.

Lee, I.-M., Paffenbarger, R. S., Jr., & Hsieh, C.-c. (1992). Physical activity and risk of prostatic cancer among college alumni. *American Journal of Epidemiology, 135,* 169–179.

Lefcourt, H. M., Davidson, K., Prkachin, K. M., & Mills, D. E. (1997). Humor as a stress moderator in the prediction of blood pressure obtained during five stressful tasks. *Journal of Research in Personality, 31,* 523–542.

Lefcourt, H. M., Davidson-Katz, K., & Kueneman, K. (1990). Humor and immune-system functioning. *Humor, 3,* 305–321.

Lehrer, P., Feldman, J., Giardino, N., Song, H.-S., & Schmaling, K. (2002). Psychological aspects of asthma. *Journal of Consulting and Clinical Psychology, 70,* 691–711.

Leibel, R. L., Berry, E. M., & Hirsch, J. (1983). Biochemistry and development of adipose tissue in man. In H. L. Conn, E. A. DeFelice, & P. Kuo (Eds.), *Health and obesity* (pp. 21–48). New York: Raven Press.

Leigh, B. C., & Stall, R. (1993). Substance use and risky sexual behavior for exposure to HIV: Issues in methodology, interpretation, and prevention. *American Psychologist, 10,* 1035–1045.

Leiker, M., & Hailey, B. J. (1988). A link between hostility and disease: Poor health habits? *Behavioral Medicine, 3,* 129–133.

Leitzell, J. D. (1977). Patient and physician: Is either objective? *New England Journal of Medicine, 296,* 1070.

Leonard, K. E. (1989). The impact of explicit aggressive and implicit nonaggressive cues on aggression in intoxicated and sober males. *Personality and Social Psychology Bulletin, 15,* 390–400.

Lepore, S. J. (1992). Social conflict, social support, and psychological distress: Evidence of cross-domain buffering effects. *Journal of Personality and Social Psychology, 63,* 857–867.

Lepore, S. J. (1995). Cynicism, social support, and cardiovascular reactivity. *Health Psychology, 14,* 210–216.

Lepore, S. J., Mata Allen, K. A., & Evans, G. W. (1993). Social support lowers cardiovascular reactivity to an acute stressor. *Psychosomatic Medicine, 55,* 518–524.

Lepore, S. J., Silver, R. C., Wortman, C. B., & Wayment, H. A. (1996). Social constraints, intrusive thoughts, and depressive symptoms among bereaved mothers. *Journal of Personality and Social Psychology, 70,* 271–282.

Lerman, C. (1997). Psychological aspects of genetic testing: Introduction to the special issue. *Health Psychology, 16,* 3–7.

Lerman, C., Daly, M., Sands, C., Balsham, A., Lustbader, E., Heggan, T., Goldstein, L., James, J., & Engstrom, P. (1993). Mammography adherence and psychological distress among women at risk for breast cancer. *Journal of the National Cancer Institute, 85,* 1074–1080.

Lerman, C., Hughes, C., Croyle, R. T., Main, D., Durham, C., Snyder, C., Bonney, A., Lynch, J. F., Narod, S. A., & Lynch, H. T. (2000). Prophylactic surgery decisions and surveillance practices one year following BRCA1/2 testing. *Preventive Medicine, 31,* 75–80.

Lerman, C., & Rimer, B. K. (1995). Psychosocial impact of cancer screening. In R. T. Croyle (Ed.), *Psychosocial effects of screening for disease prevention and detection* (pp. 65–81). New York: Oxford University Press.

Lerman, C., Rimer, B., Trock, B., Balshem, A., & Engstrom, P. F. (1990). Factors associated with repeat adherence to breast cancer screening. *Preventive Medicine, 19,* 279–290.

Lerman, C., et al. (1993). Communication betwen patients with breast cancer and health care providers. *Cancer, 72,* 2612–2620.

Leserman, J., Perkins, D. O., & Evans, D. L. (1992). Coping with the threat of AIDS: The role of social support. *American Journal of Psychiatry, 149,* 1514–1520.

Leserman, J., et al. (1999). Progression to AIDS: The effects of stress, depressive symptoms, and social support. *Psychosomatic Medicine, 61,* 397–406.

Leuchter, A. F., Cook, I. A., Witte, E. A., Morgan, M., & Abrams, M. (2002). Changes in brain function of depressed subjects during treatment with placebo. *American Journal of Psychiatry, 159,* 122–9.

Levenstein, S. (2000). The very model of a modern etiology: A biopsychosocial view of peptic ulcer. *Psychosomatic Medicine, 62,* 176–185.

Levenstein S, Prantera, C., Varuo, U., Scribano, M. L., Andreoli, A., Luzi, C., Arca, M., Berto, E., Milite, G., & Marcheggiano, A. (2000). Stress and exacerbation in ulcerative colitis: a prospective study of patients enrolled in remission. *American Journal of Gastroenterol, 95,* 1213–1220.

Leventhal, E. A., Hansell, S., Diefenbach, M., Leventhal, H., & Glass, D. C. (1996). Negative affect and self-report of physical symptoms: Two longitudinal studies of older adults. *Health Psychology, 15,* 193–199.

Leventhal, E. A., Leventhal, H., Shacham, S., & Easterling, D. V. (1989). Active coping reduces reports of pain from childbirth. *Journal of Consulting and Clinical Psychology, 57,* 365–371.

Leventhal, E. A., & Prochaska, T. R. (1986). Age, symptom interpretation, and health behavior. *Journal of the American Geriatrics Society, 34,* 185–191.

Leventhal, H. (1970). Findings and theory in the study of fear communications. In L. Berkowitz (Ed.), *Advances in experimental social psychology* (Vol. 5, pp. 119–185). San Diego, CA: Academic Press.

Leventhal, H., & Avis, N. (1976). Pleasure, addiction, and habit: Factors in verbal report or factors in smoking behavior? *Journal of Abnormal Psychology, 85,* 478–488.

Leventhal, H., & Cleary, P. (1980). The smoking problem: A review of the research and theory in behavioral risk modification. *Psychological Bulletin, 88,* 370–405.

Leventhal, H., Meyer, D., & Nerenz, D. (1980). The common-sense representation of illness

danger. In S. Rachman (Ed.), *Medical psychology* (pp. 7–30). New York: Pergamon.

Leventhal, H., Singer, R., & Jones, S. (1965). Effects of fear and specificity of recommendation upon attitudes and behavior. *Journal of Personality and Social Psychology, 2,* 20–29.

Leventhal, H., & Watts, J. C. (1966). Sources of resistance to fear-arousing communications on smoking and lung cancer. *Journal of Personality, 34,* 155–175.

Levin, I. P., Schnittjer, S. K., & Thee, S. L. (1988). Information framing effects in social and personal decisions. *Journal of Experimental Psychology, 24,* 520–529.

Levin, J. S. (1994). Investigating the epidemiologic effects of religious experience: Findings, explanations, and barriers. In S. Levin (Ed.), *Religion in aging and health* (pp. 3–17). Thousand Oaks, CA: Sage.

Levine, F. M., & DeSimone, L. L. (1991). The effects of experimenter gender on pain report in male and female subjects. *Pain, 44,* 69–72.

Levine, J. A., Eberhardt, N. L., & Jensen, M.D. (1999). The role of non-exercise activity thermogenesis in resistance to fat gain in humans. *Science, 283,* 212–214.

Levine, J. D., Gordon, N. C., & Fields, H. L. (1978). The mechanism of placebo analgesia. *Lancet, 2,* 654–657.

Levine, R. V. (1990). The pace of life. *American Scientist, 79,* 450–459.

Levy, B. R., Slade, M. D., Kunkel, S. R., & Kasl, S. V. (2002). Longevity increased by positive self-perceptions of aging. *Journal of Personality and Social Psychology, 83,* 261–270.

Levy, R. K. (1997). The transtheoretical model of change: An application to bulimia nervosa. *Psychotherapy, 34,* 278–285.

Levy, R. L., Cain, K. C., Jarrett, M., & Heitkemper, M. M. (1997). The relationship between stress and gastrointestinal symptoms in women with irritable bowel syndrome. *Journal of Behavioral Medicine, 20,* 177–194.

Levy, S. M. (1983). The process of death and dying: Behavioral and social factors. In T. G. Burish & L. A. Bradley (Eds.), *Coping with chronic disease: Research and applications* (pp. 425–446). New York: Academic Press.

Levy, S. M. (1985). *Behavior and cancer: Life-style and psychosocial factors in the initiation and progression of cancer.* San Francisco: Jossey-Bass.

Levy, S. M., Lee, J., Bagley, C., & Lippman, M. (1988). Survival hazards analysis in first recurrent breast cancer patients: Seven-year follow-up. *Psychosomatic Medicine, 50,* 520–528.

Lew, E. A. (1985). Mortality and weight: Insured lives and the American Cancer Society studies. *Annals of Internal Medicine, 103,* 1024–1029.

Lewin, K. (1935). A dynamic theory of personality. New York: McGraw-Hill.

Ley, P. (1982). Giving information to patients. In J. R. Eiser (Ed.), *Social psychology and behavioral science* (pp. 339–373). New York: Wiley.

Liberman, A., & Chaiken, S. (1992). Defensive processing of personally relevant health messages. *Personality and Social Psychology Bulletin, 18,* 669–679.

Liberman, R. (1962). An analysis of the placebo phenomenon. *Journal of Chronic Diseases, 15,* 761–783.

Lichtenstein, E., & Glasgow, R. E. (1992). Smoking cessation: What have we learned over the past decade? *Journal of Consulting and Clinical Psychology, 60,* 518–527.

Lichtenstein, E., & Mermelstein, R. J. (1984). Review of approaches to smoking treatment: Behavior modification strategies. In J. D. Matarazzo, S. M. Weiss, J. A. Herd, N. E. Miller, & S. M. Weiss (Eds.), *Behavioral health: A handbook of health enhancement and disease prevention* (pp. 695–712). New York: Wiley.

Lichtenstein, P., Gatz, M., Pedersen, N. L., Berg, S., & McClearn, G. E. (1996). A co-twin-control study of response to widowhood. *Journal of Gerontology: Psychological Sciences, 51,* 279–289.

Lichtman, S. W., Pisarska, K., Berman, E. R., Pestone, M., Dowling, H., Offenbacher, E., Weisel, H., Heshka, S., Matthews, D. E., & Heymsfield, S. B. (1992). Discrepancy between self-reported and actual caloric intake and exercise in obese subjects. *New England Journal of Medicine, 327,* 1893–1898.

Lilienfeld, A. M., & Lilienfeld, D. E. (1980). Foundations of epidemiology (2nd ed.). New York: Oxford University Press.

Lima, J., Nazarian, L., Charney, E., & Lahti, B. A. (1976). Compliance with short-term antimicrobial therapy: Some techniques that help. *Pediatrics, 57,* 383–386.

Linden, W., Chambers, L., Maurice, J., & Lenz, J. W. (1993). Sex differences in social support, self-deception, hostility, and ambulatory cardiovascular activity. *Health Psychology, 12,* 375–380.

Lindstrom, T. C. (1995). Experiencing the presence of the dead: Discrepancies in "the sensing experience" and their psychological concomitants. *Omega-Journal of Death and Dying, 31,* 11–21.

Linn, S., Carroll, M., Johnson, C., Fulwood, R., Kalsbeek, W., & Briefel, R. (1993). High-density lipoprotein cholesterol and alcohol consumption in U.S. White and Black adults: Data from NHANES II. *American Journal of Public Health, 83*, 811–816.

Linville, P. W., Fischer, G. W., & Fischhoff, B. (1993). AIDS risk perceptions and decision biases. In J. B. Pryor & G. D. Reeder (Eds.), *The social psychology of HIV infection* (pp. 5–38). Hillsdale, NJ: Erlbaum.

Lipowski, Z. J. (1986). What does the word "psychosomatic" really mean? A historical and semantic inquiry. In M. J. Christie & P. G. Mellett (Eds.), *The psychosomatic approach: Contemporary practice and wholeperson care* (pp. 17–38). New York: Wiley.

Lipton, R. I. (1994). The effects of moderate alcohol use on the relationship between stress and depression. *American Journal of Public Health, 84*, 1913–1917.

Litt, M. D. (1996). A model of pain and anxiety associated with acute stressors: distress in dental procedures. *Behavior Research and Therapy, 34*, 459–476.

Litt, M. D., Kalinowski, L., & Shafer, D. (1999). A dental fears typology of oral surgery patients: Matching patients to anxiety interventions. *Health Psychology, 18*, 614–624.

Litt, M. D., Tennen, H., Affleck, G., & Klock, S. (1992). Coping and cognitive factors in adaptation to in vitro fertilization failure. *Journal of Behavioral Medicine, 15*, 171–188.

Little, R. E. (1998). Public health in Central and Eastern Europe and the role of environmental pollution. *Annual Review of Public Health, 19*, 153–172.

Lloyd-Jones, D. M., Larson, M. G., Beiser, A., & Levy, D. (1999). Lifetime risk of developing coronary heart disease. *Lancet, 353*, 89–92.

LoConto, D.G. (1998). Death and dreams: A sociological approach to grieving and identity. *Omega-Journal of Death and Dying, 37*, 171–185.

Lombard, D. N., Lombard, T. N., & Winett, R. A. (1995). Walking to meet health guidelines: The effects of prompting frequency and prompt structure. *Health Psychology, 14*, 164–170.

Loomis, D., & Richardson, D. (1998). Race and the risk of fatal injury at work. *American Journal of Public Health, 88*, 40–44.

Lorber, J. (1975). Good patients and problem patients: Conformity and deviance in a general hospital. *Journal of Health and Social Behavior, 16*, 213–225.

Lowe, M. R. (1993). The effects of dieting on eating behavior: A three-factor model. *Psychological Bulletin, 114*, 100–121.

Lowe, M. R., Whitlow, J. W., & Bellwoar, V. (1991). Eating regulation: The role of restraint, dieting, and weight. *International Journal of Eating Disorders, 10*, 461–471.

Lox, C. L., McAuley, E., & Tucker, R. S. (1996). Physical training effects on acute exercise-induced feeling states in HIV-1 positive individuals. *Journal of Health Psychology, 1*, 235–240.

Ludwick-Rosenthal, R., & Neufeld, R. W. (1993). Preparation for undergoing an invasive medical procedure: Interacting effects of information and coping style. *Journal of Consulting and Clinical Psychology, 61*, 156–164.

Lund, A. K., & Kegeles, S. S. (1984). Rewards and adolescent health behavior. *Health Psychology, 3*, 351–369.

Lyles, J. N., Burish, T. G., Krozely, M. G., Oldham, R. K. (1982). Efficacy of relaxation training and guided imagery in reducing the aversiveness of cancer chemotherapy. *Journal of Consulting and Clinical Psychology, 50*, 509–524.

Lynch, D. J., Birk, T. J., Weaver, M. T., Gohara, A. F., Leighton, R. F., Repka, F. J., Walsh, M. E. (1992). Adherence to exercise interventions in the treatment of hypercholesterolemia. *Journal of Behavioral Medicine, 15*, 365–377.

Lynch, D. J., & Watson, P. (1992). Genetic counseling and hereditary breast/ovarian cancer. *Lancet, 339*, 1181.

Lyness, S. A. (1993). Predictors of differences between Type A and Type B individuals in heart rate and blood pressure reactivity. *Psychological Bulletin, 114*, 266–295.

Lynn, J. (2001). Serving patients who may die soon and their families: The role of hospice and other services. *Journal of the American Medical Association, 285*, 925–932.

Lyter, D. W., Valdiserri, R. D., Kingsley, L. A., Amoroso, W. P., & Rinaldo, C. R., Jr. (1987). The HIV antibody test: Why gay and bisexual men want or do not want to know their results. *Public Health Reports, 102*, 468–474.

Lyubomirsky, S., & Nolen-Hoeksema, S. (1995). Effects of self-focused rumination on negative thinking and interpersonal problem-solving. *Journal of Personality and Social Psychology, 69*, 176–190.

MacDonald, T. K., MacDonald, G., Zanna, M. P., & Fong, G. T. (2000). Alcohol, sexual arousal, and intentions to use condoms in young men: Applying alcohol myopia theory to risky sexual behavior. *Health Psychology, 19*, 290–298.

MacDonald, T. K., Zanna, M. P., & Fong, G. T. (1996). Why common sense goes out the window: Effects of alcohol on intentions to use condoms. *Personality and Social Psychology Bulletin, 22*, 763–775.

MacDorman, M. F., Cnattingius, S., Hoffman, H. J., Kramer, M. S., & Haglund, B. (1997). Sudden infant death syndrome and smoking in the United States and Sweden. *American Journal of Epidemiology, 146*, 249–257.

Macharia, W. M., Leon, G., Rowe, B. H., Stephenson, B. J., Haynes, R. B. (1992). An overview of interventions to improve compliance with appointment keeping for medical services. *Journal of the American Medical Association, 267*, 1813–1817.

MacKinnon, D. P., Johnson, C. A., Pentz, M. A., Dwyer, J. H., Hansen, W. B., Flay, B. R., Wang, E. Y. (1991). Mediating mechanisms in a school-based drug prevention program: First-year effects of the Midwestern Prevention Project. *Health Psychology, 10*, 164–172.

MacLeod, R. D. (2001). On reflection: Doctor's learning to care for people who are dying. *Social Science and Medicine, 52*, 1719–1727.

Macrodimitris, S. D., & Endler, N. S. (2001). Coping, control, and adjustment in type 2 diabetes. *Health Psychology, 20*, 208–216.

Madden, T. J., Ellen, P. S., & Ajzen, I. (1992). A comparison of the theory of planned behavior and the theory of reasoned action. *Personality and Social Psychology Bulletin, 18*, 3–9.

Maddi, S. R., Kahn, S., & Maddi, K. L. (1998). The effectiveness of hardiness training. *Consulting Psychology Journal: Practice and Research, 50*, 78–86.

Maes, M., Hendricks, D., Van Gastel, A., Demedts, P., Wauters, A., Neels, H., Janca, A., & Scharpe, S. (1997). Effects of psychological stress on serum immunoglobulin, complement and acute phase protein concentrations in normal volunteers. *Psychoneuroendocrinology, 22*, 397–410.

Magni, G., Moreschi, C., Rigatti-Luchini, S., & Merskey, H. (1994). Prospective study on the relationship between depressive symptoms and chronic musculoskeletal pain. *Pain, 56*, 289–297.

Magni, G., Silvestro, A., Tamiello, M., Zanesco, L., & Carl, M. (1988). An integrated approach to the assessment of family adjustment to acute lymphocytic leukemia in children. *Acata Psychiatrica Scandinavia, 78*, 639–642.

Maguen, S., Armistead, L. P., & Kalichman, S. (2000). Predictors of HIV antibody testing among gay, lesbian, and bisexual youth. *Journal of Adolescent Health, 26*, 252–257.

Maguire, P. (1985). Barriers to psychological care of the dying. *British Medical Journal, 291*, 1711.

Maher, V. M., Brown, B. G., Marcovina, S. M., Hillger, L. A., & Zhao, X. (1995). Effects of lowering elevated LDL cholesterol on the cardiovascular risk of lipoprotein. *Journal of the American Medical Association, 22*, 1771–1774.

Maisto, S. A., Carey, K. B., & Bradizza, C. M. (1999). Social learning theory. In K.E. Leonard & H.T. Blane (Eds.), *Psychological theories of drinking and alcoholism* (2nd ed., pp. 106–163). New York: Guilford.

Malt, U.F., et al. (1997). Physical and mental problems attributed to dental amalgam fillings: A descriptive study of 99 self-referred patients compared with 272 controls. *Psychosomatic Medicine, 49*, 32–41.

Manfredi, M., Bini, G., Cruccu, G., Accornero, N., Berardelli, A., Medolago, L. (1981). Congenital absence of pain. *Archives of Neurology, 38*, 507–511.

Mann, T., Nolen-Hoeksema, S., Huang, K., Burgard, D., Wright, A., & Hanson, K. (1997). Are two interventions worse than none? Joint primary and secondary prevention of eating disorders in college females. *Health Psychology, 16*, 215–225.

Manne, S., Alfieri, T., Taylor, K. L., & Dougherty, J. (1999). Spousal negative responses to cancer patients: The role of social restriction, spouse mood, and relationship satisfaction. *Journal of Consulting and Clinical Psychology, 67*, 352–361.

Manne, S. L., Bakeman, R., Jacobsen, P. B., Gorfinkle, K., Bernstein, D., Redd, W. H. (1992). Adult-child interaction during invasive medical procedures. *Health Psychology, 11*, 241–249.

Manne, S., Markowitz, A., Winawer, S., Meropol, N. J., Haller, D., Rakowski, W., Babb, J., & Jondorf, L. (2002). Correlates of colorectal cancer screening compliance and stage of adoption among siblings of individuals with early onset colorectal cancer. *Health Psychology, 21*, 3–15.

Manne, S. L., & Zautra, A. J. (1989). Spouse criticism and support: Their association with coping and psychological adjustment among women with rheumatoid arthritis. *Journal of Personality and Social Psychology, 56*, 608–617.

Manning, M. M., & Wright, T. L. (1983). Self-efficacy expectancies, outcome expectancies, and the persistence of pain control in childbirth. *Journal of Personality and Social Psychology, 45*, 421–431.

Mannino, D. M., Klevens, R. M., & Flanders, W. D. (1994). Cigarette smoking: An independent risk factor for impotence? *American Journal of Epidemiology, 140*, 1003–1008.

Manson, J. E., Colditz, G. A., Stampfer, M. J., Willett, W. C., Rosner, B., Monson, R. R., Speizer, F. E., & Hennekens, C. H. (1990). A prospective study of obesity and risk of coronary heart disease in women. *New England Journal of Medicine, 322*, 882–889.

Manson, J. E., Nathan, D. M., Krolewski, A. S., Stampfer, M. J., Willett, W. C., Hennekens, C. H. (1992). A prospective study of exercise and incidence of diabetes among US male physicians. *Journal of the American Medical Association, 268*, 63–67.

Manstead, A. S. R., Proffitt, C., & Smart, J. L. (1983). Predicting and understanding mothers' infant feeding intentions and behavior: Testing the theory of reasoned action. *Journal of Personality and Social Psychology, 44*, 657–671.

Manyande, A., Berg, S., Gettins, D., Stanford, S. C., Mazhero, S., Marks, D. F., Salmon, P. (1995). Preoperative rehearsal of active coping imagery influences subjective and hormonal responses to abdominal surgery. *Psychosomatic Medicine, 57*, 177–182.

Marcus, B. H., Bock, B. C., Pinto, B. M., Forsyth, L. H., Roberts, M. B., & Traficante, R. M. (1998). Efficacy of an individualized, motivationally-tailored physical activity intervention. *Annals of Behavioral Medicine, 20*, 174–180.

Marcus, B .H., Dubbert, P. M., Forsyth, L. H., McKenzie, T. L., Stone, E. J., Dunn, A. L., Blair, S. N. (2000). Physical activity behavior change: Issues in adoption and maintenance. *Health Psychology, 19*, 32–41.

Marin, B.V., & Marin, G. (1992). Predictors of condom accessibility among Hispanics in San Francisco. *American Journal of Public Health, 82*, 592–595.

Marin, G., & Marin, B.V. (1991). Research with Hispanic populations. Newbury Park, CA: Sage.

Markowitz, J. H., Matthews, K. A., Kannel, W. B., Cobb, J. L., & D'Agostino, R. B. (1993). Psychological predictors of hypertension in the Framingham Study: Is there tension in hypertension? *Journal of the American Medical Association, 270*, 2439–2443.

Marks, G., Graham, J. W., & Hansen, H. B. (1992). Social projection and social conformity in adolescent alcohol use: A longitudinal analysis. *Personality and Social Psychology Bulletin, 18*, 96–101.

Marks, G., Richardson, J., Ruiz, M., & Maldonado, N. (1992). HIV-infected men's practices in notifying past sexual partners of infection risk. *Public Health Reports, 107*, 100–105.

Marks, G., Richardson, J. L., Graham, J. W., & Levine, A. (1986). Role of health locus of control beliefs expectations of treatment efficacy in adjustment to cancer. *Journal of Personality and Social Psychology, 51*, 443–450.

Marlatt, G. A. (1983). The controlled-drinking controversy: A commentary. *American Psychologist, 38*, 1097–1110.

Marlatt, G. A. (1985a). Relapse prevention: Theoretical rationale and overview of the model. In G. A. Marlatt & J. R. Gordon (Eds.), *Relapse prevention* (pp. 3–70). New York: Guilford.

Marlatt, G. A. (1985b). Situational determinants of relapse and skill-training interventions. In G. A. Marlatt & J. R. Gordon (Eds.), *Relapse prevention* (pp. 71–127). New York: Guilford.

Marlatt, G. A., Baer, J. S., Kivlahan, D. R., Dimeff, L. A., Larimer, M. E., Quigley, L. A., Somers, J. M., & Williams, E. (1998). Screening and brief intervention for high-risk college student drinkers: Results from a two-year follow-up assessment. *Journal of Consulting and Clinical Psychology, 66*, 604–615.

Marlatt, G. A., Demming, B., & Reid, J. (1973). Loss of control drinking in alcoholics: An experimental analogue. *Journal of Abnormal Psychology, 81*, 233–241.

Marlatt, G. A., & Gordon, J. R. (1980). Determinants of relapse: Implication for the maintenance of behavior change. In P. O. Davidson & S. M. Davidson (Eds.), *Behavioral medicine: Changing health lifestyles* (pp. 410–452). New York: Brunner/Mazel.

Marlatt, G. A., Kosturn, C. F., & Lang, A. R. (1975). Provocation to anger and opportunity to retaliation as determinants of alcohol consumption in social drinkers. *Journal of Abnormal Psychology, 84*, 652–659.

Marmot, M. G. (1998). Improvement of social environment to improve health. *Lancet, 331*, 57–60.

Maroto, J. J., Shepperd, J. A., & Pbert, L. A. (1996). Dispositional optimism as a predictor of health changes among cardiac patients. *Journal of Research in Personality, 30*, 517–534.

Marteau, T. M. (1989). Framing of information: Its influence upon decisions of doctors and patients. *British Journal of Social Psychology, 28*, 89–94.

Marteau, T. M. (1995). Toward an understanding of the psychological consequences of screening. In R. T. Croyle (Ed.), *Psychosocial effects of screening for disease prevention and detection* (pp. 185–199). New York: Oxford University Press.

Marteau, T. M., Dundas, R., & Axworthy, D. (1997). Long-term cognitive and emotional impact of genetic testing for carriers of cystic fibrosis: The effects of test result and gender. *Health Psychology, 16,* 51–62.

Martelli, M. F., Auerbach, S. M., Alexander, J., & Mercuri, L. G. (1987). Stress management in the health care setting: Matching interventions with patient coping styles. *Journal of Personality and Social Psychology, 55,* 201–207.

Martikainen, P., & Valkomen, T. (1996). Mortality after the death of a spouse: Rates and causes of death in a large Finnish cohort. *American Journal of Public Health, 86,* 1087–1093.

Martin, J. L., & Dean, L. (1993). Effects of AIDS-related bereavement and HIV-related illness on psychological distress among gay men: A 7-year longitudinal study, 1985–1991. *Journal of Consulting and Clinical Psychology, 61,* 94–103.

Martin, L. R., Friedman, H. S., Tucker, J. S., Tomlinson-Keasay, C., Criqui, M. H., & Schwartz, J. E. (2002). A life course perspective on childhood cheerfulness and its relation to mortality risk. *Personality and Social Psychology Bulletin, 28,* 1155–1165.

Martin, P., Poon, L. W., Clayton, G. M., Lee, F. S., Fulks, J. S., & Johnson, M. A. (1992). Personality, life events, and coping in the oldest-old. *International Journal of Aging and Human Development, 34,* 19–30.

Martin, P., & Theunissen, C. (1993). The role of life-event stress, coping and social support in chronic headache. *Headache, 33,* 301–306.

Martin, R. A., & Lefcourt, H. M. (1983). Sense of humor as a moderator of the relation between stressors and moods. *Journal of Personality and Social Psychology, 47,* 145–155.

Marucha, P. T., Kiecolt-Glaser, J. K., & Favagehi, M. (1998). Mucosal wound healing is impaired by examination stress. *Psychosomatic Medicine, 60,* 362–365.

Marvan, M. L., & Cortes-Iniestra, S. (2001). Women's beliefs about the prevalence of premenstrual syndrome and biases in recall of premenstrual changes. *Health Psychology, 20,* 276–280.

Marvel, M. K., Epstein, R. M., Flowers, K., & Beckman, H. B. (1999). Soliciting the patient's agenda: Have we improved? *Journal of the American Medical Association, 281,* 283–287.

Maslach, C. (1982). *Burnout: The cost of caring.* Englewood Cliffs, NJ: Prentice Hall.

Maslach, C., & Jackson, S. E. (1982). Burnout in health professions: A social psychological analysis. In G. S. Sanders & J. Suls (Eds.), *Social psychology of health and illness* (pp. 227–251). Hillsdale, NJ: Erlbaum.

Mason, J. W. (1975). A historical view of the stress field. *Journal of Human Stress, 1,* 22–36.

Matarazzo, J. D. (1980). Behavioral health and behavioral medicine: Frontiers for a new health psychology. *American Psychologist, 35,* 807–817.

Matarzzo, J. D. (1982). Behavioral health's challenge to academic, scientific, and professional psychology. *American Psychologist, 37,* 1–14.

Matarazzo, J. D. (1984). Behavioral health: A 1990 challenge for the health sciences professions. In J. D. Matarazzo, S. M. Weiss, J. A., Herd, N. E., Miller, & S. M. Weiss (Eds.), *Behavioral health: A handbook of health enhancement and disease prevention* (pp. 3–40). New York: Wiley.

Maton, K. I., & Zimmerman, M. A. (1992). Psychosocial predictors of substance use among urban Black male adolescents. *Drugs and Society, 6,* 79–113.

Matthews, K. A. (1988). CHD and Type A behavior: Update on and alternative to the Booth-Kewley and Friedman quantitative review. *Psychological Bulletin, 104,* 373–380.

Matthews, K. A., & Gump, B. B. (2002). Chronic work stress and marital dissolution increase risk of posttrial mortality in men from the Multiple Risk Factor Intervention Trial. *Archives of Internal Medicine, 162,* 309–315.

Matthews, K. A., Owens, J. F., Allen, M. T., & Stoney, C. M. (1992). Do cardiovascular responses to laboratory stress relate to ambulatory blood pressure levels?: Yes, in some of the people, some of the time. *Psychosomatic Medicine, 54,* 686–697.

Matthews, K. A., Owen, J. F., Kuller, L. H., Sutton-Tyrrell, K., & Jansen-McWilliams, L. (1998). Are hostility and anxiety associated with carotid atherosclerosis in healthy postmenopausal women? *Psychosomatic Medicine, 60,* 633–638.

Matthews, K. A., Shumaker, S. A., Bowen, D. J., Langer, R. D., Hunt, J. R., Kaplan, R. M., Klesger, R. C., & Ritenbaugh, C. (1997). Women's health initiative: Why now? What is it? What's new? *American Psychologist, 52,* 101–116.

Matthews, K. A., Siegel, J. M., Kuller, L. H., Thompson, M., & Varat, M. (1983). Determinants of decisions to seek medical treatment by patients with acute myocardial infarction symptoms. *Journal of Personality and Social Psychology, 44,* 1144–1156.

Mattson, M. E., Pollack, E. S., & Cullen, J. W. (1987). What are the odds that smoking will kill you? *American Journal of Public Health, 77,* 425–431.

Maxwell, A. E., Bastani, R., & Warda, U. S. (1999). Condom use in young blacks and Hispanics in public STD clinics. *Sexually Transmitted Diseases, 26,* 463–471.

Mayer, J. (1980). The best diet is exercise. In P. J. Collipp (Ed), *Childhood obesity* (2nd ed., pp. 207–222). Littleton, MA: PSG.

Mayer, J. A., & Fredericksen, L. W. (1986). Encouraging long-term compliance with breast self-examination: The evaluation of prompting strategies. *Journal of Behavioral Medicine, 9,* 179–190.

Mayer, W. (1983). Alcohol abuse and alcoholism: The psychologist's role in prevention, research, and treatment. *American Psychologist, 38,* 1116–1121.

Mayne, T. J., Acree, M., Chesney, M. A., & Folkman, S. (1998). HIV sexual risk behavior following bereavement in gay men. *Health Psychology, 17,* 403–411.

Mays, V. M., & Cochran, S. D. (1988). Issues in the perception of AIDS risk and risk reduction activities by Black and Hispanic/Latina women. *American Psychologist, 43,* 949–957.

Mazzullo, J. M., Cohn, K., Lasagna, L., & Griner, P. F. (1974). Variations in interpretation of prescription instructions. *Journal of the American Medical Association, 227,* 929–931.

McAuley, E., Mihalko, S. L., & Bane, S. M. (1997). Exercise and self-esteem in middle-aged adults: Multidimensional relationships and physical fitness and self-efficacy influences. *Journal of Behavioral Medicine, 20,* 67–84.

McAuley, E., Talbot, H. M., & Martinez, S. (1999). Manipulating self-efficacy in the exercise environment in women: Influences on affective responses. *Health Psychology, 18,* 288–294.

McBride, C. M., Curry, S. J., Grothaus, L. C., Nelson, J. C., Lando, H., Pirie, P. L. (1998). Partner smoking status and pregnant smoker's perceptions of support for the likelihood of smoking cessation. *Health Psychology, 17,* 63–69.

McCann, I. L., & Holmes, D. S. (1984). Influence of aerobics on depression. *Journal of Personality and Social Psychology, 46,* 1142–1147.

McCann, S. J. H. (2001). The precocity-longevity hypothesis: Earlier peaks in career achievement predict shorter lives. *Personality and Social Psychology Bulletin, 27,* 1429–1439.

McCaul, K. D., Branstetter, A. D., Schroeder, D. M., & Glasgow, R. E. (1996). What is the relationship between breast cancer risk and mammography screening? A meta-analytic review. *Health Psychology, 15,* 1–8.

McCaul, K. D., Glasgow, R. E., & Schafer, L. C. (1987). Diabetes regimen behaviors: Predicting adherence. *Medical Care, 25,* 868–881.

McCaul, K. D., & Marlatt, J. M. (1984). Distraction and coping with pain. *Psychological Bulletin, 95,* 516–533.

McCaul, K. D., Monson, N., & Maki, R. H. (1992). Does distraction reduce pain-produced distress among college students? *Health Psychology, 11,* 210–217.

McCaul, K. D., Sandgren, A. K., O'Neill, H. K., & Hinsz, V. B. (1993). The value of the theory of planned behavior, perceived control, and self-efficacy for predicting health-protective behaviors. *Basic and Applied Social Psychology, 14,* 231–252.

McCaul, K. D., Schroeder, D. M., & Reid, P. A. (1996). Breast cancer worry and screening: Some prospective data. *Health Psychology, 15,* 430–433.

McCord, C., & Freeman, H. P. (1990). Excess mortality in Harlem. *New England Journal of Medicine, 322,* 173–177.

McCormick, J. (1989). Cervical smears: A questionable practice? *Lancet, 2,* 207–209.

McCoy, S. B., Gibbons, F. X., Reis, T. J., Gerrard, M., Luus, C. A., Sufka, A. V. (1992). Perceptions of smoking risk as a function of smoking status. *Journal of Behavioral Medicine, 15,* 469–488.

McCrae, R. R., & Costa, P. T., Jr. (1986). Personality, coping, and coping effectiveness in an adult sample. *Journal of Personality, 54,* 385–405.

McCullough, M. E., Hoyt, W. T., Larson, D. B., Koenig, H. G., Thoresen, C. (2000). Religious involvement and mortality: a meta-analytic review. *Health Psychology, 19,* 211–222.

McCutchan, J. A. (1990). Virology, immunology, and clinical course of HIV infection. *Journal of Consulting and Clinical Psychology, 58,* 5–12.

McEwen, B. S. (1998). Protective and damaging effects of stress mediators. *New England Journal of Medicine, 338,* 171–179.

McEwen, B. S., & Stellar, E. (1993). Stress and the individual: Mechanisms leading to disease. *Archives of Internal Medicine, 153,* 2093–2101.

McFadden, S. H. (1995). Religion and well-being in aging persons in an aging society. *Journal of Social Issues, 51,* 161–175.

McFarland, C., Ross, M., & DeCourville, N. (1989). Women's theories of menstruation and biases in recall of menstrual symptoms. *Journal of Personality and Social Psychology, 57,* 522–531.

McGinnis, J. M., & Foege, W. H. (1993). Actual causes of death in the United States. *Journal of the American Medical Association, 270,* 2207–2212.

McGinnis, J. M., & Lee, P. R. (1995). Healthy People 2000 at mid decade. *Journal of the American Medical Association, 273,* 1123–1129.

McGregor, M. (1989). Technology and the allocation of the resource. *New England Journal of Medicine, 320,* 118–120.

McGue, M. (1999). Behavioral genetic models of alcoholism and drinking. In K. E. Leonard & H. T. Blane (Eds.), *Psychological theories of drinking and alcoholism* (2nd ed., pp. 372–421). New York: Guilford.

McIntosh, D. N., Silver, R. C., & Wortman, C. B. (1993). Religion's role in adjustment to a negative life event: Coping with the loss of a child. *Journal of Personality and Social Psychology, 65,* 812–821.

McKenna, M. C., Zevon, M. A., Corn, B., & Rounds, J. (1999). Psychosocial factors and the development of breast cancer: A meta-analysis. *Health Psychology, 18,* 520–531.

McKinlay, J. B. (1975). A case for re-focusing upstream: The political economy of illness. In A. J. Enelow & J. B. Henderson (Eds.), *Applying behavioral science to cardiovascular risk* (pp. 7–18). Seattle, WA: American Heart Association.

McKinnon, W., Weisse, C. S., Reynolds, C. P., Bowles, C. A., & Baum, A. (1989). Chronic stress, leukocyte subpopulations, and humoral response to latent viruses. *Health Psychology, 8,* 389–402.

McNeil, B. J., Pauker, S. G., Sox, H. C., Jr., & Tversky, A. (1982). On the elicitation of preferences for alternative therapies. *New England Journal of Medicine, 306,* 1259–1262.

Meadows, J., Jenkinson, S., Catalan, J., & Gazzard, B. (1990). Voluntary HIV testing in the antenatal clinic: Differing uptake rates for individual counselling midwives. *AIDS Care, 2,* 229–233.

Mechanic, D. (1972). Social psychologic factors affecting the presentation of bodily complaints. *New England Journal of Medicine, 286,* 1132–1139.

Medalie, J. H., Stange, K. C., Zyzanski, S. J., Goldbourt, U. (1992). The importance of biopsychosocial factors in the development of duodenal ulcer in a cohort of middle-aged men. *American Journal of Epidemiology, 136,* 1280–1287.

Meijers-Heijboer, H., Van Geel, B., Van Putten, W. L., Henzen-Logmans, S. C., Van der Ouweland, A. M., Niermeijer, M. F., Brekelmans, C. T, & Klijn, J. G. (2001). Breast cancer after prophylactic mastectomy in women with a BRCA1 or BRCA2 mutation. *New England Journal of Medicine, 345,* 159–164.

Meissen, G. J., Myers, R. H., Mastromavro, C. A., Koroshetz, W. J., Klinger, K. W., Farrer, L. A., Watkins, P. A., Gusella, J. F., Bird, E. D., & Martin, J. B. (1988). Predictive testing for Huntington's disease with use of a linked DNA marker. *New England Journal of Medicine, 318,* 535–542.

Melamed, S., Fried, Y., & Froom, P. (2001). The interactive effect of chronic exposure to noise and job complexity on changes in blood pressure and job satisfaction: A longitudinal study of industrial employees. *Journal of Occupational Health Psychology, 6,* 182–195.

Melzack, R. (1975). The McGill Pain Questionnaire: Major properties and scoring methods. *Pain, 1,* 277–299.

Melzack, R. (1993). Labour pain as a model of acute pain. *Pain, 53,* 117–120.

Melzack, R., Taenzer, P., Feldman, P., & Kinch, R. A. (1981). Labour is still painful after prepared childbirth training. *Candian Medical Association Journal, 125,* 357–363.

Melzack, R., & Torgerson, W. S. (1971). On the language of pain. *Anesthesiology, 34,* 50–59.

Melzack, R., & Wall, P. D. (1965). Pain mechanisms: A new theory. *Science, 150,* 971–979.

Melzack, R., & Wall, P. D. (1982). *The challenge of pain.* New York: Basic Books.

Melzack, R., & Wall, P. D. (1988). *The challenge of pain.* Second edition. New York: Basic Books.

Mennella, J. A., Jagnow, C. P., & Beauchamp, G. K. (2001). Prenatal and postnatal flavor learning by human infants. *Pediatrics, 107,* E88.

Mentzer, S. J., & Snyder, M. L. (1982). The doctor and the patient: A psychological perspective. In G. S. Sanders & J. Suls (Eds.), *Social psychology of health and illness* (pp. 161–181). Hillsdale, NJ: Erlbaum.

Mercado, A. C., Carroll, L. J., Cassidy, J. D., Cote, P. (2000). Coping with neck and low back pain in the general population. *Health Psychology, 19,* 333–338.

Mermelstein, R., Cohen, S., Lichtenstein, E., Baer, J. S., Kamarck, T. (1986). Social support and smokkng cessation and maintenance. *Journal of Consulting and Clinical Psychology, 54,* 447–453.

Mermelstein, R. J. (1997). Individual interventions: Stages of change and other health behavior models—The example of smoking cessation. In S. J. Gallant, G. P. Keita, & R. Royak-Schaler (Eds.), *Health care for women: Psychological, social, and behavioral influences* (pp. 387–403). Washington, DC American Psychological Asssociation.

Meyer, D., Leventhal, H., & Gutmann, M. (1985). Common-sense models of illness: The example of hypertension. *Health Psychology, 4,* 115–135.

Meyer, T. J., & Mark, M. M. (1995). Effects of psychosocial interventions with adult cancer patients. *Health Psychology, 14,* 101–108.

Meyerowitz, B. E., & Chaiken, S. (1987). The effect of message framing on breast self-examination attitudes, intentions, and behavior. *Journal of Personality and Social Psychology, 52,* 500–510.

Meyerowitz, B. E., Richardson, J., Hudson, S., & Leedham, B. (1998). Ethnicity and cancer outcomes: Behavioral and psychosocial considerations. *Psychological Bulletin, 123,* 47–70.

Michael, R. T., Gagnon, J. H., Laumann, E. O., & Kolata, G. (1994). Sex in America: A definitive survey. New York: Little, Brown.

Michaud, C., Kahn, J. P., Musse, N., Burlet, C., Nicolas, J. P., & Mejean, L. (1990). Relationships between a critical life event and eating behaviour in high-school students. *Stress Medicine, 6,* 57–64.

Mickey, R. M., Durski, J., Worden, J. K., & Danigelis, N. L. (1995). Breast cancer screening and associated factors for low-income African-American women. *Preventive Medicine, 24,* 467–476.

Miller, M. F., Barabasz, A. F., & Barabasz, M. (1991). Effects of active alert and relaxation hypnotic inductions on cold pressor pain. *Journal of Abnormal Psychology, 100,* 223–226.

Miller, N. E. (1985). The value of behavioral research on animals. *American Psychologist, 40,* 423–440.

Miller, P., & Ingham, J. G. (1976). Friends, confidants and symptoms. *Social Psychiatry, 11,* 51–58.

Miller, R. H., & Luft, H. S. (1994). Managed care plans: Characteristics, growth, and premium

performance. *Annual Review of Health, 15,* 437–459.

Miller, S. M., Brody, D. S., & Summerton, J. (1988). Styles of coping with threat: Implications for health. *Journal of Personality and Social Psychology, 54,* 142–148.

Miller, S. M., & Mangan, C. E. (1983). Interacting effects of information and coping style in adapting to gynecologic stress: Should the doctor tell all? *Journal of Personality and Social Psychology, 45,* 223–236.

Miller, T. Q., Smith, T. W., Turner, C. W., Guijarro, M. L., & Hallet, A. J. (1996). A meta-analytic review of research on hostility and physical health. *Psychological Bulletin, 119,* 322–348.

Miller, T. Q., Turner, C. W., Tindale, R. S., Posavac, E. J., & Dugon, B. L. (1991). Reasons for the trend towards null findings in research on Type A behavior. *Psychological Bulletin, 110,* 469–485.

Miller, W. R., & Hester, R. K. (1980). Treating the problem drinker: Modern approaches. In W. R. Miller (Ed.), *The addictive behaviors* (pp. 11–141). Oxford, England: Pergamon Press.

Millstein, S. G. (1996). Utility of the theories of reasoned action and planned behavior for predicting physician behavior: A prospective analysis. *Health Psychology, 15,* 398–402.

Mintz, L. & Betz, N. (1988). Prevalence and correlates of eating disordered behaviors among undergraduate women. *Journal of Counseling Psychology, 35,* 463–471.

Miranda, J. A., Perez-Stable, E. J., Munoz, R., Hargreaves, W., & Henke, C. J. (1991). Somatization, psychiatric disorder, and stress in utilization of ambulatory medical services. *Health Psychology, 10,* 46–51.

Misovich, S. J., Fisher, J. D., & Fisher, W. A. (1997). Close relationships and elevated HIV risk behavior: Evidence and possible underlying processes. *Review of General Psychology, 1,* 72–107.

Mohr, C. D., Armeli, S., Tennen, H., Carney, M. A., Affleck, G., & Hromi, A. (2001). Daily interpersonal experiences, context, and alcohol consumption: Crying in your beer and toasting good times. *Journal of Personality and Social Psychology, 80,* 489–500.

Mohr, D. C., Dick, L. P., Russo, D., Pinn, J., Boudewyn, A. C., Likosky, W., Goodkin, D. E. (1999). The psychosocial impact of multiple sclerosis: Exploring the patient's perspective. *Health Psychology, 18,* 376–382.

Monane, M., Bohn, R. L., Gurwitz, J. H., Glynn, R. J., Levin, R., & Avorn, J. (1996). Compliance with anti-hypertensive therapy among

elderly Medicaid employees: The rates of age, gender, and race. *American Journal of Public Health, 86,* 1805–1808.

Monti, P. M., Rohsenow, D. J., Rubonis, A. V., & Niura, R. S. (1993). Cue exposure with coping skills treatment for male alcoholics: A preliminary investigation. *Journal of Consulting and Clinical Psychology, 61,* 1011–1019.

Moore, D. J., Williams, J. D., & Qualls, J. W. (1996). Target marketing of tobacco and alcohol-related products to ethnic minority groups in the United States. *Ethnicity and Disease, 6,* 83–98.

Moos, R. H. (1977). Coping with physical illness. New York: Plenum.

Mori, D., Chaiken, S., & Pliner, P. (1987). "Eating lightly" and the self-presentation of femininity. *Journal of Personality and Social Psychology, 53,* 693–702.

Morisky, D. E., Levine, D. M., Green, L. W., Shapiro, S., Russell, R. P., & Smith, C. R. (1983). Five-year blood pressure control and mortality following health education for hypertensive patients. *American Journal of Public Health, 73,* 153–162.

Morland, K., Wing, S., & Diez, R. A. (2002). The contextual effect of the local food environment on residents' diets: The atherosclerosis risk in communities study. *American Journal of Public Health, 92,* 1761–1767.

Morrill, A. C., Ickovics, J. R., Golubchikov, V. V., Beren, S. E., & Rodin, J. (1996). Safer sex: Social and psychological predictors of behavioral maintenance and change among heterosexual women. *Journal of Consulting and Clinical Psychology, 64,* 819–828.

Morrow, G. R., Asbury, R., Hammon, S., & Dobkin, P. (1992). Comparing the effectiveness of behavioral treatment for chemotherapy-induced nausea and vomiting when administered by oncologists, oncology nurses, and clinical psychologists. *Health Psychology, 11,* 250–256.

Moseley, J. B., O'Malley, K., Peterson, N. J., Menke, T. J., Brady, B. A., Kuykendall, D. H., Hollinsworth, J. C., Ashton, C. M., & Wray, N. P. (2002). A controlled trial of arthroscopic surgery for osteoarthritis of the knee. *New England Journal of Medicine, 347,* 81–88.

Moum, T. (1995). Screening for disease detection and prevention: Some comments and future perspectives. In R. T. Croyle (Ed.), *Psychosocial effects of screening for disease prevention and detection* (pp. 200–213). New York: Oxford University Press.

Moyer, A. (1997). Psychosocial outcomes of breast-conserving surgery versus mastectomy:

A meta-analytic review. *Health Psychology, 16,* 284–298.

Moyer, A., & Salovey, P. (1996). Psychosocial sequelae of breast cancer and its treatment. *Annals of Behavioral Medicine, 18,* 110–125.

Moynihan, J. A., & Ader, R. (1996). Psychoneuroimmunology: Animal models of disease. *Psychosomatic Medicine, 58,* 546–558.

Mulder, C. L., de Vroome, E. M. M., van Griensven, G. J. P., Antoni, M. H., & Sandfort, T. G. M. (1999). Avoidance as a predictor of the biological course of HIV infection over a 7-year period in gay men. *Health Psychology, 18,* 107–113.

Muller, J. E., Mittleman, A., Maclure, M., Sherwood, J. B., & Tofler, G. H. (1996). Triggering myocardial infarction by sexual activity: Low absolute risk and prevention by regular physical exertion. *Journal of the American Medical Association, 275,* 1405–1409.

Murphy, L. R. (1996). Stress management in work settings: A critical review of the health effects. *American Journal of Health Promotion, 11,* 112–135.

Murphy, S. T., Monahan, J. L., & Miller, L. C. (1998). Inference under the influence: The impact of alcohol and inhibition conflict on women's sexual decision-making. *Personality and Social Psychology Bulletin, 24,* 517–528.

Murray, D. M., Johnson, C. A., Luepker, R. V., & Mittelmark, M. B. (1984). The prevention of smoking in children: A comparison of four strategies. *Journal of Applied Social Psychology, 14,* 274–288.

Mutterperl, J., & Sanderson, C. A. (2002). Mind over matter: Internalization of the thinness norm as a moderator of responsiveness to norm misperception education. *Health Psychology, 21,* 519–523.

Myers, H. F., Kagawa-Singer, M., Kumanika, S. K., Lex, B. W., & Markides, C. S. (1995). Panel III: Behavioral risk factors related to chronic disease in ethnic minorities. *Health Psychology, 14,* 613–621.

Nadelson, C. C., Notman, M. T., Zackson, H., & Gornick, J. (1982). A follow-up study of rape victims. *American Journal of Psychiatry, 139,* 1266–1270.

Nagy, M. H. (1948). The child's theories concerning death. *Journal of Genetic Psychology, 73,* 3–27.

Nakao, M., Nomura, S., Shimosawa, T., Yoshiuchi, K., Kumaro, H., Kuboki, T., Suematsu, H., & Fujita, T. (1997). Clinical effects of blood pressure biofeedback treatment on hypertension by auto-shaping. *Psychosomatic Medicine, 59,* 331–338.

Namir, S., Alumbaugh, M J., Fawzy, F. I., & Wolcott, D. L. (1989). The relationship of social support to physical and psychological aspects of AIDS. *Psychology and Health, 3,* 77–86.

National Center of Health Statistics. "Fast Stats: A to Z" 2003 (cited 14 July 2003). Available from www.cdc.gov/nchs/fastats.

National Institute of Mental Health Multisite HIV Prevention Trial Group. (2001). Social-cognitive theory mediators of behavior change in the National Institute of Mental Health Multisite HIV Prevention Trial. *Health Psychology, 20,* 369–376.

Neale, A. V., Tilley, B. C., & Vernon, S. W. (1986). Marital status, delay in seeking treatment, and survival from breast cancer. *Social Science and Medicine, 23,* 305–312.

Neighbors, H. W. (1997). Husbands, wives, family, and friends: Sources of stress, sources of support. In R. J. Taylor, J. S. Jackson, & L. M. Chatters (Eds.), *Family life in Black America* (pp. 277–292). Thousand Oaks, CA: Sage.

Neimeyer, R. A. (2001). The language of loss: Grief therapy as a process of meaning reconstruction. In R. A. Neimeyer (Eds.), *Meaning reconstruction and the experience of loss* (pp. 261–292). Washington, DC: American Psychological Asssociation.

Nell, V. (2002). Why young men drive dangerously: Implications for injury prevention. *Current Directions in Psychological Science, 11,* 75–79.

Nelson, M. E., Fiatarone, M. A., Morganti, C. M., Trice, I., Greenberg, R. A., & Evans, W. J. (1994). Effects of high-intensity strength training on multiple risk factors for osteoporotic fractures: A randomized controlled trial. *Journal of the American Medical Association, 272,* 1909–1914.

Neumarker, K. J. (1997). Mortality and sudden death in anorexia nervosa. *International Journal of Eating Disorders, 21,* 202–212.

Newacheck, P. W., & Taylor, W. R. (1992). Childhood chronic illness: Prevalence, severity, and impact. *American Journal of Public Health, 82,* 364–371.

Newcomb, P. A., Weiss, N. S., Storer, B. E., Scholes, D., Young, B. E., & Voigt, L. F. (1991). Breast self-examination in relation to the occurrence of advanced breast cancer. *Journal of the National Cancer Institute, 83,* 260–265.

Newlin, D. B., & Thomson, J. B. (1990). Alcohol challenge with sons of alcoholics: A critical review and analysis. *Psychological Bulletin, 108,* 383–402.

Newman, S. (1984). Anxiety, hospitalization, and surgery. In R. Fitzpatrick, J. Hinton, S. Newman, G. Scrambler, & J. Thompson (Eds.), *The experience of illness* (pp. 132–153). New York: Tavistock.

Newsom, J. T., & Schulz, R. (1998). Caregiving from the recipient's perspective: Negative reactions to being helped. *Health Psychology, 1,* 172–181.

Ng, B., Dimsdale, J. E., Shragg, G. P., & Deutsch, R. (1996). Ethnic differences in analgesic consumption for post-operative pain. *Psychosomatic Medicine, 58,* 125–129.

Niaura, R., Todara, J. F., Stroud, L., Spiro, A. 33, Ward, K. D., & Weiss, S. (2002). Hostility, the metabolic syndrome, and incident coronary heart disease. *Health Psychology, 21,* 588–593.

Nicholson, P. W., & Harland, S. J. (1995). Inheritance and testicular cancer. *The British Journal of Cancer, 71,* 421.

Nichter, M., & Nichter, M. (1991). Hype and weight. *Medical Anthropology, 13,* 249–284.

Nides, M. A., Rakos, R. F., Gonzales, D., Murray, R. P., Tashkin, D. P., Bjornson-Benson, W. M., Lindgren, P., & Connett, J. E. (1995). Predictors of intital smoking cessation and relapse through the first 2 years of the Lung Health Study. *Journal of Consulting and Clinical Psychology, 63,* 60–69.

Nigl, A. J. (1984). Biofeedback and behavioral strategies in pain treatment. New York: Medical and Scientific Books.

Nikiforov, S. V., & Mamaev, V. B. (1998). The development of sex differences in cardiovascular disease mortality: A historical perspective. *American Journal of Public Health, 88,* 1348–1353.

Nisbett, R. E. (1968). Taste, deprivation and weight determinants of eating behavior. *Journal of Personality and Social Psychology, 10,* 107–116.

Noble, R. E. (1997). The incidence of parental obesity in overweight individuals. *International Journal of Eating Disorders, 22,* 265–271.

Noland, M. P. (1989). The effects of self-monitoring and reinforcement on exercise adherence. *Research Quarterly for Exercise and Sport, 60,* 216–224.

Nolen-Hoeksema, S., Parker, L. E., & Larson, J. (1994). Ruminative coping with depressed mood following loss. *Journal of Personality and Social Psychology, 67,* 92–104.

Norbeck, J. S., & Tilden, V. P. (1983). Life stress, social support, and emotional disequilibrium in complications of pregnancy. *Journal of Health and Social Behavior, 24,* 30–46.

Norris, F. H., & Kaniasty, K. (1996). Received and perceived social support in times of stress: A test of the social support deterioration deterrence model. *Journal of Personality and Social Psychology, 71*, 498–511.

Norvell, K. T., Gaston-Johansson, F., & Fridh, G. (1987). Remembrance of labor pain: How valid are retrospective measures? *Pain, 31*, 77–86.

Norvell, N., & Belles, D. (1993). Psychological and physical benefits of circuit weight training in law enforcement personnel. *Journal of Consulting and Clinical Psychology, 61*, 520–527.

Ockene, J. K., Emmons, K. M., Mermelstein, R. J., Perkins, K. .A., Bonollo, D. S., Voorhees, C. C., Hollis, J. F. (2000). Relapse and maintenance issues for smoking cessation. *Health Psychology, 19*, 17–31.

O'Donnell, C. R. (1995). Firearm deaths among children and youth. *American Psychologist, 50*, 771–776.

Ogden, J., & Mitandabari, T. (1997). Examination stress and changes in mood and health related behaviours. *Psychology and Health, 12*, 288–299.

Olbrisch, M., Benedict, S. M., Ashe, K., & Levenson, J. L. (2002). Psychological assessment and care of organ transplant patients. *Journal of Consulting and Clinical Psychology, 70*, 771–783.

O'Leary, A. (1992). Self-efficacy and health: Behavioral and stress-physiological mediation. *Cognitive Therapy and Research, 16*, 229–245.

Olbrisch, M. (1996). Ethical issues in psychological evaluation of patients for organ transplant surgery. *Rehabilitation Psychology, 41*, 53–71.

Oles, K. S., & Penry, J. K. (1987). Epilepsy. In C. S. Rogers, J. D. McCue, & P. Gal (Eds.), *Managing chronic disease* (pp. 43–57). Oradell, NJ: Medical Economics Books.

Olmsted, M. P., Kaplan, A. S., & Rockert, W. (1994). Rate and prediction of relapse in bulimia nervosa. *American Journal of Psychiatry, 151*, 738–743.

Oman, R. F., & King, A. C. (2000). The effect of life events and exercise program format on the adoption and maintenance of exercise behavior. *Health Psychology, 19*, 605–612.

Orbell, S., Hodgkins, S., & Sheeran, P. (1997). Implementation intentions and the theory of planned behavior. *Personality and Social Psychology Bulletin, 23*, 945–954.

Ormel, J., & Wohlfarth, T. (1991). How neuroticism, long-term difficulties, and life situation change influence psychological distress: A longitudinal model. *Journal of Personality and Social Psychology, 60*, 744–755.

Orne, M. T. (1980). Hypnotic control of pain: Towards a clarification of the different psychological processes involved. In J.J. Bonica (Ed.), *Pain* (pp. 155–172). New York: Raven Press.

Ornish, D., Brown, S. E., Scherwitz, L. W., Billings, J. H., Armstrong, W. T., Ports, T. A., McLanahan, S. M., Kirkeeide, R. .L., Brand, R. J., & Gould, K. L. (1990). Can lifestyle changes reverse coronary heart disease? The Lifestyle Heart Trial. *Lancet, 336*, 129–133.

Ornish, D., Scherwitz, L. W., Billings, J. H., Gould, K. L., Merritt, T.A., Sparler, S., Armstrong, W. T., Ports, T. A., Kirkeeide, R. L., Hogeboom, C., & Brand, R. J. (1998). Intensive lifestyle changes for reversal of coronary heart disease. *Journal of the American Medical Association, 280*, 2001–2007.

Ortega, D. F., & Pipal, J. E. (1984). Challenge seeking and the Type A coronary-prone behavior pattern. *Journal of Personality and Social Psychology, 46*, 1328–1334.

Orth-Gomer, K., Wamala, S.P., Horsten, M., Schenck-Gustafsson, K., Schneiderman, N., & Mittleman, M. A. (2000). Marital stress worsens prognosis in women with coronary heart disease: The Stockholm Female Coronary Risk Study. *Journal of the American Medical Association, 284*, 3008–3014.

Otten, M. W., Jr., Zaidi, A. A., Wroten, J. E., Witte, J. J., & Peterman, T. A. (1993). Changes in sexually transmitted disease rates after HIV testing and posttest counseling, Miami, 1988 to 1989. *American Journal of Public Health, 83*, 529–533.

Ovcharchyn, C. A., Johnson, H. H., & Petzel, T. P. (1981). Type A behavior, academic aspirations, and academic success. *Journal of Personality, 49*, 248–256.

Oxman, T. E., Freeman, D. H., Jr., & Manheimer, E. D. (1995). Lack of social participation or religious strength and comfort as risk factors for death after cardiac surgery in the elderly. *Psychosomatic Medicine, 57*, 5–15.

Padian, N. S., Shiboski, S. C., Glass, S. O., & Vittinghoff, E. (1997). Heterosexual transmission of human immunodeficiency virus (HIV) in northern California: Results from a ten-year study. *American Journal of Epidemiology, 146*, 350–357.

Paffenbarger, R. S., Jr., Hyde, R. T., Wing, A. L., & Hsieh, C.-c. (1986). Physical activity, all-cause mortality, and longevity of college alumni. *New England Journal of Medicine, 315*, 605–613.

Pakenham, K. I. (1999). Adjustment to multiple sclerosis: Application of a stress and coping model. *Health Psychology, 18*, 383–392.

Pakenham, K. I., Dadds, M. R., & Terry, D. J. (1994). Relationship between adjustment to HIV and both social support and coping. *Journal of Consulting and Clinical Psychology, 62*, 1194–1203.

Palermo, T. M., & Drotar, D. (1996). Prediction of children's postoperative pain: The role of presurgical expectations and anticipatory emotions. *Journal of Pediatric Psychology, 21*, 683–698.

Pappas, G., Queen, S., Hadden, W., & Fisher, G. (1993). The increasing disparity and mortality between socioeconomic groups in the United States, 1960 and 1986. *New England Journal of Medicine, 329*, 103–109.

Pargament, K. I. (1997). The psychology of religion and coping: Theory, research, practice. New York: Guilford.

Parker, J. C. (1995). Stress management. In P. M. Nicassio & T. W. Smith (Eds.), *Managing chronic illness: A biopsychosocial perspective* (pp. 285–312). Washington, DC: American Psychological Asssociation.

Parker, P. A., & Kulik, J. A. (1995). Burnout, self- and supervisor-rated job performance, and absenteeism among nurses. *Journal of Behavioral Medicine, 18*, 581–600.

Parsons, O. A. (1977). Neuropsychological deficits in chronic alcoholics: Facts and fancies. *Alcoholism: Clinical and Experimental Research, 1*, 51–56.

Parsons, T. (1951). *The social system.* New York: Free Press.

Parsons, T. (1975). *Action theory and the human condition.* New York: Free Press.

Patenaude, A. F., Guttmacher, A. E., & Collins, F. S. (2002). Genetic testing and psychology: New roles, new responsibilities. *American Psychologist, 57*, 271–282.

Patterson, T. L., Shaw, W. S., Semple, S. J., Cherner, M., McCutcheon, J., Atkinson, J., Grant, I., & Nannis, E. (1996). Relationship of psychosocial factors to HIV disease progression. *Annals of Behavioral Medicine, 18*, 30–39.

Patterson, D. R., Everett, J. J., Burns, G. L., & Marvin, J. A. (1992). Hypnosis for the treatment of burn pain. *Journal of Consulting and Clinical Psychology, 60*, 713–717.

Pavlov, I. (1927). *Conditioned reflexes.* Oxford, England: Oxford University Press.

Paxton, S., Wertheim, E., Gibbons, K., Szmukler, G., Hiller, L., & Petrovich, J. (1991). Body image satisfaction, dieting beliefs, and weight loss behaviors in adolescents girls and boys. *Journal of Youth and Adolescence, 20,* 361–379.

Payne, A., & Blanchard, E. B. (1995). A controlled comparison of cognitive therapy and self-help support groups in the treatment of irritable bowel syndrome. *Journal of Consulting and Clinical Psychology, 63,* 779–786.

Pechmann, C. (1997). Does antismoking advertising combat underage smoking? A review of past practices and research. In M. E. Goldberg, M. Fishbein, & S. E. Middlestadt (Eds.), *Social marketing: Theoretical and practical perspectives* (pp. 189–216). Mahwah, NJ: Erlbaum.

Pechmann, C., & Shih, C.-F. (1999). Smoking scenes in movies and antismoking advertisements before movies: Effects on youth. *Journal of Marketing, 63,* 1–13.

Peele, S. (1984). The cultural context of psychological approaches to alcoholism: Can we control the effects of alcohol? *American Psychologist, 39,* 1337–1351.

Peirce, R. S., Frone, M. R., Russell, M., & Cooper, M. L. (1996). Financial stress, social support, and alcohol involvement: A longitudinal test of the buffering hypothesis in a general population survey. *Health Psychology, 15,* 38–47.

Pendleton, D., & Bochner, S. (1980). The communciation of medical information as a function of patients' social class. *Social Science and Medicine, 14A,* 669–673.

Pennebaker, J. W. (1982). *The psychology of physical symptoms.* New York: Springer-Verlag.

Pennebaker, J. W. (1989). Confession, inhibition and disease. *Advances in Experimental Social Psychology, 22,* 211–244.

Pennebaker, J. W., & Beale, S. K. (1986). Confronting a traumatic event: Toward an understanding of inhibition and disease. *Journal of Abnormal Psychology, 95,* 274–281.

Pennebaker, J. W., Hughes, C., & O'Heeron, R. C. (1987). The psychophysiology of confession: Linking inhibitory and psychosomatic processes. *Journal of Personality and Social Psychology, 52,* 781–793.

Pennebaker, J. W., & O'Heeron, R. C. (1984). Confiding in others and illness rate among spouses of suicide and accidental-death victims. *Journal of Abnormal Psychology, 93,* 473–476.

Pennebaker, J. W., & Skelton, J. (1981). Selective monitoring of bodily sensations. *Journal of Personality and Social Psychology, 41,* 213–223.

Peplua, L. A. (1985). Loneliness research: Basic concepts and findings. In I. G. Sarason & B.

R. Sarason (Eds.), *Social support: Theory, research and applications* (pp. 269–286). The Hague: Martinus Nijhoff.

Perkins, K. A. (1996). Sex differences in nicotine versus nonnicotine reinforcement as determinants of tobacco smoking. *Experimental and Clinical Psychopharmacology, 4,* 166–177.

Perkins, K. A., Marcus, M. D., Levin, M. D., D'Amico, D., Miller, A., Broge, M., Ashcom, J., & Shiffman, S. (2001). Cognitive-behavioral therapy to reduce weight concerns improves smoking cessation outcome in weight-concerned women. *Journal of Consulting and Clinical Psychology, 69,* 604–613.

Perri, M. G., Martin, A. D., Leermakers, E. A., Sears, S. F., & Notelovitz, M. (1997). Effects of group- versus home-based exercise in the treatment of obesity. *Journal of Consulting and Clinical Psychology, 65,* 278–285.

Perri, M. G., & Nezu, A. M. (1993). Preventing relapse following treatment for obesity. In A. J. Stunkard & T. A. Wadden (Eds.), *Obesity: Theory and therapy* (pp. 287–299). New York: Raven Press.

Persky, V. W., Kempthorne-Rawson, J., & Shekelle, R.B. (1987). Personality and risk of cancer: 20-year follow-up of the Western Electric Study. *Psychosomatic Medicine, 49,* 435–439.

Peters-Golden, H. (1982). Breast cancer: Varied perceptions of social support in the illness experience. *Social Science and Medicine, 16,* 483–491.

Peterson, C. (2000). The future of optimism. *American Psychologist, 55,* 44–55.

Peterson, C., & Seligman, M. E. P. (1987). Explanatory style and illness. *Journal of Personality, 55,* 237–265.

Peterson, C., Seligman, M. E. P., & Vaillant, G. E. (1988). Pessimistic explanatory style is a risk factor for physical illness: A thirty-five-year longitudinal study. *Journal of Personality and Social Psychology, 55,* 23–27.

Peterson, C., Seligman, M. E. P., Yurko, K. H., Martin, L. R., & Friedman, H. S. (1998). Catastrophizing and untimely death. *Psychological Science, 9,* 127–130.

Peterson, J. L., & Marin, G. (1988). Issues in the prevention of AIDS among black and Hispanic men. *American Psychologist, 43,* 871–877.

Petrie, K. J., Booth, R. J., & Pennebaker, J. W. (1998). The immunological effects of thought suppression. *Journal of Personality and Social Psychology, 75,* 1264–1272.

Petry, N. M., Martin, B., Cooney, J. L., & Kranzler, H. R. (2000). Give them prizes, and they will

come: Contingency managment for treatment of alcohol dependence. *Journal of Consulting and Clinical Psychology, 68,* 250–257.

Pettingale, K. W., Morris, T., Greer, S., & Haybittle, J. L. (1985). Mental attitudes to cancer: An additional prognostic factor. *Lancet, 1,* 750. GET

Phillips, J. M., & Gatchel, R. J. (2000). Extraversion-introversion and chronic pain. In R. J. Gatchel & J. N. Weisberg (Eds.), *Personality characteristics of patients with pain* (pp. 181–202). Washington, DC: American Psychological Asssociation.

Pike, K., & Striegel-Moore, R. H. (1997). Disordered eating and eating disorders. In S. J. Gallant, G. P. Keita, & R. Royak-Schaler (Eds.), *Health care for women: Psychological, social, and behavioral influences* (pp. 97–114). Washington, DC: American Psychological Asssociation.

Pine, C. J. (1985). Anxiety and eating behavior in obese and nonobese American Indians and White Americans. *Journal of Personality and Social Psychology, 49,* 774–780.

Pinto, R. P., & Hollandsworth, J. G. (1989). Using videotape modeling to prepare children psychologically for surgery: Influence of parents and costs versus benefits of providing preparation services. *Health Psychology, 8,* 79–95.

Pirkle, J. L., Flegal, K. M., Bernert, J. T., Brody, D. J., Etzel, R. A., & Maurer, K. R. (1996). Exposure of the U.S. population to environmental tobacco smoke: The Third National Health and Nutrition Examination Survey, 1988 to 1991. *Journal of the American Medical Association, 275,* 1233–1240.

Pistrang, N., & Barker, C. (1995). The partner relationship in psychological response to breast cancer. *Social Science and Medicine, 40,* 689–697.

Placek, P. J., Taffel, S., & Moien, M. (1988). 1986 C-sections rise: VBACs inch upward. *American Journal of Public Health, 78,* 562–563.

Plante, T. G., & Sherman, A. C. (2001). Research on faith and health: New approaches to old questions. In T. G. Plante & A. C. Sherman (Eds.), *Faith and health: Psychological perspectives* (pp. 1–12). New York: Guilford.

Plaud, J. J., Mosely, T. H., & Moberg, M. (1998). Alzheimer's disease and behavioral gerontology. In J. J. Plaud & G. H. Eifert (Eds.), *From behavior theory to behavior therapy* (pp. 223–245). Boston: Allyn and Bacon.

Plous, S. (1996a). Attitudes toward the use of animals in psychological research and education: Results from a national survey of psychologists. *American Psychologist, 51*, 1167–1180.

Plous, S. (1996b). Attitudes toward the use of animals in psychological research and education: Results from a national survey of psychology majors. *Psychological Science, 7*, 352–358.

Poll, I. B., & Kaplan De-Nour, A. (1980). Locus of control and adjustment to chronic hemodialysis. *Psychological Medicine, 10*, 153–157.

Polusny, M. A., & Follette, V. M. (1995). Long-term correlates of child sexual abuse: Theory and review of the empirical literature. *Applied and Preventive Psychology, 4*, 143–166.

Pomerleau, O. F., & Pomerleau, C. S. (1989). A biobehavioral perspective on smoking. In T. Ney & A. Gale (Eds.), *Smoking and human behavior* (pp. 69–90). Chicester, England: Wiley.

Pomerleau, O. F., Collins, A. C., Shiffman, S., & Pomerleau, C. S. (1993). Why some people smoke and others do not: New perspectives. *Journal of Consulting and Clinical Psychology, 61*, 723–731.

Pope, H. G., Jr., Olivardia, R., Gruber, A., & Borowiecki, J. (1999). Evolving ideals of male body image as seen through action toys. *International Journal of Eating Disorders, 26*, 65–72.

Poston, W. S. C., Ericsson, M., Linder, J., Nilsson, T., Goodrick, G. K., & Foreyt, J. P. (1999). Personality and the prediction of weight loss and relapse in the treatment of obesity. *International Journal of Eating Disorders, 25*, 301–309.

Powch, I. G., & Houston, B. K. (1996). Hostility, anger-in, and cardiovascular reactivity in white women. *Health Psychology, 15*, 200–208.

Prentice, D. A., & Miller, D. T. (1993). Pluralistic ignorance and alcohol use on campus: Some consequences of misperceiving the social norm. *Journal of Personality and Social Psychology, 64*, 243–256.

Prescott, C. A., Neale, M. C., Corey, L. A., & Kendler, K. S. (1997). Predictors of problem drinking and alcohol dependence in a population-based sample of female twins. *Journal of Studies on Alcohol, 58*, 167–181.

Princeton Religious Research Center. (1990). Religion in America 1990. Princeton, NJ: Gallup Organization.

Prochaska, J. O., Velicer, W. F., Rossi, J. S., Goldstein, M. G., Marcus, B. H., Rakowski, W., Flore, C., Harlow, L. L., Redding, C. A., Rosenbloom, D., & Rossi, S. R. (1994). Stages of change and decisional balance for 12 problem behaviors. *Health Psychology, 13*, 39–46.

Prochaska, J. O., DiClemente, C. C., & Norcross, J. C. (1992). In search of how people change: Applications to addictive behaviors. *American Psychologist, 47*, 1102–1114.

Prochaska, J. O., DiClemente, C. C., Velicer, W. F., & Rossi, J. S. (1993). Standardized, individualized, interactive, and personalized self-help programs for smoking cessation. *Health Psychology, 12*, 399–405.

Prochaska, T. R., Keller, U. L., Leventhal, E. A., & Leventhanl, H. (1987). Impact of symptoms and aging attribution on emotions and coping. *Health Psychology, 6*, 495–514.

Procidano, M. E., & Heller, K. (1983). Measurements of perceived social support from friends and from family: Three validation studies. *American Journal of Community Psychology, 11*, 1–24.

Psaty, B. M., Koepsell, T. D., Wagner, E. H., LoGerfo, J. P., & Inui, T. S. (1990). Beta blockers and the primary prevention of nonfatal myocardial infarction in patients with high blood pressure. *American Journal of Cardiology, 66*, 12G–14G.

Ptacek, J. T., Smith, R. E., & Zanas, J. (1992). Gender, appraisal, and coping: A longitudinal analysis. *Journal of Personality, 60*, 747–770.

Quick, J. C. (1999). Occupational health psychology: Historical roots and future directions. *Health Psychology, 18*, 82–88.

Quindlen, A. (2002). In a peaceful frame of mind. *Newsweek*, February 4, p. 64.

Quittner, A. L., Espelage, D. L., Opipari, L. C., Carter, B., Eid, N., & Eigen, H. (1998). Role strain in couples with and without a child with a chronic illness: Associations with marital satisfaction, intimacy, and daily mood. *Health Psychology, 17*, 112–124.

Rabin, B. S. (1999). *Stress, immune function, and health: The connection*. New York: Wiley.

Rabin, B. S. (2000). Changes in the immune system during aging. In S. B. Manuck. Ed.), *Behavior, health, and aging* (pp. 59–68). Mahwah, NJ: Erlbaum .

Rabins, P. V., Fitting, M. D., Eastham, J., & Zabora, J. (1990). Emotional adaptation over time in care-givers for chronically ill elderly people. *Age and Ageing, 19*, 185–190.

Rabow, J., & Watts, R. (1984). Alcohol availability, alcohol beverage sales, and alcohol-related problems. *Journal of Studies on Alcohol, 43*, 767–801.

Ragland, D. R., & Brand, R. J. (1988). Type A behavior and mortality from coronary heart disease. *New England Journal of Medicine, 318*, 65–69.

Raikkonen, K., Matthews, K. A., Flory, J. D., & Owens, J. F. (1999). Effects of hostility on ambulatory blood pressure and mood during daily living in healthy adults. *Health Psychology, 18*, 44–53.

Rainey, L. C. (1988). The experience of dying. In H. Wass, F. M., Berado, & R. A. Neimeyer (Eds.), *Dying: Facing the facts* (2nd ed., pp. 137–157). New York: Hemisphere.

Rakowski, W., Ehrich, B., Goldstein, M. G., Rimer, B. K., Pearlman, D. N., Clark, M. A., Velicer, W. F., & Woolverton, H. 3rd. (1998). Increasing mammography among women ages 40-74 by use of a stage-matched, tailored intervention. *Preventive Medicine, 27*, 748–756.

Raphael, B., & Dobson, M. (2000). College student grief and loss. In J. H. Harvey & E. D. Miller (Eds.), *Loss and trauma* (pp. 45–61). Philadelphia, PA: Brunner-Rutledge.

Ravussin, E., Lillioja, S., Knowler, W. C., Christin, L., Freymond, D., Abbott, W. G., Boyce, V., Howard, B. U., & Bogardus, C. (1988). Reduced rate of energy expenditure as a risk factor for body-weight gain. *New England Journal of Medicine, 318*, 467–472.

Redelmeier, D. A., & Kahneman, D. (1996). Patients' memories of painful medical treatments: Real-time and retrospective evaluations of two minimally invasive procedures. *Pain, 66*, 3–8.

Reed, G. M., Kemeny, M. E., Taylor, S. E., & Visscher, B. R. (1999). Negative HIV-specific expectancies and AIDS-related bereavement as predictors of symptom onset in asymptomatic HIV-positive gay men. *Health Psychology, 18*, 354–363.

Reed, D., McGee, D., Yano, K., & Feinleib, M. (1983). Social networks and CHD among Japanese men in Hawaii. *American Journal of Epidemiology, 117*, 384–396.

Reed, G. M., Kemeny, M. E., Taylor, S. E., Wang, H.-Y. J., & Visscher, B. R. (1994). Realistic acceptance as a predictor of decreased survival time in gay men with AIDS. *Health Psychology, 13*, 299–307.

Reeves, B. R., Lang, A., Thorson, E., & Rothschild, M. (1989). Emotional television scenes and hemispheric specialization. *Human Communication Research, 15*, 493–508.

Reeves, B. R., Newhagen, J., Maibach, E., Basil, M., & Kurz, K. (1991). Negative and positive television messages: Effects of message type and context on attention and memory. *American Behavioral Scientist, 34,* 679–694.

Regier, D. A., Farmer, M. E., Rae, D. S., Locke, B. Z., Keith, S. J., Judd, L. L., & Goodwin, F. K. (1990). Comorbidity of mental disorders with alcohol and other drug abuse. Results from the Epidemiologic Catchment Area (ECA) Study. *Journal of the American Medical Association, 264,* 2511–2518.

Reiff, M., Zakut, H., & Weingarten, M. A. (1999). Illness and treatment perceptions of Ethiopian immigrants and their doctors in Israel. *American Journal of Public Health, 89,* 1814–1818.

Reinisch, J. M., Sanders, S. A., Hill, C. A., & Ziemba-Davis, M. (1992). High-risk sexual behavior among heterosexual undergraduates at a midwestern university. *Family Planning Perspectives, 24,* 116–121.

Reis, H. T., Wheeler, L., Kernis, M., Spiegel, N., & Nezlek, J. B. (1985). Physical attractiveness in social interacton: II. Why does appearance affect social experience? *Journal of Personality and Social Psychology, 43,* 979–996.

Reite, M., Harbek, R., & Hoffman, A. (1981). Altered cellular immune response following peer separation. *Life Science, 29,* 1133–1136.

Resnick, M. D., Bearman, P. S., Blum, R. W., Bauman, K. E., Harris, K. M., Jones, J., Tabor, J., Beuhring, T., Sieving, R. E., Shew, M., Ireland, M., Bearinger, L. H., & Udry, J. R. (1997). Protecting adolescents from harm: Findings from the National Longitudinal Study on Adolescent Health. *Journal of the American Medical Association, 278,* 823–832.

Rexrode, K. M., Carey, V. J., Hennekens, C. H., Walters, E. E., Colditz, G. A., Stampfer, M. J., Willett, W. C., & Manson, J. E. (1998). Abdominal adiposity and coronary heart disease in women. *Journal of the American Medical Association, 280,* 1843–1848.

Rey, M., & Rey, H. A. (1966). Curious George goes to the hospital. New York: Quality Paperback Book Club.

Reynolds, D. V. (1969). Surgery in the rat during electrical analgesia induced by focal brain stimulation. *Science, 164,* 444–445.

Reynolds, M. (1978). No news is bad news: Patients' views about communication in hospital. *British Medical Journal, 1,* 1673–1676.

Reynolds, P., & Kaplan, G. A. (1990). Social connections and risk for cancer: Prospective evidence from the Alameda Country Study. *Behavioral Medicine, 16,* 101–110.

Rhodewalt, R., Hayes, R. B., Chemers, M. M., & Wysocki, J. (1984). Type A behavior, perceived stress, and illness: A person–situation analysis. *Personality and Social Psychology Bulletin, 10,* 149–159.

Rhodewalt, R., & Smith, T. W. (1991). Current issues in Type A behavior, coronary proneness, and coronary heart disease. In C. R. Synder & D. R. Forsyth (Eds.), *Handbook of social and clinical psychology: The health perspective* (pp. 197–220). Elmsford, NY: Pergamon.

Rich, K. R. (1999). Close to the bone. *New York Times Magazine,* December 19.

Richards, J. S., Kewman, D. G., & Pierce, C. A. (2000). Spinal cord injury. In R. G. Frank & T. R. Elliott (Eds.), *Handbook of rehabilitation psychology* (pp. 11–27). Washington, DC: American Psychological Association.

Richardson, S. A., Goodman, N., Hasdorf, A. H., & Dornbusch, S. M. (1961). Cultural uniformity in relation to physical disabilities. *American Sociological Review, 26,* 241–247.

Richardson, P. H., & Vincent, C. A. (1986). Acupuncture for the treatment of pain: A review of evaluative research. *Pain, 24,* 15–40.

Rickard, K. (1988). The occurrence of maladaptive health-related behaviors and teacher-related conduct problems in children of chronic low back pain patients. *Journal of Behavioral Medicine, 11,* 107–116.

Ridker, P. M., Vaughan, D. E., Stampfer, M. J., Glynn, R. J., & Hennekens, C. H. (1994). Association of moderate alcohol consumption and plasma concentration of endogenous tissue-type plasminogen activator. *Journal of the American Medical Association, 272,* 929–933.

Ries, L. A., Wingo, P. A., Miller, D. S., Howe, H. L., Weir, H. K., Rosenberg, H. M., Vernon, S. W., Cronin, K., & Edwards, B. K. (2000). The annual report to the nation on the status of cancer, 1973–1997, with a special section on colorectal cancer. *Cancer, 88,* 2398–2424.

Rigby, K., Brown, M., Anagnostou, P., Ross, M. W., & Rosser, B. R. S. (1989). Shock tactics to count AIDS: The Australian experience. *Psychology and Health, 3,* 145–159.

Riley, J. L., & Robinson, M. E. (1997). CSQ: Five factors or fiction? *Clinical Journal of Pain, 13,* 156–162.

Riley, W. T., Barenie, J. T., Woodard, C. E., & Mabe, P. A. (1996). Perceived smokeless tobacco addiction among adolescents. *Health Psychology, 15,* 289–292.

Rimal, R. N. (2000). Closing the knowledge-behavior gap in health promotion: The mediating role of self-efficacy. *Health Communication, 12,* 219–237.

Rimer, B. K. (1994). Mammography use in the U.S.: Trends and the impact of interventions. *Annals of Behavioral Medicine, 16,* 317–326.

Rimer, B. K., Meissner, H., Breen, N., Legler, J., & Coyne, C. A. (2001). Social and behavioral interventions to increase breast cancer screening. In N. Schneiderman, M. A. Speers, J. M. Silva, H. Tomes, & J. H. Gentry (Eds.), *Integrating behavioral and social sciences with public health* (pp. 177–201). Washington, DC: American Psychological Association.

Rimer, B. K., Resch, N., King, E., Ross, E., Lerman, C., Boyce, A., Kessler, H., & Engstrom, P. F. (1992). Multistrategy health education program to increase mammography use among women ages 65 and older. *Public Health Reports, 107,* 369–380.

Rivara, F. P., Thompson, D. C., & Thompson. R. S. (1994). The Seattle Children's Bicycle Helmet Campaign: Changes in helmet use and head injury admissions. *Pediatrics, 93,* 567–569.

Robbins, A. S., Spence, J. T., & Clark, H. (1991). Psychological determinants of health and performance: The tangled web of desirable and undesirable components. *Journal of Personality and Social Psychology, 61,* 755–765.

Roberts, A. H. (1987). Biofeedback and chronic pain: An update. *Journal of Pain and Symptom Management, 2,* 169–171.

Roberts, A. H., Kewman, D. C., Mercier, L., & Hovell, M. (1993). The power of nonspecific effects in healing: Implications for psychosocial and biological treatments. *Clinical Psychology Review, 13,* 375–391.

Roberts, A. H., & Reinhardt, L. (1980). The behavioral management of chronic pain: Long-term follow-up with comparison groups. *Pain, 8,* 151–162.

Roberts, C. (1998). *We are our mothers' daughters.* New York: William Morrow.

Roberts, F. D., Newcomb, P. A., Trentham-Dietz, A., & Storer, B. E. (1996). Self-reported stress and breast cancer. *Cancer, 77,* 1089–1093.

Robertson, E. K., & Suinn, R. M. (1968). The determination of rate of progress of stroke patients through empathy measures of patient and family. *Journal of Psychosomatic Research, 12,* 189–191.

Robie, P. W. (1987). Compliance. In C. S. Rogers, J. D. McCue, & P. Gal (Eds.),

Managing chronic disease (pp. 13–17). Oradell, NJ: Medical Economics Books.

Rockhill, B., Willett, W. C., Hunter, D. J., Manson, J. E., Hankinson, S. E., & Colditz, G. A. (1999). A prospective study of recreational physical activity and breast cancer risk. *Archives of Internal Medicine, 159,* 2290–2296.

Rodin, J. (1981). Current status of the internal-external hypothesis for obesity: What went wrong? *American Psychologist, 36,* 361–372.

Rodin, J., & Ickovics, J. R. (1990). Women's health: Review and research agenda as we approach the 21st century. *American Psychologist, 45,* 1018–1034.

Rodin, J., & Langer, E. J. (1977). Long-term effects of a control-relevant intervention with the institutionalized aged. *Journal of Personality and Social Psychology, 35,* 897–902.

Rodin, J., & Slochower, J. (1976). Externality in the nonobese: Effects of environmental responsiveness on weight. *Journal of Personality and Social Psychology, 33,* 338–344.

Rogers, E., Vaughan, P., Swalehe, R., Rao, N., Suenderud, P., & Sood, S. (1999). Effects of an entertainment-education radio soap opera on family planning behavior in Tanzania. *Studies in Family Planning, 30,* 193–211.

Rogers, R. W. (1975). A protection motivation theory of fear appeals and attitude change. *Journal of Psychology, 91,* 93–114.

Rogers, R. W., Rogers, J. S., Bailey, J. S., Runkle, W., & Moore, B. (1988). Promoting safety belt use among state employees. *Journal of Applied Behavior Analysis, 21,* 263–269.

Rogers, W. H., Draper, D., Kahn, K. L., Keeler, E. B., Rubenstein, L. V., Kosecoff, J., & Brook, R. H. (1990). Quality of care before and after implementation of the DDRG-based prospective payment system. *Journal of the American Medical Association, 264,* 1989–1994.

Rohling, M. L., Binder, L. M., & Langhin-Richsen-Rohling, J. (1995). A meta-analytic review of the association between financial compensation and the experience and treatment of chronic pain. *Health Psychology, 14,* 537–547.

Rollman, G. B., & Harris, G. (1987). The detectability, discriminability, and perceived magnitude of painful electrical shock. *Perception and Psychophysics, 42,* 257–268.

Rolls, B. J., Rowe, E. A., Rolls, E. T., Kingston, B., Megson, A., & Gunary, R. (1981). Variety in a meal enhances food intake in man. *Physiology & Behavior, 26,* 215–221.

Romano, J. M., Turner, J. A., Friedman, L. S., Bulcroft, R. A., Jensen, M. P., Hops, H., & Wright, S. F. (1992). Sequential analysis of chronic pain behaviors and spouse responses. *Journal of Consulting and Clinical Psychology, 60,* 777–782.

Romieu, I., Willett, W. C., Stampfer, M. J., Colditz, G. A., Sampson, L., Rosner, B., Hennekens, C. H., & Speizer, F. E. (1988). Energy intake and other determinants of relative weight. *American Journal of Clinical Nutrition, 47,* 406–412.

Ronis, D. L. (1992). Conditional health threats: Health beliefs, decisions, and behaviors among adults. *Health Psychology, 11,* 127–134.

Rook, K. S. (1984). The negative side of social interaction: Impact on psychological well-being. *Journal of Personality and Social Psychology, 46,* 1097–1108

Rook, K. S. (1987). Social support versus companionship: Effects on life stress, loneliness, and evaluation by others. *Journal of Personality and Social Psychology, 52,* 1132–1147.

Rosario, M., Mahler, K., Hunter, J., & Gwadz, M. (1999). Understanding the unprotected sexual behaviors of gay, lesbian, and bisexual youths: An empirical test of the cognitive-environmental model. *Health Psychology, 18,* 272–280.

Rosen, C. S. (2000). Integrating stage and continuum models to explain processing of exercise messages and exercise initiation among sedentary college students. *Health Psychology, 19,* 172–180.

Rosenbaum, M., & Ben-Ari Smira, K. (1986). Cognitive and personality factors in the delay of gratification of hemodialysis patients. *Journal of Personality and Social Psychology, 51,* 357–364.

Rosenberg, M. (1965). Society and adolescent self-image. Princeton, NJ: Princeton University Press.

Rosengren, A., Orth-Gomer, K., Wedel, H., & Wilhemlmsen, L. (1993). Stressful life events, social support, and mortality in men born in 1933. *British Medical Journal, 307,* 1102–1105.

Rosenman, R. H., Brand, R. J., Jenkins, C. D., Friedman, M., Straus, R., & Wurm, M. (1975). Coronary heart disease in the Western Collaborative Group Study: Final follow-up of 8 1/2 years. *Journal of the American Medical Association, 233,* 872–877.

Rosenman, R. H., & Friedman, M. (1961). Association of specific behavior pattern in women with blood and cardiovascular findings. *Circulation, 24,* 1173–1184.

Rosenstock, I. M. (1960). What research in motivation suggests for public health. *American Journal of Public Health, 50,* 295–301.

Rosenstock, I. M. (1990). The health belief model: Explaining health behavior through expectancies. In K. Glanz, F. M. Lewis, B. K. Rimer (Eds.), *Health behavior and health education: Theory, research, and practice* (pp. 39–62). San Francisco: Jossey-Bass.

Rosenthal, R., & Fode, K. L. (1963). The effect of experimenter bias on the performance of the albino rat. *Behavioral Science, 8,* 183–189.

Roske, I., Baeger, I., Frenzel, R., & Oehme, P. (1994). Does a relationship exist between the quality of stress and the motivation to ingest alcohol? *Alcohol, 11,* 113–124.

Rossiter, L. F., Langwell, K., Wann, T. T., & Rivnyak, M. (1989). Patient satisfaction among eldery enrollees and disenrollees. *Journal of the American Medical Association, 262,* 57–63.

Roter, D. L., Lipkin, M., Jr., & Korsgaard, A. (1991). Gender differences in patients' and physicians' communication during primary care medical visits. *Medical Care, 29,* 1083–1093.

Roth, D. L., Wiebe, D. J., Fillingim, R. B., & Shay, K. A. (1990). Life events, fitness, hardiness, and health: A simultaneous analysis of proposed stress-resistance effects. *Journal of Personality and Social Psychology, 57,* 136–142.

Roth, S., & Cohen, L. J. (1986). Approach, avoidance, and coping with stress. *American Psychologist, 41,* 813–819.

Rothenberg, K. H., & Paskey, S. (1995). The risk of domestic violence and women with HIV infection: Implications for partner notification, public policy, and the law. *American Journal of Public Health, 85,* 1569–1576.

Rothman, A. J., Martino, S. C., Bedell, B. T., Detweiler, J. B., & Salovey, P. (1999). The systematic influence of gain- and loss-framed messages on interest in and use of different types of health behavior. *Personality and Social Psychology Bulletin, 25,* 1355–1369.

Rothman, A. J., & Salovey, P. (1997). Shaping perceptions to motivate healthy behavior: The role of message framing. *Psychological Bulletin, 121,* 3–19.

Rothman, A. J., Salovey, P., Antone, C., Keough, K., & Martin, C. D. (1993). The influence of message framing on intentions to perform health behaviors. *Journal of Experimental Social Psychology, 29,* 408–433.

Rothman, A. J., Salovey, P., Turvey, C., & Fishkin, S. A. (1993). Attributions of responsibility and persuasion: Increasing mammography utilization among women over 40 with an internally oriented message. *Health Psychology, 12*, 39–47.

Rotter, J. B. (1966). Generalized expectancies for internal versus external control of reinforcement. *Psychological Monographs, 80*, (609).

Rovario, S., Holmes, D. S., & Holmsten, R. D. (1984). Influence of a cardiac rehabilitation program on the cardiovascular, psychological, and social functioning of cardiac patients. *Journal of Behavioral Medicine, 7*, 61–81.

Roy, R. (2001). Social relations and chronic pain. New York: Plenum.

Rozin, P. (1996). Sociocultural influences on human food selection. In E.D. Capaldi (Ed.), *Why we eat what we eat: The psychology of eating* (pp. 233–263). Washington, DC: American Psychological Association.

Rozin, P., & Fallon, A. (1988). Body image, attitudes to weight, and misperceptions of figure preferences of the opposite sex: A comparison of men and women in two generations. *Journal of Abnormal Psychology, 97*, 342–345.

Rozin, P., & Fallon, A. E. (1987). A perspective on disgust. *Psychological Review, 94*, 23–41.

Ruberman, W., Weinblatt, E., Goldberg, J. D., & Chaudray, B. S. (1984). Psychosocial influences on mortality after myocardial infarction. *New England Journal of Medicine, 311*, 552–559.

Rubin, L. B. (1986). On men and friendship. *Psychoanalytic Review, 73*, 165–181.

Ruble, D. (1977). Premenstrual symptoms: A reinterpretation. *Science, 197*, 291–292.

Rubonis, A. V., & Bickman, L. (1991). Psychological impairment in the wake of disaster: The disaster–psychopathology relationship. *Psychological Bulletin, 109*, 384–399.

Rudd, J. R., & Geller, E. S. (1985). A university-based incentive program to increase safety belt use: Toward cost-effective institutionalization. *Journal of Applied Behavior Analysis, 18*, 215–226.

Ryckman, R. M., Robbins, M. A., Kazcor, L. M., & Gold, J. A. (1989). Male and female raters' stereotyping of male and female physiques. *Personality and Social Psychology Bulletin, 15*, 244–251.

Sackett, D. L. (1979). A compliance practicum for the busy practitioner. In R. B. Haynes, D. W. Taylor, & D. L. Sackett (Eds.), *Compliance in health care* (pp. 286–294). Baltimore: Johns Hopkins Press.

Sacks, J. J., Holingreen, P., Smith, S. M., & Sosin, D. M. (1991). Bicycle-associated head injuires and deaths in the United States from 1984 through 1988. *Journal of the American Medical Association, 266*, 3016–3018.

Safer, M. A., Tharps, Q. J., Jackson, T. C., & Leventhal, H. (1979). Determinants of three stages of delay in seeking care at a medical clinic. *Medical Care, 17*, 11–29.

Sanders, M. R., Shepherd, R. W., Cleghorn, G., & Woolford, H. (1994). The treatment of recurrent abdominal pain in children: A controlled comparison of cognitive-behavioral family intervention and standard pediatric care. *Journal of Consulting and Clinical Psychology, 62*, 306–314.

Sanders, S. H, Brena, S. F. Spier, C. J., Beltrutti, D., McConnell, H., Quintero, O. (1992). Chronic low back pain patients around the world: Cross-cultural similarities and differences. *Journal of Clinical Pain, 8*, 317–323.

Sanderson, C. A., & Cantor, N. (1995). Social dating goals in late adolescence: Implications for safer sexual activity. *Journal of Personality and Social Psychology, 68*, 1121–1134.

Sanderson, C. A., Darley, J. M., & Messinger, C. S. (2002). "I'm not as thin as you think I am": The development and consequences of feeling discrepant from the thinness norm. *Personality and Social Psychology Bulletin, 28*, 172–183.

Sanderson, C. A., & Holloway, R. M. (2003). Preventing eating disorders in college women: The differential effectiveness of primary versus secondary prevention. *Journal of Applied Social Psychology*.

Sanderson, C. A., & Maibach, E. W. (1996). Predicting condom use in African-American STD patients: The role of two types of outcome expectancies. *Journal of Applied Social Psychology, 26*, 1495–1509.

Sanftner, J. L., Crowther, J. H., Crawford, P. A., & Watts, D. D. (1996). Maternal influences (or lack thereof) on daughters' eating attitudes and behaviors. *Eating Disorders: The Journal of Treatment and Prevention, 4*, 147–159.

Sapolsky, R. M. (1992). *Stress, the aging brain, and the mechanisms of neuron death.* Cambridge, MA: MIT Press.

Sapolsky, R. M. (1994). *Why zebras don't get ulcers.* New York: Freeman.

Sapolsky, R. M. (1996). Why stress is bad for your brain. *Science, 273*, 749–750.

Sarason, I. G., Johnson, J. H., & Siegel, J. M. (1978). Assessing the impact of life changes: Development of the Life Experiences Survey. *Journal of Consulting and Clinical Psychology, 46*, 932–946.

Sarason, I. G., Pierce, G. R., & Sarason, B. R. (1990). Social support and interactional processes: A triadic hypothesis. *Journal of Social and Personal Relationships, 7*, 495–506.

Sarason, B. R., Sarason, I. G., & Gurung, R. A. R. (1997). Close personal relationships and health outcomes: A key to the role of social support. In S. Duck (Ed.), *Handbook of personal relationships: Theory, research and interventions* (2nd ed., pp. 547–573). New York: Wiley.

Sarason, I. G., Sarason, B. R., Keefe, D. E., Hayes, B. E., & Shearin, E. N. (1986). Cognitive interference: Situational determinants and traitlike characteristics. *Journal of Personality and Social Psychology, 51*, 215–226.

Sarason, I. G., Sarason, B. R., & Shearin, E. N. (1986). Social support as an individual difference variable: Its stability, origins, and relational aspects. *Journal of Personality and Social Psychology, 50*, 845–855.

Sayette, M. A. (1999). Cognitive theory and research. In K. E. Leonard & H. T. Blane (Eds.), *Psychological theories of drinking and alcoholism* (2nd ed., pp. 247–291). New York: Guilford.

Schachter, S. (1968). Obesity and eating. *Science, 161*, 751–756.

Schachter, S. (1977). Nicotine regulation in heavy and light smokers. *Journal of Personality and Social Psychology, 106*, 5–12.

Schachter, S., Goldman, R., & Gordon, A. (1968). Effects of fear, food deprivation, and obesity on eating. *Journal of Personality and Social Psychology, 10*, 91–97.

Schachter, S., Silverstein, B., Kozlowski, L. T., Herman, C. P., & Liebling, B. (1977). Effects of stress of cigarette smoking and urinary pH. *Journal of Personality and Social Psychology, 106*, 24–30.

Schaefer, C., Quesenberry, C. P., Jr., & Wi, S. (1995). Mortality following conjugal bereavement and the effects of a shared environment. *American Journal of Epidemiology, 141*, 1142–1152.

Schaefer, E. S., & Burnett, C. K. (1987). Stability and predictability of quality of women's marital relationships and demoralization. *Journal of Personality and Social Psychology, 53*, 1129–1136.

Scharff, L., & Marcus, D. A. (1994). Interdisciplinary outpatient group treatment of intractable headache. *Headache, 34*, 73–78.

Scheier, M. F., & Carver, C. S. (1985). Optimism, coping, and health: Assessment and implications of generalized outcome expectancies. *Health Psychology, 4*, 219–247.

Scheier, M. F., & Carver, C. S. (1987). Dispositional optimism and physical well-being: The influence of generalized outcome expectancies on health. *Journal of Personality, 55,* 169–210.

Scheier, M. F., & Carver, C. S. (1992). Effects of optimism on psychological and physical well-being: Theoretical overview and empirical update. *Cognitive Therapy and Research, 16,* 201–228.

Scheier, M. F., & Carver, C. S. (1993). On the power of positive thinking: The benefits of being optimistic. *Current Directions in Psychological Science, 2,* 26–30.

Scheier, M. F., Matthews, K. A., Owens, J., Magovern, G. J., Sr., Lefebvre, R.C., Abbott, R. A., & Carver, C. S. (1989). Dispositional optimism and recovery from coronary artery bypass surgery: The beneficial effects of physical and psychological well-being. *Journal of Personality and Social Psychology, 57,* 1024–1040.

Scheier, M. F., Matthews, K. A., Owens, J. F., Schulz, R., Bridges, M.W., Magovern, G. J., & Carver, C. S. (1999). Optimism and rehospitalization after coronary artery bypass graft surgery. *Archives of Internal Medicine, 159,* 829–835.

Scheier, M. F., Weintraub, J. K., & Carver, C. S. (1986). Coping with stress: Divergent strategies of optimists and pessimists. *Journal of Personality and Social Psychology, 51,* 1257–1264.

Scherer, K. P. (1986). Voice, stress, and emotion. In M. H. Appley & R. Trumbull (Eds.), *Dynamics of stress: Physiological, psychological, and social perspectives* (pp. 157–179). New York: Plenum.

Schifter, D. E., & Ajzen, I. (1985). Intention, perceived control, and weight loss: An application of the theory of planned behavior. *Journal of Personality and Social Psychology, 49,* 843–851.

Schlegel, R. P., Crawford, C. A., & Sanborn, M. D. (1977). Correspondence and mediation properties of the Fishbein model: An application to adolescent alcohol use. *Journal of Experimental Social Psychology, 13,* 421–430.

Schleifer, S. J., Keller, S. E., Camerino, M., Thorton, J. C., & Stein, M. (1983). Suppression of lymphocyte stimulation following bereavement. *Journal of the American Medical Association, 250,* 374–377.

Schneider, T. R., Salovey, P., Apanovitch, A. M., Pizarro, J., McCarthy, D., Zullo, J., Rothman, A. J. (2001). The effect of message framing and ethnic targeting on mammography use among low-income women. *Health Psychology, 20,* 256–266.

Schreiber, G. B., Robins, M., Striegel-Moore, R., Obarzanek, E., Morrison, J. A., & Wright, D. J. (1996). Weight modification efforts reported by Black and White preadolescent girls: National Heart, Lung, and Blood Institute Growth and Health Study. *Pediatrics, 98,* 63–70.

Schroeder, C. M., & Prentice, D. A. (1998). Exposing pluralistic ignorance to reduce alcohol use among college students. *Journal of Applied Social Psychology, 28,* 2150–2180.

Schroeder, D. H., & Costa, P. T. Jr. (1984). Influence of life event stress on physical illness: Substantive effects or methodological flaws? *Journal of Personality and Social Psychology, 46,* 853–863.

Schuckit, M. A. (1985). Genetics and the risk for alcoholism. *Journal of the American Medical Association, 254,* 2614–2617.

Schuckit, M. A., & Smith, T. L. (1996). An 8-year follow-up of 450 sons of alcoholic and control subjects. *Archives of General Psychiatry, 53,* 202–210.

Schulman, K. A., Berlin, J. A., Harless, W., Kerner, J. F., Sistrunk, S., Gersh, B. J., Dubé, R., Taleghani, c. K., Burke, J. E., Williams, S., Wisenberg, J. M., & Escarce, J. J. (1999). The effect of race and sex on physicians' recommendations for cardiac catheterization. *New England Journal of Medicine, 340,* 618–625.

Schulz, R., Beach, S. R., Lind, B., Martire, L. M., Zdaniuk, B., Hirsch, C., Jackson, S., & Burton, L. (2001). Involvement in caregiving and adjustment to death of a spouse: Findings from the Caregiver Health Effects Study. *Journal of the American Medical Association, 285,* 3123–3129.

Schulz, R., Bookwala, J., Knapp, J. E., Scheier, M., & Williamson, G. (1996). Pessimism, age, and cancer mortality. *Psychology and Aging, 11,* 304–309.

Schulz, R., & Decker, S. (1985). Long-term adjustment to physical disability: The role of social support, perceived control, and self-blame. *Journal of Personality and Social Psychology, 48,* 1162–1172.

Schulz, R., & Tompkins, C. A. (1990). Life events and changes in social relationships: Examples, mechanisms, and measurement. *Journal of Social and Clinical Psychology, 9,* 69–77.

Schut, H. A. W., van den Bout, J., De Keijser, J., & Stroebe, M. S. (1996). Cross-modality grief therapy: Description and assessment of a new program. *Journal of Clinical Psychology, 52,* 357–365.

Schwartz, G. E. (1982). Testing the biopsychosocial model: The ultimate challenge facing behavioral medicine? *Journal of Consulting and Clinical Psychology, 50,* 1040–1053.

Schwartz, B. S., Stewart, W. F., Simon, D., & Lipton, R. B. (1998). Epidemiology of tension-type headache. *Journal of the American Medical Association, 279,* 381–383.

Schwartz, M. D., Taylor, K. L., Willard, K. S., Siegel, J. E., Lamdan, R. M., & Moran, K. (1999). Distress, personality, and mammography utilization among women with a family history of breast cancer. *Health Psychology, 18,* 327–332.

Schwartzberg, S. S. (1993). Struggling for meaning: How HIV-positive gay men make sense of AIDS. *Professional Psychology: Research and Practice, 24,* 483–490.

Schwarz, N., Hippler, H. J., Deutsch, B., & Strack, F. (1985). Response categories: Effects on behavioral reports and comparative judgments. *Public Opinion Quarterly, 49,* 388–395.

Schwarzer, R. (1992). Self-efficacy: Thought control of action. Washington, DC: Hemisphere.

Schwarzer, R., Jerusalem, M., & Hahn, A. (1994). Unemployment, social support and health complaints: A longitudinal study of stress in East German refugees. *Journal of Community and Applied Social Psychology, 4,* 31–45.

Schwarzer, R., & Leppin, A. (1989). Social support and health: A meta-analysis. *Psychology and Health, 3,* 1–15.

Schwarzer, R., & Leppin, A. (1992). Social support and mental health: A conceptual and empirical overview. In L. Montada, S.-H., Filipp, & M. J. Lerner (Eds.), *Life crises and experiences of loss in adult life* (pp. 435–458). Hillsdale, NJ: Erlbaum.

Sclafani, A., & Springer, D. (1976). Dietary obesity in adult rats: Similarities to hypothalamic and human obesity. *Physiology and Behavior, 17,* 461–471.

Scott, J. C., & Hochberg, M. C. (1993). Arthritis and other musculoskeletal diseases. In R. C. Brownson, P. L., Remington, & J. R. Davis (Eds.), *Chronic disease epidemiology and control* (pp. 285–305). Washington, DC: American Public Health Association.

Sears, S.R., & Stanton, A. L. (2001). Physician-assisted dying: Review of issues and roles for health psychologists. *Health Psychology, 20,* 302–310.

Sears, S. F., Jr., Marhefka, S. L., Rodrigue, J. R., & Campbell, C. (2000). The role of patients' ability to pay, gender, and smoking history on public attitudes toward cardiac transplant allocation: An experimental investigation. *Health Psychology, 19,* 192–196.

Seeman, M., & Seeman, T. E. (1983). Health behavior and personal autonomy: A longitudinal study of the sense of control in illness. *Journal of Health and Social Behavior, 24,* 144–160.

Seeman, T. E., Berkman, L. F., Blazer, D., & Rowe, J. W. (1994). Social ties and support and neuroendocrine function: The MacArthur studies of successful aging. *Annals of Behavioral Medicine, 16,* 95–106.

Seeman, T. E., Singer, B., Horwitz, R., & McEwen, B. S. (1997). The price of adaptation—Allostatic load and its health consequences: MacArthur studies of successful aging. *Archives of Internal Medicine, 157,* 2259–2268.

Sagerstrom, S. C, Taylor, S. E., Kemeny, M. E., & Fahey, J. L. (1998). Optimism is associated with mood, coping, and immune change in response to stress. *Journal of Personality and Social Psychology, 74,* 1646–1655.

Segerstrom, S. C., Taylor, S. E., Kemeny, M. E., Reed, G. M., & Visscher, B. R. (1996). Causal attributions predict rate of immune decline in HIV-seropositive gay men. *Health Psychology, 15,* 485–493.

Selby, J. V., Friedman, G. D., Quesenberry, C. P., Jr., & Weiss, N. S. (1992). A case-control study of screening sigmoidoscopy and mortality from colorectal cancer. *New England Journal of Medicine, 326,* 653–657.

Self, C. A., & Rogers, R. W. (1990). Coping with threats to health: Effects of persuasive appeals on depressed, normal, and antisocial personalities. *Journal of Behavioral Medicine, 13,* 343–358.

Seligman, M. E. P., & Csikszentmihalyi, M. (2000). Positive psychology: An introduction. *American Psychologist, 55,* 5–14.

Selye, H. (1956). *The stress of life.* New York: McGraw-Hill.

Selye, H. (1974). *Stress without distress.* Philadelphia: Lippincott.

Selye, H. (1976). *Stress in health and disease.* Reading, MA: Butterworth.

Senecal, C., Nouwen, A., & White, D. (2000). Motivation and dietary self-care in adults with diabetes: Are self-efficacy and autonomous self-regulation complementary or competing constructs? *Health Psychology, 19,* 452–457.

Seville, J. L., & Robinson, A. B. (2000). Locus of control in the patient with chronic pain. In R. J. Gatchel & J. N. Weisberg (Eds.), *Person-*

ality characteristics of patients with pain (pp. 165–179). Washington, DC: American Psychological Association.

Seybold, K. S., & Hill, P. C. (2001). The role of religion and spirituality in mental and physical health. *Current Directions in Psychological Science, 10,* 21–24.

Shadel, W. G., & Mermelstein, R. J. (1993). Cigarette smoking under stress: The role of coping expectancies among smokers in a clinic-based smoking cessation program. *Health Psychology, 12,* 443–450.

Shaffer, J. W., Graves, P. L., Swank, R. T., & Pearson, T. A. (1987). Clustering of personality traits in youth and the subsequent development of cancer among physicians. *Journal of Behavioral Medicine, 10,* 441–447.

Shaffer, W. J., Duszynski, K. R., & Thomas, C. B. (1982). Family attitudes in youth as a possible precursor of cancer among physicians: A search for explanatory mechanisms. *Journal of Behavioral Medicine, 15,* 143–164.

Shapiro, A. K. (1964). Factors contributing to the placebo effect: Their implications for psychotherapy. *American Journal of Psychotherapy, 18,* 73–88.

Shapiro, D. E., Boggs, S. R., Melamed, B. G., & Graham-Pole, J. (1992). The effect of varied physician affect on recall, anxiety, and perceptions in women at risk for breast cancer: An analogue study. *Health Psychology, 11,* 61–66.

Shaw, E. G., & Routh, D. K. (1982). Effect of mother presence on children's reaction to adverse procedures. *Journal of Pediatric Psychology, 7,* 33–42.

Shedler, J., & Block, J. (1990). Adolescent drug use and psychological health. *American Psychologist, 45,* 612–630.

Sheeran, P., Abraham, C., & Orbell, S. (1999). Psychosocial correlates of heterosexual condom use: A meta-analysis. *Psychological Bulletin, 125,* 90–132.

Sheeran, P., Conner, M., & Norman, P. (2001). Can the theory of planned behavior explain patterns of health behavior change? *Health Psychology, 20,* 12–19.

Sheeran, P., & Orbell, S. (2000). Using implementation intentions to increase attendance for cervical cancer screening. *Health Psychology, 18,* 283–289.

Sheeran, P., & Taylor, S. (1999). Predicting intentions to use condoms: A meta-analysis and comparison of the theories of reasoned action and planned behavior. *Journal of Applied Social Psychology, 29,* 1624–1675.

Sheeshka, J. D., Wolcott, D. M., & MacKinnon, N. J. (1993). Social cognitive theory as a

framework to explain intentions to practice healthy eating behaviors. *Journal of Applied Social Psychology, 23,* 1547–1573.

Shekelle, P. G., Adams, A. H., & Chassin, M. R. (1992). Spinal manipulation for low-back pain. *Annals of Internal Medicine, 117,* 590–595.

Shekelle, R. B., Gale, M., Ostfield, A. M., & Paul, O. (1983). Hostility, risk of coronary heart disease and mortality. *Psychosomatic Medicine, 45,* 109–114.

Shekelle, R. B., Raynor, W. J., Jr., Ostfeld, A. M., Garron, D. C., Bieliauskas, L. A., Livy, Sc. C., Maliza, C., & Paul, O. (1981). Psychological depression and 17-year risk of death from cancer. *Psychosomatic Medicine, 43,* 117–125.

Shekelle, R. B., Rossof, A. H., & Stamler, J. (1991). Dietary cholesterol and incidence of lung cancer: The Western Electric study. *American Journal of Epidemiology, 134,* 480–484.

Sheppard, B. H., Hartwick, J., & Warshaw, P. R. (1988). The theory of reasoned action: A meta-analysis of past research with recommendations for modifications and future research. *Journal of Consumer Research, 15,* 325–343.

Shepperd, S. L., Solomon, L. J., Atkins, E., Foster, R. S., & Frankowski, B. (1990). Determinants of breast self-examination among women of lower income and lower education. *Journal of Behavioral Medicine, 13,* 359–371.

Sher, K. J., Gotham, H. J., Erickson, D. J., & Wood, P. K. (1996). A prospective, high-risk study of the relationship between tobacco dependence and alcohol use disorders. *Alcoholism: Clinical and Experimental Research, 20,* 485–492.

Sher, K. J., Trull, T. J., Bartholow, B. D., & Vieth, A. (1999). Personality and alcoholism: Issues, methods, and etiological processes. In K. E. Leonard & H. T. Blane (Eds.), *Psychological theories of drinking and alcoholism* (2nd ed., pp. 54–105). New York: Guilford.

Sherbourne, C. D., & Hays, R. D. (1990). Marital status, social support, and health transitions in chronic disease patients. *Journal of Health and Social Behavior, 31,* 328–343.

Sherbourne, C. D., Hays, R. D., Ordway, L., DiMatteo, M. R., Kravitz, R. L. (1992). Antecedents of adherence to medical recommendations: Results from the Medical Outcomes Study. *Journal of Behavioral Medicine, 15,* 447–468.

Sherman, D. A. K., Nelson, L. D., & Steele, C. M. (2000). Do messages about health risks threaten the self? Increasing the acceptance of threatening health messages via self-affirmation. *Personality & Social Psychology Bulletin, 26,* 1046–1058.

Sherr, L. (1990). Fear arousal and AIDS: Do shock tactics work? *AIDS, 4,* 361–364.

Shiffman, S., Fischer, L. A., Paty, J. A., Gnys, M., Hickcox, M., & Kassel, J. D. (1994). Drinking and smoking: A field test of their association. *Annals of Behavioral Medicine, 16,* 203–209.

Shiffman, S., Gnys, M., Richards, T. J., Paty, J. A., Hickcox, M., & Kassel, J. D. (1996). Temptations to smoke after quitting: A comparison of lapsers and maintainers. *Health Psychology, 15,* 455–461.

Shiffman, S., Hickcox, M., Paty, J. A., Gnys, M., Kassel, J. D., & Richards, T. J. (1996). Progression from a smoking lapse to a relapse: Prediction from abstinence violation effects, nicotine dependence, and lapse characteristics. *Journal of Consulting and Clinical Psychology, 64,* 993–1002.

Shiloh, S., Ben-Sinai, R., & Keinan, G. (1999). Effects of controllability, predictability, and information-seeking style on interest in predictive genetic testing. *Personality and Social Psychology Bulletin, 25,* 1187–1195.

Shinn, M., Rosario, M., Morch, H., & Chestnut, D. E. (1984). Coping with job stress and burnout in the human services. *Journal of Personality and Social psychology, 46,* 864–876.

Shipley, R. H., Butt, J. H., Horwitz, B., & Farbry, J. E. (1978). Preparation for a stressful medical procedure: Effects of amount of stimulus preexposure and coping style. *Journal of Consulting and Clinical Psychology, 46,* 499–507.

Shouksmith, G., & Taylor, J. E. (1997). The interaction of culture with general job stressors in air traffic controllers. *International Journal of Aviation Psychology, 7,* 343–352.

Shulman, N. (1976). Network analysis: A new addition to an old bag of tricks. *Acta Psychologica, 19,* 307–323.

Siegel, J. M. (1990). Stressful life events and use of physician services among the elderly: The moderating role of pet ownership. *Journal of Personality and Social Psychology, 58,* 1081–1086.

Siegler, I., Levenstein, S., Feaganes, J. R., & Brummett, B. H. (2000). Personality before and after illness onset among patients with inflammatory bowel disease: A controlled, prospective study. *Psychosomatic Medicine, 62,* 151.

Siegler, I. C., Bastian, L. A., Steffens, D. C., Bosworth, H. B., & Costa, P. T. (2002). Behavioral medicine and aging. *J Consult Clin Psychol 70,* 843–51.

Siegler, I. C., Feaganes, J. R., & Rimer, B. K. (1995). Predictors of adoption of mammography in women under age 50. *Health Psychology, 14,* 274–277.

Siegman, A. W. (1993). Cardiovascular consequences of expressing, experiencing, and repressing anger. *Journal of Behavioral Medicine, 16,* 539–569.

Siegman, A. W., Anderson, R., Herbst, J., Boyle, S., & Wilkinson, J. (1992). Dimensions of anger-hostility and cardiovascular reactivity in provoked and angered men. *Journal of Behavioral Medicine, 15,* 257–272.

Silberstein, L., Striegel-Moore, R., Timko, C., & Rodin, J. (1988). Behavioral and psychological implications of body dissatisfaction: Do men and women differ? *Sex Roles, 19,* 219–232.

Silverman, E., Range, L., & Overholser, J. (1994). Bereavement from suicide as compared to other forms of bereavement. *Omega, 30,* 41–51.

Silverstein, B., Perdue, L., Peterson, B., & Kelly, E. (1986). The role of the mass media in promoting a thin standard of bodily attractiveness for women. *Sex Roles, 14,* 519–532.

Simon, G., Gater, R., Kisely, S., & Piccinelli, M. (1996). Somatic symptoms of distress: An international primary care study. *Psychosomatic Medicine, 58,* 481–488.

Simon, N. (1977). Breast cancer induced by radiation. *Journal of the American Medical Association, 237,* 789–790.

Simoni, J., Mason, H., Marks, G., Ruiz, M., Reed, D., & Richardson, J. (1995). Women's self-disclosure of HIV infection: Rates, reasons, and reactions. *Journal of Consulting and Clinical Psychology, 63,* 474–478.

Sims, J., & Baumann, D. (1972). The tornado threat and coping styles of the north and south. *Science, 176,* 1386–1392.

Sinha, R., Fisch, G., Teague, R., Tamborlane, W. V., Banyas, B., Allen, K., Savoye, M., Rieger, V., Taksali, S., Barbetta, G., Sherwin, R. S., & Caprio, S. (2002). Prevalence of impaired glucose tolerance among children and adolescents with marked obesity. *New England Journal of Medicine, 346,* 802–810.

Skaer, T. L., Robinson, L. M., Sclar, D. A., & Harding, G. H. (1996). Financial incentives and the use of mammography among Hispanic migrants to the United States. *Health Care for Women International, 17,* 281–291.

Skelton, J. A., & Pennebaker, J. W. (1982). The psychology of physical symptoms and sensations. In G. S. Sanders & J. Suls (Eds.), *Social psychology of health and illness* (pp. 99–128). Hillsdale, NJ: Erlbaum.

Skinner, B. F. (1938). *The behavior of organisms.* New York: Appleton.

Skinner, C. S., Campbell, M. K., Rimer, B. K., Curry, S., & Prochaska, J. O. (1999). How effective is tailored print communication? *Annals of Behavioral Medicine, 21,* 290–298.

Skinner, C. S., Strecher, V. J., & Hospers, H. (1994). Physician's recommendations for mammography: Do tailored messages make a difference? *American Journal of Public Health, 84,* 43–49.

Sklar, L. S., & Anisman, H. (1981). Stress and cancer. *Psychological Bulletin, 89,* 369–406.

Skrabanek, P. (1988). The physician's responsibility to the patient. *Lancet, 1,* 1155–1157.

Slattery, M. L., Boucher, K. M., Caan, B. J., Potter, J. D., & Ma, K.-N. (1998). Eating patterns and risk of colon cancer. *American Journal of Epidemiology, 148,* 4–16.

Slattery, M. L., Schumacher, M. C., Smith, K. R., West, D. W., & Abd-Elghany, N. (1990). Physical activity, diet, and risk of colon cancer in Utah. *American Journal of Epidemiology, 128,* 989–999.

Sloand, E. M., Pitt, E., Chiarello, R. J., & Nemo, G. J. (1991). HIV testing: State of the art. *Journal of the American Medical Association, 266,* 2861–2866.

Slochower, J., Kaplan, S. P., & Mann, L. (1981). The effects of life stress and weight on mood and eating. *Appetite, 2,* 115–125.

Smeets, M. A. M. (1999). Body size categorization in anorexia nervosa using a morphing instrument. *International Journal of Eating Disorders, 25,* 451–455.

Smith, C. A., & Pratt, M. (1993). Cardiovascular disease. In R. C. Brownson, P. L. Remington, & J. R. Davis (Eds.), *Chronic disease epidemiology and control* (pp. 83–107). Washington, DC: American Public Health Association.

Smith, G. T., Goldman, M. S., Greenbaum, P. E., & Christiansen, B. A. (1995). Expectancy for social facilitation from drinking: The divergent paths of high-expectancy and low-expectancy adolescents. *Journal of Abnormal Psychology, 104,* 32–40.

Smith, J. T., Barabasz, A., & Barabasz, M. (1996). Comparision of hypnosis and distraction in severly ill children undergoing painful medical procedures. *Journal of Counseling Psychology, 43,* 187–195.

Smith, T. W. (1992). Hostility and health: Current status of a psychosomatic hypothesis. *Health Psychology, 11,* 139–150.

Smith, T. W., Pope, M. K., Sanders, J. D., Allred, K. D., & O'Keefe, J. L. (1988). Cynical hostility at home and work. *Journal of Research in Personality, 22,* 525–548.

Smith, T. W., & Williams, P. G. (1992). Personality and health: Advantages and limitations of the five-factor model. *Journal of Personality, 60,* 395–423.

Smyth, J. M., Stone, A. A., Hurewitz, A., & Kaell, A. (1999). Effects of writing about stressful experiences on symptom reduction in patients with asthma or rheumatoid arthritis: A randomized trial. *Journal of the American Medical Association, 281,* 1304–1309.

Snyder, C. R., Sympson, S. C., Ybasco, F. C., Borders, T. F., Babyak, M. A., & Higgins, R. L. (1996). Development and validation of the State Hope Scale. *Journal of Personality and Social Psychology, 70,* 321–335.

Sobell, L. C., Cunningham, J. A., & Sobell, M. B. (1996). Recovery from alcohol problems with and without treatment: Prevalence in two population surveys. *American Journal of Public Health, 86,* 966–972.

Sobell, M. B., Sobell, L. C., & Gavin, D. R. (1995). Portraying alcohol treatment outcomes: Different yardsticks of success. *Behavior Therapy, 26,* 643–669.

Sokol, D., Sokol, J., & Sokol, C. (1985). A review of nonintrusive therapies used to deal with anxiety and pain in the dental office. *Journal of the American Dental Association, 110,* 217–222.

Solomon, G. F. (1991). Psychosocial factors, exercise, and immunity: Athletes, elderly persons, and AIDs patients. *International Journal of Sports Medicine, 12* (supplement 1), S50–S52.

Solomon, Z., Mikulincer, M., & Hobfoll, S. E. (1986). Effects of social support and battle intensity on loneliness and breakdown during combat. *Journal of Personality and Social Psychology, 51,* 1269–1276.

Sorensen, G., Jacobs, D. R., Pirie, P., Folsom, A., Luepker, R., & Gillum, R. (1987). Relationships among Type A behavior, employment experiences, and gender: The Minnesota Heart Survey. *Journal of Behavioral Medicine, 10,* 323–336.

Sorensen, G., Pechacek, T., & Pallonen, U. (1986). Occupational and worksite norms and attitudes about smoking cessation. *American Journal of Public Health, 76,* 544–549.

Sosa, R., Kennell, J., Klaus, M., Robertson, S., & Urrutia, J. (1980). The effect of a supportive companion on perionatal problems, length of labor, and mother–infant interaction. *New England Journal of Medicine, 303,* 597–600.

Southam, M. A., & Dunbar, J. (1986). Facilitating patient compliance with medical interventions. In K. A. Holroyd & T. L. Creer (Eds.), *Self-management of chronic disease: Handbook of clinical interventions and research* (pp. 163–187). New York: Academic Press.

Spanos, N. P., & Katsanis, J. (1989). Effects of instructional set on attributions of nonvolition during hypnotic and nonhypnotic analgesia. *Journal of Personality and Social Psychology, 56,* 182–188.

Speca, M., Carlson, L. E., Goodey, E., & Angen, M. (2000). A randomized, wait-list controlled clinical trial: The effect of a mindfulness meditation-based stress reduction program on mood and symptoms of stress in cancer outpatients. *Psychosomatic Medicine, 62,* 613–622.

Spector, P. E. (2000). Employee control and occupational stress. *Current Directions in Psychological Science, 11,* 133–136.

Speece, M. W., & Brent, S. B. (1996). The development of children's understanding of death. In C. A. Corr & D. M. Corr (Eds.), *Handbook of childhood death and bereavement* (pp. 29–50). New York: Springer.

Speisman, J. C., Lazarus, R. S., Mordkoff, A., & Davison, L. (1964). Experimental reduction of stress based on ego-defense theory. *Journal of Abnormal and Social Psychology, 68,* 367–380.

Spencer, S. M., Lehman, J. M., Wynings, C., Arena, P., Carver, C. S., Antoni, M. H., Derhagopian, R. P., Ironson, G., & Love, N. (1999). Concerns about breast cancer and relations to psychosocial well-being in a multiethnic sample of early-stage patients. *Health Psychology, 18,* 159–168.

Spiegel, D. (1996). Cancer and depression. *British Journal of Psychiatry, 168,* 109–116.

Spiegel, D. (2001). Mind matters—Group therapy and survival in breast cancer. *New England Journal of Medicine, 345,* 1767–8.

Spiegel, D., Bloom, J. R., Kraemer, H. C., & Gottheil, E. (1989). Effect of psychosocial treatment on survival of patients with metastatic breast cancer. *Lancet, 2,* 888–891.

Spiegel, D., Bloom, J. R., & Yalom, I. D. (1981). Group support for patients with metastatic breast cancer. *Archives of General Psychiatry, 38,* 527–533.

Spiegel, D., & Kato, P. (1996). Psychosocial influences on cancer incidence and progression. *Harvard Review of Psychiatry, 4,* 10–26.

Spielberger, C. D. (1986). Psychological determinants of smoking behavior. In R. D. Tollison (Ed.), *Smoking and society: Toward a more balanced assessment* (pp. 89–134). Lexington, MA: D. C. Heath.

Spiro, A., Aldwin, C. M., Levenson, M. R., & Bosse, R. (1990). Longitudinal findings from the Normative Aging Study: II. Do emotionality and extraversion predict symptom change? *Journals of Gerontology, 45,* 136–144.

Stacy, A. W., Newcomb, M. D., & Bentler, P. M. (1991). Cognitive motivation and drug use: A 9-year longitudinal study. *Journal of Abnormal Psychology, 100,* 502–515. Personality, problem drinking, and drunk driving: Mediating, moderating, and direct-effect models. *Journal of Personality & Social Psychology, 60,* 795–811.

Stam, H. J., McGrath, P. A., & Brooke, R. I. (1984). The effects of a cognitive-behavioral treatment program on temporo-mandibular pain and dysfunction syndrome. *Psychosomatic Medicine, 46,* 534–545.

Stamler, J., Wentworth, D., & Neaton, J. D. (1986). Is relationship between serum cholesterol and risk of premature death from coronary heart disease continuous and graded? Findings in 356, 222 primary screenees of the Multiple Risk Factor Intervention Trial (MRFIT). *Journal of the American Medical Association, 256,* 2823–2828.

Stampfer, M. J., Rimm, E. B., & Walsh, D. C. (1993). Commentary: Alcohol, the heart, and public policy. *American Journal of Public Health, 83,* 801–804.

Stanek, K., Abbott, D., & Cramer, S. (1990). Diet quality and the eating environment of preschool children. *Journal of the American Dietetic Association, 90,* 1582–1584.

Stang, P., Von Korff, M., & Galer, B. (1998). Reduced labor force participation among primary care patients with headache. *Journal of General Internal Medicine, 13,* 296–302.

Stanton, A. L. (1987). Determinants of adherence to medical regimens by hypertensive patients. *Journal of Behavioral Medicine, 10,* 377–394.

Stanton, A. L., Danoff-Burg, S., Cameron, C. L., Snider, P. R., & Kirk, S. B. (1999). Social comparison and adjustment to breast cancer: An experimental examination of upward affiliation and downward evaluation. *Health Psychology, 18,* 151–158.

Stanton, A. L., Kirk, S. B., Cameron, C. L., & Danoff-Burg, S. (2000). Coping through emotional approach: Scale construction and validation. *Journal of Personality and Social Psychology, 78*, 1150–1169.

Stanton, A. L., Lobel, M., Sears, S., & DeLuca, R. S. (2002). Psychosocial aspects of selected issues in women's reproductive health: current status and future directions. *Journal of Consulting and Clinical Psychology, 70*, 751–770.

Stanton, A. L., & Snider, P. R. (1993). Coping with a breast cancer diagnosis: A prospective study. *Health Psychology, 12*, 16–23.

Stark, M. J. (1992). Dropping out of substance abuse treatment: A clinically oriented review. *Clinical Psychology Review, 12*, 93–116.

Stark, O., Atkins, E., Wolff, O. H., & Douglas, J. W. B. (1981). Longitudinal study of obesity in the National Survey of Health and Development. *British Medical Journal, 283*, 13–17.

Steele, C. M., & Josephs, R. A. (1990). Alcohol myopia: Its prized and dangerous effects. *American Psychologist, 45*, 921–933.

Stein, J., Newcomb, M., & Bentler, P. (1996). Initiation and maintenance of tobacco smoking: Changing personality correlates in adolescence and young adulthood. *Journal of Applied Social Psychology, 26*, 160–187.

Steingart, R. M., Pacher, M., Hamin, P., Coglianese, M. E., Gersh, B., Gettman, E. M., Sollano, J., Katz, S., Moye, L., Basta, L. L., Lewis, S. J., Gottlieb, S. S., Bernstein, V., McEwan, P., Jacobson, K., Brown, E. J., Kukin, M. L., Kantrowitz, W. E., & Pfeffer, M. A. (1991). Sex differences in the management of coronary artery disease. *The New England Journal of Medicine, 325*, 226–230.

Steketee, G., & Foa, E. B. (1987). Rape victims: Post-traumatic stress responses and their treatment. *Journal of Anxiety Disorders, 1*, 69–86.

Sternbach, R. A. (1974). *Pain patients: Traits and treatment.* New York: Academic Press.

Sternbach, R. A. (1986). Pain and "hassles" in the United States: Findings of the Nuprin pain report. *Pain, 27*, 69–80.

Stevens, J., Cai, J., Pamuk, E. R., Williamson, D. F., Thun, M., & Wood, J. L. (1998). The effect of age on the association between body-mass index and mortality. *New England Journal of Medicine, 338*, 1–7.

Stevens, M. M. (1997). Psychological adaptation of the dying child. In D. Doyle, G. W. C. Hanks, & N. MacDonald (Eds.), *Oxford textbook of palliative medicine* (pp. 1046–1055). New York: Oxford University Press.

Stevens, M. M., & Dunsmore, J. C. (1996). Adolescents who are living with a life-threatening illness. In C. A. Corr & D. E. Balk (Eds.), *Handbook of adolescent death and bereavement* (pp. 107–135). New York: Springer.

Stevens, V. J., & Hollis, J. F. (1989). Preventing smoking relapse, using an individually tailored skills-training technique. *Journal of Consulting and Clinical Psychology, 57*, 420–424.

Stevens, V. M., Hatcher, J. W., & Bruce, B. K. (1994). How compliant is compliant? Evaluating adherence with breast self-exam positions. *Journal of Behavioral Medicine, 17*, 523–535.

Stewart, A. L. (2001). Community-based physical activity programs for adults aged 50 and older. *Journal of Aging and Physical Activity, 9* (Suppl.), 71–91.

Stewart, A. L., Mills, K. M., Sepsis, P. G., King, A. C., McLellan, B. Y., Roitz, K., Ritter, P. L. (1997). Evaluation of CHAMPS, a physical activity promotion program for seniors. *Annals of Behavioral Medicine, 29*, 353–361.

Stewart, W. F., Lipton, R. B., Celentano, D. D., & Reed, M. L. (1992). Prevalence of migraine headache in the United States. *Journal of the American Medical Association, 267*, 64–69.

Stice, E., Chase, A., Stormer, S., & Appel, A. (2001). A randomized trial of a dissonance-based eating disorder prevention program. *International Journal of Eating Disorders, 29*, 247–262.

Stice, E., Mazotti, L., Weibel, D., & Agras, W. S. (2000). Dissonance prevention program decreases thin-ideal internalization, body dissatisfaction, dieting, negative affect, and bulimic symptoms: A preliminary experiment. *International Journal of Eating Disorders, 27*, 206–217.

Stice, E., Trost, A., Chase, A., (2003). Healthy weight control and dissonance-based eating disorder prevention programs: Results from a controlled trial. *International Journal of Eating Disorders, 33*, 10–21.

Stillion, J., & Wass, H. (1984). Children and death. In E. S. Shneidman (Ed.), *Death: Current perspectives* (pp. 225–246). Palo Alto, CA: Mayfield.

St. Lawrence, J. (1993). African-American adolescents' knowledge, health-related attitudes, sexual behavior, and contraceptive decisions: Implications for the prevention of adolescent infection. *Journal of Consulting and Clinical Psychology, 61*, 104–112.

Stokes, J. P. (1983). Predicting satisfaction with social support from social network struc-

ture. *American Journal of Community Psychology, 11*, 141–152.

Stolberg, S. G. (1999, April 25). Sham surgery returns as a research tool. *New York Times*, p. 3.

Stolerman, I. P., & Jarvis, M. J. (1995). The scientific case that nicotine is addictive. *Psychopharmacology, 117*, 2–10.

Stone, A. A., Mezzacappa, E. S., Donatone, B. A., & Gonder, M. (1999). Psychosocial stress and social support are associated with prostate-specific antigen levels in men: Results from a community screening program. *Health Psychology, 18*, 482–486.

Stone, A. A., Neale, J. M., Cox, D. S., Napoli, A., Valdimarsdottir, H., & Kennedy-Moore, E. (1994). Daily events are associated with a secretory immune response to an oral antigen in men. *Health Psychology, 13*, 440–446.

Stone, J., Aronson, E., Crain, A. L., Winslow, M. P., & Fried, C. (1994). Inducing hypocrisy as a means of encouraging young adults to use condoms. *Personality and Social Psychology Bulletin, 20*, 116–128.

Stoney, C. M., Davis, M. C., & Mathews, K. A. (1987). Sex differences in physiological responses to stress and coronary heart disease: A causal link? *Psychophysiology, 24*, 127–131.

Stoney, C. M., Mathews, K. A., McDonald, R. H., & Johnson, C. A. (1988). Sex differences in acute stress response: Lipid, lipoprotein, cardiovascular and neuroendocrine adjustments. *Psychophysiology, 25*, 645–656.

Story, M., & Faulkner, P. (1990). The prime time diet: Eating behavior and food messages in television program content commercials. *American Journal of Public Health, 80*, 738–740.

Strack, S., Carver, C. S., & Blaney, P. H. (1987). Predicting successful completion of an aftercare program following treatment for alcoholism: The role of dispositional optimism. *Journal of Personality and Social Psychology, 53*, 579–584.

Strauss, L. M., Solomon, L. J., Costanza, M. C., Worden, J. K., & Foster, R. S. (1987). Breast self-examination practices and attitudes of women with and without a history of breast cancer. *Journal of Behavioral Medicine, 10*, 337–350.

Strecher, V. J., Kreuter, M., Den Boer, D.-J., Kobrin, S., Hospers, H. J., & Skinner, C. S. (1994). The effects of computer tailored smoking cessation messages in family practice settings. *Journal of Family Practice, 39*, 262–270.

Strecher, V. J., Kreuter, M. W., & Kobrin, S. C. (1995). Do cigarette smokers have unrealistic perceptions of their heart attack, cancer, and stroke risks? *Journal of Behavioral Medicine, 18,* 45–54.

Stroebe, M. S., & Schut, H. (2001). Models of coping with bereavement: A review. In M. S. Stroebe, R. O. Hansson, W. Stroebe, & H. Schut (Eds.), *Handbook of bereavement research: Consequences, coping, and care* (pp. 375–403). Washington, DC: American Psychological Association.

Stroebe, M. S., & Stroebe, W. (1983). Who suffers more? Sex differences in health risks of the widowed. *Psychological Bulletin, 93,* 279–301.

Stroebe, M .S., & Stroebe, W. (1991). Does "grief work" work? *Journal of Consulting and Clinical Psychology, 59,* 479–482.

Stroebe, W., & Stroebe, M. (1996). The social psychology of social support. In E. T. Higgins & A. W. Kruglanski (Eds.), *Social psychology: Handbook of basic principles* (pp. 597–621). New York: Guilford.

Stroebe, W., Stroebe, M. S., & Abakoumkin, G. (1999). Does differential social support cause sex differences in bereavement outcome? *Journal of Community and Applied Social Psychology, 9,* 1–12.

Struckman-Johnson, C. J., Gilliland, R. C., Struckman-Johnson, D. L., & North, T.C. (1990). The effects of fear of AIDS and gender on responses to fear-arousing condom advertisements. *Journal of Applied Social Psychology, 20,* 1396–1410.

Stunkard, A., Sorenson, T., & Schulsinger, F. (1983). Use of the Danish adoption register for the study of obesity and thinness. In S. Kety, L. Rowland, R. Sidman, & S. Matthysse (Eds.), *Genetics of neurological and psychiatric disorders* (pp. 115–120). New York: Raven Press.

Stunkard, A. J., & Sorensen, T. I. (1993). Obesity and socioeconomic status—a complex relationship. *New England Journal of Medicine, 329,* 1036–1037.

Sturges, J. W., & Rogers, R. W. (1996). Preventive health psychology from a developmental perspective: An extension of protection motivation theory. *Health Psychology, 15,* 158–166.

Suarez, E. C., Kuhn, C. M., Schanberg, S. M., Williams, R. B., Jr., & Zimmerman, E. A. (1998). Neuroendocrine, cardiovascular, and emotional responses of hostile men: The role of interpersonal challenge. *Psychosomatic Medicine, 60,* 78–88.

Sugisawa, H., Shibata, H., Hougham, G. W., Sugihara, Y., & Liang, J. (2002). The impact of social ties on depressive symptoms in U.S. and Japanese elderly. *Journal of Social Issues, 58,* 785–804.

Suinn, R. M. (1975). The cardiac stress management program for Type A patients. *Cardiac Rehabilitation, 5,* 13–15.

Suinn, R. M. (2001). The terrible twos—anger and anxiety: Hazardous to your health. *American Psychologist, 56,* 27–36.

Sullivan, L. (1990). Sounding board: Healthy People 2000. *New England Journal of Medicine, 323,* 1065–1067.

Sullivan, M. J. L., Reesor, K., Mikail, S., & Fisher, R. (1992). The treatment of depression in chronic low back pain: Review and recommendations. *Pain, 50,* 5–13.

Suls, J., & Marco, C. A. (1990). Relationship between JAS- and FTAS-Type A behavior and non-CHD illness: A prospective study controlling for negative affectivity. *Health Psychology, 9,* 479–492.

Sumartojo, E. (1993). When tuberculosis treatment fails: A social behavioral account of patient adherence. *American Review of Respiratory Disorders, 147,* 1311–1320.

Sunday, S. R., & Halmi, K. A. (1996). Micro- and macroanalyses of meal patterns in anorexia and bulimia nervosa. *Appetite, 26,* 21–36.

SUPPORT Principal Investigators. (1995). A controlled trial to improve care for seriously ill hospitalized patients: The Study to Understand Prognoses and Preferences for Outcomes and Risks of Treatments (SUPPORT). *Journal of the American Medical Association, 274,* 1591–1598.

Sussman, S., Dent, C. W., Stacy, A. W., Burciagia, A. Raynor, A., Turner, G. E., Charlin, V., Craig, S., Hansen, W. B., Burton, D., & Flay, B. R. (1990). Peer group association and adolescent tobacco use. *Journal of Abnormal Psychology, 99,* 349–352.

Sutherland, R. J., McDonald, R. J., & Savage, D. D. (1997). Prenatal exposure to moderate levels of ethanol can have long-lasting effects on hippocampal synaptic plasticity in adult offspring. *Hippocampus, 7,* 232–238.

Sutker, P. B., Davis, M. J., Uddo, M., & Ditta, S. R. (1995). War zone stress, personal resources, and PTSD in Persian Gulf War returnees. *Journal of Abnormal Psychology, 104,* 444–452.

Sutton, S. R., & Eiser, J. R. (1984). The effect of fear-arousing communications on cigarette smoking: An expectancy-value approach. *Journal of Behavioral Medicine, 7,* 13–33.

Sutton, S. R., & Hallett, R. (1988). Understanding the effects of fear-arousing communications: The role of cognitive factors and the amount of fear aroused. *Journal of Behavioral Medicine, 11,* 353–360.

Swendsen, J. D., Tennen, H., Carney, M. A., Affect, G., Willard, A., & Hromi, A. (2000). Mood and alcohol consumption: An experience sampling test of the self-medication hypothesis. *Journal of Abnormal Psychology, 109,* 198–204.

Swindle, M. (1989). Predicting temperament-mental health relationships: A covariance structure latent variable analysis. *Journal of Research in Personality, 23,* 118–144.

Szasz, T. S., & Hollender, M. H. (1956). A contribution to the philosophy of medicine. *Archives of Internal Medicine, 97,* 585–592.

Taddio, A., Katz, J., Ilersich, A. L., & Koren, G. (1997). Effects of neonatal circumcision on pain response during subsequent routine vaccination. *Lancet, 349,* 599–603.

Talbot, F., Nouwen, A., Gingras, J., Belanger, A., & Audet, J. (1999). Relations of diabetes intrusiveness and personal control to symptoms of depression among adults with diabetes. *Health Psychology, 18,* 537–542.

Talbot, M. (2000). The placebo prescription. *The New York Times Magazine,* January 9.

Tallmer, J., Scherwitz, L., Chesney, M., Hecker, M., Hunkeler, E., Serwitz, J., & Hughes, G. (1990). Selection, training, and quality control of Type A interviews in a prospective study of young adults. *Journal of Behavioral Medicine, 13,* 449–466.

Taub, A. (1998). Thumbs down on accupuncture. *Science, 279,* 159.

Taubes, G. (1998). As obesity rates rise, experts struggle to explain why. *Science, 280,* 5368.

Tauras, J. A., O'Malley, P. M., & Johnston, L. D. (2001). Effects of price and access laws on teenage smoking initiation: A national longitudinal analysis. (National Bureau of Economic Research Working Paper 8331), Cambridge, MA.

Taylor, C. B., Bandura, A., Ewart, C. K., Miller, N. H., & DeBusk, R. F. (1985). Exercise testing to enhance wives' confidence in their husbands' cardiac capability soon after clinically uncomplicated acute myocardial infarction. *American Journal of Cardiology, 55,* 635–638.

Taylor, S. E. (1979). Hospital patient behavior: Reactance, helplessness, or control? *Journal of Social Issues, 35,* 156–184.

Taylor, S. E. (1990). Health psychology: The science and the field. *American Psychologist, 45,* 40–50.

Taylor, S. E., & Aspinwall, L. G. (1993). Coping with chronic illness. In L. Goldberger & S.

Breznitz (Eds.), *Handbook of stress: Theoretical and clinical aspects* (pp. 511–531). New York: Free Press.

Taylor, S. E., Kemeny, M. E., Aspinwall, L. G., Schneider, S. G., Rodriguez, R., & Herbert, M. (1992). Optimism, coping, psychological distress, and high-risk sexual behavior among men at risk for acquired immunodeficiency syndrome (AIDS). *Journal of Personality and Social Psychology, 63,* 460–470.

Taylor, S. E., Klein, L. C., Lewis, B. P., Gruenewald, T. L., Gurung, R. A. R., & Updegraff, J. A. (2000). Biobehavioral responses to stress in females: Tend-and-befriend, not fight-or-flight. *Psychological Review, 107,* 411–429.

Taylor, S. E., Lichtman, R. R., & Wood, J. V. (1984). Attributions, beliefs about control, and adjustment to breast cancer. *Journal of Personality and Social Psychology, 46,* 489–502.

Tedesco, L. A., Keffer, M. A., Davis, E. L., & Christersson, L. A. (1993). Self-efficacy and reasoned action: Predicting oral health status and behaviour at one, three, and six month intervals. *Psychology and Health, 8,* 105–121.

Ter Kuile, M. M., Spinhoven, P., Linssen, A. C., Zitman, F. G., Van Dyck, R., & Rooijmans, H. G. (1994). Autogenic training and cognitive self-hypnosis for the treatment of recurrent headaches in three different subject groups. *Pain, 58,* 331–340.

Terry, D. J., & Hynes, G. J. (1998). Adjustment to a low-control situation: Reexamining the role of coping responses. *Journal of Personality and Social Psychology, 74,* 1078–1092.

Theorell, T., Ahlberg-Hulten, G., Sigala, F., Perski, A., Soderholm, M., Kallner, A., & Eneroth, P. (1990). A psychosocial and biomedical comparison between men in sex contrasting service occupations. *Work and Stress, 4,* 51–63.

Theorell, T., Blomkvist, V., Jonsson, H., Schulman, S., Berntorp, E., & Stigendal, L. (1995). Social support and the development of immune function in human immunodeficiency virus infection. *Psychosomatic Medicine, 57,* 32–36.

Thoits, P. A. (1986). Social support as coping assistance. *Journal of Consulting and Clinical Psychology, 54,* 416–423.

Thoits, P. A., Hohmann, A. A., Harvey, M. R., & Fletcher, B. (2000). Similar-other support for men undergoing coronary artery bypass surgery. *Health Psychology, 19,* 264–273.

Thomas, W., White, C. M., Mah, J., Geisser, M. S., Church, T. R., & Mandel, J. S. (1995). Longitudinal compliance with annual screening for fecal occult blood. *American Journal of Epidemiology, 142,* 176–182.

Thompson, D. C., Nunn, M. E., Thompson, R. S., & Rivara, F. P. (1996). Effectiveness of bicycle safety helmets in preventing serious facial injury. *Journal of the American Medical Association, 276,* 1994–1995.

Thompson, D. C., Rivara, F. P., & Thompson, R. S. (1996). Effectiveness of bicycle safety helmets in preventing head injuries: A case-control study. *Journal of the American Medical Association, 276,* 1968–1973.

Thompson, J. (1984). Communicating with patients. In R. Fitzpatrick, J. Hinton, S. Newman, G. Scrambler, & J. Thompson (Eds.), *The experience of illness* (pp. 87–108). New York: Tavistock.

Thompson, S. C. (1981). Will it hurt less if I can control it? A complex answer to a simple question. *Psychological Bulletin, 90,* 89–101.

Thompson, S. C., Nanni, C., & Levine, A. (1994). Primary versus secondary and central versus consequence-related control in HIV-positive men. *Journal of Personality and Social Psychology, 67,* 540–547.

Thompson, S. C., Nanni, C., & Schwankovsky, L. (1990). Patient-oriented interventions to improve communication in a medical visit. *Health Psychology, 9,* 390–404.

Thompson, S. C., Sobolew-Shubin, A., Galbraith, M., Schwankovsky, L., & Cruzen, D. (1993). Maintaining perceptions of control: Finding perceived control in low-control circumstances. *Journal of Personality and Social Psychology, 64,* 293–304.

Thorndike, E. L. (1905). *The elements of psychology.* New York: Seiler.

Thun, M. J., Day-Lally, C. A., Calle, E. E., Flanders, W. D., & Heath, C. W. (1995). Excess mortality among cigarette smokers: Changes in a 20-year interval. *American Journal of Public Health, 85,* 1223–1230.

Thune, I., Brenn, T., Lund, E., & Gaard, M. (1997). Physical activity and the risk of breast cancer. *New England Journal of Medicine, 336,* 1269–1275.

Tibben, A., Timman, R., Bannink, E. C., & Duivenvoorden, H. J. (1997). Three-year follow-up after presymptomatic testing for Huntington's disease in tested individuals and partners. *Health Psychology, 16,* 20–35.

Tice, D. M., & Baumeister, R. F. (1997). Longitudinal study of procrastination, performance, stress, and health: The cost and benefits of dawdling. *Psychological Science, 8,* 454–458.

Tiller, J., Schmidt, U., Ali, S., & Treasure, J. (1995). Patterns of punitiveness in women with eating disorders. *International Journal of Eating Disorders, 17,* 365–371.

Timko, C. (1987). Seeking medical care for a breast cancer symptom: Determinants of intentions to engage in prompt or delay behavior. *Health Psychology, 6,* 305–328.

Timmer, S. G., Veroff, J., & Hatchett, S. (1996). Family ties and marital happiness: The differential experiences of Black and White newlywed couples. *Journal of Social and Personal Relationships, 13,* 335–359.

Tomar, S. L., & Giovino, G. A. (1998). Incidence and predictors of smokeless tobacco use among U.S. youth. *American Journal of Public Health, 88,* 20–26.

Tomkins, S. S. (1966). Psychological model of smoking behavior. *American Journal of Public Health, 56* (suppl.), 17–20.

Tomkins, S. S. (1968). A modified model of smoking behavior. In E. F. Borgatta & R. Evans (Eds.), *Smoking, health and behavior* (pp. 165–186). Chicago: Aldine.

Toniolo, P., Ribloi, E., Protta, F., Charrel, M., & Coppa, A. P. (1989). Calorie-providing nutrients and risk of breast cancer. *Journal of the National Cancer Institute, 81,* 278–286.

Tonnesen, P., Fryd, V., Hansen, M., Helsted, J., Gunnersen, A. B., Forchammer, H., & Stockner, M. (1988). Effect of nicotine chewing gum in combination with group counseling on the cessation of smoking. *New England Journal of Medicine, 318,* 15–18.

Tosteson, D. C. (1990). New pathways in general medical education. *New England Journal of Medicine, 322,* 234–238.

Toth, P. L., Stockton, R., & Browne, R. (2000). College student grief and loss. In J. H. Harvey & E. D. Miller (Eds.), *Loss and trauma* (pp. 237–248). Philadelphia: Brunner-Rutledge.

Triandis, H. C., Bontempo, R., Villareal, M. J., Asai, M., & Lucca, N. (1988). Individualism and collectivism: Cross-cultural perspectives on self-ingroup relationships. *Journal of Personality and Social Psychology, 54,* 323–338.

Trice, A. D., & Price-Greathouse, J. (1986). Joking under the drill: A validity study of the CHS. *Journal of Social Behavior and Personality, 1,* 265–266.

Tsoh, J. Y., et al. (1997). Smoking cessation 2: Components of effective intervention. *Behavioral Medicine, 23,* 15–27.

Turk, D. C. (1994). Perspectives on chronic pain: The role of psychological factors. *Current Directions in Psychological Science, 3,* 45–48.

Turk, D. C. (1996). Biopsychosocial perspective on chronic pain. In R. J. Gatchel & D. C. Turk (Eds.), *Psychological approaches to pain management: A practitioner's handbook* (pp. 3–32). New York: Guilford.

Turk, D. C., & Flor, H. (1999). Chronic pain: A biobehavioral perspective. In R. J. Gatchel & D. C. Turk (Eds.), *Psychosocial factors in pain: Critical perspectives* (pp. 18–34). New York: Guilford.

Turk, D. C., Meichenbaum, D., & Genest, M. (1983). *Pain and behavioral medicine: A cognitive-behavioral perspective.* New York: Guilford.

Turk, D. C., Sist, T. C., Okifuji, A., Miner, M. F., Florio, G., Harrison, P., Massey, J., Lema, M. L., & Zevon, M. A. (1998). Adaptation to metastatic cancer pain, regional/local cancer pain, and non-cancer pain: Role of psychological and behavioral factors. *Pain, 74,* 247–256.

Turner, J. A. (1982). Comparison of group progressive-relaxation training and cognitive-behavioral group therapy for chronic low back pain. *Journal of Consulting and Clinical Psychology, 50,* 757–765.

Turner, J. A., & Chapman, C. R. (1982a). Psychological interventions for chronic pain: A critical review. I: Relaxation training and biofeedback. *Pain, 12,* 1–21.

Turner, J. A., & Chapman, C. R. (1982b). Psychological interventions for chronic pain: A critical review. II: Operant conditioning, hypnosis, and cognitive-behavior therapy. *Pain, 12,* 23–46.

Turner, J. A., & Clancy, S. (1986). Strategies for coping with chronic low back pain: Relationship to pain and disability. *Pain, 24,* 355–363.

Turner, J. A., & Clancy, S. (1988). Comparison of operant behavioral and cognitive-behavioral group treatment for chronic low back pain. *Journal of Consulting and Clinical Psychology, 56,* 261–266.

Turner, J. A., Clancy, S., McQuade, K. J., & Cardenas, D. D. (1990). Effectiveness of behavioral therapy for chronic low back pain: A component analysis. *Journal of Consulting and Clinical Psychology, 58,* 573–579.

Turner, J. A., Deyo, R. A., Loeser, J. D., Von Korff, M., & Fordyce, W. E. (1994). The importance of placebo effects in pain treatment and research. *Journal of the American Medical Association, 271,* 1609–1614.

Turner, J. A., & Jensen, M. P. (1993). Efficacy of cognitive therapy for chronic low back pain. *Pain, 52,* 169–177.

Tversky, A., & Kahneman, D. (1981, January 30). The framing of decisions and the psychology of choice. *Science, 211,* 453–458.

Twisk, J. W. R., Kemper, H. C. G., van Mechelen, W., & Post, G. B. (1997). Tracking of risk factors for coronary heart disease over a 14-year period: A comparison between lifestyle and biologic risk factors with data from the Amsterdam Growth and Health Study. *American Journal of Epidemiology, 145,* 688–696.

Uchino, B. N., Cacioppo, J. T., & Kiecolt-Glaser, K. B. (1996). The relationships between social support and physiological processes: A review with emphasis on underlying mechanisms and implications for health. *Psychological Bulletin, 119,* 488–531.

Uchino, B. N., Cacioppo, J. T., Malarkey, W., & Glaser, R. (1995). Individual differences in cardiac sympathetic control predict endocrine and immune responses to acute psychological stress. *Journal of Personality and Social Psychology, 69,* 736–743.

Uchino, B. N., Uno, D., & Holt-Lunstad, J. (1999). Social support, physiological processes, and health. *Current Directions in Psychological Science, 8,* 145–148.

Ukestad, L. K., & Wittrock, D. A. (1996). Pain perception and coping in female tension headache sufferers and headache-free controls. *Health Psychology, 15,* 65–68.

Ulrich, R. S. (1984). View through a window may influence recovery from surgery. *Science, 224,* 420–421.

Unden, A., Orth-Gomer, K., & Elofsson, S. (1991). Cardiovascular effects of social support in the work place: Twenty-four hour ECG monitoring of men and women. *Psychosomatic Medicine, 53,* 50.

United Nations International Children's Eduction Fund. (1991). *Facts for life.* New York: Author.

Updegraff, J. A., & Taylor, S. E. (2000). From vulnerability to growth: Positive and negative effects of stressful life events. In J. H. Harvey & E. D. Miller (Eds.), *Loss and trauma: General and close relationship perspectives* (pp. 3–28). Philadelphia: Brunner-Routledge.

Updegraff, J. A., Taylor, S. E., Kemeny, M. E., & Wyatt, G. E. (2002). Positive and negative effects of HIV infection in women with low socioeconomic resources. *Personality and Social Psychology Bulletin, 28,* 382–394.

Ursin, H., Baade, E., & Levine, S. (1978). *Psychobiology of stress: A study of coping men.* New York: Academic Press.

Valent, P. (2000). Stress effects of the Holocaust. In G. Fink (Ed.), *Encyclopedia of stress* (pp. X–Y). San Diego, CA: Academic Press.

Vanable, P. A., Ostrow, D. G., McKirnan, D. J., Taywaditep, K. J., & Hope, B. A. (2000). Impact of combination therapies on HIV risk perceptions and sexual risk among HIV-positive and HIV-negative gay and bisexual men. *Health Psychology, 19,* 134–145.

Van Eerdewegh, M. M., Bieri, M. D., Parilla, R. H., & Clayton, P. J. (1982). The bereaved child. *American Journal of Psychiatry, 140,* 23–29.

Vertosick, F. T., Jr. (2000). *Why we hurt: The natural history of pain.* New York: Harcourt.

Vincent, C. A., & Richardson, P. H. (1986). The evaluation of therapeutic acupuncture: Concepts and methods. *Pain, 24,* 1–13.

Vincent, M., Clearie, A. F., & Schluchter, M. D. (1987). Reducing adolescent pregnancy through school and community-based education. *Journal of the American Medical Association, 257,* 3382–3386.

Viney, L. L., Walker, B. M., Robertson, T., Lilley, B., & Ewan, C. (1994). Dying in palliative care units and in hospital: A comparison of quality of life of terminal cancer patients. *Journal of Consulting and Clinical Psychology, 62,* 157–164.

Visintainer, M. A., Volpicelli, J. R., & Seligman, M. E. (1982). Tumor rejection in rats after inescapable or escapable shock. *Science, 216,* 437–439.

Wadden, T. A. (1993). The treatment of obesity: An overview. In A. J. Stunkard & T. A. Wadden (Eds.), *Obesity: Theory and therapy* (2nd ed., 197–217). New York: Raven.

Wadden, T. A., Brownell, K. D., & Foster, G. D. (2002). Obesity: Responding to the global epidemic. *Journal of Consulting and Clinical Psychology, 70,* 510–525.

Wagner, P. J., & Curran, P. (1984). Health beliefs and physician identified "worried well." *Health Psychology, 3,* 459–474.

Waitzkin, H. (1984). Doctor–patient communication. *Journal of the American Medical Association, 252,* 2441–2446.

Waitzkin, H. (1985). Information giving in medical care. *Journal of Health and Social Behavior, 26,* 81–101.

Waldron, I. (1983). Sex differences in illness incidence, prognosis and mortality: Issues and evidence. *Social Science and Medicine, 17,* 1107–1123.

Walker, E. A., Katon, W. J., Jemelka, R. P., & Roy-Bryne, P. P. (1992). Comorbidity of gastrointestinal complaints, depression, and anxiety in the Epidemiologic Catchment Area (ECA) Study. *American Journal of Medicine, 92*(1A):26S–30S.

Walker, L. S., Garber, J., Smith, C. A., Van Slyke, D. A., & Claar, R. L. (2001). The relation of daily stressors to somatic and emotional symptoms in children with and without recurrent abdominal pain. *Journal of Consulting and Clinical Psychology, 69,* 85–91.

Waller, G., & Hartley, P. (1994). Perceived parental style and eating psychopathology. *European Eating Disorders Reveiw, 2,* 76–92.

Wallston, B. S., Alagna, S. W., DeVellis, B. M., & DeVellis, R. F. (1983). Social support and physical illness. *Health Psychology, 2,* 367–391.

Walsh, B. T., & Devlin, M. J. (1998). Eating disorders: Progress and problems. *Science, 280,* 1387–1390.

Wang, T., Hartzell, D. L., Rose, B. S., Flatt, W. P., Hulsey, M. G., Menon, N. K., Makula, R. A., & Baile, C. A. (1999). Metabolic responses to intracerebroventricular leptin and restricted feeding. *Physiology and Behavior, 65,* 839–848.

Ward, S. E., Goldberg, W., Miller-McCauley, V., Mueller, C., Nolan, A., Pawlik-Plank, D., Robbins, A., Stormoen, D., & Weissman, D. E. (1993). Patient-related barriers to management of cancer pain. *Pain, 52,* 319–324.

Wardle, J., Waller, J., & Jarvis, M. J. (2002). Sex differences in the association of socioeconomic status with obesity. *American Journal of Public Health, 92,* 1299–1304.

Ware, J. E., Jr., Bayliss, M. S., Rogers, W. H., & Kosinski, M. (1996). Differences in four-year health outcomes for elderly and poor, chronically ill patients in HMO and fee-for-service systems: Results from the Medical Outcomes Study. *Journal of the American Medical Association, 276,* 1039–1047.

Ware, J. E., Jr., & Sherbourne, C. D. (1992). The MOS 36-item short-form survey (SF-36). I. Conceptual framework and item selection. *Medical Care, 30,* 473–483.

Wass, H., & Stillion, J. M. (1988). Death in the lives of children and adolescents. In H. Wass, F. M. Berado, & R. A. Neimeyer (Eds.), *Dying: Facing the facts* (2nd ed., pp. 201–228). New York: Hemisphere.

Watson, D. (1988). Intraindividual and interindividual analyses of positive and negative affect: Their relation to health complaints, perceived stress, and daily activities. *Journal of Personality and Social Psychology, 54,* 1020–1030.

Watson, D., & Clark, L. A. (1984). Negative affectivity: The disposition to experience aversive emotional states. *Psychological Bulletin, 96,* 465–490.

Watson, D., & Pennebaker, J. W. (1989). Health complaints, stress, and distress: Exploring the central role of negative affectivity. *Psychological Review, 96,* 234–254.

Watson, J. D. (1990). The human genome project: Past, present, and future. *Science, 248,* 44–49.

Watters, J. K., Estilo, M. J., Clark, G. L., & Lorvick, J. (1994). Syringe and needle exchange as HIV/AIDS prevention for injection drug users. *Journal of the American Medical Association, 271,* 115–120.

Webster, D. W., Gainer, P. S., & Champion, H. P. (1993). Weapon carrying among inner-city junior high school students: Defensive behavior vs. aggressive delinquency. *American Journal of Public Health, 83,* 1604–1608.

Wechsler, H., Davenport, A., Dowdall, G., Moeykens, B., & Castillo, S. (1994). Health and behavioral consequences of binge drinking in college: A national survey of students at 140 campuses. *Journal of the American Medical Association, 272,* 1672–1677.

Wechsler, H., Dowdall, G. W., Davenport, A., & Castillo, S. (1995). Correlates of college student binge drinking. *American Journal of Public Health, 85,* 921–926.

Wegner, D. M. (1994). Ironic processes of mental control. *Psychological Review, 101,* 34–52.

Wegner, D. M., Shortt, J. W., Blake, A. W., & Page, M. S. (1990). The supression of exciting thoughts. *Journal of Personality and Social Psychology, 58,* 409–418.

Weidner, G., Boughal, T., Connor, S. L., Pieper, C., & Mendell, N. R. (1997). Relationship of job strain to standard coronary risk factors and psychological characteristics in women and men of the family heart study. *Health Psychology, 16,* 239–247.

Weinberg, M., Schmale, J., Uken, J., & Wessel, W. (1996). Online help: Cancer patients participate in a computer-mediated support group. *Health and Social Work, 21,* 24–29.

Weinstein, N. D. (1984). Why it won't happen to me: Perceptions of risk factors and susceptibility. *Health Psychology, 3,* 431–457.

Weinstein, N. D. (1987). Unrealistic optimism about susceptibility to health problems: Conclusions from a community-wide sample. *Journal of Behavioral Medicine, 10,* 481–500.

Weinstein, N. D. (1988). The precaution adoption process. *Health Psychology, 7,* 355–386.

Weinstein, N. D., Lyon, J. E., Sandman, P. M., & Cutie, C. L. (1998). Experimental evidence for stages of health behavior change: The precaution adoption process model applied to home radon testing. *Health Psychology, 17,* 445–453.

Weinstein, N. D., Rothman, A. J., & Sutton, S. R. (1998). Stage theories of health behavior: Conceptual and methodological issues. *Health Psychology, 17,* 290–299.

Weinstein, N. D., & Sandman, P. M. (1992). A model of the precaution adoption process: Evidence from home radon testing. *Health Psychology, 11,* 170–180.

Weisner, C., Greenfield, T., & Room, R. (1995). Trends in the treatment of alcohol problems in the U.S. general population, 1979–1990. *American Journal of Public Health, 85,* 55–60.

Welin, L., Tibblin, G., Svardsudd, K., Tibblin, B., Ander-Peciva, S., Larsson, B., & Wilhelmsen, L. (1985). Prospective study of social influences on mortality. *Lancet, 1* 915–918.

Wenger, N. K., Speroff, L., & Packard, B. (1993). Cardiovascular health and disease in women. *New England Journal of Medicine, 329,* 247–256.

Wenneker, M. B., Weissman, J. S., & Epstein, A. M. (1990). The association of payer with utilization of cardiac procedures in Massachusetts. *Journal of the American Medical Association, 264,* 1255–1260.

Werner, R. M., & Pearson, T. A. (1998). What's so passive about passive smoking? Secondhand smoke as a cause of atherosclerotic disease. *Journal of the American Medical Association, 179,* 157–158.

Wetter, D. W., Fiore, M. C., Gritz, E. R., Lando, H. A., Stitzer, M. L., Hasselblad, V., & Baker, T. B. (1998). The agency for health care policy and research smoking cessation clinical practice guideline: Findings and implications for psychologists. *American Psychologist, 53,* 657–669.

Whipple, B. (1987). Methods of pain control: Review of research and literature. *IMAGE: Journal of Nursing Scholarship, 19,* 142–146.

White, A. A., III, & Gordon, S. L. (1982). Synopsis: Workshop on idiopathic low-back pain. *Spine, 13,* 1407–1410.

White, B., & Sanders, S. H. (1986). The influence on patients' pain intensity ratings of antecedent reinforcement of pain talk or well talk. *Journal of Behavior Therapy and Experimental Psychiatry, 17,* 155–159.

White, E., Jacobs, E. J., & Daling, J. R. (1996). Physical activity in relation to colon cancer in middle-aged men and women. *American Journal of Epidemiology, 144,* 42–50.

White, E., Urban, N., & Taylor, V. (1993). Mammography utilization, public health impact, and cost-effectiveness in the United States. *Annual Review of Public Health, 14*, 605–633.

Whitehead, W. E., Busch, C. M., Heller, B. R., & Costa, P. T. (1986). Social learning influences on menstrual symptoms and illness behavior. *Health Psychology, 5*, 13–23.

Whittle, J., Conigliaro, J., Good, C. B., & Lofgren, R. P. (1993). Racial differences in the use of invasive cardiovascular procedures in the Department of Veterans Affairs medical system. *New England Journal of Medicine, 329*, 621–627.

Wickelgren, I. (1998). Do 'apples' fare worse than 'pears'? *Science, 280*, 1365.

Wiebe, D. J., & McCallum, D. M. (1986). Health practices and hardiness as mediators in the stress–illness relationship. *Health Psychology, 5*, 425–438.

Wiebe, J. S., & Christensen, A. J. (1997). Health beliefs, personality, and adherence in hemodialysis patients: An interactional perspective. *Annals of Behavioral Medicine, 19*, 31–35.

Wiens, A. N., & Menustik, C. E. (1983). Treatment outcome and patient characteristics in an aversion therapy program for alcoholism. *American Psychologist, 38*, 1089–1096.

Wiggins, S., Whyte, P., Huggins, M., Adam, S., Theilmann, J., Bloch, M., Sheps, S. B., Schechter, M. T., & Hayden, M. R. (1992). The psychological consequences of predictive testing for Huntington's disease. *New England Journal of Medicine, 327*, 1401–1405.

Wight, R. G., LeBlanc, A. J., & Aneshensel, C. S. (1998). AIDS caregiving and health among midlife and older women. *Health Psychology, 17*, 130–137.

Wilfond, B. S., & Fost, N. (1990). The cystic fibrosis gene: Medical and social implications for heterozygote detection. *Journal of the American Medical Association, 263*, 2777–2783.

Willenbring, M. L., Levine, A. S., & Morley, J. E. (1986). Stress induced eating and food preferences in humans: A pilot study. *International Journal of Eating Disorders, 5*, 855–864.

Williams, A. F., & Lancaster, K. A. (1995). The prospects of daytime running lights for reducing vehicle crashes in the United States. *Public Health Reports, 110*, 233–239.

Williams, A. F., & Lund, A. K. (1992). Injury control: What psychologists can contribute. *American Psychologist, 47*, 1036–1039.

Williams, D. A. (1996). Acute pain management. In R. J. Gatchel & D. C. Turk (Eds.), *Psycho-logical approaches to pain management: A practitioner's handbook* (pp. 55–77). New York: Guilford.

Williams, J. E., Paton, C. C., Siegler, I. C., Eigenbrot, M. L., Nieto, F. J., & Tyroler, H. A. (2000). Clinical investigation and reports: Anger proneness predicts coronary heart disease risk: Prospective analysis from the Atherosclerosis Risk in Communities (ARIC) Study. *Circulation, 101*, 2034–2039.

Williams, P. G., Wiebe, D. J., & Smith, T. W. (1992). Coping processes as mediators of the relationship between hardiness and health. *Journal of Behavioral Medicine, 15*, 237–255.

Williams, R. B., Barefoot, J. C., Califf, R. M., Haney, T. L., Saunders, W. B., Pryor, D. B., Hlatky, M. A., Siegler, I. C., & Mark, D. B. (1992). Prognostic importance of social and economic resources among medically treated patients with angiographically documented coronary artery disease. *Journal of the American Medical Association, 267*, 520–524.

Williams, R. B., Jr., Haney, T. L., Lee, K. L., Kong, Y., Blumenthal, J. A., & Whalen, R. E. (1980). Type A behavior, hostility, and coronary arteriosclerosis. *Psychosomatic Medicine, 42*, 539–549.

Williams, S. S., Kimble, D. L., Covell, N. H., Weiss, L. H., Newton, K. J., Fisher, J. D., & Fisher, W. A. (1992). College students use implicit personality theory instead of safer sex. *Journal of Applied Social Psychology, 22*, 921–933.

Williamson, D. F. (1995). Prevalence and demographics of obesity. In K. D. Brownell, & C. G. Fairburn (Eds.), *Eating disorders and obesity: A comprehensive handbook* (pp. 391–395). New York: Guilford.

Wills, T. A. (1984). Supportive functions of interpersonal relationships. In S. Cohen & L. Syme (Eds.), *Social support and health* (pp. 61–82). New York: Academic Press.

Wilson, D. P., & Endres, R. K. (1986). Compliance with blood glucose monitoring in children with type 1 diabetes mellitus. *Journal of Pediatrics, 108*, 1022–1024.

Windle, M. (1992). A longitudinal study of stress buffering for adolescent problem behaviors. *Developmental Psychology, 28*, 522–530.

Windle, M., & Windle, R. C. (2001). Depressive symptoms and cigarette smoking among middle adolescents: Prospective associations and intrapersonal and interpersonal influences. *Journal of Consulting and Clinical Psychology, 69*, 215–226.

Windsor, R. A., Lowe, J. B., Perkins, L. L., Smith-Yoder, D., Artz, L., Crawford, M., Amburgy, K., & Boyd, N. R., Jr. (1993). Health education for pregnant smokers: Its behavioral impact and cost benefit. *American Journal of Public Health, 83*, 201–206.

Winett, R. A. (1995). A framework for health promotion and disease prevention. *American Psychologist, 50*, 341–350.

Wing, R. R., & Jeffery, R. W. (1999). Benefits of recruiting participants with friends and increasing social support for weight loss and maintenance. *Journal of Consulting and Clinical Psychology, 67*, 132–138.

Winkleby, M., Fortmann, S., & Barrett, D. (1990). Social class disparities in risk factors for disease: Eight-year prevalence patterns by level of education. *Preventive Medicine, 19*, 1–12.

Winkleby, M. A., Kraemer, H. C., Ahn, D. K., & Varady, A. N. (1998). Ethnic and socioeconomic differences in cardiovascular disease risk factors. *Journal of the American Medical Association, 280*, 356–362.

Winkleby, M. A., Robinson, T. N., Sundquist, J., & Kraemer, H. C. (1999). Ethnic variation in cardiovascular disease risk factors among children and young adults: Findings from the Third National Health and Nutrition Examination Survey, 1988–1994. *Journal of the American Medical Association, 281*, 1006–1013.

Winn, D. M., Blot, W. J., Shy, C. M., Pickle, I. W., Toledo, A., & Frameni, J. F. (1981). Snuff dipping and oral cancer among women in the Southeastern United States. *New England Journal of Medicine, 304*, 745–749.

Winters, R. (1985). Behavioral approaches to pain. In N. Schneiderman & J. T. Tapp (Eds.), *Behavioral medicine: The biopsychosocial approach* (pp. 565–587). Hillsdale, NJ: Erlbaum.

Winzelberg, A. J., Eppstein, D., Eldredge, K. L., Wilfley, D., Dasmahapatra, R., Dev, P., & Taylor, C. B. (2000). Effectiveness of an Internet-based program for reducing risk factors for eating disorders. *Journal of Consulting and Clinical Psychology, 68*, 346–350.

Wiseman, C. V., Gray, J. J., Mosimann, J. E., & Ahrens, A. H. (1992). Cultural expectations of thinness in women: An update. *International Journal of Eating Disorders, 11*, 85–89.

Wisocki, P. A., & Skowron, J. (2000). The effects of gender and culture on adjustment to widowhood. In R. M. Eisler & M. Hersen (Eds.), *Handbook of gender, culture, and health* (pp. 429–447). Mahwah, NJ: Erlbaum.

Wohlgemuth, E., & Betz, N. E. (1991). Gender as a moderator of the relationships of stress and social support to physical health in college students. *Journal of Counseling Psychology, 38*, 367–374.

Wolf, S. (1969). Psychosocial factors in myocardial infarction and sudden death. *Circulation, 39*, 74–83.

Woloshin, S., Schwartz, L. M., & Welch, H. G. (2002). Risk charts: Putting cancer in context. *Journal of the National Cancer Institute, 94*, 799–804.

Wonderlich, S., Klein, M. H., & Council, J. R. (1996). Relationship of social perceptions and self-concept in bulimia nervosa. *Journal of Consulting and Clinical Psychology, 64*, 1231–1237.

Wonderlich, S. A., Wilsnack, R. W., Wilsnack, S. C., & Harris, T. R. (1996). Childhood sexual abuse and bulimic behavior in a nationally representative sample. *American Journal of Public Health, 86*, 1082–1086.

Wood, J. M., Bootzin, R. R., Rosenhan, D., Nolen-Hoeksema, S., & Jourden, F. (1992). Effects of the 1989 San Francisco earthquake on frequency and content of nightmares. *Journal of Abnormal Psychology, 101*, 219–224.

Woods, P. J., & Burns, J. (1984). Type A behavior and illness in general. *Journal of Behavioral Medicine, 7*, 277–286.

Woods, P. J., Morgan, B. T., Day, B. W., Jefferson, T., & Harris, C. (1984). Findings on a relationship between Type A behavior and headaches. *Journal of Behavioral Medicine, 7*, 277–285.

Woolhandler, S., & Himmelstein, D. U. (1990). The deteriorating administrative efficiency of the U.S. health care system. *New England Journal of Medicine, 324*, 1253–1258.

World Health Organization. (1964). *Basic documents* (15th ed., p. 1). Geneva, Switzerland: Author.

World Health Organization. Maternal and Newborn Health. 2002 (cited 14 July 2003). Available from www.who.int/reproductive-health/mps.

Wortman, C. B. (1984). Social support and cancer: Conceptual and methodological issues. *Cancer, 53*, 2339–2360.

Wortman, C. B., & Dunkel-Schetter, C. (1979). Interpersonal relationships and cancer: A theoretical analysis. *Journal of Social Issues, 35*, 120–155.

Wortman, C. B., & Lehman, D. (1985). Reactions to victims of life crises: Support attempts that fail. In I. G. Sarason & B. R. Sarason (Eds.), *Social support: Theory, research, and application* (pp. 463–489). The Hague: Martinus Nijhof.

Wulfert, E., & Wan, C. K. (1993). Condom use: A self-efficacy model. *Health Psychology, 12*, 346–353.

Yarnold, P. R., Michelson, E. A., Thompson, D. A., & Adams, S. L. (1998). Predicting patient satisfaction: A study of two emergency departments. *Journal of Behavioral Medicine, 21*, 545–563.

Ybema, J. F., Kuijer, R. G., Hagedoorn, M., & Buunk, M. P. (2002). Caregiver burnout among intimate partners of patients with a severe illness: An equity perspective. *Personal Relationships, 9*, 73–88.

Yee, B. W. K., Castro, F. G., Hammond, W. R., John, R., Wyatt, G. E., & Yurg, B. R. (1995). Panel IV: Risk-taking and abusive behaviors among ethnic minorities. *Health Psychology, 14*, 622–631.

Yesavage, J. A., Leirer, V. O., Denari, M., & Hollister, L. E. (1985). Carry-over effects of marijuana intoxication on aircraft pilot performance: A preliminary report. *American Journal of Psychiatry, 142*, 1325–1329.

Yong, L.-C., Brown, C. C., Schatzkin, A., Dresser, C. M., Slesinshi, M. J., Cox, C. S., & Taylor, P. R. (1997). Intake of vitamins E, C, and A and risk of lung cancer: The NHANES I Epidemiologic Followup Study. *American Journal of Epidemiology, 146*, 231–243.

Zador, P. L., & Ciccone, M. A. (1993). Automobile driver fatalities in frontal impacts: Air bags compared with manual belts. *American Journal of Public Health, 83*, 661–666.

Zarski, J. J. (1984). Hassles and health: A replication. *Health Psychology, 3*, 243–251.

Zastrowny, T. R., Kirschenbaum, D. S., & Meng, A. L. (1986). Coping skills training for children: Effects on distress before, during, and after hospitalization for surgery. *Health Psychology, 5*, 231–247.

Zatzick, D. F., & Dimsdale, J. E. (1990). Cultural variations in response to painful stimuli. *Psychosomatic Medicine, 52*, 544–557.

Zejdlik, C. M. (1983). Management of spinal cord injury. Monterey, CA: Wadsworth.

Zelman, D. C., Brandon, T. H., Jorenby, D. E., & Baker, T. B. (1992). Measures of affect and nicotine dependence predict differential response to smoking cessation treatments. *Journal of Consulting and Clinical Psychology, 60*, 943–952.

Zhang, J., Feldblum, P. J., & Fortney, J. A. (1992). Moderate physical activity and bone density among perimenopausal women. *American Journal of Public Health, 82*, 736–738.

Zhang, S., Hunter, D. J., Forman, M. R., Rosner, B. A., Speizer, F. F., Colditz, G. A., Manson, J. E., Hankinson, S. E., & Willett, W. C. (1999). Dietary carotenoids and vitamins A, C, and E and risk of breast cancer. *Journal of the National Cancer Institute, 91*, 547–556.

Zhu, S.-H., Sun, J., Billings, S. C., Choi, W. S., & Malarcher, A. (1999). Predictors of smoking cessation in U.S. adolescents. *American Journal of Preventive Medicine, 16*, 202–207.

Zhu, S.-Y., Stretch, V., Balabanis, M., Rosbrook, B., Sadler, G., & Pierce, J. P. (1996). Telephone counseling for smoking cessation: Effects of single-session and multiple-session interventions. *Journal of Consulting and Clinical Psychology, 64*, 202–211.

Zisook, S., Schuchter, S. R., Sledge, P. A., & Judd, L. L. (1994). The spectrum of depressive phenomena after spousal bereavement. *Journal of Clinical Psychiatry, 55*, 29–36.

Zucker, R. A., & Gomberg, E. S. L. (1986). Etiology of alcoholism reconsidered: The case for a biopsychosocial process. *American Psychologist, 41*, 783–793.

Zucker, T. P., Flesche, C. W., Germing, U., Schroter, S., Willers, R., Wolf, H. H., & Heyll, A. (1998). Patient-controlled versus staff-controlled analgesia with pethidine after allogenic bone marrow transplantation. *Pain, 75*, 305–312.

SUBJECT INDEX

Earthquakes, nightmares and survivors
    of, 38
Eastern Europe
    HIV rates in, 590
    public health crisis in, 589
Eating, psychological factors and,
    278–286
Eating disorder prevention interven-
    tions, personally relevant messaging
    and, 554–556
Eating disorders, 22, 296–299
    anorexia nervosa, 296–297
    biological factors leading to, 299
    bulimia nervosa, 297–299
    dangerous effects from prevention
        programs for, 311–312
    family dynamics and, 305, 307
    personality and, 307–308
    preventing, 308–309
    psychological factors leading to,
        299–300, 302–308
    social pressures and, 302–305
Education
    and alcohol use, 238
    and coping with chronic illness,
        385–386
Educational attainment, and smoking,
    215, 216
Electroencephalogram (EEG), 429
Electromyography (EMG), 324, 325
ELISA, 477
EMG. *See* Electromyography
Emotional appeals, effectiveness of,
    526–534
Emotional support, 183–184, 200
Emotion-focused coping, 130–133, 382
Emotion-focused interventions, and
    dental procedures, 548
Enactment stage, 413
Endocrine system, effect of stress on,
    114–116
Endorphins, 322, 323
    cognitive techniques for pain control
        and, 354–355
Environmental factors, 9
Environmental pressures, and stress, 95
Epidemiologists, 25
Epinephrine, 107, 108
Esteem, or validational, support, 184
Estrogen use, health problems with, 587
Ethical issues
    animal experimentation and, 54–56
    health technology and, 16
Ethical medical decisions, making,
    575–577
Ethnic groups, social support and,
    206–207

Ethnicity
    and AIDS, 408
    and alcohol use, 238
    and cancer, 400
    coronary heart disease, 391
    and health care utilization, 488
    and pain, 331
Europe, health care in, 579
European Americans, alcohol use
    by, 238
Eustress, 112
Exercise, 59–60
    and coping with stress, 137
    and HIV infection, 421
    for pain control, 343
    and protection against cancers,
        402–403
    and social cognitive theory, 75
    and weight control/loss, 287,
        293–296
Exhaustion stage, 110
Experimental methods, description of,
    34–41
Experimental/psychological realism, 36
Experimental realism, 37
Experimental research design, key ele-
    ments of, 35
Experimenter expectancy effects, 45
Experiments, 23
Ex post facto studies, 37
External validity, 45–49
Extraversion, 167
    and health habits, 4, 151–154, 170
Extroversion-Introversion Scale, sample
    items from, 153

F

False-positive results of tests, psycholog-
    ical effects of, 477
Family
    and chronic illness, 371–372
    and eating disorders, 305, 307
    and social networks, 181
Family planning/reproductive health,
    international programs on, 588, 589
Fast food, and obesity, 286
Fast food restaurants, caloric intake
    and, 394
Fat cells, and obesity, 277
Fear-based drug prevention
    programs, 529
Fear-based health-promotion messages,
    527, 529–533
Federal Trade Commission, 572
Fee-for-service plans, 581, 582
Female physicians, and patient-practi-
    tioner communication, 490, 491

Fernald School (Boston), atomic experi-
    ments at, 51
Fetal alcohol syndrome, 240
Fetal death, 456
Fight-or-flight response, 107, 108, 114,
    121, 140, 141
Films
    alcohol use portrayed in, 249
    tobacco use portrayed in, 219
Financial stress, and alcohol use, 196
Firearms in home, and suicide, 445
Flossing teeth, 60
    and social cognitive theory, 75
    and theories of reasoned
        action/planned behavior, 67
Food advertisements, 290
Food and Drug Administration, 229
Ford, Betty, 480
Fox, Michael, 480
Fraternities, alcohol abuse and, 250–251
Freud, Sigmund, 17, 148
    patient descriptions by, 26
Friends
    and chronic illness, 371–373
    and social networks, 181
Fromme, Kim, 73

G

Gain- *versus* loss-framed persuasive
    statements, about breast self-exam,
    535–536
Gambling addicts, relapse triggers
    for, 517
GAS. *See* General Adaptation Syndrome
Gate control theory of pain, 320,
    321, 322
Gay clubs, and condom use, 544
Gender
    and alcohol use, 238
    and eating and mood regulation, 281
    and health care quality, 587
    and life expectancy, 428, 430
    and medical treatments, 493–494
    and response to stress, 140–141
    and smoking, 230
    and spousal loss, 453
    and suicide, 445, 446
General Adaptation Syndrome (GAS),
    107, 121
    model of, 108
    model of organ systems involved
        in, 109
Genetic factors
    and alcoholism, 254–255
    and obesity, 275–278
    and smoking, 262–263

K

Kaposi's sarcoma, and AIDS, 27
Kevorkian, Jack, 461
Knowles, John, 10
Kreuger, Scott, 250
Kubler-Ross, Elizabeth, 432, 433

L

Lady and the Tramp, 219
Lamaze technique, 352
Latin America, HIV rates in, 590
Latinos. *See* Hispanic Americans
Leading questions, 30, 31
Learning
  and pain, 329–331
  and placebos, 359
Learning theories, 60, 69–73
  and interventions, 541–542
  limitations with, 72
Life events, and stress measurement, 100–102
Life expectancy
  chronic illness and, 368
  disability-adjusted, 562
  increasing, 562
  optimism and, 28, 150, 151
  positive emotions and, 157
  predictors of women's health and, 586
  rising health care costs and, 13–14
  in United States, 427
Life skills training programs, and smoking, 228
Lifestyle choices, and chronic diseases, 377
Lifestyle factors
  and cancer, 401
  and eating/overeating, 284–286
Lifestyle interventions, costs of, 582
Lingering deaths, influence on grief, 440–441
Lion King, The, 219
Live for Life (Johnson & Johnson), 596
Liver damage, alcohol abuse and, 239
Living will(s)
  effectiveness of, 462, 466
  sample of, 465
Local anesthetics, 339
Loma Prieta earthquake, damage in San Francisco after, 38, 39
Longevity, racial-ethnic health differences in, 565
Longitudinal studies, 37
Long-term care facilities, death and dying in, 437

Loss-framed persuasive statements, gain-framed persuasive statements *versus*, 535–536
Lou Gehrig's disease (or ALS), 438
Low-density lipoprotein (LDL) cholesterol, coronary heart disease and levels of, 388
Low external validity, 46
Low hardiness people, quotes from, 155
Lung cancer, 9
  and smoking, 25
  in women, 586
Lung cancer surgery, and loss-framed wording/gain-framed wording, 536–537

M

Magazines, thinness norm for women in, 300
Maintenance, and stages of change, 80
Male physicians, and patient-practitioner communication, 490, 491
Malignant tumors, 399
Malnutrition, international programs on, 589
Malpractice insurance, 579, 580
Mammograms, 473, 474, 479
  cost-effectiveness and, 584
  mobile vans and, 480
  questionable benefits from, 521–522
Mammography, radiation exposure and, 477, 478
Managed health care, 581
Manning, Martha, 77
Mantle, Mickey, 577
Marijuana, 262, 263
Marital relationships, humorous look at chronic disease and, 374
Marital satisfaction, child with chronic disease and impact on, 372
Marriage
  gender and benefits from, 205
  and social networks, 181
Massage therapy, 341
Mass-media, health-promotion campaigns by, 528
Mass psychogenic illness, 483
Matching hypothesis, 199
Math performance, and swimsuit test, 302
"Maze-bright"/"maze-dumb" rats, 45
McClellan Air Force Base, organizational health center at, 596
Measles, vaccinations and decrease in, 9
Media
  screening behaviors and, 479

smoking prevention efforts by, 229
smoking promoted by, 219
thinness norm for women in, 300
Medicaid, 568, 569, 580
Medical anthropology, 19
Medical delays, 484
Medical jargon, and patient-practitioner communication, 491
Medical procedures, information needs and, 546–548
Medical psychology, 17
Medical sociology, 19
"Medical student's disease," 483
Medical technology, and health care costs, 580
Medication
  for pain control, 338–339
  patient-controlled, 498–499
Meditation, 135, 348
  and coping with chronic illness, 386
Medium-threat advertisements, 531
Melzack, Ronald, 320
Men
  alcohol use and, 238
  body image norms and, 301
  cancer types in, 398
  condom promotion ads for, 550–551
  coronary heart disease in, 390–391
  eating and mood regulation in, 281
  figure size preferences of, 306
  height/weight tables for, 269–270
  HIV routes of transmission for, 408
  life expectancy in, 428, 430
  rumination in bereavement by, 449
  screening recommendations for, 472
  smoking and, 215, 230
  social support and benefits for women and, 204–206
  spousal loss and, 453
Menopause, 587
Message framing, and health-promoting behaviors, 534–535
Metabolic rates
  exercise and increase in, 293
  and weight gain, 276–277
Mickey Mouse, 229
Midwestern Prevention Project, 532
Migraine headaches, 1, 6, 91, 317
Milgram study, 37
Military combat, and buffering hypothesis, 194
Milkshake test, 283
Mind-body dualism, 18
Miscarriages, 456
Miss America contestants, thinness norm for, 300, 301

AUTHOR INDEX